Within the fresco, the inscription reads:

TEMPLA DOMVM EXPOSITIS·VICOS·FORA·MOENIA PONTES:
VIRGINEAM TRIVII·QVOD REPARARIS AQVAM:
PRISCA·LICET·NAVTIS·STATVAS DARE·COMMODA·PORTVS:
ET VATICANVM CINGERE SIXTE·IVGVM:
PLVS TAMEN VRBS DEBET·NAM QVAE SQVALORE LATEBAT?
CERNITVR IN CELEBRI BIBLIOTHECA·LOCO·

Sixtus IV, surrounded by his nephews, appoints Platina as Vatican Librarian (1474), Melozzo da Forli, fresco, c.1477 (Pinacoteca, Vatican)

THE CIVILIZATION OF EUROPE IN THE RENAISSANCE

JOHN HALE

A TOUCHSTONE BOOK
PUBLISHED BY SIMON & SCHUSTER
New York London Toronto Sydney Tokyo Singapore

TOUCHSTONE
Rockefeller Center
1230 Avenue of the Americas
New York, NY 10020

First American Edition 1994
First Touchstone Edition 1995
Published by arrangement with HarperCollins Publishers Ltd.

TOUCHSTONE and colophon are registered trademarks of Simon & Schuster Inc.

Manufactured in the United States of America

3   5   7   9   10   8   6   4   2

Library of Congress Cataloging-in-Publication Data
Hale, J. R. (John Rigby), 1923–
The civilization of Europe in the Renaissance / John Hale.
p.   cm.
ISBN 0-689-12200-4
0-684-80352-6 (pbk)
1. Renaissance.   2. Europe—Civilization—16th century.   I. Title.
CB367.H35   1994   93-46246   CIP
940.2'1—dc20

For Sheila

CONTENTS

FOREWORD

JOHN FINISHED WRITING this book in June 1992. A month after he had delivered the manuscript he suffered a severe stroke which deprived him, for the time being, of the power to communicate. Since his intellect and personality were spared he had to bear the appalling frustration of knowing that his handicap would prevent him from seeing a book on which he had spent four years through to publication.

Although the creative work was done, no book of this scope and complexity is ready for publication when the text is completed. There were still Stuart Proffitt's meticulous editorial queries to be answered; passages had to be clarified, references and bibliography completed, proofs read, captions written to the illustrations John had so carefully chosen. If I had ever in the course of our long marriage taken John's talents and scholarship for granted I learned my lesson now. I realized that nobody short of a professional historian of the first rank, an historian who moreover understood or shared John's particular vision of his subject, would be capable of standing in for John himself.

I appealed to David Chambers, Reader in Renaissance Studies at the Warburg Institute in the University of London, and one of the editors of the *Journal of the Warburg and Courtauld Institutes*. He had been one of John's pupils at Oxford in the late 1950s, and I was aware that John admired his work; I had also often heard that his editorial skill and judgement were widely respected. Fortunately, I was too ignorant and too numbed by the shock of John's sudden illness to realize just how much I was asking of someone with numerous other demands on his time.

Nor could I have guessed at the many human qualities that could comfort and cheer John and me through the terrible months after John's stroke. David's kindness and sense of humour were not merely added bonuses, they gave us hope and reassurance at a period when I, at least, might otherwise have been broken by sorrow and worry. He was endlessly patient and generous-spirited with me. More to the point, he was determined that the book should be published as near as possible as John had written it and that John should be involved, as far as he could be, in editorial decisions. This kindness inevitably made the job even more time-consuming.

I should add that although David had no help from me, he did have the benefits of working with Stuart Proffitt, his editor Rebecca Wilson and the book's designer Philip Lewis, and he could count on the advice of Professor Nicolai Rubinstein, Emeritus Fellow of the Warburg Institute and a mutual friend of very long standing. Nicolai also read the entire typescript and shared in the proofreading, with his accustomed eagle-eyed attention to stylistic and factual detail. To resolve the problems which arose David also had, as he repeatedly pointed out, the advantage of quick access to a unique library and to colleagues with expert knowledge in different branches of the civilization of the Renaissance; if John did much of his preparatory work in the Library of the Warburg Institute, it is also largely thanks to that Institute that the book was finally completed.

SHEILA HALE
June 1993

LIST OF ILLUSTRATIONS

PREFACE

THIS BOOK IS CONCERNED with the period of European history from around 1450 to about 1620. No slice of historical time is self-contained. But what has usefully come to be referred to as the 'long' sixteenth century does have a coherence of its own. It was the first age in which the words 'Europe' and 'European' acquired a widely understood significance. It saw the emergence of a new and pervasive attitude to what were considered the most valued aspects of civilized life. It witnessed the most concentrated wave of intellectual and creative energy that had yet passed over the continent, with the culture of Renaissance Italy reaching its apogee and being absorbed or rebuffed by other vigorously developing national cultures. It was also a period in which there were such dramatic changes of fortune for better or worse – religious, political, economic and, through overseas discoveries, global – that more people than ever before saw their time as unique, referring to 'this new age', 'the present age', 'our age'; to one observer it was a 'blessed age', to another 'the worst age in history'.

I have aimed at an investigative impression which attempts to balance what was then said and done with some of the questions posterity always wants to put to the past, and perhaps to no period before the nineteenth century more concernedly than this. Just as there are loadstone cities – Paris, Prague, Venice, London – which attract visitors not only for what they are but for the associations they call to mind, there are loadstone periods, and I have tried to provide a guidebook for time-travellers to this one.

I hope it will not be thought presumptuous that my title adapts that of a book of really seminal importance, Jacob Burckhardt's *The Civilization of the Renaissance in Italy* of 1860. I have carried it for so long in my mental baggage as a talisman at once protective and provocative that this was not a journey I could undertake without it. Simply thumbing its title is to be alerted to dangers ahead. What precisely is meant by 'civilization' (Burckhardt's word was the even less definable *Kultur*)? How usefully descriptive is the term 'Renaissance'? What, indeed, did a word like 'Italy' signify to contemporaries? In temerariously extending these questions to Europe as a whole I have taken some comfort from Francis Bacon's remark that 'to desire in discourse to hold all arguments is ridiculous, wanting true judgement; for in all things no man can be exquisite', but I am aware of how far I have failed to take full advantage of the accumulation of knowledge represented in my bibliography.

For what is least *in*exquisite in the following pages I have to thank the chastening goodwill of my wife Sheila and the untiring vigilance of my editor Stuart Proffitt as they patiently reviewed the style and content of my drafts. Among the many colleagues and other friends with whom I have helpfully discussed my plan I mention only two: Nicolai Rubinstein, who urged me to stress the theme of transmission – of people and ideas; and Jane Martineau, who asked me at an early stage 'is ice hockey a part of civilization?' I also owe much to the heady juxtapositions encountered in the stacks of the Warburg Institute and the London Library, and to the opportunity to try out parts of this book given me by the Center for Medieval and Renaissance Studies at the University of California, Los Angeles. I confess my own age in admitting that I have had to send a handwritten book to be typed; but this gives me the excuse to thank Julia Cornes for remaining, like that great cherisher of manuscripts in the first generation of printing, Duke Federico of Urbino, alertly sympathetic to an outmoded form of self-expression.

PART ONE

Europe

The nether sky opens, and Europe is disclosed as a prone and emaciated figure, the Alps shaping like a backbone, and the branching mountain-chains like ribs, the peninsular plateau of Spain forming a head. Broad and lengthy lowlands stretch from the north of France across Russia like a grey-green garment hemmed by the Ural mountains and the glistening Arctic Ocean.

The point of view then sinks downwards through space, and draws near to the surface of the perturbed countries, where the peoples, distressed by events which they did not cause, are seen writhing, crawling, heaving, and vibrating in their various cities and nationalities.

THOMAS HARDY, The Dynasts, stage direction

CHAPTER I

The Discovery of Europe

THE WORD AND THE MYTH

When in 1623 Francis Bacon threw off the phrase 'we Europeans', he was assuming that his readers knew where 'Europeans' were, who they were, and what, in spite of national differences, they shared.[1] This was a phrase, and an assumption, that could not have been used with such confidence a century and a half before. It was during the period covered by this book that the word Europe first became part of common linguistic usage and that the continent itself was given a securely map-based frame of reference, a set of images that established its identity in pictorial terms, and a triumphal ideology that overrode its internal contradictions.

Though scholars throughout the middle ages had known that they lived in a continent called by classical geographers 'Europe' to distinguish it from Africa and Asia, the other land masses partly known to them, the word had little resonance. In all likelihood the great majority of those who lived in Europe and could read only with difficulty, if at all, had not even heard of the word. Their knowledge of a world beyond their local or national confines came from the stories of martyrs, missionaries and crusades and from the pulpit. The clergy harangued them as Christians forming part of the particular continent which had been chosen by divine providence to be the home of witness to the true faith: Christendom. Without spatially accurate maps, and without the mass of itineraries and travel journals to be released by the advent of printed books, Europe's identity was above all emotional: Us, uniquely privileged (and thus also punishable by wars, plagues and famines for our sins) versus Them, the godless or the erroneous believers.

As early as 1471, in a moment of enthusiastic gratitude for the welcome he was granted in Nuremberg, the astronomer Johannes Müller (Regiomontanus) praised the city as 'the middle point of Europe'.[2] For

Bacon it was always Europe; Henry VII was buried in Westminster Abbey 'in one of the stateliest and daintiest monuments' – by the Italian Pietro Torrigiano – 'in Europe'; England was involved in the 'affairs of Europe'.[3]

But the notion of Christendom was a long time a-dying. It continued to drip from the quills of those inditing peace treaties, for given man's incurable urge to fight, what better resolution to a domestic conflict than a joint Christian enterprise against the infidel? It surfaced in the prayer which a devout citizen of Milan adopted in 1565, with the advice of his confessor, for his family devotions: he prayed that God keep his family 'in perfect union and love, us and all of Christendom'.[4] Even in 1590 a conservative but travelled English squire, Sir John Smythe, alternated between referring to the countries of western 'Europe' and the 'nations of the occidental parts of Christendom'.[5] Its more personal appeal was expressed as late as 1620, when the young Cornishman Peter Mundy, labouring his way back across the Turkish-dominated Balkans after a trip to Constantinople, passed the boundary stone of the Venetian enclave of Spalato (Split): 'wee were no sooner past it, but wee entred into Christendome, then seeminge to be in a new world'.[6]

This way of expressing the relief of coming home from alien lands is as moving as it was by then rare. The sense of Christendom being a sacred sheep-fold, within which European peoples shared at least the comforting uniformity of their faith, had been subject to many erosions. Princes had struck bargains with popes, amongst other things over appointments to high clerical offices and the use of taxes levied on church lands, that anticipated the public reasons for the withdrawal of England under Henry VIII from all obedience to Rome. In 1439 an ecumenical conference in Florence had opened many eyes for the first time to the extent of the gap in doctrine and observance that divided the Catholic and the Greek Orthodox varieties of Christianity. And from the early sixteenth century, propaganda for the notion that Moscow was the Third Rome and the tsar the true leader and protector of orthodoxy drew attention to the extent and weirdness of the Russian version of the faith. Christendom, in the sense of a traveller knowing what images and services to expect when he entered a church abroad or passed clerics and friars in the street, was becoming at best 'the Christendom of Europe', as a priest put it in 1572 – and was having its centre of gravity pushed westwards.[7] The most dramatic push in this direction was the Ottomans' conquest of territories in south-eastern Europe which began well before their occupation of Constantinople in

1453; by 1529 it had brought them to the walls of Vienna, which they besieged but failed to take.

But Christendom had, until now, always been a flexible concept. It had flowed outwards to include the Byzantine Christians in Anatolia, the Coptic Christians in North Africa, even to the community of Christians, supposedly founded by the apostle Thomas in southern India, which led Vasco da Gama, when he reached Calicut in 1498, to see fanged Hindu deities as eccentrically portrayed angels and saints. Similarly, the concept had been able to shrink. After his trek across the Ottomanized Balkans, Mundy could still recognize Christendom when he re-entered the world of its customs and worship. The impact of the Turkish presence in Europe was not so much on the elastic notion of Christendom as on the increasingly concrete one of Europe.

What more convincingly shattered the idea that Christians shared membership in a club whose address was most of Europe was the Reformation, a split from the 1520s of the most piercing kind that divided non-Orthodox Christianity between Catholic and Protestant zones each emitting, especially from the 1550s, an equally hectoring and sincere call to rethink belief, behaviour and observance. Watching the process of antagonism from his headquarters in Geneva in the 1560s, Calvin, the most shrewdly observant of Protestant leaders, summed up the political and social results of the split as 'the shattering' – not, significantly, of Christendom, but 'of Europe: *Europae concussio*'.[8]

By then scores of thousands had been claimed – or allowed it to be thought that they were claimed – for Christ by missionary activity in America and Asia. But they were no longer seen as members of Christendom. The elasticity of the term was worn out. And what had, for a century, been grouched at as a sinful failing was now accepted as a fact of life: that the Christian powers would not stand up together against the Ottoman Turks for Christendom's sake. It was also in the 1560s that Matteo Bandello, a professional writer of diverting stories but also a cosmopolitan member of a new breed of Euro-watcher, inscribed one of Christendom's many epitaphs. The Turks, he wrote, have reduced Christianity to a mere 'part of Europe, thanks to the discords between Christian princes which grow from day to day'.[9] He reviewed them and concluded that 'we can affirm that few ages have seen such sudden changes as we witness daily; how it will end I simply cannot say, for it seems to me that things go from bad to worse and that the discord between Christians is stronger than ever before.' It comes as no surprise to find an entry in the *Geographical Encyclopaedia*

(1578) of the great cartographer Abraham Ortelius that simply reads 'For Christians, see Europeans'.[10]

For unexpansive minds England was different: mercifully sundered from 'transmarine nations' or, as a poet wrote in 1611, 'the CONTI-NENT'.[11] And when reviewing the Protestant isolation that followed Elizabeth's succession in 1558 to the Catholic Mary, the Spanish ambassador in London described England as 'the sick man of Europe'.[12]

That Europeans shared something other than forms of Christianity had been expressed by an editor for the first printing press to be established in Italy in 1465; he saw them as the ex-subjects and present successors of the Roman Empire and thus as 'men of the Latin world'.[13] This secularization of the attitude to those who lived in Europe led the very word to become colloquially vague. When Falstaff bragged that 'an I had but a belly of any indifferency, I were simply the most active fellow in Europe', Europe simply means anywhere.[14]

Perhaps the most striking example of the shift from Christendom to Europe comes in an oration of 1559 by the French scholar and political philosopher Louis Le Roy, for it comes in the context of a plea for the end of hostilities among Christian rulers. 'Think how far Christendom once extended and how many lands are now lost to the victorious Turk, who holds North Africa and the Balkans and has

Europa and the Bull,
maiolica dish, c. 1550
(British Museum)

besieged Vienna. Meanwhile, as though in answer to Mohammedan prayers, Europe is soaked in her own blood. What blindness there is in this! If you will not listen to me, hear the voice of our common mother Europe: "I who in the past hundred years have made so many discoveries, even of things unknown to the ancients – new seas, new lands, new species of men, new constellations; with Spanish help I have found and conquered what amounts to a New World. But great as these things are, the moment the thought of war arises, the better arts of life fall silent, and I am wrapped in flame and rent asunder. Save me from more of this: honour the arts of peace, letters and industry; and you will be rewarded by the grateful memory of mankind".' He ends with the plea, 'Do but listen to the sacred voice of Europe.'[15]

Mother Europe with a sacred voice: to an age that liked to have pictorial images of abstractions, whether it was Architecture, or Commerce, or Theology, or a Continent, how would Europe have looked to the mind's eye?

It was the only continent whose name was linked to a Greek myth. Europa was the daughter of Agenor, King of the Levantine city of Tyre. One day Jupiter, who from Olympus had noted her charms, swam ashore in the form of a white bull when she was whiling away the time with the young women of her entourage. The attraction was immediate (though the encounter was later sensationalized as a rape). The story was paraphrased in the late 1470s by the Florentine scholar-poet Angelo Poliziano, describing the relief sculptures beside the door of an imagined palace of Venus.

> On the other side of the door, Jove, transformed for love into a handsome white bull, is seen carrying off his sweet rich treasure, and she turns her face towards the lost shore with a terrified gesture; in the contrary wind her lovely golden hair plays over her breasts; her garment waves in the wind and blows behind her, one hand grasps his back, the other his horn.
>
> She gathers in her bare feet as if fearing lest the sea wash over her: in such a pose of fear and grief, she seems to call in vain to her dear companions; they, left behind among flowers and leaves, each mournfully cry for Europa. "Europa", the shore resounds, "Europa, come back." The bull swims on, and now and then kisses her feet.[16]

Jove carries her from Asia to Crete. Here he turns into a man, impregnates her, and her progeny, thus divinely sired, become the Europeans and she the tutelary deity of their continent.

Ovid's *Metamorphoses*, the source of this glowing fable, was well known to medieval writers who moralized the story to make it palatable to Christian readers. In the fourth century, Lactantius, an early Christian writer, had tried without much success to cut the legend to size by claiming that the bull was simply the name of a ship. Later, Jove's transformation into the bull was likened to God becoming man in order to be able to carry souls to Paradise, abducting them from sin and paganism. A woodcut in a 1471 treatise on the virginity of Mary shows Europa leaning chastely forward to touch the bull in an idiom that drew on earlier imagery of the virgin and the unicorn. But by the 1550s she is shown on a majolica dish sitting naked on a rock in Crete, with the shore of Tyre in the distance, while the bull firmly parts her legs with his forefoot and Cupid looks approvingly on. The contrast typifies the way in which, in a relatively short time, classical myths regained their original part-magical but also largely human resonance.

There was some hesitation in accepting so frankly pagan a founding myth. A pen-and-ink drawing (*c.* 1512), by the Nuremberg artist Peter Fischer the Younger, added explanatory labels – 'Europa', 'Jove in the form of a bull' – for those to whom the story of the abduction might still be unfamiliar.[17] But already another German, Albrecht Dürer, had caught the Italian habit of revitalizing myth and assuming a familiarity with its subject-matter. Leaving her wailing maidens, Europa, wondering but unfrightened, rides on while 'one hand grasps his back, the other his horn', across a sea peppered with reedy islets and those creatures, satyrs and sea-nymphs, through whom the Greeks had expressed their feelings about natural phenomena.

What a subject this was! Sex, violence, seascape, landscape, beauty and the beast, gestures of alarm and affection, all enriched by analogies with other increasingly popular subjects. Europa's abduction drew on representations of that of Deianira by the centaur Nessus; Europa's cosseting by her companions for what lay ahead took hints from images of the toilette of Venus before meeting Mars or of Bathsheba before obeying the summons of David. Artists rushed with pleasure towards their subject. In every medium, from painting to pottery, relief sculpture to enamel, the story soared on, never more rapturously at one with the spirit of Ovid's poem and the feeling for landscape, colour, climate and female density of beauty than in Titian's supremely

Albrecht Dürer, *The Rape of Europa*, c.1495 (Albertina, Vienna)

confident vision. Appropriately, he painted it for Philip II of Spain whose family dominated almost half of western and central Europe.

Whether Christianized, remythologized, or swept as a sugar-plum into the maw of aesthetic appetite, there is no hint that Europeans actually thought of themselves, or their continent, as owing anything material to this Europa. There were attempts to revive the more respectable medieval legend that the world had been divided between the sons of Noah: after the Flood Shem had populated Africa, Chem Asia, Japhet Europe. In 1561 a formidably intellectual Frenchman, Guillaume Postel, declared that it was indecent to pay homage to an affair between an animal and a woman who was no better than she should be, and suggested that Europe should be renamed, after Japhet, *Japétie*.[18] This had no future. The continent, like the others, had, in this age of revived Latinity, to be feminine. When the late sixteenth-century cosmographer Johann Rauw described the appearance of the continent in words, it was in the form of a woman's body, her head forming the Iberian peninsula, France and Germany her chest, Italy and Denmark

Titian, *The Rape of Europa*, 1559–62 (Isabella Stewart Gardner Museum, Boston, Mass.)

her arms, the other countries filling the rest of her legless torso[19]; and it was thus that Europe was represented in a map illustrating the work of a contemporary geographical enthusiast, Sebastian Münster. With the continent wrenched into female shape, Queen Europa's crowned head is Spain and Portugal (ruled jointly by Philip II from 1580), Sicily is the orb she holds in her right hand, the British Isles flutter from the sceptre she holds in her left.

This somewhat bizarre anthropomorphism had been influenced by another tradition of personifying Europe as a woman. While the mythological Europa became increasingly abducted back into her own, personal story, a regal and less romantic figure had risen to take her place. The two coexist in a particularly delightful painted Austrian stucco relief of the 1580s: Europa sits on the bull, but rides it as an armed empress in tranquil triumph. Ortelius, in 1570, had in the introductory text to his map of Europe, shrugged the mythical Europa impatiently and ingenuously aside: 'why Europe should be so called, or who was the first author of this name, no man as yet has found out.' But on his atlas's title-page of 1572, nonetheless, is a figure of Europe. Sternly she sits on a throne beneath an arbour. In one hand she holds the sceptre of world domination. The other extends over an orb, of globe-like dimensions, marked with the Christian cross. Below, and subservient to her, are three other female characters, a richly clad Asia, a semi-naked Africa, and a nude America holding up a human head as witness to her cannibalism.

For an expensive book dependent on the patronage of the rich as well as fellow scholars who might hope for a complimentary copy, such a display of personifications was shrewd. The realization from the early sixteenth century that America was a separate continent (even

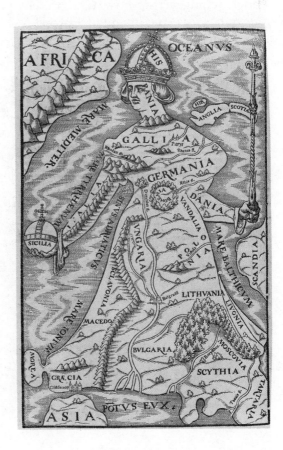

'Queen Europa', from
Sebastian Münster, *Cosmographia*
(Basel, 1588)

if its dimensions remained cartographically uncertain), impugned the
three-continents-only basis of classical authority and, with it, the tinge
of truth that had been accorded to the Jove and Europa story. It also,
save for brilliant eccentrics like Postel, knocked out the children-of-
Noah theory of continental origins. It fed the new taste for sophisticated
entertainments in which European rulers were flattered by actors representing the other continents kneeling in homage to them, as they did
in Antwerp when the city welcomed Philip as the Emperor Charles V's
heir. It was not just that Ovid's abductee lost ground to the more
striking images showing America as a naked lady whose larder was
stocked with human joints, but that an extending world view, based
on political and commercial control, wanted personifications more
congruent with reality. So 'Europe', while remaining feminine, became
a sterner, more *dirigiste* figure, keeping her breasts but losing her poetry.

In the 1603 edition of Cesare Ripa's *Iconologia*, an influential handbook telling artists how to represent personifications, allegories and
abstract ideas, the image of Europe is described as follows. She wears

Europa triumphant seated on the Bull, Hans Mont, painted stucco relief, 1580s (Butschowitz
Castle, Germany)

Europe enthroned, titlepage of
Abraham Ortelius, *Theatrum Orbis
Terrarum* (Antwerp, 1572)

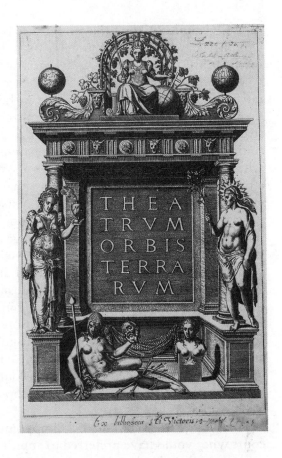

a crown 'to show that Europe has always been the leader and queen of the whole world'. Two spilling cornucopiae are beside her because 'this part of the world above all others is fertile and abundant in all those products that nature can produce.' In one hand she holds a church to represent the Christian religion, 'the truest, and superior to all others'. She points with her one hand to crowns, sceptres and coronets because 'the greatest and most powerful of the world's rulers are in Europe.' She is surrounded by a horse and weapons, wisdom's owl, and books and musical instruments because Europe 'has always been superior to other parts of the world in arms, letters and all the liberal arts'.

Now Ripa does end by saying that Europe 'took its name from Europa, daughter of Agenor King of Phoenicia, abducted and taken to the island of Crete by Jove'. But of far greater influence on his description was Strabo, whom he cites, and whose *Geography* of *c.* AD 10 was carefully studied in the fifteenth century by, among others, Christopher Columbus, who was encouraged by it to believe that Asia could be reached directly by sailing westwards across the Atlantic.

While Strabo is best known for his encouragement to overseas exploration, his influence was also great in helping Europeans to think of their continent, in spite of its smaller size, as superior to the others. He stressed its range of micro-climates and their products, its greater concentration of towns and cities, and its inhabitants' orderly, law-obeying life whether in peace or war. Seeing Europe through pre-Christian eyes at a time of new and intense respect for the authors of classical antiquity, encouraged a secular, pragmatic view of its human and natural resources. It was this that now encouraged the topographical, anthropological and historical 'Discovery of Europe' which gave Europeans the high ground of information from which they surveyed the larger, but lesser known continents with a fairly generally shared disdain.

Here, again, is Ortelius, in the English version of his atlas of 1570, *The Representation of the Lands of the World* (*Theatrum Orbis Terrarum*). Europe, with its temperate climate and fruitful soil, 'is so pleasant and so beautiful with stately cities, townes and villages, that for the courage and valour of the people and severall nations, although it be less in quantitie and circuit, yet might it be accounted, and indeed of all ancient writers hath it ever beene accounted, superiour unto the other parts of the world'.[20]

So, though possibly to the disappointment of those ladies of the court who would have preferred to appear in eastern silks and perfumes or with bodies dyed and bared to represent the rich suns of Africa or the athletic man-hunting of America, the chief role in tableaux and masques of the continents was played by a white, well-clad and stolidly commanding Europa, and the image of the 'real' Europa, the ravished Asian princess on her yearning mount quietly faded. What lingered was the image of her captor Jove, and Jupiter became for astrologers the dominant sign of Europe. It was under his planetary influence as law-giver of Olympus and God of gods that Europe's destiny was held to lie. And the nations of Europe were, following this lead, given masculine signs, Mars, Aries, Leo, Sagittarius, and Taurus itself; Europe and its components became associated with strength, with the toughest of the planets as with the most dominant of the continental queens. Was it not to Europe, and the peoples who comprised it, that the other continents, including the vast and astonishing *trouvaille* America, were being forced to bow?

Yet it was to be maps, far more than planets or images of queens, that helped to disseminate the idea that those who lived in Europe were Europeans. It was maps that made the Flemish diplomat Ogier Ghiselin de Busbecq, when he reached Constantinople in 1554, ignore the idea of Christendom and simply write that the city 'stands in Europe but looks over Asia',[21] and that helped the cartographer Francesco Basilicata in 1612, when commenting on his exquisite map of Crete, to forget the island's association with the beautiful Europa and bluntly describe it as 'on the confines of the three parts of the world, Africa, Asia and Europe'.[22]

THE MAP

The physical nature of Europe could not be assessed until the sixteenth century. Medieval maps of the world, save the most schematic, had contained geographical information but this was subsidiary to a symbolic intent: to remind the viewer that God had created a world represented by a circle of lands whose centre was His own chosen Jerusalem. The circle corralled the three continents within its circumference with little regard for their relative size or, for that matter, for which was which: the maker of the late thirteenth-century Hereford world map wrote 'Europa' across Africa and vice versa. And when, in the later fifteenth century, study of the second-century geographer Ptolemy led to the production of maps, centred on the Indian Ocean, that aimed to portray the world as it had been known to him, what a thin, waif-like extension of Asia was Europe!

Where was there room in this wisp of an image for all those microclimates, those zones of plains and mountains and forests, those cities, that all-round self-sufficiency and superiority to Africa and Asia? For those who saw more and more of them as the printing press reproduced the Ptolomaic maps, they must have seemed as purely symbolic, in their secular mode, as did the Jerusalem-centred ones.

But from the early sixteenth century, thanks to a new mathematical interest in cartographical projections that could take account of the curvature of the earth, more accurate assessments of degrees of latitude, and to the challenge of ever-expanding knowledge of the world's surface, the cartography of Europe began to enable Europeans to imagine, believably, the geographical space in which they lived. There was a succession of maps devoted to the continent that had the effect, when absorbed into world maps, of making it at least appear thicker, spatially more weighty, no longer so negligible an appendix of Asia.

Cartography in the sixteenth century became, indeed, almost a craze. The number of professional surveyor-mapmakers grew and was joined by amateurs fired by an interest in recording topographical facts in a graphic form recognizable to and usable by others. Landlords wanted estate maps, governments administrative ones for purposes of tax and toll control and the plotting of roads and canals, defensive fortifications and troop assembly points.

Statesmen used them for strategic purposes. Monarchs commissioned them as symbols of power. All over Europe they became part of the mental furniture of educated men: indeed, of their actual furniture, framed and hung, painted on walls, woven into tapestries, whole collections rolled or folded in chests and on shelves. The intuitive vision of Leonardo da Vinci which enabled him (during his employment by Florence in 1503–4 on a project to divert the river Arno from the rebel

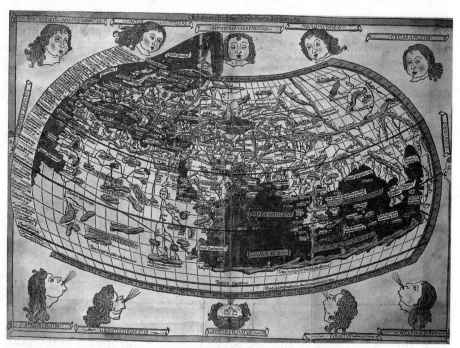

World map, in Ptolemy, *Atlas*, Ulm, 1482 (British Library)

Jan de Hervy, *View on the Zwin*, 1561 (Stedelijk Museum, Bruges)

port of Pisa) to transfer the information he had gained on the ground
to the viewpoint of an observer hovering over it like an eagle, became
something that could be learned.

Triangulation by means of compass, plane table and sight rule (the
alidade), became commonplace, with numerous illustrated handbooks
to enable amateurs to do it themselves. From hilltops and church
towers, or towing measuring wheels along the roads, the recording of
Europe's surface passed into the hands of hundreds of surveyors, highly
skilled or merely enthusiastic. Distance scales began to be incorporated into maps. Symbols for towns, cities, castles, river-crossings made
them easier to read.

The interest and trust in local maps is made clear by Shakespeare's
Hotspur. Poring over the map with his fellow conspirators against the
crown he exclaims:

> Methinks my moiety, north from Burton here,
> In quantity equals not one of yours:
> See how this river [the Trent] comes me cranking in,
> And cuts me from the best of all my land.

He proposes altering its course so that:

> It shall not wind with such a deep indent,
> To rob me of so rich a bottom here.

To which Glendower sensibly and bluntly replies:

> Not wind? it shall, it must; you see it doth.[23]

Headwaters of the river Arno, Leonardo da Vinci, drawing, *c.*1504 (HM The Queen, Windsor, no. 12277)

By then Christopher Saxton had in 1579 completed the first national compilation of regional maps. In 1602 George Owen in his *Description of Pembrokeshire* wrote of such maps that they 'are usual with all noblemen and gentlemen, and daily perused by them for their better instruction of the estate of this realm'.[24] If representations of the world, constantly adjusted to take account of new adventures and discoveries in the previously unknown, form the poetic, epic constituent of cartography, regional and national maps formed the rich prose of a Europe that was even more fascinatedly discovering itself.

In 1511 Martin Waldseemüller produced the first map of Europe that was independent both of the Jerusalem and Ptolemaic traditions. It was reissued in 1520 and soon followed by others, which in 1554 culminated in the five-foot engraved *Europe* of the Flemish mathematician and cartographer Gerardus Mercator.

Here, in the largest representation to that time of any continent, was a believably triumphalist Europe, with its plains, forests and mountain chains clearly marked, and so crammed with towns and cities that southern looked as urbanized as was northern Italy, Hungary as France,

Portugal as the Netherlands. Here at last was the Strabonic continent, stuffed with those natural resources and man-made centres of activity, that was – however small it still looked on world maps – subordinating the rest of the globe to its energies. It underlies the magnificent call of Marlowe's dying Tamburlaine:

> Give me a Map: then let me see how much
> Is left for me to conquer all the world![25]

This appearance of verisimilitude grew from the proliferation of the regional maps that were digested into the continental ones. These had begun as self-proclaimed 'new maps' interleaving late fifteenth-century and early sixteenth-century editions of Ptolemy's *Geography*.

By 1570 they had become so accurate and expressive of national

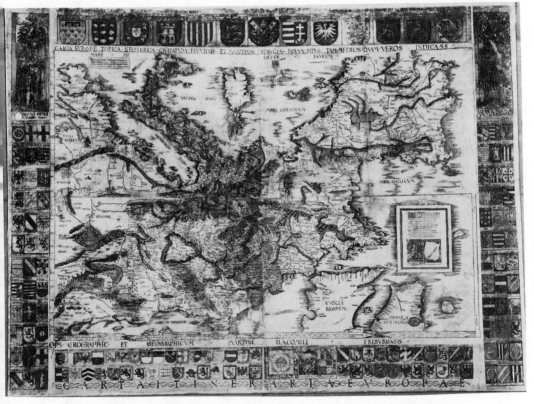

Europe, impression of 1520 after Martin Waldseemüller, *Carta Itineraria Europe* (1511)

pride that the idea of the atlas was born: Ortelius's *Theatrum* printed, in a common format, fifty-three maps, most of them of parts of Europe. It was an expensive work, probably the most costly of all books published in the sixteenth century. But its success – forty editions before the century's end – stimulated competitors who sensed a market for cheaper works solely concerned with European maps, like Mathias Quadt's *Atlas of Europe*, which was published in a smaller format in 1594 and which contained, as well as a map of Europe as a whole, fifty national and regional maps from which only Russia, Norway and Ireland were missing.

In spite of the prominence subsequently accorded to the political roles played by Italy, Spain, France and England during the sixteenth century neither atlases nor maps showed a Europe biased towards the West. Devoid of indications of national frontiers until late in the century, they were not devised to be read politically. And the busily even spread of town names did not suggest that western had any greater weight of economic vitality than eastern Europe. This even-handed appearance of uniformity owed something to cartographers' *horror vacui*, but more to their places of work and the networks of correspondents and regional map-makers radiating from them. The earlier maps of Europe were produced at Basel and Strasbourg in the upper Rhineland, and at Ingolstadt on the Bavarian Danube. Then, from the mid-sixteenth century, the production of maps and atlases of Europe moved down the Rhine to Cologne and to the establishments of Mercator and Ortelius in, respectively, Louvain and Antwerp. Though these centres took increasing note of the local maps that were now being produced in France, England and, to a lesser extent, Spain and Portugal, they were still within the traditional boundaries of the Empire, with its political reach towards the Low Countries, and Hungary, Bohemia, Poland and Lithuania in the East, and its economic interests in the Baltic; their atlases thickened with updated maps of these areas. In spite of the dramatic power games among the countries of the West, cartographic Europe retained an even deployment of information across the continental board.

Neither cartographers nor traders thought of Europe as comprising an 'advanced' Mediterranean and a 'backward' Baltic, or a politically and economically sophisticated Atlantic West and a marginally relevant East. The North Sea–Baltic maritime zone was as active as the Mediterranean, its southern coast leading through trading filaments into the rest of Europe, its ports linked by the merchant communities of the

Central and eastern Europe, 'modern' map by Barnard Wapowsky (?), after a lost original
by Cusanus, in Ptolemy, *Geographia* (Rome, 1507)

Hanseatic League whose guildhalls and major private houses shared a
recognizably similar architectural form, multi-storied and gabled, and
whose business language was a fluent jargon drawing on a common
Germanic rather than Romance base. If Mediterranean commerce was
largely concerned with expensive luxuries, its northern equivalent was
preoccupied with necessities that produced a lower profit for their
weight but supplied a larger market: timber for ships and houses, fish
for salting, seal-oil for lamps and soaps, hemp for ropes, tar for caulk-
ing, cereals and cattle drawn from low-waged hinterlands, as well as
some luxuries that were necessities to the reasonably well-off – furs to
protect against the cold, wild honey as a sweetening agent. At the end of
the fifteenth century some 200 vessels rounded the Danish promontory
every year; by the end of the sixteenth there were almost 2,000.

In 1535–6, Lübeck, the most aggressive and successful of the Hansa cities, was defeated by the combined naval forces of Norway, Denmark, Sweden and Prussia. It was the end of the Hansa's political role but the beginning of a still wider international interest in Baltic affairs. English and Dutch vessels began to take Hansa products into the Mediterranean. South German merchant dynasties, like the Fuggers, took over the direction of much Hansa commercial organization; Genoese banks established branches in Hansa ports. Swedish-Muscovite rivalry for Estonia and Livonia led to campaigns (for example the Nordic Seven Years War of 1563–70) that aroused more general interest than had the earlier conflicts amongst rulers in the Scandinavian North. The treaty of 1569 which linked Poland and Lithuania, and the desire of both to use their sparsely-harboured coastlines as trade outlets and to cut back Muscovy's desire to use Livonia for the same purpose, provided yet another element that drew attention to the North. Cartography was well prepared for the owners of maps to follow the astonishing achievement of Gustavus Adolphus and his industrialist advisers when, from 1630, they made of a previously backward and rural Sweden a major protagonist in that most Europe-wide of conflicts, the Thirty Years War.

Even-handed coverage provided, too, a context for keeping abreast of a shift in political interest towards central Europe. When in 1556 the Emperor Charles V, ailing and preoccupied with Spain, its American possessions and the Netherlands, relinquished to his brother Ferdinand and his heirs his title to the old imperial heartlands of Germany, Austria, most of modern Czechoslovakia and part of Hungary, the broken dream of a Germanic Holy Roman Empire took form again. Bohemia reconfirmed its old cultural identity. Its inhabitants became at last true 'Bohemians', confidently seeking out contacts in foreign capitals and universities. When Ferdinand's grandson, Rudolf II, chose Prague rather than Vienna as the imperial capital and made it the centre to which European intellectual and artistic talent most readily turned in the later sixteenth century, Europe was further adjusted to the evenly-spread coverage anticipated by the cartographers.

This congruence was helped, too, by the new stature of Poland. The union with Lithuania in 1569 made it the largest state in Europe. Its towns remained far-spaced and small, its central administration only shakily effective in making the union a unification. Little progress was made in binding together urban populations and rural communities dominated by rural landlords. There were ethnic minorities – Germans and Jews from the West, refugees from the Turkish-occupied lands to

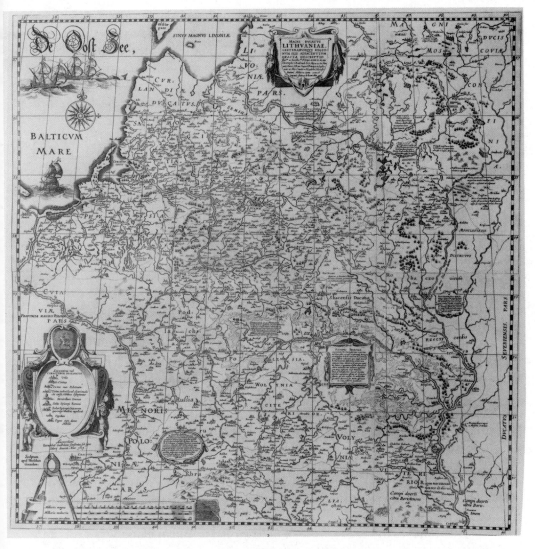

The Duchy of Lithuania, from Mikolaj Krzysztof Radziwill, *Magni Ducatus Lithuaniae* (Amsterdam, 1613)

the South and from the constantly pillaged Ukrainian lands to the East – and a warily coexisting hodge-podge of religions: Catholic, Lutheran, Jewish, Armenian and Russian Orthodox. But though seething with inner contradictions, Poland was seen from the outside as an entity to be traded and negotiated with. The use of German and Latin as the languages of diplomacy, the elective nature of the monarchy which brought French, Transylvanian and Swedish monarchs to the throne in the last decades of the sixteenth century, together with the compulsive itinerancy of Poles of good family to Germany and Italy and the corresponding resort of western Europeans to the court based on Cracow (and from 1569 on Warsaw), bound Poland firmly into the fabric of Europe.

This was not just because it was, as the inscription on a triumphal arch celebrating the election in 1573 of Henri de Valois (soon to be brought home as King Henri III of France) put it: 'Poland, Most Steadfast Fortress for the whole of Europe against the Barbarian Peoples'.[26] Lithuania, which retained the title of Duchy after the union, may have been economically more backward (as disgruntled travellers were quick to note), politically and socially more anarchic, and almost lacking in that concern for the affairs of central and western Europe that was so characteristic of the Poles. But it, too, was seen as a steadfast fortress, not so much against the Turks and Crimean Tartars but against those other westward-pressing 'barbarians', the peoples of Russia, from the Muscovite heartlands around the capital to the semi-independent Cossacks of the South. It was the interest stimulated by this European role that prompted the production of such masterpieces of devoted cartography as Mikolaj Radziwill's *Duchy of Lithuania* of 1613.

No similarly accurate and detailed map could have been made of the vast uncertainties of what 'Russia' meant. In one of the great sagas of sixteenth-century expansion, comparable to Spain's conquests in central and southern America, Muscovy had unevenly exerted its control over the northern territories between the White and Kara Seas and was pushing deep into Siberia, while a more profitable drive southwards along the Don to the Black Sea and the Volga to the Caspian brought it into contact with some of the major Asian trade routes.

These drives into Asia were of no concern to Europeans. What forced them to take notice of Russia were the westward campaigns into Livonia and Estonia which prompted Lithuanian and Swedish counterattacks. These were the aggressions by which Russia forced itself into the fretful congeries of nations which saw themselves as truly European, and raised the alarming spectre of Baltic and eastern Europe being swamped by its inexhaustible hordes. It was an alarmist fear. Russia's driving force was subdued by Ivan IV the Terrible's purges among his own warrior leaders and further emasculated by the succession crises that followed Boris Godunov's death in 1605. In 1617 Russia accepted its being barred from access to the Baltic. Yet the spectre once raised did not go away. It was reinforced by travellers' accounts of Russians' 'Asiatic' appearance – imported Persian clothing, Turkish weapons and women's garish cosmetics, their hair-trigger violence and their kow-towing devotion to the tsars, and by the tsars' own claims to be rulers of 'all the Russias', some of which 'Russias' included populations which had long been absorbed into Poland-Lithuania and had never been subject to 'Greater Russia', the Grand Duchy of Muscovy. It was here – on matters of ethnography – that the preparedness of maps to offer a context for political developments broke down; it was not that nearer Russia was *terra incognita*. Hansa merchants had known parts of it well, especially before Ivan III swept them from their eastern headquarters, Novgorod, in 1478, though no Hansa document so well conveys the strangeness of their most distant customers as does the image of a Russian merchant that hung in their guildhouse there.

Before 1500 Muscovy had received the Italian architects who designed the Kremlin, the German and Bohemian soldiers and gun-founders who made possible the conquests of populations which had courage and fine horses but no firearms, and embassies from Venice and Rome, Denmark and Sweden. The most influential description of Muscovy published in the sixteenth century, the *Commentary on Muscovite Affairs* of 1549 by Sigismund von Herberstein, was based on two embassies undertaken for imperial Germany in 1517 and 1526. Dedicating it to Ferdinand of Habsburg, he said that while he knew Hungary, Poland and Turkey, he would not write about them, for they were well known, but only about the 'habits of the Russians, which have not been brought before the knowledge of the present age'.[27]

Even nomenclature remained uncertain. The royal charter of 1555 which established the English trading company of 'the Merchants of Russia' was commonly known by its own members as 'the Muscovy Company'. In 1591 Giles Fletcher, Elizabeth's ambassador to Ivan IV, explained that Moscow was so conspicuously the centre of commerce and administration 'that not only the province but the whole country of Russia is termed by some by the name of Moscovia, the metropolite city'.[28] It was a clearer definition than most European visitors or commentators managed.

It was accepted nonetheless that classical geographers had been right; 'the very famous river the Don', Herberstein wrote, 'divides Europe from Asia.'[29] The French geographer-cartographer Antoine du Pinet was of the same mind. In 1564 he placed 'the great river the "Donk" '

Russian merchant, from coat of arms of Hansa
Merchants' Guildhouse, Novgorod (Museum für
Kunst und Geschichte, Lübeck)

as 'the boundary of Europe'.[30] But northwards of the main current of
the Don antiquity had fallen silent and contemporary cartographers
were confused. Above all: was Moscow in Europe? For some, who
drew a fairly straight line from where the Don entered the Black Sea
at Rostov and up through Nijni Novgorod to Muscovy's access to the
White Sea and the Arctic Ocean at Archangel, the answer was yes.
To others, as bewildered as were the cartographers themselves by the
problem of plotting northern distances as their longitudinal lines rushed
narrowingly towards the North Pole, it was no. Richard Eden, the
mid-sixteenth-century English collector, translator and publisher of
travel accounts, was adamant: 'if a right [i.e. straight] line be drawne
from the mouthes of Tanais [the Don] to the sprynges of the same,
Moscovia shall be found in Asia, and not in Europe.'[31] Even Ortelius
was rattled by this problem. His map of Russia, based on amateur
evidence (for Russia had no trained map-makers and visitors were
allowed only restricted freedom of movement) had its bias summed up

by an inserted representation of the Czar as a nomadic Asian potentate.

Shortage of cartographic information helped to sustain an emotional distaste for the savage manners of a people who claimed to be Christian but whose priests neither looked nor behaved as such in the eyes of those Europeans who felt themselves to be truly on the map. Like the Irish, save to the few who had access to late Elizabethan military maps of the island, Russians were left in the wings of the cartographic *Theatrum*.

For maps had become for the first time the spur to a rationally grasped personal location within a clearly defined continental expanse. And this source of self-orientation on a flat surface was given depth by the parallel development of chorography: the description in words of the topography, antiquities, customs and more recent history of the diverse regions of which Europe was composed.

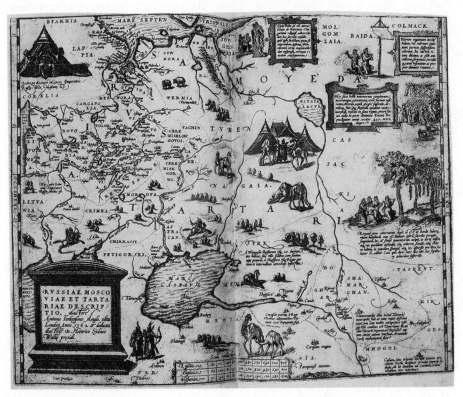

Map of Russia, in Abraham Ortelius, *Theatrum Orbis Terrarum* (Antwerp, 1572)

THE PARTS AND THE WHOLE

Ortelius explained that one of the reasons for publishing his atlas was
that every European wants to see a map of his own country 'for the love
that he beareth to his native soile'.[32] Dedicating his prose description of
England, the *Itinerary*, to Henry VIII in 1546, the antiquarian topogra-
pher John Leland had made a similar point. Having soaked himself in
'many good authors' and a 'full hundred chroniclers', he wrote, 'I was
totally inflamed with a love to see thoroughly all those parts of this
your opulent realm that I had read of'; as a result, he continued, 'I
have travelled in your dominions both by the sea coasts and the middle
parts, sparing neither labour nor costs, by the space of these six years
past, [so] that there is almost neither cape nor bay, haven, creek or
pier, river or confluence of rivers, beaches, washes, lakes, meres, fenny
waters, mountains, valleys, moors, heaths, forests, woods, cities,
boroughs, castles, principal manor places, monasteries and colleges,
but I have seen them, and noted in so doing a whole world of things
very memorable.'[33]

Leland wonderfully conveys the mood of fascination and determination that underlays the European chorographic movement. Some
chorographies started out boldly as cosmographies, universal descriptions, or, more modestly, as European ones, but what really interested
their writers was a microcosmic view of 'a whole world of things
very memorable', a world, that is, explored in terms of an extended
neighbourhood. Most of their works were concerned with areas that
they could cover on foot or horseback or by boat, with the help of
like-minded correspondents with relevant local knowledge to impart.
Chorographies were the colourful tesserae of regional self-discovery
which contributed to the mosaic of a Europe that cartographers were
enabling to be imagined as a whole.

The printing press offered a widening audience. A heightened prosperity increased the interest of the bustle and the allure of descriptions
of cities, and made the contrasts between them and the diurnal tasks
of the countryside more intriguing. The new cartography gave the
writer's eye a brighter focus. A more coherent sense of patriotism
played its part; 'Austria has no equal among the nations,' declared
Johann Cuspinian in his *Description of the Territory of Austria* of 1553.[34]
And patriotism was closely connected with the cult of classical antiquity

which encouraged writers to dig through their recent and medieval past to reveal that their country, too, had been part of Rome's magnificent outreach.

Germans, jealously aware of the wealth of *fora* and amphitheatres, temples and arches that supported Italian pride, emphasized the acknowledgement by Tacitus of their ancestors' valour. French writers, not content with the Roman remains near Avignon and at Orange, pointed to the sterling character of the Gauls as revealed in Caesar's *Commentaries*. Lithuanian writers went so far as to claim that they were descended from a boat-load of Roman legionaries blown away by a storm in the North Sea from Caesar's forces directed against England. Russians asserted that the tsars were descended from the brother of the Emperor Augustus. While maps encouraged a wide-ranging 'flat' view, and patriotism a deeper search into medieval precedents for self-esteem, the quest for a Roman past plunged the chorographers into the deepest search of all. It is from these three levels of inquiry that their works acquired their descriptive density. All came together at their most sophisticated in William Camden's *Britannia*, published in Latin in 1586 in

View of Florence, detail from Francesco Botticini's (attrib.) *Assumption of the Virgin*, *c.*1475–6 (National Gallery, London)

earnest of its author's conviction that the time had come to present Europe with a model national historical survey.

But the chorographic approach was also assimilated into more popular literary forms, such as a cobbled-together, fitfully incandescent play by the widely-travelled and feckless Elizabethan writer-of-all-work Robert Greene. His *Friar Bacon and Friar Bungay* was performed shortly before his pauper's death in 1592. It was quickly revived, printed and reprinted. Set geographically in Oxford and Suffolk, places which evoked feelings about contemporary town and country life, and historically in the time of Henry III, it makes much play with the familiar legend that Britain derived its name from Brutus of Troy, an emigré from pre-Roman times. To celebrate Henry's triumphant marriage to Eleanor of Provence, come all 'the western potentates of might', the 'glorious commanders of Europa's love' to celebrate 'The strand that gladded wandering Brute to see.' 'Thus', states Henry, summing up the island's classical foundation, political range and fruitful union of town and (through the sub-plot) country, 'glories England over all the West'.[35]

A conspicuous tendency of the chorographer was an extended and fulsome description of the capital city of his region, drawing on an earlier tradition of writing in praise of cities: in his *Panegyric of the City of Florence* (1403–4) Leonardo Bruni had asked, 'what in the whole world is so splendid and magnificent as the architecture of Florence? Indeed I feel sorry for other cities when a comparison is made with Florence.'[36] This tone recurred frequently, as when in 1505 Jakob Wimpheling in his Alsatian chorography turned to Strasbourg. Of its cathedral he wrote, 'I would say that there is nothing more magnificent on the face of the earth than this edifice. Who can admire this tower sufficiently? Who can adequately praise it? With its stone tracery, its sculptured columns, its carved statues which describe so many things, it exceeds all buildings in Europe in beauty.'[37]

With changes in artistic and surveying techniques, and the growing demand for topographical realism, representations of cities were no longer imprecise or, as in Hartmann Schedel's *World Chronicle* of 1493, interchangeable.

Francesco Rosselli's 1470s bird's-eye view of Florence reflects the new seriousness of approach in showing the artist actually at work on it. Jacopo de' Barbari's astonishingly detailed view of Venice boldly flourishes the date 'MD' to show that this is how the city actually looked – almost house by house – in 1500. In 1515 came the first

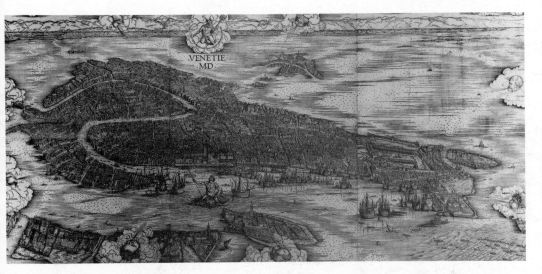

Bird's-eye View of Venice, woodcut, Jacopo de' Barbari, 1500 (British Museum)

meticulous representation of a northern city, Antwerp. From the view of Augsburg in 1521 every citizen or suburbanite could pick out his own home and garden while basking in the importance accorded to his city as a whole.

Townscapes came to encourage a broader sense of civic pride. Hans Mielich's woodcut, three metres broad, of Charles V's encampment outside the walls of Ingolstadt in 1549 linked the city to its role within the empire, and once more the artist showed himself at work, at his viewpoint from the tower of the Frauenkirche, in order to emphasize that this was a historical record.

Rulers commissioned rows of townscapes to impress visitors with the range of their authority. Philip II of Spain paid the Netherlandish topographical artist, Anton van den Wyngaerde, from 1563, to draw views of sixty-two Spanish cities throughout the peninsula. From 1575 he sent out agents from Madrid with standard questionnaires to gather information about more than 600 Castilian towns that would form a Domesday Book for the whole of Spain. From 1577 orders were sent to every town in Spanish-occupied America to 'describe the site and state the situation of the said town'. The authorities were to indicate 'if it lies high, or low in a plain, and give a plan or coloured painting showing the streets, squares and other places'.[38] None of these projects

View of Antwerp, 1515, engraving (City Archives, Antwerp)

was completed, but their scope reflects the influence of chorography
on administrative record-keeping and strategic aims.

More novel than the emphasis on towns and on information that
had a patriotic relevance (where a king had hunted, where a local saint's
relics were preserved), was a curiosity about the customs of out-of-the-
way places. In 1517 Lauren Vital noted that in parts of the northern
Spanish province of Asturias women's headdresses resembled 'the
things with which men make children'.[39] In his description of Prussian
Pomerania Thomas Kantzow in the 1530s described how vines grew
in the lowlands through which the Vistula flowed 'but the inhabitants
are so shiftless that they refuse to go to the trouble of cultivating them'.
On the other hand, in winter when the mouth of the Oder was frozen,
the indefatigable local fishermen 'cut large holes in the ice and push
the net under water with poles, drawing it back and forth'.[40] Another
writer was intrigued to learn that at Cannstadt (a small town near
Stuttgart) 'every year they have a feast called The Day of the Homely;
whoever is judged the ugliest man wins a new suit . . . and the ungainl-
iest of the women wins a girdle, a pair of gloves and other things.'[41]
As they roamed, observed and listened, the chorographers pioneered
a regional ethnography that allowed Europeans to see themselves, and
that helped others to shape descriptions of the peoples overseas with

whom Europeans were increasingly having to come to terms, and whose nature could not easily be described in traditional historical and antiquarian ways.

Regional discovery was little concerned with a political Europe that, save along a few fortified stretches of its coasts, was not yet divided by fixed frontiers. In the East, from the undrained Lithuanian marshlands to the buffer zone – some two hundred miles wide in Hungary – between full Imperial and Turkish control, though men knew which 'side' they were on, neither they nor map-makers thought in terms of fences and customs barriers. Even in the West, where political nations rubbed against one another more closely, the unbending term 'frontier' was seldom used; the words 'confines', 'borders', 'boundaries' were preferred since their vagueness allowed some elasticity for future conquests or territorial trade-offs.

There was little sense either that geographical features, save the sea, were natural frontiers. No two countries were content to be separated by a river, so natural was the bond between its banks at a time of bad roads and comparatively cheap water transport. Mountain ranges existed to be crossed, though their passes might be held on both sides. There was, however, a notion that the limits of a spoken language formed a frontier. When Michel de Montaigne travelled south from the Tyrol he spoke not of entering Italy but of entering 'the Italian language'.[42] When Henri IV seized parts of Savoy in 1601 he informed their inhabitants that 'it stands to reason that since your native tongue is French, you should be subjects of the King of France'.[43] Politically this was the frailest of arguments, for everyone knew that only historical circumstances had determined political boundaries, and that circumstances could change.

Borders, whether between England and Scotland, France and Spain and Germany, Venice and the Tyrol, were in any case porous. There were language spill-overs, jurisdictional enclaves on the 'other' side, territorial claims long-argued and unsettled. Border disputes filled lawyers' pockets, and gave rise, as in Venice, to permanent governmental bodies responsible for settling them. These deeply felt squabbles stimulated local surveying, but they made cartographers wary of incising fixed frontier lines into their copperplates, and it was only gradually that they were emboldened to add them to maps of Europe as a whole.

The compilers of maps in atlases accepted the conventions used by the cartographers with whom they corresponded, some of whom used dotted lines to indicate countries or their equivalent administrative

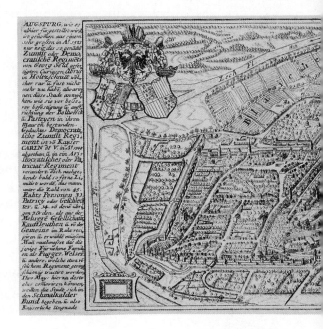

View of Augsburg,
Hans Weiditz after Jörg Seld,
woodcut, 1521
(Maximilianmuseum,
Augsburg)

areas. The revised versions Ortelius published after 1570 included more
of these lines as the convention became more widely established, but
they were more commonly used to indicate regional than political units.
Thus the Anglo-Scottish border was not shown, but English counties
were. Italy has no northern border as a whole but dots indicated the
area of Venice's control around Verona. Quadt's atlas of 1604 was the
first to make dotted country borders a feature, entitling his map of
France, for instance, 'France with its borders (*Grenzen*)'. But their use
was still not consistent, and the dots – themselves a concession to
the unreality of continuously defined 'frontiers' – were inconspicuous.
There were none on his map of Europe as a whole. Colour washes
were fairly commonly used on estate maps or to illustrate disputed
border claims, but in the very rare surviving maps of Europe with
contemporary coloration (in any case, most probably not authorized
by publishers) the washes were not intended to induce a serious reading
of the continent in political terms. They reflected the taste for maps as
decorative objects, or defined broad geographical zones. As late as 1622,
when Henry Peacham discussed the colouring of maps as part of the
education of *The Compleat Gentleman*, it was simply as an aid to remembering where the various countries of Europe were. As such, he wrote,

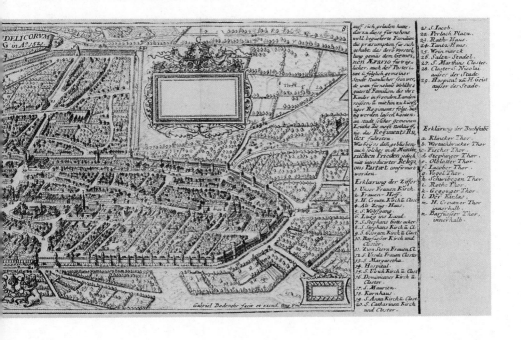

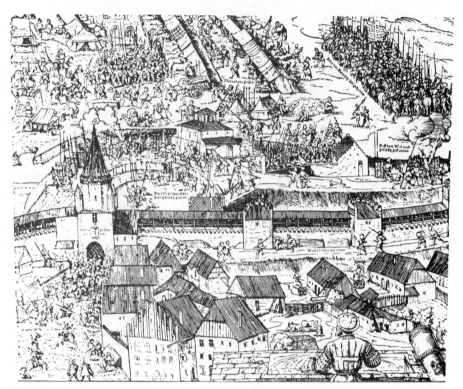

The artist's viewpoint from a church tower: detail from *The Encampment of Charles V at Ingoldstadt*, Hans Mielich, woodcut, 1549 (British Museum)

'in other countries it is the practice of princes . . . also many of our young nobilitie in England.'[44]

Unlike regional or national chorographies, maps played down the fragmentation of Europe and presented images that encouraged a continental point of view. So, gradually, did a number of historical works. During the fifteenth century the medieval chronicle, with its vivid record of local events and characters and its glances elsewhere in search of God's shaping of human destiny, had been joined by a more disciplined form of narrative that concentrated on a country's political development. Machiavelli's *History of Florence* traced the city's constitutional and territorial fortunes from the break-up of the Roman Empire to the death in 1492 of Lorenzo de' Medici, 'the Magnificent'. After that, he commented in the *History*'s closing words, 'there sprang up those fatal seeds which, none knowing how to destroy them, brought, and still bring ruin to Italy.' The leaders in the shift of approach were the Italian independent states. But it was also in Italy that from the late fifteenth century the pounding of invading armies – French, Spanish, German – led to the breaking of parochialism. 'The historical events of our times', wrote Francesco Vettori in the dedication of his *Brief Account of Italian History* (from 1511 to 1527), 'are so closely bound together that you cannot speak of those of Italy alone and omit all the others.'[45] The much more voluminous and thoughtful *History of Italy* by Francesco Guicciardini, another Florentine, but one more closely connected with international affairs as a high-ranking papal administrator, reached far into Europe, indeed, to the New World, to explain the humiliating effects of foreign intervention in the peninsula. Written in the late 1530s it was not published until 1561, but then rapidly found a European market through translations into Latin, French, German, Dutch, Spanish and English. And in the early seventeenth century Niccolò Contarini, confronting the task of writing a history of Venice during his own politically perturbed lifetime, said that he could not do this without bringing in 'many things that happened in Europe' because 'the narration of what happened to men in a single place, without a knowledge of what was happening in others, will always remain unshaded and full of perplexities. But when they are linked to distant events they will be easier to understand and more useful to those who are concerned with such issues.'[46]

'Europe' itself began to appear on the title-pages of historical works. There was a cluster from the mid-sixteenth century: Lodovico Guicciardini's *Commentary on the most notable Events in Europe* (1565), Pier Francesco Giambullari's *History of Europe* (1566), Alfonso Ulloa's *The History of Europe* (1570). It is true that for all of these, 'Europe' was merely a catchword: the first concentrated on the Netherlands, the second ran out in the tenth century, the third could have been more accurately entitled *Some Outstanding recent Military and Political Events within Europe*. There was no integrated history of Europe as it appeared on the map. Still, the acknowledgement that a single country's history was bound up with that of others became more common. The material in the Italian Paolo Giovio's *History of his Times* (1550–2) ranged from Spain and England to Poland and Russia. As one updated edition followed another, the Frenchman Jacques-Auguste de Thou's *History of his own Time* (1604–20) was considered to be as near to a complete coverage of the political and religious links and conflicts of Europe as could be looked for. There was a modest proliferation of books purporting to describe the cities and the governments of Europe as a whole.

They were most of them learned bins into which the author shovelled spadefuls of miscellaneous reading, but as part of the discovery of Europe they have some significance. A few were written by strikingly original minds and were seen as classics over many generations: in 1576 came Jean Bodin's reflections on the nature of governments (*Six Books on the Commonwealth*); Giovanni Botero's *On the Causes of the Greatness of Cities* was published in 1588. There were also thrown-together but useful compilations of leaked ambassadorial reports on countries from England to Sweden like the *Political Treasury*; first published in Italy in 1589, its subsequent editions and translations made it into a textbook for those interested in the background to international affairs. Good, vapid, or downright bad, all these books constituted a radically changed attitude to the continent. From myth and map, chorography, history and survey, Europe passed into the mind.

US AND THEM

Early in the seventeenth century an English collector of travel narratives, Samuel Purchas, made himself the spokesman for the European family of nations: 'Asia yeerely sends us her spices, silkes and gemmes; Africa her gold and ivory; America . . . [is] almost everywhere admitting European colonies.' In every department of life, whether it is the cultivation of the liberal arts or ingenuity in the mechanical ones (like 'the many artificiall mazes and labyrinths in our watches'), the palm goes to 'wee in the West', it belongs to 'us', it is 'ours'.[47] By now Strabo's distant triumphalism had worked its way again into a shared consciousness of separateness and superiority. Squeezed in physically by the alien Turkish lodgement in the south-east, extended imaginatively by increasing contacts with the other 'old' continents, Africa and Asia, and above all by the heady confidence inspired by the discovery of America, Europeans thought harder about their own identity, especially when mere curiosity about the men and manners of other continents came to be accompanied by comparisons – not always comforting – between us and them.

When in his *Utopia* (1516) Thomas More referred to political behaviour 'in Europe . . . and especially in those parts where the faith and religion of Christ prevails',[48] he was accepting that the Ottoman Turks were likely to remain the masters of Greece and the Balkans,

Charles V supported by an
angel and haunted by Sultan
Suleiman, bronze medal,
c.1530 (British Museum)

much of Albania and the whole of Bosnia. By the time Sultan Suleiman
in the 1530s added to his other titles 'Lord of Europe', they had moved
up from Bucharest, Belgrade and Budapest to within a few days' march
of Vienna. There they were held. In a medal struck at about the same
time, the bust of the Emperor Charles V was shown supported by an
angel and haunted by the turbaned profile of Suleiman. That summed
up what was to remain the status quo.

   To counter the Turkish move into Europe the idea of crusade splutt-
ered to life from time to time. But the Christian powers were all
concerned with urgent housekeeping and local enmities. And, in any
case, the late Byzantine Empire in south-eastern Europe, with its curious beards and non-Catholic form of Christianity, had never, save to
scholars of Greek, seemed a natural tenant of the continent. As for the
Holy Land itself, crusading ideas were muted by the realization that
the Turks allowed a reasonably effective tourist service to be run for
pilgrims. Indeed, the confident tolerance which the Ottomans extended
to the other beliefs they absorbed (even if Christian churches within
their domain were not allowed to sound their bells) was one of the
factors that complicated Europe's reaction to them. And as Christian
conquerors increasingly imposed their presence on overseas lands that
did not want them, the more difficult it became to deny the Turk *his*

rights of occupation. The Venetians opted for coexistence. A Franco-Turkish alliance in 1536 was explained by the French King, Francis I, in the following, only partly apologetic terms: 'I cannot deny that I very much want to see the Turk powerful and ready for war, not for his own sake, for he is an infidel and the rest of us are Christians, but to erode the power of the Emperor [Charles V] and involve him in crippling expense.'[49] Thanks to the growing, inward-looking cult of centralizing national power, Erasmus could write in 1530 – and in a book designed to shape the behavioural development of the young – that 'even if the Turk (heaven forbid!) should rule over us, we would be committing a sin if we were to deny him the respect due to Caesar.'[50]

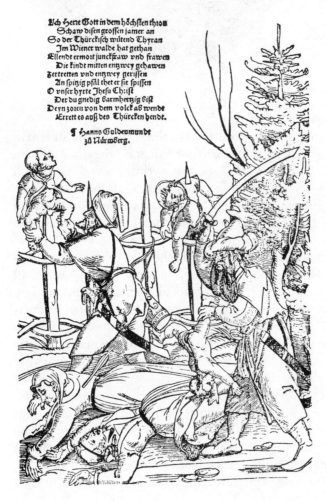

Turkish atrocities, Erhard Schoen, woodcut, 1530

Many talented Christians went to Constantinople and turned Muslim to advance their career prospects, knowing the Sultanate's distrust of promoting its own subjects to positions of military or administrative responsibility, and its need to draw on the more advanced technologies of the West. In 1581 Elizabeth endorsed trading relations with Constantinople through the Turkey Company and supported its successful operations there and in Aleppo. Nonetheless she castigated her unofficial ambassador Edward Barton for accompanying Mahommed III on his war of 1593 against Austria, 'for he had borne the English armes upon his tent . . . in the Turkes campe against Christians'.[51] In the same vein her successor, James I, shrank from the idea of accepting a formal embassy from Constantinople on the grounds that it would be 'unbecoming to a Christian prince'.[52]

In this atmosphere of double-think about Europe's alien, infidel but permanent lodger, two strands of opinion can be isolated. One focused upon monstrous inhumanity; the other on high standards of material well-being. Religion had little to do with either. The Islamic faith, spreading along the North African coast, into Asia Minor and on through the Persian Empire into India, was to most Europeans summed up as the religion of the Turks. And save for propaganda purposes, the Turks were judged as much in terms of behaviour as of belief.

To those who saw the Ottoman Empire from the outside, they were, above all, cruel. What European monarch would have all his brothers strangled – as Mahommed III had all nineteen of his – to prevent any subsequent challenge to his succession? Europeans burned, tortured and maimed: but only the Turks impaled, ramming a pointed stake up the anus and out between the collar-bones regardless of age or sex, and leaving it stuck in the ground with its skewered victim as a warning. Views by German artists of the siege of Vienna in 1529 and later Imperial-Turkish wars peppered the landscape with such writhing figures. Whenever a Turk featured in an English or French play of the later sixteenth century, he appeared laden with dread associations, however facetiously they were deployed.

To those who actually travelled in Turkey, however, this indifference to human suffering, while noticed, was diffused among more positive observations. Unlike the Russians-in-Europe, the Turks appreciated learning, the arts, and civilized comforts. The learning may have been Islamic, the arts unrepresentational, the comforts rejecting chairs and wine, but the style of life was sympathetically sophisticated. More than this, the Turks had lessons to teach Christians. In spite of their tolerance of the views of others, they took the faith and rituals of their own religion with a seriousness that was a reproach to all too many Christians. The Protestant radical Thomas Müntzer went so far in the 1520s as to say that if a devout Turk came to worship in Catholic Europe in search of added grace 'he would gain about as much as a midge could carry on its tail.'[53] The discipline and patient endurance of hardship of Turkish soldiers was often cited in contrast to the behaviour of Christian troops. Streets were filthy but the spotlessness within Turkish houses, the emphasis on personal hygiene, and the cleanliness of clothes and turbans (which provided so many highlights in Carpaccio's narrative paintings) put smelly and infrequently laundered Europeans to shame. A tiny observation made by an Italian visitor to Constantinople in 1614, Pietro della Valle, contrasts the fidgety, self-preening behaviour of Europeans at a grand reception with the decorous stillness that prevailed in Turkey. He notes that 'it seems to them very strange that we should be hurrying about like that, as if on important business, walking from one end of the rooms to another, and then returning, and then going back yet again, either alone or accompanied, with nothing else to do.'[54]

As he moved further east (he was on his way to India), della Valle continued to make comparisons. He contrasted the skilful and unviolent Persian national sport, polo, with brawling ball games like the Florentine *calcio*. The Hindu devotion to their idols 'puts us Christians to shame for the laziness with which we exert ourselves in the cult and service of the true God'.[55] And as trade and missionary work led to a flow of information about China, Joseph Hall, in his *The Discovery of a New World* of 1608, could ask 'who ever expected such wit, such government in China? Such arts, such practice of all cunning [i.e. skill]? We thought learning had dwelled in our part of the world; they laugh at us for it, and well may, avouching that they of all the earth are two-eyed men, the Egyptians the one-eyed, and all the world else, stark blind.'[56] And to move further east still, from St Francis Xavier's first mission to Japan in 1549, Portuguese, Spanish and Italian Jesuits learned the language and tried to grasp the nature of the nine religious sects they identified there in order to argue the Christian case against them. Constantly, in their letters and reports, they compared European with Japanese customs. When defecating, one noticed, 'we sit, they crouch.'[57] 'I am sending you', wrote St Francis to his superiors at home, 'a copy of the Japanese alphabet; their way of writing is very different from ours because they write their lines from the top of the page down to the bottom. I asked Paul [a convert] why they did not write in our way? He explained that as the head of a man is at the top and his feet are at the bottom, so too a man should write from top to bottom.'[58] And as the acquaintanceship deepened, so, along with surprise, did admiration. Writing of Japan later in the century, Alessandro Valignano recorded that the politeness of all classes makes them in this respect 'superior not only to other eastern peoples but also to Europeans as well'. Their children learn more quickly than ours, 'nor do they fight or hit one another like European boys'.[59]

Summing up his impressions, Valignano wrote that 'it may truly be said that Japan is a world the reverse of Europe; everything is so different and opposite that they are like us in practically nothing. So great is the difference in their food, clothing, honours, ceremonies, language, management of the household, in their way of negotiating, sitting, building, curing the wounded and sick, teaching and bringing up children, and in everything else, that it can be neither described nor understood. Now all this would not be surprising', he continues in a telling passage, 'if they were like so many barbarians, but what astonishes me is that they behave as very prudent and refined people in all these matters. To see how everything is the reverse of Europe, despite the fact that their ceremonies and customs are so cultivated and founded on reason, causes no little surprise to anyone who understands such things.'[60]

In contrast to Asia, Africa offered little challenge to reconsider the nature of Europeanness. Startling as was the achievement of Portugal in establishing trade and missionary links with West Africa, pushing across the equator in the teeth of legends about its heat burning men to cinders and, after Vasco da Gama's voyage of 1498, establishing a chain of Indian ocean bases from Mozambique to Mombasa, the European imagination was hardly stirred by information about the native peoples that were encountered. The Portuguese, already in the fourteenth century experienced discoverers and traders (the Madeiras, the Canaries, the Azores), were practical and laconic, all the more so because discussion of their overseas empire was – in the face of potential competition – severely frowned on by government.

An earlier trans-Mediterranean trade in slaves had, however, familiarized southern Europeans with a range of skin colours varying from that of Ethiopians to the paler complexion of trans-Saharan 'Moors'.

The Rialto, showing an African slave rowing a gondola, *c.*1496, detail from Vittore Carpaccio, *Healing of the Possessed Man* (Accademia, Venice)

Africans rowed gondolas for their Venetian employers, added a note of dusky exoticism to north Italian courts, and as servants were treated as pets (and lovers) in wealthy households throughout the northern Mediterranean. (The hero of the early Spanish picaresque novel *Lazarillo de Tormes* (1554) was undismayed when his mother took a negro lover.) Nor were Africans altogether unfamiliar in the North: in 1596 Elizabeth pronounced that there were too many 'blackamoores' competing with needy Englishmen for places as domestic servants.[61] While Portuguese and Spaniards exploited the domestic slave trade in Africa (and blacks had worked on whites' plantations in Madeira and the Canaries well before they were imported to work the mines and cultivate the sugar of the Americas), the shipment of Africans as labourers and military auxiliaries from Peru to Ceylon was scarcely remarked in Europe. Missionaries were uninterested in their transplanted customs and beliefs; Africans were commodity imports, irrelevant to the challenge of saving indigenous souls. Even in Africa itself missionaries took few pains to understand the men and women they hurried into baptism and whose idols they destroyed. Within Europe they were thinly dispersed and subservient. In drama their colour almost automatically established them as evil, even if, among the Magi who came to adore the Christchild on behalf of the continents of the pre-Columbian world, Balthazar was respectfully shown as a negro. Shakespeare's *Othello* was unique in building a sympathetic if alarming character between these extremes. More typical was the tissue-thin concept of Ben Jonson's *Masque of Blackness*, performed at the court of James I in the same year as *Othello*, 1605. In this a courtier representing the River Niger comes to London with his black daughters (wearing black masks, gloves and stockings) to see how – in a representative example of indifference to African geography – the English sun can 'blanch an Ethiop'. Assured that this will undoubtedly happen in the English climate, the River retires happy in the conviction that his daughters will become white and therefore in European and his own ambitious eyes, more beautiful. And as the actresses, the Queen and her ladies, remove their disguises, they do.

Of a quite different order was the intellectual energy devoted to understanding the hitherto unknown Amerindians. Introducing his account of his first voyage in 1492–3, Columbus reminded Ferdinand and Isabella of Spain of the orders they had given him. 'You commanded', he wrote, 'that I should not go to the East by land, by which way it is customary to go, but by the route to the West, by which route we do not know for certain that anyone previously has passed.'[62] While Columbus remained convinced until his death that he had done by sea what Marco Polo had done by land, his East, though still called from habit 'the Indies', rapidly came to be seen for what it was. Lopez de Gómera, dedicating in 1552 his *History of the Indies* to Ferdinand's successor Charles V, hailed the discovery of the 'new' continent as 'the greatest event since the creation of the world, excepting the incarnation and death of Him who created it'.[63] And within the intervening sixty years, Europeans had had to come to terms not only with a new continent but with new men and women. Here was an enormous landmass, unsuspected by ancient geographers, filled with societies covering a great range of organizational sophistication from the Aztecs and the Incas to the Caribs and the Tupinamba.

When the Spaniards struck at the city-building empires of Mexico and Peru they saw them as weaker versions of the empires of Alexander and Augustus, problematic enough in logistic and diplomatic terms, but, because of this analogy, not a radical challenge to rethinking the nature of political societies. Those ancient empires had been overcome. So, now, had these. It was the greater number of apparently more primitive peoples in central and southern America that aroused a crisis of conscience, public debate, and an element of self-scrutiny. Missionaries' consciences were initially troubled by two questions. The first was: do people living in a state of nature have property rights? If they do, do *we* have the right to dispossess and enslave them? The second was: do these people, who seem to live the instinctive lives of animals, have souls? If they do, should we not convert and protect rather than exploit them? This, the first pertinent and passionate discussion of abstract human rights, went on for a generation and more between settlers' needs for labour and priests' concern for potential converts. It was at last resolved in the mid-century in favour of the view that the Amerindian masses were, like their better-armed and more single-minded masters, men with legal rights and souls to save. But by then it was too late to stop a dreadful shrinkage of their numbers due to forced labour, war and the more devious pillage of lives by imported diseases, chiefly sexual and pulmonary, to which there was no native immunity. By then, too, the issue of the status of the native Americans had become naggingly repetitive. Far more interesting to those not personally concerned in its outcome was the continued adventure of the expansion of Spanish control, and its ability to produce the drug which the increasingly hectic monetary system of Europe craved: silver.

Then followed, however, what amounted to a rediscovery of the Amerindians as peoples with conventions, 'ceremonies and customs', of their own. With the Dominicans and Franciscans in America, as with the Jesuits in Japan, ethnographic inquiry was in the interest of conversion. But now it was more patient, less polemical. Instead of bullying converts, through a halting use of their language eked out by gestures, into acknowledging beliefs as weird as their own – a god who was tripartite and could be eaten and drunk by specially garbed intermediaries – languages were properly learned and native religions explored.

'In my case', wrote the historian of the Indies José de Acosta in 1590,

Amerigo Vespucci discovers America, Johannes Stradan, engraving, 1589 (Metropolitan Museum, New York)

'the realities of the Indies seemed after I had had personal experience of them to be both the same as I had heard and not the same. Indeed, I found them to be the same in that those who told me about them had not actually lied about them; but nevertheless I judged them to be very different and unlike what I had first thought.'[64] The same tone was sounded in the life work of the Franciscan Bernardino de Sahagun who from 1529 to his death in 1590 lived in Mexico preaching, teaching and trying to convert. At the same time he familiarized himself, through a disciplined course of reading and a carefully planned programme of interviews, with the language, literature and viewpoints of his enormous spiritual constituency. So great was his involvement with its members that he wrote up his findings first in their own, Nahuatl language in order to tell *them* who they had been and were within their conqueror-battered ex-empire. It was only later that he translated his work back into Spanish – a Quixotry that denied it publication in his lifetime.

As with the earlier struggle to obtain justice for the natives, the effort to understand the nature of the Amerindian societies was so single-minded that it did not throw off comparisons with European ones. That was left to the third, the intellectually weakest, most 'romantic' reaction: the wish to see them not as representatives of a New World but of the oldest world of all, that of the pre-civilized state of all mankind, unselfconscious, spontaneous and peaceful.

In 1589 a charming northern engraving showed Amerigo Vespucci discovering America. A stocky figure, armed but wearing a merchant's hat, Vespucci holds in one hand a banner with the sign of the cross, in the other his navigator's astrolabe. He has just stepped ashore from the pinnace which has brought him from his ship and finds himself immediately confronting a startled naked woman on a hammock. Leaning against one of the trees between which it is slung is her club. Strange animals roam a peaceable and otherwise deserted landscape.

This somewhat comical vision of Amerigo meeting America springs from the historical accident whereby the new lands, first shown as a separate continent in the world map published in 1507 by Martin Waldseemüller, were called – following Martin's own suggestion – not after Columbus, but after Vespucci's later voyages to South America in 1499 and 1501. At the top of this redoubtable enterprise – the map is 2.40 metres wide and composed of twelve woodcut sheets – Ptolemy ruefully considers his outmoded three-continent world and Vespucci holds the dividers which symbolize the division of America from Asia. And that Amerigo-America became conflated and accepted owes much to the irresistible appeal to Martin and others of the sensationally exoticized versions of Vespucci's own descriptions of the peoples of Amazonia and Brazil which were printed in 1504.

We shall see with what nostalgia Europeans looked back to the mythical Golden Age when men lived close to nature without the frets of business or political life, and free from the restrictions of class, laws and moral codes.[65] Akin to this was the idea of an Earthly Paradise, prelapsarianly sinless men living peaceably together with animals on the fruits of a bountiful nature. On 17 August 1498, putting out to sea after investigating the mouths of the Orinoco, Columbus noted in his journal that south of the Venezuelan coast extends 'a great continent where is located the Terrestrial Paradise'.[66]

The Vespucci account catered for a readership avid for myths and marvels and prepared to believe that while these had evaded the investigations of travellers in the old continents they would be encountered in the new. Much was made of the theme that was associated with personifications of America: cannibalism. According to his editors, Vespucci had spoken to a man who had helped to eat three hundred others, had seen salted human hams dangling for future consumption in native huts, and who remarked that it was not just enemies who were eaten but, on occasion, wives and children. The same flair for titillation marked Vespucci's discussion of sexual customs; not only were the women so lubricious that they would offer themselves freely to any male, but they envenomed the penises of their regular partners to make them swell into ever more satisfying proportions.

These were immediately catchy themes, but what most affected Vespucci's more serious readers was that, in spite of these excesses, something like an ideal society did seem to exist there. 'They wear no clothes of wool or linen or cotton because they have no need of them. There is no private property; everything is held in common. With neither king nor magistrate each man is his own master. They have as many sexual partners as they want . . . They have no temples, no religion, worship no idols. What more can I say? They live according to nature'.[67]

And while later in the sixteenth century the missionary ethnographers were realizing that to be primitive was not to be simple, and that underneath an apparently 'natural' way of life were complex religious beliefs, laws and codes of behaviour, enough reports of peaceable,

A West Indian Scene, Jan Mostaert, detail, c. 1540–50 (Frans Hals Museum, Haarlem)

unhierarchical and unmaterialistic ways of life were passed back to prompt comparisons with European ways of life.

Montaigne caught the tone perfectly. In one of the most concentrated of his usually discursive *Essays*, 'Of Coaches', he noted (with French voyages to Canada particularly in mind) that 'our world hath of late discovered another . . . no lesse-large, fully-peopled, all-things-yeelding, and mighty in strength, than ours . . . It is not yet full fifty yeeres that he knew neither letters, nor waight, nor measures, nor apparell, nor corne, nor vines, but was all naked, simply-pure, in Nature's lapp, and lived with such meanes and food as his mother-nurce affoorded him.' But since then, he went on, 'I feere that by our contagion, we shall have directly furthered his declination, and hastened his ruine; and that we shall too dearely have sold him our opinions, our new-fangles and our arts.' Broadening his target, he summed up the extinction of a Golden Age society by the imposition on it of the Iron Age values of his profit-crazed, land-hungry and war-loving fellow Europeans: 'so many goodly citties ransacked and razed; so many nations destroyed and made desolate; so infinite millions of harmlesse people of all sexes, states and ages, massacred, ravaged and put to the sword; and the richest, the fairest and the best part of the world topsiturvied, ruined and defaced for the traffick of pearles and pepper. Oh mechanicall victories, oh base conquest.'[68]

In another essay, 'Of the Caniballes' he commented 'I finde (as farre as I have been informed) there is nothing in that nation that is either barbarous or savage, unless men call that barbarisme which is not common to them.'[69] That note of bitter relativism reflects the collapse of Montaigne's own world within the feuds, from the 1560s, of the French civil wars. For the great majority, however, who did not share Montaigne's interest in the universality of human nature, the inner demons of Europe's commercial, political and religious antipathies came to pull a hood of self-regard over their imagination, enclosing it, despite continuing signals from the outside, within a shared interest in exploring the less disturbing, newly revealed world of classical antiquity and the more immediately relevant investigation of local identities and differences. By 1600 a concern for 'them' had become marginalized by a clamant interest in 'us'.

CHAPTER II

The Countries of Europe

ANTIPATHIES

While the cartographic frame within which men could think of themselves as Europeans became more clearly defined, and while those of
one country came to learn more of those of others through increased
travel and reading, there was a counter-tendency at work: to know was
not necessarily to like. Information opened minds; it also fed prejudices.

Superimposed on the objective map of Europe was a subjective
one of stereotyped national characteristics, swift identifications of folk-
loric pungency, and inherited formulations such as this from the late
medieval Spanish *Poem of Alexander*:

> The people of Spain are vital and active,
> The French we see as bold warriors,
> The English are braggarts with false hearts,
> The Italians [Lombardos] are cowards, the Germans thieves.[1]

This glib psycho-portraiture came from a vein so deep that it continued
to emerge in the writings of well-educated men, whether in the knock-
about mood (1517) of Ulrich von Hutten's 'I send you more salutations
than there are thieves in Poland, heretics in Bohemia, boors in Switzerland . . . pimps in Spain, drunkards in Saxony, harlots in Bamberg,
children of Sodom in Florence,' and so on[2], or in Louis le Roy's summary declaration of 1576 that 'on the whole the Spanish are haughty
. . . the English and Scots proud, the Greeks cautious and subtle, the
Italians wary, the French bold.'[3] An Elizabethan audience in 1596 would
have been well abreast of the spirit in which Portia ran through the list
of her suitors. The Italian – from Naples, that unrivalled nursery of
riding teachers – 'doth nothing but talk of his horse'. The Frenchman
'is every man in no man . . . if I should marry him I should marry

twenty husbands'. The Englishman 'is a proper man's picture; but alas, who can converse with a dumb-show?' The German's weakness is drink, and this permits Portia to end her review with the infallibly effective 'I will do anything, Nerissa, ere I will be married to a *sponge*.'[4]

Even at its most jocular, xenophobic name-calling reflected old fears and fancies: threats to the security of a way of life or to personal self-esteem. The map of stereotypes represented the cartography of insult, and the richness acquired in the Renaissance has been drawn on ever since.

Erasmus, for all his constant itinerancy, was not immune in his early sixteenth-century writings to the generalizing virus: Germans were easy-going and crude, the French violent under a veneer of refinement, the Italians vain and carried deviousness too far. He made Charon declare that he did not mind ferrying Spaniards across the Styx because they were abstemious, but the English were so crammed with food that they nearly sank the boat. Given Erasmus's friendships with men in all these countries, the potency of the stereotypes is clear. But in another vein, he shows how close an observer he genuinely could be. In a treatise of 1530 he is giving advice to the young on decorous behaviour.

> Amongst the Italians, some people out of respect press one foot on the other and almost take the weight on one leg in the manner of storks . . . Likewise in bowing, standards of propriety and impropriety vary from people to people. Some bend each knee equally, and there again, some do so while keeping the body erect, others while bowing slightly. There are those who, considering this to be somewhat effeminate, maintain the erect posture of the body but bend first the right knee and then the left, a gesture which is favoured among the English for the young. The French accompany a measured turn of the body with a bow of the right knee only.[5]

Indeed, it was when considering a single trait or occupation that comparative knowledge acquired about the nations of Europe was most fully – if not fairly – deployed. Portia's gazetteer had been anticipated more crudely in 1536 in Pietro Aretino's *Dialogue in which Nanna teaches her daughter Pippa to be a whore*. Nanna alerts her eager pupil to the differences in behaviour to be expected of her different clients, French, Spanish, German and Swedish as of more local ones (the dialogue is set in Venice) from different parts of Italy.[6] In 1546 the Venetian ambassador to Charles V reported on the dangers to be anticipated from the Emperor's armies in terms of the characteristics of their various components. He was brief about Charles's Netherlandish subjects, because Venice was unlikely to confront them in any numbers. In any case, 'now that the country has become commercial, and is filled with beautiful and luxurious cities, the ancient valour has degenerated.' He is fuller on the Spaniards; given the Spanish occupancy of Milan and Naples they were the most likely to attack the French-inclined Republic.

> The Spanish soldiers are very patient, and from the activity and suppleness of their movements are alert at a skirmish or at the taking of a town. They are quick of apprehension, vigilant and united amongst each other; prone to magnifying their success and to making light of their reverses; courteous in speech and bearing, especially towards their inferiors; temperate and sober; and fond of show in their dress, although they are avaricious and greedy of gain.

He was fullest on the Germans because it was to Germany that Venice most naturally looked to supplement its shrinking recruitment areas in Italy.

> The insolence of this nation is almost incredible. They are impious towards God, and cruel to their neighbour . . . They are fearless of death, but can neither foresee, nor take advantage of any passing occurrence. In the assault of a city, where much skill and dexterity is required, they are the worst people that can be: and in the case of a skirmish their interminable baggage is always in the way. They are most impatient of hunger and thirst, and will insist upon being paid at the appointed moment.[7]

For an example of how automatically rancid national characterizations could become, it is difficult to improve on the warning issued to the hero of Thomas Nashe's novel *The Unfortunate Traveller* of 1594 by an exiled English earl he met in Rome. What is to be learned in France save 'to esteeme of the pox as a pimple', in Spain save to copy a 'ruffe with short strings like the droppings of a man's nose', in Italy save 'the art of atheisme, the art of epicurising, the art of whoring, the art of poysoning, the art of sodomitry', in Holland save how 'to be drunke and snort in the midst of dinner'? 'No', concluded the Earl, 'beleeve me, no bread, no fire, no water doth a man anie good out of his owne countrey.'[8]

Soberer advice was given by the widely experienced Polish diplomat

Christopher Warszewicki a year later in his Latin treatise of 1595, *On Ambassadors and Embassies*. In general, an ambassador must be flexible and able to fit in with any society amongst whom he found himself appointed. All the same, when he turned to special cases, echoes of the stereotypes stray into the imagination of this learned and worldly man.

> The position in Moscow is suited to wary men, for there "the Greek faith" is practised, and nothing can be done without lengthy disputes . . . To Spain, individuals of a calm temperament should be sent . . . In Italy it is right that the state be represented by civilized and courteous men . . . France is a place for versatile men of speedy intellect . . . In England, handsome, high-born envoys are best suited, for the English have great respect for that sort of person, telling them apparently that it is a pity they are not Englishmen themselves. In Germany, diplomats need to keep their promises, the Germans being famed from time immemorial for their constancy and perseverance.[9]

All these strains fed a remarkable work published in 1617 in Paris by the Spanish writer-of-all-work Carlos García. It was designed to urge closer *rapprochement* between France and Spain following the insecure 1598 Peace of Vervins between those century-long antagonists. Part of García's long title acknowledged a root problem: *The Antipathy between the Spanish and French Peoples*.[10] The two greatest powers in Europe, he wrote, being neighbours, were bound to dislike one another but the devil had turned dislike into loathing. They were, after all, different in every possible way.

> The Spanish are bodily so different, and so contrasted with the French that it would be a waste of time to dwell on it, for most Spaniards are small, most Frenchmen tall; the French are blonde, the Spaniards dark; the complexion of the French is pale or rosy, the Spaniards swarthy; the French wear their hair long, the Spaniards short; the French have slim legs, the Spaniard's legs so sturdy that a Spaniard's calf is as thick as a Frenchman's thigh; the French let their beards grow unshaven from one temple round to the other, the Spaniards shave it, leaving only a moustache and a brush under the lip; the French are choleric, the Spaniards patient; the French are sprightly, the Spaniards slow to act; the former are volatile, cheerful and impetuous, the latter are ponderous, sombre and introspective; the French eat a lot, the Spanish little; the French are givers, the Spaniards savers – one could go on comparing the one with the other and find nothing but contraries.

And, in more detailed chapters, he does precisely this, comparing the different ways in which the two peoples walk and hold their bodies, speak, and react to women – the Spaniard committed once and for all in deed and thought, the Frenchman ever the servant of a roving eye.

However elaborate, this is still in the tradition of stereotypes. But García goes further, saying that the differences are so distinct that he had often wished that he had interviewed midwives in both countries to see if anything could be deduced from the ways in which the two nations' babies were delivered. He moves from physique, manners and character to mentality. The French, he says, grasp an intellectual point quickly, and then let it drop. This makes them more practical. The Spanish absorb its inference slowly, but then ponder, enjoying for its own sake a contemplation of its implications. This is why, as any French traveller will bear witness, 'there are few native Spaniards who practise mechanical skills, as weavers, cobblers, tailors' and why, to the distress of travellers, there are so few inn-keepers. 'But for the French to understand something is to turn it to practical advantage; they hate inactivity and thus immerse themselves in all sorts of manufactures.' Similarly, this mental trait makes educated Frenchmen turn to the usefulness of the law rather than to the less practical study of scholastic theology.

Having reached the brink of the impasse he had created for himself, García could see only an effective reconciliation in terms of divine intervention against the devil's divisiveness, supported by a series of marriages between the two ruling families that would at least hold the political front.

A general explanation of why the inhabitants of one country were different from others was picked up and elaborated from the climatological theories of classical geographers. 'There is no help for it', claimed Stefano Guazzo in 1574, 'but you must . . . thinke that every nation, land and countrie, by the nature of the place, the climate of the heaven, and the influence of the starres hath certaine vertues and certaine vices which are proper, naturall, and perpetuall.'[11] This is why, Giovanni Botero elaborated in 1589, 'a Spaniard doubles his energy when he goes into France, while a Frenchman in Spain becomes languid and dainty.' Geographical determinism became so pervasive that it gave a 'scientific' seriousness to the stereotyped attribution of different characters to different nations. Botero's confidence was by then typical:

Those who live in northern countries but not in the extreme north, are bold but lack cunning; southerners on the other hand are cunning but not bold . . . The former are simple and straightforward, the latter sly and artful in their ways. They are as the lion and the fox; whereas the northerner is slow and consistent in his actions, cheerful and subject to Bacchus, the southerner is impetuous and volatile, melancholy and subject to Venus . . . Mountain-dwellers are wild and proud, valley people soft and effeminate. Industry and diligence flourish in barren lands, idleness and refinement in fertile ones.[12]

This facile determinism fed the appetite for giving conduct marks to nationalities. So did the score-card of civilized behaviour. The Florentine Leonardo Bruni, early in the fifteenth century, had congratulated his fellow countryman Poggio Bracciolini on bringing back to Italy a manuscript of Quintilian from a Swiss monastery and thus 'delivered him from his long imprisonment in the dungeons of barbarians'.[13] And as men of letters elsewhere came later in the century to emulate the Italian respect for humanistic, classically based studies, they turned the taunt against their own less enlightened neighbours. This fairly esoteric test became coupled with that of respectable manners. When Erasmus noted in 1530 that it was a custom of the Spaniards to brush their teeth with urine,[14] this apparently gratuitous slur reflected the growing opposition in Spain to his own works and to the liberal Catholicism for which he stood. And throughout the century the Irish (the 'mere' or native Irish as opposed to English settlers) were coupled with the Russians as representing the parts of Europe into which the civilized virtues of decorous manners and rationally organized government had scarcely reached. And between these geographical extremes, the taint of barbarism could be caught and applied to any nation whose ways of life an observer wished to dub crude or backward.

The stereotypes projected upon one nation by others were enriched, too, by more widely discussed economic and political rivalries. In London in 1517 the Evil May Day xenophobic riot involved a two-thousand strong mob assaulting foreigners and looting their shops. Violence on this scale was rare, but ill-feeling continued to surface against real or imagined offences: low-standard price-cutting, the forging of trademarks, the seduction of honest citizens' wives. And on the other hand, foreigners were accused of keeping aloof among those they lived off; 'though they be demized or borne heere amongst us', ran a late sixteenth-century English indictment, 'yett they keepe themselves severed from us in church, in government, in trade, in language and marriage.'[15] But on the whole mercantile communities themselves operated within a system of mutual adjustment, though such generic descriptions of a north Italian merchant as Andrew Boorde's, of towards 1542, 'I am a Lombard and subtyl crafft I have /To decyve a gentleman, a yeman or a knave', added a smear to unfavourable portraits of Italians in general.[16]

Not unnaturally, the propaganda accompanying wars was rich in character assassination. During the Swabian War of 1499 Germans sneeringly referred to their pastoralist (and victorious) Swiss opponents as 'cow-herds' and 'milkers'.[17] A French poem of 1513 managed in a few lines to describe the English, who in that year invaded under Henry VIII, as hideous, loathsome, stinking and reeking tailed toads.[18] During the contemporary Anglo-Scottish war an Englishman brought a suit for defamation against his rector for referring to him as a Scot. In 1536 Thomas Cromwell was warned not to trust the Scots, for 'it is of a devillyshe dysposition of a Scottych man not to love nor favour an Englishe man.'[19] The Elizabethan campaigns in Ireland led to an endemic anti-English bitterness; loathing of the Spaniard became a habit in the northern Netherlands during Spain's campaigns to enforce religious and political obedience there from the late 1560s to 1609. And in 1603 the Duc de Sully, when on an embassy to London, warned Henri IV that 'the English hate us, and with a hatred so strong and so widespread that one is tempted to number it among the natural dispositions of this people.'[20]

Such reactions were neither representative of Europe as a whole, nor consistent within themselves. The brutal sacking of Rome in 1527 by the troops employed in Italy by Charles V, German Emperor and King of Spain, was greeted with horror throughout the peninsula. Yet Italians came to settle down without general antagonism in the 1530s under Spanish rule in the formerly independent Duchy of Milan as they had done in the Kingdom of Naples since the beginning of the century; well-to-do Italians adopted Spanish costume; in literature, resentment found but a timid outlet in portraying the classical stock type of the braggart soldier as a vainglorious Spaniard. More broadly, the increasing traffic across Europe of diplomats, merchants, scholars and artists, to which we shall be turning, led to a measure of mutual understanding. All countries employed foreigners as mercenaries and, at least among the officers within rival forces, friendships and mutual admiration did much to break down prejudice, as is clear from Pierre de Brantôme's

Lives of the Captains and, indeed, the whole range of sixteenth-century military memoirs.

Yet national prejudices, whether from deep strata of popular memory or newly stimulated, continued to surface, and not only in times of crisis. Alongside economic and political rivalries it could be the peaceable introduction of foreigners to positions of administrative privilege and power that fed national antipathies. When the young Charles of Habsburg inherited the Spanish crown in 1516 he caused virulent and lasting offence by bringing with him a corps of officials and advisers from his native Burgundy. Catherine de' Medici's lavish patronage of Italians, her former compatriots, between 1559 and 1589, caused an outburst of resentment from the disgruntled French. It ranged from aristocratic disdain of the Queen as being of mere Florentine merchant stock to accusations against Italians in general as hypocrites, corrupt, the importers into honest France of an addiction to homosexual and lesbian practices. In the 1570s Henri Estienne wrote a diatribe against the use of 'the new Italianized French language' and reprimanded courtiers for aping Italian gestures; 'the French are not by nature given to gestures and do not like them.'[21] And before this wave of prejudice had subsided, another Italian, Marie de' Medici, similarly acclimatizing herself within a circle of Italian favourites, set it gathering force again during her period of ascendancy as Queen Regent between 1610 and 1617. More dramatic still was the change from the welcome given in Poland in the late fifteenth century to Italians with useful mercantile, scholarly and artistic skills, via the sharp reservations expressed when Bona Sforza, after her marriage to Sigismund I, arrived as Queen in 1518 with her own protective *cadre* of her compatriots, to an outright italophobia later in the century. Royal attempts to exert some centralizing control over the self-patrolled anarchy of the territorial nobility were seen in terms of Italian, 'Machiavellian', political theory; Italians were denounced for effeminating native intellectual vigour and seducing Poles into wasting their substance on imported fripperies. Resentment against the economic success of Italian immigrants, exacerbated by their being granted tax exemptions on their import-export dealings, led to mockery of them as having big brains topping feeble bodies; in the face of the foreigners' exasperating success in dominating mining, publishing and the commerce in luxury goods, the face-saving Polish response was to write them off as unmanly 'lute players'. Not even the Italians' preference for farinaceous and salad foods and wine, rather than meat, game and beer went unmocked.[22]

Increasingly, Poles ceased to throng the universities of Italy and went instead to German ones.

It was from the 1570s that generalized characterizations of Italians became common. Formerly, the peninsula was seen by natives and visitors alike chiefly through the differing natures of the independent states that comprised it. Civic pride was bristlingly particularistic. In Castiglione's *The Courtier* of 1528 a Venetian's mild joke at the expense of an example of Florentine simple-mindedness was turned aside by a Florentine present who said that the story must relate to a Sienese. Travellers from abroad summarized their impressions of one region before beginning again with the next, from 'Milan the Great', to 'Genoa the Proud', 'Florence the Fair', 'Bologna the Learned', 'Venice the Rich' and so on. Ambassadors from one Italian state to another wrote home with the same wealth of investigative detail as they provided from a posting beyond the Alps. Even in the peninsula itself, 'Italy' and 'Italians' were words seldom used except in the context of a common political threat from outside or in expressions of cultural superiority to other countries. As late as 1617 an Englishman could rattle off the contrasts: 'the Milanese are said to be little jealous and to hate fat women. The Mantuans to love women that can dance. The Florentines to love a modest woman, and one that loves home. The Neapolitans to love a stately high-minded woman. Those of Lucca are said to love constantly, the Venetians contrarily, and to desire fat women with great dugs.'[23] But in spite of the persistence of this sort of catchpenny caricature, a generalized and more pervasive characterization came to be established.

It started as a domestic product. Already in *The Courtier* there is the acknowledgement that defeats at foreign hands are due to some failure of nerve that was a pan-Italian phenomenon. Giovanni della Casa, in his manual of behaviour *Galateo* of 1558, which also achieved a wide European readership in translation, referred to 'our poor country, which has been debased and humiliated in the course of events'.[24] With 'Milan the Great' and 'Naples the Noble' under Spanish control, and 'Genoa the Proud' and 'Florence the Fair' tied to Spanish political aims, the peninsula came to look more homogeneous. Only Venice could be excluded from this self-projected image, with her independence from Spanish power coupled with her shrewd avoidance of full commitment to the tauter papal control of Catholic belief and organization that was the hallmark of the mid-century Counter-Reformation. Otherwise Italy appeared to outsiders to be not only politically but religiously one.

This new 'Italy' was now the incorporated ally of England's, France's and the Netherlands' chief antagonist, Spain, a place where the Inquisition's torturers laid in wait for non-Catholics.

There was enough substance here to incendiarize traditional insult. A warning was issued in 1588 to those intending to study in its universities by Botero, an Italian writer but, as a citizen of Piedmont, then part of the Duchy of Savoy, not at heart an Italian: 'the pen there is turned into a poignard, and the inkwell into a flask and touch-paper for a gun, the disputations into bloody brawlings . . . Honesty is there flouted at and scorned, and bashfulness and modesty accounted a discredit and a shame.'[25] In 1600 an English translator of Livy warned his readers that they should stay away from the Italy his hero had recorded, 'so farre degenerate are the inhabitant now from that ancient people, so devoute, so vertuous and uncorrupt in old time'.[26] And he is echoing the opinion expressed thirty years before by Roger Ascham in his popular *The Scholemaster* that 'Italy now is not that Italy that it was wont to be, and therefore not so fit a place, as some do count it, for young men to fetch either wisdom or honesty from thence.'[27] And Ascham's most famous warning, that *Inglese italianato è un diavolo incarnato* – an Italianate Englishman is a devil made flesh – pointed the way to John Webster's two great tragedies (1612 and 1623) in which Italians poison their victims in four different ways: by the leaves of a book, the lips of a portrait, the pommel of a saddle and an anointed helmet. But Ascham's phrase was common currency. A German, Bartolomew Sastrow, quoted as a familiar proverb *Tedesco italianato è un diavolo incarnato*.[28]

In Germany, thanks to a general acknowledgement of, if not obedience to, the over-arching authority of the Germanic Empire and a shared resentment of Italian cultural pretensions, there had been a feeling of Germanness from as early as Heinrich Bebel's call to the Emperor in 1500 to defend 'Mother Germany' from the slanders of foreigners.[29] Nonetheless, there were also slogans differentiating the characteristics of German cities. There is 'a common proverb in Germany', wrote an Englishman in 1594 who had long been resident in Nuremberg: ' "the Merchants of Nuremberg, the Lords of Ulm, and the Citizens of Augsburg". Also there is a rhyme: "The Nuremberg hand Deceaves every land" '.[30] Outsiders, however, usually referred to Germans as a whole. The slander that they were humanistically unlearned had lost its sting by the 1530s. The lack of any wide appeal of their native literature, which was perceived as formless and was in any case, given the slow establishment of a recognizably 'literary' German, difficult to translate, kept alive rather longer the idea that Germans were uncultivated, in spite of an admiration all over Europe for German woodcuts and engravings. The slanders that really became part of the shorthand stereotype related, rather, to drunkenness (that 'plague from beyond the Alps', as della Casa put it[31]), uncouthness of manners and intellectual dullness.

The Italian art theorist Giovanni Paolo Lomazzo advised painters in 1590 how to portray a German: 'strutting stride, extravagant gesture, wild expression, clothing all anyhow, manner hard and stern', and to take account of the fact that they were 'filthy eaters, boring conversationalists, over-forward lovers, careful workers, faithful (though according to their own lights) soldiers'.[32] And Fynes Moryson, noting favourably that Germans 'do not make water in the streets', praised their skill as artificers but added, 'I think that to be attributed not to their sharpeness of witt, but to theire industry, for they use to plodd with great diligence upon their professions.' They are, he concludes, 'somewhat inclyning to the vice of Dullness'.[33] And considering, as did most visitors, the Swiss to be honorary Germans, in spite of their independence from the empire, he summed up their character as sober, valiant, honest, industrious and – a new and enduring note – praised them for their skill at languages.

Because east-west contacts, while increasing, were dwarfed in importance by the violent political gavotte into which the western states – the prime producers of stereotypes – were progressively involved, characterizations of the peoples east of Germany-Austria remained especially simple-minded. Hungarians were ferocious people who wore stove-pipe hats and flapped their arms while drinking. Russians were slavish, cantankerous drunks, who endured extremes of heat and cold like animals; seeking colonists to stabilize his east Baltic conquests in 1626, Gustavus Adolphus of Sweden looked for men of 'honest German habits' rather than immigrants who would reflect 'swinish Russian customs'.[34] And on the opposite fringe of Europe the Portuguese, the least visited of all European nations south of Scandinavia, were summarily written off as proudly ignorant, not even interested in the nature of the Asian peoples amongst whom they so successfully lived and intermarried, and not, until their forcible absorption into the Spanish monarchy in 1580, readily thought of as members of a European power.

It is difficult to exaggerate the broad sense in which the Alps were felt to divide a northern, transalpine world from a southern, temperamentally and culturally conditioned Mediterranean one. When the Flemish artist Hugo van der Goes died in Brussels in 1482, a brother monk said that because of his painting 'he enjoyed so great a reputation that people used to say that he had no peer this side of the Alps.'[35] And Italians used the terms *fiamminghi*, Flemings, and *tedeschi*, Germans, almost interchangeably. Netherlanders were in many respects bracketed with Germans: clean streets, sluttish personal habits, sluggish un-sun-warmed sexual appetites, above all drunkenness. When Adrian of Utrecht came to Rome in 1522 after his unexpected election to the papacy, the joke ran that a crude Fleming had become 'divino' (i.e. drunk 'di vino', from wine). Hans, the first Netherlander to be portrayed on the English stage, in the morality play *Wealth and Health* of *c.*1557, was, as the audience would have expected, a lurchingly heavy drinker. After nearly two more generations of English respect for Dutch art and music and, from 1585, co-operation with the northern Netherlands as a political ally, this stereotyped feature could still be trotted out; with no consciousness of a northern pot calling a neighbour kettle black, Sir John Smythe in 1590 claimed that this 'detestable vice hath within these six or seven years taken wonderful root amongst our English nation, that in times past was wont to be of all other nations of Christendom' – note the moralizing use of that word – 'one of the soberest'.[36] It was in vain that the Dutch represented themselves as valorous, faithful, modest and learned. Even in a quiet seat of learning, Leiden, the great French scholar Joseph Scaliger could write in 1606 that 'the Dutch are tall and slow. They wash the streets, but are dirty in their eating and drinking.' Still, he admitted that 'there are some good people,' and commended the fact that 'the country people, men and women, and almost all the servant girls can read and write.'[37]

The English did not get off any better. The Italian riposte to the *diavolo incarnato* cliché was the equally handed-about *bona terra, mala gente*: a Mantuan diplomat wrote home from London to confirm that England was indeed a paradise inhabited by devils.[38] In spite of Henry VIII's patronage of Italian artists, craftsmen and military engineers, Benvenuto Cellini, while happy to work in France, flinched from the idea of living amongst 'such beasts as the English'.[39] The medieval notion, half superstition, half belief, that the English actually had tails rolled up inside their breeches, though it surfaced in the propaganda poem of 1513, faded after the mid-fifteenth century. The new taunts

were blinkered self-esteem and, linked to this, a particularly rabid xeno-
phobia.

In 1496–7 an Italian description of England noted that 'the English
are great lovers of themselves, and of everything belonging to them;
they think that there are no other men than themselves, and no other
world but England; and whenever they see a handsome foreigner, they
say that "he looks like an Englishman", and that "it is a great pity that
he should not be an Englishman"; and when they partake of any delicacy with a foreigner, they ask him "whether such a thing is made in
their country?" '.[40] And, as was the way with stereotypes, the same
point (already repeated by Herberstein) turns up in an account of England by a German written almost exactly (1598) a century later: 'if they
see a foreigner, very well made or particularly handsome, they will
say "it is a pity he is not an Englishman" .'[41]

The Italian had dwelled on the fact that the English had 'an antipathy
to foreigners'. A Spaniard in 1554 added a variant to this already old
theme. English women actually disdained the advances of his fellow-
countrymen; however, given 'the sort of women' they were, this was
'an excellent thing for the Spaniards'.[42] A Frenchman four years later
complained that they called him and his fellows knaves, dogs and sons
of whores. The English, he concluded, were more false and lacking in
conscience than snakes, crocodiles and scorpions.[43] The note was struck
over and over again. During his stay between 1583 and 1585 the philosopher Giordano Bruno complained of being jostled and insulted.[44] A
companion of Frederick, Duke of Württemberg, recorded in 1592 that
the English 'care little for foreigners, but scoff and laugh at them'.[45] In
1581 George Pettie, the translator of Guazzo, was moved to shift the
blame for such slurs onto the changed behaviour of the English when
they crossed the Channel. England is 'the civilest countrey in the
worlde: and if it be thought to be otherwyse by strangers, the disorders
of those traveylers abrode are the chiefe cause of it'.[46] Another gibe to
have a long history was the aristocratic Italian Pietro della Valle's dis-
missal in 1615 of the English ambassador in Constantinople as 'a better
shopkeeper than a soldier'.[47]

Though by the early sixteenth century Spain was sufficiently well
known for visitors to pick up the usual differentiations between cities
– Barcelona the Rich, Saragossa the Plump, Valencia the Beautiful and
so forth – its conquests in Italy, its links through Charles V with

the German-Netherlands Habsburg Empire and the lead it took in representing the aggressive edge of revived, militant Catholicism, gave it an entirely new presence in the imagination of Europe.

Domestically, the conquest of the Moorish Kingdom of Granada and the expulsion of nearly all Jews from the whole of Spain strengthened the native emphasis on *limpieza di sangre*, uncontaminated blood. This cult of racial purity did not pass unmocked at home: in Francisco de Quevedo's picaresque novel of 1608, *The Life of Pablo Buscon* (translated as *The Swindler*), the hero's landlord 'was one of those who believe in God out of good manners and not sincerely; half-Moors they're called by the people. There's no shortage of those people or the ones who have long noses and only need them to smell out bacon. Of course, I'm not hinting at any impure blood among the aristocracy, oh no!'[48] But *limpieza* did help, outside Spain, to consolidate what was seen as a chief indicator of the Spanish character: pride. 'They suck pride in with their milk,' wrote a normally mild German traveller in the mid-century. 'They are the vainest nation I have ever seen. They have nothing but disdain for foreigners, and as they try to lord it everywhere, they are everywhere detested.'[49]

By then German attitudes had been affected by Charles V's use of Spanish troops against the Protestant cities and princes of the Schmalkaldic League. Among people who used the terms 'Mother Germany' and 'Fatherland', the atrocities complained of by Protestants were seen as insults to the German nation as a whole; and around the basic charge of cruelty clustered those of sexual licence and attempts to pervert the native honesty and decency of the German people. Such accusations were later encouraged by the remorseless sacking of cities and scorching of the earth that marked Spanish strategy against the rebellious provinces of the Netherlands; both reinforced earlier propaganda about Spain's treatment of the helpless populations of the Americas and helped to spread the 'Black Legend' of the instinctive cruelty of the Spanish character. In addition, travellers noted that, uniquely among the countries of central and western Europe, Spain had so small a mercantile and artisan class that it was forced to rely on immigrants (these in turn were accused by the Spaniards of importing over-sophisticated habits noxious to the integrity of their hosts' native character). For all the silver that flowed in from America and out again to pay for fleets and armies, in domestic economic terms, Spain came to be seen as a Lithuania or Russia of the West and the stereotype to combine dislike with disdain.

At the core of all stereotypes was a simple proposition: we are better than they, contact with 'them' jeopardizes our national integrity. It could, of course, be the result of straightforward homesickness when abroad. 'Oh! What a chasm separates the Danube from the Tiber!' mourned an Italian prelate on a diplomatic mission to Regensburg in the early 1470s.[50] 'I have much to bear', wrote an Italian artist from Brussels around 1517, 'away among foreign barbarians.'[51] Straight from the heart comes a Spanish complaint from the Netherlands wars: this is 'the land where there grows neither thyme, nor lavender, figs, olives, melon or almonds; where parsley, onions and lettuces have neither juice nor taste; where dishes are prepared, strange to relate, with butter from cows instead of oil'.[52] And a single upsetting incident could change an entire point of view: in 1517 Antonio de Beatis, chaplain to Cardinal Luigi D'Aragon, in the course of their enjoyable and objectively described tour of France, had his bag stolen at an inn. At once 'the common people' as a whole become 'as contemptible, idle and vicious as can be imagined'.[53]

It was not until around 1600 that voices were raised against the free-for-all luxuriance of snap judgement and routine prejudice. Both the need for international peace and the sense of responsibility of more widely educated men called for a less blinkered vision. The German cosmographer Johann Rauw noted in 1597 that 'the old saying is true: no country is worth three pennies more than any other.'[54] 'There is hardly a nation under the sun that has no special faults and merits,' wrote the Dutchman Karel van Mander in 1604, when recommending that painters should travel in order to widen their skills.[55] Joseph Hall in 1608 agreed that 'the French are commonly called rash, the Spaniard proud, the Dutch drunken, the English busy-hands, the Italian effeminate, the Swethens timorous, the Bohemians inhuman, the Irish barbarous and superstitious', but went on to ask, 'is any man so sottish as to think that France hath no staid man at all in it, Spain no meacock [weakling], or Germany none that lives soberly?'[56]

As with the political map of Europe, there were border zones on the mental map of national stereotypes where core national characteristics became mongrelized, picking up, as Moryson put it, 'the vices of the bordering nations . . . indeede generally the borderers of all nations are commonly the worst people'.[57] And beyond the borders were outer fringes where, as we have seen, the maps of Europe ran out of data that might have put some steadying qualifications alongside the repetitions of prejudice. In countries that were 'on the map', stereotypes were balanced by more factual appraisals, even if these did little to check the appetite for denigration. But, as in the case of Russia, lack of knowledge and the difficulty of establishing personal friendships allowed prejudice to continue its own self-sealing impulse. While diplomatic and commercial contacts with Russia multiplied, attitudes remained static, most of them recording disgust with brutal manners, sexual promiscuity, craven respect for authority, the ignorance and idolatry of the clergy, the tasteless indulgence in ostentatious luxury. A papal envoy noted in 1567 that 'the entire marketplace in Moscow offered fewer goods for sale than a single shop in Venice.'[58]

These adverse judgements concerning Russia owed something to a dislike of the climate, now over-hot, now too cold, to the restrictions placed on the free movement of foreigners, and to new standards of assessing the sincerity of religious observance and decorum of manners created by changes at home. But they also reflected uncertainty about whether visitors were dealing with a European or an Asiatic community. And this uncertainty made what was seen as 'Asiatic' more harshly judged than what was known to be uncontrovertibly Asian – and therefore judged by standards different in kind from those by which Europeans praised or blamed one another.

Simple-minded as the stereotypes were, they surfaced stubbornly in the writings of educated men. They were repeated to popular audiences by printed broadsheets and from the stage. They are usefully borne in mind not only when considering attitudes towards the wider issues of war and peace in Europe, but the attempts of governments to weld local loyalties and patriotic sentiments into a manipulable awareness of nationhood.

LOYALTIES

Through the stereotypes – which developed as characterizations of foreigners – it is easier to locate an individual's attitudes to other countries than to his own. But in all languages 'foreigner' had a double meaning: it referred to aliens but also to outsiders from perhaps only twenty miles away who came to compete for jobs or burden local charitable services. Countries were congeries of regional and local identities.

In a popular school geography textbook of 1542, the *Cosmographic*

Rudiments of Johann Honter, many times republished until the end of the century, the maps showed rivers, mountains and major cities but no borders, and the place-names – all in Latin – reflect the provinces of the Roman and medieval worlds rather than a contemporary political survey. On the map of France 'Burgundia Gallia' (Burgundy) and 'Brittania Celtica' (Brittany) are printed in larger capitals than 'Francia' itself, inscribed above 'Lutecia' (Paris)[59]; here the map was in accord with an Italian traveller's comment in 1517 that on nearing Paris one at last entered 'the real France'.[60] And this was paralleled by another writer's remark ten years later that 'London is the common country of all England.'[61]

The importance of a common mode of speech as exemplifying the inner coherence of a country was recognized as early as 1492. Presenting in that year the first grammar of the Spanish language to a surprised Queen Isabella, Antonio de Nebrija is said to have justified its adoption because, 'Madam, language is the instrument of empire.'[62] An idea of the same sort is suggested by the edict Francis I issued in 1539 to the effect that the form of French spoken in the Paris region should be the official language adopted in the whole of France. In England the need for a common language had been sounded, for entrepreneurial reasons, by William Caxton in 1490. As a printer specializing in translations, how, he asked, was he to choose 'between plain, rude and curious' forms of English? And he instanced the case of a London merchant who could not make himself understood in East Anglia.[63] The solution proposed in 1589 in a down-to-earth treatise on sound English was that as a model 'ye shall take the usuall speech of the court and that of London and the shires lying about London within sixty miles and not much above'[64].

Machiavelli lamented in 1516 that Tuscan, the classic tongue of Dante, Petrarch and Boccaccio, was challenged by those who ignored the example of Florence and who 'confound her language with those of Milan, Venice and the Romagna and with all the filthy usages of Lombardy.'[65] His concern was literary, but its vigour owed something to his distress that the peninsula's regions, foreigners to one another, could not at need unite against the 'barbarian' foreigners, France, Spain and Germany, and their invading armies. And it was not exaggerated: in 1538 a military engineer from Bergamo, Venice's subject city in Lombardy, was dismissed from Venetian service, because though skilful, his dialect was so marked that 'he had the defect of not being able to communicate his ideas.'[66]

So far as the printed word was concerned, there was a notable advance in the apparent unity of a country's language. But in the spoken language, which affected both visitors' and natives' reactions to national identity, there was little change. It was a northern Frenchman, Charles de Rouelles, who complained that in travelling across France in the mid-sixteenth century he encountered eight different ways of saying 'yes' and 'no'. Dialects were not simply a matter of aberrant pronunciation, but of divergent syntax and vocabulary. It was all very well for a German in 1597 to brag that in a journey of 'ninety-three days, provided that you travel five miles a day . . . you would walk the circumference of Germany as far as the German language is spoken', but he ignored both the differences between southern and northern German and within both.[67] When the first north German translation of the Bible was published in 1479, it had to be in double columns to take account of the Frankish and Saxon forms of the language. Even the Reformation outpouring of books and pamphlets aimed at a mass market within that whole circumference had produced little change a century later.

The sentiment of nationhood was slow to evolve because it only rang true within a country as a whole at exceptional moments of danger from outside threats. Even then, as we shall see, rallying calls from the centre faded to whispers and eventually to silence as they slowly passed along unmade roads into regions with their own forms of speech and patterns of local loyalties.

The word 'nation' itself was hardly ever used before the seventeenth century to refer to all the inhabitants of a country. It either referred to men of a particular category, regardless of their origin, as in the educationalist Roger Ascham's denunciation in 1570 of 'the barbarous nation of scholemen',[68] or it meant a body of foreigners living abroad. In universities where there were large numbers of foreign students, such as Bologna and Padua, Paris and Montpellier, the partly self-governing sections into which they were divided according to their place of origin were called 'nations'. Or, again, when the banished Italian – mostly Florentine – merchants of Lyon petitioned Henri IV in 1594 for a restoration of their privileges there, they wrote in the name of 'the Florentine nation that used to be settled in Lyon'.[69] It is true that forms of expression were used that appear to anticipate the later idea of nationhood – the 'our Germany' of Rudolf Agricola and the 'we Germans' of Luther, Guillaume Budé's homage to 'the Genius of France', the appeal to 'Italy' and 'the Italians' in the emotive last chapter of

Machiavelli's *The Prince* – but these were the words of special pleaders. Shakespeare's Henry V could cry, 'on, on, you noble English . . . Cry "God for Harry, England and Saint George"' before the storming of Honfleur, but on the eve of Agincourt, the playwright's realism led him to make Henry acknowledge those 'gentlemen of England now a-bed' who had not been stirred by the call to arms.[70] A similar regret that Englishmen had not risen to a patriotic cause had been expressed in 1517. In a court entertainment John Rastell lamented that in spite of the landfalls made by voyagers from Bristol in the late fifteenth century the credit of occupying the Americas had fallen to Spain. How much more satisfying it would have been

> If they that be Englyshemen
> Myght have ben the furst of all
> That there should have take possessyon
> And made furst buyldynge and habytacion –
> A memory perpetuall![71]

There was enough of this sort of anti-foreigner patriotism abroad to make Erasmus say, five years later, that though he had once proudly proclaimed himself in his publications to be Erasmus 'of Rotterdam' or 'of Batavia' (the Latin name of the province of Holland in which Rotterdam lay), he now preferred 'to be a citizen of the world or, rather, a stranger to all'.[72] For him, in a time of ever-renewed war and the beginnings of religious side-taking, Protestant against Catholic, patriotism, a vague sentiment, drawing chiefly on reaction to wars won or lost, became a crime against humanity. But leaving his unusual sensitivity aside, declarations of patriotism expressed on behalf of a whole country have to be judged in terms of the mood of a minority given voice by an individual. 'I think there is no man so far estranged from civil humanity which knoweth not how far every one of us is indebted to our native country', wrote Thomas Becon in 1543,

> allured unto the love and desire of the same even by a certain inspiration both of God and nature. For how glad is an Englishman, being in France, Germany or Italy or elsewhere, to know by the transmission of mutual letters what is done in England, in what case the public weal consisteth, how it prospereth . . . The love of our country must needs be great, seeing that the grave, prudent, sage and wise governors of the public weal heretofore in all their acts sought nothing so much as the prosperity and wealth thereof. What goodly sweet sentences did they instill into

the breasts of their younglings, even from the cradles, to encourage them unto the love of their country. As there are: *Pugna pro patria. Mortem oppete pro patria. Dulce et decorum est pro patria mori.*[73]

In 1543 Becon was a studious clergyman in poor health and in a poor living in Kent. He had never crossed the Channel. But he was aware that preparations were afoot for Henry VIII's expedition against France in the following year. And he was in trouble with his ecclesiastical superiors for his inclination towards a more radical Protestantism than was welcome within the Henrician church establishment. So he put his best, ingratiatingly patriotic foot forward. In its blend of real feeling and ink-horn nonsense his sentiments do, nonetheless, represent a half-way house between the patriotism of self-advantage and crisis and the still distant nationalism which awaited the will to sink regional structures and sentiments into a habitual obedience to a common authority, and the organizational ability of that authority to guide and, if necessary, compel obedience.

In all languages subjects paid dutiful homage from time to time to the idea of 'the public weal', the common good of the inhabitants of a whole country. So did governments in the preambles to laws intended to be binding on all subjects. Sir Thomas Elyot, dedicating *The Governour*, his treatise on the education of the better sort of Englishmen, to Henry VIII, had seen it as a contribution to 'the publike weale of this your most noble realme'.[74] And 'realm' certainly defined the historical dimension into which, over many centuries, the major political units had been hammered by their rulers' wars into the shape of the countries which came to be separately labelled across the early sixteenth-century maps of Europe. It was within this dimension that the stereotypes of antipathy had grown, and to this dimension that the spokesmen for patriotic feeling turned. An Englishman in the early seventeenth century went so far as to embarrass his son with the name Cassibelan, after the native King Cassivellaunus who had defied the invading legions of Julius Caesar.

The most potent focus of internal unity and of foreigners' appraisal of a country's international role, was the ruler himself. The first duty of a diplomat posted to a foreign country was to advise his government on the ruler's character, his choice of ministers, his relations with his most powerful subjects and his ability to mobilize his country's resources in war. For fellow countrymen, who carried his or – in the case of Isabella of Castile and Mary and Elizabeth of England – her image in their purses, the focus was more intense. But the immediacy of the sense of contact was blurred not only by the space and localisms that distanced prince from subject but by rulers' habit of marrying foreigners for political support against their enemies or with an eye to adding new territories to their own.

Erasmus deplored the custom. If such alliances made by princes 'would give peace to the world', he wrote, 'I would wish each of them

A candidate for Henry VIII's fourth marriage: Christina of Denmark, Hans Holbein, 1538 (National Gallery, London)

six hundred wives'.[75] But because they did not, rulers should marry a native and cultivate the interest and loyalty of their subjects. It was a hopeless plea. Princes looked on foreign states as landlords looked on estates owned by others, as territories which could be linked to the home property by marrying the heiress. That this process of accumulation could work was shown most sensationally by the multi-generational international marriage settlements which made Charles V of Habsburg by 1519 the head of something like a fifth of the population of Europe (including Germany, Spain, the Netherlands, Austria, Bohemia, part of Hungary, the duchy of Milan and the kingdom of Naples and Sicily). Even so, forced ceaselessly to invigilate his scattered properties, he wrote wearily from Spain in 1525 to his brother that 'in order to leave these kingdoms [Castile and Aragon, themselves united by the marriage in 1474 between Isabella and Ferdinand] under good order and government, I see no other remedy than to marry the Infanta Donna Isabella of Portugal.'[76] But even minor princes played the marriage market. For instance, by marrying Renée, granddaughter of Francis I, Ercole II d'Este gained an ally to support the independence of his duchy of Ferrara while Francis obtained a useful foothold in northern Italy for France.

There is no doubt that the marriage traffic focused attention on princes and their families. All over Europe the agents of princely bachelors were checking genealogies, scrutinizing nubile candidates for indications of health and fecundity, reporting on the presence or absence of facial hair, the size of breasts, indications of temperament, good or bad breath. So intrusive could these investigations be that the official responsible for the Saxon end of Henry VIII's inquiries about Anne of Cleves asked indignantly whether the King's agents would like to see her naked. Instead, Holbein's portrait of her played its part in forging this link with a useful Protestant European ally. Henry did marry, but then could not bring himself to make love to his 'Flanders mare'.

It was difficult for artists to strike the mean between what was diplomatically wanted and what was sexually acceptable. Two years before, in 1538, Holbein had been sent to make a drawing (subsequently worked up into the full length painting in the National Gallery) of another candidate for Henry's fourth match, the sixteen-year-old Christina, daughter of the recently deposed King of Denmark and already the widow of the Duke of Milan. The match foundered, as did so many of Henry's trawls among the matrimonial prizes of western Europe, on diplomatic shoals. But the expression of Holbein's sitter makes it cred-

A domestically committed Queen: Elizabeth I, contrasted with Mary, in *The Family of Henry VIII*, Lucas de Heere, 1569 (Sudeley Castle)

ible that there was some spark of independence among them; Christina is alleged to have said when approached that if she had had two heads she would be happy to offer Henry one of them. Deeper was the protest registered by Francis I's fifteen-year-old niece Jeanne d'Albret when the King insisted that she marry the Duke of Cleves whom he needed as a northern ally against the encircling power of Charles V. When the Duke nonetheless gave in to the military pressure exerted on him by Charles, Francis, to keep Jeanne available for another match, insisted that the marriage be annulled on the grounds that it had been unconsummated. Among the evidence collected was Jeanne's own statement in 1545 that she had only consented to a form of marriage 'from fear of the King [of Navarre] my father and the Queen [Marguerite, sister of Francis I] my mother, who menaced me and had me whipped by my governess . . . warning me that if I did not agree to this marriage . . . I would be beaten to death'.[77]

At a time when most marriages between influential families were based on power and property rather than free choice, royal ones turned out neither better nor worse than others. But all were warnings to subjects that their rulers' interests lay in part elsewhere; betrothals could be signed, and foreign entanglements forecast, when an heir or heiress was as young as two years old. There is little doubt that the unique intensity of the patriotic identification with Elizabeth I was due in part to her much publicized determination – following the hated marriage of her predecessor Mary to Philip of Spain – to remain if not a virgin at least a domestically committed queen.

It was not only through marriages that kings looked beyond their own realms. There were other forms of alliance, some habitual, as was Scotland's with France to check England, England's with Portugal to counter Spain, and many that were feverishly constructed and broken and renegotiated as the needs of defence and the opportunities for joint aggression came and went. And as monarchs took all initiatives in foreign policy and were reluctant to delegate much of its conduct to their ministers, Erasmus's vision of princes who thought only of their fellow countrymen could be no more than a dream. The idea remained. Indeed, it became a royal cliché: 'Kings', James I reminded Parliament in 1609, 'are compared to fathers of families, for a king is trewly *Parens Patriae*, the politique father of his people.'[78] But an estimate of how far 'love of country' was generated by feelings of loyalty to its sovereign must take account of how far such fathers were known to have non-familial matters on their minds.

Not all European countries had developed under a dynastic ruling family, and it is doubtful whether hereditary forms of leadership fostered more loyalty than elective ones. Doges of republican Venice, chairmen of a mercantile empire stretching from the borders of Milan to Cyprus, were commonly so old when voted into office that few had the chance to generate an aura of personal rule. It was the centuries-long stability of the government they represented and the protection it offered from the adversarial countries surrounding the Republic's territories, that brought respect for the doge of the moment and for the enduring image of St Mark stamped on coin, fortress and the governors' palaces in subject cities.

Popes had the advantage, however cynically gerrymandered their elections (to trade off their votes 'many cardinals met in the privies' wrote Pius II of the conclave that elected him in 1458[79]), of being God's representatives on earth in the eyes of the faithful. This did not, however, go far to help them in their domestic role as rulers of the

The Lion of St Mark, Carpaccio, 1516 (Doge's Palace, Venice)

wide swathe of territories across central Italy which formed the states of the church; and by drafting in relatives on whose fidelity they could rely as administrators, they gained for the Renaissance Papacy its reputation for nepotism. Nonetheless, the range of patronage at each pope's disposal and the fear among their subjects of being made subject to Florentine or Neapolitan rule, ensured for successive popes a degree of loyalty heavily qualified by self-interest. It was Poland-Lithuania, where the elected king had neither the support of a stable governmental machine nor a divine sanction, that the bond between subject and ruler was weakest. With a French monarch from 1573–5, a Transylvanian, Stefan Batory, from 1575–86 and a Swede, Sigismund III, from 1587–1632, the largest country in Europe had the weakest monarchical image save among the restricted electoral class of peasant-exploiting landlords. For the main concern of the Polish nobility was to choose rulers who would not interfere with their own regional interests.

To leaf further through the atlas is to confirm the impression that there was no steady identification between ruler and ruled in the parts of Europe that had been historically and cartographically defined as separate countries, and to grasp the difficulties that confronted governments seeking to gain support among their subjects for an extension of their powers.

Thus the crowns of Norway and Denmark were held jointly from 1450. In Russia, Ivan IV's determination to create a Muscovite zone within which his authority would be non-negotiable, absolute, led to his creation of the *oprichnina*, an organization of personal dependants from which the traditional aristocracy, the boyars, were banished to peripheral lands. It was the ruthless use of force this involved that earned him the sobriquet 'the Terrible', and it cut off at a blow any wider response to the tsars' claims to tap the loyalty of 'all the Russias'.

More confusing even than Italy was the accumulation of medieval traditions and interests, which cartography completed in the classical term 'Germania'. In spite of the sporadically disinterred notion of Germanness and the projection by others on to all German-language speakers of stereotyped characteristics, Germany was divided into a multitude of hereditary princedoms, prince-bishoprics, and cities to all intents and purposes independent within their walls and surrounding territories. With its local inter-urban diets which discussed matters of mutual commercial and defensive concern, its wider political alliance among southern princes and cities, the Swabian League, chiefly aimed against any extension of imperial influence, Germany was a microcosm of the independencies, alliances and antagonisms of Europe as a whole. As an English traveller remarked in 1609, 'if it were subject to one monarchy [it] would be terrible to all the rest'. As it is, he went on, 'it only serves to balance itself.'[80]

His 'one monarchy' recalled an august spectre, that of the Holy Roman Emperor, the Christian successor to the universal authority wielded by the emperors of ancient Rome. From the tenth century the

Charles V and Ferdinand, model for a medal, signed Hans Kels, 1537 (Museum für Kunst and Kunstgewerbe, Hamburg)

title, though elective, had been identified with a ruler of German stock, from the fifteenth with a member of the Austrian Habsburg family. During the intervening centuries the imperial role had dwindled from being the widely acknowledged secular protector of Christendom to that of Europe's senior chieftain, loaded with honours and associations reaching back to the empire of antiquity, but implying direct rule only within family lands and a wider influence limited to the extent to which other German princes and cities found it useful to them. It is, all the same, a significant comment on the non-domestic self-image of monarchs that on the death of Maximilian I of Habsburg in 1519, not just his territorial heir, his grandson Charles, but both Henry VIII of England and Francis I of France put themselves forward as candidates. For a foreigner, to become Emperor would bring prestige, a source of patronage through the bestowal of imperial titles (count, marquis, duke), and a special diplomatic relationship with the Papacy, the empire's spiritual *alter ego*. It would also immerse him in the thriving imbroglio of central European political discords. Yet to call Henry's and Francis's entry into the electoral competition irresponsible would be to overestimate the degree to which rulers thought of themselves simply as national leaders.

When the news of his election came to Spain Charles's chief minister said exultantly that 'God has set you on the path towards world monarchy.'[81] But Charles found that Germany, its mosaic composition still more luridly exposed from the 1520s by religious divisions, could not be dealt with; in 1556 he abdicated the imperial title in favour of his Austrian-based brother Ferdinand. But neither could Ferdinand, though he adopted German costume and wore his hair long in the old-fashioned German manner, tap any strong vein of personal loyalty among his subjects. In the late sixteenth century the Emperor Rudolf II accepted that history had detached itself from destiny and moved the imperial capital from Vienna to Prague: into the more amenable zone of the Empire's traditional reach where an emperor could function more effectively as a monarch.

What all governments had in common was a striving to extend effective control over their subjects and to link the most common contemporary meaning of the word 'state' – the power structure, that is, represented by a ruler and his ministers and chief officials – to the significance of what was then a less familiar usage: the state as a geographical catchment area of individuals owing a common obedience to central government. Whatever the terminology employed, the aim was the same: to make a ruler potent and unchallenged within his whole kingdom, to extend effective administration across it, to stimulate shared responses within a commonwealth of compatriots.

The aim was hampered by earlier and stubbornly held assumptions about government's function: to preserve, and if judged appropriate extend, territory that had been won in the past; to protect legally defined privileges while striving to ensure that all men had access to 'good justice'; to tax sparingly, for the common good and with advice; to foster the rights and influence of 'true religion'. These were conservative values. When rulers, whether a king of France or a doge of Venice, swore to observe them at their coronation or election, they vowed in effect to stop the historical process in its tracks. But, as the Italian statesman Francesco Guicciardini pointed out, any attempt to reproduce a past situation produces a novel effect because of intervening circumstances. This was particularly true of countries recovering from long periods of weak or disputed government, like France after the Hundred Years War and England after the Wars of the Roses. It also applied to those that were recovering control of lands lost in war, as was Venice in 1517. In such cases, stock-taking led to change. The result of the review of the meaning and genuineness of charters, of old claims for exemption from this or that tax or service, was not unlike that of the contemporary re-scrutiny of classical or biblical texts: the purified versions carried a changed import. And in all cases governments were forced to alter the status quo by raising more money. As the tempo of international relations quickened from the later fifteenth century, the costs of diplomacy, from ambassadors to spies, rose to match their pace. The size of armies grew: from 12–30,000 before 1500, to 85,000 in the 1570s, to 100,000 and more by the 1620s. Better cannon meant that fortresses and town walls had to be rebuilt or strengthened. And war could throw up massive extras: to redeem the sons Francis I had left as hostages in Spain after his capture at the battle of Pavia in 1525 cost the equivalent of 3.6 tons of solid gold. As all governments were forced throughout the sixteenth century to spend more on war or defence or both, resources had to rise: in France, for example, from 3.5 million *livres* in 1497 to 15 million in 1596, in Castile from 850,000 ducats in 1504 to 13 million in 1598. Overall in the course of the century state revenues rose by a factor of five. This was mainly due to the necessities of war, partly to voluntary expenditure on buildings and on lavish courts to inflate the ruler's image. It was also due to larger governmental payrolls; in Paris the Place des Vosges was built to provide housing for Henri IV's staff of civic and military engineers and cartographers. However ingenious governments were at postponing taxes by raising bridging loans from financiers, repayments, like normal expenditure, had to be met from internal revenues. And this involved extending the reach of administrative fingers into pockets previously guarded from them.

To do this, and to ensure the law and order that made administration effective, more officials had to be maintained; the non-ministerial bureaucrat pushed aside the medieval arras behind which his shadowy existence had been passed, and strode with confidence down the corridors of power, disliked, not always honest, but an essential link between ruler and subject. At the lowest level the numbers of copyists and file-clerks and bookkeepers employed by earlier governments became inflated. New tasks, notably Spain's acquisition of territories in America and Italy, involved the creation of new governmental committees, but other governments, too, enlarged the departments which had dealt with different aspects of business: finance, foreign affairs, legal issues. Above this proletariat of inky toilers there was a thickening stratum of supervisors who not only co-ordinated the work of their departments but offered advice on knotty or debatable issues. It is at this level of responsibility that their prominence in contemporary records allows them to be counted: between three and four times the number shortly after 1600 than around 1500. In absolute terms this is unimpressive. In mid-sixteenth century France, for instance, with a population of about 18 million, there were no more than three thousand or so.

Among them were men who actually bought their positions. Rulers had long rewarded loyal servants with gifts of land to which feudal titles were attached. This became a practice whereby an aristocracy 'of the sword' found themselves, to the open disdain of many of them, infiltrated by an aristocracy *de la robe* – a reference to the distinctive long clothing of the functionary. But as the need for such men, especially as tax-gatherers, grew while rulers remained reluctant to increase the immediate costs of administration, bureaucratic positions were sold for cash and even became inheritable perquisites. It was often the case that those made responsible for the collection of a specific tax mulcted its income for what they thought they could get away with. But though financially inefficient, the system reinforced the numbers of those whose status at court encouraged among their acquaintance and relations the habit of looking to the centre for profit or acclaim.

There were never enough of them, whether operating at the heart of government or in the provinces, to pump obedience along the venous system that connected a capital with a country as a whole to the extent which new legislation called for. But civil service values came to work in tandem with a growing acceptance by regional magnates and country gentlemen that their own relation with governments, whom they had long served in administering justice and by raising troops, was not so much the traditional arm's length, stonewalling routine as a matter of immediate self-interest. Where the imposition of new taxes and the diversion of judicial procedures from local to royal courts were concerned voluntary support remained grudging. But overall consent with central initiatives was eased by the formation of a common front against the volatility of the increasingly straitened poor. As landowners felt the pinch of the social antagonism and the rising prices that afflicted the age they, or at least their sons and poorer relations, found it easier to accept the honorific or cash privileges that could be obtained at court.

In his *Memoirs*, dictated in old age before his death in 1577, Blaise de Monluc, a fair example of a provincial (Gascon) but professional soldier of good birth, remarked that one must go to court from time to time 'to warm oneself as one does in the sun or before a fire'.[82]
    Traditionally a court was, and its core function remained, above all a household with a range of servants and supervisors responsible for every aspect of the lives of a ruler and his or her family. He or she had to be guarded: there were escorts to go out with, patrols to pace the corridors and watch the doors of the private apartments. He or she had to be able to work: seven thousand of Catherine de' Medici's letters have survived and when she complained of her responsibilities, the future Henri IV bluntly pointed out that 'you thrive on this labour'[83]; though Philip II loved to hunt, most of his waking hours were spent reading dispatches and writing or dictating his replies; Elizabeth I told Parliament in 1601 that 'to be a King and wear a crown is a thing more glorious to them that see it than it is pleasant to them that bear it.'[84] There were scribes and secretaries and major-domos to arrange meetings with ministers, the reception of ambassadors and visiting dignitaries. The ruler and his household had to be fed and their guests entertained with music and after-dinner shows. There had to be stables, kennels and falconry mews to support a love of sport. There were

A shower of gold coins descending from the Burgundian court treasurers. Miniature from a Book of Hours made for Lord Hastings in Bruges, *c.*1477 (Bodleian Library, Oxford)

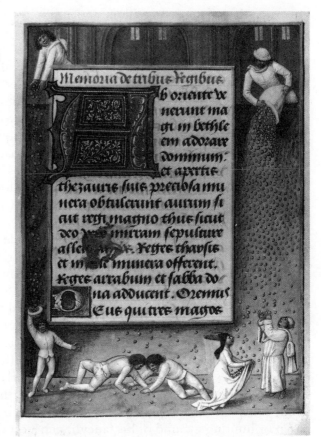

staffs to carry out maintenance work and manage the cumbersome business of transporting a ruler from one place to another. The household accounts, together with the receipts from hereditary crown lands, required a considerable staff to make sense of them. Without adding the supernumerary top-dressing of artists, dynastic historians and poets to the essential structure of household management, the numbers involved became large. Even the small court of Mantua had in 1520 some eight hundred men and women on its payroll. In the same year the papal court had two thousand, a figure matched by the French court towards 1600.

The sixteenth-century court came, however, to be much more than a mammoth household. It was also a term that symbolized government: real government, in that major decisions of policy were made by the monarch in consultation with his or her personal advisers and more formally designated councillors and heads of departments of state in the ruler's own palace, even if day-to-day administrative affairs were conducted in other buildings. It was the *locus* of personal rule in that wherever the prince was, there was the source of honours, promotions and gifts. So automatic was this latter assumption that already in the margins of a late fifteenth-century book of devotion the illuminator showed the Burgundian court treasurers at the top pouring coins down the margins into the caps and laps of eager recipients at the bottom. It was indeed above all late medieval Burgundy that had created the image of a princely court (in this case a ducal one) as being the place where great men came to add lustre to their reputations, and lesser ones to cadge a job or a free meal in memory of which they could dine out for the rest of their lives.

The court as a household, an inner-sanctum decision centre and fount of favours, a glamorous if dangerously gossip-ridden and factious club in which politically approved grandees had automatic membership and, whatever their personal interests and rivalries, came to see the advantages of governmental outreach, did not, until the second half of the sixteenth century, necessarily carry the connotation of a specific place. The court entourage of Charles V was almost constantly itinerant as the emperor diplomatized and warred across the map of his imperial responsibilities. The restless Francis I frequently called out the nearly eighteen thousand horses needed to transport the nexus of his household, complete with tapestries, silverware and overnighting tents, to a town or hunting ground of his fancy. Such a caravanserai still remained 'the court', where diversions and privileges were to be found and governmental policy discussed. Elizabeth I was often on the move, to save money by being entertained and to rally support for the crown. But by 1600 the court had also come to be a place: London, Paris, Madrid, Stockholm, Prague. With diplomatic business increasingly requiring a fixed address, and with the links between rule and region strengthened, its itinerant task was done. The warmth that Monluc wrote of came from a securely located hearth.

Life at court dealt fairly neither with political nor intellectual talent. It led to rivalries especially when leading bureaucrats acquired noble titles and lived in a style more admired than that of men who were quasi-potentates in their own remote jurisdictions. The pecking order could humiliate (which table you were seated at, whether a servant would catch your eye, whether a promised salary would be paid) as well as reassure. This led to a burgeoning literature about the court's demeaning of talent (the poet Torquato Tasso's satires were eloquent on this point) and its promotion of preening pretension – a vice neatly portrayed in the Osric of Shakespeare's *Hamlet*. Nonetheless, with its surface of grandeur and its recruitment of talent from a variety of social backgrounds, it constituted a forum of concern for national affairs.

It was also a fertile source of propaganda for the virtues of unchallenged authority. When Baldassare Castiglione in *The Courtier* described the ducal palace of Urbino as 'more like a city than a mere palace' he was not only alluding to the palace's size and appearance, diminishing that of the hill-town itself, but responding to a widespread aim among princes literally to build their image into their subjects' lives.[85] In the fifteenth century, when the Medici were the effective leaders within a republican form of government, their palace was a focus for diplomatic visits and of cultural and political patronage, but it was run as a private household, not a court. In the 1530s, shaken by crises beyond their immediate control, the Florentines accepted the leadership of the Medici as hereditary princes, and the change was quickly registered in Duke Cosimo's building programme. He left the old crowded-in-on family palace and, after first taking up residence in the palace of the Signoria, in 1560 moved into another, the former Pitti Palace. This stood on open land where it could be massively extended to house a court whose size and formality were all the greater because it was new, and had to prove itself the equal of long-established ones. He had the former official headquarters of governmental activity – henceforth known as Palazzo Vecchio, the Old Palace – redecorated to demonstrate in wall frescoes and ceiling canvases his old lineage and new authority. Next to it he cleared the space for his new offices (Uffizi) of state with their central courtyard running down to the Arno; and from them the architect, Giorgio Vasari, designed a raised covered corridor leading across the Ponte Vecchio all the way to the Pitti Palace.

So drastic an axis of power drawn across a city was unusual. But whether it was the Louvre in Paris or the extensions to Hradčany Castle in Prague, princes built not just for convenience but to impress. Visual effects were what mattered most. It was not enough that the printing press enabled princes' proclamations in their names to be nailed on church doors and on trees in village greens throughout their realms. What could not be said directly, as an order from ruler to subject, was diffused allegorically in paintings and entertainments designed for small audiences but to be widely talked about.

The role of a monarch as Jove, or as Augustus, quasi-divine protector

Hradčany Castle, Prague, Giovanni Castrucci, *pietre dure*, after 1606 (Kunsthistorisches Museum, Vienna)

of his countrymen, became a common theme in the ritualized entertainments of European courts, stressed from the 1540s by the use of stage sets whose perspective lines emphasized the central position to the audience of the ruler's throne. Using verse and dance and spectacular transformation scenes, masques allegorically referred to the ruler's power to tap the harmony of the cosmos and reproduce it on earth. Men and women uneasy about the savagery of the real world could watch the deployment of such themes as the transformation of Wild Men by Minerva and the Muses and Good Government into happily obedient subjects, or the disclosure, by theatrical sleight of hand, of a stately palace within an uncouth hill.

This reflected the narcissism of court life; it was an insurance taken out in the form of metaphors against accepting the reality of life outside. Yet James I could claim in his address of Parliament in 1609 that 'the state of monarchy is the supremest thing upon earth . . . In the scriptures Kings are called Gods.'[86] And as scholars revealed more about the powers of the emperors of ancient Rome, and as the divisions between and within countries were ever more clearly seen as complex and dangerous, political theorists pleaded the advantage of yielding old freedoms to new, decisive, unchallenged sovereign power. In his *Six Books on the Commonwealth* published in 1576, Jean Bodin went so far as to affirm that it was the sovereign's right to impose laws on his subjects 'without their consent' – unless in his judgement their resistance would unseat him.[87]

Too much can be read into a changed way of writing about authority. Resonant claims for the guidance of political action like Machiavelli's 'this is a general rule which seldom, if ever, fails',[88] or the use of the phrase 'reason of state' as a book title, as in Botero's treatise of 1589, add to the impression that authoritarianism had become more programmatic. In practice, however, both secular and clerical authorities operated, as they always had done, within the pragmatic context of getting things done. It was a man attuned to the practices of both church and state, Francisco de Vitoria, who wrote in the reign of the Emperor Charles V that rulers were necessarily compelled to 'think from hand to mouth'.[89] Theories about the nature and rights of power had to pass the conservative filter of older councillors reluctant to alter established balances between authority and consent. Whether in the case of the Venetian doge and his advisers, or of Philip II and his senior officials, brash theory was countered by the accumulated experience of men who had slowly worked their way to the top and seldom reached there before their fifties. The notion of princely absolutism – a century later to be expressed in Louis XIV's *'L'État, c'est moi'* – was in the air, but though rulers commonly had their way in external affairs, where internal, ruler–subject relations were concerned the pace of centralizing government was halting and the ideological thrust behind it open to challenge.

Palace within a Cavern, Inigo Jones, scenery design (1610) for *Oberon* (Chatsworth, Trustees of the Chatsworth Settlement)

Shortly after 1515, the year in which the young Francis I succeeded his father Louis XII as King of France, two of his subjects wrote books for his guidance about his realm and his position within it. One, Guillaume Budé, a scholar soaked in the history of imperial Rome, stressed the need for the king to strengthen his authority within the country as a whole. The other, Claude de Seyssell, a bishop and diplomatist more abreast of the recent past, reminded Francis that as his coronation oath to protect the status quo suggested, his freedom of action was subject to certain *freins*, brakes or bridles. These were the traditional rights of the church, the privileges and 'liberties' (from central interference) of towns, regions and noble families in return for services rendered in the past, bargains struck when the outlying provinces of Anjou, Picardy, Provence and Brittany came under royal control through bequest, marriage, settlement or war. Seyssell was attuned, as Budé was not, to the mood expressed at the meeting of the Estates General in 1484 by one of its spokesmen, Philippe Pot. Pot had displayed a remarkably imaginative recognition that all the provinces represented there, both those of the 'real France' and those recently acquired, formed a single country. But his message was not conciliatory. The people of France, he claimed, had a double right to determine their own concerns, first 'because they *are* their own, secondly because they are always open to victimization by [central] government'.[90] The crown did not summon so widely representative a meeting of its subjects again until 1560.

Indeed, in all countries, it was risking confrontation to call up a national assembly, the English Parliament, the Castilian and Aragonese *Cortes*, the Polish *Sjem*, the Hungarian Diet, the Swedish *Riksdag* or the Muscovite *Zemskii Sobor*, in order – almost always – to obtain co-operation in the collection of additional taxes. It was to pit efficiency and authority, as envisioned by a Budé or a Bodin, against an entrenched suspicion of novelty.

The co-operative nation state lay well in the future, and could be approached only by stealth: by the persuasion of regional magnates that co-operation was to their advantage, the sliding in of bureaucratic links between local and central authority, the grudging assent won in national assemblies with the argument that new circumstances arising from military or religious crises called for a reappraisal of old attitudes. Rulers could not force obedience. They had personal guard forces, a modest number of troops in garrisons in towns strategically vulnerable in time of war, traditional rights to organize militias and summon them to service. But none had anything like the sort of standing army that could impose their will on reluctant subjects. And any desire to equate central power with the geographical area of a country had to come to terms with the slow communications and scattered populations which also inhibited the active sharing of a sense of loyalty to authority.

Even where most densely urbanized, in the Netherlands, the Rhineland and in northern Italy, Europe consisted overwhelmingly of thinly and patchily inhabited countryside, largely self-contained environments of villages and small market towns and their inter-connecting paths and lanes. In places forests and marshes and wild hilly zones cut off even one sub-region from another. The centre may have been seen as alien from the periphery: in 1497 resentment against taxation sent 15,000 Cornishmen, all armed with some sort of weapon, as far as London before they were routed and their leaders executed. But if regionalism hampered authority it also protected it: the 1524–5 Peasants' War in southern Germany failed at least in part because men from different localities with similar anti-landlord grievances could not agree on a common strategy. Both were irruptions from the semi-sealed communities that chorographers and other travellers found so fascinating; none of these writers expressed any surprise at such dogged local conservatism, or any feeling that it should be interfered with. Even if individuals were aware of being part of great noble estates or extensive episcopal sees through agents who would, from time to time, remind them of what they owed in dues or tithes, the familiar life of tasks, kinship and acquaintances remained narrow, resisting further intrusion and disliking change. And this sense of a community's being locked in on itself was heightened by the restrictive tolls imposed by landlords on the transport of goods across the territories traditionally within their jurisdiction or along the rivers over which they had claims to riparian rights. Only the most prosperous peasant farmer could push his produce to market beyond these check-points. The great majority of men and women seldom travelled more than fifteen miles from their homes and lived in an isolation that inhibited any sentiment that can even be called patriotic save in the narrowest and most occasional of terms.

Active patriotism at a local level was chiefly restricted to educated and prosperous city dwellers who were at the same time aware that they had won and intended to maintain a constitutionally recognized position for themselves within the realm. A German student among 'the proud people of Montpellier' noted their indifference to edicts emanating from Paris: 'what, indeed, should they fear? The royal authority is so far away.'[91] *Campanilismo*, a term almost literally invoked when a character in Machiavelli's play *Mandragola* (1518) mocked another for feeling uneasy when he ventured beyond the sight of Florence's cathedral (with its landmark *campanile* or bell tower), was in Italy a symbolic expression of civic cosiness. The most heartfelt passage in Felix Fabri's *c*.1480 description of his native city, Ulm, came when he recalled the founding in 1377 of its cathedral: 'the Lord Mayor of the city descended into the pit, accompanied by other notables, in order to put in place the huge block of stone which hung suspended in the claws of a great clamp. At precisely three o'clock . . . the block was lowered, not by workmen but by the august members of the Council, some of them turning the great wheel, others guiding the ropes.'[92] There is an atmosphere of enclosure here, of the civic snugness captured also by a visitor to Calais in 1497 who wrote that 'every day in the afternoon, when the inhabitants take their rest, the gates are closed . . . at these times sentries and guards keep watch from the town's walls on all sides.'[93] This widely felt shelteredness was summed up in the Polish term for self-sufficient localities: each was a *gniazdo*, or 'nest'.

Naturally the nests resented cuckoos. When Duke Albert of Bavaria strengthened his corps of men trained in Roman law, a rural knight grumbled in 1497 that 'these men of law do not know our habits, and when they do, they are not prepared to accept our customs.'[94] And more effective central government necessarily meant not only the brushing aside of traditional legal processes but more effective pressure on pockets. As the Everyman folk-hero of the popular late medieval German tale of *Reynard the Fox* put it: 'thus our king the lion has sitting in council with him a select band of robbers, whom he holds in great honour and makes the greatest among his nobles. But let the poor wretch Reynard take a chicken, and you'll see them pounce on him . . . Little crooks are hanged, big crooks govern our lands and cities.'[95] Later hands picked up this old grudge against central power. Writing in 1531 Sebastian Franck, with the double eagle crest of the Habsburgs in mind, inveighed against 'the eagle, which signifies the life of kings and which is neither beautiful, well-formed, useful nor edible but, on the contrary, is ravenous, thievish, solitary, useless, warlike'.[96] The same note, struck more wryly, was sounded when in 1599 a character in Thomas Heywood's play *Edward IV, Part 1* said that he respects a king 'as poor folk love holidays, glad to have them now and then; but to have them come too often would undo them'.[97]

Not long after Provence was ceded by its last count, Charles III, on condition that its forms of self-government were largely to be respected, an official of the Provençal *parlement* was sent to check reports that a border district was being treated as part of 'real France'. On his arrival he found a post displaying the royal arms. Removing his hat, he knelt before it in homage. Then he had it pulled up and taken away.

Again, when King Philip II of Spain in 1566 ordered his representative in Catalonia to commandeer the services of carpenters to work on the construction of royal galleys, the answer reported to him was brusque: 'the people of Catalonia, by the liberties they have been granted are not like those of Toledo [in Castile] where any constable can order carpenters to be brought by force. Here your Majesty is seen as an individual in a contract.'[98] Shortly before, a Catalan had complained that Castilians 'give the impression that they alone are

The youthful Philip II, portrait head mounted on armour, Pompeo Leoni, Desiderius Helmschmidt and Ulrich Holzmann, 1544–56 (Kunsthistorisches Museum, Vienna)

descended from heaven and the rest of mankind are mud'. Yet Philip II, the bureaucrat-ruler *par excellence*, claimed that as he sat at his desk in the Escorial among his secretaries he could 'govern half the world with two inches of paper'.[99]

It was an understandable illusion. Rulers looked out from their courts and advisers and the diplomatic correspondence they received to a wider world represented chiefly by their opposite numbers. Knowledge of their subjects was restricted for reasons both of space and security. Similarly, their subjects knew little of them. We know far more of the personality of Renaissance rulers, the significance of the inscriptions on their coins and the meaning of the imagery deployed in their festivities, indeed about the working apparatus of their governments, than more than a few of their subjects could have known. Appeals to personal loyalty were, then, of restricted effect. There were propaganda appeals to national sentiment. In 1539, when England was threatened with invasion by the joint forces of France and Spain, Thomas Cromwell's protégé Richard Morison published *An Exhortation to styre all Englishe Men to the defence of theyr Countreye*; King Henry VIII is busily and expensively fortifying our ports: 'were it not our great shame to suffer his highnes to travaile alone?'[100] But who read such works in the restricted editions in which they were issued, probably not amounting to more than two thousand copies, and to what effect, can only be conjectured. The same is true of the works by individual enthusiasts for the history and character of their race, books like those in which in the 1570s Bernard du Haillan celebrated the 'virtue', the 'glory', the 'destiny' of France.[101] These were long books in small editions, whose authors often had an eye to court patronage; there is no doubt that patriotism existed as an idea to appeal to but little evidence that such writing quickened it.

Among Hungarian authors the revival of the Magyar language and the emergence of such leitmotifs as that Hungary was Christianity's eastern bastion and that its inhabitants were a chosen people, reflected a constant sense of immediate danger from the Turks that stimulated a merging of eddies of patriotism into something approaching a sense of nationhood. But elsewhere, threats to a country's way of life that were seen as such, rather than as crises invented by rulers for their own aggressive purposes, were intermittent. Though from 1567 four decades of armed struggle for independence from Spain gave rise to shared patriotic sentiments among the ten northern provinces of the Low Countries, expressed in common emblems on coins and medals, propaganda engravings like those showing women warriors defending the walls of their towns, and such phrases as 'The Lands of the United Netherlands', the provinces, for all their co-operative resistance, were regarded as forming a single national entity less by themselves than by others. Like the Swiss Cantons, which in 1499 won *de facto* independence from the empire by force of arms, they remained a confederation of lands with different customs, forms of speech, civic government, relationships between town and country.

The attempts of rulers to unify divisions within their countries was largely a reaction to the divisions in Europe itself and the need for income and obedience to keep abreast; the most obvious test of nationhood was the response to war. Smaller than France and Spain, and without the problems set by the assimilation of Provence and Catalonia, England is a test case for the opposing views of Budé and Seyssell.

Only in England was there anything like a monument to war's victims as opposed to the tomb effigies of commanders. It was a little frieze of archers, each accompanied by his name, in a stained-glass window in the parish church of Middleton in Lancashire. They had fallen in 1513 at Flodden. But even they were there not because they had fought for their country but because they were the tenants of the parish's patron Sir Richard Assheton. They may have been proud of being English and thought foul scorn of the Scots, but it was a landlord they fought for, not a nation. By 1588, the year of the expected invasion by the Catholic Spanish Armada, the Tudor government had done much to push power into the space notionally available to the ruler's control. It had built up a central bureaucracy. The court of Elizabeth was a focus of national interest and aspiration. Catholic Rome had been broken with and a Protestant state church had been imposed with fairly general acceptance. By the eve of the Armada's arrival in the Channel the government's organization of coastal fortification, and its early warning beacon system along the whole south coast, together with a national militia enrolment of perhaps 90,000 men (one for every eleven households in the country), were triumphs of central legislation carried into effect by co-operative local administrations. Yet of the men called up to defend England in the event of the fleet's landing the troops and cannon it carried, some found excuses to stay at home, many deserted after a few days, others were judged by their commanders to have taken no advantage of their opportunities to train themselves for a national emergency. Addressing the troops who did turn up at the

Fallen archers at the Battle of Flodden (1513): detail of the memorial window to Sir Richard Assheton, c.1524 (Middleton church, Manchester)

anti-invasion command headquarters, Tilbury, Elizabeth referred with genuine emotion to 'the loyal hearts and good will of my subjects' and to the support of 'my people'. This was a phrase she often used: 'God bles mi piple', it sounded like to a foreign visitor who heard her speaking to a crowd from a window of Richmond Palace.[102] But though it may have come from the heart, the vision it invoked was flawed.

Writing after the event, and of wars uncontroversially in the past, Shakespeare was on ground that his audience would still recognize when showing how Prince Henry's recruiter, Sir John Falstaff in *Henry IV*, was hard put to gauge a single reluctant volunteer out of Gloucestershire. Again, 'I can call spirits from the vasty deep,' claimed Glendower in the first part of the same play. 'But', came Hotspur's response, 'will they come when you do call for them?'[103] It is not surprising that when monarchs went to war they continued to rely not on 'the nation' but on those closest to them in rank and obligation who had a habit-formed following in the region where their properties lay, on less powerful men of breeding who were adventurous or anxious for advancement, on foreign mercenary professionals, and, last (and not necessarily least, for warfare occasionally produced reluctant heroes), on those natives who could not dodge the draft or thought it worth chancing an arm to lead a less restricted and perhaps more fortunate life. Here again Shakespeare gave words to covert thoughts. 'What would you have me do?' asks the pimp in *Pericles*, when reproached for the trade he had adopted; 'Go to the wars, would you? Where a man may serve seven years for the loss of a leg, and have not money enough in the end to buy him a wooden one?'[104]

CHAPTER III

The Divisions of Europe

WARS

In around 1500, Philippe de Commines, diplomat and adviser to
Charles VIII of France on foreign affairs, noted that, 'I have been as
conversant among great princes as any man of my time in France, and
not only those who have reigned in this kingdom but in Flanders,
Germany, England, Spain, Portugal and Italy . . . besides several
whom I never saw, but knew . . . by my conferences with their
ambassadors, which gave me a sufficient character of their natures and
conditions.' And the outcome of this knowledge? That Europe was
doomed to be fissured by mutual hostilities; 'God has not made any
created being in this world, neither man nor beast, nor anything else,
but He has set up some other thing in opposition to it.' Thus 'France
has England as a check, England has Scotland, and Spain, Portugal.'
And he goes on to box the compass: one Italian state against another,
Swiss against Germans, one German prince or city against a neighbour,
the Hansa ports against Denmark. 'I have spoken only of Europe', he
concludes, 'for of the affairs of Asia and Africa I am not sufficiently
informed.' But he assumes that mutual hostility is the norm 'all the
world over'.[1]

Sir Philip Sidney took his Christian name in 1554 from his godfather
Philip of Spain when the prince came to England during his brief
marriage to Mary Tudor. He died in 1586 when campaigning in the
Netherlands against Philip's forces there. In 1581, at the age of twenty-
seven, widely travelled, with many politically influential friends at
home and abroad, and disturbingly in love with the seventeen-year-old
wife of another man, he wrote in one of his sonnets to 'Stella' of
the age's insistent war-like traumas. Would the Turks – defeated at the
naval battle of Lepanto in 1571 – launch another all-out attack in
the Mediterranean? What of the Polish King Stefan Batory's chances

against Muscovy? What fortune will the Protestant armies in the Netherlands have against Philip's Catholic ones? What of Elizabeth's wars against the rebel Irish, of the outcome of the feuds at the court of Scotland?

> These questions busy wits to me do frame.
> I, cumbered with good manners, answer do –
> But know not how; for still I think of you.[2]

A further insight into the continent's feverishness comes from a monarch himself, the Emperor Charles V. In 1548, physically over-stretched by his Europe-wide responsibilities for the lands he had inherited and the Catholic faith he felt it his duty to protect from Protestant heresy, he experienced one of his recurrent fears that he would die prematurely amidst a world of adversaries. He dictated a long 'Instruction', or memorandum,[3] to guide his son Philip, accepting that 'it is almost impossible to lay down invariable rules, given the instability and uncertainty of human affairs,' but commenting on the dangers to be anticipated, from internal revolt, or foreign aggression, across the whole range of his lands from Spain itself to Milan and Naples and the Netherlands and across Germany to Austria. Philip's main difficulty would be to control a heterogeneous empire liable to spring apart either of its own volition or owing to the incitement of covetous neighbours.

He wrote sententiously

Always aim for peace. Go to war only when it is forced on you. It exhausts the treasury and causes great misery. Our Spanish subjects have supported my wars against the Protestant princes in Germany but they have had enough. Leave German affairs, as I now do, to my brother Ferdinand, but maintain contacts there, for your vigilance must be alert throughout all the possessions of our house. The most constant threat comes from France. Their kings have been and are bound to us by treaties, but remember that they are not true to their undertakings and only keep to their word when they are too poor to go to war. Never agree to renegotiate our settlements with them; that would be used as an excuse to tear them up. Keep a good guard on our northern borders with France, and maintain a fleet of galleys in the Mediterranean as a warning both to the Turks and to the French. We need to maintain good relations with Genoa because of its port, so take care for this.

He went on, from one specific problem to another,

> In the north-east I have strengthened Flanders against France by my annexation of Guelders, Utrecht and Frisia. Still, you must keep money on hand there in case there is need for a sudden mobilization; the inhabitants are reasonably loyal to us, but do not relax your watchfulness. And keep on good terms with the present King of Denmark even if you are wooed by the exiled King Christian, father of my nieces; family loyalty comes second to keeping Denmark from intervening in Flanders as it did in the past.
>
> I have settled the affairs of Savoy somewhat to the detriment of our ally the Duke, but do not help him recover the lands occupied by the French even if they are his by right. That could give the French an excuse to press south again against our Milan and if that happens our links with Genoa and Florence and our rule in Naples and Sicily could all be put at risk. Further to Italy: do not trust the Pope [Paul III], who neither honours his word nor has the general interests of Christianity at heart; keep an eye on any strengthening of the Duke of Ferrara's family relationships with the French; Venice is unlikely to form any close attachment to France, Florence is much indebted to our support of the Duke and is safe, but be watchful of Lucca and Siena. Above all, keep Milan and Naples well garrisoned with troops regularly paid to keep them loyal to us.
>
> As for the rest, remember that the Swiss covet part of our Franche-Comté; keep on good terms with England but, given the Pope's resentment against that country, very warily; with Scotland you need have little to do.
>
> Finally, you should marry again [Philip's first wife, Maria of Portugal had died three years earlier]. Nothing holds scattered possessions so firmly together as for provinces to know that their overlord has sons who might become their governors. As for choice, you must suit yourself, remembering, however, that discrepancy in age is not necessarily an obstacle, and that it is more useful to contract a match outside your own family circle.[4]

As we have seen, Philip's choice fell on Mary the new Queen of England. And from his father's death in 1558 the truth within the old Emperor's platitude about 'the instability and uncertainty of human affairs' was forced home; his reign was preoccupied with wars against the Turks, England, and rebel provinces in the Netherlands, and, on full military alert, with protecting Spanish interests during the fluctuating fortunes of the civil wars in France.

Charles's memorandum endorsed Commines's observation that the

War, the Father of All Things, Hans Weiditz (?), woodcuts illustrating an edition of Petrarch, *De remediis* (Augsburg, 1532)

European states were in a situation of constant tension. Either there was war as they rubbed up against or challenged one another, or a precarious peace. And peace was the very moment when, as a French poet phrased it in the year following Philip's accession, 'Alecto the Fury slips a serpent from her hair into the bosom of Europe.'[5] One has only to lick a finger and hold it up in the political atmosphere of the times to find it covered with fragments of such fatalistic observations.

Commines's gloomy overview owed something to the dictum of Heraclitus that 'war is the father of all things,' as interpreted in the most widely diffused of Petrarch's works, his *Remedies against both Kinds of Fortune*, – good and bad strokes of luck or chance. An illustration to a German edition of 1532 spells it out. There is conflict in the sky: wind, rain, hail, but a frizzling sun; birds fight other birds and eat small animals; animals fight one another and are hunted by men, while men fight among themselves; time, in the guise of a giant spider's web, tugs at the stability of a house; soldiers attack women while death carries off one of them from his lover's side; a cock struggles to retain his rule of the dung heap; a farmer fights to control the invasion of a nature which is already in conflict with itself. Throughout European literature the wheel of human fortune revolved with the red splash of war on its rim. Discussing the use of allegory, Karel von Mander in 1604 reminded artists of 'the common saying about the circular course of the world's way: peace brings livelihood, livelihood wealth, wealth pride, pride strife, strife war, war poverty, poverty humility, humility peace'.[6]

Every new contribution to mainstream political discourse inserted the message that for rulers war was their inheritance and might be their duty. In humanistic terms, after the universal Augustan peace into which God chose to incorporate Himself as Christ, there had been a relapse into separate political units. Each country could claim a national hero who had resisted Rome's claim to be lord of all Europe. And as embattled and defiant Protestants came increasingly to see their destinies in terms of the tribalistic Old as well as the peace-loving New Testament, they drew sustenance from the former's status as 'a book of the battles of the Lord', as an English divine called it in 1602.[7] Machiavelli's *The Prince*, written in 1513 but first published in 1532, strengthened the tendency of political theorists to think in terms of militaristic 'reasons of state'; though this was a phrase he had not used himself, he had stressed the primacy of being ready for war among a ruler's responsibilities. Commonplace, too, were arguments positively in favour of wars. They solved the problem of the wastrels and ruffianly beggars thrown up by burgeoning populations. The German soldier and scholar Ulrich von Hutten put it bluntly in 1518: 'war is necessary to get youths out of the country and keep the population down'[8]; in the possibly Shakespearean *Two Noble Kinsmen*, Arcite expressed it more picturesquely: war

> heal'st with blood
> The earth when it is sick, and cur'st the world
> O' the plurisy of people.[9]

A Russian justification for bloody and frequently unsuccessful irruptions into Livonia-Lithuania was a shrugging reference to an old saying, 'we have a lot of people.'[10] And, on another tack, war abroad was frequently advocated as a panacea for internal unrest. 'There are divers nowadays', Montaigne recorded, 'which will speak thus, wishing this

Polish–Lithuanian victory over a Russian army on the river Dnieper, 1514: anon., *The Battle of Orsha*, c.1515–20 (National Museum, Warsaw)

violent and burning emotion . . . might be diverted to some neighbour war.'[11] Giovanni Botero took up the theme: in war against a neighbouring power 'all discontent is vented on a common enemy'.[12]

These remarks cannot be dismissed as the reactions of mere writers. There were rulers who accepted the over-population and sedition arguments. Henri II of France used them to justify another intervention in Italy in 1552 – the attempt that Charles V had feared, to dominate Siena; despite the failure of that campaign the Venetian ambassador reported in 1575 that Henri III's entourage was discussing the need for another foreign war to divert the dangerous number of peasants who had assumed arms on one side or the other during France's internal conflicts since 1562.

That war, or preparedness for war, was part of the human condition was assumed by the modish debate about the rival merits of arms and letters, sword and pen. Already familiar when Castiglione gave it extended treatment in *The Courtier* and came to the usual conclusion that one was as necessary as the other, it was thoroughly hackneyed by the time Cervantes in 1604 made it the subject of a long discourse which Don Quixote pursued 'so rationally and in such well-chosen language that none of his hearers could take him for a madman just then'.[13] Indeed, the extension of literacy, the new emphasis on 'letters' as an aspect of the educational formation of the gentleman as well as the cleric, lawyer and merchant, together with the vast extension of printed books, meant that references to, or discussions of, warfare had never been so constantly crossing a reader's mind; not just from histories or books dealing directly with aspects of warfare (of which 145 were published between 1492 and 1570 in Venice alone), but from short stories, novels, etiquette books, plays and poems. The range of graphic military images in Shakespeare's works has made it tempting to see his 'lost years' between the last reference in 1585 to his youthful residence in Stratford and his emergence in 1592 as a player and playwright in London, as having been spent as a soldier in the Netherlands. Ben Jonson did serve as a soldier. So did Cervantes. Alonso de Ercilla was only one of many poets who fought and devoted whole works to their experiences. His epic *La Araucana* (1589), based on his participation in the conquest of Chile, took war for granted while mourning its consequences there as in Europe: 'must everything be battles and hardships, discord, fire, blood, enmities, hates, rancours, rages and deeds of violence . . . acts of destruction, cruelties which will weary Mars himself?'[14] Indeed, the 'wearied Mars' became a pictorial theme in its own right.

Ercilla, while doing the duty owed by an aristocrat, a member of the privileged military caste, pined for the gentler environment in which he had become an educated man, a poet and a lover. And here too literature, by reflecting life, added another note that kept the role of war alive in a reader's mind. Everywhere, save in Germany, was a fear that society's natural military leaders were preferring the arts of peace to the art of war. In 1509 a Venetian patriot who could remember the days when patricians fought in, as well as directed wars, groused at their current reliance on mercenaries and peasants while their ancestors' armour rusted on their palace walls. Later in the century a French noble noted with alarm that many of the French *noblesse* were abandoning arms and turning 'to the various branches of knowledge, to the arts and to agriculture'. And in 1600 Thomas Wilson, in his *The State of England*, acknowledged that 'gentlemen who were wont to addict themselves to wars are now grown good husbands [husbandmen], and well know how to improve their lands.'[15]

Yet by 1600 neither revulsion against the horrors of war nor a taste for cultivating one's garden could lead to a revival of the pacifistic strain that had been widely publicized through the works of the English Thomas More (*Utopia*), the Dutch Erasmus (*The Complaint of Pity*; *War is a fine Thing to those who know it not*), the German Agrippa of Nettesheim (*On the Vanity of the Arts and Sciences*), the Spaniard Juan Vives (*On the Turkish War*), or the Belgian Josse Clichthove who in his *On War and Peace* of 1523 firmly declared that he was not a patriot: 'I recognize only the name of Christian.'[16] All these, and other works of the early sixteenth century, constituted what can very loosely be called an international peace movement. It was not merely bookish. The wording of peace treaties and diplomatic correspondence shows that men of affairs at least took account of it, and there were genuine attempts to find a common ground for the long-term settlement of inter-nation antagonisms. The tenor of this pacifistic vein was, in any case, not so much that war could be cancelled within the Heraclitan scheme of things, but that individual rulers could eschew aggression and be content to housekeep within their own borders; or, if that put unrealistic strain on the aggressive instinct, at least that they should

'Wearied Mars', Lucas van Leyden, *Mars and Venus*, engraving, 1530 (British Museum)

agree – as a last resort – to deflect it against a legitimate target: the Turk.

Nonetheless, the early sixteenth-century peace movement, such as it was, had foundered by the late 1520s among wars that seemed unstoppably self-perpetuating. In 1529 Alfonso de Valdes, a loyal defender of Charles V whose armies two years before had sacked Rome, but an Erasmian at heart, wrote a dialogue one of whose protagonists was a monarch, Polidoro, presented as a good man but a victim of his age. 'Other neighbouring princes and I', Polidoro is made to say, 'engaged in such fierce warfare, and things came to such a pass that, after many years, although we all wished to live in peace, we could find no means of getting free.' He explained the dilemma in terms that could realistically be applied to Charles himself or his habitual adversary Francis I. 'On the one hand, to see my realms destroyed and the provinces over which we fought lost and virtually laid waste, so moved me to compassion that I was tempted to leave everything and live in peace; on the other hand, remembering the senseless things my enemies had done and were doing to me, and the lack of justice in everything they asserted and demanded of me, it seeming dishonourable not to carry the matter further, since I had already spent and used up so much on it, I thought it a great meanness not to pursue it to the end.'[17]

That was the mood Charles had taken for granted in his memorandum to his son. By the early seventeenth century James I of England earned mockery as 'the wisest fool in Christendom' partly because of his belief that rulers could learn to live in amity in spite of differences in their religious creeds and historical claims and grudges. In 1623 there came a belated echo from the pacifistic groundswell of a century before: 'O mortal race', mourned Virginio Cesarini, 'when death must come, why hasten it with war? . . . If you must fight, spare your native land.'[18] By that time the nations of Europe, from Spain and France to Poland and Russia, and from Sweden to Italy, were locked in the Thirty Years War.

Writing in the mid-fifteenth century, fifty years before Commines's portrait of a divided Europe, Enea Silvio Piccolomini had greeted the news of the fall of Constantinople to the Turks in 1453 with saddened resignation. Never had there been so clear a call for unity among the powers, 'but I do not hope for what I want. Christianity has no longer a head: neither Pope nor Emperor is adequately esteemed or obeyed; they are treated as fictitious names and painted figures.' Asking 'how might one persuade the numberless Christian rulers to join forces,' he reviews their overriding private concerns. Venice will not endanger its trading privileges in the Levant. Genoa is at war with Aragon over commercial control in the western Mediterranean. Castile is fighting the Moors in the Kingdom of Granada. France is too frightened of a resumption of hostilities with England after a hundred years of war to risk sending troops outside the country. England thinks only of revenge for what it has lost in France. He concludes, 'Scotch, Danes, Swedes and Norwegians, who live at the end of the world, see nothing beyond their countries' interests. The Germans are greatly divided and have nothing to unify them.'[19]

It is notable in how many cases the initial effort of starting a war created a momentum making it equally difficult to stop. Even impressive victories in the field became absorbed into the continuing texture of recurrent campaigns. It took thirteen years (1454–66) for the chief Hansa cities, with Polish help, to force the Teutonic Order to yield its claim to sovereign control over Prussia. From the French invasion of Italy and conquest of Naples in 1494–5 it took thirty-six years of renewed campaigning before an uneasy peace was restored to the peninsula, with first Maximilian's Germans, then the Swiss, finally the French dropping out of a saga that left matters much as they had been at the start, apart from the passing of the Duchy of Milan and the Kingdom of Naples and Sicily into Spanish hands. The war that started in 1562 as Sweden's attempt to check Ivan IV's advance from Muscovy into Estonia came to involve all the Scandinavian countries before it petered out ten years later. It took forty-two years from Spain's first campaign against the rebellious provinces in the Netherlands in 1567 to bring the conflict to a mere truce. When in 1593 the grumbling border strife between the eastern Habsburg Empire and the Turks escalated into open warfare it took thirteen years to bring it to a halt, with honours more or less even.

It is notable, too, how the increasing pace of diplomatic contacts made political Europe seem smaller, especially in the West. Before embarking on his expedition to Naples in 1494, Charles VIII had taken care to protect his own homeland through agreements with Maximilian, Henry VII and Ferdinand and Isabella, and to ensure the initial safe passage of his army and its supporting fleet through negotiations with Milan and Genoa. In 1509 an attack on Venice's mainland possessions was co-ordinated between France, the German Empire, Aragon, the Papacy, the Marquis of Mantua, the Duke of Ferrara and the Duke of Savoy – who was to receive as his share of the spoils the distant Venetian island of Cyprus. Henry VIII was tempted to join so

Landsknecht Battle, anon., 1514 (Universitätssammlung, Würzburg)

august an assembly but was deterred by the thought of his chief adversary, France, standing to gain so much at the expense of England's trading partner Venice.

Equally characteristic of this war-primed intercourse among the powers was the abruptness with which the alliance collapsed and changed course. On the defeat of the Venetian army in 1509, and the overrunning of its territories by the allies' troops as far as the villages along the very edge of the lagoon, the Pope, Julius II, was aghast at the preponderant share occupied by French troops. He subtracted an equally disturbed Ferdinand of Aragon from the partners and formed a Holy League – to protect Venice. This quadrille was dourly observed by Machiavelli, who replied to a notion put to him about an alliance between Italian states against their foreign aggressors, 'you make me laugh.'[20] The making and breaking of alliances as the direction suggested by rulers' opportunism changed, became a leitmotif of the period, and the cause of many of the stalemates and altered balance of forces that helped to prolong periods of warfare.

On and on went the wars throughout the century and into the next: renewed conflicts between France and the Habsburg monarchy that broke out north of the Alps – in Provence and Savoy and lower Rhineland – after the settlement in 1530 of their contests in Italy; repeated strikes of England against Scotland and France; Denmark-Norway's attacks on Sweden's mainland and island bases; Venice's Friulian war against Austria. There were wars or mobilizations for war that take their names from local crises – over Brandenburg, over Cologne – or from strategic friction points whose names symbolized the avidity with which the greater powers could spring to arms even if they did not fully exploit them: Riga, the coveted Livonian port on the Baltic; the tremblingly independent Duchy of Jülich on France's north-west border with Germany; the Valtelline (the valley linking Lombardy to the Tyrol, involving Spanish, French, German and Italian interests); the tiny Marquisate of Saluzzo, a frequently gnawed-at bone of contention between France, Savoy and Spain. Our concern is not to particularize or extend this list, but to wonder why it is already so long, and what light it throws on the political divisions of Europe.

The only power vacuums into which governments could extend their territories were in the parts of the Moldavian and Wallachian lands towards the Black Sea that were not effectively governed by the Turks. After the death of Stephen the Great of Moldavia in 1504, no ruler, in what was a zone of well-nigh tribal loyalties and subversions, survived long enough to build what could be seen as a defined country, let alone establish a dynasty to give it an enduring place on the map. Elsewhere, while there were contested or uncertain borderlands, there were no significant unorganized zones into which to expand. As Piccolomini and Commines had made clear, the countries of Europe were jammed together amidst their mutual exasperations. A country which raised enough troops could make initial inroads on the territory of an enemy. This stimulated a home guard reaction which imperilled the invader's logistic supply lines, and gave time to raise mercenaries and call up allies to check any major shift in the pattern of political power. Though the notion of a 'balance' of power within international relations had been so called from the early sixteenth century, it remained an idea rather than a programme.

So by the early seventeenth century national boundaries remained remarkably unchanged by war. Moorish Granada was annexed by

Spain, the Swiss won effective independence from the German Empire, Spain gained Milan and Naples, Tuscany absorbed Siena, Savoy-Piedmont became a more widely recognized national entity, the United Provinces of the northern Low Countries came to the brink of being a new member of the wrangling club of nations. A few German princes and cities – Brandenburg, Bavaria and Nuremberg, for example – expanded somewhat at their neighbours' expense. Overall what small return for so great an expenditure of lives, cash, misery and organizational effort, and with so little active volition on the part of the populace at large! But then, as Galileo wrote to a friend in 1610, war was a 'royal sport'.

Forward strategic planning, the search for, maintenance of, and switching among alliances, the contracting of large bodies of foreign mercenaries: these were tasks that led to a rapid development of diplomatic method. While short-term missions continued to be employed, the chief reliance came to be placed on resident ambassadors abroad, regularly replaced. Already commonplace among the Italian states in the 1460s, from the early sixteenth century the practice – stimulated by common interests in the Italian wars – spread throughout western and central Europe and was adopted by Poland in the 1560s. The links provided by the earlier occasional diplomatic missions had established contacts and provided information. But it was the resident embassies, with their staffs of secretaries, spies and long-term local informants, and the time they had to investigate not just the characters of rulers and the influence upon them of the members of their court, but the economic and military resources of their countries, that enabled rulers to feel that they knew Europe far better than had been possible in the preceding centuries.

On the whole this new flood of information about Europe, often coming in daily, undermined any inclination to think of the continent as potentially a peaceful unity. The Venetian ambassador to Rome in 1491 was quite clear about his function: 'the first duty of an ambassador is exactly the same as that of any other servant of a government, that is, to do, say, advise and think whatever may best serve the preservation and aggrandisement of his own state.'[21] Even when meeting to arrange a peace treaty, diplomats were aware of their obligation not to yield more ground than was absolutely necessary lest they narrowed the foothold from which another forward spurt could be taken. During the diplomatic skirmishes that led to the Anglo-Imperial Treaty of Bruges in 1521, Wolsey bitterly complained that his opposite number was asking for a forest when all his master the Emperor needed was seven or eight trees. All settlements, however laudatory of peace were the words that prefaced them, had, as unwritten sub-text, the possibility of a return match on better terms.

It was the assumption that international relations were fundamentally unstable that created the demand outside diplomatic channels for political news. Shortly after the coronation of Henri III in Paris in 1575 a correspondent of Sir Philip Sidney wrote to him from Venice: 'it is amazing how widely people are convincing themselves that peace has been made . . . Those who know the King better do not expect any such thing . . . and certainly not a peace which could properly be called a peace.'[22] Men of Sidney's education and standing cultivated such contacts in order to keep themselves abreast of affairs. From the 1560s business firms – the Fuggers of Augsburg, the Rožmberks in Prague – relied on networks of informants all over Europe to guide their dealings. From 1609 regularly issued news bulletins covering Europe were printed in Germany and Holland and began to be copied in France and England for a much wider audience. They dealt, of course, with crises, mobilizations, the progress of campaigns. Peace was not news. It was war that whetted the appetite to keep abreast of foreign affairs and reach for the continental map.

'Desire of glory': *The War in Picardy*, Georg Lemberger, miniature, *c.*1512 (Albertina, Vienna)

The motives that led rulers into competition with one another had been formulated by Lorenzo Valla in 1440: 'desire of glory', 'hope of booty', 'fear of incurring disaster later, if the strength of others were allowed to increase', and 'avenging a wrong and defending friends'.[23]

'Glory', for a prince's person and dynasty, was glossed as 'ambition' by historians who from the early sixteenth century became as interested in analysing the causes of war as in recording its events, and from the mid-century the motive was renamed as the search for 'reputation'. 'Honour and reputation are the things that most mark a man in the world,' wrote Charles V's brother Ferdinand in 1549[24]; in two memoranda from senior ministers urging Philip II to press the war in the Netherlands in 1577, one stressed the importance of maintaining his 'honour and prestige', the other his 'honour and reputation'.[25]

Booty for soldiers meant loot; for rulers it meant land. The ownership of territory, and the exercise of legal and fiscal rights within it, had always been the chief badge of status. We have seen that as the greatest of all landlords, princes acted within Europe as their inferiors did in the accumulation of property: reviving old claims to estates lost in times of poverty or violent occupation; linking properties through marriages. As with the widely scattered estates of medieval nobles, they were indifferent as to whether new or reclaimed lands were contiguous to the old or contained populations different in speech or custom. Centuries of conquests and dynastic marriages to foreign princesses had left a formidable residue of dormant claims. Charles VIII conquered Naples (briefly) by resurrecting a claim that extended back to the thirteenth century; Louis XII invaded Milan as 'his' by right of an ancestor's marriage to the daughter of a duke of Milan in 1389. Henry VIII's successive – and unsuccessful – invasions of France were represented as attempts to restore his inheritance from the fourteenth-century Edward III. Philip II governed and warred in the Netherlands by right of his grandfather's marriage to Mary of Burgundy in 1477. Some wars, especially those in the Baltic, did have commercial advantage as a motive, but it was never a sole one, and for monarchs it carried a stigma. Resenting Elizabeth's backing of what he saw as the provocative incursions of the Muscovy Company, Tsar Ivan reproachfully wrote, 'we had thought that you had been ruler over your land . . . but now we perceive that there be other men who do rule, and not men, but peasants and merchants.'[26] And from the English side, when Henri IV settled his war with the Duke of Savoy by asking for fiscally profitable districts rather than the prestigious marquisate of

Saluzzo, Elizabeth's agent reported that his own nobility, 'which more regard the honour of France than the profit of the king's purse, doe term it a shameful and dishonourable treaty'.[27]

'The fear of incurring disaster later, if the strength of others were allowed to increase' had led Lodovico Sforza of Milan to encourage Charles VIII's incursion into an Italy within which he felt dangerously isolated. It was the same motive that led Julius II to change sides when the French presence in Italy after the occupation of Venetian territory menaced the Pope's own power as a temporal ruler. It was fear that prompted the alliances, and the shifts in and out of them, that were the response to the polarization of international power politics from the 1530s; a response to the antagonism between the most militarily efficient and ambitious power, France, and the most extensive, the Habsburg web between Madrid, Milan, Brussels and Vienna. Fear led to the imagining of a domino effect. Duke Ulrich of Württemberg was forced into exile by his fellow members of the south German Swabian League because his attacks on neighbouring cities could have tempted them and, from their example, others, to 'turn Swiss' and fight for their independence both from the League and from the Empire that gave it some measure of protection. Similarly, it was the fear that if the Netherlands broke from Habsburg hegemony other components would follow its example, that kept Spain's military effort there alive in spite of one state bankruptcy after another.

Support for the activation of any of these considerations came from little further down than the ruler's immediate circle of like-minded magnates, ministers and chief officials, and their estimate of how much money and how many men could be raised to give a campaign a chance of success. Before coming in *Utopia* (1516) to the description of the island on which life was socially fair and as free as possible from external strife, Thomas More represents himself asking his imaginary traveller why he did not put the wisdom he had acquired from his knowledge of Utopia at the disposal of some ruler in discordant Europe. 'Well', comes the answer, 'suppose I were at the court of the French King and sitting in his privy council. In a most secret meeting, a circle of his most astute councillors over which he personally presides is setting its wits to work to consider by what crafty mechanisms he may keep his hold on Milan and bring back into his power that Naples which has been eluding his grasp; then overwhelm Venice and subdue the whole of Italy; next bring under his sway Flanders, Brabant and finally, the whole of Burgundy.' (It is worth recalling at this point that More was writing as an experienced London lawyer of forty, knowledgeable about the court and the ways in which public policy was decided and, before writing this part of *Utopia*, considering the offer of a membership of Henry VIII's council. He had just returned from a diplomatic mission to the Netherlands where he heard the news of Francis's conquest of Milan. Although, influenced by the peace-loving views of Erasmus and his humanist circle, More was exaggerating somewhat, but not seriously distorting the atmosphere of the 'royal sport'.) 'At this meeting', Hythlodaeus, More's spokesman, goes on, 'one advises that a treaty should be made with the Venetians to last as long as the King will find it convenient . . . Another thinks that a settlement should be made with the king of Aragon and that, as a guarantee of peace, someone else's [Catherine of Foix's] Kingdom of Navarre should be ceded to him. Another proposes that the Prince of Castile be caught by the prospect of a marriage alliance and that some nobles of his court be drawn to the French side by a fixed pension . . . The English should be called friends but suspected as enemies. The Scots therefore must be posted in readiness, prepared for any opportunity to be let loose on the English.'

'Suppose I proved', Hythlodaeus asks in conclusion, 'that all this warmongering, by which so many nations were kept in a turmoil on the French king's account, would, after draining his resources and destroying his people, at length by some mischance end in nought, and that therefore he had better look after his ancestral kingdom and make it as prosperous and flourishing as possible, love his subjects and be loved by them, and have no designs on other countries since what he already possessed was more than enough for him: what reception from my listeners, my dear More, do you think this speech of mine would find?' More's reply was carefully neutral: 'not a very favourable one'.[28]

In 1525 Francis was captured in battle with Charles V's army at Pavia. In 1529 he renounced all his claims in Italy. In 1535 he was again at war with Charles, this time, to general scandal, in alliance with the Turks. Peace in 1539 was followed in 1542–4 by yet another campaign against Charles. In the year before the King's death in 1547 the Venetian ambassador reported that Francis was lazy about attending to the ordinary affairs of government, 'but in all the great matters of state, matters of peace and war, His Majesty . . . insists on his will being obeyed. In this event there is no one at court, however great his authority, who dares remonstrate with His Majesty.'[29] 'Kings', as Philip II's general the Duke of Alba wrote in 1553 to one of the monarch's secretaries, 'are born to do their will, and we, their vassals and servants, are born to do their will likewise.'[30]

And kings loved to be portrayed in armour; when Charles was only twelve years old his grandfather Maximilian I fitted him out with a suit by the great armourer of Innsbruck Konrad Seusenhofer. Francisco de Holanda flattered King Sebastian of Portugal in 1571 by ingeniously portraying him as entirely embodied of military *matériel*: his crown and legs composed of cavalry and infantry combined, his arms, sword, upper chest of cavalry, his shield, lower chest and waist of pikemen, his face of artillery and his thighs of tents. This was wishful thinking; seven years later Sebastian's inability to raise a sufficiently large and loyal force in his expedition against the North African Moors led to his defeat and death in the battle of Alcazar-el-Kebir in Morocco.

Rulers could in the main rely on the greater landlord class and the higher clergy to be loyal to a sense of partnership with royal policy and play a part in persuading others to pay and serve, though we have seen through what layers of national sluggishness and indifference their persuasion had to sink. Nonetheless, once a war had been decided, it could be waged, however great the discrepancy between aim and means in implementation. Early in the sixteenth century a Venetian described the Republic's armies as 'Noah's arks' of anomalous components.[31] From the late 1560s the case-hardened core of Philip II's force fighting in the Netherlands to enforce Spanish and Catholic unity there came from Spain itself. But because of the subsequent reluctance of his countrymen to enlist, and the high desertion rate among those who did, he was forced to employ mercenaries as well; among the 17,000 men waiting in Flanders for the Armada to escort their transports across the Channel, only 4,000 were Spaniards. And when Spanish success in the South had compressed the conflict into the northern provinces which possessed the advantage of protective waterways and access to support from the sea, the 'Dutch' armies of his adversaries were predominantly composed of German, English, French and Danish troops, by no means all of whom were members of the Protestant faith let alone interested in the cause on behalf of which they were taking their pay. 'Royal sport' was a throw-away, if saturnine comment.[32] But if governments wanted war and had the money to draw on the international market of soldiers-for-sale, there was neither a religious creed nor an international authority to hamper them.

CREEDS

Whereas war had characterized the nature of European history for centuries, the fissuring of the continent by the Protestant Reformation from the 1520s was divisive on a radically different and unprecedented scale. In contrast to the saga of Christianity, gradually extending across a map of paganism, this was the phenomenon of a mostly long assured and uniform community of Christian belief enduringly split into two raggedly defined parts with astonishing rapidity and profound emotional disturbance.

The fissure occurred at a time when almost everyone believed or wished to believe that he or she played a personal role in a divine plan, initiated when God created the world and concerned more directly with the individual when God himself became a man and in this guise died under the torture of the cross for his fellows. A life unconditioned by the significance of these events had become practically unimaginable. The figures of ploughmen, carpenters and masons carved into misericords and corbels reflected the easygoing relationship of the populace with churches where workmen offered themselves for hire with the tools of their trade. In spite of Christ's driving the moneylenders from the temple, merchants arranged deals there, lovers made assignations ('did you exchange glances in a church?' was a routine question put by priests in the confessional), inscriptions and coats of arms on chapels staked a claim to secular identification with the sacred; 'you know', Savonarola told his Florentine audience, that 'they have put coats of arms on the back of vestments, so that when the priest stands at the altar, the arms can be seen by all the people.'[33]

Portrayed in altarpieces, donors knelt within scenes of the birth, adoration and crucifixion of Christ; saints stood guard over background views of the towns to which they brought their spiritual protection; the Virgin clutched her magic child within sight of an instantly recognizable local guildhall. Artists used the features of people known to them and to their audience as attendants in religious narrative, even, as Filippo Lippi did in Italy and Jean Fouquet in France, nonchalantly using the mistresses they possessed or pined after as models for Mary.

Tabernacles at street corners, crucifixes at turns in a country road, figures of saints or of scenes from Christ's Passion stamped into metal or glazed into ceramic tableware, incised into pieces of armour, moulded into oven tiles, carved into beams and furniture, forming the earliest subjects of woodcuts to be pasted or nailed up in cottages: the evidence for the naturalization of supernatural immigrants within the secular world was everywhere. The calendar came alive only with the names of saints. A Lancashire man accused in 1532 of getting a woman with child, acknowledged that he had made love to her from time to time; but not, he claimed during the critical period 'between the feast of St Mark and the feast of St John Baptist'.[34]

The clergy, the go-betweens who facilitated active relationships between the secular and the sacred, reinforced this visual connection. In the large towns of Catholic Europe the proportion of clerics (priests, monks, friars, nuns, lay members of religious orders, all identifiable by their costume) to lay men and women varied from one to three per cent of the adult population. Though they included some of the best educated members of their communities many were poorly equipped to instruct. 'A preacher who was delivering a sermon on the Annunciation said the following . . . "what do you think, dear ladies, that the Virgin Mary was doing at that time? Dyeing her hair blonde? No! Of course not! On the contrary! She had a crucifix before her, and she was reading the Book of Hours of Our Lady" '[35] This was a joke that rang true to experience. Before Protestantism challenged a fairly relaxed, because monopolistic, Catholicism, and Catholicism reacted with an effort to ensure that its clergy became models for, rather than differently clad, members of society, the relationship between theology and the practicalities of living remained in a largely unscrutinized equipoise. Bishops were also great landlords. Abbots could summon tenants to defend their property rights in arms. Rome was a salon for worldly cardinals and a marketplace of international diplomacy as well as a magnet for pilgrims; it was *Caput Mundi*, head of the world, for its admirers, *Coda Mundi*, the world's anus, for those who deplored the mercenariness of its clergy and the number of its prostitutes. All these historically induced anomalies and opinions were taken by most in their stride.

Altercation between a smallholder and his priest about the latter's right to a tithe of produce in a lean year; a burgher's negotiations to secure some relaxation of convent discipline for a daughter; the scrutiny of the *curriculum vitae* of a candidate for an archbishopric for evidence of his social status and political manipulability; Francis I's calling on Breton priests to demonstrate the strength of the men of Brittany by wrestling before his guests: all these relationships between lay and clerical worlds brought heaven, through its representatives, down to earth. Ecclesiastical punishments for such a routine offence as blasphemy were on the whole light, and absolution from most sins, save those like assaults on the clergy or the abduction of a nun, which were 'reserved' for consideration by a higher authority, could be assured to the contrite there and then in the confessional. Though the majority rarely did go to confession or took the sacrament at mass more than once a year, at Easter, as opposed to simply attending or gossiping through the Latin service, the invocation of saint-protectors, the cult of relics, the division of the day by the bells sounding from parish or monastic church all threaded a sense of security through life's uncertainties. From the churches and chapels of rural monasteries and in towns from the chantry chapels and the altars of confraternities (religious friendly societies: in 1500 there were getting on for two hundred of them in London), prayers rose to shorten the stay in Purgatory of those whose relations could pay for them. Omnipresent but not particularly insistent, for most people religion in the pre-Reformation age of faith was not a matter of strenuous or questioning belief.

Nevertheless, in moments of anguish priests were seen as essential intermediaries between God and man and true repentance as a possible guarantee against the pains of hell ('the pain caused by one spark of hell-fire is greater than that caused by a thousand years of a woman's labour in childbirth' was one way of putting it in a book of hints for confessors[36]); for God's punishments were frighteningly inexplicable. At times personal fears merged into the panics of large crowds mobbing the pulpit of a charismatic preacher; there were processions of men and women whipping one another's backs to bloody contrition for the world's sins. Nor was all at ease in the minds of the intellectuals of the church. Theologians argued about such issues as predestination, personal immortality, the efficacy of penitential works in sealing an act of contrition, the question as to how far salvation after death depended on having been as little absorbed as possible in the active life of trades and families and politics and war.

Earlier waves of heretical protest against Catholicism, its priesthood, its practices and some of its doctrines, had by the mid-fifteenth century been subdued or banished to remote places by church and state acting in concerted repression. One sect, the Czech Brethren, survived in Bohemia and its nature is described in a letter to Erasmus from a correspondent there in 1519. It usefully indicates the nature of other scattered forms of protest. The Pope and all his colleagues and officials, wrote Jan Slechta, they describe as Antichrist. They appoint their own bishops, rude unlettered laymen with wives and families. They recognize no authority but the Bible. Their ministers celebrate mass without vestments, use leavened bread and only the Lord's Prayer. They deny transubstantiation (the doctrine that the consecrated bread and wine turn, if invisibly to the eye, into the actual body and blood of Christ). Vows to the saints, prayers for the dead and confession to priests they ridicule, and they keep no holy days but Sundays, Christmas, Easter and Whitsun.

Another, less separatist, form of protest was expressed by the Brethren of the Common Life, a loose grouping of devotees of what became known as the New Devotion, the *Devotio Moderna*. Numerous in the Low Countries and Rhineland, and influential through their schools (Erasmus went to one) and books (especially the 1418 *The Imitation of Christ* attributed to Thomas à Kempis), they did not challenge the Church openly so much as imply their criticism by quietly opting out of much that it had to offer, notably what they saw as superfluous ceremonies and observances and its indifference to the subjective religious experience of the individual. Everywhere attitudes towards the Catholic Church reflected a form of double-think: acceptance of its beliefs, distrust and mockery of its personnel. Faith and anticlericalism went hand in hand in a habitual but unstable partnership. Any general picture of a European population only intermittently giving serious thought to the nature of its religion, and familiarly at home with a Church which, in spite of the splendours of its liturgy, the worldly power of its prelates and the ignorance and mercenariness of many of its ministers, was taken easily for granted as part of the order of things, has also to take account of a less readily identifiable tinder of dissatisfaction with both faith and clergy, a tinder glowing fitfully and dispersedly, but capable of being fanned. Towards 1500 a wider than usual range of paranoid outbursts and perfervid pilgrimages brought to the surface old millennarial panics that God would bring a wicked world to an end in a blaze of judgement in a year with two final zeros.

It was against this background of unease that the German priest Martin Luther, a miner's son who combined an anguished sense of spiritual uncertainty with impeccable theological credentials and an eloquently hard-hitting popular appeal, appalled the Church authorities by calling for a redefinition, a reform, of some of its most sacrosanct doctrinal positions. Tradition is correct in dating the start of the

Reformation to 1517 when Luther circulated his first challenge, if not when it portrays him as personally nailing a copy of his ninety-five theses to the door of the castle church of Wittenberg in Saxony. Nailed or not, the theses – brief heads of points to be made in the debate they invited – were quickly circulated by printers who sensed, or were told by Luther's friends, that they were the opening shot in a campaign. In spite of their number, their argument was narrow. Under licence from the Pope, Leo X, letters of 'indulgence' were being sold in Germany that promised the purchaser access to the spiritual treasury of mercy accumulated by the saints on which his soul could draw to shorten the period of its suffering in Purgatory. There was nothing new about the issuing of such indulgences, but the manner of their sale was on this occasion particularly brazen, the vendors failing to emphasize the need for a soul-searching penitence before access to the reserve of mercy could be gained. What sort of Church was this whose head implied that the God he represented could be bribed, that a man's purse was more important than his prayers? Indeed, was there any such treasury of accumulated merit on which man could draw? If not, in what other ways had the Church confused the way to salvation with misleading signposts? An excessively inept sales campaign was met by an excessively far-reaching protest.

Counter-attacks swiftly followed, first from the local Church authorities, then from the Pope, and finally in 1521 from the Emperor Charles V, intent on damping down religious controversy in his German lands. Though granted a measure of freedom from actual arrest by the protection of the Elector of Saxony, Friedrich the Wise, Luther handed tract after tract, short treatises and compilations of his letters to printers assured of a wide vernacular audience. In this race against time to get his views published, his writings acquired every now and then a hectic journalistic extravagance that did nothing to check their popular appeal. Neither did the tone of his letters to those in authority; writing to Leo X in 1520, he reminded the Pope that Rome 'is more corrupt than any Babylon or Sodom ever was . . . characterized by a totally depraved, hopeless and notorious wickedness'.[37] His associates, such as Melancthon, less spiritually creative and less personally threatened, were hard put to clarify the multiplying guidelines that were to constitute Lutheranism.

Their basis was the all-sufficiency of the Bible as a guide to belief. Luther disputed the view that popes had the power from God to declare that certain beliefs, inspired in theologically learned men, reflected the working of the Holy Ghost within the historic body of the Church and were therefore doctrinally correct, whereas others (the Immaculate Conception of the Virgin, for instance) might be important as guides to devotion, but were not beliefs binding upon the faithful.

Acceptance of this challenge to the accreting doctrine that had called forth the towering organization of the post-biblical Church was helped by the humanistic vogue for studying the ancient world in terms of the texts written in classical times and prising them loose from later interventions and commentaries. This desire to restore exactly what had been written and to see classical authors in terms of their lives and times was of clear relevance to the central Christian text, the Bible, especially the New Testament and the Epistles which themselves were written in classical times. To Luther, as to many of his less passionately radical contemporaries, a reconsideration of Christian belief through concentrating on the words and lives of Christ and those who wrote and spread the gospel close to his lifetime, led them to doubt what amounted to commentaries and inventions. Apart from the gospels' baptism and communion, the subsequently evolved sacramental apparatus – confirmation, marriage (as a sacrament as opposed to a contract) confession and penance, extreme unction, ordination – fell away, and with it the need for the miracle-aiding caste of priests that had kept it in place. And without them, the whole Catholic hierarchy, from pope to barefoot friar, became unnecessary. What also fell away – and with it the cogency of the indulgence system, for instance – was the Catholic insistence on the spiritual efficacy of penances and charitable good works. For Luther, God was moved to offer his grace, his forgiveness to a man born to sin only in response to the intensity of individual faith in his mercy. Man's justification of a wish to be saved at the Day of Judgement was reliant on what he had offered to God in his heart.

It was this belief, the one that had caused Luther the most anguish as a young man before he grasped it, that offered hope to those who felt more troubled by the Church's teaching than by the inadequacy of its clergy. A friend of the young lawyer William Roper, son-in-law of Sir Thomas More, wrote that in spite of 'immoderate fasting and many prayers' he had (like Luther) despaired of his salvation. Then he read some of Luther's works which German merchants in London had smuggled in against the ban in 1521 on their import. Reading them, Roper became 'fully persuaded that faith only did justify, that the works of man did nothing profit, and that, if man could once believe that our Saviour Christ shed this precious blood and died on the cross for our sins, the same only should be sufficient for our salvation. Then thought he that all the ceremonies and sacraments in Christ's Church were very vain'.[38]

When others took up Luther's ideas and applied them in accordance with their own inner needs, in different circumstances and through different colleagues and disciples, Protestantism took on different forms. In 1518 the priest and classical scholar Ulrich Zwingli preached in Zurich cathedral against the selling of indulgences. Also rejecting the spiritual, as opposed to the moral, efficacy of works, he proclaimed, 'we believe that by faith the forgiveness of sins is most assuredly granted to men as often as he prays to God through Christ.'[39] But he played down the notion of original sin, which Luther retained, and whereas Luther maintained a half-way position on the nature of the Eucharist, denying the transubstantiation of bread and wine into the real body and blood of Christ while accepting their actual spiritual presence, Zwingli denied any change in their nature; they were simply to be eaten and drunk as commemorative symbols of what Christ had, before his death, offered to all mankind then and for ever. These differences, once widely taught and incorporated into the words and actions of church services, established the Swiss version of reform as specifically Zwinglian.

In the same way, a new bias was set within Lutheran thought by the Frenchman Jean Calvin, another Catholic intellectual led by personal doubt to wish to reform traditional theology. Both Luther and Zwingli had largely avoided a theological conundrum that had from time to time perturbed Catholic thinkers. If God knew everything, past, present and to come, as he certainly by his nature did, then he knew each man's destiny, whether he was to be saved or damned. What, then, was the point of individual spiritual striving? Calvin openly taught that mankind had been divided between those who were predestined to salvation and those whose every God-ward effort was doomed to failure since God's first imagining the world he would create. All the individual could do was live devoutly, honour Him and His words and hope for the best – and be reverently grateful to be playing a part, however tragic, in a scheme of such transcendent mystery.

This austere vision proved a potent challenge. No other reformist idea revealed quite so sharply how many religious temperaments rejected the escort of Catholicism across the stepping-stones of the sacraments, supported by a confessor on one hand and the staff of good works in the other. It was, of course, open to some simply to assume that they, unlike their neighbours, were one of the elect, one of the chosen 'godly'. But with the publication in 1536 of his *Institutes of the Christian Religion*, Calvin's ideas became an unpermissive Calvinism, exportable to converts in the form of a single book rather than through the diffuse series of pamphlets, treatises and sermons in which Luther and Zwingli propagated their message.

Already by the 1550s the religious fissure had become defined, if not in a pattern that was yet definitive. Spain, Italy, much of southern Germany, Austria, Bohemia, Poland and Lithuania remained Catholic, though the last four had accepted the presence of Calvinist minorities. Much of northern Germany was Lutheran, as was Prussia, Denmark, Norway and Sweden. The Swiss cantons were partly Catholic; Geneva was the organizational and missionary centre of dispersed Calvinism as its adherents made headway among the municipal governments and noble families of France and the Low Countries. England, after much wavering back and forth, had become a Protestant country with a state church of Calvinist tinge. Scotland was turning to outright Calvinism. Russia, without spontaneous dissenting leaders of its own and unmissionized, retained its eccentrically Catholic Orthodox faith.

As Protestant ideas spread they opened the way for eccentrics who thought that they alone knew what righteousness meant – 'mad saints' as Luther called them.[40] There was the Netherlander Jan Beukelsz, for instance, who advocated and practised polygamy and had one of his wives killed in 1534 for playing traitor to his principles. Whole sects developed which dissented both from Catholic and the increasingly accepted reformed religions. Conspicuous among these were the Anabaptists, so-called by Zwingli because they believed that baptism had to be repeated (the Greek *ana* means again) in adulthood before it could acquire spiritual significance. Alone among Protestants, they refused to acknowledge Christ's injunction to 'render unto Caesar the things that are Caesar's', proclaiming the payment of taxes, recruitment into armies or service on magistracies as repugnant to the life of true religion. In the eyes of governments, Anabaptists who openly voiced or acted on this opinion were traitors, to be executed as such. And they were sharply criticized by the major reform movements, all of which relied on as much co-operation with the civil authorities as they could.

The religious event that most clearly revealed the coming of age of Protestant doctrine as an orthodoxy, however, was the public burning in 1553 of the Spanish theological writer Michael Servetus in Geneva, at Calvin's urging, for a crime that was formerly a Catholic monopoly: heresy. Servetus believed that Reform was insufficiently thorough. It had re-thought the forms of worship by returning to the Gospels but still accepted the post-Biblical, Catholic view of the Three-in-One nature of the Trinity, which Servetus interpreted as successive manifestations of God: as creator, as Christ and, thereafter, as the Holy Ghost, guardian spirit of the true church. Twenty years earlier his provocatively titled *Restitution of Christianity* would have been seen as just another contribution to the theology of Reform. Two years after his burning Protestantism's establishment was confirmed by a political event. In 1555 Charles V accepted in the Peace of Augsburg that he could not suppress Lutheranism in Germany by force of arms; independent cities and territorial princes were henceforward allowed to choose whichever form of religion they preferred, Catholic or Lutheran – and in some cases Calvinist.

It was the speed with which Reform spread, literally, it seemed, as an answer to prayer, that caused cities and princes to endorse it and that carried it through the waves of persecutions that began in Provence in 1545 and marked Mary Tudor's reign in England between 1555 and 1558. It was its speed and scale that established it by the 1530s as a heresy that had come to stay. It was important, perhaps essential, to this success that the founding reformers taught in towns, where preachers found ready-made audiences literate enough to follow up arguments in their written form; by 1530 German presses had turned out something like four thousand vernacular pamphlets, many in repeated editions. For this new creation of man's link with God the Beginning was indeed the Word: spoken, written, or read aloud to those whose literacy was infirm or nonexistent. Once the word was abroad its message was interpreted at different levels. For some it was enough that it was anti-papal, anti-Catholic, anti-establishment. In carnivalesque spirit Germans wiped their behinds on indulgences, one Londoner lifted up a dog as the priest lifted the wafer of God, another greeted the temporary suppression of the Mass in 1548 with bawdy vigour:

> A, good mistress missa,
> Shall ye go from us thissa?
> Well, yet I must ye kissa –
> Alack, from pain I pissa.[41]

Such antics had no staying power. Neither did the uprising of German peasant communities who saw Reform as an excuse to get their own back not just on tithe-demanding priests but rent-collecting secular landlords. More generally, Reform carried with it the appeal of the new; for centuries mountebanks had collected gaping crowds at fairs with a fresh cure for disease: here was the latest remedy for sin. In an age of extremes, of good harvests and disastrous ones, health and plague, an extreme contrast in matters of religious observance had, in the short term, an obvious appeal.

While this emotional popular support for Reform had to be taken note of by authorities responsible for law and order, it was the spread of thoughtful response to its spiritual message among citizens of substance and among a number of clerics themselves that turned heresy into a religion that could appeal to governments. The reformers were anxious to co-operate with Caesar, and their values, as far as the moral and orderly conduct of their flocks was concerned, were conservative and helpful. To be independent of the far-reaching financial and administrative structure of the Catholic church was in many cases attractive, especially where members of the ruling class did not themselves depend on clerical emoluments – bishoprics, abbacies, offices in the Roman curia – to buttress their family interests. To confiscate church and monastic property could be enormously profitable: it doubled the income of the Duke of Württemberg, it netted Henry VIII well over a million pounds. Even when taking into account the long-term costs of replacing such services as poor relief, hospices, hospitals and the stipend of ministers, there was the temptation to take advantage of a windfall. And this was especially true of those governments who saw a break with Rome as in the interest both of dynastic and foreign policy (as in Henry VIII's case) or that of freedom from interference by a higher authority, as was the case with the German princes who embraced Lutheranism. In all cases the extension of Reform was affected by the personality of its teachers and the status of the laymen who were converted to supporting its doctrine and form of worship.

It was not, perhaps, until the full doctrinal implications of Reform had been clarified in the 1540s and the monks and friars and priests had become reabsorbed into society in other guises, that the convert realized to the full what it meant to be more or less on his own with God to justify himself and hope to receive His grace. Prayers for the dead no longer rose from monasteries and the chantry chapels in cathedrals. The saints and Mary had been stripped from church and street corner.

The pious pilgrimage was ended. The giving of alms was simple charity, no more, no less. The altar and the niche where the host was reserved had lost their consoling magic and the dead died without sacramental rites. If man was now free to speak to God in his heart without the mediatorship of a priest he remained uncertain about being heard.

That one state of dissatisfied uncertainty was not succeeded by another when the initial euphoria of Reform had quieted was avoided by the building up in the meantime of support systems: a better educated ministry than the priesthood it replaced; churches bare of paintings and sculptures where concentration on pulpit or communion table was more absolute; prayers, psalms and hymns in the vernacular and in which all participated; schools where the new beliefs were taught and explained; courts to which errors in conduct or church attendance were reported. Whatever its form, from the thinned-down and politicized Protestantism of the Church of England to the Big Brother quasi-theocracy of Calvin's Geneva, the Reform reassembled formerly Catholic men and women into mutually supportive congregations and brought habits of conformity to sustain the personal adventure of the non-conformist.

The Protestant challenge to habit-ridden indifference punctuated by personal or communal panic was paralleled within Catholicism itself. 'Reformation' was originally a Catholic concept; General Councils of the Church had, in the early fifteenth century, called for a 'Reformation' of its choice of personnel and the earnestness of its pastoral care. Earlier still, religious orders had become – as with the Augustinians and Franciscans – divided between 'reformed' branches, returning to the austere demands of their founders, and those which had become more relaxed in the interpretation of their intentions. Energetic medieval bishops had tried to restore discipline in monasteries and remind the parish clergy to lead truly exemplary lives. But the flywheel of custom, the very size of the Church's organization and the docility with which its ministrations were on the whole accepted, had prevented any thorough-going reform seeming a matter of urgency. The spectacle of Protestantism, expanding fast, and finding influential protectors, changed this mood. It stimulated a programme sufficiently determined and aggressive to have been dubbed, in retrospect, a Counter-Reformation.

This had two aspects. The first was doctrinal. It was made much clearer that in Catholic eyes the sacrament of baptism washed clear the stain of original sin. Thereafter man's salvation was the result of faith

in Christ and obedience to the Church's laws, with faith being confirmed by sincerely carried out good works of penance and charity.
The importance of the other sacraments was re-stressed, with especial
emphasis on the consecrated bread and wine becoming the actual body
and blood of Christ. The essential role of an ordained priesthood, which
alone could mediate this transformation, was thus revalidated. And so
was the post-biblical power of popes, as the successors to Christ's
disciple Peter, to continue and pass on messages from God of equal
authenticity to those contained in the gospels. The practices so dear to
the mass of Catholics – the cult of relics, the invocation of saintly
intercessors, the devotion, above all, to Mary – were confirmed as
spiritually efficacious, though the procedures for establishing relics as
genuine and scrutinizing candidates for sainthood were tightened.
These declarations, worked out during successive meetings of the
Council of Trent between 1545 and 1567, contained little that was
absolutely new. But Catholicism could now be measured by a body
of definitions and requirements even more lucid and peremptory than
those explored in the successive enlargements of Calvin's *Institutes* and
at least as coherent as the statements and homilies defining the beliefs
of other Protestant faiths.

The second aspect of Catholic revitalization was pastoral. Measures
were taken to improve the educational standards of the clergy and by
means of school curricula and catechism classes to instruct laymen in
what they should believe and do. And part of this pastoral programme
was – especially through the Jesuit Order created in 1541 – directed
not only at waverers within Catholic countries, but at the re-conversion
of 'heretics' in Protestant ones. This European missionary enterprise
(often involving great personal risks), together with the domestic use
of the Inquisition to patrol adherence to belief and Indexes of Prohibited
Books to censor the reading matter of Catholics, explain the 'Counter'
label given to a call to order otherwise more accurately described as a
reformation of Catholicism. For the chief aim was not merely to correct
but to deepen faith. And the success of this effort was all the more
impressive in that missionary work from the Americas to China and
Japan diverted a considerable part of the most intelligent and daring
Catholic talent from evangelical work at home.

An era of monopolistic religion in Europe, then, with its seams of
agitation and its broad strata of laxity and near-indifference, was re-
tuned to a higher pitch by rivalry between organized faiths and by a
sense of personal urgency within each of them.

From the 1550s there came to be little change in the geography of religion. Scotland turned to Calvinism in the 1560s and thus made the union of the crowns workable, if uneasy, when the Scottish King James succeeded Elizabeth as King of England in 1603. Selective conversion to Calvinism in France during the 1560s and thereafter added an ideology to the rivalry between the great territorial magnates during a time of weak central government – which revealed how superficial the centralizing policies of previous monarchs had been in persuading French men to think of themselves as Frenchmen. During the civil wars which rent the country at intervals from 1562 until Henri IV accepted in 1593 that while he could win campaigns as a Protestant he could only gain the allegiance of the majority of his subjects by becoming a Catholic, France was in danger of becoming a 'mosaic' country like Germany or Switzerland, where the rivalry between neighbouring cities or cantons affected the choice between remaining Catholic or turning to the reformed religion.

In the Low Countries, too, as from the 1560s cities and provinces reacted in their different ways to Spain's insistence that they should remain Catholic, the earlier, scattered and voluntary reception of Protestant ideas became confused with political loyalties and regional self-interests from which the dissenting individual could escape only by flight.

The danger of interfering with religious customs had been one of the 'brakes' Seyssell had seen as limiting a ruler's power. Certainly as Protestantism spread across Germany, Switzerland and France, sinking in here and there, it emphasized the old regional divisions that hampered the development of a national loyalty. It was the same in Poland-Lithuania and the Christian parts of Hungary that were not under Turkish occupation. Noble families impatient of royal control used their embrace of the Lutheran or Calvinist faith to define their independence more strongly. It may be tempting to see governmental insistence on the unity of religious practice, as in Catholic Spain or Protestant England, as helping to bridge the gap between central government and the nation at large. Certainly religion gave a propaganda edge to pre-existing political rivalries. Reminding Londoners of the savagery of the Spanish sack of Antwerp in 1576, the anonymous author in 1602 of the play *Alarum for London* represented the consequences of a Spanish attack at home. Two little children run in panic on to the stage.

Religious controversy, a commentary on the uneasy peace between Catholics and Protestants just before the Thirty Years War (Protestant theologians and rulers on the left bank; Catholics on the right), Adriaen van de Venne, 1614 (Rijksmuseum, Amsterdam)

MARTIN:	Alas, the Spaniard's comming, what shall we doe?
LENCHY:	Alas, poore Martin, we shall both be kill'd.
MARTIN:	Alas, poore Lenchy, kisse me, prettie sister, now we must dye . . .

Enter Spaniards running with theyr swords drawne.
SPANIARDS: Kill, kill, kill!

For those who experienced a new intensity of belief it was largely a personal matter. For others the religious life centred on a church, its minister and its familiar congregation of neighbours – not a Church, nor a country.

Credal fissure produced both confusion and cruelty. In 1530, before Calvinism had further prevented Reform from presenting a united doctrinal front, Sebastian Franck expressed his despair: 'who would not rightly groan because he lives in this darkened world? . . . Behold now how many beliefs, sects and parties exist only among those who are Christians. I pass over the subdivisions of the sects into further sects and the way the parts of the various churches have nothing to do with one another'.[42] But until Geneva burned Servetus the sects harrassed and exiled rather than killed one another. When Calvinists sought refuge from persecution in France and the Low Countries a number of German cities and princes tolerated both them and Lutherans among their Catholic subjects; in some towns Calvinists and Lutherans shared the same church. It was the politicized division between Catholicism and Protestantism seen as a whole and the identification of non-conformity with treason that caused the most savage repression, whether along the chain of Inquisitorial prisons from Lisbon to Rome, or in the fires of Marian England so graphically commemorated by John Foxe in 1563 in his *Actes and Monuments* of Protestant martyrs.

In the main, however, these were symptoms of internal strains as governments decided what their subjects were to think in terms of religion. Religion was a potent exacerbator of civil war in later six-teenth-century France, as from 1642 in England, and of military action elsewhere. In 1546 Charles V explained to his sister Mary why he intended to go to war against the Lutheran Schmalkaldic League. 'If we failed to intervene now', he wrote, 'all the Estates of Germany would be in danger of breaking with the faith . . . I decided to embark on war against Hesse and Saxony as transgressors of the peace against the Duke of Brunswick and his territory . . . although this pretext will not long disguise the fact that it is a matter of religion.' In 1566 his son explained to the Spanish ambassador in Rome that he was not prepared to accept the influence of Calvinist trouble-makers in the Low Countries. 'I neither intend nor desire to be the ruler of heretics. If things cannot be remedied as I wish without recourse to arms, I am determined to go to war.'[43] Charles won his war by defeating the League in battle at Mühlberg in 1547 but eight years later lost the resulting peace with the compromise surrender of Augsburg. Philip began his war when the Duke of Alba led northwards in 1567 the first of a succession of armies that were still trying to achieve his aims when exhaustion brought the truce between both parties in 1609. But in spite of the distance over which troops had to be sent from Spain, neither of these instances can be seen as a foreign war. Charles was reaching east to restore Catholic unity in his own territories as Emperor and as ruler of the Habsburg German lands. Philip was reaching north to prevent one part of his inheritance becoming independent of the rest.

Lorenzo Valla had offered a fourth motive for a ruler's going to war: 'for avenging a wrong and defending friends'. Protestant and Catholic rulers and their advisers did express concern for the oppressed minori-ties in other countries and spoke of alliances as though there were religious as well as political motives behind them. But to go to war 'for defending friends' suggests an altruism that was almost entirely lacking. At the most, to aid embattled co-religionists abroad meant sending expeditionary forces to relieve pressure and keep up their morale. And in the sending of these (which legally fell short of an open declaration of war), as with Elizabeth's military aid to French and Netherlandish Protestants, the motives were always mixed with commercial and political considerations. It was by acknowledging this that when Émeric Crucé came in his *The New Cyneas* of 1623 to review Valla's causes of war, he concluded that 'one could add religion – if experience had not made known that this serves most frequently as a pretext.'[44] But if there were no Wars of Religion there were wars *with* religion, and this was a component that came to add savagery to their conduct and an additional problem for those who longed for an internationally peaceful Europe.

IDEALS OF AMITY

There was no lack of comment on the horrors of war.

A few days after Charles V's victory in 1547 against the Protestant Schmalkaldic League at Mühlberg, so idealistically commemorated by Titian's equestrian portrait of the armoured emperor cantering with thoughtful serenity across a tranquil landscape, a lawyer on a mission to Charles V from the Duke of Pomerania, Bartholomew Sastrow, rode past the site.

> Wherever the eye turned there were signs of the recent battle; broken lances, shattered muskets and torn-up harnesses littered the ground, and all along the road soldiers were dying of their wounds and from want of sustenance. Around Wittenberg all the villages were deserted; the inhabitants had taken flight without leaving anything behind them. Here the corpse of a peasant, a group of dogs fighting for the entrails; there a Landsknecht with just the breath of life left to him, but the body putrefying, his arms stretched out at the widest, and his legs far enough apart to put a bar between them.[45]

Again, during the hard winter of 1552–3, another civilian, serving as a doctor with the imperial forces trying to retake Metz from the French, remarked with a tone of irony quite new to the period that his patients among the wounded Spaniards in the siege lines insisted on *dying* –

Charles V at the Battle of Mühlberg, (1547), Titian, 1548 (Museo del Prado, Madrid)

'notwithstanding that each soldier had his field-bed, and a tester strewn with glittering stars more bright than fine gold, and every day had white sheets and lodged at the sign of the moon'.[46]

Another new chord, more complex because it reflected the collision between chivalrous expectation and brute experience, was sounded by the Spanish soldier-poet Francisco de Aldana who was wounded in the Netherlands in 1573. 'Nothing is seen here', he recorded, 'except, face to face, powerful squadrons attacking one another, bloody liquid staining the green grass, and people pursuing an honourable end. This is the sweet sound that is heard here: "Spain! St James! Charge, charge!"', and, as a pleasant smell which terrifies the air, the smoke of sulphur meeting blazing flames. One's sense of taste, hemmed in, seeks foul water, one's touch finds and strokes only a hard trophy of bloody steel, splintered bone with battered flesh on it, fragments of armour, torn mail. O sole noble state worthy of men!'[47]

New yet again was the poignant sense of helplessness expressed in the *Memoirs* of the Protestant François de la Noue, written in the 1580s when, after capture in battle, he had chosen imprisonment rather than the alternative offered him, that of having his eyes put out. Recalling the truce meeting in 1562 between Catherine de' Medici and the Prince of Condé and their bands of officers from both sides, Catholic and Protestant, he described how on being given permission the men mingled to greet friends and relatives.

> Each urged the other to peace and to persuade the great to listen. Some, standing a little aside, considered these things more deeply and deplored the public discord, source of future evils; and when they came to think that all the caresses then being given would be transformed into bloody murders if the commanders should give but a little sign for battle, and that the visors being lowered . . . brother would be pitiless to brother, tears flowed from their eyes.

'I was there', he went on, 'and may say that on the other side I had a dozen friends whom I held as dear as my own brothers, and they bore the same affection towards me.' Six months later, kinsman slaughtered kinsman at the battle of Dreux 'which gave some horror to the deed but did not diminish the courage'.[48]

Yet reactions of this sort were untypical. With its bear-baitings, judicial torture and witch burnings, and with rare exceptions its indifference to the welfare of peg-legged or chronically sick ex-servicemen, this was not a humanitarian age. Moreover, though armies grew in size, they scooped up hardly one per cent of a native population. The speed of recovery in at least some war-devastated zones could in retrospect be reassuring; crops were replanted, especially in countrysides near towns which could offer loans towards the produce they themselves required; industrial plant was generally small and readily renewable or, when large, as in the case of dockyards and mines, escaped destruction because they were heavily guarded or remote. Though popular revolts, whether a local uprising against the price of bread or the larger scale revolts of the 1560s in Scotland, England, Corsica and southern Spain, were affected by the engrossment of foodstuffs for armies or the interruptions to trade caused by hostilities, at the time complaints focused not on war itself but on the fecklessness of officials, the disloyalty of influential subjects, the machinations of agitators. Rulers took little account of the human toll of war: and indeed this figured, if at all, as a merely subordinate theme when projects were launched to check wars by ending the divisions of Europe.

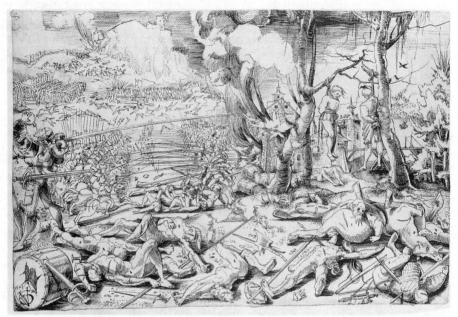

Battlefield, Urs Graf, drawing, 1521 (Kunstmuseum, Kupferstichkabinett, Basel)

In the early 1530s, some fifteen years after writing *Utopia*, Thomas More was a knight and Lord Chancellor of England, weighed down by Henry VIII's threat to slice England away from the Catholic community of Europe if the Pope would not grant him a divorce from Catherine of Aragon. He told his son-in-law William Roper, as they paced together along the Chelsea tow-path, that if he were granted three wishes he would gladly be put in a sack and thrown in the river. One, he replied in answer to Roper's obvious question, was that the divorce could be arranged amicably. Another was that 'where the most part of Christian princes be at mortal war, they were all at a universal peace.' The third was that Europe could be 'settled in a perfect uniformity of religion'.[49] None was granted, and More ended not on the bed of the Thames but on the executioner's block in the Tower of London. The divorce led to Henry's break with Rome. Princes remained at odds with one another.

This abstract, if heartfelt coupling of universal peace with uniformity of religion maintained an old hope that had been expressed early in the fourteenth century by Dante in his *De Monarchia*. The treatise was a call for a voluntary surrender of sovereign authorities to the overriding rule of a strengthened Holy Roman Empire. This supreme arbiter would bring wars to a close and produce the condition of peace within which alone men could live undisturbed and spiritually fulfilling lives. For Erasmus and his fellow peace-pleaders, the experience of the intervening centuries had destroyed faith in a universal Christian Empire. The plea was now for concord between the most effectively powerful individual rulers. In 1522–3 Erasmus dedicated his *Paraphrases* of the four Gospels respectively to Charles V, Francis I, Henry VIII and the Archduke Ferdinand, saying in his dedication of the Paraphrase of Mark to Francis, 'God sende grace that the spirite of the ghospell maye . . . ioyne the hearts of you all fower together in mutuall amitie and concorde . . . whiche have a long season [for a long time], with no lesse dishonour then slaughter and effusion of Christian blood, warred one agaynste another to the utter decay of Christes religion.'[50] In 1524 the dedicatees of Matthew and Luke (Charles V and Henry VIII) went to war against the dedicatee of Mark.

If faith in the idea of a universal monarchy had foundered, so it had in the pope as an arbiter among nations. The last grand gesture of papal arbitration was enshrined in the 1494 Treaty of Tordesillas which declared (translating the decision into modern terms) that the line of latitude 46° 37′ west of Greenwich as it ran round the globe, should define the hemispheres of Spanish and Portuguese settlement and conquest overseas. To Spain's chagrin this gave Portugal both Brazil and, on the other side of the world, the Moluccas or Spice Islands. But what was remarkable about this geo-political shot in the dark is that though flouted by voyaging Protestant nations – England, France, the Dutch – it was respected by those for whom it was intended. The Spanish instructions given to Ferdinand Magellan before he sailed in 1519 on what was to be (though he died in the course of it) the first circumnavigation of the earth, were clear on this point: 'you may discover [i.e. claim for us] in any of those parts what has not yet been discovered, so that you do not discover or do anything in the demarcation and limits of the most serene King of Portugal . . . but only within the limits of our demarcation.'[51] In his account of a later voyage round the world, the Florentine merchant Francesco Carletti noted, on arriving at Goa in 1601, that this was the headquarters of the eastern empire of Portugal 'according to the division of the world made by Pope Alexander VI'.[52]

Within Europe, though popes might offer to settle differences, their motives were suspect, especially after their immersion in the self-help politics of the Italian wars. Papal pleas for peace in the interest of crusade against the Turk were brushed aside. 'No general expedition against the Turks', Henry VIII told the Venetian ambassador who was explaining the Republic's readiness to support Pope Leo X's initiative, 'will ever be effected so long as such treachery prevails among the Christian powers that their sole thought is to destroy one another'.[53] The notion that political peace could be bought at the price of sinking differences within a shared attack on the Ottoman Empire did, however, live on, but largely in the dream world of writers flinching from the cruder facts of political life, and in that of the continuing readership of chivalric romances for whom Torquato Tasso published in 1581 his sensuous epic of the crusading mood, *The Liberation of Jerusalem*. Actual 'crusading' initiatives, like Stefan Batory of Poland's project in the late 1570s to organize a pan-European attack on the Turks with papal support (after a conjectural conquest of Muscovy) were exercises in propaganda. The extraordinary mission of the Sherley brothers, Anthony and Robert, to activate in 1600 a crusade in Europe once they had gained – as, after many adventures, they did – the support of the Turks' chief eastern adversary Shah Abbas of Persia, was the quirkish obsession of persuasive conmen, whose subsequent round of visits to guardedly interested European courts served no more than to show that the idea of unity-for-crusade had some flickering life left in it. Such flickers produced no flame. The religious aspect of peace-seeking went underground with early Reformation conflicts, to emerge in the more widely sympathized with, but still powerless, form of eirenism, the plea that all forms of sincere belief should be allowed to flourish under a peacefully unified political protection.

Firmer ground for reducing conflict seemed to be provided by multinational treaties which were designed not just to settle wars but to maintain the peace. An early model had been provided by the Peace of Lodi in April 1454. At first an agreement among the warring governments of Milan, Florence and Venice, it was rethought during the following months into the Treaty of Venice. This offered a framework for the whole of Italy to check war between states and to combine against foreign intervention. The adherence of Naples extended it to the Straits of Messina. Other independent states quickly sent their ambassadors to sign, and the Pope's assent enabled the final arrangement to be called The Most Holy League.

By January 1455 Italy had thus acquired a peace-keeping organization that was unique in Europe. Its members pledged that for twenty-five years in the first instance they would respect one another's borders, consult fellow members before taking any military or diplomatic initiative that might threaten the common interest, and maintain a force to be added to those of other members to use against any signatory who broke the terms of the agreement. Equally remarkable was the fact that not just for the initial twenty-five, but for nearly fifty years the system worked. Before the foreign invasions that started in 1494 revealed how thin was the glue holding the League together, there were only two, fairly localized, wars of any significance in the peninsula: a Papal-Neapolitan attempt to dislodge Lorenzo de' Medici from his position within Florence, and the Papal-Venetian War of Ferrara, both settled not exactly as envisaged by the terms of the Treaty, but at least by an unusual mobilization of shared diplomatic persuasion.

The merit of this system was picked up in a project of 1462 presented to the French King Louis XI by Antonio Marini, a banker-merchant of Italian extraction living in Grenoble, and more seriously by the King of Bohemia, George Podiebrad. Unlike the expressed purpose of the Holy League, they justified the imposition of a mechanism for ensuring internal peace so that war could be waged jointly against the Turks. As with Lodi, the first step was to be an alliance between a minority of powers, in this case France, Bohemia and Venice. As with the League, but on a European scale, the other powers were to be invited to join. All must promise not to make war among themselves and to maintain a common security force as well as to contribute to a crusading army. Given its larger scale, the project went further: there was to be a common law court to adjudicate members' quarrels, a general assembly of national representatives meeting regularly, and a servicing bureaucracy. It looked beyond a mechanism to push back the Turks to a permanent control of European divisiveness.

The project foundered among uninterest, suspicion and its logistic unrealism. But its general principles were to resurface in the early seventeenth century and were meanwhile reflected in the 1518 Treaty of London, which was designed to end the series of stop-go diplomatic alignments and collapses that had punctuated the political life of western and central Europe since 1494.

Like the Marini-Podiebrad plan, this one, while using the Christendom-Crusade motif as a reason for peace-making, was envisaged primarily as a permanent organization for the collective political security of the European powers. Its mastermind was Cardinal Wolsey, ambitious to leave his mark on the continent as a whole but at the time responsive to the humanistic urging of concord among princes. Its chiefly secular, political focus was nonetheless stimulated by the 1517 project for a pan-European crusade initiated by Leo X and vigorously sold abroad by his legates. Leo envisaged a general truce for five years with all the powers agreeing to accept papal arbitration over any mutual antagonism that might lead to war, and with shared contributions in cash, troops, artillery and shipping. As the legates quickly discovered, there were two major flaws in this last attempt to present crusade as a concern of all Europe (except Muscovy); the Pope was not trusted as an arbitrator, and monarchs could not agree on who was to be the commander-in-chief of the military enterprise. It was at this point that Wolsey stepped in to elaborate the 'truce' element in Leo's plan and play down the over-competitive military one. The Treaty of London was designed to settle permanently the problems of Europe, not to martialize Christendom in the short term. The aim of Wolsey, a pillar of the Church, was to cut back the emphasis on Europe's Christian mission.

As with Lodi, the core of the programme outlined in the treaty was a domestic settlement: an alliance between England and France clinched by a marriage contract between Henry VIII's two-year-old daughter Mary and Francis I's eldest son, who was still in his cradle (as a later French observer of the political scene was to observe, 'as in a comedy, so with a war: the conclusion is provided by a marriage'[54]). From this the treaty built outwards. It appealed for, and got, the adhesion of all the great powers and the lesser ones from Portugal to Guelders and Urbino. Even the Swiss, born exporters of soldiery, signed. Even the Pope accepted his position as a partner. All agreed to forbid their subjects to fight for foreign powers and to act in unison to quench local wars. Bypassing the cumbrous centralized mechanisms of the 1462 initiative, the Treaty of London extended to most of Europe a cautious optimism that divisiveness could be controlled.

Europe, however, was both too large to patrol itself and too small and too taut with past resentments to accept for long a moritorium on their renewed expression. Within two years Denmark invaded Sweden; England – in spite of the parade of amity in 1520 at the tented city of the Field of the Cloth of Gold where French and English choirs sang antiphonally at mass – arranged an attack on France in conjunction with Spain; Italy became once more the object of dynastic acquisitiveness; the spread of Lutheran belief in Germany and Switzerland made it impossible for the Pope to seek peace at the expense of the Catholic faith;

the linking of Spain to Germany and the Netherlands when Charles was elected emperor in 1519 introduced into the tenuous idea of European unity the more easily graspable notion of a dynastic axis: the Habsburgs and their supporters, versus the Valois of France and their dependants.

The drift back from concord to conflict was momentarily halted again in 1559. In that year the Treaty of Cateau-Cambrésis, based on a settlement between Spain and France, brought in the exhausted consent of every power west of Poland to an agreement that bound the signatories to subordinate their interests to an abiding general peace. But within a decade, France was at war within itself, with England sending troops to help the Huguenot faction; Sweden and Denmark were at war; following Charles V's revocation of his imperial title in 1556 the Habsburg empire, which had at least encouraged some balance of alliances around an axis reaching clear across Europe, was breaking up. Political rivalries were seconded by the ideological calls for action beaming outwards from Calvin's Geneva and Counter-Reformation Rome; the Italian states withdrew their residents from Protestant capitals; England recalled its last ambassador to Spain in 1568 and lost formal contact with Vienna; Rome ceased to be the centre of international news and views. The Europe-wide system of permanent embassies, built up during the previous hundred years, had not prevented war but it had, on occasion, facilitated peace. Now parts of it withered, replaced by an interlacing of agents of lower rank, not always accredited in the host country, information gatherers and spies rather than potential negotiators.

In 1589, thirty years after Cateau-Cambrésis, Botero reviewed the likelihood of such alliances producing lasting peace. 'As it is impossible that the interests of each of many rulers will be involved in an equal degree', he concluded, it is 'improbable that all will move with equal alacrity or eagerness, and without this equality nothing of moment can be achieved. If a wheel or weight in a clock is damaged it will spoil the whole movement, and similarly one party to an alliance who fails will throw all the rest into disorder.'[55] It was the lack of faith in alliances, and a despairing sense that Europe's divisions seemed to be perpetual, that led some thinkers, haunted by the still living idea of the Augustan Empire 'when all the world was at peace' and the late eighth-century Holy Roman Empire of Charlemagne, to forget how war-torn both these epochs had in fact been when they urged a general surrender to a beneficient superpower. Near the end of his life, in 1607, even Botero could write that, 'I believe that the human race would live happily if it were all brought under a single prince.' Warming to this hope he foresaw a Europe where all patriotisms had blended into one, where the cost of living would dip with the absence of war taxation, and where men could travel anywhere 'with the same language and the same coinage'.[56] The Italian Tommaso Campanella, one of the new wave of Utopian writers at the turn of the sixteenth century who echoed More's distress at Europe's in-fighting, saw such a leadership as belonging to Spain and then – changing his mind before the spectacle, and bitter personal experience in Inquisitorial gaols, of Catholic intransigence – to France. It is notable, however, that the country which was by then arousing the greatest general degree of admiring interest, among those who were observers of the political scene and not actors in it, was republican and isolationist Venice, whose statesmen had made it clear, in practice and propaganda, that the best solution in a divided continent was to arm for defence, stay out of trouble, govern fairly and cultivate a well-fenced garden.

After Cateau-Cambrésis, in fact, a preoccupation with international peace-making passed from the hands of politicians into the minds of intellectuals, from conference tables and attendant choirs to mental laboratories devoted to isolating the cultures of hope. This preoccupation expressed a more realistic attempt to confront fundamental problems than had the pacifistic ideas of Erasmus and his contemporaries.

The genocidal conflicts in the New World and the mounting terror in the Old of larger armies and of firearms brought to birth a novel concept, an enforceable international law, designed to restrain political violence, based on inherent 'natural' rights to life and property and on respect for the customary usages of mankind as a whole. This would replace the medieval 'laws of war' which were primarily concerned with the etiquette of formal notification of hostilities and the treatment of ransomable prisoners. Among its early theorists, international law pointed towards internationalism in the widest sense. 'For the world as a whole, being in a way a single republic, has the power to make laws just and fitting for all,' wrote Francisco de Vitoria in the mid-1530s[57]; for Alberico Gentili in 1598, the international law of war 'belongs to that great community formed by the entire world and the whole human race'.[58] Nonetheless, as men of their times, by the early seventeenth century the legal philosophers came to retreat from such generalization and to deal with the rights of subjects within sovereign nations and nations' conduct of their individual hostilities. The mature master of the subject, Hugo Grotius, made it clear in 1625 in *On the Law of War and Peace* that while it was concerned with the rights and duties of belligerents, it was not a matter for federative courts or international assemblies.

Increasingly it came to be felt that what was needed was not an organization but an atmosphere in which the notion of concord could flourish. Now that persecution on religious grounds had been extended from Jews and suspect converts from the Koran to the Bible, to men of sober and sincere Christian conscience and intellectuals themselves (the compulsively radical philosopher Giordano Bruno was burned, the Utopianist Tommaso Campanella was tortured, Grotius escaped from life imprisonment crouched in a chest of books), the first need was religious toleration, an air that would be breathed unfurtively and with confidence.

The eirenic, peace-seeking movement that spread from the mid-century through books and correspondence drew on many intellectual currents. There was the beguiling syncretism of Neoplatonism whose devotees saw God's message as permeating all forms of belief; it merely needed deciphering from the cultural codes within which it had been disguised: classical mythology, Persian Zoroastrianism, Egyptian hieroglyphics. There was the Erasmian tradition which saw the Gospels rather as a source of shared spiritual guidance for all than as an arsenal from which controversialists could pick their weapons. There was a growing belief that magical practices could tap the underlying harmony of the universe and feed it into the relations between men and nations. Turning from political and sectarian conflict there were those who adopted 'a plague on both your houses' attitude. For some this meant a resigned, stoically practical acceptance of adversity. Others took a less worldly view. 'Our fatherland', wrote Valentin Weigel in 1576, 'is not this world, or Europe . . . it is not in this or that principality . . . He who lives in God and God in him is at home in his fatherland, and can be driven out by no one.'[59] Others again saw the imperatives of internal order and diplomatic and commercial rationality as putting religious conflict in its place. Marlowe made his (unhistorical) Machiavelli burst out as Prologue to *The Jew of Malta* in 1589 with:

> I count religion but a childish toy,
> And hold there is no sin but ignorance.

And that he was picking up some groundswell of revulsion from sectarianism is shown from the plea at almost exactly the same time from political sovereignty's arch-spokesman, Jean Bodin, for religious toleration. It was a plea he cautiously left unpublished. But in 1623, in his own plea for peace, Émeric Crucé optimistically exaggerated the sensible person's retreat from sectarianism. 'We see an infinity of men who do not consider themselves obliged to believe except what reason shows them . . . The number of such people augments every day.'[60]

Simply to name such sources of opinion is to establish the diversity of their esoteric, mystical or idiosyncratic nature. And because of the erratic nature of its foundations the structure of the eirenic movement tended to drift from practical European solutions to a lightweight universalism. Learnedly attuned to all the intellectual currents of his day, Guillaume Postel, anxious as he was for peace in Europe, pressed in 1545 his reflections on the topic into a book he could not resist entitling *On Concord throughout the World*. Vainly he approached successive Kings of France, the German Emperor Ferdinand, even Venice for sponsorship. You have only, he pleaded, to urge the application of reason to the world's problems for all men to accept that divisiveness hampers men's development as physical and spiritual beings. 'Since God put men into this world to be social animals', Postel explained,

> helping one another and taking delight in being assembled together; and because it is impossible, because of the diversity of custom, languages, opinions and religions, that men should unite in one community until they first come to know each other: certainly the finest, most useful, and most necessary work in this world of accomplishing perfect human reconciliation, can only be to give men such knowledge of one another that by means of it recognizing the vice and virtue in persons or peoples previously unknown, and enduring the vice of another while approving the virtue, the world may come to a general accord.[61]

It was in similar terms that later eirenists diffused, and thereby de-fused their message: by sending it to all mankind they made it seem too abstract for individuals to grasp. The Catholic view was that all Europeans should return to being Catholic, the Calvinist that as many as possible should be converted to the Calvinist form of reformed religion. Postel, and after him the Venetian Paolo Sarpi, who in 1619 reviewed the religious and political divisions of Europe in his bitterly realistic *History of the Council of Trent*, reproached the Council (1543–63) for ignoring the ideal of conciliation in the interest of providing a programme for conflict. Similarly, the counter-Trent Calvinist Synod of Dordrecht of 1618–19 was designed not to harmonize the differences that had emerged among its international members but to reforge the faith's cutting edge. There had been some local conciliations. Polish Lutherans and Calvinists agreed to shelve their differences in 1570. The French government, with gritted teeth, accepted a degree of tolerance for Calvinist worship in 1598 with the Edict of Nantes. But imagining a general toleration that would ease the path to peace in Europe was a luxury for lonely speculators.

There was, however, a cluster of practical international settlements at the turn of the century: between the key Catholic antagonists, France and Spain in 1598, between Spain and Protestant England in 1604, between the eastern Habsburgs and the Turks in 1606, and – the most reluctant peace of all – the truce agreed in 1609 between Spain and the largely Calvinist provinces of the northern Low Countries. There was no overall programme here, simply coincidental moments of financial exhaustion and of monarchs' nervous distrust of the extent to which they had become dependent on unreliable powerful subjects or representative institutions to keep their warfaring alive. Two of the monarchs concerned, James I of England in the West and Rudolf II in the East, did have an interest in the eirenist movement, but they were known as jokers within the pack of European princes: sexually ambivalent, intellectual fellow travellers with universalist dreamers, eccentric, unsound. But the settlements did influence two blueprints for the suppression of divisions that reached back through the layers of eirenic universalism to the earlier projects for a peace-keeping organization.

Both were French and unsurprisingly so: France of all countries was the most galled in its national pride, being recently stricken by civil war, and unsuccessful in gathering allies to restore the position it had held under Francis I. Moderate opinion had been stricken by the degree of politico-religious hatred that in 1572 had led to the anti-Protestant pogrom in Paris that acquired European notoriety (save to dogged Catholics: the Pope issued a commemorative medal) as the Massacre of St Bartholomew's Day. It needed a healing time within a framework of coexistence. Writing in 1608 to the ambassador in London, Henri IV's secretary for foreign affairs wrote in by then old-fashioned terms about royal marriages that might keep France, England and Spain bound in amity. And he went on to say that if skilfully handled, these could form a base for 'a universal peace within Christendom that could last out our days'.[62] But it was Henri's senior and most trusted minister, the omni-competent Maximilien de Béthune, Duc de Sully, who extended this vague hope into a carefully analysed project for a peaceful Europe.[63] That he discussed it with Henri before the King was assassinated in 1610 is unlikely. A former soldier, the mastermind of projects for fortifications and military roads, he was advocating war with Spain up to Henri's death. Losing favour thereafter, he was dismissed and it was at some stage in his retirement, probably in the 1620s, that he inserted the scheme into the curious miscellany he called his *Memoirs*. Though its underlying motive was to ease Spanish pressure on France, its clear-cut development, which reflects his fascination with cartography and strategic planning, was the private diversion of a supremely tidy mind in enforced detachment from affairs.

Excluding 'Asiatic' Muscovy from his calculations, Sully divided the existing governments of Europe into fifteen units. Six were elective: the Papacy, the crowns of the Empire, Hungary, Bohemia and Poland and the doge and governing councils of republican Venice. Six (the crowns of England and Scotland now being joined in James I) were hereditary monarchies: France, Spain, Britain, Denmark, Sweden and Savoy. Three he characterized as mixed: Switzerland, the Netherlands, and 'Italy', by which he meant a federation comprising Tuscany, Mantua, Parma and Piacenza, Modena and Reggio, Genoa and Lucca. He proposed that Naples should be transferred from Spanish to papal rule. This is one of a number of transfers of territory envisaged as a way of establishing an equilibrium of interests. Thus Sicily was to go to Venice, Austria and the duchies south of it (Styria, Carinthia, Carniola) to Hungary, Milan and Montferrat to Savoy-Piedmont, the Tyrol, Franche Comté and Alsace to the Swiss. Spain's authority was to be limited to the peninsula, Sardinia and the Balearic and Azorean islands, and its overseas possessions would be re-vested in the Spanish monarchy at the discretion of the confederate units as a whole.

Thus adjusted, boundaries were to become true, fixed and permanent frontiers. There was to be no eirenist day-dreaming. The frontiers allowed for religious blocs, Lutheran, Catholic and Calvinist, to remain separate, and these frontiers were to be guaranteed by a general assembly of representatives from all the newly shaped units, meeting turn by turn in different countries. As the meetings of this body would for logistic reasons have to be occasional, six permanent regional councils were to be responsible in Danzig for Scandinavian and Polish affairs, in Nuremberg for German, in Vienna for Bohemian and Hungarian, in Constance for Milanese, Mantuan and Swiss, in Bologna for papal and Italian. A seventh council would alternate its meetings between the Low Countries, Britain, France and Spain.

The function of Sully's proposed federal organization was to ensure freedom of trade by land and sea and, above all, to prevent war. Each unit was to maintain a peace-keeping force to be used where necessary. War between units was only to be allowed by the assent of the Assembly and on condition that all spoils were to be shared with the noncombatant units. Sully added dutifully that a third advantage might follow: a united European opposition to the Ottoman Empire.

The hair-raising impracticality of this plan, evolved by one of the age's most experienced and hard-headed ministers of state, was an attempt to pin eirenist idealism to a template of actuality, and persuade policymakers to change the traditionalist spectacles through which they looked at their maps. It also, doubtless, owed something to his impatience with the multiplication of amateur peace projects that marked France's renewed slide into civil war in 1614 and accompanied the wider conflicts that followed as one country after another became drawn from 1618 into a renewed round of international conflict, the Thirty Years War.

Conspicuous among them for its scope was the proposal for a federal peace-keeping organization by Émeric Cruce. Cruce claimed in *The New Cyneas* that his project met Europe's needs in a practical manner. The needs were social harmony, amicable and organized international relations, and religious tolerance. And with the resulting peace would come reduced taxes and tariffs and an end to the debasement of coinages. With peace, communication between countries could be improved, especially by the international linking of seas and river systems by means of canals. 'What a pleasure it would be', he remarked, 'to see men go here and there freely, and mix together without any hindrance of country, ceremonies, or other suchlike differences, as if the earth were really as it is, a city common to all.'[64]

As for the basic requirement, peace: 'under the Emperor Augustus all the nations were pacified. And after the reign of Francis I [i.e. after Cateau-Cambrésis] peace was seen to flourish for a few years throughout all Europe'.[65] So it was a realizable aim. All the governments (and he includes Muscovy) should swear to abjure war and to cut their armed forces back to police size. All should agree to abide by the arbitration of difficulties by a general assembly of their representatives, and support majority decisions with arms if need arose. The European Council should have a fixed headquarters. Cruce chose

Venice, partly because of its position between East and West and its good communications with the northern nations, and partly 'because it is practically neutral and indifferent towards all princes'.[66] Partly too, one may guess, because of the famed social harmony between government and subjects which was part of the 'myth' of Venice, as well as the good standing of its monetary unit, the ducat, and its pronounced cosmopolitanism. For Crucé could not resist responding to eirenic universalism. He included the Sultan's representative in the Council (going so far, in his table of precedence, as to place him between the Pope and the Emperor). He even left the doors open to the invitation of emissaries from Morocco, Japan and the 'Great Mogul . . . and other monarchs as well from India and Africa'.[67]

Five years earlier, in 1618, during a meeting of representatives of the Bohemian Estates to protest against the policies imposed on the country by the absentee Emperor Matthias (who had moved his court from Prague back to Vienna), two of his leading spokesmen were thrown out of an upper window in Hradčany Castle. It was a drop of sixty feet. Miraculously the garbage filling the moat beneath absorbed the shock and they fled to tell their tale. And the speed with which the tale spread throughout the continent, from Moscow to London and from Stockholm to Rome and Madrid, illustrates the extent to which the whole of Europe had become sensitized to a crisis in one part of it. The issue of revolt and self-determination challenged authority and gave hope to minorities – especially religious ones – everywhere. As Spanish troops moved into Bohemia a Dutch observer told a German colleague of his belief that 'the Bohemian war will decide the fate of us all.'[68] As the conflict widened it offered fresh chances of intervention; central Europe became what Italy had been from 1494: a zone where territory could be annexed and national power put again to the test. It was with considerable relish that the expansionist ruler of Sweden, Gustavus Adolphus, remarked in 1628 – five years after Crucé's plan for a single peace table – that, 'all the wars that are on foot in Europe have become fused together and have become a single war.'[69]

So as the image of Europe became intellectually ever clearer, so did its divisions and the possibility of taking political advantage of them. There is no paradox here. Amity and enmity simply came to different conclusions about the knowledge increasingly available to both. And in the same way, national antipathies flourished alongside the increasing pace with which men came to know one another – Postel's failed formula for 'accomplishing perfect human reconciliation'.

CHAPTER IV

Traffic

BORDERS AND LANGUAGES

When Crucé yearned for a peaceful Europe in which men could 'go here and there freely' he was playing down the extent to which they already did. Even allowing for the inquisitorial policing of Counter-Reformation Spain and Italy, which subjected Protestant visitors to harassment and, at times, the risk of their lives, the number of people who travelled across the always porous borders of European countries was greater as a proportion of the population than ever before.

For reasons still unclear, and in a manner by no means uniform in place or time, the overall population of Europe surged: from an estimated sixty million in 1500 to eighty million by 1600, omitting Lithuania and Russia for which the demographic evidence is too patchy even for responsible guesswork. That of Germany, for instance, went up from twelve to sixteen million, of France from sixteen to over nineteen, in England and southern Italy it may have doubled, as it did in Castile from three almost to six million before there was pronounced *rallentando* throughout Spain from the 1590s. But there was little scope for the absorption of this fresh labour within an overwhelmingly tillage and pastoral economy which had by 1500 already encroached as far as was practicable into marshy, shallow-soiled and mountainous lands. The numerous scattered towns, with populations between six to twelve thousand, were too dependent on a restricted area within which to market their goods to offer many new job opportunities. The main pressure fell on cities with long established commercial and industrial bases and continuing good access to infusions of raw materials and foodstuffs. The population of London proper – the city within the walls – trebled from some 50,000 to towards 150,000; that of London as a conurbation expanded from 60,000 to something approaching 225,000.

It was the loadstone cities, the El Dorados of the dispossessed – others included Lisbon, Seville, Venice, Nuremberg, Paris and Lyon, Antwerp – which complained to governments that migrant labour, mostly native but also foreign, was wrecking welfare and social control services that were adequate only to deal with their own drop-outs: the unprotected aged, the infirm, the mentally unstable, unwanted babies, those temporarily unemployed because of a downturn in the local economy. Droves of statutes, a Europe-wide spate of books and pamphlets dealing with jobless gangs, beggars real and phoney, fetid roadside encampments, terrorized suburbs, attested to the gravity of the domestic problem and to governments' inability to deal with it. The population surge continued to push men from one country to another. With long stretches of unpatrolled borders, a multitude of fords and lonely creeks, the opportunities for furtive migrancy were legion. Many emigrants took skills or a determination that have brought their names to history's surface as taxpayers or soldiers or named criminals. Others remained, not necessarily tragically, beneath it.

In any case, given their short-staffed bureaucracies, governments limited their effective interferences with the freedom of cross-border traffic to more conspicuous targets. Merchants with goods were expected to enter through all-weather harbours or along policed highways. So were diplomatic and well-to-do private travellers; they were prepared to put up with some inconvenience for the sake of recuperating in ports or towns with good inns and the availability of regular transport (the hire of shipping or fresh horses), while they obtained the official travel permits which could save much altercation as they pressed on. All the same, as a warning sign of governmental vigilance, the issuing of passports, licences to travel, was a general if intermittent practice. Thomas Platter, a learned and eager student of 'abroad', returning home to Germany from a visit to England, transcribed the one he obtained in London from Sir Henry Cobham in 1599 before proceeding to Dover:

Whereas the bearers herof [Platter and his companions are named], highe Almaynes gentilmen and schollars come latelie over, moved with a desier to see her Mayeste and the countrey, and are nouue disirous to passe over into fraunce to the like ende: Theise are therfore to praye and requier you and everie of you whome it may concerne, not onlie to sufer them with their clokebagg [luggage for clothing] and other theire necessarie carriage quietle to passe without your or any of your lette, hinderannce or impeachment; but also to yeelde them all lawfull favor and curtesie you maye and they shall desier for their better expedicion; foreseing they carrie nothinge otherwise than becommeth. And in so doing this shalbe your warrante.[1]

This was signed by Cobham and further authenticated by Elizabeth's deputized seal in red wax.

Passports issued to nationals commonly named not just the party but the number of horses and the amount of currency being exported for travelling expenses. In time of war or international tension a time limit was mentioned and countries named which the travellers were not permitted to enter. It was, indeed, only at such times that passports were issued with any regularity, save in the case of men of rank whose recall for their services might be required by governments even in peacetime; immigration checks were in any case cursory. Platter and his friends, all Protestants, simply presented forged passports which altered their place of residence when entering Catholic territory or, in the case of their visit to Spain, passed themselves off as merchants for whom political passports were unnecessary as long as they paid duty on items in their baggage bought elsewhere; as a travel guide of 1610 pointed out, passing customs was simply a matter of pitching a bribe at the right level.

Given the porosity of borders and the corruptibility of the officials staffing their check-points, the burden of restricting undesirable immigration and movement fell on the cities. Most of those which acted as honeypots for the questing unemployed or the sectarian infiltrator were walled. When the gates were shut at dusk, not even residents could return home from a miscalculated expedition. A washed-out road, a lame horse, could leave a traveller benighted; as a result, some of the best inns and most charitably inclined monasteries were situated in suburbs. After daybreak the visitor was confronted by the gate-guard. Baggage and travel permits were scrutinized, references to citizens who could act as sponsors checked, as were certificates that arrivals had not been through areas affected by plague during the past forty days; and passes were issued to a known household or an inn which would have to return them endorsed. Weapons, a well-nigh universal part of a traveller's equipment, were, save in the case of exceptionally distinguished visitors, impounded. 'If we had only crossed the city', a visitor to Florence recorded in 1546, 'a man would have accompanied us to restore them at the other gate, but on our declaring that we were going to stay, our swords were taken from us, and the hilt provided with a wooden label, part of which they gave us to keep.'[2] Innkeepers were sometimes entrusted with these cloakroom duties as well as being required to send in daily reports on their guests to the civic authorities.

Governments encouraged their undercover agents abroad to report on their own nationals in addition to providing local information. Elizabeth's foreign affairs specialist, Sir Francis Walsingham, maintained fifty-three informants in the major towns of seven countries, including three agents in Turkey. But with the conspicuous exception of that country and Muscovy, travel conditions favoured those categories of men most able because of their education and *savoir faire* to take conscious note of their foreign experience and communicate it to others. These included, as we shall see, merchants and skilled, literate artisans, especially those who resided abroad for some time; diplomatic agents of all grades; students and scholars; men of letters, musicians and practitioners of the decorative fine arts; those who travelled in the inquiring spirit of tourists. These were at the core of Postel's belief that a sense of European community would depend on men acquiring 'knowledge of one another'.

The actual process of getting about had not changed since the Middle Ages. The cartographic revolution may have enabled travellers to imagine their route more clearly in advance, and place it on their return, but there is no clear evidence that maps were consulted en route. Few, even regional ones, showed roads, and roads, in any case, were subject to wash-outs by heavy rain and were rendered virtually unusable for months after an army had ploughed its heavy gun-carriages along them. Travellers still relied on asking locally about the most practicable way of following the itineraries, the lists of place-names that were the commonest source of directions and whose influence was reflected in the meticulous noting of stopping places and the distance between them included in journals of travel. Whenever possible they had recourse to co-nationals on the spot, or innkeepers and priests with a smattering of multi-lingual answers to stock questions or, as in the case of Venice, official guides whose function was to show visitors where to lodge and shop and what to look at.

The old pace was still observed, that of foot or horse. With all this travelling, complained a late sixteenth-century German merchant, 'I have had so little respite that my bottom has been constantly a-fire from the saddle.'[3] Journeys on horseback could quite frequently achieve a rate of fifty to seventy kilometres a day, double that or even more for a professional courier on post routes supplied with relays of fresh mounts. Political news reaching the diplomatic hub of Rome took three days at best from Florence or Naples, four from Venice, ten from Lyon, twenty-six from Madrid. In the ordinary way, a day's journey would average some forty kilometres, a pace that remained constant for travellers until the introduction of railways. Though rivers provided cheap transport downstream for heavy cargoes (boats were often sold or broken up at their destination because of the expense of towing them up again) they were seldom used by travellers because of the delays at toll stations established by riparian landlords. The canal system envisioned by Émeric Cruceé had found no support in Europe, save in Milanese Lombardy, and Turkish plans to link the Black and Caspian Seas in 1570 through a canal between the Don and the Volga got no further than did their still bolder idea of linking the Mediterranean with the Indian Ocean across the isthmus of Suez. So far as the means of transport were concerned, on well-maintained thoroughfares there were, perhaps, more carriages than hitherto – basically farm waggons with seats: Erasmus, ever groaning at the discomfort of horseriding on his many visits to friends and publishing houses, travelled in one from Cologne to Aachen in 1518. It was not a success. 'I arrived exhausted from the shaking of the carriage which was so trying to me . . . that I should have preferred sitting on my horse.'[4] Massive decorated coaches were introduced gradually from the mid-century. They were soon to be on their way to becoming symbols of social status for long-distance travellers, but for the time being were restricted to trundling impressively up and down the paved streets of cities.

Thinly populated as rural Europe was, it was seldom, even in Spain where inns were few and far between, that some sort of bed could not be found for the night. It was with surprise and dismay that a traveller in 1602 found that in Russia 'one can go for twenty or thirty miles without coming across a single town or village.'[5] That food could be bad, wine sour, lice abundant and beds shared aroused little comment. Though the frequent reports on the cleanliness of Dutch streets and houses suggests some sensitivity on the score of drainage, hygiene and stench, this was not a fastidious age. Deep potations helped. In Turkey, Ogier de Busbecq complained not about having to sleep from time to time on the ground or in a shed but about the difficulty of obtaining wine, 'the usual remedy for uncomfortable nights'.[6]

The risks grew as the population increase forced more men into highway crime. During the sixteenth century it became usual to hire escorts or wait for groups to assemble. The growing number of road-side gibbets outside towns, with putrefying robbers hanging from them, may have shown the efficiency of civic police forces but probably produced more alarm than comfort as travellers proceeded on to lone-lier stretches of road. The danger was increased by deserters from armies and those who by a campaign's end had acquired a taste for living at the expense of civilians. Fynes Moryson explained the expedi-ents that kept him reasonably solvent after being robbed on the road in France in 1617: he had sewed coins in the linings of his clothes; he had wound threads round others and stuck needles into the threads so that the cache was overlooked as a sewing kit; others he had put in the bottom of a box and coated 'with a stinking ointment for scabs' that caused the robbers to throw the box on one side.[7] Reformation con-flicts, too, bought new hazards. When Sastrow travelled from his native, Protestant Pomerania to Italy, he adopted a pilgrim's hat and badge and Italian costume (which nearly caused him to be lynched on his return through Innsbruck) and on one occasion had to feign to be dumb lest his German accent betray him.

These random examples may help to explain why contemporaries always assumed that travellers would be men. Women travelled from farmstead to market, from a German Protestant city to worship on Sunday, in a Catholic one to visit relatives. But with children and households to look after, husbands' businesses to keep an eye on or actually run in their absence, together with the insecurity of the roads, they seldom crossed national borders. Fewer than formerly went on pilgrimages further than to the familiar shrines within their own coun-tries. Only those in gypsy bands, or touring *commedia dell'arte* com-panies, or as army camp followers (as wives, mistresses, prostitutes, laundresses, food-gatherers and nurses) embraced the freedom of the road in any numbers. None left any record of her experience. Neither did the literate women who joined a merchant or artisan husband who had settled abroad or who were carried in the train of a dynastic bride. It is not surprising, in the world of bachelors and married men travel-ling on their own, that some at least were alert to note women's fashions and looks and, for example, in Switzerland and Germany to dwell on the appeal of mixed bathing establishments and the bare legs of the servant girls in taverns.

That the risks of prolonged or distant travel were appreciable (chiefly from disease rather than violent death at the hands of cut-throats or pirates) was reflected towards the end of the sixteenth century in the growth of life assurance, based by the issuing company on an anticipation – the rate depending on the destination – that the traveller might not return. Such a gamble on God's mercy was almost universally disapproved of, especially in the case of pilgrimages, but these transactions are recorded in England, the Netherlands, France and Italy and indicate the business community's awareness of the expanding volume of the movements which eirenists hoped would bring mankind together in mutual understanding.

Many of the larger towns offered the possibility of relaxing among the traveller's own compatriots. By the early sixteenth century there were Italian communities in Augsburg, Ulm, Ravensburg, Nuremberg and Trent; Bruges and Antwerp; London; Paris, Rouen, La Rochelle, Lyon, Montpellier, Avignon and Marseilles; Barcelona, Valencia and Seville; Lisbon; Geneva. Within Italy itself the German element in Florence declined but that in Lucca grew. The cosmopolitanism of Venice was a byword. In 1468 the learned Greek Cardinal Bessarion told the Doge that he was giving his magnificent library of manuscripts to the

Corporate houses of the Florentine and Genoese merchants in Bruges (16th-century print)

city because Greeks there 'seem to be in another Byzantium' and 'men come together there from practically the whole world.'[8] Thomas Coryat's nickname for the city in 1608 was 'Little Christendom'. But he accepted that even this was a restrictive phrase, for 'there you may see many Polonians, Slavonians, Persians, Grecians, Turks, Jewes, Christians of all the famousest regions of Christendome, and each nation distinguished from another by their proper and peculiar habits'[9]; Venetian place-names still record the presence of foreign communities: the Fondaco (warehouse and offices) of the Germans and that of the 'Turks' (that is, traders – Armenians, Persians and others besides Turks – from the Near East), the Fondamenta or quay of the Schiavoni (Slavs, mostly Dalmatians), the Greek church of St Giorgio, the Jewish Ghettos (itself a Venetian word). Palermo was another cosmopolitan centre. A French visitor in 1589 observed that 'one can say that the city is, apart from some native artisans, entirely populated by foreigners.'[10] And with the building up by the Medici grand dukes from the mid-century of Livorno as a well-equipped duty free port, that too became a haven for many tongues and complexions.

More significant, from the point of view of the growth of existing foreign communities and the establishment of new ones, was the increasing volume of commercial activity up and down the western and north-western European seaboards and across the oceans. 'Formerly', wrote a Spaniard in 1524 to the town council of Cordoba, urging them to improve communications down the Guadalquivir to the sea near Seville, 'we were at the end of the world; now we are in the middle of it, with an unprecedented change in our fortunes.'[11] And the same sentiment was expressed in Seville itself by a local patriot: previously our regions 'used to be the very end of the world, but now, with the discovery of the Indies, they have become its centre'. So foreign traders and bankers moved in, mostly Italian ('our Spain is the Indies of the Genoese' was a bitter native comment of 1617), but also German and French.[12] Of London, a visitor in 1545 had already noted that, 'there dwell men from most of the nations of Europe.'[13] During the first half of the sixteenth century Antwerp linked the Baltic trade in heavy goods to the Indian Ocean harvest of spices, medicinal drugs and ingredients for the dyeing of textiles. With its sophisticated harbour facilities, which included giant cranes, a bonded warehouse system, and credit facilities, Antwerp became the Venice of the North. By the 1560s, however, silting in the Scheldt was already restricting the passage of deep-draft vessels to its wharfs. And there emerged a Catholic intransigence that

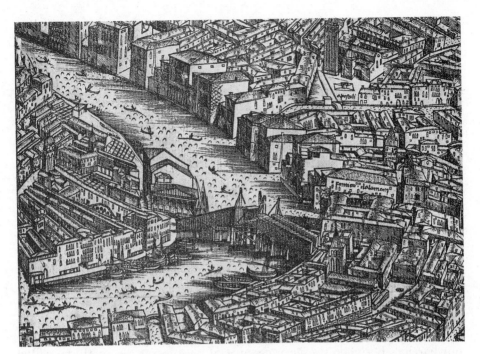

Rialto: detail from Jacopo de'Barbari's *Bird's-eye View of Venice*, woodcut, 1500 (British Museum)

made life uncertain for Protestants working in the import–export, banking, insurance and foreign exchange fields. Some moved to Amsterdam, others to those German centres which opened their gates to exiled talents: Cologne, Nuremberg, Frankfurt and Hamburg all welcomed as productive residents not only Netherlandish and French Calvinists but those Jewish and ex-Muslim Marano men of business for whom the inquisitorial and 'clean blood' purges in Spain had made life intolerable. With their acceptance of Calvinist refugees, London and the chief towns of East Anglia acquired French-speaking minorities of specialist weavers, potters and silversmiths. Religious belief joined commerce as a motive for living abroad. Most conspicuous of the cities of refuge was Calvinist Geneva. It had long been a focus for small foreign merchant communities because of its strategic position on European trade routes. By 1570 sixty per cent of its inhabitants were foreigners, mostly French, but others came from as far afield as Scotland and Crete. By the end of the century it was the most densely populated city in Europe. If Seville represented an intensification of the old, mercantile form of cosmopolitan centre, Geneva was the flagship of the new: the Noah's Ark of the refugee.

The members of all foreign communities, like the visitors who relaxed in their company, tended, with the exception of those who were particularly rich and locally well-connected, to keep to themselves, living in Little Italys of their own speech, patronizing particular monastic orders or parish churches – or, like the Florentine community in Rome or the Greeks in Venice, building one of their own. But merchants had come to chaffer and communicate, refugees to build new lives among co-religionists, and this raised the problem of language. God's confusion of languages as a punishment for the presumption of the builders of the heaven-invading Tower of Babel was a check to any easy sentiment of unity among the peoples of Europe, just as dialects cut down the sense of common background within an individual nation. Commenting on the story as it was recounted in *Genesis*, Luther broke off to give it a contemporary application: 'The Frenchman has only hatred and scorn for the German, the Italians have only hatred and scorn for all others. So we can see that this division of languages has led to divisions of habits, ways of thought and priorities that have put barriers between the very essence of peoples; it can justly be called the source of all misfortunes.'[14]

Latin was the antidote to the divisions of Babel: but as a lingua franca it had always been a learned patina on the intarsia of vernaculars and this was wearing thinner than ever. In theory nearly anyone who went to school got some tincture of Latin. It remained the most prestigious language for authors who sought a European audience. Publishers saw its market advantages. Though Castiglione's *The Courtier* was translated from the Italian fairly soon after its appearance in 1528 into English, French and Spanish, it was the Latin translation that sold the most copies. Latin enabled scholars to trail their expertise from one European university to another. It was Latin that enabled the English, through the writings of such men as Bacon, Camden, the anatomist William Harvey and the physician – and metaphysician – Robert Fludd, to re-enter as intellectuals a continent which had rejected them – with the loss of Calais in 1558 – as a political power. It was the passport which made it possible for a multilingual English poetess, Elizabeth Weston, to be lauded in Prague, where she was commemorated in a portrait of *c.*1610. But the gap between its written respectability and its practicality widened with every decade. In an Italian treatise on precautions against the plague written in 1522 the author explained that while the first part

Elizabeth Weston, c.1596,
anon. drawing (Hessisches
Landesmuseum, Darmstadt)

was in Latin for the benefit of his fellow physicians the second was in
the vernacular 'for those who have no understanding of a classical
language'. It was a tongue, as Moryson, who could in fact speak it
fluently, noted, 'living only in writing, not in practice'.[15]

Latin was to some extent the victim of its own propagandists, those
humanists who wanted to deliver it from bastard importation and
restore it to the purity of Ciceronian and Virgilian times. This was
inhibiting to those whose workaday Latin was supplemented as they
went along with words and phrases adjusted from their own native
languages. Records of Luther's conversation show him switching from
Latin when dealing with theological matters to German when applying
them to the dilemmas of ordinary, domestic life; at times the spectacle
of Latin and German words clambering over one another to convey
the rapidity of his thought reveals his personality, but obscures his
meaning. As diplomatic contacts increased, and as fewer agents were
latinate clerics, ambassadorial Latin at least from the 1520s became
restricted in the main to polite formulae of greeting and farewell,

though from the 1550s even these came to be dispensed with; inter-
preting between vernaculars became a new profession. No diplomat,
apart from papal ones, used Latin regularly for correspondence with
his government, and those – there were always some – who could speak
Latin found negotiation confusing because local ways of pronouncing it
made it difficult to catch shades of meaning. Writings on the diplomatic
function, such as Ottaviano Maggi's *The Ambassador* of 1566, came to
stress the importance of living languages. Beneath the even written
Latin surface of international agreements were native tongues translated
by interpreters and formulated by secretaries.

Few men, apart from Erasmus, had a greater love of Latin or nimbleness in manipulating it to absorb topics and nomenclatures unantici-
pated by its Augustan users than Aeneas Silvius Piccolomini. However,
writing to advise the young King Ladislas of Bohemia and Hungary
in 1450, he said that Latin, though a knowledge of it should be taken
for granted, was not enough. 'Love, no less than the sword, guards
kingdoms . . . Intercourse of language is a promoter of love . . . You
must strive to be able by yourself to hear your subjects, to understand

Maximilian, speaking seven languages, calms down his polyglot troops, Albrecht Altdorfer,
woodcut (British Museum)

them and to speak with them. Frequently some things occur which your subjects may wish to refer to you alone and which they would not entrust to an interpreter.'[16] Maximilian I proudly recorded his qualifications for his multi-lingual imperial role. He had been brought up as a child to speak German, he gained Latin at school, Saxon and Czech from his subjects, French from his wife Mary of Burgundy, Flemish from the officials in the Netherlandish parts of his inheritance, Spanish from diplomatic correspondents who were flattered by his use of their own tongue, Italian from the captains and English from the archers he enlisted into his armies.

Maximilian made a point of having one of his artists depict him resolving a mutiny among his multi-lingual troops by understanding what they were all saying. This, like other claims for his prowess in all departments of a ruler's life, has to be taken with a pinch of salt. But it is indicative. His successors in eastern Europe, Ferdinand, Maximilian II and Rudolf II also learned some at least of the languages of their scattered subjects. Rudolf's Latin was supplemented by German and Czech and at least a reading acquaintance with Spanish, French and Italian. Other monarchs, of monoglot realms, accepted the withering away of Latin. Francis I spoke an Italian that was at least comprehensible; his sons all had Italian tutors. Elizabeth I, a good Latinist, was competent in Italian and French. Philip II of Spain was unusual in sticking to his native language, as was Henri IV in an active chauvinism which made him castigate his son for learning Spanish.

School Latin was recognized as having little lasting effect. Machiavelli (who used only the odd *etiam* in his habitually vernacular writings) made fun of the lawyer in his 1518 comedy *Mandragola* for being taken in by the Latin paraded by the pseudo-doctor who was planning to seduce his wife. In 1594 Shakespeare could rely on understanding titters from the audience when his pedant Holofernes in *Love's Labour's Lost* introduced the juvenile playing the infant Hercules in the court entertainment he had devised:

> Great Hercules is presented by this imp,
> Whose club killed Cerberus, that three-headed *canis*;
> And when he was a babe, a child, a shrimp,
> Thus did he strangle serpents in his *manus*.
> *Quoniam* he seemeth in minority,
> *Ergo* I come with this apology.[17]

Five years after this, Thomas Platter, needing to use his Latin as a means of communication, commented on the difficulty he experienced in persuading either the young men at Eton or their seniors at Oxford to use it. Though Paracelsus caused a scandal by lecturing in German on medicine at his native university of Basel in 1526, some of the law lectures at the London Inns of Court were already delivered in English, and according to the statutes setting up Sir Thomas Gresham's College in 1596, the Monday lecture on medicine was to be given in Latin in the morning and repeated in English in the afternoon because 'the greatest part of the auditory is like to be of such citizens and others as have small knowledge or none at all of the Latin tongue.'[18] While universities remained faithful to formal instruction in Latin, an increasing number of institutions grew up in France, Germany and Italy for young men who wanted to equip themselves for court, diplomatic or military careers for which Latin was not a prerequisite. Around universities themselves grew fringes of 'finishing' activities; in his early teaching days at Padua Galileo doubled as a university lecturer and the holder of extramural classes for those eager to learn the new applications of mathematics to the brigading of troops and to fortification. To prepare young men of good birth 'for the service of their countrie'[19], Sir Humphrey Gilbert in 1570 proposed an academy which would maintain teachers of French, Italian, Spanish and Dutch. By 1615, when Sir George Buck represented London as England's 'third university', of more use to the state than the conservative Oxford and Cambridge, he cited the availability of teachers of these and 'divers other Languages fit for Embassadors and Orators, and Agents for Marchants, and for Travaylors'.[20]

For the upper levels of non-professional society the bias was not so much against Latin as such, as away from its weight within educational curricula. The library in Rabelais's imaginary ideal of a devout educational establishment, the Abbey of Thélème in Gargantua (1532), catered for the languages needed for Bible study, Latin, Greek, and Hebrew, but also had books in French, Italian and Spanish lest the real world be forgotten and the timbre of God's omnipresent voice muffled. The Reformation emphasis on personal religious experience, which touched Rabelais without converting him, had been expressed by Luther in 1518: 'I thank God that I hear and find my God in the German language in a way which I have not found Him up to now in the Latin, Greek, or Hebrew tongues.'[21] Sermons had commonly been delivered in parishioners' own language, but the use of the vernacular for the liturgy in Protestant countries reduced the number of those in Europe who had at least been used to hearing Latin on Sundays and saints' days.

For a number of reasons, then, the age that saw the revival of the true form of the universal language of imperial Rome also connived in its decline. A dying language could still nourish living faith. The book that had perhaps the most influence on Europe's faith and politics was Calvin's *Institutes of the Christian Religion*; it was first published in 1536, in Latin, albeit quickly translated and paraphrased for the benefit of native congregations from Scotland to Bohemia. Latin remained a medium of international exchange in matters of scholarly concern. There was a thriving neo-Latin literature whose poetry was living enough to arouse the enthusiasm of Pierre de Ronsard and his fellow poets of the mid-sixteenth-century Pléiade group. It was as a means of general communication that it lost ground.

This ground had, indeed, never – outside the most highly educated circles – been firm. For the great majority of those on the move it had never been a substitute for gesture, the display of a coin, the rapport of conviviality. Before the Reformation there was, in theory, a source of information for travellers in the person of the parish priest. In 1507 a Florentine, lost on a diplomatic mission to Munich, was relieved to meet in Überlingen a priest with 'a feeble grasp of Latin'.[22] To reduce the scandal of priests who did not even understand their own liturgy was one of the aims of the Counter-Reformation, but when the indulgence-selling priest in the 1554 anonymous Spanish picaresque novel *Lazarillo of Tormes* met a colleague who greeted him in Latin, 'he never said a word in that language so as not to put his foot in it.'[23] On the other hand Montaigne during his Italian journey found priests whose Latin was more fluent than his own book-based Italian. It was a time of hit and miss. No wonder that travellers who could afford it hired interpreters en route and nestled among their compatriots' communities whenever they could.

The issue of language becomes urgent only within the context of a demand for practical communication wider than that of basic needs. With the recognition that the practical lingua franca could not be Latin, Babel stood revealed. The interpreter now had more to offer than the humanistically educated secretary or tutor. He was employed by governments. He offered his linguistic wares in marketplaces, quaysides, in the portico of a *bourse*. (He was not necessarily to be trusted. When Busbecq inquired why an old Turk was howling as he held a glass of wine, he was told that, 'he is warning his soul to withdraw into a remote part of his body so that it will be contaminated as little as possible by the crime he is committing.'[24]) Merchants sent their sons to learn the ropes of a foreign market with a new emphasis on obtaining language skills. Some leaped at the opportunity. The sixteen-year-old Michael Behaim, while serving an apprenticeship in Breslau in 1527, was offered a place with a firm in Cracow 'so that I can learn the language'. He wrote home to say 'I would prefer Bohemia to Poland, Germans almost outnumber Poles in Cracow now . . . I will learn more if I am among non-Germans.'[25] Governments detached young men of promise from chancery chores to join foreign embassies with the same intent. Polylingualism began to be noticed and praised: a French friend of Ortelius praised his fluency in Dutch, German, French and Spanish; Marcus Perez, an emigré Marano merchant in Antwerp in the 1560s was commended by his colleagues for his enviable com-

Jacobo Strada, Titian, 1567–8
(Kunsthistorisches
Museum, Vienna)

mand of Flemish, German, French, Spanish and Italian. The international success of the Netherlandish portrait painter Antonis Mor from
the 1550s owed more than a little to his ability to speak to his subjects
and their agents in French, Spanish and Italian.

From the 1480s travellers had begun to include glossaries of useful
foreign words as appendices to their narratives. Polyglot vocabularies
were published with increasing frequency from 1477; François Garon's
Vocabulary of five Languages: Latin, Italian, French, Spanish and German
proved so popular after its publication in Venice in 1526 that by the
1546 edition it had been extended to cover eight languages. Jacopo
Strada, a scholarly collector and dealer in antiquities whose portrait was
painted by Titian, died in 1588 while working on an eleven-language
dictionary. From the early sixteenth century multi-lingual conversation
and phrase books started to appear as simple aids for merchants abroad;
from the mid-century they broadened to satisfy those who wished to
learn a foreign language in some depth. The long title of Claudius
Hollyband's *The French Schoolemaister* of 1573 suggests the new self-
culture: *wherein is most plainelie shewed the true and most perfect way of
pronouncinge of the French tongue, without any helpe of Maister or Teacher:
set foorthe for the furtherance of all those whiche doo studie privately in their
own study or houses.* The tone of some of these teach-yourself books
could be reassuringly unpedantic. Going through the parts of speech
in the parallel English and Italian dialogue columns of his *Florio, his
firste Fruites* published in 1578, John Florio wrote:

> Nowe let us come to the Articles.
> I pray you doo so sir, if you be not weery.
> To tell you the truth, I am almost weery,
> but nevertheless we wyl follow.

And the learning of declensions was cheered up, as in:

> Fayre mayde, wyll you that I love you?
> I cannot hold you that you love not if you wyl love.
> I have loved you, I love you, and will love you . . .
> I will brake my fast with you:
> We will have a pair of sasages.[26]

While this interest in learning foreign languages was intended to fill
the gap left by Latin, it accompanied an interest in the structure and
range of the vernacular language of a man's own country. Against the

reproaches levelled by German humanists at their countrymen's neglect of classical latinity, Luther claimed that there was nothing worth saying in everyday converse that could not be perfectly well expressed in German. Why waste time reviving Latin, asked Ronsard in 1589 – writing well after the publication in 1549 of his fellow-poet Joachim du Bellay's *Defence and Illustration of the French Language* – when French is so copious and flourishing? Towards the end of Elizabeth's reign Samuel Daniel prophetically asked:

> And who, in time, knowes whether we may vent [export]
> The treasure of our tongue, to what strange shores
> This gaine of our best glory shall be sent
> T'inrich unknowing Nations with our stores?
> What worlds in th'yet unforméd Occident
> May come refin'd with th' accents that are ours?[27]

But leaving this particular dream aside, the conscious cultivation of vernaculars was the product of cultural pride and administrative convenience. Save for the stimulus it gave to translators it had no intentional bearing on the problem of intercommunication. In border towns like Trent, Trieste or Ragusa bilingualism was in any case common. Spanish was a second language for the educated French of Navarre. Traditional political and military contacts between Scotland and France, Tuscany and Germany, Rome and Switzerland, Spain and the Netherlands produced pidgin forms of speech that served for practical purposes. Polish merchants travelling up the Vistula to sell their goods in Danzig could bargain in general terms using German and some Latin – retained in eastern Europe longer than in the West because of the plethora of local languages. But for native German speakers, and the Dutch, Swedes and Norwegians who traded with Danzig and the other Baltic ports, there was an adequate lingua franca of common commercial and nautical terms, just as there was throughout the trading world of Mediterranean ports. In addition, from Persia to the Moluccas Europeans made their wants known and clinched their deals in forms of communication comprising of a few nouns, verbs in the infinitive, gestures and the finger language of price bargaining.

It was the mounting volume of diplomatic exchanges that led during the sixteenth century to the beginning of the process whereby one vernacular rather than another became preferred as an internationally shared common language. In spite of the range of Portugal's empire and the importance of its trade with Antwerp, its language, to judge from the manuals, was not one that anyone sought to learn. An old Russia hand of the English Muscovy Company could declare that the country's tongue was 'the most copious and elegant in the world'.[28] But his praise fell on a respectful silence. Elizabeth's interest in the value of Russian contacts caused her to ask the Earl of Essex to learn it, which led, on the Earl's part, to no more than a dutiful humming and hawing. English itself, in spite of Daniel's crystal ball, Florio's revelation that it contained *A Worlde of Wordes* (the title of his English-Italian dictionary of 1598) and the example of Shakespeare, was no competitor in the common language stakes. As Florio himself remarked in another work, English is 'a language that will do you good in England, but pass Dover it is worth nothing'.[29]

Neither was German a competitor, in spite of the wide penetration of some of its words and phrases into the interglossa of northern commerce. Between its southern High and northern Low varieties it was later than other European languages to attain a reasonable uniformity and there was some shrinking from its very sound; for Moryson, a tolerant multi-linguist, its grating peremptoriness had the effect of 'sounding better in the mouth of Tamberlin [the ferocious tyrant of Marlowe's *Tamberlane the Great*] than of a civill man'.[30] The same internal confusions and (to others) harshness prevented the 'Dutch' of the northern Low Countries from becoming an international tongue in spite of their being so long a focus of political and commercial interest. For their own part, Netherlanders were concerned to learn the languages of their visitors and to publish handbooks to them.

The field was chiefly open to languages which, like Italian, Spanish and French, had a latinate, therefore fairly readily learnable base, and by the mid-sixteenth century the most commonly understood was probably Italian, chiefly in its Tuscan form. The Italian commercial network had long been the widest in Europe, and it continued to draw foreign merchants into the peninsula. Late in the sixteenth century a Nuremberg merchant in Lucca described how he was trying to transform a colleague's idle and prankish son into a steady young man of business: 'he fears and respects me', he reported to his wife, 'but a certain number of years must pass for a mind to mature. I have begun to dictate my Italian letters to him, a task which he gives himself readily to and performs well; it will also help him in writing and speaking Italian.'[31] The business schools for would-be merchant apprentices in Antwerp taught the rudiments of commercial Italian. The lure of the new, humanistic classical learning and the reputation of princely courts had by the 1530s peppered Europe from England to Poland with young men who had attended the universities of Pavia, Bologna and Padua or visited Milan, Mantua and Ferrara.

In the sixteenth century Italian literature came to replace the international appeal of French – or French-based – chivalrous romances. Italian authors acquired a significant foreign readership, encouraging aspirant poets in Spain, England and France to read the works of Petrarch and Ariosto in the original. The poet Queen of Navarre, Marguerite d'Angoulême, wrote in Italian to her fellow poet Vittoria Colonna. A number of the Frenchmen to whom 'the Prince of Beggars', Pietro Aretino, wrote his cajoling and bullying letters flattered him with responses in his own tongue. A glimpse of how chic Italian had become by c.1550 is offered by the lines in that language which the feeble French poet Mellin de Saint-Gelais claimed to have scratched with a diamond on a young woman's looking-glass:

> If beauties you display excell all others,
> How true t'will be of those that you conceal.[32]

Montaigne learned to speak Italian, as had his father, as a matter of course, and on crossing the Alps on his travels he changed the language of his journal from French to Italian. Returning across the Mont Cenis pass he noted with relief that, 'here French is spoken, so I leave this foreign language in which I feel facile but ill-grounded.'[33] And in an essay he explained this facility in terms which underline the convenience of a romance language as a passe-partout for wide stretches of southern and western Europe.[34] You go full tilt, he wrote, using whatever words – French, Gascon, Spanish, Latin – come to mind, but giving them Italian terminations.

Familiarity with the language was also encouraged by the general preoccupation of the western powers with Italy during the wars of 1494 to 1530 and, though less generally, up to 1559. It was not, after all, poets or merchants who determined the choice of a high-level common form of speech. Sir Thomas Hoby, who achieved fame from his quirkily energetic translation of Castiglione's *The Courtier*, had been to Italy to learn the language because, like his ambassador brother, he wanted to equip himself for a diplomatic career. And in 1559, at Cateau-Cambrésis, the French, Spanish and English chief negotiators were all fluent in Italian. Even so, in the informal discussions below the Latin surface of official deliberations on the wording of the Peace,

French (also spoken by the English and Spanish parties) appears to have been employed more frequently.

It was in fact from 1559 that French began its long career towards becoming the politician's second language. For a while there was some competition from Spanish. Spanish costume, sub-fusc but elegant, was widely copied. The great range of Spanish power was deferred to. But language did not, as Nebrijia had anticipated, march with empire; in the southern Netherlands more French than Spanish was spoken, Franche-Comté was an exclusively French-speaking area; even in vice-regal circles Spanish had little impact in Milan and Naples; in Germany, Austria and beyond, the Habsburg cousinhood baulked at the importation of a language so at odds with the Teutonic and Slavonic roots of their subjects' tongues.

In England, though Norman French had been dropped from upper-class speech by the fourteenth century, memories of it lingered in legal terminology (and the nuns of Lacock Abbey in Wiltshire were still speaking it in the 1530s); the Crown's territorial link with France, moreover, only snapped with the loss of Calais in 1558. When the Italian states had slipped from the urgent diplomatic agenda after 1559 and with the German ones largely quiescent in international affairs, France's large population, its political weight (in spite of the deadlocked confusions of its intermittent civil wars) and its geographical position all gave stature to its language in its administrative Paris-based form. For Protestants and moderate Catholics elsewhere, French universities attracted growing numbers of those who might formerly have gone to Italian ones. By 1600 the momentum that led to the international primacy of French during the country's leading role in Europe under Louis XIV was well under way. It had become the inner-circle language of cultivated German courts and Spanish diplomats had accepted the need to use it in the many negotiations with Catholic factions during the civil wars and the preliminaries of the Peace of Vervins.

The problems of verbal communication continued, however, in spite of the efforts of élites to overcome them. As indicative as any negotiating table were the rows of confessionals, with their signs for the many different languages spoken, noticed at the end of the century by a visitor to the pilgrim church of Our Lady of Montserrat. And languages remained fissured by dialects: it is doubtful whether more than five per cent of Italians spoke the Tuscan which educated foreigners learned as 'Italian'. But the energies promoting the movement within Europe of people and products were proof against the curse of Babel.

GOODS AND MEN

Some forms of traffic represented centuries-old patterns. Polish and Hungarian cattle, in herds of up to twenty thousand, were driven into east Germany and those unsold en route as far west as Strasbourg. In many parts of Europe transhumance, the practice of driving herds from summer highland to winter lowland grazing grounds and back, continued and grew with the market for meat, wool and hides. The broad Castilian sheep-runs were over four hundred miles long; with two and a half million sheep on the move and needing to be clipped, they determined an itinerant way of life for thousands of pastoralists. The sheep-runs of the Kingdom of Naples led to the development of Foggia as an important market town in the sixteenth century. Few transhumance routes crossed borders, save between Scotland and England and Pyrenean France and Spain, but as within Greece and Switzerland, all of them bore witness to the wide tracts of open land that remained even within those parts of Europe that had been productively tamed.

The later fifteenth and early sixteenth centuries were the high point of cosmopolitan pilgrimages to shrines in Europe (above all to Santiago de Compostela and Aachen) as well as to the Holy Land and – for the most energetic – Sinai. From then on numbers were severely reduced, not only because Protestants wrote off pilgrimage as an unspiritual aspect of popish superstition but also because of an uneasy feeling that pilgrimages had become an excuse for a holiday rather than an act of piety. When the Swabian Felix Fabri in 1480 consulted Count Eberhard of Württemberg, who had been to Jerusalem, about his own proposed journey there he received advice which, though heartfelt, he disregarded: there is much in common between pilgrimage, war and marriage, he was warned; all 'may begin very well and end very badly'.[35] This Dominican friar took a truly touristic approach. Not only did he produce one of the fullest and most observant travel narratives of the period but zealously prepared himself for sightseeing. 'I give you my word', he wrote, 'I worked harder in running round from book to book, in copying, correcting, collating what I had written, than I did in journeying from place to place upon my pilgrimage.'[36] The silk merchant Jacques le Saige, equally avid for non-prayerful experience en route from Douai to Jerusalem in 1518, described what he saw in memorable detail. He mentioned, for example, his embarrassment at walking into the kitchen of a French inn to hurry up his meal and finding the innkeeper's wife nude in the tub where she was washing up the dishes.

The growth of piracy in the Mediterranean and the slackening of demand led Venice to discontinue in the 1580s its long-standing provisioning and shipping service to pilgrims. In Spain they were subjected to more and more administrative harassment as they became suspected of being smugglers, illegal pedlars or common thieves in holy disguise. Mass pilgrimages became restricted to local shrines, Mont St Michel for the French, the Holy House at Loreto for Italians. Visits to the Holy Sepulchre in Jerusalem were chiefly undertaken by individuals wealthy enough to make their own arrangements. Group travel with a common aim had not necessarily led to mutual understanding; visiting in 1494 the shrines of the Holy Land, the Italian Pietro Casola noted fastidiously that, 'I always let the ultramontanes rush in front.'[37]

The age of mass migrations was long over. The medieval Germanic search for land beyond the River Elbe into Brandenburg and Pomerania and on into Prussia and Kurland had lost its urgency. So had the steadier, less dramatic drain into the previously inviting empty spaces of Poland, Bohemia and Hungary. In the sixteenth century there was a drift into central Europe of Slavonic peoples pushed up from the south-east by the conquests of a Turkish administration with which a minority could not come to terms. Most blended unnoticeably into the agricultural work-force. Others took to the roads in the West and became confused with the petty crime and the fortune-telling beguilements of gypsies, or, armed with short-bows and scimitars on stolen horses, joined the mercenary bands of light cavalry known as stradiots ('on-the-roaders'). But there were, in the West, motivations to move on a large scale. The most numerous migrants were the surplus populations of the countryside who left to try to establish a long-term niche within the work-force of towns and who presented civic authorities with problems of poverty and crime on an unprecedented scale; by the late sixteenth century twenty per cent of the populations of Hamburg and Rouen and Lyon were unemployed and considered destitute. There were the seasonal treks such as those which brought the owners of poor hill farms in the Cévennes down to help with the harvests of Provence. Their need, noted a Provençal landlord towards 1600, brings 'into the plains and warm country an infinite number of people to harvest the grain'. This recourse for 'these poor folk', he smugly remarked, was something that 'God, the sovereign housekeeper, in his providence has provided'.[38]

God's housekeeping also drew the poor from the Balkans to Italy, from the Auvergne and Gascony to Spain (where they were reviled as *gabachos*, worthless pigs), from the least productive lands of Saxony and Sweden to the alluring suburbs of Lübeck, Danzig and Revel. In such cases the distinction between the migrant needy, the voluntary self-improver and the involuntary refugee became blurred. Of the Greeks who turned up in Italy most were in search of jobs as labourers or domestic servants. Others were scholars or skilled artisans seeking better opportunities. Others were priests, rendered stipendless by Ottoman occupation, who gravitated to the Orthodox communities in the south of the Kingdom of Naples in such numbers that a late sixteenth-century bishop recommended 'throwing all of them out of the Kingdom'.[39]

Those who embarked on such unepic migrations seldom attracted so much notice. Yet they far outnumbered those who left Europe altogether. During the sixteenth century some 240,000 emigrated to the Americas, mostly Spaniards and chiefly men hoping to return with their fortunes established. Some called in the meantime for their wives. 'Here', a tailor wrote home from Mexico in 1569, 'we can live according to our pleasure, and you will be very contented, and with you beside me I shall soon be rich.'[40] About 200,000, nearly all native and male, left to try their luck in Portugal's settlements overseas. Little is known of the majority: how many died en route, how many returned, how many settled down and established families, though the Portuguese appear to have established stable relationships with local women more readily than Spaniards. While the poorest emigrants went as the domestics of men of some importance, or bound themselves to serve a merchant or the holder of a title to settle new land in return for the expenses of their passage, many appear to have paid their own way. The fare to the Americas in the mid-sixteenth century was equivalent to one to two months' salary of a skilled craftsman; beyond the savings of a peasant or urban labourer. Cities and armies at home were the New Worlds of the really poor.

Among those who could afford the voyage there were, in all likelihood, some escaping penalties for crime. If English criminals found sanctuary in Muscovy, as Elizabeth complained to the tsar in 1590, it is reasonable to assume that Iberians tried their luck in more favoured lands where no questions were asked of those with a willingness to work and some coin to show. And it is equally likely that at least some emigrants to the Americas, though not necessarily poor, had found life irksome, if not positively dangerous because of suspicion of their Jewish ancestry or because their conversion from the Muslim faith was doubted.

The problem of dubious conversion was new, and local; it dated from the reconquest by Spain of the Moorish Kingdom of Granada in 1492. The persecution of Jews was, however, an old phenomenon, and one that continued to affect the whole of Europe. In that same year, 1492, some fifty thousand Jews were ordered to leave Castile and Aragon unless they converted sincerely and evidently to Christianity. An observer watched them go. 'They journeyed with great suffering and misfortune . . . There was hardly a Christian who did not feel sorry for them, and wherever they went the Jews were invited to be baptized. Some converted and stayed behind, but very few. Instead, the rabbis went among them, urging them on and making the women and boys sing and play drums and tambourines to raise their spirits. Thus they left Castile.'[41]

For many centuries, deprived of a homeland first by a Christianized Roman Empire and then by Muslim occupation of the Levant, Jews had been on the move throughout Europe, chiefly to avoid persecution, sometimes to seek new opportunities for business skills which were seconded by a flair for languages which made them valuable intermediaries between more settled, monoglot, trading communities. Racially they had become diluted through intermarriage; hence the jumpiness even of aristocratic families in countries where Catholic inquisitorial procedures had been established. But in the main a tenacious loyalty to traditional religious observance, extending to dietary and culinary traditions, preserved both their sense of identity and provoked the antipathy of the Christians amongst whom they lived. The network of pedlars, itinerant rabbis and agents of merchants, pointed to centres – Venice, Lisbon, Antwerp, Prague – where their presence would be not only profitable but welcome. In 1520 Jews in Poland-Lithuania amounted to twenty per cent of the population assessed by poll tax. In Cracow the Jewish community was so successful that in 1595 its leaders ordered that any new Jewish immigrant hoping to break into it 'shall be excommunicated from all the holiness of Israel, shall be set aside both from this world and the life hereafter, shall have no child circumcised, and shall not be buried in a Jewish graveyard'.[42]

Given the Christian shrinking from usury, especially in its most obvious form of high interest charges on small loans, Jewish moneylenders and pawnbrokers were as welcomed as they were despised by those in temporary need of cash. 'Jews', pronounced the early sixteenth-century Venetian diarist Marin Sanudo, 'are as necessary in a country as bakers.'[43] But the self-determining alienness that kept alive their endurance as a separate organism within the body of Europe led to their being rounded on as scapegoats when wars went wrong or when food shortages pushed prices sky-high; these were times when preachers called for vengeance upon the crucifiers. Individuals might be respected for their special skills, not just as businessmen and – especially in Poland – estate managers, but as doctors, astrologers, scholarly guardians of the Hebraic background to the message of the Bible. But the need to accept the yellow patch on the chest or the yellow cap, and the curfew of the ghetto was a humiliating compromise. There were, indeed, restrictions on European Christians who wanted to make their way in Russia or Turkey or Persia. Foreign diplomats resident in Constantinople were virtually ghetto-ized within their compounds. What was exceptional was the neurotic volatility of western Christian communities.

Jews were expelled from Naples in 1501 and allowed back in 1509, from Genoa in 1516, only to return in the following year. They were driven from Florence in 1494, allowed back in 1513, banished again in 1527 and readmitted in 1531. Many of those expelled from Spain in 1492 moved to Portugal. From that uneasy environment an order of 1497 from King Manuel led to the forced baptism of some seventy thousand and the subsequent flight of some twenty thousand who followed their Spanish co-religionists either eastwards along the Islamic North African ports or the north Mediterranean Christian ones, always aware that their separateness from both worlds of faith was a passport that could be revoked at a turn of opinion. Yet others crossed the Atlantic to form the commercial element which facilitated the Portuguese establishment of a thriving colonial presence in Brazil.

While no subsequent expulsions were on the Iberian scale, Reformation fervours deepened anti-Semitic feeling and made refuges for the Jewish faith fewer and less secure. Their refusal to accept the message of the Gospel irritated Luther to the point of successfully agitating for the banishment of this 'disgusting vermin' from Saxony in 1537.[44] Calvin's own position was moderate, but many of his followers were not, taking the line that Catholic opposition offered sufficient challenge to the Protestant faith without the nagging presence of the Jewish one. Even Erasmus became concerned at the extent to which Christian scholars were paying attention to cabbala and the Talmud and immersing themselves in Hebrew studies. The vessel of renewed, evangelistic

Christianity had no room for argument about its construction; he even allowed himself to consider favourably the contention that 'it is Christian to hate the Jews' because so many good Christians did.[45] And on the Catholic side, similar enthusiasm for a revitalized and clarified religious feeling led to fresh expulsions from Tuscany and, in 1569, the forcible closing of synagogues throughout the States of the Church, except in Ancona, where the presence of the Jews was considered essential to the profits derived by the Papacy from its commerce.

This renewal of an old medieval pattern – banishment in the name of the faith, restricted permission to stay in the name of the pocket – intensified the uprootings to which Jewish communities were subject throughout the West and led to an increased migration eastwards into Lithuania and Muscovy where the special talents of the Jewish people were in shorter supply. Its intensity slackened only when from the 1570s there was a partial acceptance that the conflict between Christian faiths had reached a point of deadlock beyond which politics would have to play a greater part than evangelism. From that point the pocket's influence, aided by some disillusion with the necessity of credal animosity, could be felt more clearly. Working together, Mammon and Amity made more room for the Jews. In Prague the community increased from a few families in the 1560s to some three thousand individuals by 1600; in Frankfurt, from 420 in 1542 the Jews numbered nearly three thousand by 1613 in a city whose total population was twenty thousand. In one economic growth point after another, above all where growth had been impeded by religious faction, there was a re-opening of opportunity – seldom without a religious self-justification in terms of the enforcement of humiliating conditions affecting costume or place of residence – for Jews and those of suspect conversion to Christianity. As with Ancona, the relaxation of anti-Jewish legislation in Venice was a recognition that every source of financial skill was required to stem the dwindling economic status of Mediterranean ports, though in Venice it was also a declaration of the Republic's independence from the harrying of its religious life by Rome. Responding to similar conditions, Jews were readmitted to the Tuscan ports of Pisa and Livorno. By 1620 one can speak at last of a settled, if still selectively favoured, European Jewry.

Being on the wrong side in politics or of the law had always led to an intermittent dribble of malcontents and exiles across national borders. Charles VIII's invasion of Italy in 1494, for example, was partly prompted by the advice and information provided by displaced Italians, notable among them the Milanese Gian Giacomo Trivulzio. Having fallen out with the ruler of Milan, Ludovico Sforza, Trivulzio acted as adviser to Charles, then as commander-in-chief of his successor's army which defeated Venice in 1509; he ended by becoming naturalized as a Marshal of France. In 1598 another Italian, Francesco Tensini, was banished from Venetian territory at the age of seventeen for getting into a convent in Crema and seducing a nun. He left for the Low Countries, enlisted in the Spanish army, rose rapidly through the ranks, moved on to become Lieutenant General of Artillery to the Emperor Rudolf, and in 1617 was granted an amnesty by Venice to become the Republic's chief adviser on fortifications and a Knight of San Marco.

These examples could stand for many that were less conspicuous. Formal banishment or precautionary self-exile was, and always had been, an aspect of life's uncertainties. It was with the intensification of religious strife from the mid-sixteenth century that a Christian diaspora of the persecuted matched the scale of the Jewish one.

Some of their involuntary migrations were on a small scale. Exiled from Strasbourg for his politico-religious views in 1531, Sebastian Franck moved to Ulm where, forbidden to publish his views, he found employment as a soap-maker. Frustrated by this trade he started writing again – and was banished once more, finally moving to the more tolerant city of Basel. Others, already forced to move, had to move again, and further afield still. In St Olave's church near the Tower of London there is a figure in armour topped with a ruff within the classical arch of a wall tomb. 'Here', reads the inscription of 1582, 'lies Peter Capponi, a Florentine of ancient lineage, distinguished for his upright conversation, acceptable to the greatest princes. He endured with constancy the exile which he suffered, the victim of an unjust fate. Britain yet embraces in death him whom she took to her bosom in life. Peter Land, born at Lyons in France of Florentine parents, erected this monument of affection and grief.' Doubtless only a minority of Calvinist exiles from Lyon and other French cities were so taken to the bosom of their host country. But, like the Jews, the majority of Calvinists were town-dwellers and possessed useful skills. They moved to be able to worship in safety, but their reception was aided by their ability to transfer capital or offer a service. The numbers involved are uncertain. To contemporaries they seemed large. So many left Spanish-Catholic Antwerp for Amsterdam that a merchant immigrant there exclaimed in 1594, 'here is Antwerp itself changed into Amsterdam.'[46] The Calvinist

Joseph Scaliger, who had moved from Paris to Geneva and then to a chair at the University of Leiden, reflected angrily in 1607 on the property boom caused by well-off religious refugees, both Christian and Jewish. 'For these commodious quarters', he wrote, 'in which I have dwelt ten full years, have been sold. The present scarcity of houses in this city is so great, because of the vile medley of races immigrating hither, that tenants think they fare well if they are able to get a mere hut.' And in another letter of the same year: 'honestly, I tell you, never has so great a craze for buying possessed the minds of men. And now Leiden shall be, not a university, but a workshop or a synagogue.'[47] The press of immigrants into the Ark of Geneva was so great that housing came near to reflecting the seven-storey tenements of the Venetian Ghetto.

Meanwhile, as Europe's population grew, and a more sizable minority of the well-to-do emerged, the demand for more than the necessities of life extended and with it a stimulus to the traffic in goods and skills. In *c.* 1510 Leonardo da Vinci, on the brink of producing his visions of those hurtling whirlwinds and deluges of rain that shaped landscape and belittled the energies of man, drew a layer of storm clouds that precipitated not hail or rain but a jingling downfall of consumer objects and the tools for making them: clocks and spectacles, wine barrels, musical instruments, lamps, pots and pans, together with hammers, set-squares and pincers. Leonardo's values were not clear-cut. He deplored the savagery of war but devised weapons to make it more dreadful. He anguished over the intellectual difficulty of relating art to nature but accepted money to use his art to divert a court with emblems, pageant floats and backdrops for entertainments. He was appreciative of what decorated and gave comfort to his own way of life. But it is difficult to shrug away the significance of what he wrote below the drawing: 'O human misery – how many things you must serve for money.'

The population increase stimulated the trade in necessities: textiles, leather for shoes and belts; foodstuffs, chiefly grain but including salt (the average consumption per head in Saxony was fifteen kilograms a year, chiefly for salting fish); wood for fuel and housing; whale and seal oil for lamps; cheap beers and wines. Changes in the nature of warfare – larger armies, heavily furnished with handguns and artillery – stimulated the movement of metals, iron and copper and tin, and of

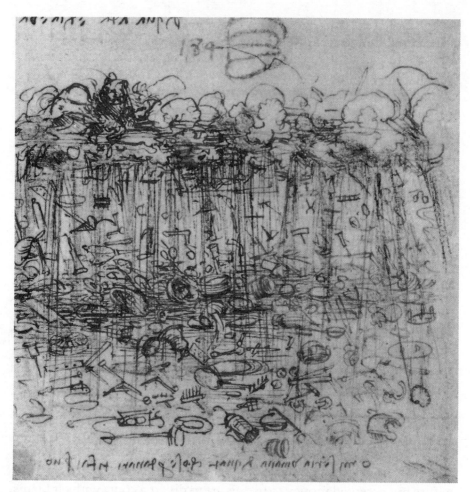

'A jingling downfall of consumer objects and tools for making them', Leonardo da Vinci, drawing, c.1510 (HM The Queen, Windsor, no. 12698)

the ingredients for gunpowder: sulphur, saltpetre, wood for carbon. The carrying trade for these bulk cargoes added their own demands: flax for rigging and sails, iron for nails and bolts and anchors, always more timber. Coastal and long distance shipping, river barges and rafts, mule trains, all responded to the needs of mouths, bodies and war. Preparing the vessels for Spain's Armada in 1588 involved English tin, Hungarian copper, German and Italian gunpowder and calls for Genoese carpenters and caulkers. Increased demand made it worth transporting over long distances products that were localized because of diverse micro-climates or the eccentric location near the surface of the soil of metalliferous ores: Baltic flax to Lisbon; Malaga wine to Bristol; Swedish copper to London; Roman alum and Sicilian sulphur to Stockholm. 'The red [smoked] herring', wrote Thomas Nashe in 1599 in his eulogy of Yarmouth, 'flyes best when his wings are dry: throughout Belgia, high Germanie, Fraunce, Spaine and Italy he flies, and up into Greece and Africa.' Italian princes imported falcons from Iceland.

It was not the plodding progress of bulk necessities along the roads, down the rivers and round the shores of Europe that Leonardo presumably had in mind, but the rain of non-necessities from the commercial skies. When Falstaff embraces Mistress Ford in *The Merry Wives of Windsor* with the cry, 'Let the sky rain potatoes!' it is not an unwontedly surreal image but a reference to the new luxury vegetable imported from America which for a while, because of its testicular shape, was considered an aphrodisiac.[48] Consumerism, responding to new money running in and out of the purses of those already or becoming well-to-do, was not about bread and fustian but about pleasing superfluities which established the status of their purchasers. The demand increased for silverware and ceramics and glass, for Persian and Turkish rugs to give a colourful glow to tables; for Flemish and French, and then Florentine and English tapestries to take the chill from walls, or for painted cloths as a cheaper substitute; for bibelots in the form of small bronze or wooden statuettes; for copper and steel kitchenware.

As more people could afford to dress well the demand for good and specialized clothing materials grew. 'Dear treasure', wrote Magdalena Paumgartner in 1591 from Nuremberg to her husband when he was on one of his business trips to Lucca, 'I ask you not to forget about my Italian coat, one like the one Wilhelm Imhoff brought his wife from Venice . . . Do not think ill of me because I always try to wheedle something out of you in every letter. I especially ask that you bring some red and saffron-coloured satin, if you can find an inexpensive measure or two.'[49] And as the taste for non-monastic herb and vegetable gardens developed, so did another aspect of far-reaching consumerism. Rabelais, on a political mission to Italy in 1536, sent back salad (lettuce) seeds from Naples to Poitou with instructions as to how to plant and cultivate them. Andrew Boorde in Spain sent home rhubarb 'seedes' imported from Africa to try their luck in an English garden.

More money meant more varied food. There was a rash of discriminating cookery books. Olive oil spread for the first time north of its climatic belt. Beer did not pass out of its own, but wine did; English

A Turkish rug gives the conference table a colourful glow: detail from *The Somerset House Conference*, 1604, artist unknown (National Portrait Gallery, London)

factors fingered the growths of Gascony and Burgundy before buying and could taste in Paris the heavy Provençal muscat shipped up from Aigues-Mortes. From London to Lübeck housewives could pick over recently arrived cargoes of Spanish, Portuguese and Italian figs, oranges, lemons and North African dates, and merchants buy the more lasting and redistributable ginger, aniseed, cumin, saffron, almonds, raisins. The Portuguese direct trade with India and the Far East, and the leakage from it that enabled Venice to collect the rich trickles that still reached the Mediterranean, put pepper and other cherished condiments on European markets with – at a price – ever more general availability. Artists painting shop and market scenes broke free from the social documentation of trades and the homely touches in religious narrative to produce full-blooded celebrations of the purchase and preparation of foodstuffs.

In 1438 the Spanish traveller Pedro Tafur had written of Bruges that anyone who has money and wishes to spend it will find in this town everything that the whole world produces. I saw there oranges and lemons from Castile, which seemed only just to have been gathered from the trees, fruits and wine from Greece, as abundant as in that country. I saw also confections and spices from Alexandria and all the Levant, just as if one were there; furs from the Black Sea, as if they had been produced in the district. Here was all Italy with its brocades, silks and armour and everything which is made there; and indeed there is no part of the world whose products are not found here at their best.[50]

A century and a half later, in 1597, Thomas Platter noticed that in Marseilles harbour 'vessels that had just berthed were discharging merchandise of all kinds in incredible quantities, rhubarb and other medicaments, monkeys, strange animals, oranges, lemons, and a thousand other products. It was a curious spectacle, to see so many people busily working everywhere and bringing news of so many distant countries.'[51] There was, then, nothing new in the traffic of exotica. It was the sheer volume of the traffic, the number of purchasers that changed.

Market Scene in Antwerp, anon., late sixteenth century (Royal Fine Arts Museum, Antwerp)

The spices and oriental luxury wares imported through Portugal's direct contact with the East led to Lisbon's becoming the third largest city in Europe and contributed to the import-export activity of Antwerp. Thanks to trade with the Americas, Seville's population grew from 49,000 in 1530 to over 100,000 by the end of the century. Discovery and settlement induced a boom in ship-building and a strong market in central and southern America for textiles, manufactured goods, oil and wine which stimulated European production in return for payment in American silver. Familiarity with western voyages led to growing colonization of the ocean as well as the land, as more vessels were built to exploit the north Atlantic fishing grounds. Though a very small element within the overall tonnage of overseas commerce, luxuries came eastwards: potatoes were joined by tomatoes, turkeys, chocolate and tobacco from America, tea and coffee from the East; sugar for the first time rivalled honey as a sweetener. There was a shift in the balance of trading activity overall from the Mediterranean to the Atlantic, North Sea and Baltic, but the only European port that grew from a small fishing harbour to a busy, cosmopolitan entrepot was Livorno in the Mediterranean. From Barcelona and Marseilles to Genoa and Venice a considerable degree of the vitality of the older patterns of commercial prosperity remained intact, as the late sixteenth- and early seventeenth-century churches and palaces in all of them amply demonstrate.

The market mechanisms which provided physically and financially for the movement of goods underwent little change. The majority of merchants continued to operate in a small way of business. Some were scarcely more than pedlars who bought local produce on credit and repaid the vendors when it reached a purchaser. Others, still operating from a static base, sent agents, in many cases their sons, to shop for local exports on a modest scale: in this way Francesco Carletti was sent to Seville in 1591 to learn about the commercial practices there and went on to trade his way round the world; the Cornishman Peter Mundy was sent by his father in 1608 to Bayonne to learn the French side of the pilchard trade and, after two years, to San Lúcar and Seville to learn Spanish and deal with the family's export of tin. At a higher level the great international families of banker merchants prospered, foundered, were replaced by others, from Medici to Fugger to Bonvisi, who kept an international oversight of commercial trends and steered credit to where it was most needed – and could most reliably be repaid. Concentrations of the credit facilities which encouraged enterprise shifted, from Florence to Genoa, from Augsburg to Antwerp, as some companies became overstretched and others flourished, but the mechanism remained. Apart from 'Moscow', the scope of the complaint of the protagonist in Marlowe's *The Jew of Malta* (*c.* 1590) would have rung true a century and a half before:

> In Florence, Venice, Antwerp, London, Seville,
> Frankfort, Lubeck, Moscow and where not,
> Have I debts owing; and in most of these
> Great sums of money lying in the banco.[52]

The great international trade fairs of late medieval commercial recovery continued to attract merchants to inspect samples of every commodity, from cloth and dye-stuffs to books and wheel-locks for pistols. The large regional fairs, Medina del Campo, Prato, Leipzig, Lublin in Poland and Geneva, all had extensive catchment areas. But the chief international gatherings came to be the fairs at Lyon and, especially, at Frankfurt-am-Main. Some indication of the range of luxuries available at Frankfurt for purchase or order is conveyed by a list of articles bought in 1495 by a merchant's agent from Lübeck: pearls, brooches, gold rings and chains, silver goblets and plates, velvet, weapons and coats of mail, spices and north Italian paper. As few merchants risked carrying large sums of cash with them to these fairs credit facilities were extended against bills of exchange, witnessed promises to pay at a future date. The novel proliferation of such familiar paper promises led to the creation of a new fair, first established at Besançon in 1536 and then, from 1579, at Piacenza, almost entirely devoted to the trading of credit notes among the representatives of the major trading and banking companies. It constituted a clearing house of debts and balances which reached, along more trails of paper, to the ledgers and strong-boxes of every major trading city in Europe.

The commercial routes were also travelled increasingly by individuals with expertise rather than goods to sell. No system of passports, no threats against those who eloped with technological secrets could staunch the flow. There was a progressive levelling-up in the European demand for industrial and other specialized craftsmen as private consumerism progressively called for 'the best'; also in the call for experts who brought talents that were locally in short supply. German miners and drainage technicians were called eastwards as Bohemia and Poland realized the value of their metalliferous seams. So many English shipwrights, cordwainers and sailmakers were attracted by the high wages paid by Ivan IV as Muscovy reached for the Baltic trade that an alarmed king of Poland, Sigismund II, protested to Elizabeth at her allowing 'artificers and skills [to] be brought unto him, by meane whereof he maketh himself strong to vanquish all others'.[53] It was a German specialist in explosives that had made it possible for Ivan to capture Kazan on his opposite, southward drive against the Tartars of the Crimea. In Lutheran Sweden, another technologically retarded country, it was agreed in 1611 that 'in the case of foreigners of another religion whose presence is desirable for economic or military reasons, permission will be given to remain in the country and follow their lawful callings.'[54] In the same way, Spain invited Protestant German gunfounders, though they were closely invigilated lest they spread their pernicious beliefs. Both England and France welcomed German gunsmiths and Italian armourers to help them stockpile the equipment that would be needed as the nature of warfare changed. Wars and religious barriers between nations hardly affected the international traffic of the arms trade and its artificers. Just as the walls of Constantinople had been breached in 1453 by Turkish cannon cast on the advice of Christian gun-founders, so, after the 1588 Armada, Sir Walter Raleigh warned the House of Commons that 'heretofore one ship of Her Majesty's was able to beat ten Spaniards, but now, by reason of our own [exported] ordnance we are hardly matched one to one.'[55]

In the skilled crafts, traditional centres retained the prestige traditionally attached to their specialized products – tapestries in Brussels, clocks and locks in Nuremberg, sword blades in Solingen, parade armours in Milan, cut velvets in Genoa, hunting crossbows in Malines, fine glass and mirrors in Venice, and so forth. All had regular contacts at the trade fairs, though travellers went out of their way to buy locally at workshop prices. Guild regulations were scrupulous about standards and vigilant to protect their monopolistic expertise. In central Europe, where the *Wanderjahr* was part of an apprentice guildsman's training, there was a regular outflow of young craftsmen. Speaking of Germany in the late sixteenth century, Fynes Moryson described how they 'use to travell through the great cittyes of Germany, Fraunce and Italy . . . These wanderers with great confidence enter the houses of the best workmen of theire trade, calling for work as if they were in theire masters houses, and living there upon their labour till they have gott money to travell further'.[56]

The *Wanderjahr* was intended to bring back enhanced skills to the home workshop. The transmission abroad of native skills was the work of master craftsmen restless at home and tempted abroad by the prospect of liberation from local guild restrictions or a higher wage. Charles VIII brought home from his 1494–5 campaign in Italy goldsmiths, an alabaster worker, a marquetry specialist, an organ maker, tailors for men's and women's clothes, a master embroiderer, a blender of perfumes, a gardener – and a black African parrot-keeper. They were joined in the next reign by medallists, stucco and faience workers, cabinet makers and advisers on the manufacture of glass wares and mirrors. The most valued imported craftsmen were given naturalization papers, adapted their names to local spelling conventions and left their businesses to their sons. From the conventions of luxury living in courts, the fashion for splendid and ingenious artefacts spread to the households of other wealthy men who either hired their own Italian stuccoist or French gardener or encouraged local craftsmen to imitate them. In England the first watches and complex clocks were made by German and French craftsmen. Then English copies of foreign mechanisms were put inside cases of foreign workmanship. But from the late sixteenth century wholly English time-pieces were being produced and a notable native development of the mechanism of their movement was under way. This process of importing skills, then copying and finally becoming independent of them was characteristic of other skills and other countries, but even by the end of the sixteenth century the specialist craftsman, especially if he had an artistic flair or a mastery of an esoteric skill like the inlaying of *pietre dure* or rock crystal cutting, could still be sure of finding employment abroad. Thomas Dallam made an organ of such ingenuity (it included a holly bush full of birds that sang and twitched their wings) that Elizabeth, who sent it as a gift to charm the Sultan into granting favours to the Levant Company, sent Dallam to explain its mechanism. He was so welcome for his skill that he was urged to settle in Constantinople. 'I answered them that I had a wife and children in England who did expect my return, though, indeed, I had neither wife nor children, yet to excuse myself I made them that answer.'[57]

Gradually, too, domestic talent replaced foreign expertise in other fields: printers, cartographers, financier-administrators (the career of the Genoese Orazio Pallavicino, naturalized as an Englishman in 1585, was an exception in this respect). A conspicuous example is that of military engineering. From the mid-fifteenth century Italian theorists and engineers worked out a solution – variants on the basic theme of the bastioned wall – to the percussive threat to defences posed by cannon. By the mid-sixteenth century Italians were designing fortifications in England, France, Spain, along the Danube, in the Spanish Caribbean and throughout the Portugese line of bases up the East African coast and down the West Indian coastline from Diu to Calicut. Thereafter the other countries of Europe learned enough to use their own subjects. Indeed, in the Italian peninsula itself, local expertise was challenged early in the seventeenth century by French and Dutch modifications of its own pioneering systems of defence.

There remained, however, an increasing flow of those who joined the traffic on the roads for travelling's own sake, for diversion and interest. The Nuremberger Gabriel Tetzel wrote a careful account of one of the earliest European journeys undertaken in a touristic spirit, between 1465 and 1467. A member of the entourage of Baron Leo of Rozmital (near Pilsen), he records how when he went to meet him Leo 'told me about his journey. He intended to visit all Christian Kingdoms, also all principalities in Germany and foreign countries, ecclesiastical and lay'.[58] Tetzel also reported the Baron's wish 'to visit the Holy Sepulchre and the tomb of the beloved St James'. In the course of a journey from Prague which circled through Germany, the Netherlands, England, France, Spain and Portugal, Italy, Austria and back to Bohemia, the tomb of the saint in Compostela was duly visited, but among so many objects of secular interest no room was left in the Baron's timetable for Jerusalem. 'Amongst the honest pleasures that men can experience', wrote Francesco Vettori in 1507 after a journey in Switzerland and Germany 'the pleasure of travelling is in my opinion the greatest. He who has not come into contact with many men and seen many places cannot be perfectly wise . . . [But] a man must be without business concerns, be free, be able to stay in a place for a fortnight at a time, to travel by land or water and not be at the mercy of any delays.'[59] Or, as Paracelsus later put it from a scientist's point of view, 'he who wishes to explore nature must tread her books with his feet. Writing is learned from letters, nature by travelling from land to land: one land, one page.'[60] And then came Thomas Nashe's airy assumption that 'he is nobody that hath not travelled.'[61] On the other hand, there were those who castigated tourism as a training school for patriotic irresponsibility and vice and instead advocated a *Wanderjahr* in the head. In 1518 Ariosto declared that he was content with a Ptolemy atlas: 'whoever wants to wander about the world may well go. Let him see England, Hungary, France and Spain. As for me, all I want is to dwell where I was born.'[62]

Doubtless, this was said with tongue in cheek. But the sentiment recurs in all seriousness in Thomas Elyot's *The Governour* of 1531; what with maps, chorographies and the records of travels undertaken by others, 'I cannot tell what more pleasure shulde happen to a gentil witte than to beholde in his owne house every thinge that within all the worlde is contained.'[63] It was to cater for this point of view that in 1600 Samuel Lewkenor published *A Discourse . . . for such as are desirous to know the Situation and Customes of forraine Cities without travelling to see them.* This difference of opinion, of course, had no impact whatsoever on would-be tourists. They were aware that with money, energy, patience and ingenuity they could go wherever reading and hearsay had suggested would be interesting or instructive. The tourist infrastructure, at least in cities, was firmly established: inns, guides to the main sites, sacristans waiting for tips to open the wings of triptychs and the doors leading to the ascent of cathedral towers and spires. In Rome in 1580 the secretary Montaigne took with him noted that, annoyed by his guide, 'he [Montaigne] set himself to become master of the trade with the help of various books and plans which he studied in the evenings, while during the day he served his apprenticeship on the spot, so that within a short time he himself could have guided the guide.' On excursions from Naples to the sulphurous ventholes of the Phlegean Fields, dogs were provided to give visitors a *frisson* as they sniffed and then fell over asphyxiated. There were guidebooks to individual countries and cities and more general works full of useful tips, such as that the travellers should keep 'an open countenance, a restrained tongue and a secret mind'.[64]

Just as pilgrimage provided a cover for adventurous variety, most tourists had a declared goal – or alibi: to learn about foreign manners; to visit princes or outstanding scholars; to acquire a foreign language; to polish such socially approved skills as horsemanship or fencing or dancing; to try the curative waters at spas; to scrutinize the remains of classical antiquity. Typical of the focusing effect of a humanistic education at the mid-sixteenth century was an entry about Rome in the journal of the nineteen-year-old Thomas Hoby, later to be the translator of Castiglione's *The Courtier*: 'After Mr Barker, Mr Parker, Whitehorn and I had thoroughlie searched out such antiquities as were here to bee seene from place to place . . . we thought it but losse of time to make anie longer abode here.'[65] Again, a little business transacted on the way could add a sense of purpose to a pleasure trip. In the course of the excursion from Nuremberg to the Netherlands in 1520–1 which Dürer recorded in watercolours and a journal, amidst entries concerned with churches and palaces, inns, meals (and their price), are notes of the engravings he sold en route and the charcoal portraits he drew, some-times by candlelight, to please or recompense the friends who enter-tained him and his wife. (To travel for pleasure with a wife was exceptional, and is explained by his immediate motive for setting off: the incidence of the plague in Nuremberg during the hot summer of 1520 and his not having a house in the country where he could leave her.)

Rozmital's grand tour became less unusual. In an impromptu and entirely secular mood, Lorenzo de' Medici's eldest son Cardinal Gio-vanni decided in 1499 to beguile the exile from Florence brought on him by the republican uprising against his family. This involved a tour intended to take him through Germany, the Netherlands, France and England (though in the event he could not face the heaving waves of the Channel). He set off from Venice with a party of friends each of whom took it in turns to settle the next day's destination. In 1517 another cardinal, Luigi D'Aragon, took a similar route in a similar spirit. According to Antonio de Beatis, in his vivid account of their voracious sightseeing, Luigi had resolved that 'not being satisfied with having several times seen the greater part of Italy, nearly all Baetica [Catalonia and Andalusia] and the furthest parts of Spain, he would also get to know Germany, France and all those other regions bordering the northern and western ocean'.[66]

Such travellers could reckon on an international aristocratic camerad-erie which entitled them, in spite of national and political differences, to a polite reception and, on occasion, aid from members of their own class. That they could also afford to have someone else write up their experiences helps to explain why many of the fullest narratives of travel record the movements and impressions of the rich. From the mid-sixteenth century, however, the literature of travel had become so gen-eral that independent travellers of humbler origin – such as Thomas Platter and Fynes Moryson – became alive to the interest of what they saw and learned, and took time at the often uncomfortable end of a tiring day in the saddle to write down something fuller than a record of miles covered and bills paid.

It is, too, in this later period that simple pleasure finds at last a full utterance. Here, for instance, is the Spaniard Eugenio de Salazar, an itinerant judge, describing what it is like to travel on a good horse with cash in your purse.

> You ride for a while on the flat, then climb the hill and go down into the valley on the other side; you ford a running river and cross a pasture full of cattle; you raise your eyes and watch the birds flying above you; you meet all kinds of people and ask the news of the places they have come from . . . There will be a pleasant encounter with some fresh village wench going to town scented with pennyroyal and marjoram, and you call out to her "would you like my company, my dear?" . . . A peasant will sell you a fine hare to make a fricassée, or you may buy a brace of partridge from a hunter. You see in the distance the town where you intend to sleep or stop for a meal, and already feel rested and refreshed by the sight.

But beneath the surface of this constantly enriched literature, the decline of organized pilgrimage meant that fewer men of modest means crossed national borders for diversion and self-education. More merchants, scholars and diplomats wrote up their impressions as they went along, but the extensive self-educative tour became more than ever a luxury for the privileged. It was for them that the guidelines of what to look for and learn from became more elaborate and imperative. Francis Bacon summed them up in 1597 in his essay *Of Travel*. A serious tourist, he laid down, needs a smattering of foreign languages, a tutor-guide, a map and a book describing each country. He should avoid his fellow countrymen but not become over-influenced by foreign manners.

> The things to be seen and observed are: the courts of princes . . . the walls and fortifications of cities and towns . . .; antiquities and ruins; libraries, colleges, disputations and lectures, where any are; shipping and navies; houses, gardens of state and pleasure near great cities; armouries, arsenals, magazines; exchanges, burses, warehouses; exercises of horse-manship, fencing, training of soldiers, and the like; comedies [i.e. plays], such whereunto the better sort of persons do resort; treasuries of jewels and robes, cabinets and rarities: and to conclude, whatsoever is mem-orable.[67]

This is challenging. It was written by a man with a universalist mind who had never got further from London – and then as a very young man – than France. But from his copious library it draws on a widening body of opinion. And though it cuts out the sense of fun and adventure, of sexual escapade, and of interest in landscape and local and popular oddities of appearance or behaviour that recur in travel narratives, Bacon's essay represents not unfairly the novel consensus that independent travel should seriously broaden the mind to an understanding of what was common to and distinctive amongst other nations of Europe. In its range and definition it requests a new strand in the civilized awareness of the nature of the continent.

Europe remained a composite of mini-economies which could survive the temporary cutting of links with the main traffic of commercial interchange. The movements of armies, though devastating locally, were threads and pockets compared with the spaces left open to travellers to whom roads in any case were often no more serviceable than tracks. War, or an outbreak of plague, complicated movement but did not check it on any large or lasting scale. How far did this rich, and more or less continuous, traffic affect the individual's attitude towards living within a multi-national Europe?

There was an undoubted increase in knowledge among those who traded and travelled and took their skills to other countries. But a firmer grasp on the nature of the continent did not create Europeans. Of course, underneath what was written, more was said, repeated, colloquialized into gossip and so, as far as evidence is concerned, evaporated. But the written word does not suggest any change of heart among the great majority; national stereotypes were still passed from pen to pen, wider interests were at odds with patriotisms and nationalisms, and both were strengthened by political and religious divisions. Cultural blinkers could be as occluding as ever, and the number of those who crossed borders was still very small compared with the vast majority who seldom, if ever, moved more than a long day's journey from home. There is, though, no doubt that the forms of traffic in all their increasing variety contributed to a vitalizing of curiosity, and an opening of the aperture through which individuals viewed what was being thought and made elsewhere. Without them, Europe would not have been irradiated with the cultural changes which have given rise to the term Renaissance.

PART TWO

Renaissance

Some think it the historian's business . . . to grasp in a single intuition the 'spirit' or 'meaning' of his period. With some hesitation, and with much respect for the great men who have thought otherwise, I submit that this is exactly what we must refrain from doing. I cannot convince myself that such 'spirits' or 'meaning' have much more reality than the pictures we see in the fire . . . The 'canals' on Mars vanished when we got stronger lenses.

C. S. LEWIS, *English Literature in the Sixteenth Century, excluding Drama* (1954)

CHAPTER V

Transformations

UNFROZEN VOICES

In the course of the voyage imagined by Rabelais in the 1552 version
of the fourth book of *Gargantua and Pantagruel*, 'Pantagruel suddenly
jumped to his feet, and took a look about him. "Can you hear something, comrades?" he asked, "I seem to hear people talking in the air.
But I can't see anything. Listen". . . . So as to miss nothing, some of
us cupped the palms of our hands to the backs of our ears . . .; the
more keenly we listened, the more clearly we made out voices, till in
the end we could hear whole words.' Greatly alarmed, Pantagruel's
party was told by the ship's captain that what they were beginning to
hear were the sounds of a great battle which had been frozen by winter
and were now beginning to thaw. Some, indeed, fell on deck; where
they 'looked like crystallized sweets of different colours . . . when we
warmed them a little between our hands, they melted like snow, and
we actually heard them'.[1]

This is no bad analogy for the recovery of the sounds of classical
antiquity after the long medieval winter that closed in with the loss of
Rome to the barbarians. It was the warming of texts by devoted editing
from the fourteenth century onwards that allowed their authors' voices
to speak clearly again, and the consequential extension of interest in
the world they had lived in that made their battles real again. Though
the preliminary work had been done in Italy, by the time Rabelais
wrote educated men and women throughout Europe had come into
repossession of an Old world – an instructive, recognizably relevant
alter ego – that was to most of them of far greater interest than the
New. Far in the past, but nearer to their own concerns than the medieval centuries, was a society like their own, lacking only stirrups, the
compass, printing, gunpowder, the papacy and the Americas: a society
which, thanks to time's tendency to winnow its trivial sources and

monuments more thoroughly, appeared to have been peopled by an intellectual and creative master-race. Whatever there was to do, in philosophical speculation, political action or cultural achievement, appeared to have been done, and done with a supreme vigour and accomplishment, among a people whose history not only had the clarity of distance in time but the wholeness of a completed cycle, from obscurity through world empire to barbarian chaos.

Text by text, as the imaginative reconstruction of the ancient world proceeded, the relevance of this *alter ego* became clearer. Their words no longer obscure, their personalities restored, replaced in the context of their own society, the appeal of the authors the middle ages had read but not really heard – Plato, Aristotle, Virgil, Cicero and Ovid – became stronger than ever, and they were joined by a host of others. The impact of so many minds on men who read them not merely with admiration for their knowledge or their particular expertise, but as models from whom to learn about statecraft, the waging of war, the creation of works of art and the more important art of bearing up under adversity: this impact made the study of the ancient world into a cultural force. It was not simply the perusal of neglected manuscripts but purposeful communication with a race of illustrious forebears.

There is nothing fanciful about the notion of communication. 'I am never less solitary than when alone,' wrote Alberti in the 1430s, referring to the authors of his favourite classical texts, serious and eloquent or humorously diverting.[2] In 1513 Machiavelli explained in a letter to a friend how, dismissed from his chancery post and 'mouldering' in his family's isolated farm, he found the solace which enabled him to write *The Prince*. 'When evening comes, I return home [from the local tavern] and go into my study. On the threshold I strip off my muddy, sweaty, workaday clothes, and put on the robes of court and palace, and in this graver dress I enter the courts of the ancients and am welcomed by them, and there I taste the food that alone is mine, and for which I was born. And there I make bold to speak to them and ask the motives of their actions, and they, in their humanity, reply to me. And for the space of four hours I forget the world, remember no vexation, fear poverty no more, tremble no more at death; I pass indeed into their world.'[3] And this sense of rapport came to spread well beyond Italy. The Greek Plutarch died around AD 120. Reaching down his volumes of Plutarch's *Works* fifteen and a half centuries after his death, Montaigne felt instantly, appetitively, at ease with him. He is 'so universal and so full', he wrote 'that upon all occasions, and whatsoever extravagant subject you have undertaken, he intrudeth himself into your work, and gently reacheth you a helpe-affording hand, fraught with rare embellishments, and inexhaustible of precious riches . . . He can no sooner come in my sight, or if I cast but a glance upon him, but I pull some legge or wing from him'.[4] In 1600 Philemon Holland, a country doctor who spent more time with his books than his patients, dedicated his translation of Livy to Queen Elizabeth. 'Reach forth your gracious hand', he begged, as though introducing a foreign friend, 'to T. Livius, who having arrived long since and conversed as a mere stranger in this your famous island . . . humbly craveth your Majesties favour to be ranged with other free denizens . . . to live under your princely protection.'[5]

Some listened to the voices of antiquity in a mood of nostalgia for a time when it had been possible for Europe to be at peace and men to be unshackled by a preoccupation with sinfulness: amidst the briar-covered ruins of ancient Rome, Poggio Bracciolini wrote in about 1430, 'surely this city is to be mourned over which once produced so many illustrious men and emperors, so many leaders in war: which was the . . . parent of so many and such great virtues, the mother of so many good arts, the city from which flowed military discipline, purity of morals and life, the decrees of the law, the models of all the virtues, and the knowledge of right living.'[6] But the prevailing mood in which the ancient past was studied was not wistfully romantic. Its deeds and achievement acted, rather, as a challenge and an encouragement. This was not just an us-and-them source of wry comparisons with Turks and Amerindians but a confrontation with heroic ancestors. Twenty years after Bracciolini, Cyriaco of Ancona said that it was the responsibility of the present 'to restore the dead . . . to revive the glorious things that were alive to those living in antiquity but had become buried and defunct . . . to bring them from the dark tomb to light, to live once more . . .'[7] And the survival of their tongue, Latin (in parts of southern Italy, Greek too) brought them close to those who read their works or about their times.

By the early sixteenth century the influence of classical scholarship, and its popularization through translations and paraphrases, had acquired a critical mass which produced unstoppable chain reactions. There was hardly a branch of inquiry, from jurisprudence to mathematics, military science and the arts, that was unaltered by the stimulus of a relevant text, artefact or record of historical experience. Introducing the next work he wrote after *The Prince*, his *Discourses on Livy*,

Machiavelli in 1519 referred to 'the general respect for antiquity'. He referred to what lawyers had learned from the *Corpus of Civil Law* of the sixth-century Emperor Justinian and physicians from Galen and Hippocrates. He referred to how often 'a great price is paid for some fragments of an antique statue . . . to give to artists who strive to imitate them in their own works'. Now he has resolved 'to open a new route, which has not yet been followed by anyone' – a model, derived from Roman example, of the methods to be adopted by constitutional-ists, statesmen and generals.[8] At nearly every point, antiquity offered a comparison to be made with the long inheritance of chivalrous, feudal and Christian values; indeed, both Reformers and Counter-Reformers dipped their pens into the vast pool of classical ink. Rome had achieved greatness first as a republic then as an empire. So both would-be abso-lutist rulers and fervent republicans could cite ancient arguments and exemplars to support their case. Sir Francis Walsingham pointed out to a friend how flexibly the new knowledge could be used. Study that in the experience of antiquity, he urged, which can be usefully applied 'to these our times and states, and see how they may be made serviceable to our age or why to be rejected'.[9] Writers and artists, philosophers and men of science, pundits on agriculture, manners and domestic life, all turned to antiquity in the same spirit: what could use-fully be learned? And as they so turned, a new release of adrenalin flowed into the intellectual and creative life of Europe, all the more strongly for the ebullience of contemporary talent that could take advice from the past in its stride.

It was through the reinvigoration of already existing talent and sense of purpose that the revival of interest in the ancient past made its most creative mark. Challenged to cover the huge space, one hundred and thirty-eight feet across, left open at the crossing of the cathedral of Florence, Filippo Brunelleschi studied the construction of domes like that of the Roman Pantheon. Nonetheless, by its completion in 1436 his adaptation of ancient methods led to his cupola having a radically different appearance from anything created in antiquity. It is striking that when Hernán Cortés set off with his small band of Spanish adventurers to the conquest of Mexico in 1519 he exhorted them not to model themselves on the heroes of the romances of chivalry, the staple reading of his noble class, but to imitate the deeds of the Romans. Whereupon, his chronicler Bernal Diaz (who was there, though he wrote after the event) recorded, 'to a man we all responded that we would follow his orders, that the die was cast for good fortune, as

The Pantheon, Rome

Caesar said at the Rubicon.'[10] Both the race of ideas and the linguistic storms they threw up that characterized Rabelais's writing from the 1530s, owed their apparently anarchic idiosyncracy as much to his classical erudition as to his love of spoken and written French.

This was a revival which depended, however, on the grinding persistence of narrower enthusiasms. The driving force behind the study of antiquity was scholarly, an intellectual excitement in the recovery, collation, criticism and publication of texts. From the fourteenth century the process of thawing and explaining the voices had been a heavy commitment for dedicated men. Early in the sixteenth century Guillaume Budé complained of the 'sacrifice' involved in taking time off from his work to get married. Behind the beneficiaries of the revival were those who fed them with the dispatches from the past they found inspiring: men who, as Postel said, describing his own labours, had to breathe into their inkpots to keep writing during hard winters. And while the texts were being published and translated (over half a million copies of Virgil in both forms by 1600) and paraphrased for popular consumption, references like the Rubicon of Cortes's companions were plucked out and bandied about in converse, so that a familiarity with the present's *alter ego* was promoted by changes in European educational curricula.

It was from the fifteenth century Italian 'umanista', the man who used the texts to teach the 'literae humaniores', the branches of study most concerned with the secular human condition (grammar and elo- quence, history, poetry and moral philosophy), that the word 'human- ism' was invented in the nineteenth century to describe the conditioning of ideas that drew on a knowledge of classical antiquity. In *c.* 1402 Pietro Paolo Vergerio wrote his manifesto of liberal education *On the Conduct of Honourable Men*. While the body was to be kept fit by exercise, lessons were to shape the pupil's character and prepare him for a life of useful service. Grammar was to enable him to master the exemplary texts that would make his speech and writing easy and adaptable to different themes and audiences. History would provide him with examples of behaviour to shun or follow, poetry with a desire to imitate the virtues of the heroes of epic literature. Moral philosophy was to stress the high standards of personal behaviour that were expected of the responsible citizen.

Vergerio wrote his treatise while acting as tutor to Ubertino da Carrara, son of the ruler of Padua, and the few schools that followed his prescription most closely were all city-based and connected with centres of authority. Vergerio's pupil Vittorino da Feltre opened one in Mantua at the invitation of its ruler Gianfrancesco Gonzaga. Guarino da Verona taught at Ferrara after being brought there as tutor to the son of the Marquis Niccolò d'Este. The first humanist school in Spain was run by Marineo Siculo who, illiterate until the age of twenty-five in a small Sicilian town, had all the zeal of the self-taught. The school was for the benefit of Queen Isabella's court, and in 1492 Marineo wrote to a friend that 'I have my home crowded all day long with these ebullient young nobles. From the empty pastimes to which . . . they have been accustomed from their childhood, they are already turning little by little to the love of letters.' He pushed his students as quickly as possible through the rote-learning of grammatical rules to the texts themselves, to the personalities of their authors; in this way, he claimed, 'they will certainly advance more, and become not gram- marians but Latinists.'[11] Erasmus was of the same mind: education was to ease the contact with the past which would enrich life in the present. It was in direct collaboration with Erasmus that John Colet, Dean of

St Paul's, founded St Paul's School in 1509 – another school at the centre of political power.

Such programmatically humanist schools were few and – despite educationalists' protests that this was far from their aims – class-ridden. Medieval schools had been perfectly competent to prepare boys for mercantile occupations and for the universities which turned them into priests, lawyers and doctors. But as bureaucracies expanded, diplomatic business increased and courts played an ever-growing role in national life, the relationship between educational supply and demand changed. Though the diplomat and friend of Erasmus Richard Pace claimed in 1517 to have met a gentleman who exclaimed 'by God's body, I had rather have my son hanged than that he should be studious . . . the study of literature should be left to the sons of peasants,' his spokesman was becoming out of date.[12] The publications of educational theorists and the influence of tutors in private households (the classical scholar John Cheke was tutor to King Edward VI and gave lessons to the future Elizabeth I) did as much to promote a liberal education as the few model schools. The printing press made the labours of classical scholars more and more conspicuous in booksellers' shops. Phrase books and compilations of quotations, like Erasmus's *The Abundance of Words and Ideas* of 1512 and his enormously popular *Adages*, reissued in one edition after another, assumed that the educated person would want to pepper his writings with classical tags and allusions. The fashion grew for a rounded competence which, if amateurish, was agreeably different from the rigid professionalism and uncertain social background of the medieval university specialist.

The European fame of Baldassare Castiglione's *The Courtier* that swiftly followed its publication in Venice in 1528 was due to the courtly setting. In its pages men of high birth and political responsibility discussed in the ducal palace of Urbino, sometimes seriously, sometimes jokingly, the qualities required in the active man of affairs who bore classical learning lightly and was at ease in the company of women, poets and musicians. It was the quintessential portrait of an exclusive society which actually subscribed to the values of Vergerio's educational philosophy; for Castiglione purported to be writing down what was actually said. And these were, after all, the values cherished in antiquity itself. The educated man, as Cicero, the most widely read of ancient authors, had written, should 'have a theoretical acquaintance with the topics of philosophy . . . it is also desirable that he should not be ignorant of natural philosophy . . . nor, while he is acquainted with the divine order of nature would I have him ignorant of human affairs. He should understand the civil law . . . he should also be acquainted with the history of past ages . . ., to be ignorant of what occurred before you were born is to remain always a child.' Or again, 'antiquity', Quintilian had written in the first century A D, 'has given us all these teachers and all these patterns for our imitation, that there might be no greater happiness conceivable than to be born in this age above all others, since all previous ages have toiled that we might reap the fruit of their wisdom.'[13] Feeding on such sources, humanism became ever more convincing as a teacher for *this* age.

Much of its influence spread informally, after school and outside universities. It infected both but had a broader, independent life of books, tutors, informal study groups, gossip: the routes along which any intellectual fashion travels towards orthodoxy. On the whole, universities were chary of changing syllabuses and teaching methods that had served Europe well for centuries. What did come to influence them was the humanist emphasis on the bearing of education on conduct, on the importance of seeing authors in the round rather than as providing snippets for discussion, and, above all, on the need to return not only to the sources of secular literature but to those of Christianity.

In 1496 Colet's lectures at Oxford on St Paul's *Epistles* to the Corinthians broke radically with the traditional methods of the divinity teacher. Instead of approaching his subject through medieval Latin commentaries, thus reminding his auditors that the church represented an accumulation of interpretations as well as of dogma, he used the Greek text directly. He explained how the form and language of the epistles were conditioned by St Paul's view of the men to whom it was directed. He placed Paul himself within the context of Roman civilization and the early years of Christianity. And by locating him clearly in place and time Colet enabled Paul to speak almost as directly to the students of Oxford as he had spoken to the Corinthians – to bear witness from the beginnings of the church and to encourage personal reflection instead of being used as the excuse for a display of erudition. Perhaps even more impressive as exemplifying the humanistic desire to return to the sources was the desire to see the Bible in what was essentially the language of God and Christ, Hebrew. Its pioneer student was the independent German scholar Johann Reuchlin, who formulated its rules so that others could study it. This led to the accusation that he was supporting the Jewish in opposition to the Christian faith. His humanist friends published in 1514 by way of open testimonial a collection of letters written in support of his views, *The Letters of Famous Men*. Two of his defenders, von Hutten and Crotus Rubeanus, were not content with this and in the following year published a pendant, *The Letters of Obscure Men*. This purported to be a selection of letters written to one of Reuchlin's chief adversaries, Ortvinus Gratius, a theologian at the University of Cologne, by *his* admirers. With considerable skill and great relish these 'admirers' made it clear that Ortvinus was an immoral and pettifogging ignoramus. They celebrated his sordid amours, praised his ability to determine such weighty matters as whether the eating of an egg containing an unhatched chick on a Friday were a venial or a mortal sin, and, above all, they impugned his learning. 'When I was in your study at Cologne', wrote one of them in mock respect, 'I could see well enough that you had a multitude of volumes, great and small. And there you sat, with a whisk in your hand, to flap away the dust from the bindings.'[14]

On the whole, however, the attack on scholasticism, the matter and manner of medieval university teaching, was restricted to its emphasis on training the mind without affecting the heart. Too much time, humanists claimed, was devoted to ingenious riddles, such as 'whether we are bound by the law of love to deliver a neighbour from oppression, infamy or death, when we cannot do so without danger or hurt to ourselves, and if it is against his will'. But partly out of self-interest, because some wanted chairs for themselves, or at least to be unharried if they set up in university cities as private teachers, and partly out of genuine respect for the continued vitality of traditional learning, their attacks never became systematic. The Spaniard Juan Luis Vives, a passionate advocate of the humanistic framework for education, movingly described in 1519 the wrench he felt when turning from the tradition within which he had once felt at home. Only after long reflection could he accept changing 'the old for the new . . . often I turned my thoughts from better things [humanist studies] back to the old [scholastic] ways, to try to convince myself that I had not wasted so many years in Paris.'[15]

Though humanism presented the merits of a pagan civilization to a Christian one, it became naturalized with little strain. Yet Pico della Mirandola's assertion in 1487 that God had spoken as relevantly, if not as directly, through the mouths of pagan seers as through those of biblical prophets, led to his condemnation by Rome; when, after a period of tactful self-exile in France, he returned to Florence, it was on the understanding – rather as in the later case of Galileo – that he should stay at home and keep quiet. When the humanist Konrad Celtis dedicated in 1502 a mythology-ridden poem to the nun Caritas Pirck-heimer, famous herself as a Latin scholar, she rebuked him in sound terms. He must, she wrote back, 'give up celebrating the unseemly tales of Jupiter, Venus, Diana and other heathen beings . . . make the saints of God your friends by honouring *their* names and *their* memory.'[16] Some humanists, when taking holy orders, as many did, felt a pang of compunction. 'We ministers of God', wrote Bartolomeo Fonzio in 1510, 'certainly *can* publish whatever we composed when we were still laymen, but whether we *should* with a clear conscience I do not know.'[17] The church authorities in Spain were as repressive as they could manage to be, given the royal protection extended to Italian humanists. The Protestant authorities in Prague banned all perform-ances of 'pagan plays' from 1535. But this was most probably due to the liberties taken by the leading actor in a performance of Plautus's *Miles Gloriosus* in that year, for which he was clapped into prison.

On the whole, however, there was felt to be little potential conflict. Humanist moral teaching emphasized the obligations of honourable individual conduct and the pursuit of the collective good in terms that contradicted neither the Ten Commandments nor the Sermon on the Mount. There was in any case a strong tendency among theologians themselves to divide the aspect of truth that was ascertainable by reason and community experience from that of spirituality and revelation. 'Surely the first place is due to holy scripture', wrote Erasmus in his widely read dialogue *The Religious Banquet*, 'but sometimes I find some things said or written by the ancients, by pagans and poets, so chaste, so holy, so divine, that I am persuaded a good genius enlightened them. Certainly there are many in the communion of saints who are not in our catalogue of saints.'[18] Luther's gratitude for humanist studies as aiding a linguistic understanding of the Bible was such that he adopted a Providentialist view of this aspect of the rebirth of knowledge. 'Formerly', he wrote, referring to the previous century, 'no one knew why God caused the languages [Latin, Hebrew, Greek] to be revived, but now for the first time we see that it was done for the sake of the Gospel . . . To this end He gave over Greece to the Turk in order that the Greeks, driven out and scattered, might disseminate their language and provide an incentive to the study of other languages as well.'[19] Calvin was shaped by and endorsed humanistic studies and also – as long as the texts were carefully chosen and the teaching of them vigilant – the classics-based school curricula that were becoming standard in

Andrea Mantegna, *Trial of St James*, destroyed fresco, *c.* 1450–4 (Eremitani church, Padua)

Europe for the preparation of ministers as well as merchants, courtiers and lawyers. The Jesuits accepted the educational importance of good Latin learned from serious classical authors. The Council of Trent reaffirmed the sacrosanctity of the traditional, non-humanistic text of the Bible, the Vulgate, because so much Catholic doctrine flowed from it. But the Counter-Reformation accepted that humanism was an extra hand on the clock of scholarship and pulpit eloquence that could not be set back. When the great Vatican obelisk, originally erected in Alexandria by the quasi-divine Emperor Augustus, was laboriously winched upright in front of St Peter's in Rome in 1586, Pope Sixtus V thought putting a fragment of the true cross on top would suffice to exorcise its pagan significance.

While humanism implied an admiration for the ideas and deeds of the ancients, the antiquarianism that accompanied it was a more dispassionate form of curiosity. Mantegna, an inventively creative artist with an academic turn of mind – his patron Isabella d'Este referred to him as her 'expert in antiquities' – placed religious subjects in studiously meticulous classical settings. But this was in the spirit of historical accuracy, not of confrontation; he had many humanist friends to advise him but his was not a humanist art. Nonetheless, the collecting of Roman and Greek coins and classical gems and vases and statues that spread from Italy from the fifteenth century, though pursued largely with a historically biased acquisitiveness, buttressed an admiration for the qualities that had produced them. Brought into courtyards and displayed in gardens, the past mingled with the present in a manner far more provocative than was the presence in churches of images of men and women who had been martyred almost equally long ago.

Coming towards the educated public from so many directions, it is not surprising that antiquity became fashionable. Over baptismal fonts clergymen resignedly intoned such 'Christian' names as Julius Caesar, Camillus, Aeneas, Hector, Achilles, Flavia, Livia. As with all fashions, some fun was poked. In the early 1540s Niccolò Boldrini produced a woodcut showing the revered and influential classical group of Laocoön and his sons as writhing monkeys; Niccolò dell' Abbate's portrait of the warrior Francis I showed him wearing a frock because the goddess Minerva was the emblem of intelligently used force. Andrea Palladio's devotion to classical architectural features was guyed in some anonymous verses:

Niccolò Boldrini, *Caricature of the Laocoön*, early 1540s

> Palladio does not visit prostitutes;
> Or, if he likes to visit them sometimes,
> He goes to exhort them to undertake
> An antique atrium for their brothel.[20]

But something of the potency a mere name from antiquity could convey is reflected in Hamlet's rueful observation of the Player's immersion in the tale of Priam's death,

> What's Hecuba to him or he to Hecuba
> That he should weep for her?[21]

In the fifteenth century scholars had described the ruins of classical antiquity and sought to explain their original form and function. Artists – Pisanello in the 1430s, for instance – drew them. Architects measured and sought to learn from them. In the sixteenth century, however, apart from the collector's respect for antique vases, bronze and silver objects, sarcophagi carved in deep relief, free-standing busts and other statues and well-preserved inscriptions, the imaginative familiarity with the culture of antiquity was such that its more conspicuous remains were treated as though the Vandals had come again. Useful as material for modern buildings, it was enough to have them in the mind's eye.

Even as early as *c.*1450, without protest from his architect Leon Battista Alberti, the student of Vitruvius, and one of those who had measured Roman buildings, Sigismondo Malatesta of Rimini had commandeered ancient marbles by the cartload for classicizing works in the church of San Francesco. In a report drawn up in 1519 for Pope Leo X, the authors warned that 'all this new Rome which we see today, great as it is, so embellished with palaces, churches and other buildings, is built with mortar made from ancient marbles.' Stop this pillage, they urged, preserve what evidence is left of those 'divine spirits' who founded 'the glory and the [very] name of Italy'.[22] The plea was vain. Bramante's new St Peter's was fed from the Forum; the buildings of ancient Rome remained for generations a quarry for their classicizing successors. Pope Paul III forbade others to pillage in 1540, but only to obtain a monopoly for the work on St Peter's. The philosophy was that what was new was best. It was in vain that the few men of the temper of polymathic scholar Claudio Tolomei pleaded for conservation: 'A ruined arch, a dismembered temple, a fallen theatre, a gateway thrown to the ground', he wrote, 'are of far greater worth than any of the undamaged modern houses, tall palaces, broad streets, new places of worship and elegant gardens.'[23] In 1596, by when France had become a major contributor to humanistic studies, a visitor severely commented on the state of the Roman amphitheatre at Nîmes: 'several houses have been built in this space in recent years, a very regrettable thing, for the preservation of this monument, of its kind the most complete in existence, and respected by both Goths and Saracens, ought to be considered a matter of importance.'[24] Only in Verona, subject from 1405 to Venice but anxious to maintain any signs of its earlier, Roman, independence, were Roman arches and the Arena respected and new buildings constructed which referred stylistically to its classical remains without looting them.

Humanism, as it branched into topic after topic from the stem continuously nourished by textual scholarship, certainly added glamour to the world that rehabilitated Antiquity. In 1492, while Mantegna was working on his carefully researched and resplendent *Triumph* canvases, his patron the Marquis Francesco Gonzaga proudly wrote of 'the

Andrea Mantegna, *The Triumph of Julius Caesar* (canvas VI: Bearers of coins, plate and armour trophies) *c.* 1500 (HM The Queen, Hampton Court)

Triumph of Julius Caesar [which] he is painting for us in images that are almost alive and breathing, so that the subject seems not to be represented, but actually to exist'.[25]

Without Sir Thomas North's translation of the *Lives* by Montaigne's favourite author, Plutarch, in 1579, Shakespeare could not have sent Antony into the Venus fly-trap of Cleopatra's embrace. But humanism's influence was above all practical. It drew the attention of artists and writers to classical models. At the same time its fashionable endorsement by patrons reaffirmed the status of their activity and thus promoted a desire to adapt the models rather than simply copy them.

Historians adjusted both their manner and their material to the models offered by Livy, Tacitus and Polybius, pushing God to one side of the chain of causes and effects and subordinating miscellaneous detail to political and military narrative. Lyric poets seemlessly absorbed fragments from Ovid and Catullus and Tibullus, changing the tenor without losing the impetus of their own voices. Others responded to the structure of the classical epic while retaining – as did Ariosto and Tasso and the Portuguese Luis de Camoens in *The Lusiads*, his epic of overseas expansion of 1572 – much of the entertainment value of the chivalrous romance. Plays influenced by classical examples, notably the comedies of Plautus and Terence and the tragedies of Seneca, joined the stream of performances that carried forward the medieval love of theatre. They were staged from the later fifteenth century, as were new Latin ones based on them. The success of these entertainments, first in Italy and then elsewhere, led to the writing of plays in the vernacular which, while following the formal five act structure and the unity of time and place that characterized ancient Roman comedy, spoke more directly to contemporary audiences. Machiavelli's *Mandragola* of 1518 is set in a precise year, 1504, and place, Florence, and nothing in its plot or characterization rang false to either. Even when classical plots were recycled, as in Bernardo Dovizi's *La Calandria* of 1513, which conflated the intrigues of Plautus's *Casina* and *Menaechmi*, the sense that comedy – as its practitioners emphasized – was holding up a mirror to the manners of the present was unobscured by smoke from the lamp of scholarship. And as the classically rule-based play travelled abroad and was shaped by different hands to fit the talents of different companies and the traditional expectations of audiences, it underwent the adaptations deplored by the priest in Cervantes's *Don Quixote*. 'Our dramatists', he grumbled, 'pay no regard to the place or time in which their action is supposed to occur. I have seen a play whose first act opened in Europe, its second in Asia, and its third ended in Africa. And if there had been four acts, the fourth no doubt would have finished in America, and so it would have been played in all four quarters of the globe.'[26] Shakespeare, however, who knew the conventions of classical drama perfectly well, was expressing himself as an actor who knew audiences when he had Hamlet introduce the travelling players as 'the best actors in the world, either for tragedy, comedy, history, pastoral, pastoral-comical, historical-pastoral, tragical-historical, tragical-comical-historical-pastoral, scene individable, or poem unlimited'.[27] And Lope de Vega, Shakespeare's contemporary and Spain's first dramatic genius, wrote of his own work in terms that might have been levelled at Cervantes's priest. 'When I write a play', he explained, 'I lock away the [classical] precepts with six keys and I banish Terence and Plautus from my study . . . Though they [his plays] might have been better if written in another manner, they would not have found the favour they have enjoyed.'[28]

Similarly, once scholarly editions had called attention to the classical dialogue form as used seriously by Plato and Cicero and for humorous purposes by the second century Greek satirist Lucian, it was popularized by such works as Erasmus's *Colloquies* and Castiglione's *Courtier*; by 1600 it had been used to descant on the nature of love and government, on warfare, art, mathematics and metallurgy: there was hardly a topic, high or low, that had not been manipulated into dialogue. With the dialogue as with the drama, the stimulus of revived antiquity travelled far from its sources: from first hand, to second and third hand and on by osmosis to the merest reference to the parent stock of texts. Humanism could not have become a movement if it had remained close to the study and classroom of the *umanista* – or had not moved, in parallel homage to ancient achievement, to texts which lay outside his original brief. Lecturing at the university of Copenhagen in 1574, the astronomer Tycho Brahe referred enviously to the precocious mathematical knowledge of his classical forebears, 'while we, unfortunately, have to spend the best years of our youth on the study of [their] language and grammar, which they acquired in infancy without trouble.'[29]

From the hydraulics of Archimedes, the agriculture of Marcus Terentius Varro, and the geography of Ptolemy and the diagrams in Aelianus Tacticus's treatise on military formations, to the voices of poets and prose writers and the portraits of warriors and statesmen given by historians and biographers (conspicuously Plutarch and Suetonius), the humanistic syllabus came to offer access to examples and information relevant to all educated walks of life, and recognition signals – a quotation, a name – that could be exchanged between them. Only two sources of information about the ancient world were lacking. Women, secluded in the home by classical convention, were glimpsed solely as empresses, priestesses or prostitutes, or as the objects of a poet's feelings. Here there was no helpful or reassuring voice to listen to. If anything, the clearer view of Greek and Roman society helped to confirm the growing tendency to restrict the role of women above the shopkeeper class to the care of household and family. On the other hand, with access through printed books to the humanist curriculum, girls and women with supportive families could now become as learned as most men. In the late fifteenth century the Venetian Cassandra Fedele's reading in Latin and Greek, and skill as a public orator in Venice and at the University of Padua, brought her widespread fame while still young. Angelo Poliziano, tutor and friend of Lorenzo de' Medici and, with Ficino and Pico della Mirandola, the leading Florentine scholar, wrote to tell her in 1491 of his admiration for Pico, 'than whom there never was a mortal more brilliant nor, I judge, more excellent in all branches of knowledge. Now behold, I begin to revere you, Cassandra, immediately after him, and even perhaps alongside of him'.[30] She was invited by Queen Isabella to join the Aragonese court, but the Senate refused to allow her to leave the city her reputation enhanced. Thereafter, though regarded somewhat indulgently by men as interesting prodigies, humanism could parade a roll-call of highly-cultivated women like the tragic victim of royal intrigue Lady Jane Grey, briefly queen of England before her execution in 1554, and her contemporary, the French poet Louise Labé.

The second voiceless zone of antiquity was that which had been occupied by the merchants and businessmen. Yet in fifteenth-century Italy, the scholarly core of the humanist movement had been supported by the patronage of merchant oligarchs and financially aware condottiere rulers. Had it not been so, the pervasiveness of humanism as a cultural influence, a shared cast of thought, in Europe then and later would have been delayed. The subject in the *umanista*'s curriculum which bridged this silent zone was moral philosophy, the spirit of the ancient world in its guise as councillor to men who wanted reassurance that they could live honourably as well as actively and prosperously. The teaching derived from the *Ethics* of Aristotle (not a neglected text, but re-read with a new sense of its relevance), the *On Public Duties* and *On the Orator* of Cicero, parts of Plutarch's *Moralia* and Seneca's moral-philosophical tracts, contained warnings against immoderate ambition and displays and taking unfair advantage of others. It did not, however, share the Church's condemnation of profit-seeking or its disapproval of an immersion in civic affairs. It presented a reasoned and demanding code of self-control, moderation and public service which appealed to those in the best position to sponsor the literary and artistic aspects of the revival of interest in antiquity.

Humanists in fifteenth-century Italy also devoted their attention to the other, the more abstract, metaphysical side of ancient philosophy, above all reappraising (and translating) Plato. Ficino's work on Plato and his successors, especially the third century AD Plotinus, achieved

Sandro Botticelli, *Primavera*, *c.*1477 (Uffizi, Florence)

a wide-ranging synthesis and accord with Christianity, systematic enough to be dubbed Neoplatonism. Some of its ideas – the relationship between knowledge and knowability, the ethical significance of beauty and love – were absorbed by poets (Lorenzo de' Medici, Pietro Bembo) and by the devisers of subjects for such paintings as Botticelli's *Primavera*. To establish the refinement of the court of Urbino, Castiglione ended *The Courtier* with an oration on the nature of love, put into the mouth of Bembo and much influenced by Ficino's publications, that culminated on a note so mystically ecstatic that when he had finished Bembo was left 'looking towards heaven, as if dazed. And then the signora Emilia, who together with all the others had listened to all he had to say with the utmost attention, plucked the hem of his robe and said "Take care, Pietro, that with these thoughts of yours you too do not cause your soul to leave your body".'[31]

For though metaphysics had much to offer the speculative mind, what most men and women wanted was an intellectual support system for dealing with the values and predicaments of everyday life. The tone of Pico's celebration of the dignity of man can be traced throughout the writings of the Renaissance, but it was double-edged, for to be uniquely privileged man was also uniquely burdened. Man might be 'in action how like an angel! in apprehension how like a god! the beauty of the world! the paragon of animals!' and yet, to a troubled Hamlet, he was still a 'quintessence of dust'.[32]

Philosophy in the sixteenth century lost much of the earlier contact it had had with basic human concerns through its cohabitation with theology. Those for whom it was a professional concern devoted themselves to sorting the newly emerging classical texts into schools, Pythagorean, Epicurean, Sceptic, Stoic, and exploring the links between them, as well as to amending the existing Aristotelian and Platonic systems in the light of access to neglected or previously unknown ancient commentators. There was a falling-out between them; 'pigs, dirty swine', was how the German Cornelius Agrippa of Nettesheim described those who did not agree with him.[33] And as the Church became Churches each insisted the more on the priority of its own teaching as opposed to that of the ancients. Cicero himself came to be more valued for his style than for his thought. While edition followed edition of Petrarch's accessible fourteenth-century *On Remedies against both good and bad Fortune*, the man who wished to consider himself a 'philosopher' in the sense of being armed by knowledge against life's accidents, turned his back on academic publications. As Stefano Guazzo made one of the characters in his *Civil Conversation* of 1574 say, 'the more bookes of philosophy we have at this day, the fewer philosophers we have.'[34] It was not until the next two decades of the century that the Netherlander Justus Lipsius, one of the most influential if not one of the most profound minds of the Renaissance, evolved an accessible philosophy that spoke directly to the personal anxieties of the age in the tones of a revived Stoicism.

Writing his *Essays* in the 1570s and 1580s, when political and religious conflicts caused the countries of Europe to be in 'a crazed, troubled state as is ours at this present', Montaigne rejected the intellectual play of metaphysics as irrelevant: 'it is man with whom we have always to doe – whose condition is marvellously corporall.'[35] He turned, among moral philosophers, to the Stoics, and, among them, increasingly to Seneca, 'from whom I draw unceasingly, forever dipping and emptying my pitcher'.[36] While the students of other philosophies, chasing the mind-matter issue into ever more esoteric circles in the empyrean of speculation, led to a distrust of man's reasoning faculty, Stoicism put it at the centre of its view of his place in creation. There were certain virtues – notably distinction between right and wrong, self-control over the passions, courage as opposed to recklessness – which could be intellectually explained and developed through education. The Stoics were interested in practical psychology, in learning how not simply to observe and categorize phenomena but how to endure them. Their ideas had been absorbed by Cicero and thus passed, though as a flavour rather than a doctrine, into medieval thought and humanist moral philosophy. It was the religious and political disarray of the second half of the sixteenth century that gave them a closer relevance to men who wanted a stance of some dignity even as helpless spectators of events. 'It is a noble and lofty thing', wrote the poet Tarquato Tasso in 1594, the year before the end of his tragically puzzled life, 'to observe decorum in adversity, and to be not only intrepid but constant in meeting the blows of fortune.'[37] Stoicism, with Seneca (a longer-lived contemporary of Christ) as its spokesman, was an attitude whose appeal was strengthening. 'Its voice', Seneca had written, 'is for peace, calling all mankind to live in harmony.'[38] This was the note that sounded continuously in Lipsius's ear as he sought to systematize the inchoate body of works by the Stoic school of philosophers.

Lipsius was born in Catholic Flanders in 1547. By the time he moved to his first professorial chair at the newly established Protestant University of Leiden in 1575 the Netherlands was the leading European centre of humanistic studies. Prosperity had attracted scholarly printers; accounting for his move from France to Antwerp Plantin explained that 'no other place in the world could furnish more convenience for the trade.'[39] Fugitives from the French civil wars and exiles of conscience, like Scaliger, found a measure of tolerance, and readers and students were prepared in Latin in schools which were among the best in Europe. But from the Spanish intervention in 1567 to impose Catholic uniformity and political obedience, the Netherlands had also become, in a well-worn phrase of the time, a School of War. 'Behold', Lipsius wrote in 1584, 'we are driven hither and thither by war, we are tormented not only by external wars, but by civil wars, not only by civil war but by war among ourselves. For we have not only two parties, but new parties springing up within them. O my country! What salvation will preserve you? To these ills are added pestilence, famine, forced contributions [payments to soldiers to buy them off looting and pillaging], robbery, murder and – worst of all ills – tyranny and repression not only of the body, but of the spirit. What do we see in the other countries in Europe? War or fear of war amid supposed peace, and shameful servitude under petty rulers, which is hardly preferable to war itself.'[40]

The generalizing nature of this condemnation was a device for deflecting ecclesiastical censorship from his main concern, the religious divisions between the Protestant northern and the Catholic southern provinces of the Low Countries and the sectarian factionalism in the former. A Catholic by upbringing and perhaps at heart in spite of his intellectual eirenism, Lipsius left Leiden three years later; after years of uncertainty and a host of offers from France, Italy – including one from the Pope – and Catholic German princes, he chose his homeland and accepted a chair at Louvain in 1592. There he wrote and taught, amidst renewed censorship wranglings, this time with the Jesuits, who deplored his lack of doctrinal commitment, until his death in 1606. It is to one of his favourite students there that we owe two painted likenesses. Philip Rubens, the artist's elder brother, was a scholar deeply affected by Lipsius's classical studies and one of the first to be affected by his exposition of a Christianized Stoicism. When the brothers and

Pieter Paul Rubens,
*Rubens, his brother Philip and
Jan van der Wouwere with
Justus Lipsius*, c.1615
(Pitti, Florence)

Pieter Paul Rubens and
workshop, *The Death of
Seneca*, *c.*1615 (Museo del
Prado, Madrid)

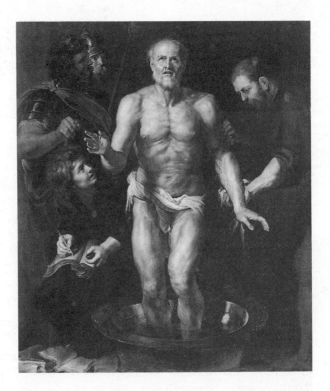

some friends met in Italy in 1602 it was natural that they should discuss
their impressions of the country, and that Lipsius (who had never been
to Italy) was in their minds is shown by his inclusion in the group
portrait of himself and the others that Peter Paul Rubens painted as a
record of their meeting. Philip, indeed, was offered his chair at Louvain
when Lipsius died in 1606. When he in turn died in 1611, and four
years later a posthumous volume of his works coincided with a new
edition of Lipsius's *Seneca*, the artist's *in memoriam* took the form of
another imaginary meeting, this time between the brothers, a mutual
friend, and Lipsius. There are books on the table. The Palatine Hill in
Rome appears in the background. Lipsius, as mediator and sage, points
to an open page while in a niche above him is a bust of Seneca in a
three-quarters profile that echoes his own.

Rubens had already produced a moving painting of Seneca steadfastly
enduring the judicial suicide to which he was condemned by the
Emperor Nero on a trumped-up charge of conspiracy. His works were
among those he had read to him while he worked in his studio as he

grew older. It seems likely that, as man of affairs and diplomat as well as busy artist of genius, he was one of the many who found in the Neostoicism expounded by Lipsius a stabilizing influence which supplemented that of the church whose mass he attended every day when in tolerable health.

On Constancy in a Time of Public Evils, the work of 1583 in which Lipsius mourned the dissensions of his age, is a dialogue in which a Stoic sage dissuades a fearful young man (as the author presents himself) from escaping adversity by flight. Where to? There is no escape from the world's evils save in facing them actively with firm self-knowledge and self-control, with constancy. An English translation, *Two Bookes of Constancie . . . containing principally, a comfortable Conference in common Calamities*, was published a year after the original edition. The book was an instant and widely translated success.

Lipsius was no mere sage. One of his pupils at Leiden had been Prince Maurice of Nassau, one of the leading spirits in the reforming of the armies of the northern Provinces so that they could stand up to the hardened forces of Spain. Changes in sixteenth-century military practice – a greater reliance on infantry, the minimizing of casualties caused by gunpowder weapons by adopting smaller and better disciplined tactical units – made modern armies increasingly resemble Roman ones. Through his *Roman Warfare* of 1595 Lipsius became a military pundit, consulted by the reformers, including Maurice, on points of detail even when he had moved to 'Spanish' Flanders. And the relevance of his immense knowledge of the political institutions of the ancient world made his 1598 *Politicorum sive civilis doctrinae libri VI*, translated into English as *Politicke Discourses*, another influential work, with an appeal not so much to the private individual, as was that of *On Constancy*, but to the directing political class of the time. Within ten years over twenty-two thousand copies in Latin had been printed; and it was widely translated, the French version alone being reprinted ten times before 1613.

In addition to its interest as a compendium of information and of quotations from classical authors, the *Discourses* was a work with a clear message. For the development of the individual, order was needed. To enforce it, authority was required, and this, if exerted in a manner seen to be reasonable, had the right to command the disciplined support of individuals, whose active co-operation was needed to keep the institutional structure sound. In return for obedience the ruler must govern fairly, especially where justice and taxation are concerned. He has a contract of honour with his subjects, both parties being part of God's plan for life in communities. The guiding principle of a sound political structure was, then, self-control within state control. Moreover, given the importance of order, Lipsius took up some of the ideas that had given Machiavelli such a bad name. The ruler should not seek peace by remaining neutral while others grew stronger by war. Deception was a permissible weapon to use against evil men. There was a morality derived from the emergencies of statecraft. The philosophical man should accept this. In Lipsius's eyes, Machiavelli was a man who had seen the intellectual light without being illuminated by the divine one.

For his readers this tone of voice, emerging in the respectable garb of antiquity, was congenial and reassuring. Firm government, supported by a co-operative populace, fitted snugly into the ideals of almost all higher organizational systems, whether political or religious. And though Lipsius was calculatingly vague about religious practice, he doubled the respectability of his ideas by presenting them as fostering the Christian values of fortitude, service and spiritual self-development. He wrote from a Catholic seat of learning, but it was a Lutheran theologian, David Chytraus of Rostock, who, lecturing on *On Constancy*, said, 'buy it and read it, students, because no such book on philosophy has been written or seen in a thousand years.'[41]

In his *Stoic Philosophy* Lipsius provided a self-portrait which, in addition to his letters and the circulation of his books, suggests something of the respect humanist scholarship could command if it spoke directly to a thoughtful public. 'I could almost exclaim, with Livius Drusus, that "to me alone no holiday has fallen from boyhood up". I get up in the morning. "Here are letters, answer them". Having done that, I turn to other things. My servant comes to say that some nobleman has called, or a youth from France, Germany or Sarmatia [Poland, or perhaps used in the more general sense of eastern Europe], wishes to pay his respects . . . I have hardly recovered my breath when one of my Belgian friends appears. "Hello, there! I've just written a poem – or pamphlet – and I want you to read it". "Anything more?" "Criticize it and correct it" . . . Then I think I'm really free: but someone else comes in and wants an epitaph . . . or else an inscription for a house or an arch or an altar. Then what about my students? . . . Still, from time to time I return to myself, and I turn over in my mind something beneficial and profitable. A little superficially and maybe incidentally; yet I do turn it over.'[42]

Lipsius was not the originator of a new approach to philosophy, as Spinoza (a Dutchman) and Descartes (a Frenchman) were to be in the next two generations. But of all the humanist scholars of the Renaissance he was the one who best taught men how to be 'philosophical'. It was this personal appeal Fynes Moryson had in mind when, on passing through the Netherlands, he had found no opportunity to meet 'Lipsius, whom I love for his Booke of Constancy'.[43]

Moryson was a Fellow of Peterhouse, Cambridge, and he wrote the account of his travels, in which this remark occurs, in Latin before translating it into English. Obviously the voices spoke most directly in their own tongue, and humanists renamed themselves to demonstrate their receptiveness: Lips became Lipsius as before him, Bredekopf (Broad-head) had become Laticephalus, Sommerfeld Aesticampanus and Bauer (Peasant) Agricola. To latinize a name was to make for a linguistically consistent title-page, but it was also a form of self-promotion within the ranks of socially approved learning. From its initial patronage by men of standing, and the adoption of the classics-based syllabus that remained the staple of well-bred education well into the nineteenth century, to a gleaning of classical learning from translations, humanism involuntarily made an acquaintance with ancient culture a badge of caste. Lipsius's message for those perturbed by the convulsions within society was addressed to those who played a responsible part in it. By his generation, humanistic values had become a distinguishing feature of the 'civility' to which we shall turn and which had its own agenda for separating itself from the ever-growing number of those with dirty hands and pleading stomachs.

There is no conflict here with the liberating effect of the voices as they thawed. Humanistic enthusiasm lasted so long because its core of energy, the historical reality of antiquity, was uncontroversial (save when an assassin pleaded the example of Brutus or a paganizing faddist mocked the Christian faith), and because the scholarly excitement about the need to exploit the achievements of the Greek and Roman past was sustained by evidence that it could be done. But as writers reviewed the offered models and took encouragement from or issue with them, they came to hope more self-consciously that their work would, as Milton was to put it, 'fit audience find, though few'. The popular culture of stories, ballads, proverbs and the vivid phraseology of gossip towards which Montaigne loved to turn an ear, retained its own energy. Yet apart from the linguistic voracity and the inclusive humanity of Rabelais, few authors in the sixteenth century accepted its sayings and

turns of phrase save when, in a play or picaresque novel (the anonymous Spanish *Lazarillo de Tormes* of 1554, for instance), authors went
deliberately slumming. The authors of the torrent of writing that
reacted to the lure of print and the growth of a literate audience, at times
looked up to and passed on to their readers Latin tags or mythological
references. At the level of consciously crafted literary forms, humanism
supported the division between those who had a say in the way the
world was run and those who had not.

CHANGED APPEARANCES

Vital and pervasive as were the ways in which humanism altered the
ways in which men wrote and thought, it is the arts that evoked a
different picture of them and their times. From around 1400 men and
women acquire a three-dimensionality of body and an instantly
decipherable play of facial expression that makes them appear different
in kind from their flatter, more passive medieval forebears. They stand
in groups as though they could move in a moment into a different
relationship with one another. Instead of seeming to be merely superimposed on a background, the manner of rendering a room, a street
or a stretch of countryside puts them at ease within its space.

To achieve this congruence between art and reality was a deliberate
aim. It was stressed by the few artists – Alberti and Leonardo are
conspicuous examples – who wrote about what the goal of the painter
and sculptor should be. Giorgio Vasari, a highly successful painter
himself, as well as the first historian of Italian art from around 1300 to
the 1560s, summed up the change: 'we see that at that time accomplished artists were setting themselves to the intelligent investigation
and zealous imitation of the true properties of the natural world.'[44]
They were sustained by an active welcome from non-artists for an art
that mirrored life. Describing the sculptural reliefs on the façade of the
cathedral at Orvieto in the mid-fifteenth century, the future Pope Pius
II recorded in his memoirs that 'the faces stand out from the marble as
if alive, and the bodies of man and beasts are so well rendered that art
seems to have equalled nature. Only speech is lacking to make them
live.'[45] Over and over again travellers seeking a way in which to praise
works of art eked out the routine 'lovely' and 'very fine' with 'as if
it were alive'.[46] 'Every figure looks as though it were alive', noted

Hieronymus Müntzer of the van Eyck altarpiece in St Bavo, Ghent in 1495. For Antonio de Beatis in 1517 the same work was 'done in oils with such perfection and truth to life both as to the proportions and colouring of the parts of the body and to the use of light and shade that one has no hesitation in saying that this is the finest painting in Christendom'.[47]

Jan van Eyck, *Adam and Eve*, panels from upper wings of *The Ghent Altarpiece*, 1432 (St Bavo, Ghent)

Leonardo da Vinci, *The Last Supper*, fresco, 1495–8 (Santa Maria delle Grazie, Milan)

This appetite to see art once more falling into step with life was so strong as to lead Antonio, on his return to Italy, to make a striking assumption about the *Last Supper* of Leonardo, whom he had actually met and listened to in France, at Amboise. 'The figures in the painting', he recorded, 'are portraits, from the life, and life-size, of various court personalities and Milanese citizens of the time'.[48] The comment was wide of the mark. The anatomical drawings Leonardo had shown him were a means to make idealization carry conviction not to make his apostles resemble friends and acquaintances. Yet his comment is also a revealing one. He saw the fresco in the company of his master, the sophisticated Cardinal Luigi of Aragon, in the course of a tour of the sights of Milan they were given by the city's notables, and Antonio's opinions commonly deferred to those of his betters. Writing a decade before, in 1508, and with reference to painting in Germany, Christoph Scheurl wrote that it 'has only now been brought back to life again'. For him the hero of this rebirth was Lucas Cranach, and by turning rhetorically to address this artist, who was by no means a straightforward copier of nature, he makes it clear that what he meant by life was life-like. He reminds him that 'once in Austria you painted grapes on a table in such a natural way that after you had left a magpie flew by and was so annoyed at the deception that it hacked at the work with beak and claws; the stag that you painted at Coburg made dogs bark when they caught sight of it.'[49] By then, it is true, Pliny's anecdotes about the art of antiquity, among which were stories of birds pecking at painted grapes and stallions neighing at painted mares, had come to be handed about as part of the small change of humanistic comment on aesthetic matters. But it did not take a knowledge of Pliny to realize that artists had mastered the description of nature. Writing in 1535 of a new plant discovered in America, the Spaniard Fernandez de Oviedo noted that words were not enough: 'it needs to be painted by the hand of a [Pedro] Berruguete' – the Spanish painter and sculptor who died in 1508 – 'or some other excellent painter like him, or by Leonardo da Vinci or Andrea Mantegna, famous artists whom I knew in Italy.'[50]

All these remarks were made by men who were well aware of the wealth of descriptive, naturalistic details in the medieval carvings and paintings amidst which they worshipped and on the pages they turned of illuminated manuscripts: plants and animals, meticulously rendered costumes, the tools employed by craftsmen and peasants. Though it was primarily interest in the way in which the human face and body was painted that caused art to be seen as having been brought back to life again, that perception drew on an awareness that the figures were related to their setting in a way that made them appear at home there. Antonio de Beatis thought of Leonardo's apostles as being portraits because surely the people sitting at so naturalistically laid a meal at so realistic a refectory table in such a believable architectural space, and interreacting, group by group, in such a credible manner, must be taken from the real life to which the painter was referring.

For Vasari the 'renewal', the 'restoration', the 'rebirth of art was above all due to artists' acknowledging 'the debt they owe to nature, which constantly serves them as a model'.[51] For him this fresh overview of artists' approach to their subjects came – after its anticipation by Giotto in the early fourteenth century – to be established irreversibly in the early fifteenth by Masaccio for painting and Donatello for sculpture. At the same time, Jan van Eyck was transferring the colours, spaces and fully realized people of the world of nature to the panels of his Ghent altarpiece with its 'truth to life'. And Claus Sluter in Dijon was bringing to sculpture a physiognomical pungency and a grasp of bodily weight and structure that had only been hinted at, here and there in Europe, before. As in Italy, this grasp of natural appearances formed an enduring base for the changed appearance of paintings and statues, not just in the fifteenth and sixteenth centuries but until the twentieth. The whole-heartedness of the change in both the South (initially in Florence) and the North (initially in the 'Belgian' provinces of the Netherlands), is remarkable. Earlier scattered hints were absorbed into a revolutionary completeness that only an intense single-mindedness could achieve.

Masaccio's fresco *The Tribute Money* in the Brancacci Chapel of the Florentine church of Santa Maria del Carmine was painted in *c.*1427. It is a multiple narrative. Christ and the Apostles have arrived at Capernaum. This is a Roman city and they are asked to pay an entrance toll or tribute. As Jews, in their own homeland, they argue – in the central episode – about the rights and wrongs of this imperialist imposition with the gatekeeper, whose back and arms eloquently declare his surprise at their obstinacy. Christ, intent on his mission, cuts the argument short. He tells the indignant Peter to cast a line in the lake of Galilee – as he does in the episode on the left, flushing with the exertion as he crouches to haul it out – 'and when thou hast opened his mouth, thou shalt find a piece of money: that take, and give unto them for me and thee' (Matthew 17: 26). In the third episode Peter angrily dumps the coin in the gatekeeper's hand. The story is enacted on the outskirts of a credible (if not credibly classical) town, where buildings soar up

Masaccio, *The Tribute Money*, fresco, *c.*1427 (Brancacci Chapel, Santa Maria del Carmine, Florence)

beyond the picture's frame. We watch a group whose expressions all follow the same argument and whose bodies are spaced believably over a firmly imagined tract of ground; we look past buildings and figures into a landscape of lake, trees, hills and cloudy sky which do not just hint at reality but show it. All lines not parallel to the picture's edges recede to a common vanishing-point; the landscape does not take a series of leaps backwards from one equally clearly defined zone to another but recedes evenly, changing in tone and clarity. Figures are defined not just by outline but by the play of light and shade which builds up a sense of their volume. The application of these rules, plus a personal taste for simple, naturally falling drapery and rugged but unquirkish faces, gives *The Tribute Money* a 'reality' heightened by the intellect above the reality perceived by the normally restless eye.

To move from the open countryside to a single room, Jan van Eyck in his *The Betrothal of the Arnolfini* of 1434 bears witness to the real world in a double sense. Giovanni Arnolfini, a merchant from Lucca who spent much of his business life in Bruges, where he came to know Jan, holds his young wife-to-be's hand in his left and lifts the other to pledge his troth to her in a ceremony before witnesses that had the full force of marriage, even though it was conventional to confirm the contract sacramentally in a church. He looks towards his witnesses to ensure their attention. There are two, reflected in the convex mirror on the end wall: tiny figures, suitably dressed for the occasion in bright colours, one of whom is almost certainly Jan himself – above the mirror he has written 'Jan van Eyck was present.' The mirror itself is witness to the reality of the room. It shows the top of the chest, otherwise hidden by Giovanni's fur-trimmed coat. It shows another window where the room extends in front of him, and the doorway in which the witnesses of the act stand, to be joined, year after year, by as many others as come to stand in front of the picture; he is happy, clearly, to have his oath endlessly renewed. Everything in this room (the best bedroom was also used for entertaining close friends, not just for sleeping in) is an exact transcription of reality: the bottle glass in the window, the apples on the chest, the wooden sandals for outdoors use, the grained floorboards, the gathering up of the fiancée's dress in the fashionable pregnant look then current in France, where she was brought up. Some objects are chosen as symbols: the single candle in the chandelier, representing the single choice the pair have made, the little dog, emblem of domestic fidelity, the statuette of St Margaret, patron saint of childbirth. But there is nothing obtrusive about their

Jan van Eyck, *The Betrothal*
of the Arnolfini, 1434
(National Gallery, London)

presence. The mirror is more likely to represent the artist's skill than
the concept of art's holding a mirror up to nature, but by extending
the room towards a succession of spectators it is an apt, if not intentional, symbol of space and time. Real and solemn, the *Betrothal* is
much more than an exquisitely rendered slice of life.

These two considered documents of a new age of realistic perception,
which differed more in approach than intention, are all the more
remarkable for their breaching a popular and highly respected style that
was at the height of its brilliance. During the fourteenth century a
gracefully decorative, unemphatic manner of painting and illuminating
had been evolved that was so widespread in Europe that it has been
called International Gothic. The label plays down the variety of means
by which artists from France across Germany to Bohemia, and from
the Netherlands to Spain and Italy, had absorbed a lively interest in

Limbourg brothers, detail of miniature in the *Très riches heures* of the
Duke of Berry, 1411–16 (Musée Condé, Chantilly)

everyday details into compositions which if they lacked both intellectual and spatial depth, had a charm which was by no means superficial.
And while Masaccio and Jan were at work the style showed no signs
of faltering. There was nothing tentative or *fin de siècle* about the series
of illuminations showing the labours of the months which the Flemish
brothers Paul, Jean and Herman de Limbourg produced for the Duke
of Berry from 1411 to 1416. Skies were never so piercingly blue, nor
castles quite so lofty, so raised as though by wizards rather than masons,
as those before which peasants carried out their tasks or fashionable
men and women rode out in festival guise to the sound of trumpets.
But the castles are defensible. The men and women are lightly individualized. The peasants hunch with effort or, stooping, show their
pants beneath their jerkins. And divided by walls and fences and roads,

the countryside they work in has an extensiveness which alludes to increasing distance without analysing it. Nothing is out of key. Nothing has been rethought.

Radically different in scale and richness, Gentile da Fabriano's large altarpiece *The Adoration of the Magi* was painted in 1423 for one of the wealthiest men in Florence, Palla Strozzi, and for one of the city's most fashionable churches, Santa Trinita. Yet it, too, drew on a tradition of incorporating naturalistic detail into an overall pattern that did not pay much attention to simulating the weight and volume of bodies or objects, or to inviting the observer to enter the pictured space. All Gentile's talents are, as it were, in the shop window. Within the arches at the top of this jostling celebration of Christianity's most joyous moment, there is a curlicue of narrative; on the left the three kings sight the star from a mountain top; in the middle they and their

Gentile da Fabriano, *Adoration of the Magi*, 1423 (Uffizi, Florence)

energetic entourage wheel towards one of the cities they passed through by day; on the right they file into one of the towns they came to at dusk. Then, as though they had slid downhill, they appear in the right-hand foreground, gesturing, grimacing, trying to remember the importance of the occasion. Birds fly and fight, monkeys gibber, a camel looks down his nose, a lion's head looks like a man in a lion mask. With fashion-plate elegance the standing king quiets this mood. From his central axis his colleagues fall into attitudes of deepening adoration. They bend into what is almost another picture. Isolated by the rock which shelters the ox and the ass, Joseph and Mary look gravely down at the gestures in which the work's meaning culminates, the reciprocal acts of homage and blessing. And it is a mark of Gentile's genius that this moment is both ritualistic and natural. The child is doing what no newborn baby could do, yet his hand touches the old man's head with something of an infant's automatic exploratoriness, and while one foot goes forward dutifully to be kissed, the other curls up as though afraid of being tickled. The picture is full of such inventiveness. Though the surface is held together by the restrained splendour of its colour, this is not a work to be read as a whole but to linger over, detail by detail. Much of the detail (for instance, the David-like page holding the horse and the huge sword, with his sturdy legs-apart stance and eager expression) has so much energy, incorporates so much fresh observation, that it casts doubt on the acceptability of the conventions that contain it. Gentile continues the old double standard for the size of buildings and human beings. The upper landscapes have an unnatural clarity and end against an unvarying gold sky. The figures on the right are less a company of individuals than a pile of faces. Much, indeed, has been observed. As with the Limbourg illuminations nothing has been rethought.

Shortly after the completion of Gentile's *Adoration*, work began in the Brancacci Chapel. Not long after Masaccio's rigorous reassessment of the painter's attitude to the natural world in *The Tribute Money*, his influence was registered in *The Deposition from the Cross* by a cloistered artist, the Dominican Fra Angelico, who without it might have painted the epitome, rather than a rejection of much that was characteristic of the International Gothic. *The Deposition* was commissioned by Gentile's patron, Palla Strozzi, and for the same church, Santa Trinita. It was intended to complement the *Adoration*. Yet for all the persistence of Fra Angelico's love of bright colour, surface pattern and sharp, shallow details, of making everything appear newly minted, in this work he

quietly distanced himself from that long tradition. The view of Jerusalem in the left-hand arch is based on a real flair for the analysis of
geometrical solids, a flair enhanced by their three-dimensionality. There
is a suggestion of mathematics, too, in the symmetrical grid formed
by the two ladders on either side of the Cross in the centre; and as the
topmost man stoops to let Christ down, his halo stoops with him. The
landscape, beyond the stage area of flowery grass, moves uninterrup-
tedly back to the horizon, and there, as in nature, the sky darkens.
Among the figures, there is a shared, intent concentration on the central

Fra Angelico, *Deposition from the Cross*, *c.*1432–43 (Museo di San Marco, Florence)

tragedy or – for this painting is an aid to meditation, not an attempt to record an event as it actually might have been – the symbols associated with it. And the faces are moulded into relief by the light that falls across them from a common source on the left. Everything is gentler, prettier, more insinuating than in Masaccio, but the hints of analytical rigour and consistency are his.

Another *Deposition*, almost exactly contemporary (*c.*1435) with Fra Angelico's, shows how thoroughly the convention of Gothic art had been rephrased by Netherlandish artists other than Jan van Eyck. Rogier van der Weyden (in his picture at the Prado) accepts the traditional curving sway for the body of Christ and the bending figures of St John and the Magdalen which bracket the scene. He rationalizes the familiar preference for a shallow, packed foreground by boldly dropping a solid wall on to the hill of Golgotha, leaving only enough room for the ladder to be reared behind the cross. He maintains the fashion-consciousness of the chivalric taste for carefully studied costumes contributing to a colourful ensemble. But Antonio de Beatis might well have expected these figures to be taken from known individuals. Their faces reflect thought and feeling. Beneath their clothes are living bodies, supple, like the Magdalen's, strong like the central figure who rests Christ's weight on his thigh. Though there is a Gothic fancy in the fluffs of drapery blowing out – in this windless scene – from the side of the young man on the ladder he is a triumph of the art of transcribing into paint a real person as he performs a task. The rendering of hands alone across the picture demonstrates the consolidation of a new approach to the relationship between art and nature. And in the Netherlands as in Italy, the approach was – for all the many variations that were to be played upon it – fundamental to the changed appearance of Renaissance art.

The power behind the change came from the individual genius of the artists who promoted it. But their choice of direction, and its being echoed and sustained by lesser talents, owed much to local conditions that were widely shared. In both the Netherlands and Italy there was an accumulating desire on the part of sections of the clergy to rally the faithful, as they took fresh heart from their recovery from the panic caused by the Black Death of the mid-fourteenth century, by making the Gospel story as real as possible to them. This was achieved chiefly through anecdotal and story-telling sermons and homilies, but literary realism was building up a pressure which other influences would release from words into paint. One was financial recovery in both areas after the Black Death. Commercial life became more intense, the personalities who influenced civil life more watchfully scrutinized. New building projects stimulated pride in the urban environment – some of the earliest accurate city-views are to be seen through the windows of the religious paintings by Jan van Eyck, Rogier van der Weyden and their contemporary The Master of Flémalle. Simultaneously, as the leading figures in Church and State – and both came from the same aristocratic background, based on landlord power or mercantile success – came to reassess their position in the control of public events, they wanted manuscript histories whose illuminations showed battles and sieges, diplomatic meetings and grand entertainments in readily imaginable terms. And as panel painters worked in close proximity to illuminators, and could be employed in both capacities, sharing the patronage of the same men, their portraits and altarpieces came to adopt a common intention.

This was particularly true in the Netherlands. In Italy there was less demand for chronicle illuminations showing historical events. But there, where humanism was working its early way among the patrons of artists of repute, there was a compensating inclination towards painters who could bring the art of antiquity to mind by an allusion to a classical setting or to the 'life-like' appearance of ancient sculpture. Both elements were present in Masaccio's fresco *The Trinity* of *c.*1427 in the Florentine church of Santa Maria Novella; figures as fully realized in the round as those of *The Tribute Money* are shown in a chapel with a classically coffered ceiling that is curved to run back from the arch of its pillared and pilastered façade. The weighty quality of Masaccio's figures drew on the sculpted figures of contemporaries like Nanni di Banco who were aiming at a classical appearance for their works. In *c.*1413 Nanni had produced a shrine of re-evoked antique statuary. Within a Gothic niche on an outside wall of the church of Orsanmichele stand the marble figures of *The Four Crowned Saints* – Christian sculptors who were martyred by the third-century Emperor Diocletian for refusing to carve the statue of a pagan deity. In a relief below the niche Nanni shows them at work as though they were working in his own times as members of the guild of stoneworkers who had commissioned the whole work. So one of them builds a stone wall, two others carve the Gothic architectural details that were still in lively demand (a twisted column and a boss) while the fourth, as a specialist sculptor, chips away at a burly and very un-Gothic *putto*. Above them the martyrs, draped like actors bringing them to life from Diocletian's

Nanni di Banco, *The Four Crowned Saints*, c. 1410–15 (Orsanmichele, Florence)

times, discuss with reticent dignity the timeless significance of their death. The disciples in *The Tribute Money* take in the significance of Christ's words in a mood very similar to the one created by Nanni di Banco.

Though the relationship between painting and sculpture was as close in the North as in Italy, it was the classicizing strain in Italian sculpture that compensated for the greater avidity with which Netherlandish artists interpreted the world in terms of observation. It was this strain, added to the Italian bias towards theoretical means of bringing art and nature together, notably the analysis of spatial representation through colour values and mathematically worked out sight-lines (the narrowing perspective lines that made the chapel in Masaccio's *Trinity* appear to extend behind the wall on which it was painted), that created the different approaches within the common appetite for the real presence of the world in art.

From the 1430s, then, as commercial prosperity increased the flow of orders and the competition between workshop and workshop and the artists of one city with those of another, the pattern – whereby the International Gothic style originating chiefly in France had radiated to all points of the compass – changed. Henceforward the generators of changed appearances were the Netherlands and Italy, with artists in other countries taking from either what they were ready to absorb. This usually involved combining what was new and fashionable from either source within a style that was congenial because regionally familiar. But in *c.*1450 the most eagerly responsive of French artists, Jean Fouquet, acquired a remarkably steady balance between both models. In his portrait of Estienne Chevalier with his patron saint and martyr St Stephen (holding one of the stones with which he was pelted to death), there is an Eyckian minuteness in the rendering of textures and surfaces: the hair and clothes of the two men, the veined marble slabs in the wall behind him. But it was Fouquet's visit to Italy in the years shortly before he began this work that accounts for the fall of light that reveals the structure of the saint's neck and face and that sets both figures so naturally within the space they occupy.

This balance is all the more remarkable for the lack in the 1440s of any obvious 'Italian' model for a foreign painter to seize upon. Whereas in the Netherlands change was slow after the 1430s and resulted from

Jean Fouquet, *Estienne Chevalier with St Stephen*, detail from altarpiece, *c.*1450, (Staatliche Museen, Berlin-Dahlem)

the temperament of successive masters rather than from any radical stock-taking, in Italy the mid- and later fifteenth century was a time of restless experiment. The interest in working from a theoretical base led to the creation of paintings which, however marvellous, contained an emphasis on perspective (Uccello), anatomy (Pollaiuolo) or delicate draughtsmanship (Botticelli), isolated within their proponents' idiosyncracies. The harshly selective realism of Castagno, the fevered grace of Cosmè Tura, the metallic finish of Crivelli's decorative fantasies: over and over again there was a quirkiness or the drenching of a subject in a personal style that rebuffed imitation. The influence of International Gothic persisted – in an individual, like Pisanello, in a whole school, like that of Siena. Indeed, the much later notion of 'schools' of painting reflects the differences between the appearance of the art produced in various regions of Italy. Within each there were artists of sharp individuality. And with so many alternatives in the air and so many uses to which a sympathy with antiquity could be put, or put aside, the course of an artist's approach to his commissions could vary in a manner unthinkable before the fifteenth century. Without a knowledge of his career as a whole it would be difficult to accept that Donatello's *St George* of *c.*1415–17 and his *Magdalen* of *c.*1453 were the work of the same man, or that the tenderly classicizing *Annunciation* of the 1430s was from the same hand as the unguarded emotionalism of the San Lorenzo pulpit reliefs of the 1460s. For one artist, Mantegna, antiquity was something to reconstruct, as in his feigned marble and bronze classical reliefs. For another, the sculptor Adriano Fiorentino, a classically generalized face was something useful to add dignity to a slight, girlish bronze figure clearly studied from a naked model posing in his workshop.

Amidst so much diversity, there was as yet no generic Italian – or, for that matter, Milanese, Florentine or Venetian – style whose settled principles eased its assimilation by others. There was an occasional work which appeared to restate the achievements of Masaccio as though they had become a norm. Such a work was the brilliantly accomplished fresco of 1477 by Melozzo da Forlì, *The Appointment of Platina as Librarian of the Vatican*. In a deep classical hall, Pope Sixtus IV appoints the kneeling humanist Bartolomeo Sacchi [Platina]. Melozzo's geometrically defined space and solid, personalized figures have a confidence suggesting a norm that no longer calls for renewed heart-searching. But this was an isolated pause in a continuing search for solutions.

It was this lack of an assured base that kept Italian artists aware of

onatello, *St George*, c. 1415-17
Museo Nazionale del Bargello, Florence)

Donatello, *St Mary Magdalen*, c. 1453
(Baptistery, Florence)

what was to be learned from the North. From the 1430s painters in a country which was used to fresco on walls and the ungleaming, flattish effect of tempera on panel, had experimented with oil-based colours. It was with Antonello da Messina, however, who in the 1460s had studied works by van Eyck and Rogier van der Weyden in the collection of King Alfonso of Naples, that the Flemish use of oil paints to heighten the definition of details, to enhance tonal depth with glazes, enabling the artist to overlap and modify work in progress, was mastered. In a work like Antonello's *Portrait of a Condottiere* of 1475 it was the fusion of the Italian ability to build anatomical structure from within, with the Flemish technique of surface tonal contouring through the use of oils, that influenced the artists of Venice (where Antonello painted this portrait), and especially the most influential of them, Giovanni Bellini. It was not just in technique that Italians still confessed themselves to be learners. It was in *c.*1478 that the huge *Adoration Altarpiece* by Hugo van der Goes arrived in Florence, sent by Tommaso Portinari, who had commissioned it while working for the Bruges branch of the Medici bank. From the effect it had on the artists who – in the most sophisticatedly vital cultural centre in Italy – were influenced by it, we can see that there was not yet any agreed upon local style. An altarpiece (for the Portinari family chapel in the church of San Egidio), it was also an exhibition piece, demonstrating the calm development that had carried forward in the Netherlands the work of Jan and Rogier. While not achieving the overall balance of composition that was becoming cherished for Florentine altarpieces, it was studded with lessons: the boldly informal suggestion of a space bounded on the left by a massive classical pillar beside which the ox and ass munch at their manger and on the right by an open wooden framework; the emotive isolation of the Christchild, lying flat on his back on the floor; the meticulous rendering of the different costumes of the three groups of kneeling angels; the contrasting cluster of almost jarringly homespun shepherds, their rough features somehow etherealized by their devotion: the leit-motif of prayerful hands; the *trompe l'oeil* still-life of vase and jar and sheaf of straw in the foreground; the linking of the triptych's wings and central scene by a landscape common to all of them. These, singly, or in combination, were among the features that established the Netherlands as the chief source of borrowings by European artists up to the early sixteenth century.

Fouquet was exceptional among visitors to Italy in his ability to sense the idealized realism to which Italian experimentalism was to

Hugo van der Goes, *Portinari Altarpiece, c.* 1475–8 (Uffizi, Florence)

lead. Most reacted only to the real antiquities they saw or the classicizing details or settings used by Italian artists. When the Antwerp painter
Jan Gossaert had been to Italy in 1508, these were what lingered in his
memory as he painted *St Luke drawing the Virgin* in *c.*1515. The result
was a skilled and attractive worst-of-both-worlds hybrid. The purely
Flemish elements, the Virgin and Child and the saint, have lost their
native volume and, despite their spreading robes, become mere cut-outs
applied to the 'classical' architectural vista which clamours for attention.
'Classical' rather than classical, Gossaert flourishes his newly acquired
knowledge but mixes Gothic with Roman frames for the sculptural
reliefs, invites the eye through a classically pillared and columned and
coffered vestibule to a Gothic fountain. He invokes Italian mathematically planned perspective but irritatingly gets it wrong while rejecting
the perfectly convincing observation-based recession from foreground
to horizon of his own inheritance.

By then, however, Italy was on the verge of offering to the rest of
Europe a succession of readily comprehensible styles for imitation or
emulation within which the raw bones of experiment had been suppressed. Though Vasari's view of the fifteenth century was biased by
his own practice as an artist in the mid-sixteenth, when he wrote his
account of Italian art, his summary of its qualities rings true. While
not grudging in his appreciation of individual artists, he complained
that 'the excessive study' they applied to their individual approaches
had led to a 'dry, hard, harsh style', lacking the 'inspired grace' that

Jan Gossaert ('Mabuse'), *St Luke drawing the Virgin, c.*1515 (National Gallery, Prague)

came from a mastery of all approaches; the true, 'fine style' that established Italian leadership in Europe followed the use of this mastery to select, imitate and adjust 'the most beautiful things in nature' to the goal of art. It was this mastery, hidden within a graceful harmony of composition and colouring and giving an impression that was both 'realistic' and 'unforced', that opened the new period of achievement 'which we like to call the modern age'.[52]

These qualities were exemplified for Vasari in the work of Leonardo and Raphael, both of whom, he wrote, were among those who turned back 'to learn the art of painting' from Masaccio's frescoes in the Brancacci Chapel. Of the two it was Raphael who first represented to non-Italians a style which was seen as authoritatively and assimilably Italian. Despite his painstaking preparation by means of compositional sketches and drawings from models, his large compositions had a radiant certainty of intention and effect. No other artist – including the Leonardo of *The Last Supper* – had invented imaginary worlds which were so easy to enter. Whether it is that of the philosophers of antiquity conferring in a classical architectural setting whose spaciousness and conviction supports the quality of their thought, or that of the amorous water-gods and gravity-defying disciples of Cupid (who appraises their performance from within a cloud) encircling the sea-nymph Galatea, the effect is the same: Raphael issues an invitation to the worlds of learning and myth and steps aside. There is no nudging, no insistence, no exaggeration or loose end that reminds the spectator that this is a construct based on much labour. It was this ability to use his own imagination to liberate the spectator's that made Raphael's paintings appear to float free from the busy world of Italian inventiveness. Among his most influential works were the full-size, coloured designs for episodes from the lives of Saints Peter and Paul which were sent to Brussels to be made into tapestries in 1517. For those that saw them in that much visited city, or stood before the tapestries when they were sent to hang below the wall frescoes in the Sistine Chapel in the Vatican, they revealed another aspect of Raphael's talent: his gift for putting monumentally conceived figures into realistic narrative interaction while preserving an overall air of enhanced naturalness.

It was an approach to painting that lent itself to copying and black and white reproduction through the means we shall turn to in the next chapter. And it was sustained by Raphael's assistants, some of whom, like Giulio Romano, became highly successful independent artists. Others, outside his immediate circle, also prolonged his influence: Correggio, Parmigianino – who, Vasari wrote, 'strove to imitate him in all things, but above all in painting'[53] – and, because the blend of strength with charm in his work was readily transferable to other media, the sculptor Jacopo Sansovino. It was not so much the hand of Raphael but the Raphaelesque style that entered the stream of choices open to artists outside Italy. And it was the ease and life-likeness of the style that made it fly further than that of the more wrestled-with profundity

Raphael, *Galatea*, c.1514
(Villa Farnesina, Rome)

of Michelangelo's figures on the Sistine ceiling which he produced when both artists were working for Pope Julius II. It was, moreover, Raphael who, in a work left unfinished in a few details at his death in 1520 (at the age of thirty-seven), *The Transfiguration*, struck a yet newer manner that was to be reflected from Italy across the arts throughout most of Europe. Tenebrous or sharply arbitrary in colour, declamatory in gesture, spatially resistant to rational analysis, *The Transfiguration* would be simply a sign that Raphael had become impatient with the Raphaelesque were it not for others who wanted to bend the rules of calmly harmonious composition, the naturalistic depiction of the human figure, and the logical organization of what was near and far.

Such a one also was Rosso Fiorentino. Three years after Raphael died in Rome, he painted *Moses and the Daughters of Jethro* in Florence. The text from *Exodus* that he was called on to illustrate seems a fairly mild one: 'Now the priest of Midian [Jethro] had seven daughters: and they came and drew water, and filled the troughs to water their father's flock. And the shepherds came and drove them away: but Moses stood up and helped them, and watered their flock.' Rosso interpreted this brief story with dervish-like intensity. Moses, the berserk central figure, helps by wrenching and pounding. The fallen figure in the right foreground is deliberately difficult: the parallel arm and thigh, the pelvis heaved up by the crossed legs to provide a previously unattempted vista of belly and inner thigh seen beyond an escarpment of ribcage. The difficulties here, and in the other nude figures, are solved with an almost ruthless (though not unsensual) professional fervour, while the parody of their alignments provided by the cluster of sheep's heads shows the emotional distance between the painter and his subject. The

Raphael, *Transfiguration*, c.1517–20 (Pinacoteca, Vatican)

Rosso Fiorentino, *The Daughters of Jethro*, 1523–4 (Uffizi, Florence)

shepherd storming in from the left, hand histrionically outflung and cloak artificially stiffened upwards, is another academic exercise, as is the frozen, balanced figure of Jethro's better-than-naked daughter. Her face is doll-like, the hands mincing, the coiffure jauntily out of keeping with the theme, but the exposed breast, the shoulder and extended arm proclaim the Florentine tradition of defining by outline and modelling by light. In spite of its over-elegances and shrilly unnatural colours the painting is a tribute to the humanistic, sculptural, rationally analytical strain Rosso had absorbed as a 'Fiorentino' through the very intensity with which he rejects it.

Seven years later Raphael's admirer Francesco Mazzola, Il Parmigianino, started work – in the town, Parma, from which his commonly used nickname is derived – on the painting that has come to be known as *The Madonna with the Long Neck*. It could with equal justice be called the Madonna of the Long Fingers, or of the Extended Torso, or, more briefly, of the Nipple or of the Navel, so many are the features that distingush her from other Madonnas, let alone from real women. There is nothing ultra-personal or undescriptive about the colour here. The child is scarcely winning, but his size is a conventional reminder of the dead Christ, who will be supported on that same lap. The Bacchus-Baptist youth, whose wine jar will then be replaced by the new wine of the Redeemer's blood, represents a concept hardly more far-fetched than was a good deal of contemporary religious imagery, nor is the contrast between the reference to a time of refined paganism and Old Testament prophecy, and the contemporary foreground, unduly

Parmigianino, *Madonna with the Long Neck*, 1530–40 (Uffizi, Florence)

strained. But here the more-or-less conventional comes to a stop, to be overtaken by the urge, at any cost to the reality of appearance or the truth of feeling, to be exquisite. The orthodox stabilities have gone. There is no way of measuring the distance between the Virgin's dais, the withered prophet and the unusually shaped column. The supporting characters are all crammed into one side. The artist aims not to convince the faithful but to surprise and ravish the connoisseur.

One of the qualities Vasari looked for in an artist's work was, indeed, his *maniera*, the manner in which he expressed himself. In these two paintings manner takes precedence over matter. Art, instead of concealing skill, flaunts it. Mannerism offered a holiday from *The School of Athens*. Throughout Italy in the 1520s and 1530s and in much of Europe thereafter, a number of painters and sculptors, however versed in the techniques of copying nature and reducing its idiosyncracies to order, moved towards artifice: 'artificial', as opposed to 'natural' became a term of praise. Reality, once mastered, became something to play with.

Mannerism's early connotations of energetic academic sabotage, as in *Jethro's Daughters* or cool preciousness as in Parmigianino's careful extrapolation from the Raphaelesque norm, became blurred as its influence simply became a licence to do old things in a new way. Italian influence was direct in the case of the French School of Fontainebleau and the contemporaneous, gracefully self-conscious sculpture of Jean Goujon. This was because Italian artists who favoured its style – Rosso and the Mantuan Primaticcio (a master of the *svelte* elegance that could be teased from it) and the sculptor Benvenuto Cellini had been invited to work in France. More independently, artists broke their own traditions. Whether expressed in the personal approaches of the suavely erotic Frenchman Jean Bellange, or the Netherlander Pieter Aertsen, who pushed gospel episodes into the background of genre scenes of contemporary everyday life, or the tranced spirituality of the Spaniard-by-adoption El Greco, the Mannerist mode became a third choice; by the mid-sixteenth century European artists could follow this fanciful route, or the soberer alternative of Netherlandish realism, or Raphael esque idealized and ordered naturalism, both of which retained their appeal as models.

It was not until the end of the century that another alternative model appeared. Its initiator was Caravaggio. Again, a personal approach became an imitable style only because it was quickly picked up and modified for ready assimilation by others. Genius alone did not create movements. The two greatest painters of the mid-century were the Netherlander Pieter Breughel and the Italian Titian. There was nothing about Breughel's technique that was particularly individual. It was his vision of nature's pitiless indifference to the men who ploughed and harvested and hunted across its immensity, his sympathy with underdog tasks and crude diversions (his first biographer described him and a friend going to country feast-days 'disguised as peasants'[54]), his politicized anger against war and religious intolerance that kept his status to that of a respected phenomenon. Discriminating admirers bought his pictures, but no Breughelesque style emerged. Titian, for all his imaginative daring, had no temperamental difficulty in pleasing the chiefly rich and powerful patrons of his portraits, religious works and mythological scenes. In his *Diana and Actaeon* of 1559 female nudes came alive as never before in European art: warm, breathing, palpable, discovered as patiently by light, colour and brushstrokes as they were suddenly revealed to the startled Actaeon. Every realistic care has gone into the painting of water, trees, sky, the pillar with its foreboding trophy of a stag's skull, yet the air is heavy with enchantment. The story was a familiar one, told over and over again in paint: the virgin goddess of the hunt is stumbled upon while bathing by a human hunter. To punish him for having seen her nakedness she sets his own hounds on him, and they kill him. Titian's scene is so rich in colour, from the red robe hung up to dry on the left to the purple velvet on which Diana sits and the striped pink and white dress slipping from her black servant's shoulder, and so enduring in its overall convincingness, that the stab of tragedy Titian introduces is shockingly unexpected. It is achieved by Diana's abrupt gesture, dramatically at odds with previous representations of the tale. In the moment of Actaeon's sudden appearance, a time too short for the woman drying her mistress's leg to realize what is happening, Diana snatches up a cloth not to conceal, with a human's modesty, her crotch or her breasts, but the crescent emblem of her divinity on her head. She lets a man see what men want to see, and dooms him for it.

This painting, as was the most dashingly splendid of all evocations of *The Rape of Europa*, was done for Philip II and sent to Spain. Yet in spite of his international fame, and the number of assistants who helped him turn out copies and variants of his works for clients who could not gain access to his full-time commitment, Titian did not introduce the Titianesque. This, as with Breughel, was not because his technique was inimitable. He exploited, it is true, the oil medium's

Titian, *Diana and Actaeon*, *c*.1559 (National Gallery, Edinburgh)

ability to be piled up and manipulated. An observer of his late work
recorded that

> the final stage of his last retouching involved his moderating here and
> there the brightest highlights by rubbing them with his fingers, reduc-
> ing the contrast with the middle tones and harmonizing one tone with
> another; at other times, using his finger he would place a dark stroke in
> a corner to strengthen it, or a smear of bright red, almost like a drop of
> blood, which would enliven some subtle refinement; and so he would
> proceed, bringing his living figures to a state of perfection. And as Palma
> [Giovane] himself informed me, it is true to say that in the last stages
> he painted more with his fingers than his brushes.[55]

But this, if not the exaggeration of an enthusiast, did not apply to
most of the finest of his works. Titian's way of painting followed an
imaginative route that others, whether in Italy or abroad, admired but
did not feel moved to follow. His works were turned to often; by

Rubens, for instance, later by Rembrandt. But there was no Titianesque movement, no *Tizianisti* as there came to be *Caravaggisti*.

Caravaggio's *The Supper at Emmaus* suggests, economically and powerfully, the nature of the fourth transfiguring style. The five disciples who, while walking to the village of Emmaus, came upon Jesus after he had risen from his tomb and invited the apparent stranger to eat with them there, only recognized him as Christ when 'he took bread and blessed it.' Then 'their eyes were opened and they knew him.' While the innkeeper follows Christ's words without sensing their significance, the disciple on the left hunches spontaneously forward, the other flings his arms wide apart. With this gesture he not only supports St Luke's narrative while reaching for the spectator's attention but precisely measures the depth into which Caravaggio has compressed the episode. In the same way, the contrast between the delicate hovering of Christ's right hand over the bread and the out-thrust right

Caravaggio, *Supper in Emmaus*, *c.* 1602 (National Gallery, London)

hand which tells of its sacramental significance, has both a rhetorical and a technical purpose. The artfully angled light illuminates details of intense realism: the tear at the crouching disciple's elbow, the sticking-up legs of the chicken, the basket of fruit overlapping the tablecloth, the anachronistic pilgrim's cockleshell on the jerkin of the disciple on the right. Dramatic contrasts of light and shade; intense but never eccentric or modish colour; no hesitation in using models from street or tavern; a driving belief in the liberation of spiritual truth through realistic means: these, allied to a superb command of every device to which an artist might wish to have recourse, led to his work becoming an object of emulative fascination to other painters. By the 1620s there were *Caravaggisti* in much of western Europe. Some, like the Spaniard Juan Bautista Maino, were scarcely more than agreeable copyists, others, notably the Frenchman Moise Le Valentin, were led towards personal genius by their innate sympathy with Caravaggio's approach and its effects.

The 'model' styles both led and released. They released a reappraisal of the relationship between the activity of making works of art and an interpretation of the world of human experience and natural facts. Though the demand grew for routinely recognizable portraits and land-scapes and attractive female bodies and illustrations of how machines worked, the search for a creative form of realism did not merely involve learning how to copy. Artists earned their repute by offering patrons what they were prepared to accept, but the initiative lay with them. It was they who prepared the way for the northerner Rubens (who caught what he wanted from Raphael and Titian) and the Spaniard Velázquez (who turned both to Caravaggio and to Flemish neo-realists like Aertsen) in the 1620s and 1630s to make other changes in appearances. Meanwhile, they had made their Renaissance age appear more real to posterity than the equally alive one that had preceded it. And Manner-ism, whose transplants from Italy thrived so well in the hot-beds of lingering Gothic fantasy elsewhere, continued to acknowledge the methods that made illusion seem real by perverting them. Referring to the mathematical basis of proportion and perspective, 'the artist's thinking', wrote Federico Zuccari in 1607, near the end of his long career as a painter in the Mannerist style, 'must be free as well as lucid, and his mind must be liberated and not restricted by a mechanical dependence on such rules'.[56]

A decade earlier, the Flemish Bartholomeus Spranger, working in Prague, had drawn on the preciousness and cool eroticism of Parmigi-

Bartholomaeus Spranger,
Triumph of Wisdom, 1595
(Kunsthistorisches
Museum, Vienna)

anino to produce a masterpiece of skilled rule-breaking, *The Triumph of Wisdom*. Minerva, goddess of war-like force intelligently employed, stands in smoothly provocative *contrapposto* holding a spindly lance that would have snapped if used. Offered the victor's crown and palm by winged boys, she treads with an elegant sandal on the throat of ignorant barbarism, a bound nude youth sprawling on his back. In the left foreground Bellona, goddess of war and savagery, leaves the scene. Opposite her, Clio, the muse of history, prepares to add another campaign to the record. Learning, represented by the astrolabe held up on the left, and the arts, indicated by the architect's dividers held up on the right, are free to carry on their pursuits again. The work is a tribute to the successes of Spranger's patron, the cultivated Emperor Rudolf II, against the Turks. The personages are taken from mythology. But here the painting's classicism stops. Nothing could be less like anything from the ancient world that remained to be seen or was recorded in a written description than this squeezed but indeterminate space, these vaguely related clusters of effetely beautiful faces or the short-skirted legs-apart pose of wisdom's goddess, whose breasts are so much more succulently offered to the spectator than through the classical device of the slipped chiton, the long robe fallen from one shoulder.

The influence of humanism on the changed appearance of the world as registered through the arts was, in spite of the pervasiveness of its appeal, by no means universal. Northern realism from Jan van Eyck to Hugo van der Goes and on to Aertsen owed nothing to it. Masaccio added to the narrative realism of Giotto the figural weight and volume sculptors were imitating from antique carvings, but there was no antique model for the reality of the space in which his figures stood or moved across, nor had the feeling behind his haunted Adam and anguished Eve any need for hints from the Roman past. Raphael worked in a Rome where classical statues were being unearthed and eagerly collected as the city grew. He worked for popes, Julius II and Leo X, whose courts were foci of humanistic studies. But his portraits of both owe nothing to the accumulating shelves of realistic Roman busts. Working from living models, looking at real faces and postures, refining from his master Perugino the meadows and vistas in which he placed his Madonnas: even when immersed in a classical subject like *The School of Athens* or *Galatea* it was his own eye and mind that measured space and his own instinct for form that determined the harmony of his compositions.

Obviously, with no classical paintings to look at, and with written descriptions of them open to interpretation, the painter was not as directly challenged by the evidence of antiquity as was the sculptor and architect. And for all the arts the notion of rebirth, with which Vasari so closely identified Raphael, was, after all, about giving new life to antiquity, not to reproducing it. Raphael's own swing in middle age to Mannerism indicates the freedom artists felt to invent their own aesthetic canons. Titian's mythologies followed classical stories but he painted them with the approach he carried forward from his master Giovanni Bellini and his youthful colleague Giorgione. No degree of pressure can make a humanistic label adhere to the work of Caravaggio. This is not to say that painters abstained from displaying a knowingness about antiquity. They might allude to and produce variants on known ancient sculptures and buildings, or aim at an overall *all' antica* effect.

Masaccio, *Adam and Eve*, detail from fresco
(Brancacci Chapel, Santa Maria del
Carmine, Florence)

But painting, as it turned from Gothic forms, was not exposed as was
sculpture to the hand-holds on new ones proffered by ancient statues
and reliefs. But even sculptors showed an impatience with a Gothic
style whose juice had run thin, and their rivalry with colleagues, their
impulse to carve and model by their own lights, were as important as
the models that challenged them and more stimulating than the antiquarian taste of humanistic patrons. Work by work, from the stricken
pathos of Donatello's wooden *Magdalen* of *c.*1453 and the wholesome

charm of Luca della Robbia's contemporary terracotta Madonnas, to the well-nigh abstract anatomy of Jacopo Sansovino's marble *Neptune* of *c.*1560 and the balletic lift of Adrien de Vries's bronze *Hercules, Nessus and Deianeira* of 1603 (for sculpture, too, had its Mannerist movement), sculptors made works that would have been looked at askance in the Roman forum.

We have seen that at the height of humanistic fervour in Italy the ruined buildings in that forum were cannibalized rather than protected or restored. Yet of all the arts, architecture was most closely identified with the revival of interest in classical antiquity, with the most obvious rout of the Gothic style, and with the most prestigious way of associating the owner of a palace and house or garden with the ancient way of life. The most eye-catching change in appearances was the classicizing of buildings.

The process began, naturally enough, among those who saw themselves most directly the Romans' successors. In *c.*1402 Filippo Brunelleschi and his fellow sculptor Donatello paid their first visit to Rome itself. It was a time calculated to make the city appeal to Brunelleschi's imagination. He had just lost to Lorenzo Ghiberti a competition for a set of bronze doors for the Florentine Baptistery, which was then believed to have been built in antiquity, notwithstanding its difference from any building that existed from that era. There was a wave of patriotic pride that Florence, as a republic founded before Rome became ruled by emperors, had held off the armies of the aggressive Duke of Milan, Giangaleazzo Visconti, represented in Florentine propaganda as a tyrant. And now that the popes, who had resided in Avignon from 1307 to 1377 because of Rome's lawlessness, had returned and gradually made the city safer, it was possible for private individuals to wander at will through the ruins of a civilization to which their own owed so much. Though Brunelleschi continued from time to time to work as a sculptor, what he saw there turned his imagination towards architecture.

What he and other designers of buildings who made study-visits to Rome learned was of little direct relevance to contemporary building practice. The use and purpose of the Roman forums were hopelessly obscured by decay and the strata of soil and rubbish deposited over centuries. The columned Roman temple was the symbolic antithesis of the Christian church; it also lacked the audience space required by a preaching ministry. When Pope Pius II in 1458 commissioned the construction of a new town on the plateau above his village birthplace Corsignano, the palaces reflected the classicizing features that were by then becoming popular, but the cathedral was firmly Gothic. When architects did turn to ancient models for churches, as from Leon Battista Alberti's San Francesco in Rimini of the early 1450s, it was to apply to façades a slice of the spiritually neutral Roman triumphal arch. Of the other ruins whose functions could be discerned, the house-over-shop building type of, for instance, Trajan's forum, because of its logical commercial and domestic function, had been so long in use in Italian cities that it did not have to be reinvented. For all their impressiveness the Colosseum and the Arena at Verona were irrelevant to an age without the state-sponsored public cult of gladiatorial and animal combats. Revered the ancient Romans may have been, but only with respect to the rural villa did modern Italians want to live like them. And the villa, as it developed from Lorenzo de' Medici's Poggio a Caiano of

Leon Battista Alberti, San Francesco, Rimini, early 1450s

Palladio, Villa Rotonda, Vicenza

the 1480s to the symmetrical Villa Rotonda with its four temple-front porticoes designed by Andrea Palladio in the 1550s, was the Tuscan or Lombard farmhouse classicized rather than a reconstruction of any actual ancient example.

What Brunelleschi and his successors learned as they measured and analysed the effects they admired in Roman buildings was partly a matter of engineering. Contemplating the great hemispherical dome of the Pantheon and looking up at the lofty expanses of coffered vaulting in the Baths of Caracalla, they had no wish to copy buildings for which there was no contemporary use, but worked out methods of covering large spaces without the need for the prominent external buttresses which were so characteristic of Gothic structural methods. Brunelleschi's solution to the problem of covering the gaping hole over the crossing of Florence's over-ambitious cathedral was a dome that did not look Roman; but it could hardly have been conceived without his identifying the problem as one Roman masons would have solved.

The second source of fascination was the way in which Roman architects had given variety and relief to surfaces by the use of vertical elements – columns, half-columns and pilasters, and to horizontal ones by using different types of masonry divided into tiers by entablatures and other strongly marked mouldings stretching right across the surface. As this visual vocabulary was mastered, it became apparent that, whether in intention or effect, it was far from abitrary, the relationships between the details contributing to a harmonious and dignified composition. It also became clear that the Romans had used their most obvious trademark, the different 'orders' of base, column and capital, in a logical manner, putting on the outside of the Colosseum, for instance, the more obviously weight-bearing orders, Tuscan and Doric, at the bottom, and the more open and fragile-looking Corinthian forms of capital in the upper tiers.

The speed with which this vocabulary was acquired and applied was due not just to the bias of humanist architectural patrons and the interpretative genius of Brunelleschi, but to the survival in Italy of buildings in the early medieval Romanesque style, which had carried forward elements from ancient practice, and the absence of Gothic buildings of the soaring, flamboyant confidence being built elsewhere in fifteenth-century Europe which might have challenged an aesthetic based on a return to Rome.

Save for details, Brunelleschi's pioneering and influential loggia of 1419–24 in front of the Hospital of the Innocents owed as much to his acquaintance with round-arched Romanesque cloisters as to what he had seen in Rome. Alberti's classical façade for San Francesco in Rimini was the less difficult to create for his being familiar with that of the *c.* 1100 San Miniato in Florence where, with the help of Vitruvius and his own experience, he worked out the ideas expressed in his treatise

Filippo Brunelleschi, Loggia of the Innocents, Florence

On the Art of Building of 1452. It was Vitruvius whose influence was paramount. His book *On Architecture*, written in the first century AD was the only work on the subject surviving from antiquity and therefore a compelling authority. It became known in a reasonably clear text from the early fifteenth century. Vitruvius helped enthusiasts for classical details to see how they used to give harmony and an expression of function to buildings of different types; religious, domestic, festive or defensive. And by providing such a rationale, he helped to rally anti-Gothic sentiment. 'Proportion', Vitruvius had written, 'consists in taking a fixed module . . . both for the parts of a building and for the whole, by which the method of symmetry is put into practice.' 'I shall define beauty', echoed Alberti, 'to be a harmony of all the parts . . . fitted together with such proportion and connection that nothing could be added, diminished or altered but for the worse.'[57] A hundred years later Vasari could look back with satisfaction on a *fait accompli*.

San Miniato al Monte, Florence

Leon Battista Alberti,
Palazzo Rucellai, Florence

Our Italian buildings, he wrote, have acquired 'the qualities of good rule, order, proportion, design and style'.[58]

Thanks again to the return of prosperity after the generations that recovered from the Black Death of 1348, Italian merchants, at a time when such principles were becoming accepted, were able to commission palaces which took advantage of them. Thanks, too, to a quelling of the faction fights between rival civic interests, windows could be larger, doorways more spacious: both offering decorative opportunities for builder-designers. As a result new palaces, first from the 1440s in Florence, then in Rome and Milan, and somewhat later, around 1500, in Venice, ceased to look Gothic. Windows and doors no longer had pointed but flat or semi-circular tops. Façades, instead of being blankly practical street fronts, acquired a more individual personality and invited aesthetic appraisal. As so many of their designers were themselves artists – Michelozzo (who planned the mid-fifteenth century Medici palace), Raphael, Michelangelo, Giulio Romano, Vasari and Bernardo Buontalenti were among them – the variations that were invented to compose a surface and to ring changes on the appearance of cornices, string-courses and window embrasures were legion. Ancient Roman architecture was already eclectic compared with the austerer Greek forms from which it was derived. When from the 1520s secular architecture went through its own Mannerist phase of fantasticated window and door surrounds and deliberate constructional illogicalities, Renaissance classicizing led to a further degree of eclecticism, leaving non-Italian designers free to follow or break the rules of proportion as it suited their native traditions and their patrons' taste.

In Italy there was a continuity of contact with the works of antiquity, a shared approach to their characteristics and a constant experimentation with them by architects in one city well aware of what was being built in another. The diverse Italian forms of classicism reached the rest of Europe in the form of fashionable hints not so much as how to build *all' antica* but how to allude to what had already become in Italian hands a variety of allusions to the classical past. In spite of the wide distribution from 1537 of illustrated handbooks to true classicism, like Sebastiano Serlio's *General Principles of Architecture in Concordance with the Teaching of Vitruvius*, it was Italianate rather than classical architecture that found lodgement within regional styles. Because of expense, climate and the different ways of living indoors that governed the exterior appearance of a building, architecture outside Italy was the most conservative of the arts, preferring the enlivening effect of a brooch of classical roundels or a necklace of classical statues in niches to a full change of national costume. Few non-Italian architects were as prepared to echo such examples of Italian practice in their own countries as Serlio's Burgundian château of Ancy-le-Franc, which he designed in c.1546 during his residence in France.

And not only were national styles resistant to outside influences; they were being actively developed in the sixteenth century by native architects of powerful individuality: Pierre Lescot and Philibert de l'Orme in France, Juan de Herrera in Spain, Robert Smythson in England. The tall, gabled merchant house of northern and central Europe yielded nothing but some occasional surface classical motifs to the flat-topped Roman-Italian model. It took an imported Italian work-force to prevent the design of the Italianate palace built in 1536–43 for the

Sebastiano Serlio, Château of Ancy-le-Franc

Duke of Bavaria-Landshut from relapsing into the habits traditionally favoured by local masons. And for architects and master-masons prepared to respond to influences outside the development of their own vernaculars there were, besides, handbooks of French and Flemish designs which competed with Italian ones; Smythson, for instance, drew on both.

It is in fact notable that the Italian building form that was adopted most eagerly and without major modification throughout Europe and wherever Europeans settled overseas, was the bastioned type of fortification. But the challenge from cannon was equal in all countries, local living habits were irrelevant, and methods of construction were straightforward and identical wherever old walls were modified or new ones built *alla moderna*. The new fortifications which transformed the appearance of towns' perimeter walls and turned tall strategic castles into squat, often star-shaped fortresses, used geometrical principles to establish the maximum fire-power from the cannon mounted on the bastions, whether to hit an advancing enemy force at a distance or to protect a neighbouring bastion from his advanced storming or mining parties. The trace, or outline, that determined the relationship of one bastion to another, and each part of the defensive system to its whole circumference, was an exercise in rationally worked out pro-portion – adjusted, naturally, to the lie of the land. In this process the military engineer was drawing on the mathematical bias that had enabled architects to analyse in the buildings of Rome the modules which Vitruvius had identified. Brunelleschi himself designed a bastion at Pisa. His intellectual successor Giuliano da Sangallo designed fortifi-cations as well as churches; so did Bramante, the first architect of the new St Peter's in Rome; so did Michelangelo, whose vestibule to the Laurentian Library in Florence was a landmark in architectural Manner-ism and who carried forward the work on St Peter's; so did the designer of churches and palaces Michele Sanmicheli; so did Buonta-lenti. This list of names reaching from the early fifteenth to the late sixteenth century could be extended. As it stands, it suggests the link between the necessarily mathematical base of fortification plans and the approach to domestic and ecclesiastical buildings. Without this there could not have occurred the most startling of Italian attacks on Euro-pean architectural tradition; the driving of Gothic from its own temples.

Gothic churches had become naturalized as the settings for prayer and liturgy in Italy since the early thirteenth century, and for all their harking back to some extent to features of the Romanesque, the prin-ciples introduced c.1421 by Brunelleschi in his design of San Lorenzo in Florence were as bold as they were novel. Interior spaces were not to be rushed up on shafts and dissipated in loftily arched roofs. They were to be articulated through rows of columns and pilasters ruled across with unbroken bands of moulding and, through the use of a single module, or measurement, that determined through a system of ratios the relationships between nave columns and aisle chapels, the breadth and height occupied by both. Space thus determined invited a calm calculation of its effect rather than a subjective empathy with it. And this sense of an enclosed theorem was strengthened by a flat, boxing-in ceiling to the nave. Decorative features, moreover, were to be reticent. Capitals were to be identical rather than eye-catchingly individualized by the story-telling fancy of the masons. Statuary was no longer to pour into porches, sprout from ribs and arches or gesticu-late from rooflines. The aim of the new canon of beauty was clarifi-cation and lucidity. Working on a much smaller scale in his design some ten years later for the Pazzi Chapel in the cloister of another Florentine church, Santa Croce, Brunelleschi was able to demonstrate the canon with an even more manifesto-like precision. Here, in an

Filippo Brunelleschi, San Lorenzo, Florence

extended cube under a round dome, structure became its own decoration, calling only for blue-ground terracotta roundels to echo the sky
seen through the dome's porthole windows.

Though there is no record that the Pazzi Chapel became for architects
what the Brancacci Chapel came to be for painters, Brunelleschi's
calmly calculated austerity, and the way in which it went to the heart
of what established the conceptual difference between the appearance
of classical and Gothic buildings (however unlike his constructions
were from those of ancient Rome) resonated on through the work of
Florentines who grew up with them like Giuliano da Sangallo and
Michelangelo. It spread – through the late fifteenth century work of
Mauro Coducci – into the last Italian city to remain loyal to Gothic
forms, Venice. In the greatest of that city's Renaissance churches, the
Redentore (begun in 1576), Palladio drew on his own researches into
the construction of the impressive and then still largely roofed baths
of 'Roman' Rome. But the spare and luminous space he created from
files of columns below and rounded voids and solids above echoed, if

Filippo Brunelleschi, Pazzi Chapel, Santa Croce, Florence

with a richer dignity, the intention of early Florentine anti-Gothic: to enlist mathematics in the service of worship. And while Brunelleschi concentrated on getting his interiors right (San Lorenzo still lacks a finished façade) and avoided direct reference to actual Roman monuments, other architects such as Alberti, for example, in Rimini or in his Sant' Andrea of 1470 in Mantua, put such classical references literally up front. Perched high on the pediment of the meticulously worked out but bravura temple arcade of the Redentore, the statue of Christ holding his cross cuts a wan, if not downright incongruous, figure. It was the existence of these two derivations from Rome, the cleanly rational inside, and the overtly classical façade, that separately or in combination enabled Italianate ecclesiastical architecture to modify, at times to transform, church building habits beyond the Alps.

CASH AND CULTURE

Admiring the carved choirstalls in the church of St Michael in 1520, Dürer noted that 'in Antwerp they spare no expense for such things because there is enough money.'[59] Nearly a century later, in 1617, Jan Breughel displayed in his *Allegory of Sight* a lavish inventory of what could be bought because it appealed to the eye, from the peacocks and

Palladio, The Redentore, Venice

fountain in the garden to the flowers in a vase indoors; from tapestry, rug, cabinet, dishes, medals, antique busts, candelabrum, to an astrolable and telescope made as much for admiration as use; from portraits and other paintings (including one of the most moving of all Titian's works, the *Allegory of Alfonso d'Avalos*), to chains and other goldsmiths' work. This assemblage of objects is not far different in spirit from the paintings of the 1560s by Joachim Beuckelaer with their slithery slopes of wet fish, serried hooks-full of game, kitchen tables loaded with joints of meat, and toppingly piled vegetable stalls, all thrust at the spectator with such succulent surface verve as to over-satisfy the appetite rather than awaken any prickle of guilt. Revisiting Italy in 1590 a traveller noted, 'I am now in Rome but I cannot recognize the place. Everything appears new: the houses, the streets, the aqueducts, the obelisques and many other marvels.'[60] When Hardwick Hall in Derbyshire was completed in 1597 its lavish fenestration contained more glass than had ever been inserted in a secular building. By his death in 1598 Philip II had amassed over one thousand paintings in addition to the five hundred-odd that he had inherited. In 1600 the library of the French historian Jacques-Auguste de Thou contained around six thousand books. These

Jan Breughel, *Allegory of Sight*, 1617 (Museo del Prado, Madrid)

Joachim Beuckelaer, *Fish Market*, 1560s (Royal Museum of Fine Arts, Antwerp)

random examples indicate that for those with purchasing power this was an age of 'more'.

They span a period when there was more money in more hands to be spent on things shaped by mind and hand for the pleasure of a reasonably discriminating body of purchasers, things surplus to basic requirements: comforts, conveniences, luxuries and beguiling ostentations that enhanced the sense of the purchaser's well-being – physical, social, intellectual. Nothing changed so far as the basic money relationship between society and its culture was concerned. Cash from monastic rents and endowments had supported the scriptoria which produced illuminated manuscripts. Cathedrals had risen from a base of wages. Altarpiece and reliquary, brooch, tapestry and horse trapping: whatever consumed time and materials had had to be paid for. The role of the personal or institutional patron, with a large-scale or long-term commitment to a project, or to the fostering of a valued personal talent, broadened, but in essence it remained what it had been in the Europe of the middle ages. The greatest change that came with the Renaissance was the increased number of simple customers: those who shopped for culture, paying as they went. In spite of booms and bankruptcies, even of long, punishing wars, the European market for cultural artefacts became and remained more extensive than in previous centuries. The purchasing of non-essential objects new to a household's traditional shopping-list, or which replaced those that came to seem outmoded by changes in technique and style, became a more habitual aspect of amenity, status and informed acquisitiveness. More cash, more wares – the equation itself is obvious enough. But it has little cultural significance save in the context of the nature and quality of what producers were moved to make and what customers were conditioned to accept.

The Renaissance popularizing of classical myth broadened the market for paintings and statues and cupboard friezes of Minerva, Mars and Venus, the Herculean Labours, Cupids and Amazons, Bacchus and Pan. And with such imagery coming to be the staple of secular public festivals, humanism wafted a flavour that could almost unconsciously be absorbed by non-learned spectators – or read about by others, in printed descriptions of them which explained the arcane references. With mythological imagery painted on ceilings, carved into fireplaces, placed in garden vistas and paraded in masque and ballet, the leakage into the fine and decorative arts from humanistic scholarship was the more widespread for its coinciding with the general utilization by artists of their knack for creating an illusion of reality. Whereas a representation of Venus in the denatured guise of *Luxuria* or Concupiscence would have maintained a static market for moral abstractions, to obtain a Venus *toute entière* as Racine, inheriting a deluge of enticing images, was to put it, extended the impulse to buy something suggestively attractive.

Once Lucas Cranach had produced, in his *Venus Restraining Cupid* of 1509, the first frontally nude goddess in German art, he and his workshop were kept busy turning out variants of this archly provocative subject. Whereas changes in the appearance of works of art did not affect the demand for religious paintings, whose use was habitual and whose subjects readily identifiable from their context however unlife-like they were, the effects of realism caused a popular – and condemned – spread of lascivious imagery. Realism created a new demand for the record of real occasions: an actual, rather than a symbolic battle, a politically significant festivity, such as Henry VIII's celebration of amity with Francis I at the Field of the Cloth of Gold. It offered a fresh impetus to the decoration of house façades, from that of the soldiers and well-dressed men and women portrayed on

Lucas Cranach, *Venus restraining
Cupid*, 1509 (Hermitage
Museum, St Petersburg)

Maximilian I's 'Golden House' in Innsbruck and Giorgione's figurative
frescoes on the Fondaco dei Tedeschi in Venice, to the new streets built
to encourage settlement in Livorno; 'their houses', Peter Mundy wrote
in 1617, 'painted without-side in Stories, Landskipps, etc., with various
coulors, makeing a verie delightfull shewe'.[61] It notably extended the
market for prints, whether deliberate connoisseur's pieces, such as the
engravings for each of which Lucas van Leyden expected to get a gold

Lucas van Leyden, *Self-Portrait*
(Herzog Anton Ulrich
Museum, Braunschweig)

florin, or the crude propaganda of the 'fowle picture' of Queen Elizabeth reported by an English agent as being circulated in Paris, 'she
beinge on horsback . . . with her right hand pullynge upp her clothes
shewing her hindpartes'.[62]

The aspect of art for which a realistic aesthetic caused the most
general extension of demand was, however, the portrait. Now whole
groups could be as accurately commemorated as individuals: a patron's
friends witnessing the Adoration, the members of a Venetian magis-
tracy or the officers of a Netherlands militia guild. During the fifteenth
century the portrait had come to be played upon by a number of
influences; the Roman coin and bust, the technique of taking wax masks
from the life, the experimentation of artists studying themselves for
self-portraits which necessitated, as they glanced into a mirror, their
breaking from the earlier, static models of full face or pure profile.

Portraiture came to withstand a careful scrutiny. In 1498 Isabella
d'Este wrote to Cecilia Gallerani, a Milanese noblewoman, now married but formerly a mistress of Duke Lodovico Sforza of Milan: 'today

we happened to be looking at certain fine portraits by the hand of
Giovanni Bellini and we came to discuss the works of Leonardo . . .
Remembering that Leonardo has painted your portrait' – the *Lady with
the Ermine* now in Cracow – 'we ask if you would be good enough to
send us your portrait by this messenger so that we may be able not
only to compare the works of the two artists but also to have the
pleasure of seeing your face again.'[63]

Cecilia's reluctant agreement is also revealing. She hesitated because
in the intervening few years her appearance had slightly changed from
the record Leonardo had made of her.

There were few fifteenth-century Venetian portraits, but in the sixteenth century Vasari noted that 'it became customary in that city that
every man of any note should have his portrait painted either by Giovanni [Bellini] or by some other,' and that 'in all the houses of Venice
are many portraits.'[64] More revealing still is a comment by Pietro

Leonardo da Vinci, *The
Lady with the Ermine*, c.1490
(Czartoryski Museum,
Cracow)

Aretino that 'it is the disgrace of our age that it tolerates the painted portraits even of tailors and butchers.'[65] And, indeed, in *c.* 1530 a goldsmith persuaded Lorenzo Lotto to paint him, in one work, not only full face but in left and right profile. Whether in the traffic in portraits of prospective princely wives or husbands or in the exchange of miniatures that spread from the 1520s and joined medals as gifts and mementoes, the wish for a true likeness became more marked. Sitters or their friends came to want, moreover, portraits that revealed not just features but temperament. There was more interest in a transient expression (Mona Lisa could not smile all day), on the spontaneity that a drawing could give, or, notably in France, the effect of a play of thought or mood on a face that chalk or crayon revealed. And the increasingly popular family group broadened the scope of fifteenth-century man and wife portraits, which had commonly shown them in separate paintings. These came to celebrate a relationship rather than commemorate a nuptial contract.

The availability of works of art that gave pleasure because of their realism coincided with a taste for domestic comfort and the building of houses which contained more rooms. Leon Battista Alberti's *On the Art of Building* of 1452 noted the change. 'The husband and wife', he wrote, 'must have separate bedrooms, not only to ensure that the husband be not disturbed by his wife, when she is about to give birth or is ill, but also to allow them, even in summer, an uninterrupted night's sleep whenever they wish. Each room should have its own door, and in addition a common side door, to enable them to seek each other's company unnoticed. Off the wife's bedroom should be a dressing room, and off the husband's a library.'[66] The search for privacy led increasingly to the separation of living from entertaining spaces and the addition of such comforts as separate summer and winter bedrooms and long galleries for taking exercise indoors. Already established in Italy by 1500, this wish to extend the number of rooms appeared in England and France from the mid-sixteenth century, both in the building of new houses and the refashioning of old ones. And the prosperity which encouraged the liking for domestic privacy allowed for their furnishing.

There was an unprecedented demand for desks, tables, sideboards, sets of hanging shelves and cupboards, all suited to the housing and display of new possessions. The lofty medieval great hall was felt, as Leonardo put it, to give 'an impression of melancholy', and without it, it was possible to add a mezzanine, a floor within the same space.[67]

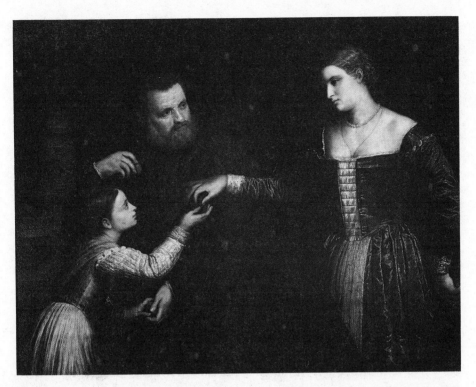

Paris Bordone, *Family Group*, *c.*1547 (Chatsworth, Trustees of the Chatsworth Settlement)

Larger fireplaces and bigger windows, with clear glass replacing semi-opaque oiled paper, made for lighter rooms in which paintings and tapestries could be properly appreciated.

Some families, even rich and noble ones, continued to live austerely; overall, however, the social pressure to use surplus money to furnish and embellish was an infectious part of the age of 'more'. At its extremes, superfluity was literal: an especially fine table called for a protective carpet and that in turn for a protective cover of cloth. Alongside the commissioning of important individual works of art, the workshops of painters, sculptors, goldsmiths and cabinet-makers turned out speculative products for which they could anticipate a purchaser with reasonable confidence. From the mid-sixteenth century, inventories of house contents made for valuation purposes reveal a clutter compared with the spareness of earlier rooms. Quite typical of the eclecticism that was becoming commonplace was the juxtaposition, in an Antwerp inventory of 1552, of 'A picture in oil showing our dear Lord carrying the Cross' with 'An alabaster relief of Venus and Cupid'. Italian inventories show that the plea of the Florentine sculptors' guild in their carnival song did not go unheeded: 'Who wants some elegant little statue for their delight? You can put it above your head or on a little stand. Our figures make every room look good.'[68]

In the fifteenth century it was chiefly politically important merchants, whose palace-houses stood cheek-by-jowl with the silversmiths, cabinet-makers and painters whose wares they dealt in as well as bought, who influenced the princes and ambassadors they entertained. Thereafter it came to be princely spending patterns that carried a seal of approval in the eyes of the inflating number who attended courts and imitated the taste of rulers. Thus Elizabethan nobles vied in providing the Queen on her progresses about the country with the Italianized architecture, the Frenchified gardens, the Flemish tapestries and portraits with which she was familiar at Hampton Court. Intermarriage between merchants and aristocratic families needing an infusion of ready money; social promotions of members of the legally or financially accomplished urban class; in these ways luxurious modes of living affected town-bred men and women. 'A London alderman might be too proud to marry a daughter outside his guildmaster circle, but not wish to be embarrassed by his lack of silver-gilt table furnishings, wall-hangings of stamped leather or tapestry and portraits when entertaining a courtier. The Lithuanian noble may have scorned to replace his wooden manor house with a stone palace, but he bought the carpets, glassware and paintings that his agents told him were *de rigueur* in the Artushus, the merchants' club in cosmopolitan Danzig. The process of discriminating accumulation was helped by the relative openness of merchants' art collections and those of the great princely ones which were made available to visitors.

It was probably access to the Spanish royal collections, which contained works by Rogier van der Weyden and Bosch alongside those of Jacopo Bassano and Titian, that permitted Francisco de Quevedo, who knew the court at Madrid well, to expect the readers of *The Swindler* to grasp what his narrator meant when he said of a company of beggars getting ready to wring public sympathy, that 'even Bosch's twisted postures can't compare with what I saw.'[69]

Until the 1530s in Protestant countries, and continuing thereafter in Catholic ones, as important as the diffusion from above of the fashion for buying works of art was the persistence of a more traditional pattern: for individuals, families or guilds had presented to churches and were used to seeing there works of art at all levels from great altarpieces to the most modest of *ex votos*. Even when working on religious commissions, the artist's freedom to express a personal style in painting or carving within conventional subject matter had been little hampered by a customer's conservatism or public disapproval; Vasari's account of the stylistic changes between 1300 and 1550 in Italy would hold good if every secular work he mentions were to be ignored. It was with an eye used to the variety of styles and periods represented in what amounted to ecclesiastically approved collections that the new generations of customers went shopping.

It is tempting to wonder about the role of women in the purchasing extravaganza of the Renaissance. The outstanding case of Isabella d'Este's purchase of paintings was also quite exceptional. She was the daughter of a prince, Duke Ercole I of Ferrara, who was himself an informed patron of artists, and the wife of another, the Marquis Gianfrancesco Gonzaga of Mantua, who left the government of the court and the state in her hands during his prolonged absences as a soldier. Even so, all her known purchases were restricted to her own private apartments in the palace-castle of Mantua, and not to her husband's rooms or those used for public occasions.

When the patrician Alberti, thoroughly immersed as practitioner and theorist in the world of painting and sculpture, wrote of household management in the 1430s, he had made it clear that the wife's role was restricted to the day-to-day running of family life, the supervision of servants and foodstores, the serving of meals. Objects of value were the husband's province. While the man went out and about, chaffering and making deals and extending his acquaintance, the woman's part was to remain as the fulcrum of orderliness at home. During the rest of the fifteenth and throughout the sixteenth centuries there were both real and theoretical changes to the relative positions of married men and women. In the 1560s the important Bohemian mint at Kutná Hora was run by Susanne Erker as 'manager-mistress'. But by then opportunities for women to run businesses on their own or with their husbands had become rarer. Women continued to run the ferries across the Rhône at Lyon, worked all over Europe in markets and shops, but as in both northern and southern Europe guild membership progressively came to be withheld from women, their earning power and freedom of action declined within the sort of households where nonessentials were bought. Women of the purchasing classes came to be restricted to domestic duties in the home and to the management of charitable organizations, such as hospices and almshouses, on a voluntary basis. There was, then, little challenge to Alberti's views. Published in Latin in 1529 and translated in the course of the century into Spanish, English, French, German, Italian and Dutch, the *Education of the Christian Woman* by the Spanish humanist Juan Luis Vives also emphasized that a woman's role should be restricted to the home and not overlap with that of men. In 1589 *The Common Welth of England* by Sir Thomas Smith, a twice-married man who had painted and sculpted in his youth and was interested in domestic architecture, took the same line: women were 'those whom nature hath made to keepe home and to nourish their familie and children, and not to meddle with affairs abroade.'[70]

Meanwhile, Protestantism was exalting the married state as the ideal environment for godly living: if Luther explained the width of women's hips as a sign of their being destined to home and childbirth this was simply part of his revulsion from the unnatural celibacy of monks and nuns. And Catholic teaching, too, came to emphasize the dignity of the married state for those for whom celibacy was not manifestly a gift of God. The monkish preoccupation with the unpleasantness of women's bodily functions died away, but sexual prejudice did not disappear. An early sixteenth-century seat in the Hanseatic town hall of Reval in Estonia reminded its merchant members with vivid carvings of the medieval themes of how the wise Aristotle had crawled on all fours while his paramour rode him in triumph, and how Delilah had ruined the besotted Samson at the height of his powers with her gelding scissors. The Polish adaptor of Castiglione's *The Courtier* in 1566 explained that he had cut out the female characters in the dialogues because his readers would not credit their participation in such a cultivated debate. When the great Danish astronomer Tycho Brahe died in 1601 at Prague, Europe's most cultivated court, his funeral eulogist praised him for 'keeping his sons to their studies and his daughters to spinning and sewing'.[71]

Yet these sentiments count for little against the abundant evidence that more women were gaining an education at home through printed books, and that of the incidence of love and trust within marriage which was probably little influenced by economic or ideological change. It was well before the Reformation idealization of marriage that the German Ludwig von Diesbach wrote on his wife's death that 'I would give God Almighty a hand and a foot from my body if he would let me have my wife back in joy and sorrow until we both grow old.'[72] To give but one more example: Queen Mary of Bohemia constantly wore a jewel found on the body of her husband Lewis II after his death in battle against the Turks in 1529. She explained its significance to her in her will. 'Since the death of my husband, the King, I have worn on myself a golden heart which he had worn to the end of his life. I hereby order that this heart, along with the small chain on which it hangs, be melted down and distributed among the poor. It was the companion of two persons who were never separated in life from each other in body and inclination until their death, and therefore let it be annihilated and let it change its form as have the bodies of those who loved one another.'[73]

It is, then, only reasonable to assume that women, whether real, as in the amused and alert *Woman of the Hofer Family* of *c.* 1470, or the Olivia imagined by Shakespeare in *Twelfth Night*, played a part in the furnishing of the homes in which they spent their lives. Their taste for fashion and quality in clothes was the despair of moralists, and we have seen the merchant's wife Magdalena Paumgartner's plea to her husband, when he was negotiating for cloth in Italy, to forgive her 'because I try to wheedle something out of you in every letter'.[74] Tycho Brahe's girls might have been sentenced to sewing, but books on embroidery, like that of Giovanandrea Vavasori of *c.*1545, discussed furnishings as well as clothes. If even a fairly modest Venetian court-esan, Julia Lombardo, could furnish her house in the 1530s with can-opied beds, mirrors, chests, brass fire-dogs, small sculptures, porcelain, majolica and glass and paintings both profane and religious, it is unlikely that 'good' housewives showed less interest in their homes. Even negative opinions point in this direction. Be careful, Ariosto warned a friend, not to marry above your station or your wife will bring luxurious habits that will ruin you. Women's greed, the Duke of Northumberland warned his son in 1609, was such that you must 'never suffer your wife to have power'; keep her to instructing the servants, caring for the linen and bringing up children: these should be her occupations except 'when great personages visit, to sit at the end of a table and carve handsomely'.[75] More representative of the averagely prosperous urban home was the account given of his parents' way of dealing with their mutual competitiveness in their Cologne home by Hermann von Weinsberg. His father would say, 'Wife, let's come to an arrangement; one week you rule over the house and hold authority and the next week I will rule.'[76]

Whether decided on by the husband alone or with his wife the cost of fine and decorative art objects, based on time, materials, transport,

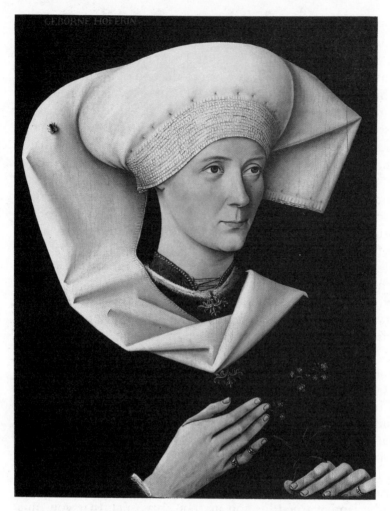

Anon., *Woman of the Hofer Family*, c.1470 (National Gallery, London)

the fame of the maker and the generosity or urgency of the person giving the order, is difficult to generalize about; even when records of prices have survived it is not easy to relate them to income or to other living costs. Two comparisons are at least suggestive. When Lorenzo de' Medici's possessions were valued after his death, a portrait by Pollai-uolo was assessed at four florins, an embroidered wool bed canopy at sixty; he had paid one hundred for an Arab horse. In 1573 Sir Francis Willoughby paid forty-six shillings and four pence for a silver box to contain sugar and thirty shillings for a pair of portraits of himself and his wife by a painter, George Gower, of sufficient renown to become Serjeant Painter to Queen Elizabeth. It can be fairly safely said that as far as the fine arts were concerned, prices did not move ahead of inflation, and that those who prospered kept ahead of them, and were able to maintain the impetus of 'more'. In real terms, for instance, the four hundred ducats Caravaggio received in 1607 for his altarpiece *The Acts of Mercy* (a high price for the day) was similar to the one hundred and ninety florins Fra Angelico was offered for an altarpiece, a more complex structure, in 1433. Prices do not contradict Fernand Braudel's conclusion that by the middle of the sixteenth century, culture had become a major industry.[77] He wrote of Italy, but this holds good for Europe as a whole.

Music, too, was caught up in the culture of 'more'. The sixteenth-century emphasis on harmonic rather than contrapuntal composition, and on dramatic sensuous effect, led to the enlargement of choirs and orchestras. Town bands became more numerous and more skilled, no longer simply fulfilling their traditional role of enlivening civic processions and welcoming important dignitaries, but giving public concerts which drew on a broadening repertory of scores. Humanistic interest in the sort of accompaniment that had heightened the effect of verse among the Greeks – evidenced by Nicola Vicentino's *Ancient Music Accommodated to Modern Practice* of 1555 and *Dialogue Concerning Ancient and Modern Music* of 1581 by Galileo's father Vincenzo – encouraged the idea that any occasion that might call for words, a wedding, a treaty, the birthday of a ruler or a lover, was also an occasion for a set of verses and a musical composition to enhance them. There was an outpouring of settings for single voice songs and for the new Italian musical form, the madrigal (not only an entertainment but a laboratory for compositional experiment).

More than ever before, music, and music that had to be bought and learned, became part of the texture of festival and ceremony, worship and leisure; that one of the figures in the 1533 group portrait by Cornelis Anthonicz of members of the Amsterdam crossbow militia holds a score, for instance, shows that this was no traditional guildsman's drinking song. All these developments, and the stimulus given to their diffusion as they became absorbed within the flux of fashion, involved expenditure. Even though home music remained an amateur enthusiasm, alertness to change increased the consumption of scores and there was a steady demand for instruments that were beautiful as well as serviceable, such as elaborately painted keyboard cases. With the larger numbers of salaried singers and instrumentalists employed by towns, courts and cathedrals, the cost of music-making increased to an extent that cannot be usefully quantified but which certainly rose markedly between the mid-fifteenth and the early seventeenth centuries.

It was, however, books that were the most pervasive cultural wares. The broadened literacy of the age owed much to the cash available to produce, market and buy them. Between the introduction in the mid-fifteenth century of Johannes Gutenberg's pioneer press and the beginning of the sixteenth century something like 28,000 editions had been produced. A newly extensive middle class readership was identified and aimed at. 'Beside the raskall multitude and the learned sages', the English translator of Cicero's *Tusculan Disputations* pointed out, 'there is a meane sort of men: which, although they be not learned, yet, by the quickness of their wits, can conceive al such poyntes of arte as nature could give.'[78] In peak years nearly 1,000 different titles were being issued annually in France before 1600 and by 1611 Thomas Coryat was complaining that 'methinks we want rather readers for bookes than bookes for readers.'[79]

More revealing than de Thou's exceptional collection of books is the earlier and smaller library of six hundred left on his death in 1528 by Georg von Frundsberg, not a scholar at all, but a busy and pugnacious professional soldier. It included chivalrous romances, tournament books and travel accounts, but also medical, legal, and theological works and the most familiar classical texts. Revealing, too, of the audience for books who had more interest than time or stamina, was the number of epitomes and cribs that purported to give all you needed to know in boiled-down form. De Thou's detailed *History of His Own Times* ran to many volumes, emerging at intervals from 1604; a decade earlier, Mathias Quadt had written a one-volume digest of the history of the whole world prefaced with a reassuring word to the reader:

> You need not any longer now
> Peruse great tomes with furrowed brow;
> You save yourselves much strain, and may
> Employ your time another way.[80]

And book prices, though soaring for finely printed or heavily illustrated ones, permitted an occasional purchase for those who had little money to spare: in the 1530s in France a twenty-four-page pamphlet cost as

Cornelis Anthonicz, *Members of the Amsterdam Company of Crossbowmen*, 1533 (Historical Museum, Amsterdam)

much as a loaf of low quality bread, a New Testament a labourer's daily wage. In conjunction with the press, reading or being read to became for the first time a popular cultural pleasure alongside talk and music.

Printing also moved more men and women to write, and to write with care: a deeper literacy led to a more alert literariness. Thanks to the availability of printed books the writer received a wider range of imaginative stimuli and was made more aware than hitherto of the contribution by others to the genre to which he or she was attracted. While Petrarch and Chaucer and François Villon remained revered exemplars for authors in Italy, England and France, and Virgil, Tacitus and Cicero universal models, the desire to find a personal literary voice and let it be heard acquired a potent stimulus. And amidst the verbal chatter that accumulated in the alleyways of publication, such voices sounded in greater number: the promise of a wider audience tempted closet writers into the open. It was this that moved the French poet Louise Labé to exhort women in the introduction to her *Works* in 1555 to make their mark on the age by writing. In this way, she claimed, they would not be lost to the historically featureless procession of performers of household tasks and wearers of jewels, but achieve a personal impress: 'the honour that knowledge will give us will be entirely ours, and it will not be taken from us by the thief's skill . . . or by the passage of time.'[81]

The lure of the wider audience offered, however, no automatic appeal to some of the most deeply committed of writers. Both Machiavelli's *Prince* and his *Discourses on Livy* circulated as manuscripts before they were printed after his death. Guicciardini lavished his literary care on the successive reshapings of the *Ricordi*, meditations engendered by his political career, but he was content with the narrow audience of his own family and kind. Neither of the most original autobiographies of the age, Benvenuto Cellini's and Girolamo Cardano's, was published in the author's lifetime. Spenser's publication of *The Faerie Queene* was as much in the spirit of the presentation copy of a manuscript to a patron as in that of a bid for wide acclaim. Authors were not paid a royalty, and often no fee; any appreciable profit came, as Erasmus was quick to realize, from glowing dedications which might bring a cash reward or some assistance with a career from the recipient. In 1586 Emanuel van Meteren wrote to his cousin Ortelius about what he might expect from the publication of his recently completed *Belgian History*. Ortelius replied that 'as far as my experience goes, authors seldom obtain money from their books, but usually receive a few printed copies.' This is all the payment he received himself, he went on, from Christopher Plantin, and he even knew other authors published by the Plantin Press, who 'seeing that their work was printed elegantly, presented him with a silver dish'.[82] And with exceptions like Tasso, creative writers seldom found patrons to support them. Cervantes was only one author of genius who died poor. The press provided an income for editors, translators and sometimes pot-boiler writers, but thoughtfully creative authors were no freer than their predecessors had been from a dependence on an income from other sources. The capital on which Shakespeare retired to Stratford as a comfortable property owner owed nothing to the patchy publication of his individual plays, save perhaps to the publicity they gave to the company he wrote for and part owned.

Drama itself had always relied more than any other literary form on money. The enormously popular passion enactments and miracle cycles of the later middle ages, sometimes lasting as much as a week or more, played all over Europe in open fields or streets and market squares to audiences of up to twenty thousand. Part drama, part religious ceremony (attendance at some plays qualified the spectator to an indulgence, a remission of years in purgatory similar to those available at pilgrimage churches) and part fair, the cost of their sets, costumes, instrumentalists and singers, and the policing of crowds and refreshment stalls, had been provided by the guilds whose members took part and by the sponsoring civic and ecclesiastical authorities. The authors or, rather, the revisers of the traditional texts, were unpaid. From the later fifteenth century these theatrical leviathans became an endangered species. Something of their populist rough-and-readiness began to suffer: in York from 1476 the actors had to attend auditions to ensure that their words would be clearly heard. The demand grew for more elaborate stages and more telling effects: in 1501 in Mons the effigies switched at the last moment into the place of actors representing martyrs sentenced to be burned were stuffed with animals' bones and entrails to give the smoke the stench of reality. These were moves pointing to performances to smaller audiences in enclosed spaces, where, in addition, admission charges could be imposed. For rising costs, as well as an increasing distrust of large crowds and a change towards a less crude religious sentiment, meant that the great days of subsidized popular religious drama were over by the 1530s. Thirty years later, indeed, it had been banned as controversial and provocative throughout France, and elsewhere had been confined to merely local festival occasions.

From the 1420s, however, morality plays, religious in intention, but enacting conflicts between vices and virtues rather than bringing to life stories from the Bible and the lives of saints, had also become popular. Original scripts were written, at times by authors of note; Lorenzo de' Medici composed one. Some, as in his case, were performed by religious confraternities which bore the cost. Others were toured by small semi-professional groups who expected a contribution from the onlookers whether they performed in a church, an inn yard or a nobleman's house. It was from these groups, and those who toured with more miscellaneous entertainments – playlets and recitations, dances and juggling – that the full-time acting companies of the Renaissance developed. It is true that as passion and miracle plays withered, other centrally subsidized theatrical experiences came to flourish: civic processions with actors declaiming verses in praise of a new mayor or visiting dignitary along the route, princely interludes and masques for members of a court. And individual institutions, Oxford colleges, French, Netherlandish and Italian convivial clubs, paid for the performances of secular plays, often written by their members. But while it was within these subsidized *ad hoc* performances that play-writing became more sophisticated and absorbed the influence of the classical drama, and while the halls they used emphasized the advantages, for players and audience, of enclosed formalized settings, it was the touring companies who took these lessons forward to the professional repertory companies and the purpose-built theatres for which Shakespeare, Lope de Vega and Alexandre Hardy wrote.

Such theatres, whose doors allowed admission to be charged, opened in London from 1576, in Madrid in the 1580s and began in Paris in 1599. An impresario put up the capital, shared the profits with the actors and hired bit-players when a large cast was called for. (Some companies took their name from a distinguished patron: not, however, to obtain financial backing but support in high places when the company ran into trouble with political censorship or magistrates who disapproved of the playhouses on moral grounds.) At the large commercial theatres in London (the Globe opened in 1599), with their covered tiers of galleries rising around an open space for standing room, one penny was charged in the arena, from two to six, according to the proximity of benches to the stage, for the galleries. In smaller, indoor, weatherproof theatres admission varied from six to thirty pence. When a penny was a day's wage for a skilled worker, the fact that London's theatres by 1605 could accommodate over eight thousand men and women at any one time points to drama's ability to retain an audience after the introduction of charges. Indeed, the anticipated audiences were larger than ever. The London commercial theatres were open daily except in Lent. Nor was there any serious restriction of the social range of audiences. In *c.*1618 the Mayor of Exeter sniffed that 'those who spend their money on plays are ordinarily very poor people.'[83] He was referring to travelling companies performing in inn yards on the pass-the-hat principle. But in 1609 the playwright Thomas Dekker had written of the London theatres that 'your stinkard has the same liberty to be there in his tobacco-fumes which your sweet courtier hath, and . . . your car-man [carter] and tinker . . . sits in judgement on the play's life and death.'[84] The preface to the posthumous first collected edition of Shakespeare's plays in 1623 was a tribute both to a more general literacy and to the range of the audience for plays; it was addressed 'to the great variety of readers, from the most able to him that can but spell'. Even though the gap between the really and the fairly and the breadline poor was widening in England as elsewhere in Europe, the conditions which supported the outburst of dramatic vigour and genius that above all constitutes England's Renaissance, owed much to the enabling function of cash.

There is little evidence for how much of this passed to the writers of plays themselves. Many, like Plantin's authors, wrote for pleasure and were glad if their work got an airing; none of the creators of Italian Renaissance comedy – Machiavelli, Ariosto, Bernardo Dovizi (Il Bibbiena), Aretino – wrote for a fee. Shakespeare could count on his share, as actor and playwright, of the money paid at the door, but his position was unusual. Judging from the number of plays some free-lance authors produced the profits from each must have been small. His contemporary Thomas Heywood claimed to have written or collaborated in two hundred and twenty between 1596 and 1633. By his death in 1635 Lope de Vega had written over five hundred plays which still survive out of a reputed output three times that size. His French contemporary, Alexandre Hardy, was claimed to be the author of at least seven hundred.

Something more is known about the earning power of artists. Though the records of their income are such a gappy maze of fees, subventions, salaries and perquisites and unquantified expenditures that no overall estimate can emerge, it is clear that at least some of those who were especially sought-after were better off than their medieval predecessors could have hoped to be. We have noticed the cash lures that tempted a few to live and work abroad. Dürer acted as his own publisher and shrewdly used trade fairs and agents to sell his prints from early in his career; he became able to buy one of the finest houses in Nuremberg. Lucas Cranach's house in Wittenberg was so grand that when the deposed King Christian II of Denmark visited the city with his train in 1523 the Council asked the painter to accommodate him. Titian was able to live in comfortably bohemian style by neglecting ill-paid commissions for more lucrative ones, by encouraging his literary friends to praise him in print, by focusing on Italian princely patrons and the Habsburg rulers, Charles V, Mary of Hungary (Charles's regent in the Netherlands) and Philip II, as well as by putting his assistants to turning out copies. Other artists' houses, Giulio Romano's in Mantua, Vasari's in Arezzo, the buildings and grounds Rubens bought in Antwerp in 1610 and started embellishing six years later: these were all the products of careers that were rare in their success, even rarer in the extent to which success was well managed. Perhaps the nearest to a more representative one that can be established, because of the fullness of the surviving accounts, is the trading experience of the superbly gifted, if eccentric Lorenzo Lotto. Born in Venice in 1480, he painted for noblemen and great churches. But his records also reveal the width of the markets for his works, especially for portraits, among individual friars and parish priests, merchants in a small way of business, even a number of artisans. He sent religious works to the trade fairs in Venice and Brescia where paintings were offered among other products, natural and manufactured. He sent them abroad, speculatively, with merchant friends to hawk on his behalf. In 1550 he organized a raffle in Ancona for forty-six uncommissioned paintings. He also exhibited, for sale, preliminary drawings for finished works for which he had already paid. He died in 1556 or 1557, still working, but depending on charity for his maintenance.[85]

What writers and artists earned is of intense autobiographical interest: it was to them and their dependants, it must be to us. But overall the interest is subsumed within the larger relationship of cash to quality. Capital investment in printing presses, theatres and workshop and studio space responded to demand and quickened productivity. Prosperity stimulated demand. Demand offered opportunity which attracted talent. But we must remember that there was no *necessary* connection between the economy and creativity, between money and genius. In the Florentine generations of Botticelli, Leonardo, Raphael, Michelangelo, Ficino, Pico della Mirandola and Machiavelli, nearby Genoa was as commercially active but produced no artist or thinker of note. The prosperity that built great country houses and filled the theatres left Elizabethan England a net importer of fine and decorative arts. Thanks to its monopoly of trade with the Spanish Americas, sixteenth-century Seville became the most prosperous of Spain's cities while artistically remaining deeply conservative; on the other hand, from the end of the century, the so-called Golden Age of Spanish art and literature (to which Cervantes and Lope contributed) coincided with the first issues of a copper coinage, the symptom of a specie-starved and slack economy. But overall, taking into account the greater purchasing power of Europeans in a period of lively commercial activity, social and educational change, and an intense concern with status and fashionableness, the power of money helps to explain the increased consumption that gave works of genius a better chance of being produced and appreciated than ever before.

The problem, indeed, is to imagine quantity alongside quality. Time has dealt far more kindly with art than with writing by destroying much of what was routine and second-rate. Yet there remain enough wooden portraits, gawky mythological subjects (the *Magnanimity of Alexander* in the Hermitage is a useful reminder of how poor Italian fifteenth-century painting could be) and clumsy sculptures to persuade us, if we can see past the charm that survival has given them, that Renaissance culture is not only to be assessed in terms of masterpieces. Vasari saw the distinction between quantity and quality clearly enough: 'one should not use the fineness and excellence of a single work to prove that everything was perfect.'[86]

CHAPTER VI

Transmissions

'TH'INTERTRAFFIQUE OF THE MINDE'

In 1492 the thirty-three year old chorographer, humanist scholar and first German poet laureate Konrad Celtis delivered his inaugural lecture at the recently founded University of Ingolstadt. Speaking to a youthful audience, he urged them to learn new things and think new thoughts, for they belonged not just to Germany but, as he said, to 'the commonwealth of letters'.[1]

By this he meant not the static internationalism of the common texts and syllabuses that had long been studied in European universities, but novel and personal attitudes to the process of learning and the forms of self-expression. The commonwealth was still a-building. Most of its representatives were Italians; he had encountered a number of them on a journey across the Alps. Others, university and school teachers or independent scholars and gifted amateurs, were Germans he had met in his travels across the Empire. There were also, outside his acquaintance, scholars in France, England and the Netherlands, who were becoming similarly attuned to the new learning. All were just beginning to be linked by personal contacts, correspondence, printed books and translations. Their fourteenth-century forebear had been Petrarch who, in disturbed times, kept in touch from one temporary eyrie after another with spirits he suspected of being akin to his own, in their wish, that is, to establish a real rather than a rote relationship with the authors of classical antiquity. Not long after Celtis's death in 1508 Erasmus was to establish himself through the international range of his correspondence and the distribution of his books as the informal president of a commonwealth increasingly sure of itself as a non-institutionalized support system for like minds. His pacifism and humane appeal to the universalist kindness of Christ's message were from the 1520s overtaken by more bitter political and religious rivalries.

Hans Baldung, *Erasmus shortly after his Death*, drawing (Offentliche Kunstsammlung, Basel)

In Catholic countries his works were proscribed. But the ground-swell that had come to encourage the idea of pan-European contacts proved irrepressible.

In 1574, four years after the first publication of his *Theatrum Orbis Terrarum*, Ortelius began to keep his 'Book of Friends' or autograph album. By 1596 one hundred and thirty-three men and one woman (the Flemish poet Caterine Heyns) had signed or written verses in it, either at his house in Antwerp or as he took it around on his travels. This number represents only a fraction of his correspondents, but by itself the album is a moving symbol of what the commonwealth had become. It is not the geographical range of the signatories – England, France, Spain, Portugal, Italy, Germany as well as the southern and northern Low Countries that is so remarkable; it is the variety of occupations and intellectual interests that they represent. There were lawyers, diplomats, statesmen, clerics both Protestant and Catholic, doctors, as well as classical scholars and antiquarians, poets and printers and wealthy merchants like Nicholas Rockox, the patron of Rubens and Van Dyck. The English contingent included the historian William Camden, the scholar-diplomat Thomas Smith (who sent a message and his coat of arms from Richmond) and the mathematician-astrologer John Dee. Other signatories represented calligraphy, numismatics, botany, cosmology, music and architecture. Artists who signed included Pirro Ligorio, Lucas de Heere and Hendrick Goltzius. Ortelius cheated in the case of Pieter Breughel, who had died in 1569, writing him in as homage to an old and cherished friendship. And there were, of course, fellow cartographers. Indeed, the idea of the album might have derived from a field trip of 1560 when Ortelius, Mercator and other friends together carved their names on a druidic standing stone near Poitiers.

Given the frequent campaigns in the Low Countries and the disrupted state of civil war France, it was remarkable how many foreigners turned up to sign during the pauses in hostilities. In 1591 Ortelius complained to his nephew that the reprint of the *Theatrum* had been held up because 'two years ago I ordered paper from France, but the roads are now so unsafe that it is difficult to get any merchandise thence.'[2] No wonder a German friend wrote in the album 'we shall never be done with misery until government is in the hands of philosophers.'[3] It was this sense of a philosophical new look at mankind, incorporating a range of interests that united intellectuals well beyond the confines of universities and war-like appeals to patriotism, that in 1603 prompted Samuel Daniel, greeting the publication in England (by that Italian living in London, John Florio) of the essays of Montaigne, to write:

> It being the proportion of a happy pen
> Not to be invassall'd to one monarchie,
> But dwell with all the better world of men
> Whose spirits all are of one communitie,
> Whom neither oceans, desarts, rockes nor sands
> Can keep from th'intertraffique of the minde . . .[4]

By then the traffic connected not only individuals and intellectual coteries in the West but led across western Europe to the Prague of the Emperor Rudolf which, until stifled by the noose of the Thirty Years War, remained the outstanding cosmopolitan centre of the world of learning and its alliance with the literary and figurative arts. So great was the expectation that members of the commonwealth would make their way there that in 1604 Scaliger wrote resignedly from Leiden to a friend: 'Last evening our [mutual friend] Mylius informed me that he had learned from your letter that I was dead in Prague. I do not suppose, my dear Welser, that I am dead somewhere else, so long as I am alive here.'[5]

The universities, however slow to accept changes in the content of their courses, remained the recruitment base for the commonwealth and the source of vocational qualification for the church, law and medicine, and they continued to cater for the sizeable minority who wanted to study abroad. In the early sixteenth century forty-one per cent of the students at Cracow were foreigners, including Scandinavians and Scots. Six thousand and sixty Germans graduated from Padua in the second half of the century. There was no university city, even those as small as Bourges and Saumur, whose streets did not resound with non-native voices. Parents accepted their sons' wish to leave home, making reciprocal arrangements with families abroad to save the cost of food and lodging. Even the London College of Physicians, set up expressly to give Englishmen an opportunity to study medicine without going to Padua or Montpellier, admitted foreign students from 1518 – for a double fee.

At the majority of universities, visiting teachers could be licensed to teach for degrees while supporting themselves on payments made directly to them by students. In this way fresh approaches to learning insinuated themselves alongside the traditional curricula. And especially in the first half of the sixteenth century, a certain number of non-nationals were given stipendiary positions. This was easiest in institutions that were new, like the body set up outside the framework of the Sorbonne by Francis I which became the Collège de France. Among its founding professors were two Italians, a Fleming and a Luxemburger wooed away from his chair at Cologne. But even in Oxford the statutes of 1516 of Corpus Christi College allowed the election to the Fellowship of a foreigner as long as he was clearly superior to native candidates, though this concession was made only to men whose origin was Greece or 'Italy beyond [i.e. south of] the Po'. At Cambridge some college statutes allowed their fellows periods of study leave; it was by taking advantage of such a clause that Fynes Moryson spent the years of 1590–5 on his indomitable travels throughout Europe.

It is probably true that for many, perhaps most, students the benefits of study away from home were blinkered by the more-or-less uniform core curricula and by voluntary isolation outside the latinate lecture hall, within the linguistic world of their 'own' nations, the self-governing institutions which regulated the social welfare and academic interests of minorities. The 'nations' could be broad. The 'northern' one at Padua included Germans, Hungarians, Poles, Bohemians, Netherlanders and English. They could be restrictive; the Scots had their own 'nation' at Montpellier, at Orleans the French themselves were divided among 'nations' serving those from Normandy, Picardy and students from the rest of the country. But for some at least the student life of shared lectures, joint contempt of townsmen, carousing and scrapping and excursions into the surrounding countryside, gave a clear impression that there was more to being abroad than mere escape from family ties and degree-chasing. When the young Polish poet Jan Kochanowsky was a student in Padua in the 1550s he was so fired by the French lecturer Antoine Muret's extra-curricular enthusiasm for Ronsard that he set off to Paris to meet him. John Kay (Caius), leaving Cambridge to study medicine at Padua, managed to get lodging in the house of the university's outstanding anatomist, the Fleming Andreas Vesalius. Thence, armed with introductions he moved on elsewhere in Italy and through Germany and France. When he had crowned his subsequent career by becoming in 1555 President of the London College of Physicians he obtained for it, on the Italian model, permission to use the bodies of executed criminals for dissection.

The experience of university study abroad created the habit of remaining in touch with foreign friends and mentors and their ideas, even though political and religious intolerance cut at these contacts. In 1534 King Sigismund forbade his Polish subjects to leave for foreign universities. The prohibition was largely ignored. Spanish subjects were forbidden to study outside Spain, Portugal or Italy in 1559, and most Spaniards, in any case the least peripatetic of Europeans in the cause of learning, obeyed. Fewer Protestants came to seek formal enrolment in universities in Catholic countries, but many came to listen to the talented voices on their fringes. Unofficially the life in and around universities was not radically changed as far as its stimulus to the life of the intellectual commonwealth was concerned.

Printing in its first century, while making knowledge and opinion ever more available, did little to check the tradition of the learned pilgrimage undertaken in order to sit at a master's feet or consult an outstanding fellow-scholar; print-fame, indeed, reinforced it. In the 1480s and 1490s, for instance, though his Neoplatonic works were published and though he protested that he was in no sense a formal

teacher, Marsilio Ficino's reawakening of the spirit of Platonic philosophy brought to him in Florence a steady stream of young men from
beyond the Alps. Looking back on his own pilgrimage, Georg Herivart
of Augsburg described it as 'the happiest days of my life'.[6] Such visits
could also affect the development of a scholar's work. It was when he
was in England that Erasmus's contact with Thomas More and John
Colet (a correspondent of Ficino's) led to his concentration on the
language and thought of the Church Fathers and his belief in the self-
sufficient relevance of the Gospels to everyday life. The publications
to which this new turn in his studies led evoked an international fame
that brought lucrative invitations from the Duke of Bavaria and the
kings of France, Spain and England. Preferring a footloose independence, Erasmus refused them.

Useful and stimulating as learned itinerancy was, it is difficult to
avoid the feeling that for some, as before and since, self-improvement
was linked to restlessness. Konrad Celtis wrote an elegy in praise of
wandering in search of knowledge; this was after he had run away
from home and spent ten precarious years flitting from school to school
and university to university and, indeed, mistress to mistress. There is
a suspicious relish in Paracelsus's account of his intellectual formation.
'For many years I studied at the universities of Germany, Italy and
France, seeking to discover the foundations of medicine. However, I
did not content myself with their teachings and writings and books,
but continued my travels to Granada and Lisbon, through Spain and
England, through Brandenburg, Prussia, Lithuania, Poland, Hungary,
Wallachia, Transylvania, Croatia, the Wendian Mark [part of Livonia],
and yet other countries which there is no need to mention here . . . I
went not only to the doctors, but also to barbers, bathkeepers, learned
physicians, magicians and women.'[7] While these travels helped to form
the independence of his views, his taste for drink and low life and his
combative nature also delineate him as a learned *picaro*, one of those to
be diagnosed by an Italian author in 1591 as 'men on whom a certain
decree of the heavens has imposed a life of wandering about the provinces of the world'.[8]

New subject matter called for pilgrimages to its pioneer exponents.
Just as Ficino's contemporary, Pico della Mirandola, had travelled in
the 1480s to improve his Greek and learn Hebrew and Arabic from
native speakers before grammars and vocabularies became available in
print, so students of botany, applied mathematics, and of chemically
serious alchemy, felt their way along the grapevines of foreign contacts.

It was during his peregrinations from Cambridge to Prague, seeking contacts on the fringes of universities and at the courts of princes hospitable to his brand of magico-science, that John Dee turned up in Antwerp to sign Ortelius's album. But as new approaches and information worked their way into publications represented in private, university and princely semi-public libraries, the need to travel to keep abreast diminished.

It was largely to cope with the growing interest in the natural sciences, humanist and vernacular philology, and aesthetic theory, literary and artistic, that the fringe life of universities became increasingly drawn away to new fora for the discussion of common intellectual interests: loosely constituted 'sodalities' or discussion groups, or, from the mid-sixteenth century, more formally structured academies with strict rules and seriously conceived programmes of research. These bodies attracted both scholars and interested amateurs, and while some were little more than local convivial societies glossed with a nit-picking parade of learning, others, like the scientific Accademia dei Lincei in Rome (founded in 1603), were true scholarly institutions, welcoming like-minded visitors and actively keeping in touch by correspondence with foreign researchers and their publications.

Additional centres for discussion were provided by the major printing establishments. Alongside the typesetting and the squeals and thuds that reassured authors that their manuscripts were going to be reborn as books, and the resident staffs of scholarly proof-correctors, illustrators and translators, were other visitors, sometimes lodging in the printer's house or nearby, who could be sure of meeting congenial spirits. The Venetian printing shop of Aldus Manutius set the tone. Aldus himself complained in 1514 about the success his attention to scholarly editing, his distribution network and the wide appeal of his convenient small-format editions of the classics had brought him. 'Apart from six hundred others', he wrote in his introduction to one of his best-sellers the pseudo-Ciceronian *Rhetorica ad Herennium*,

> there are two things in particular which interrupt my work. First, the frequent letters of learned men which come to me from every part of the world and which would cost me whole days and nights if I were to reply. Then there are the visitors who come, partly to greet me, partly to see what new work is in hand, but mostly because they have nothing better to do. "All right", they say, "let's drop in on Aldus!" . . . I say nothing of those who come to recite a poem to me or a piece of prose, usually rough and unpolished, which they want me to publish for them.[9]

The centres multiplied: Cromberger in Seville; Gryphius in Lyon, to whom Rabelais's early career as a doctor owed as much – as editor of classical medical texts – as it did to his university classes; Oporinus in Basel, the publisher of Vesalius and generous host to religious radicals and unorthodox universalists like Postel; Robert Estienne, whose Parisian corps of editors outshone the philological expertise of the Sorbonne. In Antwerp the 'Golden Compasses' printing plant of Ortelius's friend Christophe Plantin, with its twenty-two presses, one hundred and sixty workmen and numerous fonts for different languages and formats was, with its quiet courtyards and guestroom extensions, as much a hospice for itinerant intellectuals as it was a book factory and the home of Plantin's family. By 1570 the presses of Venice had produced half the books made in Italy as a whole; there, as in Lyon or London or Frankfurt, the existence of numerous presses created the atmosphere in which popularizing authors mediated between the learned and the wider literate worlds.

As the circles of ideas widened the correspondence linking men and women of a learned turn of mind grew in volume. Because of their heavy foreign enrolment, many large universities from the early fifteenth century had provided organized postal services of their own. These continued to function, as did the service provided to friends by the international trading companies. From the later fifteenth century there was an additional service offered by the relay routes of posthorses organized under contract for governmental diplomatic use but sometimes available, for a fee, and at the discretion of couriers, to private individuals. Using the service organized by an emigré Italian firm in the Netherlands, letters from Brussels in 1500 reached Granada in eighteen and Naples in fourteen days. Through the organization set up by the Italian Prosper Provana in the mid-sixteenth century, couriers left Cracow on Sundays, reached Vienna on Wednesdays and got the mail to Venice on the following Tuesday.

Off the few main routes, correspondence was still a matter of using the waggoners who plied between markets, and travelling friends. When Leonardo da Vinci died at Amboise in 1519, his companion and literary heir Francesco Melzi wrote to the artist's brothers in Florence about his will 'which I would have forwarded to you had I found someone I could trust. I am waiting for an uncle of mine to come to see me, and he will be returning thereafter to Milan. I shall give the will to him and he will ensure a safe delivery'. For the brothers' less confidential response, however, he added, 'Send your reply to me via the Gondi' – a banking firm with branches in France.[10]

Even the commercial systems were not infallible. In 1581 a Fugger correspondent wrote from Cologne to the office in Nuremberg that the courier from Antwerp had been robbed: 'all the letters he had received were taken from him, partly opened and torn up, or thrown into the fields. What has become of the courier himself it is impossible to say.'[11] Nonetheless, when encyclopaedic authors, like Vasari in compiling his history of art, or Paolo Giovio while writing the political and military history of his own times, broadcast an appeal for information they could be reasonably confident that it would arrive. Ortelius printed a message to his readers asking for fresh information and promising to mention their contributions by name. Robert Estienne asked for new words and usages for the second edition of his French–Latin dictionary. An appeal for additions to his *Popular Errors* of 1578 concerning health and medicine brought Laurent Joubert 456 responses within a year. Over 3,000 letters to and from Erasmus have survived. Lipsius had sent and received 4,300 letters to and from some seven hundred correspondents before his death in 1606. Grotius sent and received around 7,600. Such juggernaut correspondences tapped into the less capacious ones that linked orthodox scholars with political and religious radicals, as did the correspondence from his home in Aix-en-Provence of Nicolas Fabri de Peiresc, the friend of Camden and Bacon, Lipsius, Grotius and Scaliger as well as of the more contentious Paolo Sarpi, the flagellator of Tridentine Catholicism, and the heterodox Utopian Tommaso Campanella.

Numbers and names cannot reveal the personal warmth that permeated the commonwealth. Paintings enabled distant friends to see as well as hear from one another. Erasmus and his friend Peter Gilles, the scholarly town clerk of Antwerp, commissioned portraits from Quentin Massys in 1517 to send from the Netherlands to Thomas More in London. This, Erasmus wrote to him, was 'so that if fate should carry both of us off, we can, in some form at least, be with you'.[12] In the same vein, the twenty year old Philip Sidney had his portrait painted in 1574 by Veronese in response to a plea from his much older friend and mentor Hubert Languet. When they parted in Frankfurt, with Sidney continuing his European tour to Italy, Languet had pleaded for one: 'though your likeness is so engraven on my heart as to be always before my sight, yet I beg you kindly to indulge me'.[13] Shared interests, even when not sustained by actual meetings, stirred affection. Repu-

Quentin Massys, *Erasmus*, 1517 (HM The Queen, Hampton Court)

tations attracted fan mail. Men who knew Erasmus only from his books
wrote letters of anxious inquiry as to his health and diet. Having heard
of his preference for the wines of Burgundy, an Antwerp merchant
wrote to assure him that if only he would visit his admirers there 'we
will see to providing you not only with Burgundy but with Persian
and Indian wine if there were any need for that.'[14] Ortelius received a
dedicatory letter which suggests the mood in which fellow practitioners
of non-university based subjects too, in this case mapping and cos-
mography, had come to regard one another.

> Dearly beloved Ortelius,
>   Neither the daily shaking of the continual fever, with a double
> tertian, neither the looking for present death, neither the vehement
> headache without intermission could put the remembrance of my

Ortelius out of my troubled brain, wherefore I send you my *Wales*
[part of a larger description of Britain that was published post-
humously] . . . Take therefore this last remembrance of thy
Humphrey and for ever adieu, my friend Ortelius. From Denbigh,
in Gwyneth or North Wales, the XXXth of August 1568. Yours
both living and dying, Humphrey Lluyd.[15]

Ortelius noted on the letter that Lluyd had died the next day. It is in
no way uncharacteristic of the nature of the commonwealth that the
two men had been introduced by a sympathetic Welsh financial agent
of a London firm while they were all in Antwerp.

That printed books became crucial currency within the commonwealth goes without saying. They obviated the laborious process of
copying by hand and, if lost on the way to a recipient, could be
replaced. They facilitated discussion over distance because page
numbers and diagrams could be cited from identical copies. Unprotected by effective copyright, pirated editions could triple their circulation.
Their dedications and forewords carried messages and acknowledge-
ments that brought princes and scholars together in a world of learning
most of which lay outside that of university teachers. From Aldus on,
printer-publishers had inserted their wares into the familiar channels
of international commerce, and the Frankfurt book fair, which con-
vened each year towards the end of Lent and in the late summer, was
not only a meeting place and a centre of distribution through orders
based on advance copies, but constituted the nearest equivalent to a
deadline that then existed: Sebastian Münster complained to his correspondents in Prussia that if he did not receive their contributions to his
Cosmographia of 1550 before 'the next Lent book fair at Frankfurt' he
would be ruined.[16] Scaliger grumbled in 1597 at the domestic circumstances that would make his current book miss the next fair. From
1564 catalogues of the books on offer there were published. Of the
nearly 30,000 titles advertised between then and 1600 sixty-five per
cent were in Latin. At a time when authors were increasingly using
the vernacular to express their ideas to a national audience, this figure
shows the continuing vitality of Latin as the scholarly commonwealth's
basic tongue; in the correspondence that linked its members across
borders its predominance is overwhelming. Indeed, Latin had seldom
before been handled with such conversational ease, from the copious
spontaneity of Erasmus's letters to the pellucid charm of Scaliger's.

It was also, however, the first great age of translations. By 1528

Thucydides, Xenophon, Caesar, Livy, Suetonius and Sallust were available in French. By 1558 Nicholas Grimshaw's preface to his translation of Cicero lamented the backwardness of the English in not having already done for their country what 'Italians, Frenchmenne, Spaniards, Dutchmen and other foreigns have liberally done for theirs'.[17] The reproach was echoed, with more bite, in Henry Billingsley's translation in 1570 of Euclid. He hopes that this will 'excite and stirre up others learned to do the like . . . By meanes whereof, our Englishe tounge shall no lesse be enriched with good Authors then are other straunge tounges: as the Dutch, French, Italian and Spanishe, in which are red all good authors found amongest the Grekes or Latines. Which is', he goes on to say, 'the chiefest cause that among them do florishe so many cunning and skilful men in the inventions of straunge and wonderfull thinges, as in these our daies we see there do'.[18] This was very much in the utilitarian vein that was also part of the spirit of the commonwealth: practical application in the case of Billingsley, who was a London merchant interested in the use of mathematics in navigational techniques, exemplary moral relevance in Thomas North's translation in 1579 of Plutarch's *Lives*; with little Greek himself, he was able to take advantage of the more advanced 'foreigns' and based his work on the French translation of 1559 by Jacques Amyot.

By no means all authors who hoped for an international hearing used Latin. In the case of languages like Flemish, Dutch and Czech, it was essential, and authors who were not fluent Latinists sought translators. But some were shy of the wider exposure. Richard Mulcaster, referring to his plea for a more practical, vocational education for boys, his *Elementarie*, wrote in 1581 to Ortelius that 'if our English public approves of it I will send it to you in Latin, but if it is not approved, I desire my errors to be confined to my own island.'[19] Paracelsus was a rare example of an author with a subject of pan-European interest who refused to consider Latin, truculently claiming that German was just as refined and dignified a language. It was a more general sign of the concern to find a wide audience that many authors who did write in Latin were also anxious to become known in their vernacular tongues and engaged translators or left it to their publishers to find one. Publishers often took the lead. The first printed editions of the early and mid-fifteenth century histories of Florence by Leonardo Bruni and Poggio Bracciolini, for instance, were posthumously translated in 1476 into Italian from the Latin manuscripts. It was printers, not the author, who hustled Sigismund von Herberstein's *Commentary on Muscovite Affairs* into Italian, German and Czech within a few years of its publication in Latin in 1549.

The rendering of a foreign vernacular into their own could appear to translators as a positive mission. Castiglione's *The Courtier* was first published in Italian in 1528. Latin, French, Italian and German versions followed, and Sir Thomas Hoby, who translated it into English rather late in the day in 1561, declared that it was his duty to make available to his fellow-countrymen so necessary a guide to useful, learned and polite accomplishments. The appeal of translation owed something, too, to its being seen as a contribution to the translator's own national literature at a time when writers were conscious of helping to develop their native vernaculars into becoming ever more apt for literary expression, especially when the non-canonic status of dictionaries justified inserting a degree of personal flavour through paraphrase or actual invention. Hoby's *Courtier* was prefaced by a letter from Sir John Cheke, the leading English scholar of Greek (and translator of Sophocles and Euripides into Latin), which indicated the linguistic flux challenging the translator. 'I am of this opinion', he wrote, 'that our own tung shold be written cleane and pure, unmixt and unmangeled with borrowing of other tungs, wherein if we take not heed by tiim [in time], ever borrowing and never payeng, she shall be fain to keep her house as bankrupt.'[20]

There was nothing absolutely new about translations from one vernacular into another. From the mid-fourteenth century the marvel-filled *Travels* attributed to Sir John Mandeville had been translated not only into Latin, English, German, Spanish and Italian but even into Czech, Danish and Irish before it began a new career in printed form. But there was certainly no medieval anticipation of the sheer volume and variety of sixteenth-century translation which the shrewd printer Etienne Dolet recognized when in 1540 he published his book on 'the way to make good translation from one language to another'. Luther's hymns, the satirical polemics of the shoemaker–*Meistersinger* Hans Sachs appeared in English; Castiglione, Ariosto and Tasso in Polish; the Spanish novel *Lazarillo de Tormes* in Latin, English, German, Italian and Dutch; Matteo Bandello's collection of short stories, the *Novelle* (chiefly written during his residence in France) in Spanish; Montaigne's *Essays* in Italian and English. And if we add the freedom with which authors of different nationalities quoted and paraphrased one another (Raimond de Fourquevaux's *Instructions on the Conduct of War* was largely an unacknowledged version of Machiavelli's *The Art of War*), something can be grasped of the range of 'Th'intertraffique of the minde' and the unprecedented speed with which ideas, and ways of expressing them, were now absorbed and exchanged.

MIGRATING STYLES

The very phrase 'International Gothic' implies the transmission of artistic ideas from one centre to another. The frescoes of the Catalan Ferrer Bassá in the 1340s, for instance, reflected the influences of his distant contemporary the Sienese Simone Martini. Simone himself had become familiar with the style in which French artists were working when he was invited to Naples by its king Robert of Anjou, Count of Provence. Invitations to artists whose fame travelled the diplomatic and clerical networks; pictures commissioned abroad for display in churches at home; the movement of illuminated manuscripts: by these means artists and patrons in one country became aware of what was happening in another. But from the mid-fifteenth century they become more visible as the traffic in works of art increased and more evidence for it survived. Patrons cast their nets more widely, collections were assembled, artists travelled not only to fulfil commissions but to learn, printing enabled specimens of an individual's style to be broadcast with a facility that was entirely new.

   In artistic terms, Europe was drawing in on itself. With the Turkish advance, Byzantine influence in Italy, which had been particularly strong in Venice, petered out. So did the Moorish arch shapes and decorative filigree that had embellished Portuguese and southern Spanish architecture; what lingered on there did not reflect taste so much as convenience in a near-African climate: coolly tiled interiors, courtyards with water tanks, pierced shutters. And elsewhere Islamic imports of ceramics, glasswares and metalwork were increasingly treated as exotica that required some Europeanization – with a lid, a handle or mount. In response to this isolationism, by the middle of the sixteenth century Near Eastern artificers were exporting wares that copied European forms. Only carpets, as yet unreproducible by domestic technology, and some Iznik pottery, continued to bring Islamic motifs into European homes. The time for the influence of the arts of the countries overseas that Europeans were so rapidly penetrating lay far in the future. Dürer applauded the craftsmanship of the Mexican

Michelangelo, *Madonna and Child*, c.1504–5 (Notre Dame, Bruges)

gold and silver objects he saw in Brussels in 1520, to the extent of saying that 'all the days of my life I have seen nothing that gladdened my heart so much.'[21] They were, all the same, melted down. And fresh imports that escaped the furnace and entered princely collections were gathered as inert curiosities. Commercial and political rivalries kept merchants and statesmen alert to Europe's reach overseas. We have seen that reports about 'them', whether Amerindian or Asiatic, stimulated reassessments of the nature of 'us'. But as far as the mainstream of cultural awareness was concerned, too many fresh indigenous literary and artistic impulses and too excited an awareness of the common Roman past played within and across Europe to prompt more than cursory glances outside. In the arts, as in scholarship (in which Arabic learning had played so vital a part in the middle ages), the continent became an increasingly sealed world of its own, and this very isolation added an alacrity to the migrations of styles within it.

The presence of foreign artists, especially if resident for some time and working with native colleagues, was a significant and often, as in the case of the Italians – Rosso Fiorentino, Primaticcio, Cellini – invited to France by Francis I, a crucial influence on the change of direction within national style. The traffic in objects also played a part alongside the migration of men. The fame of Michelangelo's giant *David*, which had been manoeuvred into position in front of the Palazzo Vecchio in Florence in 1504, moved a visiting Flemish wool merchant to buy his marble *Madonna and Child*.

But it was to be a generation after its installation in the Church of Our Lady in Bruges before it was seen as an exemplary work of art as well as an object of devotion. Indeed, because merchants imported works in response to the local fame of the artist at least as much as for the appeal of their work to their own taste, which had been formed in a different cultural environment, the arrival of foreign masterpieces could be particularly stimulating. We have seen how, after trade contacts with Flanders had introduced works by Jan van Eyck and Rogier van der Weyden, the *Adoration Altarpiece* of Hugo van der Goes arrived in Florence. It was installed in 1483 in Tommaso Portinari's family chapel against a background of frescoes by some of the most innovative of Italian mid-fifteenth century painters, Domenico Veneziano, Andrea del Castagno and Piero della Francesca, all of whom represented stylistic tendencies strikingly at odds with Hugo's. It was partly the discordance of this setting that accounts for the stimulus it gave local artists, from Domenico Ghirlandaio to Leonardo, who saw it there, and who took from it aspects they found congenial to their own work.

The picture arrived safely after a long voyage by sea. Not all purchases were so fortunate. Agnolo Tani, also, like Portinari, a Medici agent in Bruges, commissioned from another artist of genius and regional fame, Hans Memlinc, what is arguably his most beguilingly painted and deeply felt work, a triptych of the *Last Judgement*. This too was destined for a family church in Florence. But the ship carrying it was captured by a Danzig pirate who presented it as a trophy to the cathedral there. Merchant purchases of works of art, whether personal,

Nuno Gonçalves, *St Vincent Altarpiece*, *c.*1470 (Cathedral, Lisbon)

as in these cases, or speculative investments analagous to the tapestries and engravings which were a reliably saleable import from north to south, were transmitters of style, potential or immediate in their effect. Without such landings of imported wares on foreign soil it would, for example, be difficult to account for the organizing power of the composition and the humane psychological immediacy of the figures within the crowded polyptych that Nuno Gonçalves painted in *c.*1470 for the chapel of St Vincent in the cathedral of Lisbon. It was the Lisbon trade with Flanders that enabled Nuno to soar above the somewhat wooden provincialism of his native country.

Because on the whole southern merchants were more familiar with the market for luxury furnishings than were their northern colleagues,

the balance in the import-export business favoured the flow of works of art from northern Europe to the south until the beginning of the sixteenth century: a traffic that encouraged painters to use linen or canvas that could be rolled up for easy transport rather than wooden panels. Thereafter it came to owe more to cultural diplomacy and the personal initiative of patrons and collectors. In 1502 the Florentine government, dependent on French military assistance in its war against Pisa, commissioned a bronze *David* from Michelangelo and dispatched it by sea to Florimond Robertet, the French King's principal adviser on foreign affairs. By then, moreover, the horses, weapons and suits of armour that princes traditionally gave one another were being joined by medals and portraits. Usually combining a realistic portrait on one side with a propagandist image or self-revealing emblem on the other, medals, reproducible and easy to transport, were also condensations of the style of the centres from which they were sent abroad. They were personal gifts that were also cultural transmitters.

And the same could be true of painted portraits. The Wittenberg workshop of Lucas Cranach the Elder was paid in 1533 for turning out no fewer than sixty pairs of portraits of the newly acceded Elector of Saxony, John-Frederick, and his wife Sibilla for distribution to his political contacts. When in 1550 a toadying Milanese official wrote to beg Charles V's chief minister Cardinal de Granvelle for a portrait by 'your most excellent painter'[22], Antonis Mor, what he got was a copy by a studio assistant. Nonetheless, portraits, even if they were not originals, spread artistic styles abroad with more directness than did many translations of works of literature.

The plaster casts of antique sculptures in Italy that were imported into France affected the work of the classicizing Pierre Bontemps, who was responsible for the tomb of Francis I, and of the most elegantly refined of French sixteenth-century sculptors, Jean Goujon. The copies and variants of famous paintings, like Leonardo's *Virgin and Child with St Anne* (1508–10), which were turned out by pupils in the absence of any commissioners' or artists' property rights, found their way far afield. But the most widely infective multiples came from the press – not the printed word, but the printed illustration.

Giovanna Tornabuoni, bronze medal by Niccolò Fiorentino, *c.*1486 (British Museum)

In one respect printing had hampered the transmission of styles that could be fully appreciated at a glance by cutting back the production of illuminated manuscripts; black and white could not convey the effect of light Piero della Francesca learned from illuminations from the circle of his French contemporary Jean Fouquet. The printed books that were found most useful for blending foreign into native styles were above all illustrated works on architecture, from Serlio's work of 1537 on the order and Giacomo da Vignola's *Rules for the Five Orders* of 1562, via Andrea Palladio's *Four Books on Architecture* of 1570 and Jacques Androuet du Cerceau's *The Finest Buildings in France* of 1579 to Vincenzo Scamozzi's *The Idea of a Universal Architecture* of 1615. These showed what had and should be done, and the illustrations could be used as models even by those unable to read the texts. For painters, sculptors and workers in the decorative arts, from the mid-sixteenth century there were encyclopaedic handbooks illustrating personifications (as we have seen in the case of Europa) and other shorthand symbolic methods of communicating ideas; bees swarming in a cast-away helmet as a fairly straightforward image of Peace for instance: industrious life resuming after the interruptions of war. In his *Iconology* of 1611 Cesare Ripa managed to symbolize so complex an idea as Reason of State: an armoured woman keeps the lion of force tamed by the pressure of one hand while the other brandishes the sceptre of rule; she treads on a book: it is labelled IUS (Justice) and is half hidden by her skirt because statecraft demands that the ordinary processes of law should be covered over in times of emergency. This figure was copied intact as part of the iconographic argument on the title-page of a book published in Venice in 1624.

The Frankfurt book fairs acted as a distribution centre for engravings and art woodcuts – those not simply dashed off for an audience wanting popular news broadsheets or devotional images. An acquaintance of Dürer's friend and patron, Willibald Pirckheimer, wrote to him in 1520 expressing surprise that there were so few of the artist's works 'at the fair, whereas the engravings of the Dutchman Lucas were so numerous'.[23] But Dürer had by then set off on his journey to the Netherlands where he disposed of his prints on his own account, selling some, exchanging others – as in Antwerp with those of Lucas van Leyden himself and trading the works of his German fellow-printmakers like Hans Baldung. And this interchange between German and Netherlandish graphic ideas which Dürer had begun to absorb as a young man through the engravings of Martin Schongauer which were influenced by both, was paralleled, to even greater effect, by the circulation of German prints in Italy and vice versa. In the mid-sixteenth century Vasari paid reluctant homage to the influence of German engravings and woodcuts. He saw them as affecting an interest in and the actual treatment of the countryside (he remarks huffily that 'there is not a cobbler's house without a German landscape'[24]) and as introducing an undecorous note of spontaneous emotionalism: contaminating, that is, the essentially Italian genius for tending what was harmonious and ideal within the inchoate mass of natural appearances and psychological quirks. Writing of Pontormo's works from the 1520s, he mourned that the artist, having been attracted to Dürer's manner, 'captured it so strongly that the charm of his own early style . . ., full of sweetness and grace, was greatly changed by that new intensity and effort, and much damaged by his chance encounter with that German style; in all these [later] works, therefore, beautiful though they may be, there is recognizable only a little of the graceful excellence he had up to then given his figures'. This carried on the older prejudice that had earned the Venetian engraver Jacopo de' Barbari, on returning from working in Germany in the early sixteenth century, his unflattering sobriquet 'of the Barbarians'. All the same, throughout the first and second generations of sixteenth-century north Italian painters, from Giorgione, Titian, and Pordenone to Lotto and Gaudenzio Ferrari, the influence of northern prints was strong. Vasari himself, indeed, used a greatly enlarged copy of a Dürer woodcut, *The Siege of a Town*, as the background to one of his historical paintings in the Palazzo Vecchio in Florence. And it spread through the booming majolica industry's avid search for fresh narrative imagery with which to enliven the plates and dishes produced for the tables and sideboards of the well-to-do.

In return, Italy transmitted northwards fewer engravings that were self-contained works of art, but instead images which publicized the work of major painters by giving the simplified essence of their styles. It was with Marcantonio Raimondi's prints after Raphael in the 1520s, and those commissioned after Michelangelo in the 1540s by the Roman printer Antonio Lafrery particularly in mind that Vasari praised Italian engravers. 'They have given circulation', he wrote in his life of Marcantonio, 'to many subjects and manners of painters for those who cannot visit the places where the chief works are, and have given an understanding to those beyond the Alps of things of which they were unaware.'[25] And Italian prints of decorative borders and motifs joined the Germanic stock of printed models for woodworkers, plasterers and gold and silversmiths that offered ideas to craftsmen throughout Europe.

Collecting contemporary works of art for their own sake, rather than buying them for devotional purposes or as domestic furnishings, was stimulated in Italy by the interest in acquiring ancient gems and coins, vases and sculpture. By the 1470s Giovanni Rucellai, the Florentine patron of Leon Battista Alberti, was expressing a proto-art collector's mood when he noted 'that we have in our house' – the palace Alberti designed for him – 'many objects of sculpture and painting and wood inlay by the hands of the best masters who have existed for a good while back, not only in Florence but in Italy as a whole'.[26] In 1502 Isabella d'Este, the wife of the Marquis of Mantua, wrote that 'we desire to have in our *camerino*' – a room on the ground floor of the Gonzaga Palace – 'pictures with a [narrative] story by the excellent painters now in Italy.'[27] Using the Este family and diplomatic agents outside Mantua, there was hardly an outstanding painter she did not approach – Mantegna, Giovanni Bellini, Perugino, Leonardo, Titian and Francesco Francia, Giorgione, Raphael and Michelangelo – not always with success.

Though by then Italians were beginning to see the Flemish works they had bought because they liked them as also witnessing to the conscious breadth of their taste, it was from the contact with Italy of the invading French kings Louis XII and Francis I that non-national accumulations were deliberately aimed at elsewhere. For Louis the transfer of antiquities, manuscripts and paintings from Milan and Pavia may well have been akin to the mood in which the Venetians had brought home works of art from their conquest of Byzantium in 1204, primarily as trophies. But Francis was more discriminating in his acquisitiveness; it was a foretaste of attitudes to come when in 1528 he commissioned Battista della Palla to collect in Italy 'large numbers of antiquities of every sort, that is, marbles and bronzes, and paintings by masters worthy of his Majesty'.[28] Della Palla's activities were roundly condemned by Vasari as cultural rape, and were passionately and successfully denounced by the widow of Pier Francesco Borgherini who discovered that he was chaffering to buy their marriage bed because it had been decorated with paintings by Pontormo, Andrea del Sarto, Granacci and Bachiacca, being itself, indeed, a collection as well as a collector's piece. But though to her della Palla was 'a most vile dealer . . . a cheap salesman' devoted to 'dismantling the decorations of gentlemen's bedrooms', he managed to ship to Marseilles no less than forty crates of antiquities, sculptures and paintings through purchases and commissions for new works and copies of old ones.[29] This consignment buttressed the growing French interest in the antique. It also reinforced the view that Italian contemporary art was above all Florentine. And through the inclusion of such works as Rosso's *Moses and the Daughters of Jethro*, it emphasized the taste for the Mannerist bias in the work of the artists Francis paid to work for him at Fontainebleau and other royal residencies.

Later collectors, especially princes whose international contacts kept them aware of who was being most talked about, became more eclectic. Philip II of Spain valued works by Joachim Patinier and Hieronymus Bosch as well as those of Titian. Spain's territorial links to the Netherlands and Italy were shaping influences on his taste, but the artistic accumulations of Rudolf II, like his assemblages of curiosities of nature and technological ingenuities, followed no political guidelines. Rudolf had been brought up at the court of Philip II, his uncle, and he provided studio and workshop space in Hradčany Castle in Prague for painters and sculptors from Italy, Spain, France, the Netherlands, Germany and Switzerland to work both on their own account and for him. The vogue from the late sixteenth century for paintings of collectors' cabinets and reception rooms shows how many modes, past and present, were available for consultation in these encyclopaedias of styles and how widespread the traffic in works of art had become.

Some artists travelled chiefly to learn, by meeting colleagues, studying their works and accepting commissions to pay their way before returning. Others, like those of Rudolf's *équipe*, were hired to stay and work outside their own countries. The contributions they made to the migration of styles were naturally idiosyncratic. Breughel rejected what was proffered on his tour through Italy in the 1550s. El Greco, in Italy in the 1560s, threw off the icon-based tradition he had practised in his native Crete but, on moving to Spain, came to obey a personal vision which owed progressively less to either. Later in the century the northern sculptors Jean Boulogne (his name naturalized to Giovanni Bologna during his long employment in Florence) and Adrien de Vries gave themselves up with such abandon to the seduction of Italian style that for all their expressive power as individuals they can be seen as honorary Italians. And not all of those who worked abroad communicated their own manner, but, rather, lapsed into a tranquil working relationship with those they were surrounded by. Cumulatively, nonetheless, artists who travelled to learn or find employment stimulated the rephrasing of the regional varieties of Gothic into the changed styles associated with the Renaissance.

Apart from the mid-European *Wanderjahr*, which took the young Dürer to Switzerland and across the Rhine to Strasbourg and Colmar, and such rarer cases as when shortly after the mid-fifteenth century the ruler of Milan, Francesco Sforza, had sent his court painter Zanetto Bugatti to improve himself in the workshop of Rogier van der Weyden, the school-route for artists most commonly led from north to south. It was especially from the Low Countries that artists, reacting against the painstaking immaculacy of their own traditional approach, travelled to explore other conventions. Lodovico Guicciardini's recognition of the transformations Italy had produced in the work of such painters as Jan Gossaert (Mabuse), Jan van Scorel and Maerten van Heemskerck and the sculptor and architect Cornelis Floris, and their subsequent transmission of them to local colleagues, led him, in his *Description of the Low Countries*, written in 1561 after a long residence there, to boast of Italy's pedagogic role within northern art.

Self-portrait of Maerten van Heemskerck in Rome (Fitzwilliam Museum, Cambridge)

After giving a list of names he went on to say that

> almost all the aforementioned painters, architects and sculptors have been
> in Italy; some in order to learn, others to see works of ancient art and
> to make the acquaintance of people who excel in their profession, others
> to seek adventure and make themselves known. After having satisfied
> their desires, they return in most cases to their native country with new
> experience, ability, and honour; and from there they spread, having
> become masters, to England, all over Germany, and particularly through
> Denmark, Sweden, Norway, Poland and other northern countries,
> including even Russia, not mentioning those who go to France, Spain
> and Portugal.[30]

This diaspora of Italianized as well as Italian artists, and the seemingly
inexhaustible self-renewal of the approaches to style generated in the
peninsula itself, long kept Italy's tutorial role paramount. Of Rubens's
journey from Antwerp in 1600 his nephew wrote that he 'was seized
with a desire to see Italy and to view at first hand the most celebrated
works of art, ancient and modern, in that country and to form his art
after these models'.[31] From the West it was chiefly from Spain, and
then before the frequent residence of Italian artists called in by Philip
II, that there were pilgrimages to the unfraught naturalism and classical
allusiveness which were the liberating aspects of Italian styles. These
transformed the work on their return home of visitors like the painter
and sculptor Alonso Berruguete – who also caught the early tremors
of Italian mannerism – and Pedro Machuca who, like his chosen model,
Raphael, was both painter and architect. There is some irony in the
coincidence that Machuca's Italianate arcaded courtyard for Charles V's
palace at the Alhambra in Granada was begun in 1527, the year in
which the emperor's troops sacked Rome.

Artists who asked for or were offered salaries to work abroad were,
like mercenaries, little concerned about their employers' religious or
political roles. Gentile Bellini spent 1479–81 in Constantinople, whither
he had been invited to paint the Sultan's portrait. The sculptor Guido
Mazzoni of Modena was working in Naples when Charles VIII's invading army took the city by storm in 1495. Introduced to Charles, and
flattered by being knighted by him, he followed the king back to France
where he designed his tomb at St Denis and, after his death, served his
successor invader of Italy, Louis XII. On his own death, shortly after
returning home, his tomb was decorated with the lilies of France. From

Courtyard of the Palace of Charles V in the Alhambra, Granada

richer evidence something more can be gleaned of the motives and feelings of the Italian artists who followed his example over the next two generations. One attraction was the luxury of a fixed stipend. In 1516 Francis I had 'collected' the wearying sixty-three-year-old Leonardo da Vinci and installed him, as genius and curiosity, in a suburb of Amboise for a retainer of seven hundred crowns a year. Little was demanded of him, though, as Antonio de Beatis remarked, in spite of a recent stroke 'he can still draw and teach.'[32] Benvenuto Cellini, for his more active service with Francis I from 1540–5, was offered the same sum, and the generously salaried Florentine sculptor Giovanni Rustici, who died at Tours in 1554, wrote with some complacency that 'men who toil the whole day, that is, those who work for a living rather than for honour, are actually workmen; works of art cannot be executed without long reflection'.[33] For Rosso there was a radical change of personal status; 'living in the style no longer of a painter but a prince', Vasari noted, 'he kept very many servants and teams of horses, and he had his house furnished with tapestries and silver and other valuable furniture and fittings.'[34] If Rosso in 1540 committed suicide, the first artist known, or assumed on good grounds, to have killed himself, this was not due to lack of favour but to the exacerbation of an unstable temperament by a financial success that led him into overwrought litigation. Andrea del Sarto, on the other hand, though earning more in France than in Florence, was persuaded by his wife to return home within two years, and Francesco Salviati was so unhappy there that he, too, left before two years were up and told Vasari 'how well he [Vasari] had done not to go to France, recounting things that would rob anyone of the wish, no matter how intense, to go there'.[35]

Salviati's stay in 1554–6 coincided with the exhaustion of the French treasury from war and growing factionalism at the court of Francis's successor, Henri II. From 1562 began the disturbances of the civil wars and the growing unpopularity of the Italian Queen Mother, Catherine de' Medici. But it was not simply political confusion that spelled the end of the great period of Italian influence on the arts. By then its lessons had been absorbed and its intellectual principles grasped to the extent that suited French tastes. In a parallel rhythm fewer Netherlandish painters went to Italy, as Rubens and after him Van Dyck still did, to learn, but accustomed already to naturalized Italianate styles at home, they travelled to the peninsula looking for work and some were accepted as sympathetic colleagues and employees. It was high praise when Vasari extolled a portrait of his hero Michelangelo by the Flemish painter and printmaker Giovanni Strada (another foreigner whose name, Jan van der Straat, became naturalized), for those cherished Italian qualities 'rich inventive power, great knowledge of design, and infinite grace'.[36] Both the landscape painters Mattheus and Paul Bril were patronized in the later sixteenth century by popes who lived amongst the works of Raphael, Michelangelo and Giulio Romano. The thoroughly Italianate intarsia panels of towards 1600 in the sacristy of the Certosa di San Martino, Naples, are signed 'Lorenzo Ducho, Frisian' – from the northern Low Countries and 'Teodoro de Vogel, Fleming'.

As with 'Giovanni Bologna', the name of the prominent French portraitist Corneille de Lyons conceals his origin, which was Dutch, just as that of the Spanish painter Alejo Fernandez obscures his German origin. Isaac Oliver, the chief follower of the only English painter of genius in the sixteenth century, the miniaturist Nicholas Hilliard, was French. Indeed, we know the features of Henry VII from the tomb sculpture by Pietro Torrigiano, who had fled from Florence after punching Michelangelo on the nose, and who ended his life in a Spanish inquisitorial prison. We see Henry VIII and the prominent Englishmen and women of his time through the brush and pencil of a Swiss, Hans Holbein the Younger, Mary through the eyes of the Dutchman Antonis Mor, Elizabeth chiefly through those of Lucas de Heer, Hans Eworth and other Flemings and their studio copyists. It was not until the appointment of the feeble Robert Peake as painter to James I's son Henry, Prince of Wales, that a native was formally entrusted with images of royalty in England.

For a few artists, the learning and transmission was aided by their being enlisted into diplomatic entourages. Rodrigo Borgia, later Pope Alexander VI, brought back Italian fresco painters to work in the cathedral of Valencia in 1472. Jan Mostaert's art was radically reformed on his accompanying the Bishop of Utrecht to Rome in 1508. It was on a visit to England in the suite of Philip II that the Italian medallist Jacopo da Trezzo produced the first classically inspired image of an English monarch, Mary Tudor. His influence on the medallists he met on further tours with, or on minor diplomatic missions on behalf of Philip, took the tradition he had derived from Pisanello, Matteo de' Pasti and other Italian medallists of the fifteenth century to Flanders and to France, where even the greatest medallist of his day, Guillaume Dupré, derived inspiration from Jacopo's work. Yet other opportunities for the interchange of ideas came from the grand collaborative projects where scale and timetable called for a wide trawl through the domestic and foreign employment markets: Francis I's Fontainebleau, Duke Cosimo I's lavish redecoration of the Palazzo Vecchio in Florence during the 1560s, the furnishing from the 1570s of Philip II's enormous palace-monastery, the Escorial.

All the same, none of the most powerfully innovative and influential artists (with Leonardo as a mysterious exception) chose to leave the native atmosphere in which their imaginations – and profitable studios – flourished for more than occasional journeys. Botticelli, Raphael, Michelangelo, Giovanni Bellini, Correggio, Titian, Tintoretto, Annibale Carracci, Caravaggio (though a short stay in Malta left the starkly brooding *Beheading of the Baptist* in the Cathedral of Valetta); Bosch and Breughel; Grünewald, Altdorfer and Cranach; Jean Fouquet and Jean Perréal (though both were influenced by visits to Italy, in c.1450 and c.1500): all stayed at home or worked nearby and let foreign agents come to them, and the list could be prolonged. Even Dürer's two spells of learning and working in Venice, during the winter of 1494–5 and between 1505 and 1507, were but breaks in his long working life in Nuremberg, from his apprenticeship in 1486 to his death in 1528. But once artists and their patrons had come to admire an alien style, as in France from the mid-sixteenth century, it was more naturally absorbed through the works produced by local practitioners of talent rather than of genius, and through imported works that represented an alien manner but gave time to take stock of its implications.

The major artists of the International Gothic had established the technical and stylistic base for personal expressiveness. By the turn of the fifteenth and sixteenth centuries a whole network of artisan artists – a class generally slow to change its traditional ways – were still working in a manner that could be called the International Naïve. From Switzerland and Germany and northern Italy to Denmark and Finland, itinerant fresco painters in village churches and rural castles, and the illuminators of local chronicles and popular works of devotion, were using common conventions: vapid or caricatural faces, sketchily defined drapery, hard outlines, scant concern for colour as a modelling agent, a vigorous if clumsy sense of narrative. It was not just self-educating artists who were on the move.

For all the vitality of the visual arts, however, it was music that exerted the most universal appeal. To play an instrument was a common aristocratic accomplishment. Henry VIII played lute and virginals, sang from scores at sight and composed masses and songs. The Flemish Clemens 'non Papa', Clemens not-the-pope, was distinguished in this way from another amateur composer, Pope Clement VII. When the diplomat Richard Pace took time off in 1516 from an arduous mission to bring the Swiss and Maximilian into an alliance with England against France, he took refuge in a public bath in Constance where, secure from interruption, he wrote his first scholarly work, De Fructu. In this he recorded that as a schoolboy at Winchester his studies had been dominated by 'a proficiency in music far beyond my age'; only the intervention of the Bishop of Winchester himself, who 'sent me to pursue the study of literature into Italy, to the school [university] at Padua', diverted him from continuing to indulge his passion.[37] At about the same time as the bishop's intervention, in Italy, and lower down the social scale, Benvenuto Cellini was battling with his music-loving artisan father to be allowed to become an artist while 'his greatest ambition as far as I was concerned was to turn me into an accomplished musician; and I was never more miserable than when he used to talk to me about it, saying that I showed so much promise that if I wanted I would outshine anyone in the world.'[38] Again at about the same time, de Beatis recorded in Bruges that 'most people are fond of music' and

Jan Breughel, detail from *The Sense of Hearing*, [?] 1617 (Museo del Prado, Madrid)

in Antwerp that 'everyone goes in for music, and they are so expert at it that they play even handbells so harmoniously and with such full tone that the handbells themselves seem to sing.'[39]

Cellini's father was a member of the town band of Florence, playing at civic receptions and on processional or festival occasions. Such bands, comprising trumpets, fifes and drums, were commonplace in European towns of any size, in some cases giving regular evening concerts. And when Erasmus expressed the hope that New Testament stories would be sung at the spinning wheel and the plough this was no mere sentimentalism; a German prayerbook of 1509 had taken it for granted that 'when two or three come together they have to sing, and they all sing at work in house and field, at prayer and devotion, in joy and sorrow, mourning and feasting.'[40] This may have been stretching a point too rosily, but there is no doubt about the widespread opportunities to listen to music, in church, at weddings and dances, at markets and fairs. And when one of the many itinerant troupes of beggar-musicians turned up, they were adept in their ballads at picking up fragments of the local language and making reference to local events. Soldiers, students and tradesmen – quite apart from the formally organized guilds of Mastersingers – had convivial songs of their own. A Spanish manuscript anthology of *c*.1500 tapped a wide range of traditional European sources and put aristocratic songs alongside popular ones. A German miniature illustrating a Nuremberg pageant float in 1519 contrasted the wind instruments which drew attention to its passing by, with the strings quietly entertaining the patrician men and women sitting on it round a table in a feigned garden. The theme of musicians playing while their betters picnicked was to recur in art for the rest of the century.

From the lullaby crooned in a hut to the prowess of Isabella d'Este on the lute and clavichord there was a familiarity with, and a widespread ability to perform musical works with voice or instrument. Dürer noted in Venice that during a concert the viol players were moved to tears by the beauty of the composition they performed, and no description of the feelings induced by looking at a work of art had quite the intensity of Andrea Calmo's reaction to the performance of a song composed for lute accompaniment by one of Isabella's protégés, Marchetto Cara: 'as for the manner of singing, I have never heard anything better. God! what a beautiful voice, what style, what fullness, what diminuendoes, what suavity that would melt the hardest heart.'[41] One of Pope Leo X's chapel masters (Leo himself was another potentate-composer), the devout Fleming Elzéar Genêt, went so far as to renounce secular music altogether because of the danger of its arousing worldly passions.

It was then that music was becoming split into its linked but distinct international worlds: that of composers, and that reflecting the cult of vocal 'canaries' and virtuoso instrumental performers. Until the mid-sixteenth century, composers and the styles they represented flowed from north to south, while the movement of singers and instrumentalists tended to be in the opposite direction. The competition among Italian courts to offer their visitors the most sensuous of sounds issuing from throat or instrument led to outstanding performers being paid more than university professors, and to contracts more binding on them than any set for an artist or man of letters, regularly broken as they were to obtain still better terms elsewhere. It was during a visit to Henry VIII's court, with its Italian organists, brass and woodwind players that an Italian judged the music he heard there to be 'more divine than human'.[42] Francis I engaged – and offered French citizenship to – Italian sackbut, cornet, lute and hautboy players. The Florentine emigré Luigi Alamanni wrote verses to be set by his fellow-countryman Francesco dell'Ajolla, who had been wooed to settle as an organist in Lyon. It is unlikely that this scattering of talented performers did anything to improve the quality of the background music which brayingly accompanied banquets. Nor did it moderate the celebration of public festival occasions with mere noise – when Charles V came to meet Pope Clement VII in 1529, for instance, 'so great were the sounds of voices, trumpets, drums and artillery, that it seemed that Bologna was turned upside down.'[43] It was the taste for music to be listened to with

Lorenzo Costa, *A Concert*, c.1488 (National Gallery, London)

care, whether religious or secular, that determined the north-south flow of the compositional styles that executants were called on to interpret.

These had been evolved early in the fifteenth century among the inter-communicating composers of northern France, the Low Countries and England; the works of the English composer John Dunstable, who died in 1453, have largely to be deduced from continental copies of his manuscript compositions. In the late fifteenth century the leaders of northern styles, Jacob Obrecht, Alexander Agricola and Heinrich Isaac, all spent time in Florence. The Flemish composer and musical theorist Joannes Tinctoris worked from 1474–95 at the court of Naples. All were brought south by the word spread along diplomatic and commercial networks that the best music, like the best tapestry, was being fabricated in the North. When Charles of Burgundy became King of Spain in 1516 he brought with him a whole choir of Flemish part-singers and their scores.

Whereas the greatest visual artists stayed at home and sold their wares abroad, composers, who were not financially dependent on workshops, travelled freely, scattering their spores from one centre to another. Some years after the death of the Florentine Antonio Squarcialupi in 1470, Lorenzo de' Medici (who commissioned a monument to him in the cathedral where he had been the director of music) called Isaac from Flanders. Yet before Lorenzo died, Isaac had moved on to Vienna as director of music to the imperial court. His ability to give his own impress to the local styles he moved amongst is shown by the popularity of the Italian, German and French verses he set to his own compositions. The boast of Isaac's German pupil Ludwig Senfl that he 'is known throughout the world' was hardly an exaggeration[44]: manuscript copies of his music have been traced from Portugal through Baltic Germany to Poland. In similar vein was the career of a still greater Flemish-born composer, Josquin des Prez, which was largely spent in Italy and France. Castiglione had one of the characters in *The Courtier* remark ironically that once 'when a motet was sung [at Urbino] it pleased no one and was considered worthless until it became known that it had been composed by Josquin.'[45] A firmer tribute came from Germany, from Martin Luther: 'he is master of the notes; others are mastered by them.'[46]

The sacred music – settings of the Mass – of Josquin and Obrecht were among the earliest to be published by the Venetian inventor of printed typesetting for musical scores, Ottaviano Petrucci. Introduced in 1510, and soon taken up by others, Petrucci's process did not at once replace manuscript scores, especially the large-format, often illuminated ones, easily readable from some distance, which were propped on huge lecterns for cathedral choirs. But it did obviate the mistakes incorporated in copyists' versions and, by forcing written music into universally comprehensible black and white symbols, gradually abolished the colour coding of noted values that had been developed regionally. Such scores were seldom so rigidly complete as to ignore the existence of *ad hoc* assemblages of instrumentalists or the taste for improvisatory display on the part of player or singer. But printing hastened the transmission of styles beyond national borders and broadened the repertory of music-making at home.

Orlandus Lassus, who worked in England, France, and Germany as well as Italy before his death in 1594, was one of the great composers of masses and religious motets of the century. This instance of his flexible attitude towards the secular musical innovations of Italy shows little beyond the adaptability of Flemish styles previously anticipated in the works, both religious and secular, of Josquin's time. It was the compositions of the first generation of Italians of comparably authoritative genius in the later sixteenth century that pressed the advantage from the South back across central and northern Europe: Andrea Gabriele, his nephew Giovanni and Palestrina. Richly sonorous and readily intelligible, their work made its way through pupils and scores, and influenced those who still crossed the Alps from the North but who came now chiefly to learn from the brilliant solemnity of Italian works for massed choirs and the emotional poignancy of the secular madrigal. Though Italian styles were forced to sidle round entrenched positions (like the Lutheran church music of German Protestant states and the continuing Spanish preference for variants on Flemish polyphony) and to some extent sank within native traditions – as in France and England – that had been exploring similar directions with less generative impact, by 1600 they had become frames of reference for innovative composers throughout Europe. And when the long preoccupation with the support of poetry by music had led to the invention of opera, Italy's musical hegemony was assured for over a century to come.

Nowhere was the Italian influence so surprisingly direct as in Europe's south-western extremity. Among the deeds and consequences of overseas exploration the pioneering contribution was Portugal's. By 1473, probing, trading and gathering information as they went, its maritime expeditions had crossed the equator and, by returning to tell the tale, doubled the imaginable size of the habitable globe. By rounding the Cape of Good Hope in 1498, Bartholomew Dias also rounded off the shape of a continent whose extent had from classical times been wrapped in a fog of conjecture. Though Columbus four years later reached landfalls that turned out to be the pickets of America, the arrival in Lisbon of the cargoes of spices that followed Vasco da Gama's arrival in 1498 via the Cape in India caused major tremors through the European commercial world, well before the import of American precious metals.

The monarch who dispatched Vasco, Manuel I, took a royal cut from the sale and transhipment of spices and presided over the most buoyant phase of Portugal's economy before the exploitation of the riches of Brazil in the early eighteenth century. There is no evidence that Manuel, who reigned from 1495 to 1521, paid more than lip service to the idea that a motive for exploration was to gain souls for Christ, but like any other merchant venturer of the time he was convinced that, given the risks involved both for men and investment, prayer for protection should be offered at the start of an enterprise and grateful thanks offered to God at its conclusion. He knew that the greatest risk-takers, his mariners and their families, would expect it; and prayers were considered most efficacious when offered in churches, and their momentum best guaranteed by professional intercessors, monks. Manuel was generous to a number of monastic foundations. He especially favoured the Hieronymite community at Belèm, the assembly point on the Tagus (whose north bank then reached almost to the monastic church's walls) whence his fleets left on their voyages, and the foundation at Tomar, north of Lisbon, of whose Order of Christ he was, by royal tradition, the Grand Master. At both he fostered building works of striking, indeed strident individuality, so much so that the style they represent has been dubbed Manueline.

Begun shortly after 1500, the white limestone monastic church at Belèm exemplifies every possible opposing aesthetic factor to those then ruling in Italy. The windows are round headed, but obscured by ogival mouldings. Other mouldings, in long horizontal strips, simply run into one side of the windows and re-emerge on the other in no deliberate relationship to the openings' differing height in the wall. Buttresses shoot up like extended pocket telescopes, adding discursiveness to the wall surface rather than expressing their structural function of transferring weight down from the internal vaulting system,

Belèm, monastery church

Belèm, monastery cloister

Tomar, West window (exterior) of the monastery chapter-house

which here, in fact, needs no such assistance. The main arch of the south portal is rounded, but it encloses two flattish-headed doors each surmounted by a pointed lunette. Surrounding this portal complex is a dense projecting cluster of sculpted shafts whose different lengths give the impression of being the pipes of an external organ. The frame of the west door includes projecting lacework canopies and deep stage-sets for statues and New Testament scenes. The double-level monastic cloister is built out from the north wall. Here again simplicity has been eschewed. Though square in plan, the corners of the cloister have been pulled forward to take the starkness out of the ninety degree angles. The arcades on both tiers have suppressed rounded arches but their radii in each tier are different. So is the tracery within them, supported by sharply individualized columns. Again there are buttresses, square below, columnar at the upper storey; in both cases they are there less for support than as excuses for more surfaces to decorate.

Not even at Belèm, however, is decorative exuberance more dramatically displayed than in the extensions Manuel sponsored to the monastic buildings at Tomar. Here the west window of the new (1510) chapter house has on the inside a dividing shaft crawling with ropes, basket work and artichokes. Outside, where the effect aimed at is broader, it is dwarfed within a thickly embossed panel whose motifs include armillary spheres (Manuel's personal emblem), ropes and floats, cork-oak roots, fictive curtains, columns, urns and tassels, a fusion of things naturally solid and limp. It is grotto furniture applied to a façade, the most strutting stylistic trademark pinned on any European building of the time.

Manuel's patronage opened a Pandora's Box-ful of influences which united in this uniquely flavoured exuberance: the late-Gothic flamboyance of France and Flanders with the broken-arch outlines and scribal details of Islamic, *mudéjar* workmanship and, as on the columns of the church at Belèm, a light peppering of Italianate motifs, putti and urns, derived probably from printed sources and certainly without any humanistic impulse or concern for developments in Italy. The style represents neither renewed respect for classical achievements nor rebirth in its other sense, a revival of native talent; the directing, building and sculptural teams were multinational, French, Spanish and Portuguese, and the workforce was even more heterogeneous. The product of a local melting pot, stirred by an individual in a transient phase of financial euphoria, its export elsewhere was out of the question. Yet the Manueline moment is inescapably part of the sum of new achievements to be embraced within the time-span of 'Renaissance'.

From 1529, however, the term *al Romano*[47] begins to appear in Portuguese building records, and in the 1530s Joâo de Castilho, builder of the Gothic vaulting of the church of Belèm, dramatically changed his style and produced one of the purest examples of the classical spirit anywhere in Europe: the casket-like Chapel of the Immaculate Conception on a small hill within sight of the Tomar monastery. Free-standing, equally carefully finished inside and out, this small building, with its Corinthian columns and pilasters supporting barrel vaults, its rectangular windows whose outer frames and pediments are reflected in full relief on the outside of the walls, and its reliance on clarifications of volume rather than on decoration, rivals such a model of refinement as the Pazzi Chapel. And then, from 1554, came the rebuilding of the main cloister of the monastery, hard up against the Manueline flank of the church. While the Chapel of the Conception reflects the fifteenth-century spare phase of Italian anti-Gothic the architect of the cloister, Diego de Torralva, gave the cloister the later, more histrionic and openly classical references that had been explored by Giuliano da Sangallo and Bramante. Yet apparently no Italian was directly involved, nor had humanism acquired in Portugal a status that would influence architectural commissions. This remained true of the next marriage of a classical to a Manueline structure, the breaking through in 1571 of the east end of the church at Belèm by Jerònimo de Ruâo (son of a French sculptor) to add an austere mausoleum sanctuary. Here Manuel lies with his wife and their immediate successors in heavy plain sarcophagi borne on elephants' backs in a space defined by smooth marble panels separated by double columns topped, in two tiers, by scrupulously correct Ionic and Corinthian capitals.

With these exceptions, religious architecture outside Italy in the sixteenth century was slow to reflect the basic rethinking of church design set in train by the practice of Brunelleschi, the theory of Alberti, the authority of Vitruvius and the ease with which ancient structures could be studied, generation by generation. In Spain Charles V's and Philip II's personal and political connections with Italy led to the introduction of Italianate classical features, but these were chiefly prominent in secular buildings. Church architecture preferred the internal atmosphere produced by the Gothic, and externally, classical ornament in Spain was in competition with the exuberant irrationality of the native Plateresque, 'silversmith-like' style. In France it was, again, secular buildings that responded most readily to Italian influences. In contrast to the multiplicity of new *châteaux* that were built before the civil wars, there was a backlog of unfinished Gothic churches to complete, and when the wars came in the 1560s church building came virtually to a halt. Caution and controversy, indeed, checked the building of new churches whenever there were Reformation tensions: throughout England, the Netherlands, Germany and Switzerland, Italian influence was chiefly limited to the design of monuments and (in Catholic churches) altars in existing structures. When appearances next changed on an international scale it was after the Thirty Years War closed with the Treaty of Westphalia in 1648 and when England in 1660 joined France as a country living with tensions but without civil war. With religion

Tomar, Chapel of the Immaculate Conception   Belèm, Mausoleum Chapel, monastery church

reasonably settled, area by area, the designers of churches could turn with a more thorough intellectual preparation to the lessons of ancient Rome itself and with less regional defensiveness to considering their response to a new set of Italian variations, those of the Baroque.

THE VAGARIES OF GENIUS

In spite of the originality and influence of Netherlandish artists from the early fifteenth century, it is Italy that has traditionally been seen as representing the cultural tone of Renaissance Europe. It was there that scholars first put the present in touch with the life of classical antiquity, there that contemporary achievement in learning, literature and the arts was most consciously seen as a re-emergence of long-buried talent. And though other Europeans were also sharply aware that their times were notably different from those of their medieval forefathers, it came to be posterity's admiration for the unflagging creativity of Italian artists and thinkers that seized first on Vasari's reference to the rebirth of the arts, then extended it to characterize Italian culture as a whole, and finally applied the term Renaissance to a period of European history.

So much glamour has accrued to the term, with its implication that mankind can heave itself free from the dragging weight of centuries and make a fresh, born again, start, and so great is its convenience in directing attention to the dovetail connecting one phase of a particular country's experience to the next, that to reject it is artificial. As long, that is, as it is accepted that its use is also artificial; it implies that the achievement of a few men of genius can represent the circumstances of the many: it would be hazardous to put the formative agents of cultural change, as contributors or patrons, at more than a thousandth part of the population of Europe. And while it draws on the example of the continually self-renewing creative energy of Italy, the word Renaissance loses much of its appropriateness when transplanted from peninsular soil. It becomes a medal used to congratulate the acceptance of an Italian flavour within another country's culture ('the Renaissance in Spain') or simply the achievement of a largely native peak of creative ebullience ('the English Renaissance').

Certainly, as the European transmission system speeded up and purses and minds were opened wider, more Europeans looked to what was being made and thought in Italy. Towards 1500 the emigré Antonio Bonfini wrote of his patron King Matthias Corvinus, who had received a humanist education and married a daughter of the King of Naples, that 'he strove to transform Pannonia [Hungary] into a second Italy.'[48] A century later, in 1609, returning from a revelatory visit to Italy to his native southern Low Countries, the travel writer Daniel L'Ermite visited the court at Köthern, near Dessau in northern Germany, of the princeling Ludwig of Anhalt. Ludwig's palace was surrounded by gardens planted from imported seeds and trees in an Italianate fashion, and there in 1617 he founded a literary society, based on the Florentine Accademia della Crusca, to purify the German language on the lines of the Crusca's great *Dictionary* of 1612. Meanwhile L'Ermite noted that 'when I came to Prince Ludwig I really thought that I had already returned to Italy; so much was everything about this prince formed on the Italian model. His very servants at court are quite Italian in their language, clothes and manners; even the architecture of his palace is not, like ours, without delicacy. You would find nothing about the prince himself which would yield to an Italian, whose virtues, however, not whose vices, he embodies. He marvellously combines easy Italian grace with German seriousness.'[49]

Leaving such *parti pris* laudations aside, there were sixteenth-century echoes of Italian taste in architecture and sculpture from Granada and Hampton Court to Uppsala and Cracow and the Kremlin, of Italian painting from Seville to Antwerp; there were few poets in Europe who did not recognize Petrarch and Ariosto as desirable models, few scholars who did not use classical texts prepared by Italians or the approach to them pioneered by Italian humanists. Castiglione's *The Courtier* was a continental handbook of correct social comportment and a model for the range of interests of the educated gentleman, Machiavelli was the notorious 'Machiavel' of Innocent Gentillet's *Contre-Machiavel* of 1577 and in 1589 of the Prologue to Christopher Marlowe's *The Jew of Malta*: 'though some speak openly against my books, Yet they will read me.' But imports from Italy no more transformed a country's indigenous culture than did the spices imported from Venice add more than an exotic flavour to its tables.

As with a chain of whispers, the original messages of literary or artistic ideas acquired a different import as they were passed along. They traversed regions which distorted or drowned them. They became confused by being mingled with messages passed along other chains. In the early 1520s, for instance, the Toledan Pedro Machuca painted his masterpiece, *The Deposition*. The basic structure of the composition – the highlighted central triangle and backing verticals of ladders and cross – owes much to Italy, as do the slumped anatomy of Christ and the turned head of the turbaned woman beside the Magdalen. The compressed group of Jews debating the significance of the Crucifixion with the Good Centurion on the right, and the curlicued banner above them, derive on the other hand from northern tradition, while the unifying brooding, nightfall sense of a mystery that was also a historical reality is the product of Machuca's own background and temperament.

Sir Philip Sidney's meandering prose romance *Arcadia* was improvised and written at speed; in 1590 he reminded his sister that it was 'done in loose sheets of paper, most of it in your presence, the rest by sheets sent unto you as fast as they were done'.[50] It shows how many influences, classical Greek, medieval French, more recent Italian and Spanish, jostled in the mind of an Englishman who had received a sound humanistic education and had studied in Italy. Again, men looked back as well as outwards. Spenser's sympathies, for all the

Pedro Machuca, *Deposition*, 1520–5 (Museo del Prado, Madrid)

ancient and neo-Latin authors he had absorbed, leaned markedly towards the chivalric tradition of knights-errant, dwarfs, hermits and maidens in distress. Sidney drew on his knowledge of classical literary theory when writing his *Defence of Poesie* in 1591, but in it he confessed that 'I never heard that old song of Percy and Douglas that I found not my heart move more than with a trumpet.'[51] Shakespeare sounded a similar note. 'That piece of song', the love-sick Orsino in *Twelfth Night* tells the disguised Viola,

> That old and antique song we heard last night:
> Methought it did relieve my passion much;
> More than light airs and recollected terms
> Of these most brisk and giddy-paced times.

Such occasional nostalgia for what was old and familiar was universal. The turning back of artists to find a congenial foothold for a fresh advance, the working through by the press all over Europe of the long backlog of unpublished medieval texts: little perished from the past until it had entirely lost its savour. Cultural traditions, social requirements and intellectual appetites differed from country to country. There could be no uniform pattern of consumption as far as learning, literature and the arts were concerned.

Even humanism, as it rapidly fanned out from Italy from the late fifteenth century and provided Europeans with a common reference point in the classical past, was chiefly a tool for the reshaping of their own preoccupations and ways of expressing them. Nor was the new range of examples it offered to writers necessarily congenial. In spite of the availability of a wide repertory of ancient love poetry, for example, authors in one country after another chose to go no further back for inspiration than to Petrarch. This was in part because his verse exemplified how feeling could be expressed in a vernacular. It owed something to the lessons that could be learned from his technical virtuosity and the beauty of the sound patterns it shaped. But it was also because Petrarch's rueful exploration of the personal psychology of love arose within a fourteenth-century religious and social environment that gave his verse a continuing poignancy that could not be felt or communicated so relevantly by drawing on the poets of the classical, pagan world.

Whatever was brought to the surface from the deep strata of antiquity was interpreted by individuals in their own terms. Whatever was made in Italy in the fifteenth and sixteenth centuries was subject elsewhere to local adaptation and met two major obstacles: personal genius and shared temperament – the stereotypes of national character were not just the scathing inventions of inter-country rivalry. El Greco exemplifies the self-expressing individual of genius. Coming to Italy as a Cretan icon-painter in the 1560s, he recorded his debt to what he saw during his residence there by including portraits of Titian, Raphael and Michelangelo in a corner of the *Purification of the Temple* which he painted in Rome; they are made to appear as though they were the donors of the gifts he used in painting it.

Once in Spain from 1577, however, he burned away most of his discipleship in the flame of his own vision. Even his first major work there, *The Disrobing of Christ*, revealed a new steadiness of artistic purpose, with an equilibrium between the inner and the observing eye that establishes it as one of the outstanding works of painting not just in

Spain but in Europe, anticipating both the naturalism of Velázquez and the spiritually illuminated earthiness of Caravaggio. Then his art became more inwardly personal. In the large *Adoration of the Shepherds* he painted shortly before his death in 1614 for his own tomb, every device known to Renaissance painters, save perspectivally based illusionism, is used and transformed. Three of the shepherds raise their hands as if to warm them at the light that beams outward from the child. The Virgin's hands bless what they reveal. The fourth shepherd folds his arms, and with them the significance of the event, to his heart. A scene instantly recognizable as rooted in everyday observation is manipulated into a unique way of seeing by the interplay of colour with colour, the use of light to support the rippling outlines of legs and arms; what is known to be stillness is rendered as movement. And above, what is known to be in movement, the soaring angel and the brilliantly foreshortened swarm of angels, is given a sense of permanence; while men's faces age and their bodies are subject to change, and other men take their places as worshippers, spiritual beings of impassive, unchanging beauty are there from the moment of Christ's birth until the end of time. It is a painting of dazzling technical virtuosity. But this is a Mannerism of the mind, not of ingenious rule-breaking or a search for novelty, a style without a dominating source and which could have no progeny.

The obstacle provided by national temperament in Europe to the influence of a classicized and Italianized culture was nowhere more strikingly demonstrated than in Germany from the 1480s to the 1530s. The initial enthusiasm for humanism of the generation of Konrad Celtis was motivated as much by rivalry with the repute of Italian scholarship as by interest in antiquity for its own sake; it lost that interest still further with the Lutheran call to moral order in the present. Nor from amidst the mass of treatises, pamphlets, poems and plays that flowed from German presses did any individual literary voice emerge to catch the attention of writers elsewhere or, for that matter, at any later time. Brant, Luther and Sachs spoke with direct force to their fellow Germans, but there was no Ariosto, Ronsard, Sidney, Cervantes or Kochanowski. Germanic expressive genius, especially in southern Germany and the Rhineland and in German-speaking Switzerland, was concentrated in the work of sculptors and painters. In the very decades when Italian art was becoming most 'Italian', across the Alps, in the hands of a remarkable cluster of men of exceptional talent, it was becoming more 'German' than ever before. When the full-size model of Verroc-

El Greco, *Disrobing of Christ*,
1577–9 (Cathedral, Toledo)

chio's burly and compact equestrian statue of the *condottiere* Bartolommeo Colleoni arrived in Venice to be cast in bronze, Felix Fabri the
Dominican friar from Ulm commented that the Venetians were 'imitating the custom of the pagans'.[52] No such comment could have occurred
to any observer of Bernt Notke's contemporaneous *St George*. The
vividly polychromed (over wood) horse rears up over the jagged frenzy
of the stricken dragon. The saint rises in his stirrups to bring down
the finishing sword-stroke not with Colleoni's scowling concentration
on the job in hand, but with a calm confidence that the blow will be
directed less by his own arm than by that of his coadjutor, God. Equal

in genius, even allowing for the difference in subject matter these horses and riders are conceptually worlds – or at least the Alps – apart.

From then, *c.* 1480, there was only an occasional echo of Italian art's conscious aestheticism, its suppression of ragged outlines, its decorum of expression and gesture, its seeking for an overall grace and harmony, its dislike of the ugly side of reality and of 'low' subject matter. Germanic artists continued to respond to the angularities and emotionalism of their own version of late International Gothic. They welcomed the untidiness of nature just as they were fascinated by the lives of peasants and soldiers. In work after work there was a direct and unfastidious empathy with what things felt like: the crushing weight of the Christ-child on St Christopher's shoulders, the depth of the wound in Christ's side as measured by Thomas's probing fingers, the gasp of a soldier

Bernt Notke, *St George*, 1470 (Cathedral, Stockholm)

Hans Baldung *Mourning over the Dead Christ*, *c*.1513 (Ferdinandeum, Innsbruck)

when a pike goes home in his throat, the jerking bodies of pilgrims in the throes of religious hysteria at a shrine. There was a spontaneous subjective identification with past experience, from the sexual advances between Adam and Eve when in a state of prelapsarian sinlessness, to the howls of execration as his torturers jammed the crown of thorns on to Christ's head. Some of these strands are present, without excessive emphasis, in Hans Baldung's *Mourning over the Dead Christ* of *c*. 1513. Christ's awkwardly slumped body is pushed towards the spectator. The distraught Magdalen clutches the toes of one of his inordinately stretched-out legs. St John's robe flutters in resonance with his grief. Behind is no Jerusalem but a local landscape of farmstead and distant mountains and a nearby forest which has provided living crosses for the malefactors, only whose feet are included (a single foot in the case of the one on the right). In contrast to the sallow flesh of Christ and the paler, disquietingly bloodstained cloth in which he is to be wrapped, the colours are eye-catchingly bright. The painting is meant to disturb, to make belief believable.

Its non-Italian flavour is mild, however, in comparison with Jörg Ratgeb's *Resurrection*, where the everyday and the supernatural meet in a ferocity of conviction. The soldiers are flung back – in a genre litter of up-to-date weapons, wine flask and jug, and the playing cards with which they had been gambling before falling asleep – by the almost audible blast with which an incandescent Christ is projected outwards and upwards from his rock-tomb. And no work so commands the whole intense range of Germanic feeling as the three triptychs which Mathias Grünewald's huge *Isenheim Altarpiece*, completed *c.* 1515, was ingeniously hinged to deploy as they were opened in succession in accordance with the stages of the liturgical year. With its command of perspective, easy knack with still-life detail and (at times) weightily

Mathias Grünewald, *Crucifixion*, detail from the *Isenheim Altarpiece*, *c.*1515 (Unterlinder Museum, Colmar)

realistic treatment of drapery this work is intellectually abreast of advanced practice elsewhere whether Netherlandish or Italian. But it could not have been produced outside a personal and communal taste for pathos verging on the horrific, for the high-pitched subjective use of colour of Grünewald's homeland. Christ's lash-spotted body has the yellowish-green of decay. Though the mouth gapes in an exhaustion beyond recovery, the fingers twist upwards from the sagging crossbar to which His hands are nailed and blood glistens at the tips of His clubbed and claw-like feet. And the pointing finger of the Baptist, himself resurrected by the artist from his execution by Herod, consults the book of the future and from it declares, in the inscription beside him, 'He must increase.' Neither in colour, nor in its treatment of historical time any more than in its scale – compare the size of the Magdalen with the group of St John supporting the ashen Virgin – could such a work have occurred to an Italian.

With painters and sculptors working over some forty years in centres stretching from Cologne to Basel and from Strasbourg to Nuremberg, and in an artistic world never closed to outside influences, the term 'Germanic' covers a multitude of impulses. Yet for all these distances, debts and personal idiosyncracies, a body of work was created that was above all nationally *sui generis*.

A few artists turned – as Cranach frequently did – to mythological subjects, though commonly these were restricted to woodcuts, and the classical feeling for them was seldom easy or natural. In the Swiss Niklaus Manuel's *The Judgement of Paris* of *c.* 1517, for instance, Paris is an up-to-date young man, Juno a *Hausfrau* and the simpering Minerva is more provocatively naked than Venus and, indeed, wears the ostrich feather head-dress associated by other artists with army prostitutes. Though Dürer once reproached his fellow-countrymen for producing work 'like a wild and unpruned tree'[53] and paid two thoughtful visits to Italy, only his late (*c.* 1526) *Four Holy Men*, with its compact composition and massive, simplified drapery, looks at first sight as though it could have been produced in the South.

Generally, Germanic artists found borrowed Italian clothes uncomfortable. In *Christ Shown to the People* by Urban Görtschacher the stage which contains the figure is, if quirkily, 'Renaissance' in the Italian mode: the relief carving at the end of the staircase, the mouldings of the central arch and the perspective view of the arcaded corridor beyond it, the pilastered round-headed opening above it and the burlier columned arcade glimpsed on the left: all this recalls a minor Quattrocento

Niklaus Manuel, *The Judgement of Paris*, c.1517 (Kunstmuseum, Basel)

mise-en-scène. But once the characters are included the mood is transformed. The gesticulating crowd with their strained expressions, the figures boozing or lounging on the staircase, above all the cramped, crouching, awkwardly hand-bound figure of the main actor, Christ, place this at once far away from Italy, as do the fluttering ribbons of inscription which add a verbal comment to the pictorial message of the episode.

A work like this is a reminder of the multitude of minor painters, many of them named only after the impress of a particular work, or from the city or region where they lived, who were satisfying local demand. For a further reason why Italian styles, as they flowed up to the West through France and to the East through Poland and changed the manner of artists in the Netherlands, failed to make significant inroads into this middle zone, was productivity of such high and widespread quality that patrons felt little need to shop elsewhere, and of such a pungent and confident character of its own that its practitioners were happy to reinvestigate and maintain their own purely native approach.

Nationalistic conservatism played some part in this. Maximilian I, arch-propagandist for the German empire and his role within it, would employ no foreigner among the teams of artists he employed to celebrate his deeds and destiny. Duke Wilhelm of Bavaria, though choosing a cycle of classical battles to decorate his summer palace, appointed only local painters. How his confidence was rewarded can be seen by comparing Altdorfer's contribution, the deeply pondered, at once exquisite and apocalyptic, *Battle of Issus* (Alexander the Great's defeat of Darius, King of Persia) of 1529, with the blandly expert accumulation of classical motifs in Giulio Romano's *Battle of Constantine* in the Vatican of a few years before.

From the 1530s the full distinctiveness of Germanic art, however, began to collapse. The Protestant iconoclastic movement hit artists'

Albrecht Dürer, *Four Holy Men* (Apostles?), *c.* 1526 (Alte Pinakothek, Munich)

earnings. Reformation politics cut at some of them more directly. Ratgeb was executed in 1526 for having taken the underdog side in the Peasants' War. The same crisis brought the sculptor Tilman Riemenschneider's career to a close with imprisonment and torture. Grünewald's Protestant sympathies led him to flee from his position in Mainz as a court painter to the Archbishop of Brandenburg to Halle, where he died two years later in 1528. He continued to paint there, but, in the case of the persecution of Barthel and Hans Sebald Beham, political invigilation robbed artists of the freedom of interpretation which was very much part of the Germanic impulse to paint and sculpt. Though demand slackened, some artists of genius worked on unharassed: Dürer until his death in 1528, the sculptor Veit Stoss until 1533, Altdorfer until 1538, Baldung until 1545, Cranach, increasingly as an automa-

Urban Görtschacher,
Christ shown to the People,
1508 (Kunsthistorisches
Museum, Vienna)

Albrecht Altdorfer, *The Battle of Issus*, 1529 (Alte Pinakothek, Munich)

ton, until his death in 1553. It was not so much religious politics
that brought the Germanic artistic contribution to the Renaissance age
practically to a close: churches banned art only in parts of Germany
and Switzerland, the demand for portraits, for mythological and
historical subjects grew. It was, rather, a fluke: the absence of a new
generation of artists of genius. And after having been kept waiting
in the wings, Italianizing understudies took over a stage vacated by
its leading actors.

As applied to the cultural life of Germany, 'Renaissance', then, has little significance unless the word is leached free from any association save that of a surge of shared advance on what had gone before in this single, visual, and not long-lived aspect of native creativity. In France it is possible to speak on the one hand narrowly of a French Renaissance, not in this case a visual but a verbal phenomenon: the shared contribution of a group of poets who created a notable advance on native literary tradition, and on the other (and far more broadly than in the case of Germany) of the Renaissance in France.

In the long period (1307–1377) during which the Papal court took refuge in Avignon from the baronial unruliness of Rome, humanism established a French base during its formative stage; Petrarch worked in Provence until he was forty-nine. Thus naturalized, humanism remained in the French intellectual bloodstream with the ease of reference to its texts and ideas that emerged with such instinctive facility in the essays of Montaigne. In painting, though the Sienese painter Simone Martini came to work at Avignon when at the height of his career in 1339, and though artistic relations between France and Italy continued – both Jean Perréal and Jean Bourdichon, the leading French painters around 1500, went to Italy – the vagaries of genius were such that no Frenchman in the later fifteenth or the sixteenth century emerged to be stimulated by Italian achievement or to build on the earlier talent of the Limbourg brothers or Jean Fouquet. The presence of Rosso and other Italians jolted into existence the fragile School of Fontainebleau painters, but native painting, as best represented from the 1550s by the careful draughtsmanship of François Clouet and Corneille de Lyon, never flourished as it had done in Germany. This was not yet France's painterly moment. It was, however, though not in the sense of a consistent 'school' of European pre-eminence, the moment of a number of sculptors, from Jean Goujon in the 1540s to Germain Pilon in the 1580s.

These were men whose obvious intelligence underlies the mastery with which they drew the grace of late Gothic French sculpture into a clearly understood relationship with the classical inspiration behind the work of the Italians who, like Cellini, worked in France, or with the ancient works, or casts from them, imported by Louis XII and Francis I. And it was, in the same qualified sense, the moment of French architects. And again, in a Europe peppered with Italian-classical motifs thrown at façades and perched uneasily on roof-lines, the key to the success of the French hybridization of native styles was a sensibility that was highly intellectualized. The mid-sixteenth century designs of Jacques Androuet du Cerceau and Philibert de l'Orme represent a deliberate attempt to understand the principles expounded by Vitruvius, open to inspection in the classical remains of Rome (both had been there), and interpreted by Sebastiano Serlio, who died in France in 1554 after designing the Château of Ancy-le-Franc, a perfect marriage between the prescriptions of his treatises and what a French patron was prepared to accept. A later Italian art theorist, Giovanni Paolo Lomazzo, wrote sourly in 1584 that Serlio's written works had produced 'more hack architects than he had hairs in his beard', but this did not hold true for France.

It is not, however, the easy passage of humanist interests from Italy to France or the adaptive intelligence of native sculptors and architects that constitute the French Renaissance. This was a genius for the use of words; in the prose of Rabelais and Montaigne, but above all in poetry.

In *c*. 1530 Jean Clouet (the father of François), an artist who looked as much to the Low Countries as to Italy for his inspiration, produced a portrait of an unknown Frenchman holding a small volume labelled 'Petrarcha' – the *Man with a Petrarch*. Thirty years later such a subject would have been more likely to hold one of the equally small and personally precious volumes of the first pocket editions of the collected poems of Pierre de Ronsard, published in 1560. By then French poets, especially those of the Pléiade group, had absorbed Italian and classical models into voices of their own which were to be listened to and emulated throughout western Europe from Spenser to Jan Kochanowski, 'the Polish Ronsard'.

The term 'Pléiade', which Ronsard himself employed, refers to the group of stars within the constellation of Taurus named from the seven daughters of Atlas. Only six of the stars could in fact be seen before the introduction of the Galilean telescope, so the analogy suited the body of friends who studied and exchanged ideas in Paris: Ronsard and du Bellay, Jean-Antoine de Baïf, Rémy Belleau, Pontus de Tyard and Etienne de Jodelle. In 1550 they were respectively 26, 27, 18, 22 and 29 and 18 years old. They then referred to themselves as a 'brigade', a like-minded radical sodality. And this sense of a common enterprise was fostered by their contacts with other groups of tradition-challengers in Lyon and at the University of Poitiers. As in the atmosphere of a 'school' of painters watching one another's work, or in the observant rivalries of the later London theatre, the sense of closeness

Jean Clouet, *Man with a Petrarch*, *c*.1530 (HM The Queen, Windsor Castle)

within a minority acted as a stimulant. And by then Paris was the settled abode of a previously itinerant court at which, as in the subsidiary salons that came to surround it, aristocratic birth or inherited money gave the members of the brigade an entrée. Verse was popular in polite circles for its role in flirtatious (and not so discreet) love affairs and for its shorter forms being commonly set to music. Paris before the ugly factionalism that grew with the civil wars, towards the massacre of St Bartholomew's Day was a congenial and encouraging place to be youthful and a poet. Well educated, they could share the interest in the then fashionable Italian and Latin poets and share the pleasure taken in the mythological conceits of court entertainments. But for them the native poetic tradition was a source of national pride, and to bring it abreast of Italian repute was particularly intriguing under an Italian Queen Mother, Catherine de' Medici.

What saved the Pléiade poets from being a coterie and made their approach into a movement was the energy and talent with which they sensed change and promoted it in theory and practice. Consciously an avant-garde, they turned on their immediate predecessors as not having exploited the promise of their own tongue. They detected in them a reluctance to keep abreast of change, a failure of nerve: 'today', a French author had stated resignedly in 1529, 'the language is changed in a thousand ways from what it was fifty years ago.'[54] Ignoring the creative use made of this state of flux by Rabelais and the poet Clémont Marot, who had died in 1544, du Bellay turned in 1549 to the wider debate about language in order to claim a new starting point.

The humanists' revival of correct and elegant, as opposed to what they dubbed 'refectorial Latin', had also challenged the literary status of vernaculars.[55] 'Because many depraved and distorted things had later been composed by many in that language', Pietro Bembo in 1525 wrote in defence of the Italian of Dante, Petrarch and Boccaccio, 'no longer mindful of its correct and proper usage in writing, it seemed, therefore, that in a short time, unless someone came to its aid, it would so far decline as to remain for ages without honour, without splendour, without any reverence or dignity.'[56] Luther's concern with German was more direct; to communicate ideas to a wide audience, he said, 'one must look people in the mouth.'[57] Patriotism played a strong part in Juan de Valdés's defence of Castilian in his 1535 Dialogue on Language. Just how widespread this interest in vernaculars, and particularly their suitability for poetry, had become fifty years later can be seen from Sidney's Defence of Poesie: 'The Italian is so full of vowels that it must ever be cumbered with elisions; the Dutch so, of the other side, with consonants, that they cannot yield the sweet sliding fit for verse; the French in his whole language hath not one word that hath his accent on the last syllable saving [but] two, and little more hath the Spanish, and therefore very gracelessly may they use dactyls. The English', he roundly concluded, 'is subject to none of these defects.'[58]

The 'Defence' of Sidney's title was picked up from du Bellay's Defence and Praise [Illustration] of the French Language, the Pléiade's linguistic manifesto. Du Bellay's concern, too, was with poetry as the highest use of the resources of language. The lexical pool of French, he emphasized, is rich; all the same, the poet's ear and learning will show him what to adapt from Italian or Latin usage while being careful not to mongrelize the native stock. There is a strong emphasis on the poet's mission: to dispel ignorance, raise taste and exemplify the genius of the country. This is what the vernacular should be improved to do; 'I cannot blame too strongly the rashness of some of our countrymen who, being anything rather than Greeks or Latins, deprecate and reject everything written in French.'[59] Moving from words to works, he deplores some of the metres and structures used by his predecessors. 'Sonne moy des beaux sonnetz,' he says with a deliberately provocative play on words: 'let me hear fine sonnets, an Italian invention no less erudite than pleasing.'[60] It was part of the Pléiade's challenge both to themselves and to their followers that they combined linguistic nationalism with an admiration for such forms as the Italian sonnet sequence and the Latin ode and eclogue. Most of them, indeed, kept abreast of learnedly fashionable taste by writing Latin verse, thus giving their authorship and sponsorship of French poetry a respectable aura. They were not to know of the latinate Milton's patronizing reference to Shakespeare's 'native woodnotes wild', but they were determined not to be slighted as naïve regional artists.

In a sonnet of 1552 Ronsard speaks of how tiny particles, tumbling in random trajectories through space, came to cling together in forming the world.[61] So, he went on, an accumulation of random incidents has created love in his heart. When it dies, will it be dissipated into the four elements of earth, air, fire and water? No, thanks to his voice, it will sound throughout the universe for ever. With its reference to the Lucretian atomic theory and the medieval idea of man as microcosm of the cosmos, and the twist he gave to a cliché almost as old as verse itself that the poet's words outface death, the poem suggests how the Pléiade generation from the 1550s to the 1570s manipulated a variety of atoms into substances that were musically new and structurally firm. Thus in one of his sonnets Belleau, with his opening words, 'If you want me to die between your arms, my love', sets the reader wondering how the familiar conceit of orgasm as a little death will be resolved.[62] The poet goes on to point out that to make this possible his love must remove her clothes so that he can twine himself as closely to her as does ivy about the elm – an image lifted directly from one of the Pléiade's most admired neo-Latin poets, the Dutchman Johannes Secundus. Then the poem broadens to the contemporary scene: some seek death in the flanks of a bastion, in a skirmish, in battle, but I,

Belleau concludes, seek glory in another way, 'for I, my love, risk my life within your lips'.

Conceits that are not merely clever, a compression of ideas that does not squeeze them dry, a range of allusions that are absorbed, with a skilled nonchalance, into a personal tone: these are some of the qualities that account for the appeal of the Pléiade's lyric verse. Another is their rephrasing of themes of universal relevance. Poets, ancient and medieval, had long expressed the loneliness of exile and the joy of seeing again the smoke from one's own chimney; the solace of the countryside as opposed to the hectic pursuits of the town; the fearful hurrying past of the years and the pathos of a withered carcass still tremulous from the sparks of youthful passion; the enormity of destiny and the littleness of man; the feverish extreme yet the sense of purpose given by love – all were amply recorded aspects of the human condition but each was readjusted to suit present feelings and stimulate the contemporary ear.

Of all their themes, love was of course the most hackneyed. Yet when Louise Labé (who remained in the subsidiary sodality of the Lyon poets, but whose freshness of utterance has made her an honorary member of the Pléiade) had flared out at the start of a sonnet with a description of how the snows of the Caucasus thaw 'when Phoebus has completed his great O' (she was no heliocentrist), a new touchstone for the reader's immediate or imagined experience came to be established in what followed:

> There was a time when sad and doubting still
> You craved the warmth of my unready fire.
> But now that you have sated your desire,
> And held me bound and captive to your will,
> You have, to quench your flame, found some device,
> And if I once was cold, you now are ice.[63]

And another was offered when Ronsard, normally so ready in his affections, so tenderly sensuous, broke out in execration against a woman who nightly so exhausted herself with her dildo that she had no welcome left for him.[64]

Family and court connections kept the Pléiade poets aware of the wider religious and political issues that were to lead to the civil wars. Du Bellay, visiting Rome as diplomatic secretary to his relation Cardinal Jean du Bellay, was disillusioned both with the capital's political cynicism and its religious slackness. Watching the Tiber he longed for the Loire. Confronted by marble palaces and grandiose courtyards he regretted leaving the slated houses of Anjou and their modest yards. These sentiments occur in one of the most famous of all the group's poems, 'Heureux qui, comme Ulysse, a fait un beau voyage . . .' – and then comes home. The sequence in which it is placed is called as a whole Regrets.[65] Throughout it is the feeling (perhaps occasionally over-indulged) that for him the times are out of joint. For Ronsard the contrast between the present 'age of iron' with its wars and greed and quarrels with 'the age of gold' in which men had lived on easy terms with one another and with nature became a steady refrain. Sadly, in a poem addressed to his literary companions he referred – in 1553, before the civil wars had begun – to 'Poor Europe . . . Europe on whom the Gods No longer deign to turn their eyes.'[66]

While an eloquent master of all the lyric themes handled by the movement, Ronsard was by far the most immersed in public ones as well. From his youth as a page at court and a minor diplomatic envoy, his livelihood, until from 1565 he received a steady income from ben-efices (taking minor clerical orders did nothing to inhibit the celebration of his love affairs), depended on patronage; as with other authors, his publications brought him fame but not money. He had therefore to turn out congratulatory verses and song-settings for individuals, even love poems on behalf of those whose passion was not matched by their literacy; and he became the unofficial poet laureate of the Queen Mother during the short reigns of Henri II, Francis II and Charles IX. He commemorated victories, peace treaties, alliances; after the Franco-English agreement (the Treaty of Troyes) of 1564 Robert Cecil was sent a volume of his poems, including an 'Elegy to Her Majesty of the Realm of England', to pass to Elizabeth. Characteristically this elegy forecast that she would bring back to life 'the lovely age of gold'.[67] He was much engaged in writing diatribes against the Huguenots who, in court eyes, were responsible for making the age one of iron.

No poet had produced so much verse on so many occasions and covering so many topics of personal and public concern. Yet Ronsard was neither a Panjandrum of Poetry nor a verse machine. He was seldom facile or mechanical. Though called on now to praise peace, now to drum up support for war, his rhetorician's zeal on either side bore the conviction that poetry could enhance the validity of any senti-ment, any point of view. While as a technician of sound-forms and structures Ronsard was a poet's poet – at a time when this was considered a virtue – he was also a man whose whole attitude to life expressed itself naturally, if artfully, in verse; there is little he wrote, even to order for a lover or a politician, that did not sound some note of personal commitment to the process of writing it. It is in his work, and that of his fellow stars within the constellation of Taurus, that the genius of the French Renaissance, blending ancient example and Italian influence with a long native tradition, is most purely manifested.

In 1586, Elizabeth's commander of the English forces supporting the opposition of the northern Low Countries to Spain, the Earl of Leicester, was given a civic welcome to Leiden. As a prominent feature of it, he attended a lecture by Lipsius on Tacitus. His forces included his nephew Philip Sidney, who struck up a friendship with Lipsius that led to an invitation to come to England in that same year, presumably to a university chair: 'I know', Sidney wrote, 'that you would be very welcome to our Queen and to many others, yea to all others.'[68] Later that same year the author of the *Arcadia* and the *Defence of Poesie* died of a gunshot wound received at the Battle of Zutphen. The next year saw the first production in London of two plays, Christopher Marlowe's *Tamburlaine* and Thomas Kyd's *The Spanish Tragedy*, which were still being performed into the 1630s in spite of intensely varied challenges from the greatest number of talented dramatists – from 1590 including Shakespeare – who had ever worked in the same city in a comparably short period. If Lipsius had accepted the invitation he would have arrived in the early burgeoning of the native English Renaissance within the italicizing Renaissance in England.

As in France, humanism in England had become readily acclimatized. At the beginning of the sixteenth century Erasmus congratulated his English friends on their learning. It had become widely naturalized within higher education and intellectual life well before William Camden wrote his Latin history *Britannia* in 1590 and Thomas North added to previous English translations of classical authors in his *Plutarch* (1579), which was to be the prime source for Shakespeare's Roman plays.

Other Italian influences had flowed readily past insular, Protestant prejudices. Italian words and literary devices were shopped for freely. The Italian language was respected if Italian behaviour was not; breaking into the play within the play when the actor taking the part of Lucianus pours poison into the sleeping King's ear, Hamlet loudly comments to the watching court that 'the story is extant, and written in choice Italian.'[69] William Harrison, in his 1586 *Description of Britain*, felt called upon to claim that 'if ever curious building did flourish in England, it is in these our days, wherein our workmen excel and are in manner comparable with old Vitruvius, Leo Baptista [Alberti] and Serl[i]o.'[70] Yet the first building that actually demonstrated a true over-all grasp of Italian principles was the Queen's House at Greenwich, designed by Inigo Jones in 1616. In spite of Henry VIII's early patronage of Italian artists, there was a dearth of vigorous native talent either to use their example or to counter it. Monumental sculpture was still allowed in post-Reformation churches, but nothing came to rival Pietro Torrigiano's tomb of Henry VII and his wife in Westminster Abbey of 1512. And without any serious challenge from native painters, the uninformed taste of patrons turned to works that took the easy route across the North Sea.

Even the most humanistic of subjects produced in England, Elizabeth disconcerting Venus, Juno and Minerva by confronting them not with Paris's apple but with the regnal orb, was the work of an immigrant Fleming, Hans Eworth. More justifiable than Harrison's claim was the confidence, buoyed up by the literary music of the voices of Sidney, Spenser, Shakespeare and (in his opinion, if not posterity's) his own earlier works, that led Michael Drayton in 1613 to regret England's geographical isolation:

> O that Ocean did not bound our style
> Within these strict and narrow limits so;
> But that the melody of our sweet isle
> Might now be heard to Tiber, Arne, and Po;
> That they might know how far Thames doth outgo
> The music of declined Italy.[71]

Nonetheless, and granted the prestige of Italian architectural ornament, *novelle* and poetry and the number of translations from that language (for instance, Sir John Harrington's 1591 version of Ariosto's *Orlando Furioso*); despite, too, the range and quality of England's own poetry, from the expansive, ruminative tread of Spenser's stanzas in the *Faerie Queene* to the tension within Donne's lyrical-philosophical verse, and despite the talent of its outstanding composers (William Byrd, Orlando Gibbons and John Dowland died within three years of one another between 1623 and 1626), it is the extraordinary vigour and range of the playwrights that above all justifies reference to 'the English Renaissance'.

Hans Eworth (attrib.), *Queen Elizabeth I as Paris*, 1569 (HM The Queen, Hampton Court)

Fifteen ninety-one was a year which saw the first production of Shakespeare's formally inventive and wittily ironic *Taming of the Shrew* and the anonymous real-life melodrama (a wife and her lover murder her husband) *Arden of Faversham*. Both, in response to popular demand, were frequently restaged. In the same year John Florio, born in London to Italian parents and a prominent interpreter of Italy to England, published his instructional dialogues in both languages. One concerned the lack of attention paid by English dramatists to the classically-based rules observed by their Italian opposite numbers. 'After dinner', the student suggests, 'we will goe see a plaie.' The teacher crushingly remarks that 'The plaies that they plaie in England are not right comedies.' Bravely the student refers to the popularity of the theatre:

'Yet they doo nothing else but plaie every daie.'
'Yes, but they are neither right comedies nor right tragedies.'
'How would you name them, then?'
'Representations of histories [stories], without any decorum.'[72]

Florio may have been unaware of, or misunderstood the stance of the learned John Lyly who in 1588 put into the mouth of the Prologue to his comedy *Endymion* the deliberately goading announcement that 'we present neither comedy, nor tragedy, nor story, nor anything, but that whosoever heareth may say this: Why, here is a tale of the Man in the Moon.' Certainly he wrote before he could have witnessed in 1603 the failure of Ben Jonson's classically structured tragedy *Sejanus*.

While Plautine comedy and Senecan tragedy were drawn on by others besides Jonson, the very number of new plays (two hundred and seventy-five at least between *Tamburlaine* in 1587 and Shakespeare's *Henry VIII* in 1613) and their range of style and subject matter, shoulders to one side the impact of classical and Italian models. From subtlety to bombast, wit to heavy moralizing, native and classical historical settings to those of the domestic, 'citizen comedy' of London and its suburbs like Thomas Dekker's *The Shoemaker's Holiday* and Jonson's *Every Man in his Humour* in which Shakespeare, as a working actor, performed: the drama splits every explanatory mould save those of genius, skill, demand and opportunity.

'Holla, ye pampered Jades of Asia!'[73] Long before Marlowe's *Tamburlaine* opened the lungs of English dramaturgy with the revitalizing force that Masaccio's Brancacci Chapel frescoes imparted to Florentine painting, there had been an addiction to the telling of stories by actors over a social range from courtiers to Bottom the Weaver. Apart from the homespun seasonal ritual of morality cycles, *ad hoc* groups entertained noble households and toured the inn yards and market places of provincial towns, while Oxbridge students staged and adapted classical plays, and schoolboys, such as those from St Paul's for whom *Endymion* was written, played at court or in private houses. From the 1570s the licensing of permanent companies and the founding of purpose-built playhouses in London established a theatrical machinery that both responded to and increased the number of spectators and dramatists. By 1605 there were three public open-arena theatres (The Theatre, The Globe and The Fortune) and two indoor ones. With the former each providing room for some two thousand spectators, standing in the centre or seated in the galleries, and the latter with seats for about four hundred, they could together cater in a single day for up to eight thousand playgoers. Repeat visits were thus a commercial necessity: hence the repertory system, which meant that an actor might have to memorize thirty roles in a season, and which led to a voracious demand for new scripts. During the boom period for the production of new plays, 1600–10 (for Shakespeare this ran from *Hamlet* to *The Tempest*), the places available each year in the commercial theatre, discounting Sundays and Lent, may have topped a staggering two million when the population of London was two hundred and fifty thousand. Never before in Europe had there been so heavy a vote of confidence in a single form of cultural activity. Nor, it might be added, so great a tribute of protest. Complaints culminated in a petition to the city magistrates in 1619. Thanks to the theatres, 'there is daylie such resort of people, and such multitude of coaches, where of many are Hackney coaches, bringinge people of all sortes, that sometymes all our streetes cannott containe them.' In Ludgate, for instance, 'the inhabitantes there cannott come to their howses, nor bringe in their necessary provisions of beere, wood, coale, or haye, nor the tradesmen or shopkeepers utter [sell] their wares, nor the passenger goe to the common water staires without danger of their lives and lymmes.'[74]

Inevitably there were empty seats. But this spurred rivalry among companies, between dramatists, between the smaller indoor theatres, fostering a wittier, more formally structured appeal to a well-educated or at least well-off and fashionable audience, and the public ones where there was a broader expectation of what constituted a pennyworth. But the taste for play-going and actor-fancying was such that the audiences of the comfortable and more private theatres also attended performances in the jostling, weather-smitten public ones. 'Groundlings' may have been Hamlet's word for those who stood rather than sat, but *Hamlet* was not written only with them in mind. Indeed the relish for word-play within a dramatic story – and the apprehension of life itself as dramatic, full of political plots, murders, witchcraft, wars, sexual scandals, sudden inexplicable deaths, must be taken into account – was well-nigh universal. With boys playing women's parts (and those of men of all ages in the indoor theatres) and with little consistency aimed at in settings and costumes, the appeal to an audience's ability to lose themselves in a performance was not so much manipulated as rawly voluntary, affected less by consistent illusion than by the varieties of response to story, acting, style, echoes of personal experience, and language. The vocabulary and phraseology of English was in a state of vigorous flux, whether at the level of the convoluted *Euphues* which Lyly wrote with his non-dramatist hand, or the inventive jargon of London's vagrant underground of thieves and conmen. Between 1580 and 1623 nearly 11,000 new words appeared and stayed in the vocabulary of English, adding nearly one quarter to the previous resources of the language; many others were doubtless coined, spoken and lost sight of.

It is, then, not surprising that writers turned to the stage. Some managed a single play and expired. Others turned from one to another with little pause; Thomas Heywood claimed to have written or collaborated in two hundred and twenty between 1596 and 1633. Of the recorded new plays performed in 1611, for instance, two were by men of genius, Shakespeare and Jonson; six by men of outstanding skill or individuality, Francis Beaumont and John Fletcher in collaboration, Fletcher on his own in two cases, Dekker, Cyril Tourneur and Thomas Middleton; five by more facile men, John Cooke, Nathan Field, William Rowley and two by Heywood. In addition there were revivals of tried favourites. Altogether the appetite for theatrical dialogue and effects was so constant as to enable a playwright to indulge his own aspirations short of flagrantly inviting political and religious censorship; bawdiness was let slip with a shrug, a contributory reason for the Puritan criticism which led eventually, in 1642, to the order that the theatres should be closed altogether, an order honoured almost as much in the breach as in the observance.

Though Shakespeare may have won favours for his poems, his income depended on his career as an actor and business partner in his company, The Lord Chamberlain's Men, renamed The King's Men on James I's accession in 1603. That he should have ended his career as a prosperous and respected Stratford owner of land and property without having alienated his socially diverse audiences through the stretch of imagination and language in his plays is striking evidence for the peculiarly English addiction to theatrical experience. Quite unlike the creators of the Manueline style, the patron-fostered major painters of Italy, the Low Countries and Germany, or the private-income poets of the Pléiade, Shakespeare was reliant on popular support, as were his fellow playwrights. English drama was in this respect different in kind from other peaks of national creativity.

Apart from firing off a squib or two against the stylistic gaucheries of his predecessors and the *ad hoc*, unregistered companies who provided, outside the theatres, instant dramatizations of shock news stories – 'the quick comedians', who, as Cleopatra says with such scorn, 'extemporally will stage us and present our Alexandrian revels'[75] – Shakespeare took no side in the debate about stagecraft that other authors frequently referred to in their prologues. While fully aware, as in *The Comedy of Errors* or *Julius Caesar*, of the canonic classical structure for comedy and tragedy, he stayed within his own mental universe of dramatic forms, responding to the suitability for development of stories he found personally challenging or useful to the finances of The King's Men. Yet there is hardly a contemporary genre, apart from domestic melodrama, that was not echoed or anticipated in his work. There was a supremely confident ease in the relationship between his own responses and his professional awareness of the theatrical world he had identified himself with. More remarkable still is the facility with which his mind aligned for poetic utterance in the relevant register for his dramatic and verbal purpose the whole range of his knowledge and experience.

Our knowledge of Shakespeare is scant for three reasons: the thinness of documentary evidence for his life; the avoidance of overtly personal viewpoints in his plays; and the perennial mystery of the nature of genius. But something can be glimpsed. The range of the sources of his plots, or parts of them, is large: classical drama, probably not at first hand; Italian *novelle* in translation or retailed in discussion; English chronicles; earlier plays; contemporary novels (Robert Greene's *Pandosto* for *A Winter's Tale*, Thomas Lodge's *Rosalynde* for *As You Like It*); North's Plutarch. But apart from plot sources, some rhetorical devices – it is unlikely that formal orations like 'Friends, Romans, countrymen', did not owe something to the popular classical treatise on public speaking the *Ad Herennium* – and a few instances where a phrase or train of thought seems directly attributable to a book, as in an echo in *The Tempest* of Florio's translation of Montaigne's essay 'Of the Caniballes', there is the indelible impression of the non-traceable, skimming manner of the swift reader who seeks suggestion rather than statement. And it would be impossible to get even near to the sources of his inspiration without seeing him as a lip-reader of the conversational encyclopaedia that London represented, with its range of educated acquaintance open to a fashionable actor and author, its tavern raffishness, its status hovering between that of island and continent for those engaged in trade, diplomacy and soldiering, its foreign communities which could provide the local colour for *The Merchant of Venice* and the Franglais of Hal and Katherine's wooing scene in *Henry V*, and encourage the 'Boscos thromuldo boskos' mumbo-jumbo of Parolles's presumed Muscovite captors in *All's Well That Ends Well*.[76]

It was not just verbal appetite and emotional empathy with his characters' reactions to the situations he confronted them with that promoted Shakespeare's leadership within the active hive of English drama. It was also his squeezing use of the London of court, city, waterfront and constant traffic for ideas and information which, through some instant storing and sorting process, passed into the language of his plays. It is through the work of Shakespeare and his fellow dramatists that we can see most clearly why contemporaries' alertness to the dense fabric of events and achievements that for them constituted, as we shall see in the Epilogue, 'Our Age', has to qualify any retrospective view of 'Renaissance' either as a classical revenant in Italian clothes stalking across Europe in search of devotees, or as identifying scattered peaks of national creative achievement.

PART THREE

Civilization

Civilization has to be defended against the individual, and its regulations, institutions and commands are directed to that task.

SIGMUND FREUD, *The Future of an Illusion* (1928)

CHAPTER VII

Civility

THE NORMS

In March 1772 Boswell called on Dr Johnson as he was preparing
the fourth edition of his great *Dictionary*. Fertile as usual with bright,
up-to-date ideas, Boswell suggested the inclusion of the word 'civilization'. This, he thought, would be a useful general term to oppose
'barbarity' because 'civility' was more socially narrow. The lexicogra-
pher would have none of it; 'he would not admit *civilization*, but only
civility.'[1] To civilize, in the sense of extending the values of civility to
those not irredeemably barbarous, was acceptable as a verb, but the
process had not gone so far that civilization could be used of society
as a whole. Nowhere else did Johnson show himself more directly the
heir of the social and intellectual values of the Renaissance.

The medieval view of European society had been that it constituted
a stratified Christian co-operative. According to its model of the Three
Estates, the masses of the Third laboured for the Second Estate of
warrior leaders who protected them, and for the clerical members of
the First, who prayed on behalf of both. From the fourteenth century
this simple model had come under strain. Knights had become estate
managers as well as warriors. Members of the Third Estate had become
ever more widely differentiated in status and activity. From the mid-
fifteenth century the pace of challenge to the model increased. The
proportion of well-off and socially conspicuous commoners grew with
commercial prosperity, the enhanced status of the legal and medical
professions and the extending bureaucratic reach of central and municipal governments. The clerical Estate became less clearly defined, in
perception if not in function, by the Reformation, by suppression of
monastic prayer-houses and the loss of the clergy's quasi-monopoly of
learning. The image of the Second Estate became further blurred by
marriages between blood and wealth, reliance on court service and a

form of education akin to that of the non-noble. In the sixteenth century there were complaints about English knights who could not ride, Spanish *hidalgos* who could not shoot, Italian *conti* and *baroni* whose swords only left their scabbards in personal quarrels. Only in and beyond the eastern German marches were the descendants of a *Graf* or *Ritter* likely to remain unreconstructed members of the military caste, and even there the influence of major Habsburg courts at Vienna and Prague and lesser ones at Innsbruck and Graz had a taming effect. It was not that aristocrats felt less conscious of their birth, or that commoners withheld deference from their rank, but that the Estate to which they belonged had lost something of its separate clarity.

These changes led to the notion of the Three Estates becoming archaic and formal, as in the representation in the English Parliament of Bishops, Lords and Commons. In ordinary usage 'estate' came to refer to a man's position in society regardless of what Estate he belonged to. The uncertainty caused by greater social flux led to reiterated attempts to pin people down; everyone, ran an Augsburg ordinance of 1537, must wear clothing suitable to their station in order 'to be recognized for whome he or she is'. And it led to renewed emphasis on the need for hierarchy. The very homeliness of the imagery used by Sir Thomas Elyot in his *The Governour* of 1531 suggests the need to put the conservative message clearly. 'Where all thynge is commune', he wrote, 'there lacketh ordre; and where ordre lacketh, there all thynge is odiouse and uncomly. And that have we in dayly experience; for the pannes and pottes garnissheth wel the ketchyn, and yet shulde they be to the chambre none ornament. Also the beddes, testars and pillowes besemeth nat the halle, no more than the carpettes and kussyns becometh the stable.' Could a potter or tinker administer justice, he went on, a ploughman or carter respond to an ambassador, a weaver lead an army? Without due regard to rank and the custom of obedience to superiors, 'it can be no more said that there is a pub-like weale, than it may be affirmed that a house . . . is well and sufficiently furnished.'[2]

With the three-tier model of social organization appearing less and less usefully descriptive, recourse was had to a still older two-tier one, simpler yet more flexible, ancient and pagan, yet better suited to an analysis of contemporary Christian society. This was the 'civility' that Johnson valued so much, and the division the term implied between those who did and did not subscribe to its values.

Aristotle had explained society in terms of man's being, uniquely, a 'political' animal, programmed by his nature to cluster into families and communities where alone his potential as the only animal endowed with reason could be realized. Unlike the Christian, providential view of the purpose of human life and of a social organization designed above all to prepare men to meet their Maker at an ever-imminent Last Judgement, the Greek view was biological in its starting point and open-ended as to the historical consequences of human associations. Yet Aristotle's ideas and methods of argument had been absorbed on so broad a front into medieval Christian philosophy that his claim that the highest form of life was *politikos*, political (or, in its more familiar Latin translation, *civilis*, civic), was taken in their stride even by men who set a high value on unworldly spiritual contemplation. Besides, both royal and baronial households with their chivalrous codes, and monasteries with their cloistral forms of decorous behaviour, represented his association-seeking impulse in thoroughly respectable guise.

What encouraged the Aristotelian seed to grow within the Christian Estates model was the increasing attention paid by humanists from the fifteenth century to other classical authors. In Greek and Latin poets, from Homer's near contemporary Hesiod to the Roman Lucretius writing in the first century B C, more romantically intriguing accounts were found than Aristotle had given of the origins of society: a story of man's evolution from lonely wanderings to organized communities via the harnessing of fire, the working of metals, the need for mutual defence from wolves and lions and depraved men. Their surmises had been handily condensed in Vitruvius's treatise on architecture:

In the olden days men were born like wild beasts in woods and caves and groves, and kept alive by eating raw food. Somewhere, meanwhile, the close-grown trees, tossed by storms and winds, and rubbing their branches together, caught fire. Terrified by the flames, those who were near the spot fled. When the storm subsided, they drew near, and, since they noticed how pleasant to their bodies was the warmth of the fire, they laid on wood; and thus keeping it alive, they brought up some of their fellows, and, indicating the fire with gestures, they showed them the use which they might make of it. When in this meeting of men sounds were breathed forth with differing intensity, they made these chance syllables customary by daily use. Then, giving names to things more frequently used, they began to speak because of this fortuitous event, and so they held conversation among themselves. Since, therefore, from the discovery of fire a beginning of human association was made, and of union and intercourse; and since many now came together in one place, being endowed by nature with a gift beyond that of the other animals, so that they walked, not looking down, but erect, and saw the magnificence of the universe and the stars, and moreover, did easily with their fingers whatever they wished; some in that society began to make roofs of leaves, others to dig out caves under the hills; some, imitating the nests and constructions of the swallows, made places into which they might go out of mud and twigs. Finding, then, other shelters and inventing new things by their power of thought, they built in time better dwellings.[3]

And so they progressed to the building of towns and cities, the organization of their government and the establishment of social distinctions. As Cicero became the most read of all the authors of antiquity, especially after the discovery of a complete text of his *On the Orator* in 1421, it was increasingly clearly realized that everything he was revered for, whether as a moral philosopher or master rhetorician, took active civic life for granted. Moral philosophy for the Romans represented the art of observing the highest ethical standards while living usefully and enjoyably within a large community. The rigorous educational formation of the political orator and legal pleader was to enable him, as Cicero wrote, 'to operate amid all the bustle of city life'.[4]

From the historian Tacitus, another cult figure among the fifteenth-century resuscitators of classical literature both for his style and subject matter, more could be learned of the civilizing influence of cities. In the account of the life of his soldier-administrator father-in-law, Gnaeus Julius Agricola, Tacitus described the attempt to tame the inhabitants of Britain. 'To accustom these dispersed and ignorant, and consequently war-like men to the pleasures of a tranquil and stable existence, he privately encouraged and officially helped them to build temples, markets and dwelling places . . . And he had the children of the important men educated in the liberal arts.'[5] In author after author the adjective *civilis* was encountered as an ideal attribute, and *civilitas* as the noun which summed up the virtues of the sophisticated urban life of antiquity. And from the later middle ages circumstances were conspiring to shift attention to the quality of life in towns. They grew more populous, nobles built palaces there, rulers spent more time in their capitals. As *civilis* made its way into vernaculars (the Italian *civile*, the French *civil*, the English civil), commonsense observation of contemporary power structures made it easier to see the point of the classical emphasis on cities as the models for what should be valued in human development even while the Christian bias continued to assert itself.

'Man is subject to a double regime,' wrote Calvin in his *Institutes of the Christian Religion* of 1536; 'one is spiritual . . . the other is political or civil, through which man is instructed in the duties of humanity and civility'.[6] In 1583 an author could say of the parts of America to the north of Spanish settlements in Florida that 'God hath reserved the same to be reduced unto Christian civility by the English nation.'[7]

Alongside urban civility as a test of a society's development, another legacy from antiquity affected the appraisal of the condition of mankind as a whole. Aristotle had declared that 'just as some are by nature free, so there are by nature slaves, and for these latter the condition of slavery is both beneficial and just.'[8] This rationalization of the slave base of ancient economic life passed intact into sixteenth-century discussions of social organization. One of the speakers in Castiglione's *The Courtier*, with whose opinions the author on the whole identified himself, pointed out that 'there are many men concerned solely with physical activities, and these differ from men versed in the things of the mind as much as the soul differs from the body. As rational creatures, however, they share in reason to the extent of being able to recognize it; but they do not possess it themselves or profit from it. These, then, are essentially slaves, and it is more advantageous for them to obey than to command.'[9] Again, referring to the natives of Peru, Juan de Matienzo remarked in 1567 of their crude habits that 'it is more beneficial for them to serve than to rule. As Aristotle says, nature has given stronger bodies and less understanding to those born to serve, while those who are free have less physical force and greater understanding.'[10]

The discussion of slavery was shot through with inconsistencies. Even Busbecq, who regretted semi-seriously that 'we can never achieve the magnificence of the works of antiquity, and the reason is that we lack the necessary hands, that is, slave labour', went on to refer to 'the means of gaining knowledge of every kind which was supplied to the ancients by learned and educated slaves'.[11] The conquistadors who hacked their way to dominating Peru were not men with bulging brains and feeble bodies. But in conjunction with the Ciceronian emphasis on intellectual training and emotional self-control, and with the contemporary distinction between 'citizens' with municipal rights and duties and mere city dwellers, the class bias of ancient society strongly influenced the meaning of civility, and promoted its limitation to an educated élite.

The workers-for-others, especially the peasants and urban labourers who constituted between eighty and ninety per cent of European mankind, were excluded from this new model of a civility within society. It complicated the inclusion of the clergy unless their education and way of life had a secular polish. As for the warriors of the Second Estate, late in the sixteenth century Pierre de Bourdeilles, Seigneur de Brantôme, in his *Lives of the Great Captains* fought a rearguard action on behalf of their order as an essential component of a nation's civility. But he acknowledged the notion of civility when he added fastidiously, 'I have no desire to speak of ignoble people whether from the fields or in the towns, that being far from my aim; it is for those who are outstanding that my pen flies.'[12]

Whereas the Greeks and Romans had dubbed barbarians those who lived (like Tacitus's Britons) outside their politico-cultural worlds, the tendency grew in the sixteenth century to distinguish between those in a single country who did, or did not, subscribe to the norms of civility. As the sixteenth century ran on, chorographers ceased to pay attention to the quaint customs of the commonalty. Above all, civility came to be seen as the result of a process whereby man was tamed and disciplined. Lipsius defined it as the 'rod of Circe which tameth both man and beast that are touched therewith, whereby each one is brought in awe and due obedience where before they were all fierce and unruly'.[13] In the last phrase he is quoting Livy, yet another voice from antiquity that shaped the notion of what *civilitas* meant. But neither the widening interest in classical criteria, nor the extent to which they were picked up as relevant to current changes within society, suffices to explain the widespread acceptance of the idea of civility by around 1600 without a further look into the influence of the 'us' and 'them' strand in European self-awareness.

Though travellers to the Ottoman Empire continued to condemn the faith of Islam and to cite examples of Turkish cruelty, observation became more clear-sighted as the Christian steam that had clouded their vision evaporated, allowing them to particularize the qualities that matched those of sophisticated European behaviour. Among them were literacy and education; personal self-discipline; the rational exploitation of human labour and natural productivity; an emphasis on domestic comfort and decorum; skill in the arts both of war and peace; the rewarding of intelligent ambition; above all, an emphasis on firm government and respect for the law. In 1551 an Italian author who had lived in Constantinople as a member of the Sultan's household since his capture at sea at the age of twelve, warned in a book *On the Manners and Way of Life of the Turks*, that a Christian monarch contemplating a crusade against the Turk 'would do well to put aside the current myths about his incivility and barbarity'.[14] In the same way the Chinese and Japanese came to be judged primarily by the secular criteria of European civilization. Of course they too followed an erroneous faith. But by now belief in a higher being and an organized form of religious observance were in themselves seen as aspects of civility. Quite different to Turks and Orientals were African negroes, described in 1554 by the chronicler of an English voyage to Guinea as 'a people of beastly living, without a god, lawe, religion or common wealth'.[15]

This was also an early reaction to the Amerindians: living *sans roi*, *sans loi*, *sans foi*, as a French commentator rhymed it,[16] they were, as we have seen, initially looked on as irrational, without intellectual organizing power, and were thus if not exactly animals (though they were on occasion likened to monkeys) certainly natural slaves and probably incapable of comprehending the Gospel. Both issues aroused a strenuous debate among on-the-spot missionaries and home-based lawyers and theologians as to what degree of *policia*, the Spanish term for civility, could be attributed to them. As the discussion moved on from monkeys or men to what sort of men, the yardstick of *policia* was increasingly used. And as it was conducted chiefly among the clergy, it is interesting to see the growing hold on their world view of the secular standards by which God's creation was now assessed.

Looking back on his early experience as a companion of Hernán Cortés, the conqueror of Mexico, Bernal Diaz wrote that even the marketplace of Tenochtitlan had aroused their admiration so much that 'some of our soldiers who had been in many parts of the world, in Constantinople, in Rome and all over Italy, said that they had never seen a market so well laid out, so large, so orderly, and so full of people.'[17] But it was not the Mexicans and Peruvians who caused the debate. Like the Turks and Chinese they lived in stable architectural settlements, had governments whose laws were recognized and obeyed, had priesthoods and places of worship. It was the peoples of the West Indies, the Isthmus and northern and north-eastern South America, with their spider-eating and cannibalism, nakedness and sexual promiscuity and their apparent lack of any forms of social and commercial organization, who caused the controversy.

By the time their status as enslaveable beings was debated formally at Valladolid in 1550, enough had been learned of them to raise the issue to a better informed and more charitable plane. And whereas much information about them had previously been guarded as a secret of state, an account of the proceedings at Valladolid was published and entered the bloodstream of the wider consideration of what constituted a civilized being. Both the issues and the sources of the evidence presented were confused and polemical (the chief antagonists were the passionately pro-Indian missionary Bartolomé de las Casas and the natural-slaver Juan Ginés de Sepúlveda), but with all allowance for special pleading and shades of meaning, there was a measure of agreement that *policia*, or the capacity to achieve it, involved possessing the following credentials: rationality; laws spiritual and governmental and obedience to them; settlement in communities, especially in towns; the use of money and an understanding of trade over and above the natural economy of theft and barter; the exploitation of nature rather than merely living off it; the possession of a structured language susceptible to analysis and translation; costume and diet that reflected choice and decorum rather than instinct; an awareness, subsuming all these categories, of right and wrong.

Two decades before, the Spanish international lawyer Francisco de Vitoria had noted of the Amerindians that, 'I for the most part attribute their seeming so unintelligent and stupid to a bad and barbarous upbringing, for even among ourselves we find many peasants who differ little from brutes.'[18] And to see how instinctive the classical division between civilized and barbarian, brutish men became, we can look at the way in which Christian Europe's own Amerindians, the Irish and the Russians, were described. George Turberville, who knew Ireland well, linked both in a poem of 1568. The Irish had been famous for their contribution to the early fortunes of Christianity in the British Isles, but now the poet remarks that he had never seen a

> people so beset with saints, yet all but vile and vain:
> Wild Irish are as civil as the Russies in their kind:
> Hard choice which is the best of both, each bloody,
> rude and blind.

So he warned his readers:

> If thou be wise, as wise thou art, and
> will be ruled by me,
> Live still at home, and covet not these
> barbarous coasts to see.[19]

On the other hand, those who urged Queen Elizabeth to offer land grants in Northern Ireland saw barbarousness as a positive invitation to cross the Irish Sea. Such grants, it was urged, would 'bring the rude and barbarous nation of the wild Irish to more civility of manner' and tame them into becoming 'good and obedient subjects', notably by encouraging them to live in settled communities.[20] Fynes Moryson in 1617 accepted that the 'wilde or meere Irish' had long ago maintained a fine bardic tradition, but now 'alas how unlike unto Orpheus, who with his sweete harpe and wholesome precepts of poetry laboured to reduce the rude and barbarous people from living in woods to dwell civilly in townes and cittyes, and from wilde ryott to morall conversation'.[21] And five years earlier Sir John Davies, a man who knew the country and strove to be fair-minded, found himself exasperatedly referring to Irishmen's 'contempt and scorn of all things necessary for the civil life of man . . . I dare say boldly that never any person did build any brick or stone house for his private habitation . . . Neither did any of them in all this time plant any gardens or orchards, enclose or improve their lands, live together in settled villages or towns'.[22]

These views reflected domestic experience. In c.1530 Thomas Starkey saw the orderliness of urban life as offering a civilizing remedy for the lawlessness that afflicted the country at large. He described how in early times 'men were brought by lytel and lytel from the rude lyfe in feldys and wodys to thys cyvylte wych you now se stably stablyshd and set in al wel rulyd cytes and townys.' He deplored the stubborn preference of men of birth for life in the country (the same reproach was levelled by Italians against the French), and wrote that 'our gentylmen must be caused to retyre to cytes and townys' and build fine houses there so that 'they may not contynually dwel in the cuntrey as they . . . dyd before ther was any cyvyle lyfe knowen or stablyshyd among us.'[23] Within eighty years this plea came to sound like a prophecy. By 1616 James I noted that London attracted so many men of substance that he feared for the effectiveness of regional administration. He complained to the Star Chamber council that 'all the country is gotten into London, so as with time, England will onely be London and the whole country be left waste . . . let us in Gods Name leave these idle forreine toyes and keepe the old fashion of England.' His desire that all houses be destroyed save those of 'courtiers, citizens and lawyers' had, it goes without saying, no effect.[24]

If salvation from sin meant aiming for eternity in the New Jerusalem, the city of God, salvation from the taint of barbarism during life was to be sought in London, or Nuremberg, or Prague. The wayfarer may have noted the landscape through which he passed and the country inn where he spent the night, but towns and cities were the goals, the havens of comfort and congenial society. It was in them that the journal writer reviewed his impression of the region in which they lay. In a corner of each of the county maps of John Speed's *Theatre of the Empire of Great Britain* of 1611 was a reassuring bird's-eye view of the principal town. With their universities and cathedrals, hospitals and poorhouses, town halls and guildhalls, their streets of luxury crafts and markets selling more than local produce, their printing presses and bookshops, their visible if not particularly effective systems for policing crime and exerting some control over water supply, sewage and the paving of streets and squares, cities hardly needed 'civility' to establish them as the representatives of a non-barbarian way of life, even if, as they became ever more populous, a sullen and desperate barbarism loured within them. This simply added a fastidiousness based on real experience to the impression derived from what was known of the social divisions in the Greek *polis* and the Roman *urbs*. 'Urbanity', indeed, became a synonym for civility.

For increasingly not just the job-hungry but the erstwhile settlers of cultural and behavioural ideals were coming to town. Instead of remote monasteries being islands of learning and disciplined community life, the highest prestige was accorded to the urban units of the monastic orders. The choice made by monarchs to cut back the time spent in progressing through their realms with a caravanserai of administrative and judicial staffs further increased the drawing power of the cities they made their permanent headquarters. In a book whose title, *On the Causes of the Greatness of Cities*, indicated the hold of centres of civility on the minds of his contemporaries, Botero pointed out in 1588 that once a ruler had chosen a place as his capital, 'all matters of importance have recourse to that place, all princes and all persons of account, ambassadors of princes and of commonwealths, and all agents of cities that are subject, make their repair thither. All such as aspire and thirst after offices and honours run thither.'[25]

He might have added merchants. Commerce and the use of money was a test of the civility of the Amerindians because it was taken for granted as a sign of an advanced state of society in Europe. Britain, as Spenser wrote in *The Faerie Queene*,

In antique times was savage wildernesse,
Unpeopled, unmanurd, unprov'd, unpraysd . . .
. . . ne was sought
Of marchants farre, for profits therin praysd,
But was all desolate.[26]

Praising peace in a poem of 1538, François Sagan coupled the advantage that education and learning could flourish again with the ability of merchants once more to move freely.[27] And in a post-Armada pageant Elizabeth's glory 'Shall honour Europe whilst there shines a sunne', in a poem ending with the refrain

Religion, arts and merchandise
Triumph, triumph!'[28]

For like every other concept lifted from the past, *civilitas* underwent a sea-change as it became moulded into 'civility'. Merchants had become far more respected and influential members of society than they had been in the ancient world (at least, as it was then understood) and they could not be excluded from those who were 'civiled'. It was merchants and bankers who facilitated the accumulation of the material evidence of having left barbarism far behind: houses and furnishings, gardens, distinctive clothing, books, tutors for children, funds for voluntary travel to spas or further abroad. While the cash basis of civilized life had always existed, it was in this period that it became openly acknowledged as a distinguishing mark of civility. By the mid-fifteenth century the merchants to whom we shall turn had become exemplary representatives of how civilized status could be attained by those who come neither from the First or Second Estates. Before his downfall on trumped-up charges of peculation in 1453, the French royal financier and diplomatic agent Jacques Cœur had been ennobled and had built in his native Bourges a house which still demonstrates his taste as well as his wealth. When Cosimo de' Medici died in 1464 he had not only founded a line which was to control Florence until the eighteenth century; he had gained Italian fame as a patron of artists and scholars and international respect as a merchant banker who was also a shrewd diplomatist. In the early sixteenth century the acceptability in princely circles of members of the Fugger family of Augsburg was due to their cultivated way of life as well as to their ability to advance gigantic loans – as they did when Charles of Habsburg was squaring the electors who created him the Emperor Charles V.

By the late sixteenth century the notion of civility had become the organizing principle of an overview of Europe's population. Its impact on the vocabulary of appraisal was international. We can see this in the frequency with which the phrase 'civil conversation' was used in the sense of discussion amongst civilized people of civilized subjects. For Spenser, himself of necessity a courtier, it was

> . . . in Princes hall
> That vertue should be plentifully found,
> Which of all goodly manners is the ground
> And roote of civil conversation.[29]

For the Italian Stefano Guazzo, whose *Civil Conversation* of 1574 was aimed at a wider audience (and was soon translated into French, English, German, Spanish and Latin), the reach of civility could be broader. In answer to a leading question in his dialogue: 'What meane you by that woord Civile?', the response was that 'to live civilly is not sayde in respect of the citie but of the quallities of the minde', and this quality could be attained in the countryside by 'gentlemen' and even by those who 'ought to be put in the middest betweene gentlemen and clownes'.[30] And this outreach, which drew on the impulse to attribute civility to Turks and Amerindians, was sustained in the Dutchman Johann Althusen's *Two Books of Civil Conversation* of 1611. 'Civil conversation', he wrote 'may be defined as the art of applying appropriate behaviour, or as the art of making behaviour conform to propriety and right reason.'[31]

So as classical influence and the observational relish that accompanied the 'discovery of Europe' washed away at the analysis of society according to the Christian Three Estates, a double impulse came to be at work. On the one hand, there was the desire to extend the ability to be considered civilized as widely as possible in the interest of public order. Defining *civilisé* in 1599, a popular French author, Lancelot Voisin de la Popelinière, said, 'that is to say, governed and organized according to certain political forms rather than living in a savage state'.[32] On the other hand, there was the commoner tendency to identify civility with city-based values: sound education, polite manners, the discriminating use of money and a social standing which enabled its owner to play a part in public affairs. On the whole, the test of civility was most generously applied to non-Europeans; more grudgingly to the European fringes (Giles Fletcher's account of his experiences in Russia in 1591 accepted that, though barbaric, the masses there were capable of being 'civilled and brought to more understanding of God and good policie'[33]); least inclusive when considering those whose growing numbers posed a threat to the civility of the privileged, the urban poor, the 'clownes' of the countryside.

In whatever context it was used, the key element within the notion of civility was the imposition of rational principles of nurture on an originally untamed nature. In a frequently repeated phrase, it was the role of government 'to bridle the people'[34]; in a sculpture of 1548 Leone Leoni showed an armoured Charles V standing over a naked and chained figure representing man in his natural, insurgent state.

Within civilized society itself each new generation needed to be

Leone Leoni, *Charles V triumphs over Savagery*, bronze sculpture, 1548 (Museo del Prado, Madrid)

'firmly disciplined', as a Venetian law of 1551 extending the scope of public education put it.[35] The emphasis on good manners, evidenced in hundreds of books on social decorum, was, behind its veneer of etiquette, intended to suppress among the privileged their natural inclination to fart and brawl and thereby to blur painfully evolved social distinctions. An account of Lorenzo de' Medici's visit to a rural site near Vallombrosa, where he wanted to build a villa and gardens, referred to his wish to reclaim it 'alla civile'.[36]

For every desirable civilized norm was about taming, whether it related to the body politic, morals, education and manners, an un-exploited site in the upper Arno Valley or the painting style of Dürer's contemporaries which, as he lamented, was 'like a wild and unpruned tree'. And because only a minority could claim to be part of civility, an emphasis on its norms was kept alive by the threat of the incalculably tamed majority in the countryside and the volatile unwashed within the walls. Patriotism and religion were allowed their heroes and martyrs. Men in many walks of life sought and acquired distinction. But the norms themselves did not encourage individualism. Civility had been hard won, was protective of the status it had acquired, satisfied that it had regained the ground lost by Greece and Rome to the barbarians, and determined to keep it. Its most cherished values favoured conformity. And they were endangered from within by the merchandising which had itself become a norm and by civility's self-proclamation in terms of the display of personal possessions and diversions. The passage in which Tacitus described the civilizing of the Britons went on with a warning: 'and, little by little, men drifted towards the pleasures of vice: porticoes, baths, elegant banquets. Among the naïve this was known as "civilization"; it was nothing but a form of servitude.'

To civilize was to spread the values of civility. And it was the commercial and cultural aspects of civility that took the chief blame among those who saw their society as being too civilized for its own good, especially when threatened from outside. 'It is evident', wrote Machiavelli in 1513 in *The Prince*, 'that if rulers concern themselves more with the refinements of life than with military matters, they will lose power'.[37] In the later *The Art of War* he deplored the fact that 'our Italian princes, rather than accepting the blows of foreign war, thought it sufficed for a ruler to cogitate in his study a neat riposte, to write a fine letter, showing subtlety and quickness of wit' while he degenerated amidst comforts and pleasures.[38] Even Castiglione allowed one of his spokesmen to criticize an over-refinement that tends 'to corrupt the

young and lead them into dissolute ways. And the consequences are
that the name of Italy is brought into disgrace and there are few who
have the courage I shall not say to die, but even to take a risk'.[39] Late
in the century Michel de l'Hôpital expressed his concern that so many
aristocratic Frenchmen were abandoning arms and turning 'to the various branches of knowledge, to the arts and to agriculture' that it would
be necessary to engage foreign captains to defend the country against
Spain.[40]

From the mid-sixteenth century the effeminating effect of civility
was fairly widely deplored. The inhabitants of the southern Netherlands, the Venetian ambassador Bernardo Navagero observed in 1546,
used to be vigorous and courageous; 'but now that the country has
become commercial and is filled with beautiful and luxurious cities,
the ancient valour has degenerated.'[41] Educational theorists came to
place more emphasis on practical instruction and less on the study of
the humanities. Indeed, in 1580, the headmaster of Merchant Taylors'
school, Richard Mulcaster, saw culture as sapping the social exclusive-
ness that preserved civility. Too many boys were encouraged to have
aspirations above their status; 'they will not be content with the state
which is for them, but because they have some petty smack of their
book they will think any state, be it never so high, to be low enough
for them.'[42] Montaigne, who sat and wrote among his books with a
perfumed handkerchief at hand to wipe his moustache, became disillusioned with the use of paper which perpetuated animosities, rather than
healed them ('when writ we ever so much as we have done since our
intestine troubles?'). He was moved to claim that 'the mightiest, yea
the best settled estate that is now in the world, is that of the Turkes,
a nation equally instructed to the esteeme of armes and disesteeme of
letters. I find Rome to have beene most valiant when it was least
learned.'[43]

It was the failure of civility to reduce life's discontent that sustained
the medieval fascination with the Wild Folk. These naked denizens of
forests and remote valleys, jealous protectors of their unlawful wives
and unbaptized children, were liable to spring from among the trees
with a lifted club to batter travellers unwary enough to threaten their
lairs. It was disillusion with civilized niceties that supported the pastoral
mood in art and literature. 'Woodland songs carved on the rugged
barks of beeches', wrote Jacopo Sannazaro in his 1485 *Arcadia*,

Albrecht Altdorfer, *Wild Man's Family*, drawing, 1510 (Albertina, Vienna)

no less delight the one who reads them than do learned verses written on the smooth pages of gilded books. And the wax-bound reeds of shepherds proffer amid the flower-laden valleys perhaps more pleasurable sound than do through proud chambers the polished and costly boxwood instruments of the musicians. And who has any doubt that a fountain that issues naturally from the living rock, surrounded by green growth, is more pleasing to the human mind than all the others made by art of whitest marble, resplendent with much gold?[44]

Montaigne was thinking on these lines when he wrote that 'there is no reason art should gaine the point of honour of our great and puissant mother nature. We have so much by our inventions surcharged the beauties and riches of her workes that we have altogether overchoaked her: yet, where ever her puritie shineth, she makes our vaine and frivolous enterprises wonderfully ashamed.'[45]

This was the civilized mood of nostalgia for the Golden Age when man was not yet civilized. It drew on the vision of medieval millenarianism: a world of restored simplicity in which man, naked amidst the ruins of his pomps and institutions, awaited judgement. It was quickened by reports of the Amerindians who 'seem to lyve in the goulden worlde . . . wherin men lyved simplye and innocentlye', as the English translator in 1553 of Peter Martyr's *On the New World* phrased it,[46] and was sustained by what was seen as the corruption of an originally natural way of life. The Myth of the Golden Age came to be hymned by court poets at ease within their sinecures, and was embodied at great cost by the devisers of princely pageants. It evoked from Montaigne a deeply felt nostalgia for a lost state of nature; it induced Cervantes, and not only for comic effect, to make Sancho Panza resign the cares of the governorship of which he was at first so proud; and it produced (mediated through Florio's translation of Montaigne's essay *On the Cannibals*) Gonzalo's anti-civility speech in *The Tempest*:

> Had I plantation of this isle, my lord . . .
> And were the king on't, what would I do? . . .
> I' the commonwealth I would by contraries
> Execute all things; for no kind of traffic
> Would I admit; no name of magistrate;
> Letters should not be known; riches, poverty,
> And use of service, none; contract, succession,
> Bourn, bound of land, tilth, vineyard, none;
> No use of metal, corn, or wine, or oil;
> No occupation; all men idle, all;
> An women too, but innocent and pure . . .
> All things in common nature should produce
> Without sweat or endeavour: treason, felony,
> Sword, pike, knife, gun, or need of any engine,
> Would I not have; but nature should bring forth,
> Of its own kind, all foison, all abundance,
> To feed my innocent people.[47]

The fashion for this sort of yearning was already so diffused by 1566 that the French political philosopher Jean Bodin judged that it warranted a snub; he pointed out that it was subversive and foolish, undermining civilized values. It romanticized a time 'in which men were scattered like beasts in the fields and the woods and had as much as they could keep by means of force and crime, until gradually they were reclaimed from that ferocity and barbarity to the refinement of customs and the law-abiding society which we see about us'.[48]

UNDER MERCURY

In 1564 the city council of Nuremberg licensed a printed version of its charter and legal code. On the allegorical title-page Respublica, the figure of a woman representing the body of citizens and their government, points upwards with one hand towards God, who is blessing the city from the sky. Her other hand rests on the shoulder of Liberality, representing the wise use of money. Liberality, too, raises one hand. Over it is draped a purse which acts as a hive for the bees swarming round it. These represent the citizens who work for the common productive good, in concord among themselves and obedient to their King (the sex of the chief bee was then assumed to be male) or lawgiver. What they produce is coin. It tumbles down from the hive into a tray she holds on her lap. This is divided into two compartments, one for the profit accruing to the honourable merchant, the other for the deserving poor. On Respublica's other side sits Justice, who ensures an equable distribution of the city's gains, thus enabling Peace, leaning back against Republica's legs, to slumber on.

That an intelligent manipulation of money came to be accepted as an aspect of settled and civilized life owed something to the extra demand for goods generated by the population rise in the fifteenth century, and an increased volume of cash and credit transactions. But as a consciously expressed ingredient it owed much to overseas discovery. In the East, Europeans chaffered with merchants as shrewd and profit-minded as themselves. But in the parts of Africa untouched by Arab trading skills the value attached by the native inhabitants to beads and baubles spelled barbarism. And when an understanding of the use of exchange media beyond the local limits of barter and gift was applied as a test to the Amerindians, both government and the Church openly acknowledged the importance to civility of financial enterprise.

Of the transatlantic voyages, Busbecq remarked, 'religion supplies the pretext and gold the motive.'[49] Brown breasts and buttocks called

Good Government and the benefits of profit-making: titlepage from Nuremberg Statutes, woodcut, 1564 (British Museum)

for Christian clothing. Settlers wanted home comforts: the eastwards flow first of gold and then silver linked most of Europe to the production of goods needed in America. When Richard Hakluyt showed in 1598–9 with his massive *Principal Navigations, Voyages and Discoveries of the English Nation* that a compilation could also be a patriotic epic, he unhesitatingly coupled the saving of souls for Christ with the conviction that Elizabeth's encouragement of colonization would 'enrich her cofers'.[50] And because the increased costs of courts, diplomacy, officialdom and wars were meanwhile making nonsense throughout Europe of the medieval assumption that rulers should quietly live on the income from their own estates and traditionally accorded taxes and tolls, the fiscal devices of governments further emphasized the political role of money. John Donne was led to compare the cumulative impact of taxation to that of love:

> And though each spring doe adde to love new heate,
> As princes doe in times of action get
> New taxes, and remit them not in peace,
> No winter shall abate the springs encrease.[51]

Though the industrial base of the European economy broadened with the demand for manufactured goods, it was above all by the purchase and distribution of these and of raw materials that the economy was characterized. Contemporaries saw it in terms not so much of the maker, but of the merchant. When Charles V visited Antwerp in 1520, the year after his election as Emperor, one of the tableaux lining his route showed him embracing Europe while the other continents knelt pleadingly before him. On another, figures representing Philologia (learning) and Mercury (commerce) triumphed over the vanquished figures of Ignorance and Barbarism. It was this sort of confident connection between trade and civility in an international context that led Spenser to confirm the barbarity of early Britain in terms of its being unfrequented 'of marchants farre'; it prompted at about the same time a versifying French man of business to celebrate the economy with a *Hymn to Commerce*.

While in mythological narrative Mercury was the messenger of the gods, astrologically he had come to be connected with advanced artisanal skills. In an Italian miniature of *c.*1460 for instance, his 'children' are shown at work: a scribe, a painter, a clockmaker, a sculptor, an armourer, a musical instrument maker, a potter. By 1500 the developing interest in the nature of the economy as a whole led to the disinterment of his identity within the Roman pantheon as the patron of merchants. In Jacopo de' Barbari's 1500 *View of Venice* Neptune looks upwards from the lagoon, whither he has safely led the merchant ships anchored there, to Mercury, hovering in the sky and surrounded by an inscription: 'Mercury the illustrious teacher of this fortunate emporium'.

In 1515, five years before Charles V's visit, Mercury was similarly shown presiding over a woodcut view of Antwerp. To celebrate the opening of the new town hall in Augsburg, Adrien de Vries was commissioned in 1596 to make an over-life-size figure of Mercury to top the fountain erected in front of it. But it was again in connection with

Skilled artisans, the children of Mercury, miniature, *c.*1460

Antwerp the boom city *par excellence* as the volume of trade and financial transactions shifted from the Mediterranean to the Baltic and Atlantic, that Mercury was celebrated, with a maximum of iconographic
panache, as the tutelary genius of trading.

In the foreground of Jost Amman's woodcut *Allegory of Commerce*
of 1585 bales and barrels are being packed and given their merchants'
marks while clerks check and record the contents, and, in inner rooms,
merchants discuss prices and exchange rates and cast their accounts.[52]
In the middle ground goods are loaded into wagons which haul them
off to the warehouses and shipping on the distant Scheldt, Antwerp's
river lifeline to the world at large. In the sky, flanked by the coats of

arms of Europe's leading commercial centres, Mercury flies forward from the Zodiac. In one hand is the caduceus, his emblem as messenger and teacher, from the other hangs an enormous pair of scales which dominate the composition. One pan is labelled 'credit' the other 'debit'; between them, on a pillar rising from the basin of a fountain filled by capital and distributing profit if all goes well, is Fortune, partly bald, partly long-haired – inviting the merchant to 'seize opportunity by the forelock' – and teetering gracefully on the unstable globe of chance. As a plethora of labels makes clear, the merchant can use every nuance of calculating and accounting procedures (Amman's programme was set by a professional book-keeper) but is engaged in the riskiest, as well as potentially the most profitable, branch of business. The dilemma is summed up in a group at the foot of the composition. Sturdy males personifying Prudence, Integrity and Linguistic Skills surround a female figure. She stands amidst emblems of power: orb, crown, a sack of coin, and the civilized luxuries that cash can buy: musical instruments, books, works of art. But she, too, is perched on an unstable sphere; the success she promises is based on luck. And, in accord with another, moralistic, strain in contemporary attitudes to material gain, alongside the sack of coin nestles a skull.

For all the fingers-crossed cautions and moralized flinching from the over-materialistic implications of commerce, the sophisticated use of trade and money was openly asserted as a civilizing influence. When the two sons of the Emperor Maximilian II visited Milan in 1563 the governor of the city resolved to put the benefits of Spanish rule over the duchy literally in the shop window. 'The Duke of Sessa,' a citizen noted in his journal, 'commanded by public cryer that all the shops in Milan be opened' – they were normally closed on St Sylvester's Day, 31 December – 'and that everyone put on display all the most beautiful things he had to offer so that the said two might see the beauty of the stores of Milan.'[53] The accounts of travellers of all backgrounds give the highest praise to centres of civilized life that were also thriving emporia of goods. Educators took numeracy seriously, with textbooks aimed at the schoolmaster and the autodidact. There were multiplication tables which could be cut out for ready reference and learned by heart. There were problems related to loans: X lends A, B and C different named sums at ten per cent on dates D, E and F. When on date G he calls in all loans and interest, how much should he get? Others related to the recurrent problem of reconciling the values of different currencies. As early as 1458, William Wey in his handbook

Jost Amman, *Allegory of Commerce*, woodcut, 1585 (British Museum)

for pilgrims had warned them to get rid of local coin before moving on, 'there be so many dyvers chaunges of them in dyverse lord-shyppes'.[54] By 1614 four hundred different types of coin flowed in and out of the Netherlands. Merchants valuing them were catered for by printed conversion tables. But just as navigator's tables of declinations had to be adjusted in the light of fresh astronomical observations, the conversion tables were subject to error, chiefly caused by governmental decision to reduce the precious metal content of a coin or enhance it. So in spite of the increasing use of paper for cash transfers, the weighing and assaying of coin remained a conspicuous element in the mercantile craft.

For Thomas Mun, writing *England's Treasure by Forraign Trade* in the 1620s, the merchant's understanding of the forces affecting the world of business (assisted by his language skills) made him the key exemplar of useful knowledge. But there was no Copernicus of the financial cosmos. The observations of Elizabeth's experienced financier Sir Thomas Gresham led him to pronounce the 'law' that bad (debased) money will drive out good if both are circulating at the same time, but governments remained locked in a quasi-Ptolomaic stage of economic theory: free trade was dangerous, a country's wealth depended on the precious metal coins entering or circulating within it. Neither was it a time of financial inventiveness. Double-entry book-keeping – celebrated in Amman's woodcut – had been introduced in the early fourteenth century. It was still used only patchily in the sixteenth. Insurance, partnerships, affiliates, transferable shares in capital ventures: these were all devices that were further developed but were not new. Speculative dealing in 'futures', the forward prices of the coming herring catch or the demand for whale oil, for instance, were extensions of the familiar practice of forestalling the anticipated price of cereals. Monopolies and cartels acquired a novel and controversial prominence, but there was nothing new about the drive to corner a market and set a price. The entrepreneur who brought production, processing and sale under a common financial umbrella, as in the cloth trade, or gathered bands of mercenaries in order to hire them out to governments preparing for war, made or lost larger fortunes than formerly; but he was still exploiting medieval expertise. The use of paper instead of cash as both a convenience and a security measure, did facilitate transactions on a novel scale and encouraged a truly mercurial intellectualization of business affairs, but its origins lay in the promissory notes and bills of exchange of the later middle ages. And again, when governments used every means they could imagine might work to cajole or bully tax coin from private purse to treasury, and went on to bridge the inevitable delays between legislating for a tax and actually receiving it by selling offices of state, raising loans on the international money market and issuing redeemable bonds on public debts, the impact on political opinion and personal careers was great but the input of fresh ideas was minimal. This impact was especially marked when from the later sixteenth century the mercantilist notion developed that governments should regulate commerce and manufacturing in the interest of the national economy as a whole. Like the state bankruptcies that underlay what was seen as the need for such regulation (the Papacy in 1521, France in 1558, Spain in 1557, 1575, 1596 and 1607), mercantilism both in theory and practice sharpened the attention paid to the processes of getting and spending.

The acceptance of financial enterprise as a civilizing agent still had its embarrassing side. In his *Adages*, the most widely distributed of his books, Erasmus declared that, 'indeed, it is against nature, as Aristotle said in his *Politics*, for money to breed money . . . Nowadays the rage for possession has got to such a pitch that there is nothing in the realm of nature, whether sacred or profane out of which profit cannot be squeezed.'[55] He was repeating a long-established belief, enshrined in the Church's canon law, that over-concern with material gain endangered the soul, and that to make a profit over and above a notional just charge for a commodity or a loan was sinful. The puritanical strain in the Reformed religions accepted this increasingly neglected aspect of Catholic moral teaching and tried to revive its force. In a pamphlet of 1520 Luther castigated the philosophy of 'pay up or give interest for I must have my profit!'[56] Excessive commercial profit, he argued, was a form of theft. Profit should barely cover raw material, labour and transport. He reminded his readers that St Paul had plainly set down in his first Epistle to Timothy that 'the love of money is the root of all evil, which, while some coveted after, they have erred from the faith.' Though less peremptory, Calvin was equally clear about adhering to the just charge and to the spiritual dangers of over-much striving to be prosperous; there was little hint in sixteenth-century Calvinism of the later idea that wealth might be a sign of God's favour. And from the mid-century the Counter-Reformation's own brand of puritanism reaffirmed Catholicism's lapsed responsibility to denounce practices that could be considered usurious.

The profit motive, then, was lectured at, antiphonally from the pulpits of both faiths; and the press, while with one hand producing primers for calculating interest of an entirely non-judgmental nature, with the other supports the moralists with tracts and broadsheets. German prints denounced the mercenary marriage, the extortions practised on the poor and the unpreparedness of the proudly prosperous to face their Maker when death tapped them on the shoulder.

A print based on Breughel's drawing *The Battle of the Strong Boxes and the Money Bags* showed the strong-boxes puncturing the money-bags and the bags splitting the staves of the boxes to capture an intestinal spillage of coin; money fighting money for still more loot.

In another print, designed by Maerten van Heemskerck, a bedizened Queen Money rides with her servitor Robbery in a chariot drawn by Fear and Danger and accompanied by Folly and Envy; beneath her cloak she shelters Robbery; her chariot is followed by Pandemia, the thoughtless multitude. The early German novel *Fortunatus* (1509) borrows the magic and derring-do of the chivalric romance but has a

Jan Galle after Pieter Breughel the Elder, *Battle of the Strong Boxes and the Money Bags*, woodcut (Kress Library, Harvard University, Cambridge, Mass.)

Dirck Coonhert after Maerten van Heemskerck, 'Queen Money' and Robbery followed by
the multitude, from *The Unhappy Lot of the Rich*, woodcut (Albertina, Vienna)

merchant as the hero of a story that ends in misery and blood. In
Thomas Kirchmeyer's play of 1540, *The Merchant*, the hero is the illegitimate offspring of a coupling between Gain and Capital and the plot
concerns the efforts of Conscience to persuade him to think of higher
things than profit before it is too late to save his soul. Ten years later,
in a moralizing work by the Dutchman Dirck Coornhert, the familiar
medieval figure of Everyman now becomes a rich merchant converted
by the blandishments of Money and Falsehood to a life of spiritual
blindness. 'Good morning to the day!' exclaims the power-mad miser
Volpone in the opening speech of Jonson's play: 'and next, my gold!
Open the shrine that I may see my saint'.

At times such strictures reflected political instability rather than
moral flinching. An extreme example was the exclusion from communion in 1581 of bankers – along with acrobats and brothel keepers
– in the Protestant northern provinces of the Low Countries, then in
need of God's aid against the armies of Spain. But more generally,
routine disapproval was given a practical edge by the consequences of

inflation. This made the issue of prices more sensitive because more socially divisive. It also stimulated the old abuse of forward buying and – because prices did not rise evenly – the gambling appeal of purchasing in one part of Europe to sell in another. Inscribed in 1531 on the façade of the new Antwerp bourse, the meeting place for commercial news and deals, was 'For the service of merchants of all nations and languages'. By the mid-sixteenth century rivalry among its members led to the passing and re-passing of ordinances threatening heavy fines or the amputation of fingers for assaults with insults, fists or swords, and there were cases of merchants hiring cut-throats to murder commercial adversaries in the streets outside. Almost equally scandalous was the number of traders who went bankrupt or absconded without arranging a settlement of their debts. Mere bribery and peculation could be accepted more shruggingly; they were equally rife at court and in the pay and provisioning of armies. But they strengthened the moralists' conviction that a preoccupation with money endangered the Christian basis of society.

Caught between wider opportunities and louder warnings, merchants pleaded risk, fluctuations in exchange rates, the time-lag between paying out and getting back to justify their prices or interest charges. Later in life, by then a cardinal, the Jesuit Robert Bellarmine looked back on his experience as a confessor in the Netherlands in the 1570s dealing with such ingenuities as one of the least pleasant stages in his career. But merchants took comfort from the dignified setting of their guild and livery halls and the respect accorded them by governments. They comforted themselves within the decent values of responsible family life. If another old habit, that of heading an account book or even a bill of exchange with a cross and a JHS. MA (Jesus, Mary) died away they still, in Protestant as in Catholic countries, left bequests to pious or educational or charitable institutions.

Like that other religious bugbear, sex, money drove men either to get it and keep it quietly at home or go Don Juanizingly accumulating its trophies for the sake of the chase: asked in old age whether the time had not come to stop speculating and relax amidst his gains, the leading merchant banker of his age, Jacob Fugger of Augsburg who died in 1525, was reputed to have replied that 'he had no intention of doing so, but wished to make a profit as long as he could.'[57] How far, then, did financial passion and acumen fuse itself into civility in the guise of 'capitalism', the deliberate, intellectualizing search for more?

Simple material possessiveness was a long familiar trait. Reminding his prince not to meddle with the private property of his new subjects, Machiavelli pointed out that 'men sooner forget the death of their father than the loss of their patrimony.'[58] Some of the symbols of possessiveness, like the deep-cut 'LAU. R. MED' incised into Lorenzo de' Medici's antique hardstone vases, sound a new note, but reflect a mood no different from the careful inventories of cherished possessions in medieval wills. Overseas discovery offered scope for grander gestures. The Portuguese erected pillars at their African landfalls to proclaim ownership on behalf of their monarchs. But the Venetians had installed columns or reliefs displaying the image of St Mark on towns they had taken over on the Italian mainland from the early fifteenth century. When the Spanish conquistador Bernardo de Vargas Machuca in 1599 used as a frontispiece to his account of Spanish military enterprise in America an engraving of him measuring a globe with a pair of compasses, the inscription, 'To the compass and the sword, More and more and more and more', was not a hymn to personal gain but a burst of imperialist triumphalism.[59] The change of tone in personal acquisitiveness was expressed in less flamboyant remarks. 'Because the Florentines are devoted to trading and the pursuit of gain', wrote Machiavelli's friend Francesco Vettori, commenting on Giovanni de' Medici's election as Pope Leo X, 'all were thinking of the need to profit from the pontificate.'[60] The Flemish diplomat Busbecq deplored 'self-interest, the ruling principle of these days'.[61] The well-born merchant Michael Behaim ruefully commented to a cousin in 1534 that, 'although I too am a Behaim of Nuremberg, my family and coat of arms have been of no help to me. I tell you this so that you will not presume on the same, for people truly attach no importance to such things. Today it is no different in Nuremberg than elsewhere in the world: one who has money advances, while one who has nothing gets little in addition. People observe that one has nothing; they do not ask who one is.'[62]

It was not only merchants who stepped on the profit escalator powered by population growth and rising prices. The aristocratic enclosure of land for sheep in order to take advantage of the demand for wool was castigated in More's *Utopia*. French nobles, while disdaining trade, were quick to capitalize on mineral deposits on their estates. Polish and Bohemian titled landlords set up brickworks and distilleries and eagerly sold their grain crops for shipment to the Baltic. In these cases, however, though money was sought with a new vigour, it was used to build finer houses, to buy luxuries, to enhance the respect due from others, rather than to be recycled into new sources of profit. State lotteries also drew attention to gambling with money without associating it with calculated profit seeking: in Zurich and Cologne they were, it is true, part of the publicity attached to trade fairs which benefited local commerce; but those of Venice were to raise money for war finance, those of Antwerp and Amsterdam to fund public works or objects of charity like the madhouse financed by the Amsterdam lottery of 1610. Greed for cash, land and a prestige impossible to attain at home were motives for risking lives in Mexico and Peru, but to be a conquistador was not to be a capitalist any more than to be a pirate was.

What can be said is that increased opportunities for making money enlisted more men to take advantage of them and that profit-oriented occupations acquired a self-conscious seriousness of purpose. Aldus's petulance at his friends' interruption of his working day in his Venetian printing press was a symptom of this.[63] An English book on accountancy of 1553, claiming to be as necessary to merchants as 'is meate or drinke to hym that dooeth thirst or hunger', emphasized the importance of gainfully employed time; its dedication ended with:

> Sith [since] knowledge, then, is of such price and grace,
> And time ones loste wyll not agayne renew,
> Learne well this booke, while you have time and space,
> That you the lacke dooe not lament and rewe.[64]

For those who, like Jacob Fugger, found the manipulation of money an obsessive source of delight for its own, unavaricious sake, or who, living in a commercial hub like Antwerp, were drawn into the heart of its busyness, the always imprecise term 'capitalist' can be applied without any sense of anachronism. Such men relished the pursuit of gain beyond its immediate return and psychologically thrived on risks and finding ways of mitigating them.

The denunciation by Aristotle and the medieval Church of profit that outstripped the value of the service offered, simply reveals the universal truth that men and women who trade in goods or coin-changing want to make money for themselves from their deals. But with the Renaissance came a new explicitness about the satisfaction as well as the profit itself to be gained from a successful transaction. The French merchant and banker Jacques Coeur, ennobled for his financial services to the French crown in 1448, chose for his coat of arms the

motto, 'To the valiant heart nothing is impossible.' In the following
year the merchant republic of Genoa reminded its citizens that cash
gains should not be locked up in possessions but reinvested in business
'which can produce great fruits and great utility'.[65] While the military
demand for iron was growing and before American silver came to be
imported in quantity from the mid-sixteenth century, the literature
devoted to the technology of mining in central Europe was rich in
beckonings to investors. Thanks to this book, said a character in one
of the earliest examples of the genre, which was written in dialogue
form, 'I shall be given a reasonable understanding of which mines can
be worked gainfully so that my investment will not be wasted but will
show a profit.' God had planted the ores in the earth, wrote another
author, and it is men's duty 'to avail themselves of the universal creation'. There was risk involved, accepted a third, writing in 1530, but
'no one, truly, with an abject or timid soul ever did anything, or,
indeed, ever will do anything.'[66]

It was mining again, with its long chain of processes linking the deep
ore to the finished nail or gauntlet, that led to the clearest description yet
written of the means of extracting a profit from inert 'universal creation'. It comes, suitably enough, at the start of deliberate governmental
mercantilism, in Botero's *Reason of State* of 1589. As opposed to silver
he pointed out that

> the earnings from iron mines are not enormous. But a great many people
> live on profits from processing and exchanging this iron: those who
> mine it, who refine it, who smelt it, who sell it at wholesale and retail,
> who use it to make war machines and arms for defense and offense and
> innumerable tools for use in agriculture, architecture, and all sorts of
> crafts, for daily needs and for the innumerable necessities of life, to which
> iron is as important as bread. Thus if you compare what the owners
> earn from the iron mines with the profits made by the craftsmen and
> the merchants through their industry – which also greatly enrich the
> prince through custom fees – you will find that industry far surpasses
> nature. Compare raw marbles with statues, colossi, columns, friezes,
> and the infinite numbers of works made from it. Compare timber with
> galleys, galleons, ships, and other vessels of every sort – warships, freigh-
> ters, and pleasure craft – or with statues, household objects, and all the
> innumerable things that are made with the plane, the chisel, and the
> lathe. Compare colours with paintings, and the price of the one with
> the value of the other, and you will see how much more valuable labour
> is than material. You will also see how many more people live by their
> trades than from the immediate benefits of nature.[67]

This emphasis on investment, manufacture and commerce at the expense of agriculture reflects something of the urban bias of civility, its respects for the man-made rather than the ready-made product, for skill rather than mere labour. The Renaissance was an age with capitalists – from Cosimo de' Medici and Jacques Coeur to Jacob Fugger and on to the great armaments barons of the late sixteenth century, Louis de Geer of Liège and Elias Tripp of Dordrecht – rather than of capitalism. All the same, the special flair of such men arose within an increasing general appreciation of the ways in which natural products and work could be changed into money. There were, too, new and larger examples of capital investment in the products of others' labour; the clustering artisanal dockyards satisfying the boom in merchant and naval shipping, the twenty thousand labourers and craftsmen working in and around the iron mines at Schwaz in the Tyrol, the forty thousand workers in the armaments plants of the Val Trompia, near Brescia in northern Italy by 1600. Exceptional careers and industrial plants do not add up to an overall change in the medieval liking for profit. The Venetian dockyard, the Arsenal, employed up to four thousand men in exceptional years in shipbuilding and the manufacture and handling of naval stores. But throughout the sixteenth century respect for traditional civil and religious holidays kept the working year to around 265 days. The economies of the future which can be short-handed as capitalistic were only slowly on their way to being so defined.

The great majority of money-handlers, in any case, either lived away from the mainstream of commercial and banking services or were too morally sensitive or under-capitalized or simply untalented to be seen in such terms. The overall business mood cannot be assessed in terms of dramatic interest rates, but of a plodding and conservative industriousness, heedful of such tags as Brant's

> The man who's careful when he borrows
> Has but few cares and fewer sorrows[68]

and Luca Pacioli's 'regular accounting preserves long friendships'.[69] There was a widespread reluctance to switch from Roman to Arabic figures and an inclination to salt away capital surplus to routine trading needs into annuities or bonds of small but sure yield. Well before 1500 those who relied on such investments were nicknamed *Ledichganghers* or idlers in the Netherlands. Reflecting on Venice's lacklustre showing in the wars of the League of Cambrai in the early sixteenth century,

Girolamo Priuli claimed with bitter exaggeration that 'our ancestors were brave, fierce, impatient of injuries, quick to strike, prone to fight. Now we are of mild mind, meek, long-suffering, shy of a blow, shrinking from war. And this, I take it, because in olden times we all lived by trading and not on fixed incomes.'[70] And as war finance came to produce more opportunities in France, Italy, Spain and some of the Low Countries provinces to invest in public debt bonds, and everywhere the purchase of land was pursued as bringing dependable income as well as prestige, over the generations the flight of capital from the counting house became increasingly marked.

As his prominence grew, the merchant attracted criticism for social pretension.

In around 1450 a drawing by Rogier van der Weyden showed peasants diverted from their natural tasks to shovelling up chairs and tables. Towards 1500 a French writer attacked wives who wanted their daughters to dress like aristocrats (he suggested a costume divided down the middle into different styles). Preachers attributed visitations of the plague to 'that greedy and devouring serpent of covetousness', as an

Rogier van der Weyden (attrib.), 'Peasants diverted from their natural tasks, shovelling up chairs and tables', drawing, c.1450 (Robert Lehman Collection, Metropolitan Museum, New York)

English cleric put it in 1551.[71] The outward display of wealth, raged Philip Stubbes in 1583, makes it 'verie hard to know who is noble, who is worshipful, who is a gentleman, who is not'.[72] The complaints run on to Eméric Crucé's anti-merchant gibe in 1623 that 'so long as he will see the tinsel of gold and silver glitter on the clothes of the nobles, he will rather mortgage all his worth, than not wear them.'[73] When Agostino Chigi, among the richest of Roman bankers and, as a patron of Raphael and builder of the delightful Villa Farnesina, the most cultivated of them, proposed himself in 1512 to the wife of the Marquis of Mantua as a suitor for the hand of her husband's illegitimate daughter, she commented: 'he pleases me entirely, except for his being a merchant and a banker, which unfortunately seems to me unbecoming to our house.'[74] A similar reproach was to be levelled against the two Medici queens of France, Catherine, wife of Francis I, and Henri IV's wife Marie, for their coming from a family of mercantile origins.

It is true that a merchant could make vulgar slips of taste; the Italian Gaspare Ducci, at a dinner he gave for the 1550s Governor of the Netherlands, Mary of Austria, had the oysters gold-plated. But varied as were the forms and expressions of mercantile wealth, the most representative way of life remained that described by Machiavelli in his comedy *Clizia*. Complaining of her husband's infatuation with a young girl, his wife explains that,

> Anyone who knew Nicomaco a year ago and came across him today couldn't help being amazed by the great change that's come over him. He used to be thought dignified, responsible, sober. He passed the time worthily; got up early in the morning, heard Mass, ordered the day's food, and then saw to whatever business he had in town, at the market or the commercial magistrates' office. If not, he either discussed some serious topic or other with a few friends or shut himself in his study at home to balance and tidy up his accounts. Then he ate happily with the family . . . Then he went out and spent the rest of the day either in business or in some sober and respectable recreation. Every evening, he was home by dusk, stayed with us a while by the fire if it was winter, and then went into his study to look over his affairs, and three hours after sunset he had supper in the best of humours.[75]

It was the sort of life to be found everywhere among trading societies of the middling sort. Erasmus described them in the Netherlands. 'If you look at the manners of everyday life, there is no race more open to humanity and kindness or less given to wildness . . . It is a straightforward nature, without treachery or deceit and not prone to any serious vices except, that is, a little given to pleasure, especially to feasting.'[76]

For amidst the resentment and the sniping there was a steady growth of confidence among the mercantile community as a whole. Their skills were needed, they were a crucial part of the interconnectedness of Europe. Personally or through agents they were unusually abreast of news and affairs. They were more numerate, in some instances more cultivated, than many of their social betters. If they connived at the restrictive practices of the guild system, it was the better to define their position by dominating it and excluding outsiders. While devout, they were, of all sections of society, the most tolerant at a business level of those of differing faiths with whom they dealt. There was a touch-iness on the score of the usury issue and of its possible association with the pawnbroking, small loan and secondhand clothes dealing of the Jews.

There is something defensive about Quentin Massys's tender and serious portrait of 1514 of a merchant weighing coin watched by his wife, who holds a leaf of her prayer book open to reveal a miniature of the Virgin and Child; the just weight implies the just dealing of which the Church approves and which puts no strain on the honourable standards of Christian family life.

But later portraits, like Dürer's intent Danzig merchant Bernhard von Reesen of 1521, or Holbein's self-assured Hermann Wedigh of Cologne, painted in London in 1532, or Christoph Amberger's resolute Matthäus Schwarz, the proud head book-keeper to the Fugger (he commissioned a number of portraits of himself inscribed 1542): all of these dispense with the paraphernalia of the businessman's craft to concentrate on his character and bearing.

The importance of his role within society was recognized with a novel clarity. In a negative sense, this was made especially clear in Spain, where discriminating taxation, the hounding of merchants with Jewish blood and the pervading aristocratic ethos were believed to have emasculated native commerce and manufacture. In his 1600 survey of what was needed to restore the country's economic vitality, González de Cellorigo took for granted that merchants were part of 'the natural order of things'. Our country, he complained, 'has come to the extreme contrast of rich and poor, and there is no means of adjusting them to one another. Our condition is one in which we have rich who loll at ease, or poor who beg, and we lack people of the middling sort, whom

'Just dealing': Quentin Massys, *The Banker (or Merchant?) and his Wife*, 1514 (Musée du Louvre, Paris)

neither wealth [in land] nor poverty prevents from pursuing the rightful kind of business enjoined by natural law'.[77]

By 'the middle sort', Cellorigo did not mean either non-aristocratic members of the professions, lawyers, physicians, bureaucratic officials (of whom there were plenty in Spain), or the providers of day-to-day services like shopkeepers and innkeepers, however useful and worthy these might be. He meant men who were economically productive: wholesale merchants, importers and exporters on a large scale, bankers, manufacturers of goods in more than local demand. 'All the people which be in our countrie', wrote the English headmaster Richard Mulcaster, in 1581, 'be either gentlemen or of the commonalty. The common is divided into marchauntes and manuaries [labourers and artisans].'[78] But the meaning of 'merchant' was still vague. The French 'bourgeois' was not yet available as a blanket term for the middling sort; Thomas Platter, hearing it for the first time as he travelled across France in 1599, explained that it signified 'a man who can live on his rents' rather than working for a living.[79] The multifariousness of money-making activities made categorization difficult. In all but accepted rank 'marchaunts' could live in a style indistinguishable from that of a gentle-man or noble, or from that of an artisan head of a craft workshop. On the other hand, military entrepreneurs like Georg von Frundsberg in the 1520s and Sebastian Schertlin von Burtenbach, who died in 1577, could derive fortunes from supplying mercenaries to government that compared with those of the great merchant bankers. We have seen that artists could be successful traders.

Any generalized definition of the European 'merchant' escapes either over space – he could be a member of the ruling class in Venice or Augsburg but not in Paris or Naples, part of a burgeoning social

Albrecht Dürer, *Portrait of the Danzig Merchant, Bernhard von Reesen*, 1521 (Gemäldegalerie, Dresden)

component in France, a declining one in Spain – or dissolves over time; to follow a given merchant family over more than three generations is commonly to encounter either movement via marriage, court favour or estate purchase out of a world that can usefully be called mercantile – or fallen fortunes. Jacques de Beaune, from a modest merchant family, was able to lend the French crown 240,000 livres in 1518. In 1523, richer than ever, he was appointed chief financial officer of the kingdom. In 1527 he was hanged for peculation. On Jacob Fugger's death in 1525 the family firm was worth nearly two million gold florins. Within two more generations it had declined, within four vanished. Ducci's fortune did not long survive the oysters.

Such dramatic examples were rare, but the volatility was not. The ineptitude – or lack – of an heir, a shift in demand, an unwise trust in creditors: these, as well as winds and wars, greased the slippery globes on which Amman's mercantile Fortune figures balance. Nonetheless the broadening sweep of the money manipulators, with the ennobled financiers on one flank and Machiavelli's routine-ridden Nicomaco on the other, did not falter overall, nor did the lure of profit fail to tempt recruits like the youth from Basel who later recorded (in 1530) that 'when I saw that [Joannes] Hervagius and other printers had a good business, and with little work made a good profit, I thought "I should like to become a printer" '.[80] Between them they earned more that was surplus to livelihood than had been available in earlier centuries. So not only did they contribute to the veining of the notion of civility with money, but their spending habits acquired a new cultural prominence alongside the traditional ones of rulers, aristocrats and princes of the church. Under Mercury, to mingled admiration and alarm, Queen Money rode alongside Queen Europe.

THE STATUS OF LEARNING AND THE ARTS

In 1584, at the age of eighty, the French court historian André Thevet published his *True Portraits and Lives of Illustrious Men*. The work of a man who had travelled in the Americas and the Levant as well as in Europe, where he had an extensive circle of correspondents, it was the fullest *Who's Who* and *Who Was Who* of the European sixteenth century. He employed a group of Flemish artists for the two hundred and thirty-three engraved portraits that accompanied his short biographies, leaving blanks where he was not satisfied that he had located a true likeness. He included, however, not a single artist's life. There is no sculptor, architect or musician. Men of letters do little better. Joachim du Bellay and Ronsard get a line each in the life of someone else. Rabelais is referred to as 'a man of unusual knowledge'.[81] Thomas More's administrative and diplomatic career is described, culminating in the trial for treason in which he was pronounced ' "Githy", which is to say in their language, "worthy of death" ', but there is no mention of *Utopia*.[82] The qualifications for inclusion were political, military, theological and legal, or, in the case of the socially useful branches of knowledge, navigational, historical and cosmographical, and medical. Thevet also admitted 'some artisans who by their ingenious labours discovered very beneficial secrets necessary for the support of the public good', but printing, alchemy and mathematics were commemorated not by contemporary practitioners but through their inventors, Gutenberg, Jabir ibn Haijan and Pythagoras; once established, their utility could be taken for granted. This was a personal view. By modern criteria it is a distortion of 'Renaissance'. But in its indifference to the role of literature and the arts it is not unrepresentative of the Renaissance age itself. Some twenty years previously the mathematician, physician and astrologer Girolamo Cardano had published the horoscopes of one hundred outstanding men of his century. Only one, Dürer, was an artist.

There was, it is true, no inclusive word for culture that might have prompted a wider survey. Florio's Italian–English dictionary of 1598 rendered *cultura* as 'husbandrie, tillage, manuring, ploughing'. Bacon wrote metaphorically of 'the culture and regiment of the mind'. But this is as far as the Latin *cultura* got towards the wider significance the term acquired in the nineteenth century. Similarly restricting was the absence of a term for the 'fine arts' as a group, so they were thus left on the margin of discourse about man's evolution from barbarism to civility. And marginalization was encouraged by the common meaning of 'art' as skill, whether at the artisanal level (the Italian for craft guild was *arte*) or that of the application of organizational ability in a wider context, as in Machiavelli's *The Art of War*. Also inhibiting to the acknowledgement of creativity as being among the norms of civilization was the hangover from the use of the term 'liberal arts' as defining the secular curriculum of medieval university education: grammar, rhetoric, logical argument, arithmetic, geometry, astronomy and mathematically based musical theory. All these were concerned with understanding and conserving the intellectual roots of civilized life rather than embellishing or challenging them. In contrast, the handicraft element in painting and sculpture placed them among the guild- and workshop-based mechanical arts. Even in Florence, artists were not formally released from membership of a guild until 1571. Imaginative literature was poised – under the label 'poetry' – uncertainly between the two categories, its respectability as an element within civility owing most to its repute in classical antiquity. Even Thevet included a life of Homer and one of 'Sappho Lesbienne', strenuously denying any connection between that honourably married poet and the 'other' Sappho, 'the horror of whose crime it rather behoves me to suppress than to mention here'.[83] Again, the cultural vocabulary was restrictive. 'Letters', as in the frequently involved comparison between 'arms' and 'letters', implied well-educated literacy and the possession of learning or the ability to appreciate it in others. The 'lettered man' was not yet 'the man of letters'.

Thevet's view, however, corresponded to that of his equally culti-vated contemporary, the official historian of Venice, Paolo Paruta. His lifetime (he died in 1598) witnessed the fame of Venetian architects and artists, among them Palladio, Titian, Veronese and Tintoretto, but also an international admiration for the way in which the Republic had almost perfected the stabilizing religious, political and social aspects of civilized life. Concentrating on the latter, he wrote off letters and the arts as, in comparison, 'matters of slight concern'.[84] It is true that in an earlier and more personal work, his Discourses, he had lumped together fortification, ship design, medicine, sculpture and painting 'and every other noble discipline' as aspects of human endeavour which 'we see perfected every day through new initiatives',[85] but, like Thevet, his instinct was to marginalize what was not essential for the preservation of civility's core. For those concerned with defining the difference between civilized and savage society, literature and the fine arts played not so much a formative as an honorific, indeed dispensable role. What really mattered was the learning from which the barbarian mind was excluded, and the architecture which symbolized the power and sophis-tication of a socially and politically organized way of life.

Naturally men who were themselves learned praised learning, all the more because they found themselves the appreciated legatees of a classi-cal inheritance to which their medieval predecessors had paid little attention. The enthusiasm for contact with the learned civility of the ancient world was expressed as early as the 1330s, when Petrarch exclaimed, 'I am alive now, yet I would rather have been born in another time,' and wrote eloquent letters to the heroes he could only meet through their works.[86] By including examples of these among his widely circulated correspondence, he encouraged others to see the part learning had played in antiquity, whether in the person of a Cicero, who was both philosopher and participatory man of affairs, or of a Livy who recorded public events as an inspiration to posterity. And as governments from the late fourteenth century came to employ scholars to supervise and add dignity to their own correspondence, the link between learning and rule became closer. When Cardinal Bessarion decided in 1468 to bequeath his library to Venice he could address the Doge and Senate with confidence that his gift would be appreciated. 'Books', he wrote. 'are full of the voices of the wise, full of lessons from antiquity . . . so great is the power of books . . . that without them we would all be rude and ignorant. Without books, we should have almost no memory of the past, no examples to follow.'[87]

In Florence in the 1430s, Matteo Palmieri wrote in his *Della Vita Civile* – on civic, or 'civil' life – 'now indeed may every thoughtful spirit thank God that it has been permitted to him to be born in this new age.'[88] But this contemporary of Donatello, Brunelleschi and Filippo Lippi, while mentioning the revitalization of the arts as part of the recapture of classical attainments, stressed above all the importance of 'philosophy and wisdom' being at last 'drunk from the pure fountainhead'. He was writing for a politically responsible class for whom learning was more important than diversion. And this was the emphasis that was taken up in the North from the early sixteenth century. When Celtis urged his fellow Germans to show the world that they were not cultural barbarians he spoke not of the arts but of learning. For Erasmus in 1517 'all over the world, as if on a given signal, splendid talents are stirring and conspiring together to revive the best learning', but it was for their blindness to learning, not the arts, that he castigated the 'Philistines'.[89] Steadily, learning, or at least a more than superficial education, came to be taken for granted by those for whom it was not a vocation. 'Alas, you wyll be but ungentle gentlemen,' Pettie urged his readers in 1581, 'yf you be no schollers: you wyll doo your prince but simple service, you wyll stande your countrey but in slender steade.'[90] As for the prince himself, Botero in 1589 repeated the medieval quip: 'an unlettered prince is a crowned ass.'[91]

From at least *c*.1441, when the tough condottiere Francesco Sforza authorized Pisanello to commemorate him with a medal which showed on the reverse of his profile a cavalryman's horse and sword together with a book, the notion that sword and pen, arms and letters went together, became axiomatic. Would Julius Caesar be remembered if he had not written of his military deeds? Rulers supported scholarly eulogists and court historians. And learning, diluted into an educational programme that still allowed generous time for 'the servyce of the wylde goddes'[92] (the euphuism for hunting and hawking employed by the tutor to the son of Henry VIII's chief minister Thomas Cromwell), became part of civility's self-protection. A warning was given in 1507 by the biographer of a German aristocrat that his caste had neglected learning, 'whereas the children of peasants have taken to study and thereby come to large bishoprics and high legal offices . . . so that, as the common proverb says, the chairs have jumped upon the table'.[93] Education was similarly urged in *c*.1530 on the nobility of England, 'where gentylmen study more to bring up gud hounds than wyse hey-rys; [heirs]'.[94] The plea for the absorption of learning through education was uphill work; Montaigne noted despairingly of his well-born companions on his visit to Italy that all they had gained from being schooled and sent to college was 'a hatred of books, like almost all our men of noble blood'.[95] But whether accepted or rejected, the idea was abroad that learning should accompany political and social status.

It was helped as the subjects studied by the ancients came to be

'The sword and the pen': Pisanello's medal of the condottiere Francesco Sforza, *c*.1441 (British Museum)

seen as relevant to a view of the human and natural world which was non-vocational (as were medieval educational syllabuses) and graspable by the non-specialist. When Dürer's friend Willibald Pirckheimer, a patrician man-of-affairs, asked in 1517, 'Why should a man live if he cannot study?' as a riposte to doctors who warned him not to burn the candle at both ends, he was responding to an idea of learning as a free activity, a badge of the sensible use of leisure by a civilized man. And when he remarked that, 'it is a gift of God that we live, but of philosophy that we live well,'[96] he was using 'philosophy' not as a self-contained branch of academic inquiry but in the developing sense of an informed general outlook, the sense used by Hamlet when he indulgently chided his student friend:

> There are more things in heaven and earth, Horatio,
> Than are dreamt of in your philosophy.[97]

When every man (but not Everyman) could be a philosopher, then learning became all the more an aspect of civilized life that was taken for granted. Printing, cheaper books and more of them, helped to incorporate its image. From the mid-fifteenth century Italian citizens of means began to have small studies built into their existing houses or provided for in new ones. This was partly to store private family papers, but above all it was to provide a sanctuary where the head of a busy household could retreat to read his favourite books, often at night when others were asleep.

With their desks, reading stands, lamps, braziers and bookshelves, these were the models that artists – Gozzoli, Botticelli, Colantonio, Carpaccio, Dürer and others – used in depictions of the bookish retreats of the scholar-saints Jerome, Augustine and Gregory. The habit spread. In the mid-1530s the scholarly John Leland, venturing through the politically uneasy north of England, rejoiced to find in the tower of a castle belonging to Henry Percy, Earl of Northumberland, a study-room with desks and book-rests called 'Paradise'.

From the fifteenth century serious students had been allowed to borrow books from the collections of the Medici in Florence and from the Vatican in Rome. In the sixteenth century a municipal library was established in Nuremberg which by the 1550s contained some four thousand volumes, manuscript and printed. In 1537 the first copyright library, with the obligation on all printers to supply copies, was set up by law in France. This was only partially implemented, but the notion

Niccolò Colantonio, *St Jerome in his Study*, *c.*1450 (Museo di Capodimonte, Naples)

that an educated citizenry was advantageous to government was gathering force.

A combination of personal ambition for self-improvement at a time of enhanced but competitive job opportunities, and of the humanistic emphasis on education, meant that more pupils were in any case going to schools whose teaching methods became less lackadaisical; by the mid-sixteenth century parents were already complaining about the expense of buying revised educational primers. The result of improved schooling, of the aristocratic acceptance of education as carrying a civilized cachet as well as being a means to advancement at court, and of the refusal of guilds to accept an apprentice 'unless he can write and read', as the London goldsmiths' company ruled in 1478, was that

Europeans became more literate.[98] This was most marked in towns. By the mid-sixteenth century some fifty per cent of Londoners could in some measure read and write; figures for the majority of other European cities, ignoring immigrants from the countryside, suggest a comparable or slightly smaller proportion. In rural areas, outside the homes of the rich, the rate remained very low, though it would be a rare village of any size where there was not a man able to read aloud from printed books bought from the itinerant chapman, defined in 1611 as 'a paltry pedlar' whose bag, 'which he carries for the most part open and hanging from his neck before him, hath almanacs, books of news or other trifling wares to sell'.[99]

In England, those accused of crimes were entitled to plead 'benefit of clergy' in order to gain access to a lighter sentencing procedure for a wide variety of offences. It involved passing a basic literacy test: the ability to sign with a name rather than a cross and to puzzle through a line or two of scripture. Originating as a palliative to governmental

The Vatican Library: anon. fresco, showing Sixtus IV and Platina, c.1478 (Hospital of Santo Spirito, Rome)

claims to bring the clergy within a uniform secular legal system, its continuance after the Reformation owed something to a growing distrust of the illiterate masses. It was certainly an incentive to gain at least a veneer of education. Of two thieves who burgled the Earl of Sussex's house in 1613 one was hanged, the other, who passed the test, was merely branded on the thumb. If judged by this test, the rate of literacy in Europe probably did not alter much between the mid-fifteenth and late sixteenth centuries. What did change was the proportion of those with the ability to write freely and to understand, retain and judge what they read. It was this aspect of popularized learning that led Richard Mulcaster to see civility as being threatened by those who wanted to climb beyond their station in life. It was the socially broadened access to ideas that led, as we shall see, to governments turning to the censorship rather than the collecting of books.

There was, however, no controversy about the primacy of architecture among the arts. Alberti had written on painting and sculpture as well as architecture. But it was for the architect that he reserved his highest praise in 1452: 'He ought to be a man of fine genius, of a great application, of the best education, of thorough experience . . . It is the business of architecture, and indeed its highest praise, to judge rightly what is fit and decent . . .'[100] Three years later Pope Nicholas V justified his embellishment of the Vatican and the Lateran 'not for ambition, nor pomp, nor vainglory, nor fame, nor the eternal perpetuation of my name, but for the greater authority of the Roman Church and the greater dignity of the Apostolic See'.[101] His successor-but-one, Pius II, actually thanked his architect Bernardo Rossellino for over-spending on the cathedral and papal palace of Pienza: 'You did well, Bernardo, in lying to us about the expense involved in the work.'[102] In his treatise *On Magnificence* of 1498, Gioviano Pontano, humanist and former adviser of Alfonso II of Naples, spoke only of architecture as suited to the patronage of men of high status. Town planning came to reflect a new emphasis on the rational organization of exemplary civil life. And what Alfonso had in mind was explained by another member of his scholarly entourage. This writer, Pietro Summonte, recorded how 'in my time the Lord King Alfonso II', who was driven out of Naples by the French in 1495,

was so fond of building and so anxious to create something magnificent that, had not misfortune toppled him from his throne quite so soon, he would have unquestionably adorned this city very richly indeed. He intended to divert a far-off river along huge aqueducts to flow into the city, and . . . he wanted to replan the principal thoroughfares so that they would run direct from one wall to the other, demolishing porches, awkward angles, and anything else that blocked the way, and at the same time straightening the roads which crossed them. The resulting symmetry of roads and streets, and the fact that it slopes naturally from north to south, would have turned our city into the cleanest and most elegant in Europe . . ., the least shower of rain would have caused it to shine more brightly than a burnished silver coin . . . In addition he was going to build a truly sumptuous church . . . together with a vast palace . . . where the law courts were to be installed . . . All these noble, sublime schemes were halted . . . by the sudden barbaric invasion of King Charles VIII of France.[103]

The anti-barbarian theme sounded by Summonte had been touched on in the context of individual buildings by Giovanni Rucellai in 1473. He thanked God for allowing him the circumstances in which he could live 'as a rational creature and not . . . a barbarian'. He went on to record that of all his achievements he was proudest of his architectural projects, which included the façade of Santa Maria Novella, 'because in part they serve the honour of God as well as the honour of the city and the commemoration of myself'.[104] In a similar vein, when Duke Cosimo I of Florence commissioned a portrait of himself as patron of the arts some ninety years later, it was to show him, in spite of his patronage of sculptors and painters, surrounded chiefly by architects with their drawings and models.

As cities became more law-abiding and prosperous, there was more play for individuality in the design of palaces that did not have to double as fortresses, and a consciousness that they were not only expressions of personal rank but contributions to the variety and dignity of the urban fabric. Civility from the mid-fifteenth century acquired a structural as well as political and social significance. Aristocratic town houses, the mid-sixteenth century 'New Street' of patrician palaces in Genoa, French and German guildhalls, the towering merchants' houses of early seventeenth-century Amsterdam: all these were expressions of secular confidence as they rose among the bell-towers and spires of the First Estate. All fed the pride of civic eulogies. By the early seventeenth century the civilizing role of urban architecture was being commemorated in analogies between the structure of government and the components of a building.

In Italy, architectural theory drew inspiration, as we have seen, from the fabric and the building styles of ancient Rome, the exemplar first of republican then of imperial civility. And the repute of a classicizing style and of the architects who promoted it, owed something to the identification of the Gothic with barbarism. But within the northern Europe of the 'Goths' themselves the word had positive connotations of native vigour and independence. The 'Goths', after all, had resisted and finally overwhelmed Rome. It was their architecture that had conquered Europe and was still conducting a lively rear-guard action in Genoa, Milan and Venice throughout the fifteenth century. So while the core values of civility came to be equally cherished in the North, Italianate building styles were adopted more slowly.

But what did more to promote the image of architecture as the art closest to civility itself, in the North as in the South, was that the only surviving classical treatise devoted to any form of art was the *On Architecture* of Vitruvius, which linked architecture firmly to learning. In his opening chapter Vitruvius wrote that 'the architect should be equipped with knowledge of many branches of study and varied kinds of learning, for it is by his judgement that all work done by the other arts is put to test' – that is, challenged by their setting. 'Let him', he went on, 'be educated, skilful with the pencil, instructed in geometry, know much history, have followed the philosophers with attention, understand music, have some knowledge of medicine, know the opinions of the jurists, and be acquainted with astronomy and the theory of the heavens.'[105]

Practising architects took this with a grain of salt, just as they broke or followed his rules very much as it pleased them. But Vitruvius's influence helped to associate architecture closely with the liberal rather than the mechanical arts. This can be seen as early as 1468 in Luciano Laurana's contract to work on Duke Federigo of Urbino's new palace:

> We judge those men worthy of honour and commendation who are distinguished by intelligence and outstanding skill, and most of all with that expertise which has always been prized among both the ancients and the moderns, that of architecture, founded as it is on the arts of arithmetic and geometry, which are the chief among the liberal arts because they are nearest to the demonstrable truth of things and have that scientific and intellectual element which we greatly value and esteem.[106]

This wording has all the more force in that Federigo himself took a close interest in the building's construction and plan. It is clear why allegorical figures of Architecture commonly held a pair of geometrist's dividers as their distinguishing attribute. Indeed, the idea of Architecture remained more vivid than the image of the Architect. There was no formal apprenticeship and training. Men with a reputation for design, from the goldsmith Brunelleschi and the painter Bramante in the fifteenth century to the designer of costumes and stage sets Inigo Jones in the early seventeenth, produced exterior and floor plans to be interpreted by experienced master builders and their teams. Even princes might join in: Henry VIII 'devised' fortifications on the Channel coast and around Boulogne; Giovanni de' Medici, by profession a soldier, submitted a design for the unfinished façade of Florence's cathedral in 1587 in competition with the sculptors Giovanni Bologna and Bernardo Buontalenti, who had come to architecture from miniature painting and who continued to be known, perhaps best known at the time, for his designs for masques and other Medicean court festivities. Palladio was a rare example of a specialist, the earlier sixteenth-century Sangallo family a rarer example of a full-time domestic and military architectural practice.

Sir Francis Willoughby chose Robert Smythson to build Wollaton Hall in Nottinghamshire for him in the 1580s because he wanted a country seat that combined references to the castle of earlier prestige with the arrangement of rooms that reflected the civility of the urban palace. But save for patrons and others with local knowledge, buildings were not seen as so much the products of individuals of genius as contributions to the most conspicuous material expression of civilized life. It was seldom that travellers in Europe thought more about who had designed them than did the conquistadors on encountering the edifices of the Incas and Mayas. Squares, bridges, covered markets, canal embankments and warehouses, fountains: all received comparable attention as contributing to the built image of civility.

Whereas the designers of houses and Christian temples had direct contact with ancient Rome through surviving monuments and the imprimatur of Vitruvius for their works, and sculptors had at least the example of ancient statuary that had survived or was being uncovered by ploughmen and construction workers, painters had no models of the figural or narrative art of antiquity; it was then buried in the mud, ash and lava sealing Pompei, Herculaneum and Oplontis. In 1512–13 Dürer expressed his regret that no ancient treatise on painting had survived.

Many hundred years ago there were several famous artists, such as those named Phidias, Praxiteles, Apelles, Polycleitus, Parrhasius, Lysippus, Protogenes, and the rest, some of whom wrote about their art and very artfully described it, and gave it plainly to the light; but their praiseworthy books are, so far, unknown to us, and perhaps have been altogether lost . . . Often do I sorrow because I must be robbed of the aforesaid masters' books.[107]

There is some disingenuousness here. Dürer was preparing a primer for young artists, for which the need was all the greater because of the disappearance of the 'aforesaid masters' books'. And the names of those he cited were all taken from one he did not mention, the richly informative description of the arts of ancient Greece and Rome contained in the encyclopaedic *Natural History* compiled by Pliny the Elder in the first century A D. The relevant chapters not only recorded the careers, repute and works of painters and sculptors, but contained anecdotes that could be, and were, taken up from the fifteenth century as grounds for aesthetic rules. Dürer went on to write that 'no single man can be taken as a model for a perfect figure . . . You, therefore, if you desire to compose a fine figure, must take the head from some, and the chest, arm, leg, hand, and foot from others.'[108] Pliny had written that Zeuxis, wishing to paint an image of Helen for a temple at Agrigento in Sicily, 'held an inspection of maidens of the place paraded naked, and chose five for the purpose of reproducing in the picture the most admirable points in the form of each'.[109]

Pliny had mentioned Pamphilus, 'the first painter highly educated in all branches of learning, especially arithmetic and geometry, without the aid of which he maintained art could not attain perfection'.[110] This was welcome evidence that painting could be associated with the liberal arts. Alberti drew on it in his 1436 *On Painting* in order to stress the role in art of mathematics (for perspective – 'without perspective nothing can be done well', Leonardo was to write[111]) and of rhetoric (for the selection of subjects from poetry and history and for deploying them with variety and decorum). From Pliny, too, came the news that in antiquity works left unfinished on an artist's death could be 'more admired than those which they finished, because in them one sees the preliminary drawings left visible and the artist's actual thoughts'.[112] And this hint that the artist possessed a creative personality that distanced him from the mechanical skills of other guildsmen, surfaced in Dürer's remark about the artist's ability 'daily to pour forth and make

Wollaton Hall, Nottinghamshire, 1588 (City of Nottingham Art Gallery)

many new figures . . . which had not been seen before nor imagined by any other man',[113] and in Michelangelo's that 'an artist paints not with his hand but with his mind.'[114]

Nonetheless, by turning to concentrate on the arts in his encyclopaedic work which, as he proudly announced, contained 'twenty thousand matters worthy of consideration' including botany, zoology, agriculture, minerals and medicine, Pliny was not representing a consensus of ancient opinion. Seneca had placed painting well in the margin of what mattered to honourable citizens. Lucian, another ancient author of influence in the fifteenth century, had remarked fastidiously that while one might appreciate the works of sculptors one would not wish to be a sculptor oneself. In antiquity, as in the age that looked to it for so much of its definition of civility, there was a discrepancy between on the one hand the respect for artists and the demand for their works, and on the other the status accorded to the arts they practised.

Much of the contemporary evidence for an interest in the achievements and personalities of artists comes from Italy. In this respect it is clear that Italians, particularly Florentines, were exceptional and precocious. As early as the 1330s the Florentine chronicler Giovanni Villani cited painters among the names on the city's roll of fame. By the late fifteenth century patrons discriminated amongst artists more or less as a matter of course. In c.1490 an agent of the Duke of Milan in Florence reported on the outstanding painters available for commissions: Botticelli's works had 'very good organization and balance'; Filippino Lippi was not as skilful as his father, Filippo; Perugino's air was 'very gentle'; Domenico Ghirlandaio was a good all-rounder in panel and fresco 'and he is very expeditious and does a lot of work'.[115] By the 1530s discrimination had gone beyond a consideration of alternative manners, technical accomplishment and the likelihood of delivery dates. The Marquis Federico Gonzaga of Mantua instructed his agent in Rome to beg for anything Michelangelo might be prepared to offer: 'and should he by any chance ask you what subject we want, tell him that we desire and long for nothing but a work from his genius.'[116] And the cherishing of what had been acquired became more explicit. 'Though I am poor', wrote Sabba di Castiglione in his memoirs of 1549, 'I adorn my little study with a bust of St John the Baptist at the age of fourteen, sculpted in the round from Carrara marble by the hand of Donatello, which is very beautiful. Its quality is such that, if one could find no other work by him, this is enough to make him eternal and immortal in the eyes of the world.'[117] It was in Italy towards the mid-sixteenth century that artists of high talent and with influential patrons could, like Cellini, commit crimes of violence with a measure of impunity or, as in the case of the sculptor Leone Leoni, literally get away with murder. And it was Vasari's *Lives*, first published in 1550 and extended in 1568, that offered not only the first mass of information about artists' lives and works but the first methodical account of how they had saved the arts from barbarism and led them first to emulate and then to surpass the achievements of their classical ancestors.

This respect for individual artists was paralleled, independently, in the North. Jan van Eyck was not only sought after by wealthy Burgundian patrons but was entrusted in the 1420s with diplomatic missions to Portugal and Spain by Duke Philip the Good. It was the local fame of his Netherlandish successors, Rogier van der Weyden and Hans Memlinc, that led Italians to commission works from them; before his death in 1494 Memlinc had become a man of significant wealth. Two decades later, Lucas van Leyden married an aristocrat and thus, as his biographer mourned, 'lost much time in banquets and high living'.[118] In France, an Italian resident of Tours wrote in 1477 that when comparing in the church of Notre Dame 'representations of the saints from older times with modern ones . . ., I reflect how much Jean Fouquet excels the painters of all other centuries in his art'.[119] In 1511 Jean Perréal was described in a contract as 'painter and private secretary to the King our Lord' – Louis XII.[120] In Spain, Michael Sittow, an Estonian trained in the Netherlands, was employed as court painter by Queen Isabella at a salary higher than those of all but four other court employees.

In Germany Martin Schongauer was praised in his lifetime as the most glorious of painters. Dürer rose from the modest artisan status of his parents and of his resentful wife to the admiring friendship of such aristocratic intellectuals as Pirckheimer. When Peter Vischer and his sons finished the elegant Gothic shrine of St Sebald in 1519, the poet Helius Hessus wrote that 'not even the Muse would be capable of such labour or of doing justice to this immortal work, which neither Praxiteles nor Myron nor Polycletus nor Chares nor Scopas could duplicate. Although fame commends these masters . . . greater glory shall fall to our times'.[121] In 1538 the city council of Basel agreed to continue to pay most of Holbein's salary to his widow during his prolonged stay at the court of Henry VIII 'since he is famous beyond other painters on account of the wealth of his art'.[122] In c. 1600 Nicholas Hilliard, regretting that England still had no Dürer or Holbein, Raphael or Rosso, wrote that he had heard it said that islands 'seldom bring forth any cunning man, but when they do it is in high perfection; so then I hope there may come out of this our land such a one, this being the greatest and most famous island of Europe'.[123]

Certainly no Englishman had figured in the remarkable lists compiled in 1548 by the Portuguese Francisco de Holanda (so called from his father's native province) of 'the renowned men who in Europe stand out in painting, sculpture and architecture in our times'.[124] He begins with the twenty-one painters he called 'the eagles' of art, then he lists illuminators, sculptors, architects, engravers and medallists. Altogether there are fifty-five names, ten Spanish (or identified with Spain), three Portuguese, three Netherlanders, one French and one German; the rest are Italian, commencing with the four greatest 'eagles': Michelangelo, Leonardo, Raphael and Titian. Taken with what has gone before, Francisco's conspectus can give the impression that the arts were, after all, firmly placed within educated views about the nature of civility.

Indeed, with such evidence in mind, and the transmission of sought-after artists' works across Europe, it comes as no surprise that when in 1563 the first formal academy of art, the Accademia delle Arti del

Disegno, was established in Florence, it was taken under the patronage of Duke Cosimo I. Among its members were Vasari, the court painter Agnolo Bronzino and sculptor Bartolomeo Ammannati; in the following year the academicians organized Michelangelo's obsequies in a ceremony which was as much a homage to the arts themselves as to the man. For Michelangelo from boyhood had been drawn to painting much against the wishes of his well-born family who wanted him to study for a career that was respectable. But his passion grew to such an extent that, as his disciple and biographer Ascanio Condivi wrote, 'it led him to abandon learning his letters altogether. This brought him the disapproval of his father and his father's brothers, who hated the art of design, and very often he was outrageously beaten: as they were ignorant of the excellence and nobility of the art, it seemed shameful to them that it should be practised in their family.'[125]

At roughly the same time – in 1561 – observers were praising the amateur painting skill of Philip II's French wife, Elisabeth, while professional Spanish artists were producing works for patrons who equated their status with that of carpenters and masons. Even when Raphael was treated as a social equal by Roman cardinals and Titian cherished the patent of nobility he was granted by Charles V, save for artists of unusually fashionable talent or personal charm or – as with Perréal – a usefulness outside their profession, the taint of manual labour remained: the painstaking apprenticeship of colour grinding and canvas sizing, the handwork of brush or chisel. Even in Italy, Lodovico Dolce, in his *Dialogue about Painting* of 1557, was having to argue the case for painting on the grounds that since antiquity it had been 'held in high esteem by kings, emperors and men of greatest discernment'.[126]

Many artists, probably the majority, were little concerned at being bracketed with the mechanical crafts. Most purchasers looked to skill without worrying about the nature of genius, and membership of a guild implied works of quality, whether they were original, or copies of other men's masterpieces or shrewd forgeries, as with the artificially aged and falsely inscribed works by Bosch which were such a tribute to his repute. The apprenticeship and workshop system coped adequately with radical changes in artists' aims. In any case, purchasers generally took what they were offered by artists they respected. It was this permissiveness that allowed the extraordinary spectrum of experiment that characterized the period as a whole: artists were free to respond to one another's work and to react against or modify tradition. It was the few who sought status for their activity as well as

Raphael, Portrait of Baldassare Castiglione, 1516 (Musée du Louvre, Paris)

success for their works who pushed the claim of painting and sculpture to be seen as intellectually abreast of the liberal arts. It was Vasari and his colleague who pressed the idea of an academy upon Cosimo, they who petitioned to plan the celebratory funeral rites for Michelangelo. It was, again, Vasari who contrasted the artists of his own age with those of the fifteenth century who would agree to paint banners or decorate furniture 'without shame, as would be the case today'.[127]

In books dealing with the intellectual formation of the civilized man an appreciation of the arts might be included; on occasion this was coupled with a recommendation to learn how to draw.

Castiglione, whose friendship with Raphael led to the artist's sensitive portrait of him, remarked that 'a knowledge of painting is the source of very profound pleasure'.[128] But he felt bound to stress the utilitarian side of this knowledge: its assistance in judging the arts and artefacts – vases, cameos, intaglios – of antiquity, and in producing sketch maps when planning a military campaign. More representative of received opinion was the advice Thomas Elyot gave in his 1531 *The Governour*. If a child, he wrote, 'be of nature inclined (as many have ben) to paint with a penne or to fourme images in stone or tree, he shulde nat be therfrom withdrawen . . . but, puttyng one to him whiche is in that crafte wherein he deliteth excellent, in vacant tymes from other more serious lernynge he shulde be in the most pure wise enstructed in painting or kervinge'.[129]

There is some retrospective irony in the fact that painting and sculpture were not considered 'serious' activities during a time when the arts in Europe were demonstrating an unprecedented range of invention and achievement, when portraits of the Virgin believed to have been painted by St Luke himself were objects of devotion, when a pope, Julius II, could – according to Vasari – pummel a bishop who had been uncouth enough to say of Michelangelo 'that such men were ignorant creatures, worthless except for their art',[130] when it was fairly common knowledge that Alexander the Great had so admired Apelles that he had rewarded him with his favourite concubine, when heads of state were beginning to accumulate collections and competing with one another in order to do so. And to some extent the discrepancy does reflect the lack of an organizing concept which could bring the fine arts firmly within definitions of civility.

Unlike music, which was not only popularly appreciated but legitimized by being among the medieval liberal arts, and unlike poetry, which was heavily represented among the classical Muses, there was no conceptual niche for painting and sculpture. Lacking one, wrote Leonardo de Vinci, painting 'was left without advocates'. In his notebooks he repeatedly challenged the primacy accorded to poetry. 'Painting serves a nobler sense than poetry and represents the works of nature with more truth than the poet . . . It is a nobler profession to imitate the things of nature than to imitate in words the actions and speeches of men.'[131] But when occasions came for recapitulations of the cultural pursuits that could flourish again when civility's hatches were reopened after being battened down against the barbarisms of war, the arts were still the artificers rather than the objects of celebration. One of the set pieces in Lyon, when the inhabitants were rejoicing in the 1559 Peace of Cateau-Cambrésis, was a thirty foot high figure of Mars. It was set on fire. As it collapsed, a tableau of Minerva and the Muses was seen within it, 'demonstrating', as an observer wrote, 'that the death of Mars is the resurrection and the life of Minerva, goddess of wisdom and the liberal arts'.[132]

However, by the turn of the century – despite the cultured priorities of Thevet and others – there is evidence that a niche for the visual arts had at last been provided north of the Alps. Even so, it only applied to works approved by a ruler who was uniquely open to conferring prestige upon those who fed his omnivorous interests as patron and collector. In a bronze relief by Adrien de Vries the Emperor Rudolf II rides in triumph in the centre of the composition. In the background a last barbarian wields his club. Under the hooves of Rudolf's mount a defeated Bellona, the war goddess, writhes in ignominy while Fame prepares to lift her trumpet in homage to the conqueror. With the palm of

Lucas de Heere, *The Liberal Arts in Wartime* (Turin Pinacoteca)

Adrien de Vries, *Rudolf II as Protector of the Arts in Peacetime*, bronze relief, 1610 (HM The Queen, Windsor Castle)

victory in one hand, the Emperor bends to offer renewed encouragement to the supple naked ladies who represent the culture of peace. Music and Poetry are there, the latter with a book symbolizing learning in general and a child clinging to her to show that education can tranquilly begin again. But they are pushed to the left. Next to the Emperor, and the only figure presented frontally, is Architecture with her set square and dividers, but prominently entwined with her are women holding a palette and brushes and a chisel and statuette. And in another Rudolfine work, a painting by Hans von Aachen, a languorously seductive Peace holds up an olive branch above the trophies of war while offered sustenance by Ceres, goddess of seasonal plenty, and embraced by a youth who (with remarkable aplomb) holds in one hand an astrolabe with a sword running through it as a symbol of universal concord protected by arms, and in the other an emblematic confection signifying the fine arts: palette and statuette.[133]

These were late and idiosyncratic cases of special pleading. Generally speaking, throughout Europe the arts were still seen as embellishments to civility's political, religious and economic core. The attention paid to them in Italy from Villani onwards was exceptional. Working in the chief cities of small states their practitioners were familiar to men of wealth and status. The particular intensity of the rapport between Italians and the prowess of ancient Rome bolstered respect for those who successfully emulated the artists of antiquity. Among European patrons it was above all Italians who showed the greatest understanding of what distinguished the great artist from the competent hack. It was in Italy during the sixteenth century that interest grew in the rival merits of painting and sculpture, and in the competing effects of poetry and painting, issues that brought the nature of art as such into the repertory of subjects discussed by thoughtful men. Yet even in Italy Paruta could shrug aside the arts when considering the values that had created civility and ensured its preservation. Learning was indispensable: history to inform and guide; poetry and eloquence to describe the highest form of conduct and incite men to emulate it (the point was frequently made that captains needed eloquence to sustain the morale of their troops); philosophy and theology to keep fear of the inchoate at bay. The enthusiasm of some of those who bought works of art as a source of private pleasure cannot be doubted; neither can the belief in their usefulness for winning prestige, serving political propaganda and buttressing religious belief. Nonetheless, given the threats to civility to which we are to turn, they were seen as delightful and useful but expendable. Like weatherhouse figures they could come out when the sun of tranquillity shone, go inside when the political or social climate darkened. In spite of our own homage, they were not then thought of as part of the equipment that kept civilized mankind barbarian-proof.

THE RETREAT TO UTOPIA

For those pedlars of social engineering blueprints the Utopianists, civility was becoming corrupted. Endorsement of the pursuit of gain was creating new rifts and resentments within the structure of society. The pervasive lure of the arts was not only sapping man's moral fibre but positively dehumanising him: such, at least, was the view of Calvin, himself a Christian Utopianist: 'many are so delighted with marble, gold and pictures that they become marble, they turn, as it were, into metals, and are like painted figures.'[134] But those who advocated an escape from civility's constricting norms, and praised the ease and the honest spontaneity of men and women in a primitive state, were mistaken. What was needed, according to the Utopianists, was a rethinking of civility's norms on drastically disciplinarian lines.

They were reacting to a chorus of criticism of contemporary *mores*. 'Money is king among us,' mourned Willibald Pirckheimer to a friend with reference to Nuremberg.[135] The reply from Vienna was that it was the same everywhere. Bodin in 1574 attributed the rise in the cost of living in France to the extravagant style in which the rich lived. Under Mercury corruption became so rife that a fresco of about the same time in the town hall of Geneva showed a bench of judges all of whom had had their hands cut off as a sign that justice should not accept bribes. In 1527 Jean Bouchet deplored gardens and houses devoted to 'wantonness and sensuality, which seem the homes of venereal and lascivious rather than martial and honest men'.[136] Niccolò Zen wrote in 1539 of Venice's poor showing against the Turks in the recent war in terms that recalled Tacitus's description of what civility had done to the Britons. Formerly valiant people, he complained, 'when one, two and three generations have passed . . . think only of idleness and pleasure, and then they value architects, songs, music, players, palaces, clothes . . . Miserable is that city, that prince who enjoys such entertainments, because he will be subjugated by vile and ignoble people'.[137] These and other complaints were summed up in 1550 in a Dutch engraving which shows a young man representing the honourable citizen being bound while he helplessly watches a demon painting on the replica of a human heart the devil's coat of arms: a crown and coronet, a naked woman and a sack of money.

More's *Utopia* was published in 1516. His portrayal of an ideally devout, rationally organized and stable society was not intended as a goal but a warning. The egalitarianism of More's Utopians, their proscription of money, their scorn of superfluous luxuries (gold was restricted to chamber pots), their tolerance of differing sincere religious beliefs: these traits were in the main intended to make the reader rethink the values of his own world, not seek to recast it on Utopian lines. The book, however, was not free from an addiction to social planning for its own rigidly intellectual sake, and More clearly relished his – that is, the Utopians' – ingenuities: 'they breed a vast quantity of poultry by a wonderful contrivance. The hens do not brood over the eggs, but the farmers' – exactly forty of them in each rural commune – 'by keeping a great number at uniform heat, bring them to life and hatch them. As soon as they come out of the shell, the chicks follow and acknowledge humans as their mothers.'[138] Something of More's manipulative intransigence was taken over, indeed exaggerated, by those who shared his moralizing challenge to contemporary society. For once the new approach to the nature of society had been accepted, and the nation of civility isolated and explored, a number of writers were tempted to become dieticians to the body politic, advising a less self-indulgent regimen, a cutting-down of luxuries and privilege in order to prolong its health. The genre of ideal commonwealth depictions became a rich one, through Francesco Patrizi's *The Fortunate City* of 1551 which, being written when he was only twenty-two, suggests the extent to which Utopian speculation was already in the air, to Tommaso Campanella's *The City of the Sun* (begun in 1602 but not published until 1623) and Bacon's *The New Atlantis* published in 1627. All illuminated the self-protective norms of civility by seeing them as essential disciplines of the self and of the community.

Utopian writers derived their principles from the complex life of cities even if, as with More and Bacon, they depicted isolated islands. All sought to simplify the social and economic complexities that put citizens at the mercy of lawyers who, as More put it, 'cleverly manipulate cases and cunningly argue legal points'.[139] His Utopians banned them. In his *Education of a Christian Ruler* of 1543 Mambrino Roseo inserted a description of an ideal commonwealth, Garamantia, which he pretended that Alexander the Great had come across in the course of his Indian campaign. The Garamantians only had seven laws – and they reveal the dehumanizing neatness to which Utopianism was prone. The first law was that the other laws should never be changed; the second, that only two gods should be worshipped, one the lord of life, the other of death; the third, that everyone should be dressed in identical clothing to avoid envy and ostentation; the fourth, that any woman having more than three children should be killed; the fifth, that anyone detected in telling a lie should be put to death; the sixth, that all inheritances should be split into equal parts; the seventh, that no man should be allowed to live for more than fifty and no woman more than forty years. Roseo was writing in 1543, but the draconian solution to problems of current European concern, such as religious controversy, social rivalry, contested wills and overpopulation, had already been given European currency through the inclusion of an account of the aforementioned in a far more widely distributed and translated work, the Spaniard Antonio de Guevara's *Mirror of Princes* of 1529, which appeared in English in 1557.

For most authors the model for the governance of an ideal city was not so much the *Republic* of Plato, though that lay alongside More's *Utopia* as a spur, but the monastery. Responding to current competitiveness in sartorial display and the complications of sumptuary laws, Utopianists, from More's 'as for clothes, these are of one and the same pattern throughout the island and down the centuries', to Campanella's insistence on plain overalls, saw the advantage of the uniform monastic habit.[140] Secularized, the monastic timetable was adopted so that everyone in Utopia was doing the same thing at the same time and was known to be doing it. Meals were to be taken in common at set hours to ensure equality of consumption and to enable the magistrates to adjust the demand for foodstuffs according to their availability, a point emphasized by Lodovico Agostini in his *The Imaginary Republic*, written between 1575 and 1580. It was Agostini who – in the interest of preserving law and order – forbade his citizens to wander the streets or gather in the piazza during communal mealtimes or after nightfall.

Monastic, too, was the common emphasis on the distrust of personal possessions. The inhabitants of the City of the Sun, wrote Campanella, 'assert that extreme poverty makes men liars, false witnesses, thieves, outlaws – cunning, cowardly and deceitful – while wealth makes them insolent, haughty, ignorant, disaffected, treacherous, and presumptuous. But public ownership of goods makes them all rich and poor at the same time – rich in that they possess everything, poor in that they do not have possessions to serve, while all possessions serve them. On this point they have high praise for the tenets of Christianity and for the lives of the Apostles'.[141] Whether the recommended social organization was straight-forwardly communistic, or allowed for a slave or serf class to labour in the countryside and perform menial tasks in the city, or distinguished between a directing class of citizens and an obedient class of non-citizens, there was a common emphasis on avoiding extremes of poverty and wealth as being the chief threat to civilized order. Praising his minuscule native state of San Marino in Utopian terms, Lodovico Zuccolo in 1625 put its tranquil condition down to 'a certain economic mean among the citizens'.[142] Apart from More's prohibition of the use of money, and the suggestion of a luxuries tax in the Utopian essay in Robert Burton's *The Anatomy of Melancholy* of 1621, there is no mention of how this happy state of affairs was to be brought about. Utopias in general, however, were not concerned with the transition from real, historically conditioned commonwealths to the ideal ones they describe.

A striking instance of the race from problem to solution is the remedy for the sins, crimes and unhappiness arising from marriage conventions and sexual appetite. Identifying strongly with the high-mindedness of his Utopians, More likened sex to the 'agreeable sensation [which] occurs when we discharge faeces from our bowel',[143] but recognized the dislocatory power of extramarital passion: 'the reason why they punish this offence so severely is their foreknowledge that, unless persons are carefully restrained from promiscuous intercourse, few will contract the tie of marriage, in which a whole life must be spent with one companion and all the troubles incident to it must be patiently borne.'[144] To give physical compatibility a chance, then, prospective couples were, suitably chaperoned, allowed to see one another naked before confirming their choice, for why should human breeding be treated more lightly than that of horses? Bacon's spokesman for the customs of Atlantis remarked that his colleagues had read of this 'in a book of one of your men, of a feigned commonwealth', but preferred their own practice of allowing friends to report on the couple after observing them bathing naked in each city's 'Adam and Eve pools'; for it was essential to have satisfying and eugenically sound marriages in a society in which 'there are no stews, no dissolute houses, no courtesans' and no recourse to the substitute satisfactions of masculine love.[145] The Utopianists' concern for sound marriages and healthy children who would not be a burden to the state reflected the infidelities and foundlings and cripples of the real world. At the same time, with their interest in the optimum ages and times and methods (slowly, to increase the final sperm count) for making love, it legitimized a heartless prying into private lives that was not much at odds with the endorsement of euthanasia in the cause both of dealing with terminal pain and purging the state of useless mouths.

The ruthless planning zeal of Utopianists was by 1552 a target for irony in the ideal commonwealth described in Anton Francesco Doni's The Worlds of 1552. Within the perfect symmetry of his circular city, with its hundred streets radiating out from a central piazza, each street was devoted to a single craft, each segment of countryside beyond the walls to the cultivation of a specific crop. All hot food had to be fetched from communal kitchens. All citizens were equal in wealth and lived in uniform houses, identically and simply furnished. All were dressed in identical clothing whose colour denoted the decades of their age. Doni's solution to the marriage problem was to abolish it, and to promiscuity to permit it. When in either case there were children, if they were sickly or deformed they were drowned, if healthy they were fostered after weaning by the state. 'Oh happy country', exclaimed the character in Doni's dialogue to whom this solution was explained, 'which abolishes the sadness of the death of a wife, of fathers, mothers, children and relations, where there is never cause for weeping.'[146]

However tongue in cheek Utopias might be, however consciously Utopianists fed on their predecessors or wilfully tuned their stringencies still higher, all saw the need for a drastic tinkering with the dangerous messiness of a civility flawed by historical accidents, conflicting beliefs and personal idiosyncrasies. The norms of civilization needed rewriting on a clean slate, and common to all Utopian panaceas was an insistence – variously described as far as its mechanism was concerned – on the voluntary and unquestioning acceptance of pure standards of social hygiene, purged of the troublesomeness of ambition, introspection and the aberrant love of privacy and personal taste. Life was to be cheerful, active, healthy, egalitarian, co-operative – and invigilated. In the City of the Sun it was not just foreigners who 'are well supervised; there are informers who report to the state about everything'; among the natives themselves, 'it is wonderful to see that men and women always go about in squads, never alone, and that they always obey their leaders without the slightest displeasure.'[147] The point of a Utopia was that everything was given, uniform, and for ever. The plague of the old, and the threat to the new norms of civility, was individualism. And leaving aside Bacon's Atlantis, which harboured a research institution to advance scientific knowledge, the last thing that was needed in Utopia was questioning and non–utilitarian creative thought.

So most Utopians avoided discussing the place of learning in their ideally static societies. More praises it as a benign recreation for many, as a preparation for diplomacy or high office for a few. Only Bacon sees learning as prompting questions and leading to discoveries, and then in fields restricted to the domain of the natural scientist. With this partial exception, there was no room in Utopias for original or speculative ideas – or for the private diversion provided by the arts. Patrizi said that comedies and love poetry should be kept away from children's eyes and ears. Otherwise there is silence on the topic of literature in Utopias. Music is allowed within limits. Patrizi favoured it when its mood was solemn or cheerful, not when it aroused other, less usefully social emotions. For Doni and Campanella it served the purpose of communal relaxation and morale-raising. After dinner in the City of the Sun 'the people give thanks to God with music and

. . . sing aloud the deeds of the Christian, Hebrew and Gentile heroes of every nation; they also sing hymns in praise of love and wisdom and every virtue.'[148]

Nor, with a ban on luxury goods and insistence on uniform housing, furnishings and clothing, was there much scope for architecture or painting and sculpture. More, who only allowed statues of famous men to be displayed, 'as a spur and stimulus to virtue', found himself wincing at this aspect of the power of his non-cash-based and egalitarian vision, which, he agreed, 'utterly overthrows all the nobility, magnificence, splendour and majesty which are, in the estimation of the common people [elsewhere], the true glories and ornaments of the commonwealth',[149] but put aside this rare instance of his nostalgia for non-Utopian mores. Painting was largely ignored, save for didactic purposes. This was a stance taken over from non-Utopian shapers of civilized character. Writing in c. 1510 of the furnishings suitable for the household of an ideal young cardinal, Paolo Cortese proposed that he should see on waking in his bedroom paintings representing virtuous acts to predispose him to imitate them during the day. A few years later Erasmus, writing of the palace of an ideal young prince, said that its pictures should show the Magnanimity of Alexander (as he set free the captured womenfolk of his defeated foe Darius) and the Continence of Scipio (who returned a captured girl to her lover) and other 'wholesome pictures . . . instead of those which inculcate wantonness, vainglory or tyranny'.[150] In the only extended mention of the place of art in a Utopia, Campanella described how the inside of the wall surrounding the city of the Sun was covered, for the purpose of public instruction with a pictorial encyclopaedia; painted maps, animals, examples of the mechanical arts, portraits of great warriors, statesmen, religious figures and inventors. These heroes were not only to serve as examples to the young but, through the power of sight, to serve a eugenic function: 'for upon these the shapely women devoted to the perpetuation of the race gaze in order to improve their offspring.'[151]

For the Utopianists, imagining an ideal society safe from the dangers that threatened it in the real world, it was necessary, as Plato had found, to limit the role of learning, literature and the arts to one of social and moral usefulness, and to keep civility from becoming too civilized for its own good.

CHAPTER VIII

Civility in Danger?

THE VOLATILITY OF HUMAN NATURE

Biblical and medieval animal lore had praised the industrious ant, the ingenious spider, the monogamous elephant, the obedient bee and the faithful dog. But from the fifteenth century the orderliness essential to civilization was emphasized by the repeated definition of man as an animal endowed with reason, and the distinction between irrational and disciplined behaviour. It was very much in line with Utopianist thought that a German moralist, Johann Agricola, wrote in 1528 that 'Our Lord wishes people to conform to rule in external matters no less than in their thoughts. Each must do what is right and proper for one of his estate and order. If this is not done we shall become no better than beasts and irrational animals.'[1]

At about the same time, an Italian medallic portrait of Attila the Hun, the arch–representative of instinctual barbarism, represented him as entirely composed of intertwined animals. Anatomically animal, spiritually flawed by disobedience in the Garden of Eden, but gifted with the ability to chose between the instinctual behaviour of toads and wolves or the etherealized intelligence of angels, human nature was inevitably volatile. When in 1608 George Chapman had a character in his *The Tragedy of Charles Duke of Byron* reflect, 'O of what contraries consists a man!',[2] it was an observation obvious enough at any time to men and women of ordinary powers of observation of their neighbours. But as civility came to be more clearly defined it was an issue that increasingly perturbed clergy, philosophers and, above all, legislators.

In a proclamation to be posted in marketplaces and on parish church doors throughout England, Henry VIII's Council in 1513 summed up the problem set by human nature to the ideal of obedience and orderliness.

'Instinctual barbarism':
a bestial portrayal of Attila,
anon., bronze medal
(British Museum)

Forasmuch as it is often seen that man's reason, whereby he should discern the good from the evil and the right from wrong, is many times by seduction of the Devil, worldly, covetous and sensual appetites, repressed and vanquished, whereupon commonly ensue discords, murders, robberies, divisions, disobedience to sovereigns, subversions of realms and destruction of people, so that where these reign victory in time of war and justice in time of peace be utterly damped and exiled; therefore emperors, princes and government of the time past, for refraining of such inordinate appetites and punishment of those folks which rather eschew to offend for fear of bodily pain or losses of goods than for the love of God or justice, full wisely and politicly ordained divers laws serving to the same purpose as well in time of war as peace.[3]

When in 1580 Montaigne took his aches and pains to the quiet spa at Plombières in eastern France, he copied down the regulations, posted in French and German. No one was to be admitted whose body bore the marks of contagious disease (plague or syphilis). It was forbidden to bring arms into the bathing areas or, whatever the status or place of origin of a visitor, 'to utter words that were provocative or inciting to quarrels'. It was forbidden 'to all prostitutes and women of light behaviour to come nearer the baths than one hundred paces on pain of being whipped at the four corners of the establishment'; men who solicited their company were to be fined and imprisoned. No blasphemous language was to be tolerated.[4]

Violence, sexual licence and disrespect for religion: these were the chief infections arising from undisciplined human nature which endangered the orderliness of states and spas alike. They always had done. But a new sensitivity to what distinguished civilized from savage society, a more determined attempt by governments to pin down disorder, and by revitalized churches to patrol the behaviour of the faithful, changed attitudes if not facts. And the printing press and realistic pictorial imagery made public opinion sensitive to these issues to an unprecedented extent.

The most habitual threat to order was instinctive violence. That tempers were short is clear from a multitude of criminal legal cases dealing with peasant and artisan woundings and murders after a swift escalation from words to deeds. The quick-tempered Paduan artist Niccolò Pizzolo was murdered in 1452. Mantegna, that devout and scholarly painter, hired thugs to beat up rivals who filched his designs. The Swiss artist Urs Graf's spells of voluntary military service were escapes from the legal consequences of his bouts of brutal quarrelsomeness. Michelangelo's broken nose was the result of an altercation with a fellow sculptor. Christopher Marlowe was murdered. Ben Jonson killed the actor Gabriel Spencer in a tavern brawl. The popularity of fencing lessons in the sixteenth century reflected not just the fashionable adoption of a new form of costume sword, the rapier, but the need to be prepared for a higher incidence of the violence that could follow a jostling on the street. Throughout Europe, legislation tried to prevent the carrying of arms in towns or other places of public resort, such as country taverns, and assumed their spontaneous use in case of altercations arising from a gambling loss or sensitivity to a presumed insult; the motivation of a 1611 interdiction on the carrying of arms between dusk and sunrise in the small French market town of Laon was 'to avoid henceforward the populace from killing one another for the slightest quarrels'.[5] Francis Bacon recorded how James I told him 'that when he goeth abroad he seeth himself royally attended with many goodly noblemen and gentlemen, and taketh great joy to see them and think on them. But again it grieveth him much more that he is not assured of the lives of any of them four and twenty hours, for if they discourse but a few words the lie is given, the lie begets a challenge, and a challenge death'.[6]

Cruder forms of self-help were commonplace, the punching of a debtor until he agreed to pay up, the employment of assassins in family vendettas and of armed bands to avenge real or fancied wrongs. In his autobiography, written in the 1540s, the German Götz von Berlich-ingen described thirty feuds he had carried out either in the pursuit of personal vengeance or in the pay of others. In 1555 a student at the university of Montpellier recorded that,

> I often saw, in front of the shoemaker's shop, a man in a long cloak, who had had his nose cut off and who dragged himself along painfully on two crutches. He had been a handsome fellow once, a writer [official scribe] in Nîmes, and had been the lover of the wife of a doctor of law named Bigottas. The husband, with several masked students, surprised the young man in bed with his wife. They choked him with a cord, and after cutting off his genitals and his nose, threw him thus mutilated into the street. The victim recovered, however, and came to Montpellier to drag out the remainder of his wretched life.[7]

A snarling sixteenth-century inscription under the male figure carved into a niche of classical design in the Grocers' guildhall in Stralsund reads: 'if you are not a grocer, then keep out or I will hit you across the mouth.'[8] It reflects the mood of the initiation rites which the Hanseatic merchant guilds of Bergen imposed on journeymen aspirants to full membership. First they were hoisted feet first up a chimney until nearly asphyxiated. Next they were thrown three times from a boat far out in the harbour and pushed back until the last moment each time they tried to climb back. Last, naked in the guildhall, they were whipped until bloody and then had to sing a comic song to round off the enter-tainment.

In his autobiography Bartholomew Sastrow describes how his father, a brewer and corn merchant of Greifswald, was forced to move to Stralsund after killing a man during a dispute over a business deal. Bartholomew studied law at the university of Rostock and went on to have a reasonably successful and humdrum career as a notary. Indeed, he wrote his memoirs in order to encourage his children to follow his example. The work's fascination, however, lies in his depiction of life amidst the inter-family and inter-city feuds during a time when Hanse-atic prosperity was threatened by the Baltic rivalries of Sweden and Denmark. It is a story of brutal parental discipline, of schoolboy quar-rels leading to the free use of knives, of brawls in the streets and bandits in the country, of corrupt magistrates, carelessly cruel punishments (of one execution Sastrow noted that 'in spite of his unquestionable insanity the murderer was broken alive on the wheel') and a stubborn nursing of grievance. It describes a society unbending in its prejudices and animosities, utterly materialistic save for its crude superstitions and its prurient scrutiny of the private lives of its Lutheran ministers. When Sastrow heard that his father's old adversaries had fallen on hard times he commented, 'Yes, the Almighty has comforted me, he has permitted me to see the scattering of my enemies.' Such a peacetime background does not seem so very remote from his experience of the anti-civilian atrocities of Charles V's Spanish troops he encountered during the Schmalkaldic war of 1546; 'women and girls suffered the most terrible outrage. As for the men, after having suspended them by their genitals, the barbarians tortured them to make them reveal the places where they had hidden their money . . . Every house was deserted, the dwellings of the nobility as well as the peasants' farms . . . In one house we found a *membrum virile*.' After congratulating himself on having had this decently buried, he describes how on discovering that his horse had been stolen, 'according to the usages and customs of war, I chose the best nag at hand, and bridled and mounted it in the space of a few minutes'.[9]

Sastrow's Pomerania may have been particularly unruly, but it had no monopoly of violence. It was an age when standards of behaviour were set by the old and flouted by the aggressive young. And these were in the majority. Half of the population, possibly more, was under twenty. Apart from free-lance prostitutes and licensed market stall-holders, girls and young women, whether married or not, were kept at home or went out with a chaperone or in a group. The bulge in the population was most provocatively composed of male adolescents, teenagers and young bachelors. Complaints about their insubordination and reckless peace-breaking were a Europe-wide commonplace. Their gangs terrorized mature citizens, whether in Switzerland, where in 1477 they bullied and robbed in the name of the 'mad life', or in late fifteenth-century Florence, where Savonarola's bands of youthful vigilantes abused their moralistic brief to keep men from gambling and nag women out of making a display of their jewellery and insufficiently covered breasts. In France their inter-village ritual combat games led to woundings and killings before which the law could do little but shrug away the inevitable consequences of youthful excitement. In 1554, a year of challenge to Elizabeth's succession to her Catholic prede-cessor, Queen Mary, London aldermen were ordered 'to have a vigilant eye . . . to the inhabitants and specially to the young'.[10] Even in calmer times an English statute of 1563 referred to 'the licentious liberty of youth', and accepted that 'until a man grow unto the age of twenty-four years he . . . is wild, without judgement and not of sufficient experience to govern himself.'[11]

Peasant boys worked in the fields from the age of eight or nine and urban adolescents took up an apprenticeship at thirteen or fourteen, often far from home. However loving and concerned parents were about the conduct of their children, at an impressionable age the young were chiefly in the company of one another or of older unmarried men. Social rank made little difference. University students were notoriously obstreperous outside the lecture room. The practice (which declined during the sixteenth century) of sending well-born boys to be groomed as pages in larger or more aristocratic households involved their spending as much time with stablemen and servants as learning the niceties of polite behaviour. Though there were, of course, studious, timid or dutiful exceptions, it is reasonable to accept that most men, between childhood to maturity, passed through a phase in which violent behaviour was taken for granted. And this conditioning was possibly further tainted by exposure to a callous cruelty to animals that were not pet dogs or valued horses (the game of throwing stones at cats buried up to the head, the baiting of bulls and bears) as well as to the public and much appreciated spectacle of the maiming or execution of criminals. In 1556 a student in France recorded the progress to the gallows of a man who had robbed and murdered a canon of the cathedral:

> After the judgement had been read aloud, the executioner put the man on a cart, where he was laid on the lap of the executioner's wife. He then began to pinch him with red-hot tongs, and this treatment continued until they came to the canon's house. There the executioner cut off both the man's hands on a block placed on the cart for that purpose. The woman held him with his eyes blindfolded, and as each hand was cut off she pulled a pointed linen bag over the stump, from which shot a jet of blood, and tied the bag on tightly to stop the bleeding.[12]

Before quitting Turkish for Venetian territory in 1620 Peter Mundy came to Valjevo. At the gate he saw the bodies of two impaled 'men on stakes, throwne downe, halfe eaten with Dogges and Crowes'. And he went on to remark casually that 'heere we had Cherries at a farthing a pound.'[13]

It was not only in remote Bergen that manners were rough. Erasmus,

writing of schools known to him in the more sophisticated Low Countries, condemned 'initiation ceremonies fit for executioners, torturers,
pimps or galley-slaves' and cited the case of a boy who was forced to
eat excrement before being hoisted up by ropes and 'savagely beaten
on all sides until he nearly died'.[14] Referring to life in France in the
1580s, Botero wrote of 'the multitude of thieves and murderers', the
need 'for watchmen of the vineyards and orchards; gates, locks, bolts
and mastiffs about the house'.[15] Giles Fletcher's comment on Russia in
1591 would not have made Moscow seem very different from Seville
or Naples or parts, at least, of London: a man, he wrote, will be robbed
in the street 'if he goe late in the evening, and yet no man to come
forth out of his doores to rescue him though hee heare him crie out'.[16]

In spite of the Commandment 'thou shalt not kill', the Christian
attitude towards acts of violence was not without its equivocations.

When Titian in the 1550s painted on the ceiling of San Spirito in
Isola in Venice the tremendous second blow with which Cain killed
Abel, and created the illusion of his toppling down into the body of
the church, this was not only a reminder to the congregation of the
danger to society of crime; God had both cursed and protected Cain
through the 'mark' he carried into his banishment. Without violence
the Catholic Church would have lacked the martyrs whose fates sustained the prayers of the devout. Popes and Protestant preachers
endorsed violent punishments for those they pronounced to be slaves
to erroneous beliefs and commended or fulminated against wars in
accordance to what they judged their rightfulness to be. Secular authority itself, guardian of civility's values, was not innocent; 'considering
its origin carefully', Francesco Guicciardini wrote in about 1525, 'all
political power is rooted in violence.'[17]

For most observers the concern with violence was on an everyday
level, and it was growing. This becomes apparent not just because
more records have survived but because the level of violence increased,
or at least was perceived to increase by those who deplored it, as wealth
flowed into fewer hands and the proportion of the population who
turned to violence for gain or the release of resentment increased. The
extending commercial cultivation of land left families without food
from their own plots. Competition for jobs in the swelling populations
of towns at a time when guild memberships were frozen in the interest
of keeping profits high, led to a proliferation of wage-earners who
could hope for no promotion within the concern they worked for –
the 'prentices' of whose trouble-making propensities civic magistrates

were so wary. While not in themselves an indication of increased violence, something of the social attitudes that could prompt it can be
gleaned from off-hand remarks. The poor 'are not so beautiful to look
at as the higher groups,' wrote the Florentine Antonio Filarete in the
early 1460s;[18] to the military governors of besieged towns who pushed
them out to the enemy's guns lest they ate their betters' dwindling
stores of food, they were 'poor and useless', 'useless mouths', 'useless
people';[19] for Thomas Nashe in 1599 – himself a debt-ridden if talented
scribbler – they were 'the rubbish menialty'.[20] Mid-fifteenth-century
plans for rationalizing the medieval clutter surrounding St Peter's in
Rome provided for three new streets, one for the rich, one for the
reasonably well-to-do, one for the service-rendering poor. Leonardo's
ideal town plan provided upper walkways for the 'gentlefolk' to protect
them from the infrastructure used by *la poveraglia*, the plebs.[21]

Sebastiano Serlio's woodcuts of 1545 for ideal stage settings distinguished between the classical grandeur suitable for the noble personages

Stage designs for tragedy (left) and comedy (right), from Sebastiano Serlio, *Architettura*,
Lib. II (1545)

of tragedy, and the barbarous Gothic fitting for the plebeian characters of comedy. Equally revealing of the consciousness of social imbalance was the question Shakespeare put into the mouth of Jack Cade, leader in 1450 of a peasant revolt against the crown, in *Henry VI, Part 2* of 1594. Interrogated by a notary after his capture, Cade, girdingly speaking in the name of the underdog whose only signature was an illiterate's cross, asks, 'Dost thou use to write thy name, or hast thou a mark to thyself, like an honest plain-dealing man?'[22]

From cur's bite to eagle's stoop, there was, as always, ample evidence that animalistic violence could break through civility's norms at any social level. But an awareness of the split between privilege and want (there was a Spanish proverbial saying: 'There are only two families in the world: the Haves and the Have-Nots') drew a more alarmed attention to man's latent aggressiveness. It had been to protect themselves from this instinct, wrote Juan de Mariana in 1599, that when primitive men turned from killing beasts to becoming predators on their own kind, they 'began to draw themselves together with others in a mutual compact of society and to look for someone outstanding in justice and trustworthiness . . . In this manner', he went on, 'from fear and frailty . . . the civil societies in which we live well and happily were born.'[23] But by the time he produced this bland formula it was all too obvious that many did not accept that the conditions in which they lived were outstanding in justice and trustworthiness. And the centuries' wars produced a stream of investigations into the links between personal and public violence. Pierre de la Primaudaye summed up their contradictory findings in 1577. On the one hand, men's characters, under the influence of war 'are greatly changed from their natural disposition and become savage'. On the other, it is from the 'quarrels and dissentions among men from whence seditions and private murders proceed, and in the end civil and open wars'.[24]

There was also a heightened preoccupation with the danger to civilized public order that arose from man's animalistic sexual urges.

Crimes of passion following adulteries or rejections; rapes; fisticuffs, knifings and thefts in red light districts; problems of inheritance arising from illegitimate births: these had all been long familiar issues in the courts. The reprinted stories of Boccaccio and the new ones of Marguerite de Navarre (published in 1559) only gave shape to still earlier anecdotes about the sexual incontinence of monks and nuns. The gleeful communal ceremony of putting bride and groom to bed, the rich vernacular repertory of words for sexual organs and activities, the lack of

Man's divided nature: *Hercules at the Crossroads*, attrib. to Girolano di Benvenuto, *c.*1500 (Ca' d'Oro, Venice)

privacy in cramped and crowded homes, ensured that at least the facts of sex and sexual appetite were unmysterious. That readers of chivalrous romances would decode their idealism to find the underlying sexual charge had long ago been taken for granted by Dante; reading *Lancelot* together, there came the point, which brought them to Hell, when Paolo and Francesca 'read no more'. Vivid denunciations of sodomy, especially when crop failures or wars were explained in terms of God's anger with this most unnatural use of the body, brought into the pulpit knowledge that was familiar enough in folk-tale and the street. In one of Pietro Aretino's dialogues of the 1530s an experienced prostitute advises her daughter that to warm up a sluggish customer she should put on his clothes. 'No sooner does the gentleman see you transformed from a woman into a man than he will leap on you as hunger does on a hot loaf.'[25] Erasmus would not have allowed a reference to convent lesbianism to appear in his *Colloquies* (widely distributed and used in schools) if he had anticipated that it would come as a disturbing surprise to his readers.

It would be hazardous to suggest that sexual appetites changed or that sexual behaviour actually became more of a threat to the structure of civilized society. There is a remorseless familiarity about what the sources reveal. In 1476 a complaint was levelled against a priest who exposed 'his private parts to many women in the parish'.[26] In 1530 Joan Martyn of St Ives in Huntingdonshire accused Robert Blundell of breach of promise. He had said, 'I will marry thee iff thowe wylt lett me have adoo with thee,' and she had replied, 'certayn I will never have noon but you,' and 'upon that', noted the clerk to the church court, 'they had adoo together.'[27] They were sentenced to be married on pain of excommunication. In 1540 the warden of an orphans' home in Zwickau in Lutheran Saxony sexually abused a nine-year-old girl in his care. The girl complained and the case was examined. The offender was executed. The girl, because contaminated though innocent, was given half a florin and cloth for a shift and driven from the town. The physician Girolamo Cardano, in a book published in 1550, noted that some 'individuals will achieve erection only when they beat, even whip, another person.'[28] While in Rome in 1580, Montaigne was told about the wedding services held for homosexual couples in the church of San Giovanni a Porta Latina, a practice continued until 'eight or nine Portuguese of this fine sect were burnt'.[29]

None of these aspects of behaviour would have come as a surprise to a medieval magistrate or confessor. But there was a new alertness to the nature of sexuality itself. This was due in part to the more vigilant scrutiny of morals by Catholic clergy and the strenuous demands made by Protestantism on sexual conduct. In parts of the 'Merry England' of Elizabeth I the holier-than-thou aspect of Protestantism led to neighbour accusations of fornication, adultery, buggery, incest, bestiality or bigamy being levelled against one in seven of the local population. Army commanders in the field had learned how the resentment of sexual predation could alienate communities on whom they relied for produce, transport and guides; military codes were published to warn soldiers and itemize the sexual misdemeanours that would be punished

Albrecht Altdorfer, *Soldier paying a Prostitute*, c.1508 (Private Collection, London)

with death. Overseas discoveries drew attention to the sexual habits of non-Europeans and the appetite with which colonists took advantage of them; and not only overseas: Giles Fletcher warned Elizabeth that the agents of the Muscovy Company spent so much on their Russian mistresses that they were forced to embezzle Company funds. As more men came to travel, new grapevines of sexual gossip led to the stews of Hamburg or the bath-houses of Switzerland or the classier charms of Venetian courtesans. Writers on Turkey catered for day-dreamers with bold guesswork as to the nature of harem life and elaborate accounts of the sensual joys awaiting the faithful in the Islamic paradise.

Moralists publicly lamented that printed vernacular translations of Ovid's love poems could corrupt 'tender youths and delicate maidens' now that their texts were presented as reflecting real, as opposed to spiritually allegorized affairs (the Venetian Church authorities in 1497 forced a publisher of the *Metamorphoses* to remove illustrations of 'naked women, phallic deities, and other unclean objects'[30]). The continuing demand for literature with an erotic content, but now with a more psychologically believable treatment does suggest a heightened sexual self-consciousness. The idea – current from c.1500 – that the function of comedy was 'to hold a mirror up to nature' produced not only a wealth of humorous sexual by-play, a thwarted lover consoling himself by masturbating, for instance, but also, with the anonymous Italian *The Venetian Woman* of about 1518, a movingly sincere expression of a female sexuality that earlier literature had either ignored or treated with ostentatious decorum. The message of Horace's '*Carpe diem*', 'seize the day', had been familiar to medieval poets. Lorenzo de' Medici gave it a freshly pointed invitingness in his 1470s carnival song:

> How lovely is youth –
> Yet it slips away;
> If you would be happy, be so.
> There is no certainty about tomorrow.

With Pierre de Ronsard it acquired an emotional depth of personal feeling. In his 'when you are old' sonnet of the 1550s he urges his love to yield before

> I will be underground. Boneless with those
> Ghosts in the shade of myrtle I'll repose;
> You by the hearth a stooping old housewife,
> Regretting my love and your proud disdain.
> I urge you, live! Forestall tomorrow's pain,
> Gather today the rosebuds of your life.[31]

No earlier poet had so movingly described the emotional content of the act of sex as Ronsard did in another sonnet, 'When I lie prone above your lovely face . . .'.[32] And none had made such enticing play on an old theme as did his predecessor Clément Marot in his ode to the breast: beware, he wrote, 'The joy that taste and touching brings – You'll want to move to other things.'[33]

This development of the erotic in literature, which moved Torquato Tasso to include in his epic hymn to Christian heroism of 1575, *The Liberation of Jerusalem*, the love scenes and stories that kept the poem popular for their own sake for generations to come, was in itself no index of actual sexual behaviour. Writers were making sexuality appear more alarming to moralists by attuning it more suggestively to contemporary sensibility. Whereas what was simply obscene – like the cheerful bawdy of the Polish Mikolaj Rej's book of poems of 1562, *Little Frolics*, or the jokes recorded by Béroalde de Verville in a book of *c*.1610 ('I wish my pussy were a holy water stoup', said a lady, 'so that everyone would put their fingers in it'[34]) – could be tittered at or condemned almost unthinkingly, eroticism implied a sexuality of savour and intention that might lead from fantasy to behaviour. For Brantôme, an indifferent love poet himself, even the private poring over reprinted medieval romances in Spain and France, especially the most warmly realistic of them, *Amadis of France*, resulted in girls being 'moved, polluted and made wanton'.[35] But the public danger of erotic literature (read, after all, within the literate confines of civility's guardians) was not explored as was the connection between the aggressive instinct and crime and war. When books were censored in parts (as was *The Decameron*) or banned (as were Pietro Aretino's brothel conversations) it was more with readers' thoughts than their acts in mind. This was also true of the more overt, and far more novel element of the erotic in art. Artists' growing mastery of anatomical exactitude and three-dimensional illusionism, and their use of naked models, led to an extending market for figures which were believable in terms of current national standards of unclothed female and masculine attractiveness.

Just as a flexibility in the handling of vernacular language enabled writers to match contemporary feelings with a new directness of expression, so changes in the technique of pictorial descriptions permitted artists to produce a sexual imagery that was abreast of fact or dream. As with the nude in Dürer's engraving *The Idler's Dream of 1498*, a symbolic Temptation at last became visibly tempting. Savonarola's denunciation in the 1490s of religious images that awakened the wrong emotions might be dismissed as a celibate's paranoia were it not, for instance, for the evidence that the *St Sebastian* of his fellow Dominican, the painter Fra Bartolomeo, was later removed from Savonarola's own church, San Marco in Florence; 'the friars found out by the confessional that women had sinned by looking at it because of the comely and lascivious realism with which Fra Bartolomeo had endowed it.'[36] After keeping it out of the public eye for a while they sold it to an agent of the King of France. Leonardo da Vinci claimed that 'the painter can even induce men to fall in love with a picture that does not portray any living woman. It once happened to me that I made a picture representing a sacred subject which was bought by one who loved it – and then wished to remove the symbols of divinity in order that he might kiss it without misgivings. Finally his conscience prevailed over his lust and he . . . removed the picture from his house altogether.'[37] Leonardo was stressing the power of painting as opposed to that of sculpture. But we cannot assume that a statue, whether Donatello's caressingly nude bronze David, even Michelangelo's unrealistically large marble version of the same subject, installed in 1504 to commemorate Florence's sling-shot triumph over the Goliath of Medicean ascendancy, were protected by their symbolism from a more direct appraisal. By 1545, and probably since 1504, Michelangelo's giant had been supplied with 'gilded leaves'.[38]

Humanistic studies revealed the ancient Roman taste for sexual subject matter; Suetonius's description of Tiberius's pleasure palace in Capri, for instance. Enhanced technical nimbleness extended the reper-

'Imagery abreast of fact or dream': anon., *Woman with the red Lily, c.*1540s

Noble-headed but lascivious: bronze medal of Pietro Aretino (British Museum)

tory – and the knowingness – of the clumsily obscene images carved for medieval corbels and roof-bosses.

An Italian medal of Aretino showed his own, ennobled head on one side and, on the reverse, that of a satyr entirely composed of penises and testicles; a roughly contemporary northern engraving by Hans Sebald Beham showed a scene of lesbian titillation. Some of these works acquired considerable notoriety. The engraved series of sixteen sexual positions by Raphael's favourite engraver Marcantonio Raimondi were condemned to be destroyed in Rome but clandestine copies had a European currency. Versions were circulated at the court of Henri III of France in the 1580s and they were knowingly alluded to by Ben Jonson in his plays *Volpone* (1606) and *The Alchemist* (1610). Prints like the *Lascivious Scenes* of the 1590s by the highly respected painter of religious works, Agostino Carracci, give some idea of what Henry Peacham had in mind when he complained in 1612 that it was lewd art that 'was oftener enquired after in the shops than any other'.[39]

In his book of 1550, Cardano, ever anxious to promote the balanced temperament, advised scholars, because 'study dissipates the animal spirits', to adopt an anti-Utopian regimen of 'reading love stories and putting up pictures of beautiful maidens in their bedroom'.[40] When the lord in *The Taming of the Shrew* decided to see how the drunk and sleeping Christopher Sly would react to waking in circumstances of luxury, he ordered his servants to

> Carry him gently to my fairest chamber,
> And hang it round with all my wanton pictures.[41]

Where to hang such pictures was a matter of serious concern to the early seventeenth-century author, Giulio Mancini, of *Reflections of Painting*. Mildly lascivious ones, he concluded, should be put in rooms not usually visited by guests, and really erotic works in extremely private ones.

Given this background (and bearing in mind such details as the naked woman the French court enamellist Bernard Palissy modelled in the bottom of a sauce-boat) it would be ingenuous not to see the many such formal nudes as Titian's *Venus of Urbino* and its variants, or Lucas Cranach's slyly smiling full-frontal Venuses, as being as deliberate in intention as desired for their effect.

Patrons played the international art market to satisfy their tastes. France was not without competent native painters when Francis I wrote to Duke Francesco Gonzaga of Mantua requesting 'nude figures of a Venus' by Lorenzo Costa or when Duke Cosimo I of Florence sent him Bronzino's chillily provocative *Allegory of Venus*.

'The formal nude': Titian, *Venus of Urbino*, 1538 (Uffizi, Florence)

'Chillily provocative': Agnolo Bronzino, *Allegory of Venus*, 1540s
(National Gallery, London)

Rosso and Primaticcio at Fontainebleau skilfully caught the local, fashionable taste for seductive androgyny. The languorously self-displaying figure of Argus in Paulus van Vianen's silvered plaquette of 1610 was a virtuoso essay in satisfying the demand for homosexual images.

Giovanni Paolo Lomazzo, repeating in his treatise on art of 1584 the old truism that art had power to affect feelings, chose the otherwise unlikely word 'wife' when he stated that a painting can 'cause the beholder . . . to desire a beautiful young woman for his wife when he

A homosexual image: Paulus van Vianen, *Mercury and Argus*, silvered plaquette, 1610 (Rijksmuseum, Amsterdam)

seeth her painted naked'.[42] For the institution most at risk from sexual desire was marriage. We have seen the concern of the Utopianists either for making this lynchpin of civility effective or abolishing it as unworkable. As with violence and sexuality itself, the unstable marriage was a fact of life which became a matter of increasing open concern. From the fourteenth century the nuclei of parents and children had gradually detached themselves from their extended families. Increasingly, those who were reasonably well-off felt themselves, and were perceived by others, emotionally and financially, to be separate units. Increased urban prosperity led to greater mobility – from country to town and from one town to better opportunities in another – which drew the ambitious individual away from the settled kinship group into a house of his own and a self-sufficient way of life. It was a tendency encouraged by administrations which for purposes of taxation, and the imposition of labour and military service, found it convenient to think in terms of separate 'hearths' or households. There was in addition clerical pressure from both faiths to conflate the once adequate secular agreement to marry with the added solemnization of that contract in front of an altar. All combined to mould the image of the single family.

There was a flood of publications from the 1530s which idealized marriage and catered for it with advice. It was at the same time mocked in art and literature by the motifs of male infidelity, the cuckolding of husbands by rampant wives, the wars between the sexes as they fought for hegemony within marriage's walls. Shakespeare's young heroines (the Rosalind of *As You Like It*, the Kate of *The Taming of the Shrew*, the Beatrice of *Much Ado about Nothing*) play the lively verbal games of their last days of independence for an audience whose marriages might not have remained so diverting and secure as those of the merry wives of Windsor. After marriage, as graphic artists as well as writers showed with such vim, came the battle for who would wear the trousers, the moment when brilliant repartee was transformed into nagging, verbal fencing into physical beating. In Hans Sachs's play for the Nuremberg carnival of 1533 a friend slips a word into the ear of a disillusioned husband:

> Go ahead and act like a man!
> Otherwise she'll end up riding you,
> And before long she'll
> Deprive you of your pants, your purse and your sword,
> Which will make us all ashamed of you.
> Do not give her too much rein
> But rather take an oak cudgel
> And beat her soundly between the ears![43]

This sort of bitterness, reflected in a copious roll of matrimonial law cases, alarmed moralists.

The proportion of secure, mutually supportive marriages probably remained unchanged. But the novel publicity accorded to unhappy ones drew not only on centuries of distrust of Eve's disturbance of primal sinlessness, and of celibates' dislike of the natural functions of women's bodies, but on real problems that arose within marriages. Some five per cent of mothers died in childbirth. After producing enough healthy children (death in infancy was at a similar rate) to ensure extra earnings as they grew up and, for the well-off to pass on an inheritance and make useful marriages, each possibility of conception raised for those who were not well off a practical problem. Could the child be afforded especially were it to be a girl in a world where women

outnumbered men (a problem exacerbated by the abolishing of convents in Protestant countries)? Though methods of avoiding conception
were used – mutual masturbation, coitus interruptus, anal intercourse,
the employment of dubiously concocted pessaries, urination immediately after sex, prolonged breast-feeding – all were potential sources of
uncertainty and guilt for the devout or merely superstitious. Abortion
was widely practised. It was often successful, but it was feared as a sin
which even the most easy-going priest or minister found difficult to
absolve, and it was known through farmstead and tenement gossip to
be physically hazardous. Unwanted babies might be killed by neglect
or – to use the common colloquialism – by 'overlaying', smothering
in the crowded conjugal bed. More commonly infants were left, in
sadly increasing numbers, on the steps of charitable foundations, but
even this was not a recourse which newly pregnant women could view
dispassionately.

Reproduction put a strain on marriage and not only for those in
straitened circumstances; the well-off had to think hard about dowries
for daughters and the division of inheritances. This may in part account
for the high proportion of those who remained single – perhaps as
many as twenty per cent in Protestant England, where the clergy could
marry and there were no nunneries. A common solution was the postponement of marriage until between twenty-three to twenty-five for
women and twenty-eight to thirty for men, thus giving males time for
saving up for a separate household and, in the case of craftsmen, gaining
a mastership, as well as cutting down for both the reproductive years
of wedlock. But while postponement may have stabilized marriage,
the high proportion of bachelors and unmarried young women multiplied the disturbances and moral problems raised by illicit sex and the
publicity accorded to it. In Catholic countries convents remained open
for those whose families could afford the entrance fee. But everywhere
a proportion of girls and young women drifted into prostitution.[44] In
places where the conventions of inheritance passed down the line of
eldest sons the problem was compounded. Some fifty per cent of
Venetian men of good birth remained unmarried to protect the family
fortune. The number of prostitutes there (and, in parallel, the punishment of the active partners in homosexual relationships) was, unsurprisingly, especially high.

The feverish effect on the body politic of violence and, to a less
measurable extent, of sexuality was thought to be compounded by
another aspect of human nature that caused an ever mounting alarm:

Hendrick Goltzius, *The Love Match versus the Mercenary Marriage*

man's inclination to be idle. Everyone in Utopias had to work for the common good as well as their own spiritual benefit. The rational use of shared labour resources would cut down working hours – six for More, as low as four in *The City of the Sun* – but the medieval condemnation of the vice of sloth remained a governing principle behind the surveillance of work and leisure alike in ideal communities. The issue was much in the air. Alongside pulpits' continuing emphasis on the devil finding work for idle hands, men of secular learning debated the proper use of the *otium*, leisure, that was one of the gifts offered by settled, civil life, and administrators strove, at times in panic, to deal with what was a double problem: the unemployment of those who could find no job, and the trouble caused by the temperamentally work-shy.

The debate about the use of leisure inspired such portraits as Matteo Bandello's fictional description of the prosperous and sensual Zanina who spent her days in bed reading the *Decameron* and Ariosto's *Orlando*

Furioso, with its deeds of valour and dreamy love episodes. The short stories and comedies of the sixteenth century include a notable cast of deplorable characters, some derived from classical literature: the parasite, living off others by his wits; the bragging soldier, too cowardly to fight; pompous schoolmasters who had never bothered to study; doctors who invented their own credentials; pimps who lived off their women; idle servants; fake astrologers who exploited the fears of the ignorant; beggars. What all had in common was the motto ascribed to them by a Spanish author: 'we want to live without working.'[45]

It was the last named, the beggars, who caused the most practical concern. The urban undergrounds they constituted had their own hierarchies and specializations: those who faked wounds and sores; those who ran gangs of importuning boys and pre-teenage tarts; apparent devotees who cut purses in church; those who pretended to be on pilgrimage as penance for an involuntary sin which made a good whining story. Twenty-five such categories were distinguished by the Basel magistrates. A London magistrate described a Fagin-like school for pickpockets. Beggars seemed at times to threaten every foothold civilized life had won with their crime and noise. With reference only to children, citizens of Lyon complained of their crying and hooting from hunger and cold day and night throughout the town, making a marvellous racket in the churches, disturbing the devotion of the people: '. . . oh, what confusion, heartbreak and scandal'.[46] And almost equally perturbing was the Europe-wide addiction among honest citizens to reading about the tricks and habits of the very underclass that threatened them. The literature of London low-life was particularly rich, but it was the Spaniard Francisco de Quevedo who, opening in *c*.1608 his novel of jauntily heartless violence, scatology and exploitative cunning, *The Swindler*, recognized this demand most frankly:

> Here you will find all the tricks of the low life which I think most people enjoy reading about: craftiness, deceit, subterfuge and swindles, born of laziness to enable you to live on lies: and if you attend the lesson you will get quite a lot of benefit from it. And even if you don't, study the sermons [which described such activities in order to denounce them], for I doubt whether anyone buys a book as coarse as this in order to avoid the inclinations of his own depraved nature . . . Praise the genius of its author who has enough commonsense to know it is a lot more amusing to read about low life when the story is written with spirit, than about other more serious topics.[47]

Common to the aggressive, libidinous and slothful aspects of undisciplined human instinct was its psychological volatility. Fears of crop failure or of other indications of imminent catastrophe or divine punishment were communicated across whole regions by market gossip, wandering pedlars and self-appointed itinerant preachers in a few weeks, producing hysterical crowds whose mood could turn them into mobs searching for scapegoats; landlords and merchants holding out for higher prices, the God-offending Jews, the devil-controlled witch.

In a sermon at York in 1596 the priest called for prayers and repentance: 'our July hath been like to a February, our June even as an April . . . our years are turned upside down . . . our summers are no summers, our harvests are no harvests.'[48] This was obvious enough to his congregation. Moreover, few would not have read, or had read to them, the annual astrological forecast given in the cheap almanacs that since the introduction of the press had become almost the most widely distributed of all printed works: by the year of the sermon they were to be found in nearly one out of every three English households. They were often wrong, and known to be; above the calculable motions of the planets was a God with his own estimate of when and where man's sinfulness called for a summer that was no summer. But the almanac, together with prognostications that explained the significance of such portents as comets and shooting stars, a murrain among livestock, a monstrous birth of a child half human, half pig, had the power in difficult times to exacerbate the fears of the rational and the irrational alike.

Real or precautionary belief both in astrological influences and the mysterious workings of divine punishment were common to poor and rich, ignorant and educated alike. That tough general and military entrepreneur the Count of Wallenstein (1583–1634) wore an amulet inscribed with astrological signs. In times of dearth or war governments regularly called on the churches to preach repentance and organize processions of the devout to invoke God's pardon for whatever transgressions (sodomy, blasphemy, lax church attendance, uncharitableness towards the poor and the afflicted) were in need of correction. The civilized saw themselves as intelligently conniving with, rather than superstitiously surrendering to, the lure of astrological prediction. Omens and portents were another matter. Critical historians linked comets and bolts of lightning to the deaths of princes and military defeats. The patrician diarist Marin Sanudo described what he thought to be a revealing moment in Venice in 1509. The Republic's army had been defeated. The Great Council was digesting the news. The proceedings were lengthy, the issues complex and dire. After some hours the elderly Doge, presiding over the assembly, slipped from his throne to go to the lavatory. Heads were shaken at this unprecedented breach of civic decorum. It was for the plebs to obey their bladders, not the wise, least of all a head of state. It was seen as an omen of wider catastrophes to come.

Barred from comprehending the apparent injustice of the human predicament as explained by theologians, the scarce-schooled lived in terms of a view of life based on tradition and observation: the fortunes and misfortunes of individuals, the incidence of good and bad years for crops and animals, of epidemics and health for men. All were incalculable. In such circumstances, seemly conduct and prayer were less important than propitiation. Saints were more prominent in the uneducated imagination than Christ, saints who protected the places where they had died or the crafts and trades they had practised before their martyrdom. In a late fifteenth-century joke, a man when his son's life was in danger after an accident, prayed to a painting of Christ as a youth disputing with the scribes. When the boy nevertheless died, the disgusted supplicant turned on the picture and said, 'I promise that I shall never again have anything to do with you or with other children, for he who gets mixed up with children can only expect childish behaviour!'[49] It was a joke told to be laughed at by sophisticated people. Its interest lies in its acceptance that there was a large segment of the population who looked to religion to provide direct answers to personal crises. It drew on cases when images which failed to produce what was expected of them were tossed into rivers or whipped. Soldiers turned to St George or St Andrew, potential plague victims to St Sebastian or St Roche, cobblers to St Crispin, women in childbirth to St Margaret, travellers to St Christopher. Intermittent religious feeling, flaring in moments of anguish, sought to invoke, touch whichever representative of the divine was most appropriate. Relics, too, had this power to comfort, not so much the more esoteric ones which strained even unsophisticated belief, like the Virgin's nightgown in Aachen or the water in which she had washed Jesus's baby clothes in Cairo, or his foreskin, cut off at his circumcision (Calvin, not a widely travelled man, had seen three of them), but bits of bone and fingernail and hair that passed the current of hope directly between worshipper and protector, whether calendared saint or local martyr scarce known outside a neighbourhood covering a few score square miles.

If this were a sign of uninstructed irrationality, such superstition was widely shared. Princes collected holy bits and pieces. The Elector Friedrich, the protector of Luther, had over 19,000, including a piece of the burning bush and some soot from Daniel's fiery furnace. Cathedrals enshrined them in silver-gilt and jewelled reliquaries. Fear was a social leveller, even if educated men saw homage to relics in terms of just-in-case while the frightened poor saw them in terms of all-or-nothing. The same link within social divisions applied to pre-Reformation pilgrimages. Educated men combined this act of contrition with a lively intellectual curiosity about the scenes and manners encountered en route and rarely flung themselves into pilgrimage out of mere desperation. Numbers of simpler men did.

In around 1520 an artist depicted the paroxysms of devotion in which many of them writhed in front of the miracle-working statue of the

Michael Ostendorfer,
Pilgrimage to the Beautiful Virgin of Regensburg,
woodcut, 1520
(Germanisches
Nationalmuseum,
Nuremberg)

Virgin in Regensburg. In that year local craftsmen turned out 109,108 clay and 9,763 silver mementoes of the statue; souvenirs for some, for others amulets of enduring reassurance. How far Catholic and Protestant attempts to deprive men and women of touch-wood, 'superstitious' comforts in times of adversity cannot be measured, nor the extent to which they were replaced by a recourse to magical spells and pre-Christian protective spirits, nor the extent to which the Reform of both faiths lowered the threshold over which alarm stepped into the mind. What is certain is that superstition, in the sense of surrender to the irrational, was only pushed to one side.

A devout Italian shopkeeper described in 1509 a salesman of good-luck prayers who climbed into a baker's oven and emerged unscathed whereas the dough he took with him was cooked through. 'I have not seen a greater miracle than this, if', the diarist cautiously added, 'it *is* a miracle.'[50] The Lutheran Sastrow with no flicker of doubt reported how a kitchen maid of his mother's had suddenly taken to throwing around the saucepans and frying pans while screaming, 'I want to get out, I want to get out.' She was, of course, he went on, possessed by a devil. And there was an obvious explanation. 'Her mother had bought a cheese at the market. In her absence the daughter had opened the cupboard and cut out a large piece. On her return the mother had expressed the wish that the devil might take the perpetrator; and from that moment dated the possession.'[51] Francis I was to use the divinity inherent in his consecration ceremony to touch the heads of nearly 17,500 of his subjects who knelt before him to be cured of scrofula – chronic swelling of the lymphatic glands. English kings, Catholics and Protestants alike, did the same from the reign of Edward IV to that of James I, and even beyond, to Queen Anne. For the Calvinist intellectual James, this was done more as homage to a traditional attribute of kingship than out of a superstitious belief that he could actually cure his subjects. At the same time he was a convinced persecutor of witches.

The belief that certain individuals, through their surrender to Satan, were not only enabled to carry out such malicious tricks as curdling milk, raising storms and making men impotent but to blur the wavelengths on which God communicated to mankind, was centuries old. As an example of the way in which heresies could blight true faith, by the fifteenth century witchcraft had been defined and punishments ranging from penance to death had been worked out. But it was only from the sixteenth that the victims – some 100,000 were killed throughout Europe, eighty per cent of them women who as widows or spin-

Urs Graf, *Witches' Sabbat*, drawing, 1514 (Albertina, Vienna)

sters were loners in their communities – multiplied. It was all very well for Montaigne to point out that 'it is putting a very high price on one's conjectures to roast a man alive for them', but those who denounced, investigated under torture and burnt witches did not see that Satan's ability to chose accomplices was a matter of conjecture. It was part of his role as enemy of God and corrupter of His creation.

It is probably no mere coincidence that witch persecution grew alongside the churches' whittling down of other, homely means of coming to terms with life's uncertainties. It became tempting to blame an unpopular neighbour rather than a recalcitrant saint for the sickness of a child or a horse. Moreover, to accuse a neighbour of witchcraft was to show a solidarity with the new, disciplined orthodoxy of both faiths, which might contribute to the accuser's standing. Many, if not most, accusations were at this personal and local level, and James I brought with him to the fairly easy-going English form of Protestantism the narrower and more authoritarian Calvinism of his native Scotland, where witches had been sought out with a determination foreign to his new realms. There were, however, more wholesale purges. Between 1587 and 1593 three hundred and sixty-eight persons were burned as witches in and around Toulouse. In 1611 and 1612 two hundred and sixty witches were killed in the small south German town of Ellwangen. In some cases the hunt was up – as in the case of Jewish persecutions – for scapegoats accountable for catastrophic food shortages. In others (as at Ellwangen), self-generated panics led to escalating accusations, nourished by nightmare imaginings of witches flying through the air to Sabbat congregations where, amidst sexual entanglings amongst themselves and with their devil-masters, they plotted against decent men and women. Scare fed scare, poisoning an atmosphere in which some of these accused actually saw themselves as having for their sins been chosen by Satan, and voluntarily connived with their punishment.

Other manifestations of popular nervous instability were treated as the political revolts they sometimes, if unintentionally, became. 'In the year of our Lord 1476', a Bavarian chronicler reported,

> there came to the village of Niklashausen a cowherd and drum player . . . The whole country, he said, was mired in sin and wantonness, and unless our people were ready to do penance and change their wicked ways, God would let all Germany go to destruction. This vision, he said, was revealed to him by the Virgin Mary . . . Thus it came to pass that great numbers of people went to Niklashausen to pray in the church of Our Lady there. All Germany seemed in commotion. Stableboys ran from their horses, taking away the bridles. Reapers left their reaping, carrying their scythes. Women ceased haying, coming with their rakes. Wives left husbands, husbands wives. As it happened, the grape harvest had been excellent and abundant, and wine was cheap that year. Taverns were set up in the fields.

The drummer preached against sinfully extravagant clothing and 'many men and women took off all their clothes and left them in the church, going away naked except for their shifts.' He also 'preached violently against the government and the clergy . . . so vehemently against the priests that the pilgrims of Niklashausen made up a special song which they chanted along with their other hymns. It went:

> O God in Heaven, on you we call,
> Kyrie eleison,
> Help us seize our priests and kill them all,
> Kyrie eleison.

Getting to hear of this, the bishop of nearby Würzburg, who was also the chief political authority in the city, sent out troops. Many peasants were killed and captured. The sequel is reported as thus:

> In Würzburg the towers and dungeons were filled to overflowing. Later, however, most were pardoned. Only the drummer and one or two others were burned at the stake and their ashes thrown into the river Main so that no superstitious cult might be made of them. All the same, a few of the faithful succeeded one night in digging up some soil from the spot where the drummer had been burned. They carried this to their homes and treasured it as a sacred relic.[52]

It was this sort of spontaneous volatility, throwing up political slogans as it spread, that aroused the greatest alarm to those intent on defending the civilized values by which they judged behaviour that was, or was not rational. And they saw themselves as manning an archipelago of reason and justified privilege within a vast sea, heaving with instinctual currents of violence and covetousness, represented by the peasantry who formed the overwhelming majority of the European population.

In a Dutch allegorical print of 1550, one of a series showing society as a horse unbridled by reason, Justice is bucked off by her recalcitrant mount. Above her toppling figure is the inscription 'Good justice wants to ride the foolish world, but it will not permit her to do so'. In his prose romance *Arcadia*, Sir Philip Sidney described what happened when the irrational populace was given charge of its own destiny. The poor townsmen wanted cheaper corn and wine, but 'the ploughmen, vine-labourers and farmers would have none of that. The countrymen demanded that every man might be free [given citizen's rights] in the chief towns: that could not the burgesses like of. The peasants would have all the gentlemen destroyed; the citizens . . . would but have them reformed. And of each side were like divisions.'[53] Typical of the fears of ordinary men of substance was Jean de Tavannes's bitter reflection in his memoirs, written in the 1580s, that ignoring any rational organization of society, 'the people want, specifically, equality.'[54]

With notable regional exceptions – such as late sixteenth–century

'Justice toppled': from Maerten van Heemskerck, *The Allegory of the World as an Unbridled Horse*, 1550 (Albertina, Vienna)

Holland, where nearly fifty per cent of the population lived in towns or in the suburban villages around them – the rural population of the continent was seen as its most dangerous element. This population was by no means homogeneous. There were differences in wealth between farmers and labourers, in role (there was an infrastructure of factors, bailiffs and rent-collectors who linked labourer to landlord), in occupation: rural clergy, wheelwrights, millers, blacksmiths, the carriers whose waggons and mules took produce to markets, the travelling brokers who offered credit secured on cottages and farm implements and against the sale of unripe crops. There were many in the country who were poor without being peasants. In *c.*1620 Tristram Risdon described the life of the tin miner of Devon and Cornwall; his 'apparel is coarse, his diet slender, his lodging hard, his drink water and, for want of a cup, he commonly drinketh out of his spade or shovel. His life is in pits . . . and in great danger, because the earth above his head is in sundry places crossed over with timber to keep the same from falling'.[55] Elsewhere, as in Friesland and the Tirol, peasant freeholders even had a representative to speak for them on local government bodies. To townsmen, however, and to those educated members of the land-lord class whose financial and administrative roles brought them to cities and courts, the countryside could easily be seen in times of rural hardship as a wilderness of ignorant, crudely toiling but potentially rebellious 'peasants'. Neither the familiarity of the town-based owner of rural property with his tenants, nor the rural aristocrat's close know-ledge of the families whose labour he relied on, checked the impulse to see them as savages in smocks.

Luther, a rural miner's son, turned against 'peasants' as a class when in southern Germany they threatened the social hierarchy he relied on to endorse his programme of Reform. Erasmus, who for all his romanticisation of the psalm-singing ploughman had probably never met one, warned his young readers who wished to be identified with civility from imitating the unreclaimed crudeness of peasants who wiped their noses on their clothes. The Spanish jurist Francisco de Vitoria reminded his readers, as we have noticed,[56] that while we may deplore the habits of non-Europeans, 'even among ourselves we find many peasants who differ little from brutes.' A deluge of town-based jokes helped to mock and distance the threat that the minority faced from the immense reserve of rustic outsiders, for as more countrymen came looking for work in towns, and more merchants diversified their investments or sought enhanced social status by purchasing country properties, the figure of the peasant became an increasingly familiar one. Sebastian Brant mourned in 1494 that

> Now city folk from peasants learn
> Great wickedness in their turn;
> From peasants springs all knavery –
> Each day a new discovery.[57]

In a few anecdotes the naïve peasant gets the better of the townsman (in Machiavelli's short story *Belfagor* a peasant even tricks a devil); most present them as butts. A peasant comes home from town with half of his beard shaved off and proudly recounts that he had got the better of the barber by only offering him half his fee. A group of peasants ask an artist for a picture of Christ. Asked whether they want him shown living or dead, they reply, 'alive, for then if we don't like it we know very well how to kill him'.[58] Such jokes are only worth repeating for the supercilious contempt they display. The rougher side of Italian

Christoph Murer (attrib.), *Peasants Dancing*, woodcut, early sixteenth century

anti-peasant feeling comes out in the plays written in the mid-1520s by the Paduan Angelo Beolco for patrician audiences in Venice (many of whom relied on the exploitation of these same peasants for the income from their country farms), inviting them to laugh at his all too realistic portrayal of rural brutality, poverty and hopelessness. A spate of early sixteenth-century German prints satirizing peasants as they clumsily imitated the fashions and diversions of their betters was taken up later in the century in the Low Countries. Below one of Christoph Murer's anti-peasant engravings illustrating the uncouth abandon of a peasant dance, is this inscription: 'As far as the court is from the sheep-fold, so is the courtier from the peasants. This bawdy round dance will soon teach you that. But thus do the different sides of life manifest themselves.' Shakespeare's Sir John Falstaff wrote off the yokels he contemptuously recruited into the king's wars, as born to be shot, they were 'food for powder, food for powder; they'll fill a pit as well as better'.[59]

It was not so much the number of such references as the edge on many of them, sharpening from scorn to hatred, which gives the impression that town-based civility was felt to be precarious. In eastern Europe the independence of the great landlords from effective royal

control, and their virtual monopoly of local police and judicial power, led to a heartless exploitation of the peasantry in the interest of maximising the profits on the export of agricultural produce. In Poland the days on which the peasant was forced to work for his lord rather than for himself and his family rose from one a week to six during the sixteenth century. Landlord insistence on receiving rents in kind prevented tenants from taking advantage of any rise in the price of produce they did not need for their own families. Similar changes – resulting in a return to the conditions of early medieval enserfment – affected the peasants of Hungary and Lithuania. In Transylvania a peasant could not even call a Sunday his own. Tied to service, forbidden to travel, largely unschooled and ignorant, poor and without recourse against the whips and clubs of his overseers, the eastern European peasant was not seen as a threat to the way of life of castle complex or city: he was referred to with confident disgust rather than with the mockery that masked alarm.

In the West the demand for agricultural labour after the Black Death of 1348 had led in the opposite direction. Peasants were wooed away from their original lords or released from labour services to persuade them to remain. Disadvantaged but legally free, able to buy land when they could afford it, able to enter the market with their own produce and animals on however small a scale, with access for some, even if only for a few years of childhood, to schooling, the peasant was not only more visible to those plying between the more numerous towns of the West, and more thought and written about, but was potentially socially mobile himself. Some became priests. It was from among the peasantry that Andrea del Castagno rose to fulfil governmental and ecclesiastical commissions for frescoes in Florence and Konrad Celtis became an influential professor at Ingolstadt. This background was borne in mind when from the later fifteenth century the position of the peasantry worsened in parts of the West. Traditional landlords enclosed land for broad sheep pastures; new ones from a mercantile background enforced their rights and ignored old concessions. Peasant misery and resentment grew. And among civility's warning antennae were some tuned to give the alarm at any perception of change.

NEW INSECURITIES

All lands into disgrace have got
And none's contented with his lot,
And none remembers now his sires:
The world is full of fool's desires.[60]

This mourning of the passing of the good old ways comes, again, from Sebastian Brant's *Ship of Fools* of 1494. Its tone was echoed in a rich international literature of regret that lasted throughout the following century. In 1587 William Harrison, in his *Description of England*, complained that what with ear-ringed men and doubletted women passing him in the London streets he had become confused as to 'whether they were men or women', for 'it is now come to pass that women are become men, and men transformed into monsters.'[61] Such complaints about the times being out of joint were far from new. As long ago as the thirteenth century a Latin song ran to the effect that 'Youth will no longer study! Learning is in decay! The whole world is topsy-turvy! The blind lead the blind and hurl them into the abyss, birds fly before they are fledged . . . What was once outlawed is now praised. Everything is out of joint.'[62]

A similar desire to cling to past traditions rather than accept, let alone positively look for change, motivated not only the 1505 Statute of Nothing New (*Nihil Novi*) forced by the Polish nobility upon King Alexander I, but was characteristic of the demands for a return to the old ways continually made by rebels, whether peasants or aristocrats, against innovating authority throughout sixteenth-century Europe. A conqueror, wrote Machiavelli in *The Prince*, should certainly displace and expunge the former ruling family, but he must not alter the laws to which their subjects had become habituated. 'If novelties have to be introduced', Botero advised eight decades later, 'let this be done gradually and almost imperceptibly.'[63] There were many for whom the search for innovation in practical, spiritual or intellectual and creative life was a creed. But even among humanists and reformers and natural scientists the attraction of the new was accompanied by the conviction that in most cases it was also a return to traditions that had been lost sight of, whether it was the wisdom and achievements of antiquity or the ideals of early Christianity; if they saw further it was partly because they stood firmly on the shoulders of their predecessors. It was above all the great majority who lived on or near the breadline who saw change as loosening their grip on a life that was already insecure.

Volatile breaches of the norms of behaviour by acts of violence, incontinent sexuality and panicking crowds were familiar enough, but in the Renaissance they came to be more amply recorded because the order they threatened was more consciously defined, and because they were exacerbated by additional pressures on the individual. Governmental interference with ways of life that had become stabilized by habit, played a part. More disturbing were impersonal forces, demographic and economic, and the massive upsetting of traditional attitudes towards religion: what it offered and what it expected from the individual.

As the population of Europe rose, there were many years in which agricultural productivity and distribution were far from being able to keep pace. The effect of food shortages on so drastically enlarged a number of mouths may be gauged by a casually told anecdote in a Neapolitan chronicle: 'a few days ago [April, 1601] . . . a peasant, along with his wife, so as not to see their three sons perish from hunger in front of their eyes, locked them in the house and set out in the name of heaven. After three days had passed, the neighbours, not having seen them, decided to knock down the door, which they did. And they found two of the sons dead, and the third dying with straw in his mouth, and on the fire there was a pot with straw inside which was being boiled in order to make it softer for eating.'[64] The poor were seldom so passive. 'The sea shall be dry when the poor man has a friend'[65]; such proverbs may have been resignedly bandied around, but the sources are fuller of armed bands invading their lords' fields and barns or streaming to towns, at times exhaustedly begging for bread, at others violently and concertedly demanding it.

The situation was aggravated by the pressure on the populations within the towns themselves. By 1600 those of Rome, Palermo, Vienna, Nuremberg, Augsburg and other northern cities – Hamburg, Danzig – had doubled within the century. Those of Lisbon and Seville and Messina had trebled. The population of Lyon grew by one-third between 1530 and 1535. London had four times as many inhabitants by 1600 than it had had when Henry VIII came to the throne in 1509. The result everywhere was shacks and noisome tenements, 'dark dens for . . . thieves, murderers and every mischief worker',[66] according to a London observer in 1592, and an intensification of the familiar problem of urban poverty and street violence. And as the growth in population pressed ever harder on the food supply, prices naturally rose and made life harder than ever for the poor.

Population growth contributed to price inflation by increasing demand. The dramatic infusion of silver from Mexico and Peru probably had an inflationary effect as it worked its way into the monetary system of Europe. The diversion of manufactured goods to satisfy the demand of settlers overseas may have led to higher prices being charged for those available in Europe. So did the manipulation of the bullion content of coins by governments tiding themselves over a succession of temporary monetary crises; merchants adjusted prices upward to meet the lower precious metal content of the cash they received. To a friend in Spain, where prices had risen fivefold during the previous century, Lipsius wrote in 1603 that 'the New World, conquered by you, has conquered you in its turn.'[67] Other targets were easier for victims of the rise to grasp. In 1523 a German pamphleteer had concentrated on monopolistic merchants and mercantile associations whose cornering of the manufacture or import of products made them more expensive; the result was that 'it's the poor man who pays for it all.'[68] An English preacher in 1549 seized on greedy landlords who so increased their rents 'that poor men, which live by their labour, cannot with the sweat of their face have a living, all kinds of victuals is so dear'.[69]

Both the simplicity of contemporary explanations and the complexity of subsequent attempts to find better ones reflect the significance of this phenomenon. In France the purchasing power of wages fell by forty per cent (in Normandy – for inflation was always patchy, if cumulative overall – by seventy per cent). In the English midlands it has been estimated that the gap between average wage and average price increased by fifty per cent. In the second half of the sixteenth century, while the wage of unskilled and semi-skilled workers in Germany's largest city, Augsburg, became adjusted upwards by forty-seven per cent, prices rose by nearly seventy per cent. In 1568 Jean Bodin, a political philosopher and a careful observer, wrote that 'the price of things fifty or sixty years ago was ten times less than at present.'[70] What perturbed him was what the future seemed to hold in store: more peasant uprisings induced by scarcity, more tumults in market places, the roads ever less safe because of the increase in those who took refuge in banditry, more spontaneous and widespread support for malcontents of all social orders who sought a following against the real or imagined injustice of authority. Acting in consort, the impersonal agents of population increase and inflation put the haves of Europe on a new level of alert against the threat from the have-nots. Robert Wilson's play of c.1590, The Cobbler's Prophecy, warned the rich, those of 'Chimneys so many, and alms not any', that the time would come when 'These poor that cry, Being lifted up on high, When you are all forlorn, Shall laugh you to scorn.'[71]

Governments themselves widened the split as all over western Europe central administrations tried to extend their grasp on resources of men and money. Larger armies meant wider recruitment, voluntary or forced. And to many contemporaries this was not seen as alleviating social distress by the offer of a wage, but as increasing the turmoil within the population of the deprived, which was the chief source of troops. Of the new soldiers removed from their families and neighbourhoods in the 1520s, a German wrote that they 'learn and become habituated to all kinds of vice . . . they learn whoring, adultery, rape, gluttony, drunkenness, and beastly things such as stealing, robbing and murder. These things become their daily bread, and they commit them against poor people who have never harmed them'.[72] Though this is the voice of a moralist, there is ample evidence that once given arms and detached from the normalizing conventions of their communities, the enlisted peasant or poor townsman turned ferociously upon the vulnerable members of his own economic background abroad. He brought home the bullying anti-social behaviour learned while foraging

The Venetian doge
approves cash for war:
maiolica plate inscribed
'action not words', c.1495
(Fitzwilliam Museum,
Cambridge)

from camp or while on the march or when occupying surrendered towns.

To pay for wars, diplomacy and courts, governments did their best to increase taxes. Their success was patchy. This was a change welcomed by no one, whatever their status. It is true that while bureaucracies grew in size there were never enough officials to ensure that the full expectation of a tax yield could be garnered.

All the same, whereas artists before the mid-sixteenth century illustrated the handing out of public money to grateful soldiers, sailors and the poor, thereafter they showed glum or resigned citizens bringing their taxes to offices stuffed with clerks and files.

In a late sixteenth-century French drawing, men and women trudge in to pay at a desk over which is the admonition 'Fear God, Honour the King', and in a contemporary painting by the younger Pieter Breughel taxpayers humbly confront disdainful clerks who preside over an avalanche of papers. These taxes were levies on property and – less frequently – income; but the rates of both were commonly lowered from the original demand by bodies representing the monied interests of a realm, or by lawyers representing aggrieved individuals who could afford to pay them. The most reliably yielding taxes were those on commodities: on firewood, grain, wine, meat, oil, salt and cloth, for instance. And outside rural areas, where transactions often remained within a barter economy, it was on the most determinedly volatile element of the community, those who had just enough to resent the rise in prices, that the impact of commodity taxes fell most heavily. Reporting in 1595 on his experience of the States of the Church as Venice's ambassador in Rome, Paolo Paruta drew his government's attention to a situation (which they would recognize as akin to their own local one) of endemic banditry, recurrent famine 'and continued taxation that is collected with all rigour'. These factors, he remarked, 'have given birth in the soul of the Church's temporal subjects to a deep dissatisfaction with their government, and a profound desire for change in the hope that whatever else happens, they might improve

'Fear God, Honour the King': *The Tax-Collector*, anon. drawing, late sixteenth century (Musée du Louvre, Paris)

their present most tormented condition'.[73] The change he had in mind was a return to the time when the exactions of both landlords and government bore more lightly on tenants and subjects.

In addition to the strains induced by population growth, price rises and governmental fiscal policy, the emotional stability of Europe had to undergo Trial by Reformation. During the first generation of the spread of Protestant ideas in southern Germany, Switzerland and parts of France, popular proselytism was often rowdy. Congregations began to challenge and catcall during services. Arguments spilled out into streets and taverns, leading to fights and looted shops. Large crowds of the sort that had always put local authorities on edge, flowed from Catholic towns and villages to hear Protestant preachers addressing open-air assemblies. There was a vogue for paintings of St John preaching in the wilderness as a commemoration of the second propagation of the true gospel. And just as Catholic missionaries in America destroyed images of faiths that had, for the true God's sake, to be supplanted, so outbursts of image smashing marked the more hectic roundings on the painted and sculpted evidence of Catholic superstition. The 'Martin Luther' scratched into Raphael's eucharistic fresco *The Triumph of the Sacrament* in the Vatican by a German soldier during the Sack of Rome in 1527 was no more than a scratch compared with the wholesale hammering and burning that destroyed works of art while Protestants were baying for ascendancy in Swiss and German cities, in England in the 1540s and in the Netherlands from the mid-1560s. Erasmus, who had settled in Basel to be near its scholarly printing presses and because of its atmosphere of tolerance, watched the outburst of early 1529 in horror: 'not a statue had been left in the churches, in porches, on facades, or in the monasteries. Everything frescoed is lost under coats of whitewash. Whatever would burn has been thrown into the pyre, everything else hacked into small pieces. Neither value nor artistry prevailed to save anything.'[74] On the first of April the city magistrates approved the outburst: 'we have no pictures in our churches, either in the city or the country, because they formerly gave much incitement to idolatry . . . Hence in future, by God's help, we will set up no pictures.'[75] On April 13th Erasmus left to spend the rest of his life in Freiburg-im-Breisgau. In other Swiss cities, in Zurich, for instance, the process of cleansing the temples was more moderate; it involved dismantling, storing or selling rather than destruction. Nonetheless artists, unable to live on portraits and secular subjects alone, emigrated or turned to other occupations.

To honour afresh the second Mosaic Commandment not to worship graven images was both an affirmation of obedience to God's word and an expression of loathing directed against the superstitious bedazzlements that ensnared the victims of the Catholic Whore of Babylon. The setting for Protestant worship was to be undistracting. Statues were removed, paintings replaced by texts, the Ten Commandments conspicuous among them. Stained and painted windows were remade in plain glass. Altars were dismantled, their stones at times being used to re-flag chancel floors which were lowered to reduce the contrast between the clergy's privileged podium and the nave. Rood-screens, which further emphasized the separate spaces occupied by priest and congregation, were taken down. Embroidered altar frontals and vestments were banned. Bells and candlesticks, the portable furniture of catholic liturgy, were sold or stolen. The leading reformers – Luther, Zwingli, Calvin – endorsed these changes, though none supported the artistic terrorism that too often accompanied them.

Arguably, this clearing away of images in order to provide a changed decor for worship could be both doctrinally and liturgically justified. But what alarmed men like Erasmus was the mindless vandalism, the jealous revenge on objects that represented privilege and oppression, that took purely instinctual advantage of the justification. Instead of being levered from their niches and disposed of, for instance, all but one of the two hundred and sixty-two statues decorating the Alcock chantry in Ely cathedral were smashed or mutilated. As in the case of the drummer of Niklashausen, spiritual leadership released pent-up frustrations of wider import. The incidence of savage iconoclasm was erratic. In contrast to the St Albans mob, the parishioners of St Laurence, Ludlow, on the other side of England, accepted the changes in religion, reign by reign, with resignation. They dismantled their rood-screen in 1548, replaced it in 1554 when Henry VIII had been succeeded by the Catholic Queen Mary, took it down again in 1559 when the rules changed once more under Elizabeth. Once the initial fervours had passed, both in England and on the continent, religious pictures and statues remained under doctrinal ban, but here and there chancel steps were reintroduced and personal monuments, even memorial altars were brought back or remade. Elizabeth forbade any further defacement of images; those that still remained in parish churches and cathedrals could be lived with peaceably as relics of a past era.

Interrupted services, vandalized and looted churches, neighbouring

parishes reviling one another's practices, divided families: these manifestations of strain passed. But even when the agitation caused by a
choice between versions of the Christian religion had been taken out
of the hands of most individuals by governmental decisions, personal,
introspective tensions remained.

The result both of Protestant zeal and reactive Catholic rigour was
to increase the awareness of sinfulness among the sensitive of both
faiths. For fear of contamination and to parade their own orthodoxy
neighbours turned informer to an increasingly over-worked Inquisition. A Brescian was denounced to the Inquisition for having claimed
that the motive of the writers of the Bible was simply to make men
frightened, and of remarking that 'he loved a fine boy while having
sex with him more than God.' Another Italian, a shoemaker, was
reported to have pronounced that the sacramental wafer was just 'a bit
of food which one puts in one's mouth and comes out of one's arse'.[76]
Such remarks were no longer safe within the formerly harmless context
of goading the straitlaced or making a risqué joke. Individuals who
untroubledly held eccentric opinions as to the nature of creation or the
role of angels, were forced from their usually remote rural homes
towards the civic fires of uniformity. Even within the doctrinally
reasonably easy-going Elizabethan form of Protestantism (which nonetheless killed Catholic missionary priests like Edmund Campion when
it could locate them), a rigidity developed which showed as little mercy
towards weak friends as towards professional ideological foes. In 1608
the Englishman John Molle was arrested in Rome while acting as tutor
to a young nobleman and imprisoned by the Inquisition. After three
years of diplomatic approaches that failed to secure his release, his wife
remained more concerned for his conscience than for his life. 'Your
deare wife', wrote a friend on her behalf in 1611, 'preferres your faith
to her affection, and in a courage beyond hir sex, contemnes [despises]
the worst miserie of your losse, professing she would redeeme your
life with hirs, but that she would not redeeme it with your yieldance
[i.e. if Molle turned Catholic in order to be freed]; and while she lookes
uppon those manie pawns of your chast love, your hopefull children,
wishes rather to see them fatherlesse than their father unfaithfull.'[77]

It may be that Molle responded to this appeal to a higher loyalty.
He was still in prison when, much later, he died. But a firmer structure
of belief did not calm the inner tensions of all. It was the jumpiness
and inflexibility within the tautened religious convictions of both Protestants and Catholics that brought the denunciation and burning of

witches to epidemic proportions. Psychological depression, characterized as 'melancholy', was a condition that medical literature had discussed since antiquity. But never before had so much attention been paid to this expression of hopeless, undealable-with inner confusion, and the suicides that have been attributed to it, as in the generations that followed the introduction of the Reforms. Robert Burton's *The Anatomy of Melancholy* in 1621 surveyed with almost inordinate copiousness every aspect of this 'epidemical disease that so often, so much, crucifies the body and minde',[78] but was nowhere more concerned than when dealing with the causes and symptoms of religious despair.

Personal inner tensions, however, were of no concern to national governments or regional and municipal administrations. It was the drummer's followers; the armed northern English rising of 1536 which, because of the protest it contained against Henry VIII's suppression of the monasteries, was euphemistically dubbed 'The Pilgrimage Grace'; the defiant bands of six thousand and more who brought weapons with them to hear Calvinist preachers in the Catholic Netherlands in 1566: these, and the scattered cells of splinter sects like the Anabaptists who defied the authority of both Church and state, were the threat. Manifestations of this sort, which acted as foci for social and political protest, added a religious dimension to fears that civility was in danger.

CHAPTER IX

The Control of Man

THE DISCIPLINES OF STATE AND CHURCH

A stealthy rise in population; a more obvious gap between prices and wages; a not always welcome challenge to spiritual self-confidence: these offered fertile ground for agitation. They coincided with a growing unease between defensive haves and resentful have-nots. And time after time, when demanding higher taxes or recruiting for larger armies, governments found that their pursuit of tightened control over their subjects' desire outran performance.

Fear of insurrection was a steadily nagging irritant within the lives of those with power or property to lose. It was in response to this fear that writer after writer resurrected the classical analogy between the body politic and the human body. Sometime between 1532–4 Thomas Starkey, by no means an automatic conservative save on the issue of social hierarchy, wrote

> To the head with the eyes, ears and other senses therein, resembled may be right well the under offices by princes appointed, for as much as they should ever observe and diligently wait [watch] for the weal of the rest of this body. To the arms are resembled both craftsmen and warriors which defend the rest of the body from injury of enemies outward, and work and make things necessary to the same; to the feet the ploughmen and tillers of the ground, because they by their labour sustain and support the rest of the body.[1]

An observer of the northern Pilgrimage of Grace of 1536, a rising in which a composite of anti-governmental grievance rode on the back of protest against the dissolution of the monasteries, wrote to Thomas Cromwell, 'would it not be foolish and unheard of for a foot to say it wanted to wear a hat just as the head does, or for a knee to say it wanted to have eyes?'[2] This was the mood which led European observers to forgive much to the infidel Turks because of their civilized acceptance of their rulers' authority. And the fear was as present to municipal as to national governments. A spokesman in Annibale Romei's *The Courtier's Academy*, which was translated into English soon after its appearance in 1585, put the analogy firmly into an urban setting:

> Now a city being nothing else but a body of men united together, sufficient of itself to live, it is necessary that like to a human body it be compounded of unlike members the which, in goodness and dignity among themselves unequal, all notwithstanding concur to the good establishment of a city. Whereupon as it would be a thing monstrous and incommodious to see a human body wholly compounded of heads, arms, legs or of other members . . . so would it be altogether as disproportionable . . . if all men in a city were artificers, husbandmen, soldiers, judges or of one self condition and quality.[3]

The complacency with which such jejune pieties could be repeated is a warning that while respecting the desperation that made subjects rebel, it is unwise to exaggerate the overall incidence of revolt within Europe. To look for attacks on the status quo is to find them. There were plots to supplant rulers. Whole areas rose in rebellion, though in the most dramatic cases – the Swiss cantons' rejection of the imperial and northern Low Countries of Spanish authority – these make less sense as rebellions than as wars of independence. There were mass risings against what was seen as a misuse of what was nonetheless accepted as legitimate authority. There were local riots in towns and rural areas against immediate conditions of hardship. But though there were some general causes of uprisings, mostly related to living standards and local religious preferences, there was no general pattern. Europe was too large, its regional communication networks too restrictive, its political and religious uniformities too fragmented for generalizations from general causes to be useful either across space or time. Fractious or charismatic individuals could trigger resentments that would otherwise have lain dormant, hunger riots were led by men who had never gone hungry. Regional and urban authorities varied in their powers to quash or placate unrest in its early stages. In other instances, causes of unrest were absorbed within communities all too practised in the sullen arts of endurance. However truculent and vicious rebellious subjects could be when mobilized, their demands were very rarely revolutionary in any change-the-system sense.

Most alarming were threats to heads of government themselves. The last case of an armed take-over of a large state was the *condottiere* Francesco Sforza's self-appointment as ruler of Milan in 1450, and of small ones the *coups d'état* that changed the ruling families of Württemberg in 1498 and of Ansbach in 1515. 'Uneasy lies the head that wears a crown,' said Shakespeare's ageing, sleepless Henry IV. In 1595 his *Richard II* described the deposition of a king as long ago as 1400. But Richard's offences were also those of contemporary centralizing monarchs:

> The commons hath he pilled with grievous taxes
> And quite lost their hearts: the nobles hath he fined
> For ancient quarrels and quite lost their hearts.[4]

In 1569 the hitherto quasi-independent nobles of northern England had risen in rebellion against Elizabeth. In 1583 another plot, named after one of its protagonists, Francis Throckmorton, was uncovered. Both drew on nobles' irritation with the bureaucratization of government and on a fairly widespread hankering after a return to the old Catholic faith. Hailed before the Privy Council to explain why they had put on such a provocative play, Shakespeare's company defended their choice of subject on the grounds that Richard's reign lay so far in the past that no contemporary parallel could have been intended. They were let off with a caution, but thereafter the censorship of plays prior to production or publication was tightened. The very success of historical plays, not just Shakespeare's, showed how long were residual memories and how audiences liked to have them revived. In 1610 came another abortive rebellion, this time centred on a man Elizabeth had not only favoured with promotions but made it clear that she was attracted by, Robert Devereux, Earl of Essex. After Essex's execution, the Queen went through the lists of records kept in the Tower of London with their keeper, the lawyer and antiquarian William Lambarde. Coming to those of Richard's reign, 'I am Richard II', she said pointedly; 'know ye not that?'[5]

Dread of domestic nobles' disaffection and, given the religious and political divisions of Europe, their ability to obtain covert support from abroad as well as a following at home among those 'pilled with grievous taxes', led a fear of plots to become endemic among heads of state. Standing armies, permanently established military forces which could patrol insurgent regions, were kept small, not just because they were expensive but because the most lasting damage to power structures, whether dynastic or republican, could be achieved by a strike at the centre. In 1599, in his book on kingship, the Spaniard Juan de Mariana affirmed that 'the insurrection of people is like a torrent; it is swollen but for a short time.'⁶ This was too dismissive, but to guard the palace was seen as at least as important as to police the realm. Money flowed to royal guards and escorts. Protocol – who was permitted to be where in princely residences – served the function not only of enhanced dignity but added security. It was in the corridor leading from the kitchen to where Elizabeth was at supper that some of the most daring participants in the Essex plot were overpowered.

Such precautions stopped well short of the paranoia displayed by earlier rulers, Duke Filippo Maria Visconti of Milan (d. 1447) or King Louis XI (d. 1483) of France, for instance, who at times made themselves literally the prisoners of their own suspicions. Monarchs showed themselves among their subjects, hunted, attended public festivities. But precautions mounted. Innkeepers were required to report any whiff of conspiratorial talk. The use of spies and informers proliferated. The Florentines under Duke Cosimo I, reported the Venetian ambassador in 1561, lived in terror of being denounced as disloyal. This was to some extent disingenuous; his own government, through the Council of Ten, which was responsible for state security, maintained a lengthy payroll of secret agents both at home and abroad, as did Elizabeth's. Treason, conspiracy to supplant the leaders of governments, was watched for with at least as much concern as were risings against their policies.

Apart from Utopian dreams of social justice, there was no serious writing about the remaking of society. But there was a growing body of thought that advocated not just passive disobedience to rulers thought to be tyrannous but their death. For Pietro Paolo Boscoli and his fellow conspirators of 1513 in Florence, to kill the leading members of the dominant Medici family was to assume the mantle of Brutus – portrayed with such stern dignity by Michelangelo. For the writers in France in the 1570s who came to be known as the *Monarchomachi*, or king-killers, it was justifiable to replace by force a persecuting government with one tolerant of religious minorities. In a country where at least fifteen per cent of the population were Protestants, such apparent invitations to attack at the top rather than agitate for change from the bottom were important matters of state. In 1604 an English traveller Thomas Dallington, who was well aware of the popular discontents in his own country, focused on the Frenchman's tendency to speak ill 'of their owne state and king himselfe . . . which insufferable vice of theirs, I heere put in the first place because I holde it of all others the most disloyall and unlawfull'.[7] In 1610 the king himself, Henri IV, was not just criticized but stabbed to death by the redheaded fanatic François Ravaillac, a Catholic who saw the monarch's tolerant attitude to religion as treachery to the true faith.

To take up the contemporary analogy, it is in contrast to such thrusts to the heart of civility that fevers within the body of society can be seen as to some extent justifying Juan de Mariana's complacency in his book already mentioned.

There were entire regions where all classes, landlords and merchants, farmers and artisans, combined against the coercive thrust of central authority. In 1520 the towns of northern Castile, at first with support from local nobles and their tenants, rebelled against the subordination of their independence to the lawyers and fiscal officials of central government. Within a year, however, the evidence that a rebellion against the crown was disintegrating into a social war against rural and urban landlords and *their* legal pretensions and fiscal demands, led the nobility to crush the revolt of the *Comuneros* in the king's name. Or a single city might rebel against the depersonalizing of its historic identity by the intrusions of a centralizing monarchy. In 1539 the citizens of Ghent expelled the representatives of Charles V and called on neighbour cities to follow their example. None did; in the following year an imperial army forced the municipal government to recant and, in symbolic recognition of its treachery, to surrender its bells and artillery and destroy tracts of the walls within whose shelter they had defied a greater authority. In a reference by then familiar, they and other towns that had been tempted to join them were accused of wanting 'to create cantons for themselves, as in Switzerland'.[8] The rebellion in the southwest of England in 1549 followed others: in Yorkshire in 1489, in Lincolnshire in 1536. As with the Comunero revolt, a combination of royal troops and local changes of mind as to what was to be gained, led tempers to simmer down, if not to be forgotten.

Like the deposition of kings, popular revolts lingered alarmingly in the memory. One was the English Peasants' Revolt of 1381, with its troubling refrain, 'When Adam delved [dug] and Eve span, Who was then the Gentleman?' Another was the armed clamour in 1378 for a voice in government from Florence's disenfranchised urban woolworkers, the *Ciompi*. For a few months they succeeded. The lingering trauma of this débâcle helped to bias a city which felt it had some claim to have pioneered the notion of civility, into so guarded an attitude towards the potential enemy within that in the fifteenth century its well-to-do inhabitants accepted the dominant, Mafia-like influence of the Medici family, and in the sixteenth closed ranks still further about a princely, ducal, head of state. The extent to which civic violence got out of hand in London's Evil May Day of 1517 was a recurrent spur to magistrates and substantial citizens to impose curfews, strengthen the watch, confiscate arms and keep apprentices within doors during later outbursts. Nourished by the broadsheets and pamphlets that accompanied them and the niches they found in civic chronicles, revolts and riots built up in the memory to produce ever more conservative overreactions. In the aftermath of a storm-in-a-teacup riot by London apprentices in 1595 it was claimed that they planned 'to robbe, steale, pill and spoile the welthy . . . and to take the sworde of aucthorytye from the magistrats and governours lawfully aucthorized'.[9]

The most lurid early-warning signal to the beneficiaries of civility was set off by the south German Peasants' Revolt of 1524–5. This followed earlier revolts by peasants and artisans who rallied under the emblematic *Bundschuh*, the thonged shoe of the labourer, against the exactions of secular and ecclesiastical landlords: in 1502 a crowd of some thousand, stiffened by unemployed soldiers from the same background, was broken up before it could reach the towns and castles it intended to storm. The confessions of the ringleaders, though extorted under torture and not fully to be trusted, suggest why such uprisings caused such alarm; 'they said that the principal reason for their entering this association of the *Bundschuh* was their desire to abolish every remaining yoke of servitude, and, following the example of the Swiss, to gain their liberty through the use of arms . . . they confessed that it was their intention to annihilate all authority and government.'[10]

The revolt of 1524–5 sprang from the same resentment against land-lords whose legal advisers cited as precedents much earlier 'rights' to exploit peasants' labour and restrict their freedom of movement and choice of marriage partner. During the competition for labour after the Black Death these had been allowed to slip and their reimposition after so long a lapse was seen as a radical break with practices that had become traditional. The mood of revolt was inflamed by a mistaken impression: peasants saw the Lutheran Reformation as a revolt against authority in general, an offer to the poor of revenge against the rich – a position Luther himself furiously denounced. Moreover, the sum-mons to arms was not spread merely by word of mouth but by printed exhortations and statements of grievances. Less on account of its scale than the free use of weapons both by the insurgents and the troops called in to check and butcher them, this has been called a Peasants' War rather than a revolt. And, as with the settlement of a war, the peasants in some areas did win concessions in return for downing their arms, enough, at least, to check the slide into neo-serfdom which similar outbreaks in eastern Europe failed to check.

No country in Europe was spared occasional spurts of popular resentment during the rest of the century. Some were savage but short. Others got no further than threats: in 1596 the English carpenter Bartholomew Steere told a crony that 'there would be such a rising as had not been seen a great while' in which 'he would cut off all the gentlemen's heads',[11] but he failed to attract a following before the authorities got to hear of his threat and arrested him. In the south of France scattered peasant revolts between 1593 and 1595 did, however, gather support from poor townsmen. There were attacks on rural nobles who failed to protect their tenants from pillaging soldiers in the last convulsions of the civil wars. There were others on towns where magistrates heavily taxed others while living fatly themselves: 'they seek only the ruin of the poor people, for our ruin is their wealth.' The claim made by the nobles who raised troops against the rebels that 'they wished to overthrow the monarchy and establish a democracy on the pattern of the Swiss' reflects fear rather than reality, but the spectre of social war that had been raised in 1524–5 loomed behind these later and less pervasive revolts.[12] It was in this charged atmosphere that Botero gave a general warning that authorities should be prepared to make some initial concessions to insurgents 'because they may become increasingly embittered and alienated, and though they may at first only feel resentment, they will eventually rise in open rebellion'.[13]

Not least because food shortages so often prompted violent protest, the urban were as liable to insurrection as the rural poor. They terrorized their betters from time to time whether in Naples or in London or Paris. But civic riot was generally repressible by local law and order agencies when coupled with promises of amelioration and the threat that if the disturbance continued professional troops would be called. It was the peasantry, widely dispersed and armed with swords or knives for the watch and ward of their hamlets or with the sickles and scythes they used in the fields, who were seen as the greater threat. Yet their petitions and demands, written by literate sympathizers, artisans or clergy, reveal little that was more contentious than calls for a return to the good old days when fair play and respect for tradition was the basis of law and social habit. Folk stories reveal the modesty of their ambitions. One such tale, reflecting the dreams of a populace prone to debilitating illness, told of a peasant 'who while ploughing came across a golden vessel full of liquid. Thinking it to be rainwater, he washed his face and drank. His body and goodness, his spirit and wisdom were strengthened, and from ploughman he became – one of the King's porters'.[14]

Scattered across Europe as they were, it is probably true to say that territorial rebellions and rural and urban riots, known at home, and heard about or read about from abroad, drew attention to the dangers inherent in the changes in European society especially where change was most noticeable, in the West. At the level of popular disturbance it was not the Jove-like figure of the monarch that was at risk but the devotees of Mercury, whether landlord or merchant or bureaucrat. Higher prices, increased taxes: these were perceived as the dominant indicators of social unfairness. Even when the cause of a revolt was ostensibly religious, as during the riots in the southern Low Countries in 1579, a deeper aim was discerned: 'to seize the wealth of the rich'.[15]

On the whole, however, the religious reform movements seconded governments' concern with the obedience of subjects. In his *Spiritual Exercises* of 1536, the Spanish ex-soldier Ignatius de Loyola, founder of the Jesuit Order, anticipated the mood of Catholic Reform as it was to be defined by the Council of Trent. 'We should put away completely our own opinion', he wrote, 'and keep our minds ready and eager to give our entire obedience to our holy Mother the hierarchical church.'[16] The published forms of Calvinist worship and organization were called *Books of Discipline*. By 1550 a copy of Thomas Cranmer's *Book of Homilies* had been placed in every English church; prominent among the sermons to be read from it were those 'On Obedience' and 'On Rebellion'. By the 1559 Elizabethan Act of Uniformity church attendance on Sundays and the Holy Days selected by government was made compulsory. In 1583 the Archbishop of Canterbury, John Whitgift, emphasized the importance of there being 'a settled order in doctrine and discipline' to avoid 'disobedience to the Queen and law'.[17] In both Protestant and Catholic countries, pulpit exhortations had never been so open to prompting by the state. Both had long seen the church courts' punishments for sin and the secular courts' penalties for crime as symbiotic partners in the defence against the errant aspects of human nature. From the mid-sixteenth century this co-operation became closer than ever. The churches relied more on state support in their drive to keep faiths monolithic. Even in Venice, of all Catholic states the most wary of full co-operation with the Papacy, a doge referred in 1564 to 'the public utility which springs from the protection of the Catholic religion'.[18] In countries of either faith, the clerical network was an invaluable supplement to those of provincial administrators and paid informers in giving advance warning of political as well as doctrinal heresies. Never before had thought control been more pervasive. Never before had neighbours felt encouraged to pry too busily into others' conduct or to denounce them so readily to priest, pastor or magistrate.

It was in Germany, where printing was pioneered, that censorship was first introduced. In 1475 the University of Cologne, jealous of the freelance expression of ideas, obtained from the Pope the right to grant licences for the publication of books and to punish those who produced or read unauthorized ones. In 1496 a similar censorship was set up within the archdiocese of Mainz, this time reflecting fear of the spread of unorthodox religious notions, and five years later Pope Alexander VI extended the practice to the whole of Germany. Bishops or those they deputed to the task were to punish the printers of unauthorized works dealing with the Christian faith by excommunication and fine. Similarly in Italy, religious censorship was introduced first in individual dioceses – Treviso in 1491 – and in 1515 extended to the peninsula as a whole. By then the flood of books and the realization that a new, less instructed and more excitable audience for them was being reached, moved a number of European secular authorities to insist on manuscripts being submitted to them before printing.

With the spread of Lutheran pamphlet literature the battle between idea and control was fully joined. In 1520 Luther's works were publicly burned in Cologne and Louvain while he organized similar bonfires of papal edicts and decretals in Wittenberg. In the following year Charles V prohibited the printing, possession or reading of any works by Luther, while the Reformer on his part did his best to persuade the Elector of Saxony to ban those written by Protestants with whom he did not agree. As governments came to protect one or other form of reformed religion, censorship to preserve their adopted faith came to run in parallel with the ecclesiastical machinery in Catholic states; this reached its mature range with the publication of the Tridentine Index of 1564, a list of books in print which the Catholic faithful were peremptorily forbidden to read if they valued body and soul. Thereafter no book of any sort was to be printed without explicit permission from the relevant governmental or ecclesiastical authority.

'Erasmus censored': defaced
portrait in a copy of Sebastian
Münster, *Cosmographia*, 1550
(Biblioteca Nacional, Madrid)

For by then it was realized that the title of a book did not necessarily
alert attention to the nature of its opinions. What is more, books had
come to be seen as potential threats to political and moral as well as to
doctrinal values. So Machiavelli, as well as Luther, became a totally
banned author. Bawdy books jostled occultist ones on the list, works
of 'classic' literary status had to be bowdlerized, the *Decameron* being
purged of anticlerical and explicitly sexual stories and passages. *The
Courtier* had its section on jokes emasculated and its reference to the
role of Fortune in human affairs replaced by reference to that of God.
In seminary libraries banned books might be preserved but handled
only by those judged to be immune from infection. When Thomas
Platter saw a copy of the Calvinist Geneva Bible in the Jesuit College
at Tournon in 1595, 'my companion Dr Collado wanted to open it,
but one of the fathers angrily forbade it, saying that it was a work of
the damned.'[19]

Naturally there grew to be a thriving smuggling trade. Printers also
falsified their imprints, in Catholic cities giving Protestant places of
origin for banned books and vice versa, a practice already familiar

enough to be guyed by a Lutheran broadsheet which purported to be printed in 'Bethlehem on the Nile'. In a few cities – such as Venice or Basel – thanks to a combination of civic confidence and a desire to foster the book trade, censorship remained light. So in spite of growing repression it was possible for determined readers with money and some courage to secure much of what they wanted, the printed versions of the Index itself giving a useful survey of what was enticingly heterodox or *risqué*. There were never enough censors to deal thoroughly with manuscripts submitted for publication. But censorship did force intellectual dissidents into secret conspiracies and pre-print methods of communicating disaffection through messages and correspondence.

Inquisitors – another overworked corps of repressors – rarely showed more interest in convincing unimportant suspects of their doctrinal errors than in swiftly and if necessary cruelly extorting blanket vows of obedience: 'I confess and believe', ran one formula to be sworn to, 'that the Holy Roman Church is the true church and communion of the faithful, outside of which there is no salvation.'[20] But Hebrew studies were suppressed; in 1553 all copies in Italy of the Talmud were ordered to be sought out and burned and none was henceforward to be published. Disturbing philosophical speculation and astronomical theories affecting the biblically established centrality of the earth were monitored not just through successive revisions to the Index but in the prisons where Campanella spent much of his literally tortured life, or in the flames of the bonfire on which in 1600 Giordano Bruno paid for his challenging the Catholic view of man's place in the universe. And while speculation was forced to obscure itself within the language of an apparent orthodoxy or was driven underground, new university chairs of theology were established, including, as at Bologna, the scholastic theology which had previously been ridiculed by Christian humanists throughout Europe.

In both Catholic and Protestant countries prints were censored along with books, changes in the copperplates being enforced on occasion to render nude figures less provocative. It was the Council of Trent in 1563 that first established guidelines for painting (no 'seductive charm') and a licensing procedure for new religious works of art which might be considered 'unusual' treatments of their theme.[21]

The prohibition was not only against sensual suggestiveness but also narrative detail that distracted from the work's doctrinal import – it was the diverting lavishness of detail in Veronese's *Last Supper*, not a display of flesh, that caused him in 1573 to be summoned before the

Inquisition. Given three months to 'improve and change it',[22] he simply altered the title to *The Feast at the House of Levi* mentioned in St Luke's Gospel. It was a comparable attitude that caused the long-respected masterpiece of Nuno Gonçalves, the *St Vincent Altarpiece* of *c.*1466, to be removed from its convent church and placed in storage because its wealth of realistic portraits was held to divert attention from the saint himself. As with prints and books, the guidelines were interpreted with different degrees of strictness; few censors went so far as Johannes Molanus in the Catholic Netherlands who objected to the Christ Child being shown naked. The rules, moreover, and the mood of caution which they induced in the treatment of secular and mythological subjects, did not inhibit the artists from working for private patrons. Distrust of the nude meant that in Spain, where the Inquisition was allowed the greatest freedom to enforce the spirit of the Tridentine reforms, tortured martyrs kept their clothes on and mythological subjects were few. Nonetheless, Philip II, though having a scarf arranged round the loins of Cellini's naked marble Christ when it arrived for installation in the church of the Escorial, continued to enjoy Titian's glowingly physical mythological scenes in his other palaces. And it was not only in the South that art was affected by politico-religious pressures. Pieter Breughel's anti-war and populist stance led him to advise his wife to destroy any works remaining in his studio on his death. In 1551 the Muscovite state church forbade the import of western religious works of art and any departure on the part of native artists from the traditions of Orthodox icon painting.

In both Protestant and Catholic countries the repression of freedom of expression was more concerned with ensuring doctrinal uniformity and political obedience than with morals. In England, while printed accounts of political news were banned if events were 'over-slenderly', or 'untruly or amiss reported',[23] the drama censors looked, as in the case of *Richard II*, only for threats to government and its policies; they let through bawdy expressions and such themes as adultery, rape and incest. Deplorable as sexual animality might be, it was of far less concern than aristocratic conspiracies against heads of state, regional threats to 'go Swiss' and covetous social protests.

In 1565 it was government and church in co-operation that essayed the most dramatic attempt to enforce obedience on subjects. Since the conquest of the Kingdom of Granada in the late fifteenth century, the forcible conversion of the Moorish population who had chosen to stay had aroused doubts; was the Christianity they henceforward professed

Paolo Veronese, *The Feast at the House of Levi*, 1573 (Accademia, Venice)

sincere? Were they in treacherous contact with Spain's Muslim enemies in North Africa? The flavour of the measures proposed in 1565 to deal with the problems raised by the Moriscos, as they were termed, is well conveyed in their spokesman's protest. 'When the naturals [natives] of this kingdom were converted to the Christian faith, there was no regulation compelling them to abandon their dress, language or customs,' Francisco Nuñez Muley pointed out. 'The dress of our women is not Moorish but merely provincial, just as in Castile and other regions . . . If the 200,000 women of this kingdom are to change their dress from head to foot where will they find the money? . . . To require our women to unveil their faces is only to provide opportunity for men to sin after beholding the beauty of those they are attracted to, while the ugly will find no one to marry them.' He cited the Christian merchants from Syria and Egypt who were accepted as such when they traded with southern Europe, even if they dressed like Turks and spoke Arabic. As for us, he went on, how can old men learn Castilian, or

the young, without sacrificing the time they need to employ in earning a living? 'How can a language be taken away from a people, the natural language in which they are reared?' Already, he summed up, 'we are persecuted by the ecclesiastical and secular courts; yet we are all loyal vassals, obedient to His Majesty . . . Never could it be said that we have committed treason from the day we surrendered.'[24]

King and the Cardinal responsible for the church in the region, Diego de Espinosa, were unmoved. It took two years of savage warfare to impose their policy of integration. Even then its success was not trusted. Only after another long campaign of search, skirmish and arrest, lasting until 1614, could Spain rest after ridding itself by death or deportation of some 270,000 potential traitors to King and Christ.

At a cost in military wages, equipment and the hire of transport that no other country could or would have thought of expending save in wartime, Spain had demonstrated the power of government at home. By this flagrant breach of Machiavelli's warning not to meddle with subjects' traditional routines, Spain's ideological victory over unwanted customs was achieved with the loss of the subjects themselves at a time when alarm was being expressed at the fall in the population of Iberia. And the circumstances were unique to Spain. Elsewhere, the most dramatic examples of successful interference with ways of life were achieved not by national but by civic governments, and in the sphere of public health. Methods of checking recurrences of the plagues involved, as we shall see, draconian measures. By the second half of the sixteenth century all large Italian cities had acquired permanent public health boards which revived previous *ad hoc* legislation and extended it. They closed off streets, barred houses with suspected men, women and children inside them, shut down shops and inns, drove stall-holders to distraction by forbidding the sale of a wide variety of goods in markets, determined where and how burials were to take place, forbade social gatherings and church attendance save for selected services of intercession. Returning from one in 1576 the Milanese schoolmaster Giambattista Casale, who had left, as he thought, his household in good health, was ordered to go straight home because the health inspectors had cause to think it infected: 'they are waiting for you and will shut you up too.' During the days that followed a fire broke out and 'none of the neighbours would come to help us.'[25] Giambattista, a docile, pious and educated man, was one of many who accepted the need for such drastic interventions. Many others resisted them, testing the police resources of municipalities as much as did the dispersing of riotous assemblies. Effective control over subjects was far more clearly demonstrated in towns than in the administrative functions of national governments. All were long familiar with the routines of regulating guilds and markets and self-defence forces, adept at keeping abbatoirs and middens down-wind, street fountains and open drains running freely, at maintaining walls and gate-guards and supervising brothels and inns and the comings and goings of strangers. They had on their payroll customs clerks, night-watchmen, town-criers, gaolers and, in large cities, torturers and executioners. And as population growth and inflation led rural families to try their luck in towns, and because it was in towns that religious and social protests were most prominent, governments increasingly left the responsibility for social policing to urban governing bodies which had the means of control more readily available.

Help was at hand here from the higher moral standards demanded by Reform. In both Catholic and Protestant countries the old structure of church courts and clerical parish visitations was revitalized. 'For what', Calvin asked, 'will be the consequence if every man be at liberty to follow his own inclinations? But such would be the case, unless the preaching of the doctrine were accompanied with private admonitions, reproofs, and other means to enforce the doctrine.'[26] And because most sins (covetousness, envy, theft, sexual licence, blasphemy – which implied disrespect for authority – murder) had social connotations, magistrates co-operated with Catholic priests and Protestant ministers. When the artist brothers Sebald and Barthel Beham were accused in 1525 in Nuremberg of irreligion, as well as their opinion of the Bible and the Eucharist being investigated, they were asked whether they accepted the authority of the magistrates over their possessions and the determination of their civic status.

The sentences imposed by church courts were mild: public confession, the wearing of penitential sackcloth with bare legs and feet, token fines, being banned from church attendance and shunned by the devout. These were appeals to conscience, but also to humiliation in the eyes of neighbours. When shame did not act as a deterrent, civic authorities offered public exposure in the stocks. And when the sin had obvious public relevance, as in the case of crimes against property or the person, including rape, the secular courts, with their powers of banishment, imprisonment, maiming and execution took over if they had not already taken the initiative. Short of dealing with crimes of this nature, the church courts acted as a forum for nagging offenders against decency and social decorum into toeing the respectable norm. 'Everyone', Calvin had added, 'should study to admonish his brother'. As towns became more crowded and edgy it became ever clearer, as accusations flowed into the church courts, how low in the pecking order of Christian values came Christ's exhortation 'thou shalt love thy neighbour as thyself'. Even so, some deplored the moderation of the sentences imposed on sinners. 'The punishment appointed for whoredom now', complained the Puritan Philip Stubbes in his *The Anatomie of Abuses* (1583), 'is so light that they esteeme not of it; they feare it not, they make but a jest of it. For what great thing is it to go two or three days in a white sheet before the congregation, and that some tymes not past an howre or two in a day, having their usual garments underneath as commonly they have?'[27]

In some cities – Augsburg and Geneva were conspicuous examples – magistrates sensitive to anything that might lead to a breach of the peace concerned themselves directly with the discipline of morals, both within marriage (even habitual quarrelling between husband and wife could be punished) and outside it. Everywhere moral policing was made all the more time-consuming when easily patrolled red-light districts were closed down and prostitution took to the streets. The censorship of books printed locally, and the searching of imported ones was another onerous aspect of moral control, far more rigorous control than by national systems. The fear of volatile crowds produced bans on traditional street theatre and a tightened regulation of fairs, cattle markets and public sport and feast days with their service element of drink stalls and their legacy of broken heads and vendettas. Dancing, a taste almost as widespread as the music that accompanied it, was equally suspect. Lutheran Greifswald forbade it even at weddings because, as a citizen noted in 1551 of his own wedding, 'the manner in which the men whirled the matrons and damsels round and round

Urs Graf, *Feathered Soldier*, drawing, 1523 (Kupferstichkabinett, Kunstmuseum, Basel)

had become indecent'.²⁸ And in the widely read *Introduction to a Devout Life* (1609) of François de Sales, the author warned the Catholic laity that 'balls and dances are not objectionable in themselves, but the way in which they are normally conducted is a strong incitement to sin.'²⁹ Such views promoted the non–body–contact formality of the licit form of dance practised at court and imitated by manners-conscious townsmen, from which the artifice of ballet emerged.

Assemblies, private or public, whether without or within walls, were easier to police than the love of personal display. There was nothing novel about sumptuary ordinances designed to cut down the use of imported foreign luxury cloths, to prevent a socially exacerbating display of wealth and to reduce the inflammatory effect of partially exposed breasts and genitals emphasized by cod-pieces. They had never been fully effective. At a time when the European economy was prospering they had, though endlessly reprounced, less chance of being obeyed than ever. The very councils that issued these regulations took advantage of modes of entertainment and dress that distinguished them from the ruck of the less privileged. The cult of fashion was irresistible to those who simply wanted to be respected by their peers. Even common soldiers, who accepted their outsider status, defiantly flaunted down-at-heel and deliberately ripped versions of the high style of their employers.

Male attacks on female vanity – the use of cosmetics, tweezers and hair bleaches – were almost as old as Jezebel herself. But Leonardo da Vinci had both narcissistic men and women in mind when he wrote that 'among the simple-minded one single hair out of place presages to the wearer high disgrace . . . and such as these keep only a mirror and comb for their counsel and the wind is their principal enemy . . . Human folly ever increases.'³⁰ His own interest in hair and head-dress styles and costumes was acute, as was that of his contemporary Dürer, who annotated his costume drawings as to where and when he had drawn them. As Christoph Weiditz moved from Germany to Spain and on to the Netherlands in 1531–2 he kept a portfolio of coloured drawings of the costumes he encountered, province by province and class by class. There was something of the chorographers' interest in local customs here, but increased travel and travel literature, and the circulation of tailors' guides to the making of foreign styles, all fostered an interest in fashion for its own sake. It was not just an abstract anthropological fascination that led to the adoption in court entertainments of exotic costumes or to translations of such works as Jost

Amman's *Theatrum Mulierum* of 1586 which appeared in English as *Gynaecum; or, the Theatre of Women: wherein may be seen the Female Costumes of all the Principal Nations, Tribes and Peoples of Europe.*

And though costume-books were chiefly preoccupied with women, the moralists' target remained a broad one.

> Shameless and fickle I do brand
> Style-slaves who live in every land,[31]

wrote Sebastian Brant. Andrew Boorde commissioned a much-remarked-upon woodcut showing a near-naked man with a pair of shears in one hand and a length of cloth in the other. Underneath was the verse:

> I am an English man, and naked I stand here,
> Musyng in my mynd what rayment I shal weare;
> For now I wyll were this, and now I wyl were that;
> Now I wyl were I cannot tell what.[32]

Taste in costume was unaffected by its convenience to the wearer or by differing climatic conditions; borrowings, from Spain to Bohemia or Italy to England, whether of furs or taffetas, were simply a matter of style. Everywhere in courts and cities fashion drew attention to changing aspirations and enhanced an awareness of social distinctions. Even when an adopted style was sober, as in the case of the rich gravity of Spanish noble attire, the gap was emphasized between the wardrobes of the well-off and the standardized work clothes of the poor whose single holiday outfits, however lovingly and carefully made, retained almost unaltering regional traditions.

In times of reasonable prosperity, distinctions of rank, even when more complexly orchestrated through cut and colour, aroused moral outrage rather than social resentment. And on the whole, apart from war's interruptions, the urban economy throve. There was industrial and commercial growth, building and rebuilding, more households requiring servants; an ability to absorb a fair proportion of the increase in the domestic population. It was the price of food rising against wages, coinciding with a sharp increase in rural immigration that from the 1540s brought to a head an intensifying threat to law and order and, with it, the problematic relationship between repression and amelioration.

Familiar mechanisms existed for keeping the price of bread to affordable levels. There were civil emergency stores. There was legislation
against dealers who bought crops before harvest and merchants who
bought grain to store until shortage put its price up. But as inflation
made the familiar temptation to forestall and engross – the English
terms for these abuses – more and more attractive, and because corn
merchants carried weight within municipal governments and could
plead that financial enterprise was an ingredient of civic progress, price
control became progressively less effective. This form of amelioration
was, as a result, shifted into a more general and more debated area: the
respective roles of charity and welfare in relieving distress and assuaging
discontent.

The importance of charitable concern for the disadvantaged had long
been axiomatic: Charity, along with Faith and Hope, was one of the
prime Christian virtues. In a multitude of paintings and statues *Caritas*
offered her breasts to hungry children. Care for the poor was among
the much illustrated Acts of Mercy, derived from the words of Christ
in the Gospel of St Matthew, that helped a man to gain salvation; it
was a theme so familiar that in the greatest of all renderings of it,
Caravaggio's painting of 1606 in Naples, the artist could rely on the
spectator sorting out who represented what Act in his jostling, tenebrous street scene.

Though medieval institutionalized charity – doles at monastery
doors, homes for orphans and foundlings, alms houses for the decrepit,
hospices for the sick – had responded to a mixture of protective love
and society's preference for tucking its casualties out of sight, the more
common form was those individual 'good works', hand-outs at street
corners, church doors or after weddings or funerals, that Reformers
decried as useless bribes to obtain grace. Catholics saw the poor as an
opportunity to display their charity: 'the poor are on the cross of adversity', ran a characteristic utterance of 1531, 'as much for the salvation
of those that aid them charitably as for their own salvation.'[33] When
the city of Ypres, an early victim of mass immigration, tried in the early
1530s to replace private charity with municipally sponsored welfare
schemes, the Dominicans and Franciscans there proclaimed that 'forbidding [anyone] to ask for alms . . . is evil, vicious, and in conformity
with a principle of Luther which has been condemned'.[34]

By then, however, personal charitable gifts had begun to be channelled into centrally run distributive agencies both in Protestant cities,
where the secularization of Catholic monasteries and other pious

foundations had forced empty stomachs to turn to government, and in Catholic ones under siege by the destitute. It became ever clearer that the newcomers were arriving in numbers not to be deterred by gate-checks, floggings or red-hot brandings as undesirables. By 1600 the notion of such institutions as the Central Charitable Agency (Aumône-Général) of Lyon, the hospice-reformatory of San Lazzaro in Venice, or the model reformatory-workhouse of Amsterdam, were accepted as the most effective palliatives for a plague of mouths for which, for all its resilience, the European economy could produce no cure.

And this quasi-solution aroused resentment. There were printed forms to fill out before receiving relief payments, house-to-house calls by officials vetting the number of dependants and the validity of claims to be unwillingly unemployed. Visits by relatives were restricted to institutions designed to isolate men and women so that they would learn to repent their sins or their idleness and learn a productive skill. These irritating by-products of officialdom did little to enable a practical intention to become an acceptable solution. The system was, in any case, overwhelmed both by sheer numbers and the proportion of the poor who preferred begging and crime to patrolled rehabilitation. In its turn, the problem of the congenitally work- and institution-shy contributed to making more obvious the division between the poor and the secure members of urban society. There had long been a distinction made between the deserving poor, the *poveri vergognosi* or 'ashamed poor' of Italian parlance, who reflected the 'I cannot dig, to beg I am ashamed' of St Luke's parable of the unjust steward, and those who offended St Paul's warning to the Thessalonians: 'When we were with you, this we commanded you: that if any would not work, neither should he eat.' And while charity retained, as it always had done, an element of humanitarian concern, it was the Pauline strain that led municipalities to incarcerate or expel the determinedly indigent.

Central governments did, if belatedly, realize that the problem of the cities was related to misery and restlessness in the country. Measures were passed – in 1531 for the Spanish Netherlands, in 1566 for France, in 1563 and 1576 and, most comprehensively, in 1598 for England – that ordered local administrations to pass back vagrants to their place of origin and rural parishes to provide for them and punish any renewed inclination to leave. But they were only marginally effective. While citizen bodies drew greater strength from systems of corporate and familial discipline, the burden continued to fall on the towns.

COMMUNAL AND SELF-CONTROL

Fears that witches belonged to covens and thieves and beggars to fraternities were exaggerated: but it was natural enough to imagine such outsiders belonging to them at a time when society at all levels was linked into forms of association and deferred to their corporate purposes.

Behind their walls the inhabitants of cities and large towns had affiliations with groups of various kinds that extended the contacts within families and among friends and between neighbourhoods into civic life as a whole. Neighbourhood ties were close, if sometimes quarrelsome and malicious. They were the closer for being centred on parish rituals and on urban subdivisions – 'wards', 'Vierteln', 'sestrieri': whatever the vocabulary, the principle was the same throughout Europe – responsibility for street patrols, fire-watching and the reporting of such offences as the blocking of drains by rubbish or the harbouring of criminals. Crafts were commonly concentrated in single streets. This, and the habit of living over the shop, kept the life of work and the hours of leisure localized in a village-like intimacy. Neighbourhood links were frequently confirmed by intermarriage, especially before the churches from the 1530s came to stress the forbidden degrees of cousinship. There was little privacy, within or out-of-doors, and thus magistrates got to know where to move when trouble was brewing and whom to arraign.

The sixteenth century saw no slackening in the economic and social purposes that had created the medieval craft and service guilds. Statutes were amended to make it more difficult for 'foreigners' to gain access to the privileges of membership or undercut prices. But the old hierarchies of masters, journeymen, apprentices, and labourers hired to carry in raw material and deliver finished products, remained. The guilds continued to petition and lobby municipal government in order to protect their quasi-independent status, to provide charitable assistance to needy members or their families, in Catholic cities to maintain and embellish 'their' chapels and altars in the churches traditionally associated with members' births, marriages and deaths.

Some guilds were linked to larger religious and charitable confraternities whose headquarters varied from the magnificence of the richly endowed 'scuole' of Venice with their dignified boards of governors, to quite humble meeting places in a priest's house or the back room of a tavern. The steadying civic role of confraternities is well conveyed by the terms of association of that of San Ildefonso at Valladolid, which emphasized its charitable function and enjoined that prior to formal meetings all quarrels should be settled and that 'those who are not on speaking terms with one another' should promise to sink their differences.[35] In the guildhalls and militia company headquarters of the North – the group portraits of whose officials by Hals and Rembrandt followed a tradition established in the 1530s – as in the assemblies of southern confraternities, the expected mood was one of shared amity, whether the business was financial, devotional, or convivial. Personal kinship and clientage ties wove a tissue of relationships that made for stability.

In the countryside, clientage – the offering of services and loyalty to a superior in return for his protection – was a non-contractual variant on the dissolving forms of feudal dependence on a lord. Under these, land grants had been made by rulers to nobles, and by them to lesser tenants, in return for aid in case of national and, less licitly, local emergency – as when, during the Wars of the Roses in the second half of the fifteenth century, sub-tenants supported their immediate feudal superiors against the crown. By c.1500 an enhanced effectiveness of royal power and a dwindling acceptance of the idea that the tenancy of land should involve the commitment to risk life and limb, led to fallen-in tenancies being renewed without the obligation of military service. At the same time, landless men of good birth offered to serve in noble households as – in effect – mercenaries in exchange for board and lodging and a measure of support if their way of life got them in trouble with the law. Such 'affinities' were some compensation to nobles of the old type who were used to a personal following; but as die-hard values changed, and as regional political life became more stable, these too withered away.

Yet feudalized relationships had tapped and catered for deep psychological and practical needs. The weak needed the protection of the strong and the prestige of the strong was helped by having a mini-empire of supplicants and supporters some of whom possessed useful military, financial, legal or ecclesiastical power of their own. By c.1550 such part-time clients of a dominant regional family had taken the place of the affinities (which, displaced, became the model for brigand bands). These clientage relationships reached their acme in the French civil wars, when rival territorial clans, seeking to control the policies of a monarchy weakened by youthful incumbents, drew support not only from traditional landlord loyalties but also from those individuals and whole towns and regions who sought support either for their new, Calvinist, beliefs or for those of their revitalized Catholicism.

In the countryside clientage was a means of retaining status while surrendering a degree of independence. In towns the impulse to seek and enjoy dependency operated in ways which demonstrate how basic this exchange of services was. Few examples are as clear-cut as that of the fifteenth-century Medici, who carefully sustained a power base which reached right down from their own circle of bankers and international traders, through the confraternity of the Magi to which they belonged (Botticelli painted an *Adoration* showing members of the family among the onlookers) and the parish whose church – San Lorenzo – they patronized and embellished, to the local gangs of plebeian youths who could turn out to support them with weapons and cheers. This form of boss-ism, which secured them votes in municipal councils on issues they were known to favour, was established not by contractual political ties, which were illegal in Florence, but by favours: a debt might be forgiven, a loan advanced, a dowry paid, a job reference written, a marriage proposal given influential support, a surrogate kinship relationship established through the role of standing godfather to a client's child. It was a system whose effects were never precisely calculable. It generated an exhausting burden of correspondence and meetings with petitioners – all the more so because its purpose included a genuine streak of paternalism. It was a sign of radically changed times when Cosimo I de' Medici, installed in 1537 as Duke, came to clear the desk of his assured authority from the clutter of clientage. But by then Florence had passed from the municipal to the princely phase of its history.

Elsewhere, in less politically important European cities, competition to play a part in municipal government and maintain a controlling role in guilds and livery companies led to comparable forms of clientage. From a shrewd choice of marriage partner and a set of useful relatives-in-law, men of business reached down for supporters among the masters of workshops and the leaders of the neighbourhood organizations responsible for law and order and worship. The more prosperous a city and the more gentleman-like the comportment of its leading families, the more strongly these links were pursued. The result was a growing solidarity within urban society above the swelling ranks of the most immediate victims of market fluctuations, the journeymen (the semi-skilled artisan paid by the day – the *jour*) and the really poor. Old modest shifts of status continued: the industrious apprentice of both myth and reality climbing to mastership and guild rank; the bankrupt merchant relying on modest doles from his fellows as he dropped from the historical record. There was, nonetheless, a widening of the gap. More aristocrats than formerly coveted a marriage alliance with a wealthy commoner; more commoners of wealth and confidence responded to the cachet of living – by acquiring land or state office or simply by conducting themselves 'nobly' in their town houses – like aristocrats so far as a niceness of manners was concerned.

For 'manners', as ran the motto of Winchester College, reflecting its fourteenth-century founder's belief in the power of nurture to tame nature, 'makyth man'. And manners, conscious adjustments of behaviour in order to be respectful of oneself and pleasing to others, became a form of emollient that eased the adjustment of roles among those with territorial, commercial or bureaucratic influence. They also helped to consolidate among them a common stance towards those who threatened their shared civility.

It was the increased mingling in centres of power of men from diverse backgrounds that led Giovanni della Casa to stress the importance of good manners. His *Galateo*, a treatise on polite behaviour first published in Italian in 1558 and rapidly translated into French, Latin, Spanish, German and English, was aimed at the *arriviste*, for whom manners had to compensate for a lack of traditionally inculcated manner. 'For as each one of us,' he comfortingly wrote, 'is daily obliged to meet other people and converse with them, we need to use our manners every day. But justice, fortitude, and the other virtues of the higher and nobler sort are needed less frequently. We are not required to practise generosity or mercy at all hours, nor could any man do so very often. Similarly, those who are endowed with courage and strength are seldom called upon to show their valour by their deeds.' And he went on: 'no one need doubt that a person who proposes to live in a civilized place among other men, rather than in a desert or a hermitage, will find it most useful to live with courtesy and tact. Furthermore, other forms of virtue need greater resources and are of little or no avail without them. But manners are rich and powerful in themselves, although they are made up of nothing but words and actions.'[36]

Della Casa drew on two main sources. The chief was Cicero, whose *De Officiis (On Public Duties)* emphasized the need for the responsible citizen to think as consciously of the use of his leisure as of his business hours; agreeable conversation and whiling away the hours in shared pastimes were an aspect of civilized life that had an ethical justification if kept within the bounds of physical and verbal decorum. This prime authority for Roman moral philosophy legitimized, therefore, a pre-occupation with manners. Della Casa's second source was Castiglione's *The Courtier*, itself impregnated with the teaching of the *De Officiis*, which dealt extensively with the rules of agreeable conversability suit-able to a court society of men and women of mixed national and occupational backgrounds. Here the idea that polished manners, based on real accomplishment, could sustain and improve social rank, reached its early apotheosis.

This preoccupation with top-dressing talent with niceties of behaviour was widely shared. Independently of Castiglione a very dif-ferent character, the dourly intellectualizing Florentine statesman Fran-cesco Guicciardini, wrote in 1528, the year in which *The Courtier* was published, that 'when I was young, I used to scoff at knowing how to play, dance, and sing and at other such frivolities. I even made light of good penmanship, knowing how to ride and dress well, and all those things that seem more decorative than substantial in a man. But later, I wished I had not done so . . . Skill in this sort of entertainment opens the way to the favour of princes, and sometimes becomes the opening or the reason for great profit and high honours. For the world and the princes are no longer made as they should be, but as they are.'[37] And Erasmus in his 1530 *De Civilitate* admitted that 'I do not deny that external decorum is a very crude part of philosophy, but in the present climate of opinion it is very conducive to winning goodwill.'[38]

Written by a man of aristocratic birth, a soldier and diplomat as well as an educated man of letters, *The Courtier* could be read by his social equals throughout Europe without any fear that by following his pre-cepts they would lose prestige. In his discussion as to whether birth or talent was the better qualification for courtier-ship the bias ran in favour of birth. But his message that neither birth in itself, nor professional competence with the sword, was enough to procure influence at court without education and a calculated ease of manner, was easy to accept; it was recognized as being in practice timely, and conceptually it was little more than updating of the traditional chivalric code of bravery and loyal service allied to a gentleness and flexibility of demeanour off the battlefield or tournament ground. One of the most frequently quoted and adapted passages in *The Courtier* was a lady's advice to a man-at-arms who could only talk of battle even when dancing, that he should be greased and put in a cupboard until war broke out again. Later in the century this was echoed by an aristocrat who was a soldier himself; in his *Discourses* on military affairs, François de la Noue wrote that soldiers should not – 'like artisans' – have nothing to talk about save their craft. 'And in this connection', he went on, 'I remember a response that was made at court to a man who, even in peacetime, could only speak of war: "when that returns, you will be useful again".'[39]

Castiglione's advice again caught the changing mood of the times in his emphasis – taken once more from Cicero – on the role of anecdote and jokes in lightening and harmonizing polite society. Medieval preachers had sugared their exhortations with anecdotes and popular proverbial expressions; from the 1430s manuscript collections of such sayings began to circulate. Then, with the extension of education among men of rank, the anecdote began to be supplemented by the pun and the verbal quip. A Florentine in 1497 wrote to his brother to send him 'eight or ten' witty sayings to help him hold his own in court circles in Rome.[40] The fashion caught on so well that Lord Burghley in 1590 found it necessary to warn his son that 'I have seen many so prone to quip and gird as [if] they would rather leave their friend than their jest.'[41]

The Courtier could also be read as an etiquette book, an aid to social climbing. In his comedy *La Cortigiana*, printed in 1534, Pietro Aretino mocked a provincial bumpkin who believed that by reading such a book he could become a courtier and a cardinal and have a noblewoman as his mistress. In Elizabethan England dramatists assumed that even the groundlings would not be bemused by a character's being called 'Castilio Balthazar' in 1602 or a reference to another in 1604 as 'the absolute Castilio'. In 1604 the authors of *Westward Ho!*, Thomas Dekker and John Webster, thought it appropriate to put into the mouth of the procuress Mistress Birdlime the catty comment on a merchant's wife that 'she hath read in the *Italian Courtier* that it is a special ornament to have a skill in painting.'[42] By then Castiglionesque behaviour had become in some circles a byword for place-seeking and a socially divisive code of manners.

For some, then, self-grooming for success could suppress the animal in man only to turn him into an ape of his betters. But there was a more serious aspect of the discipline imposed on natural man by manners, one that Castiglione took for granted and that contributed to the success of his and Della Casa's books and those of their numerous imitators.

The earliest, thirteenth-century, works on correct deportment had been written by clerics. They arose from the conditions of life in closed monastic communities, where the extravagancies of gait and gesture that characterized the disorderly behaviour of the layman were deemed unsuitable. Monastic manners were intended to correct the irritating effect of mannerisms. There, in the echoic spaces of chapel and refectory, the belch, the hawking up of phlegm, the noisy expulsion of intestinal gases, disturbed concentration on worship or the silent listening to the reading aloud during meals of the lives of saints. It is this mood that Erasmus caught up in his *De Civilitate*, a book of social advice to the young that went through some ninety editions between 1530 and 1600. Don't sneeze in other people's faces, he warns. If your clothes smell, change them before a meal. Don't spit indigestible bits of food on the table; catch them in your hand and throw them nonchalantly to one side. Don't snort in company, 'although we must make allowance for heavy breathers who are afflicted with asthma'.[43] Della Casa followed suit: 'when you have blown your nose, you should not open your handkerchief and inspect it, as though pearls or rubies had dropped out of your skull.'[44] This extrapolation of refectory-based codes of conduct to lay circles indicates the persisting existence of crude behaviour as well as the continuing influence of clerical upon secular manners. We have an early seventeenth-century assessment of the achievement of clerical *mores*. 'One cannot exaggerate', wrote the Spaniard Juan de Grijalva around 1600, with reference to the native inhabitants of Central and Southern America, 'what the three orders [Franciscan, Dominican and Augustinian] have achieved in this kingdom, since not only does one owe to them the promulgation of spiritual doctrine but that they taught the Indians moral and civil behaviour, in short everything necessary for human life. For these people used to be so savage that they did not even know how to eat properly, how to cover themselves or converse with each other in a courteous and civil manner. But all this the three orders in this region have taught so thoroughly that it now compares favourably in religion and civility with the whole of Europe.'[45]

Courtly and monastic manners had long been meshed. The abbots and abbesses of important foundations were, conventionally, aristocrats themselves and their monasteries and convents entertained the travelling rich as well as offering doles to the poor; lessons in deportment were not learned from the by-way institutions whose uncouthness of manners and morals were the despair of the episcopal authorities who occasionally visited them and the relish of short story writers from Boccaccio onwards. All over Europe, too, the large households of prelates of the church, with their staffs of chaplains and administrators, were crossroads for the traffic of secular and clerical manners, each conscious of the need for self-discipline in the interest of mutual respect and personal advancement.

For all the conduits – ecclesiastical, aristocratic, humanistic – that fed the reservoir of manners had in common the notion of the disciplining of instinctive behaviour by civilized conventions of self-control. In a letter of 1589 to Sir Walter Raleigh prefacing *The Faerie Queene*, Spenser wrote that within his towering allegory was the concealed intention 'to fashion a gentleman or noble person in vertuous and gentle discipline'.[46] As a poet he cited others as his sources for examples of decorous behaviour and the high principles that motivated it, even-handedly combining classical with contemporary models, Homer and Virgil, Ariosto and Tasso. From both worlds, he went on to explain, he had tried to portray in his central character, Arthur, an exemplary hero who personified the ethical and political wisdom of ancient time as adapted to Christianized and chivalric values.

It would be a mistake, however, to see the preoccupation with manners simply in terms of influential books and centres of courtly and ecclesiastical power. There were other forms of organization which, while lacking a prescriptive literature, had long represented the need for self-control: the meetings of councils and magistracies, the governing bodies of charitable institutions and of guilds. More novel was the growing emphasis on good manners in the reasonably well-off family which reflected a heightened concern for proper conduct in both Protestant and Catholic communities. The domestic table was to be a school. 'Do not snort like a pig,' admonished the text of a 1534 German broadsheet bearing a picture of a family at a meal; 'be moderate, do not fall upon your plate like an animal,' 'do not lick the corners of your mouth like a dog,' 'do not rock back and forth on the bench lest you let loose a stink.' And it ends: 'Now you rise from the table, wash your hands and diligently to your business or work; thus sayeth Hans Sachs [the author of the text], shoemaker.'[47]

Crude as it was, such advice, multiplied by scores of cheap pamphlets and books, reflected the need for families of middling status to associate themselves with the mores of their betters. They emphasized the need to control not just table-manners but the spontaneous facial expressions, shouts, bursts of laughter and broad gestures that marked the culture of uneducated toil. The values they preached, sobriety, moderation, orderliness, deference to age and authority, were aimed to establish respectable social rank. They were also aimed to demonstrate respectability of another sort: that of the godly household where good manners represented good morals. Both strands deferred to the values of civility. Both responded to an intensifying of governmental reliance on the heads of the single cells within the honeycomb of urban organizations, the family and its head, commonly male, to take the initiative in controlling instinctual behaviour. After Cosimo de' Medici's death in 1464 the inscription on his tomb in the family's parish church of San Lorenzo included the title, *Pater Patriae*, 'the father of his country', which had been voted by public decree. Thereafter, rules and civic authorities increasingly proclaimed themselves to be the fathers of their subjects or communities. And such 'fathers' looked to real ones, blaming them for a 'want of government' when the young men for whom they were responsible roamed the streets breaking windows and pelting the watch.

The overall effect of the newly advertised and more widely accepted cult of manners can only be guessed at. It did not tame the violence of those of gentle birth, witness the duel and the treasonous plot. It produced Osrics at court. Those who rose from Hans Sachs's table and

'Bovine Man': from Giovambattista della Porta, *De humana physiognomia*, 1586

washed their hands were still prone to using a knife in a quarrel or having to face a church court for getting the maid who had served them with child. In the upper level of society the acknowledgement of intellectual attainment as a feature of the well-mannered person aided a more understanding respect for women; below that level the enhancement of the image of the family patriarch tended to reduce it. While not challenging society's hierarchical structure, manners, whether those of Castiglione or Erasmus or Hans Sachs, supported order, endorsed the values of civility. Above all, they gathered in the privileged and the respectable into a shared wariness of the threat posed by those who lacked manners, who preyed rather than prayed and who took advice not from books but from their stomachs and the wails of their children.

HOLIDAY

When Olivia's puritanical and order-loving steward Malvolio in *Twelfth Night* reprimanded Sir Toby Belch for his noisy drinking, Shakespeare provided the tipsy knight with a celebrated retort: 'Dost thou think, because thou art virtuous, there shall be no more cakes and ale?'[48] It was a reply to delight an audience aware that even by attending a play they were incurring Malvolian disapproval.

The Protestant suspicion of 'vain pleasures' arose from a desire to keep morals abreast of manners and to honour God both outside and inside church. Sunday was to be observed as a Holy Day rather than as a holiday from work which just happened to include a church service. Just as vice could lead to extremes, so could virtue: Sabbatarianism led to a more general attack on worldly pleasures throughout the week; and affordable books – Testaments, catechisms, saints' and martyrs' lives – were now conveniently at hand to replace the suspect recreations of taverns and evening walks in the countryside. And iconoclasm was not restricted to the breaking of popish images. There were popular festivities to be quashed which smacked if not glaringly of pagan origins at least of Catholic endorsement: maypoles, ritual tumblings in the summer hay or (in Piedmont) winter snow, the fêting of Boy Bishops and proletarian Lords of Misrule.

A puritanical strain was an aspect of both Protestant and Catholic Reform. It was more marked in Protestant countries because theirs was a faith that had to prove itself and which, whether in its Lutheran,

Zwinglian or Calvinist form, was not so established by the early seven-teenth century that there were not those within it who held themselves responsible for keeping up the pressure towards total godliness. And secular authorities cautiously supported them; Malvolianism coincided with the growing fear of rowdiness, crime and social resentment. Even the diversions of the privileged acquired in the sixteenth century an apologetic note. The relevance of hunting to war had long been acknowledged before Machiavelli stressed it in 1513. In peacetime the Prince, he wrote, 'should always be out hunting, so accustoming his body to hardships and also learning some practical geography . . . This kind of ability teaches him where to locate the enemy, how to lead his army on the march and draw it up for battle and lay siege to a town to the best advantage'.[49] What is interesting is the increasing frequency with which the point is made. To give but one example, 'hunting is a military exercise,' Lodowick Lloyd explained to the readers of his *The Practice of Policy* in 1604: 'the like strategems are often invented and executed in warres against soldiers as the hunter doeth against divers kindes of beasts.'[50] Joust, tournament, running at the ring or quintain (charging to put a lance-point through a dangling ring or to knock aside a pivoted board without getting struck as its other end whirled round): all these came to be justified as politically useful. 'Every form of mounted game of skill and combat', an Italian author wrote in 1600, 'has real combat as its end and purpose.'[51] Even chess, essentially a board game for gentlefolk, was justified by its theorists if not by its practitioners, in terms of its social symbolism. Rulers, king and queen, in conjunction with the Church (the bishop), supported by the military caste (the knight) and the powers entrusted to the officials they sent the length and breadth of the kingdom-board (the castles), worked in close conjunction with the Third Estate (the pawns). In Spain the pawns were common soldiers who could earn promotion at the end of a faithfully followed campaign. In Switzerland and Germany they were divided into a cross-section of the whole Third Estate: merchant, doc-tor, lawyer, innkeeper, civic watchman, blacksmith, peasant and the equivocal messenger who kept everyone in touch with one another but, as an instinctive gambler, was not to be trusted.

As with hunting, which barred tracts of countryside when there were more who needed its firewood and game, and the joust, which was becoming, at a time when cavalry was playing a smaller part in war-time, little more than an energetic parade of social rank, the litera-ture of chess (commended by Castiglione to his courtier) contained few ideas that did not have medieval precedents. It is the constant repetition which suggests that the notion of justifying behaviour in terms of what was suited to the civilized commonwealth was not restricted to the middle ranks of society.

These were all diversions that had self-regulating rules and formalities. More disturbing to State and Church were the recreations which were personal, immediate holidays from care. Gambling was deplored for the quarrels and changes of fortune it produced. But nobles bet on the prowess of a falcon, merchant companies kept wager-books recording, as did that of the Hanseatic traders in Danzig, bets on the price of the herring catch, the outcome of a military campaign, the identity of the father of an illegitimate child. Dice and cards were ubiquitous. Artists showed them among the possessions of the damned or on the ground beside the sleeping soldiers deputed to keep watch over Christ's tomb. Both, vainly, were forbidden by ship-board regulations and military codes; clerics thundered against the cause, but punishment, save in the case of those who made a trade of cheating the gullible, was directed against the consequences of loss: violent crime or theft. It was the same with drink, for which Noah's shameful drunkenness provided a ready text (*Genesis* 9, 20–27) for pulpit scolding. The licensing of taverns in towns was, as in Elizabethan England, made stricter, but the aim was more to keep an eye on drinkers than to stop them drinking. For the most part the taverns of Renaissance Europe were refuges for travellers and the equivalent of working men's clubs where gossip and argument were as important as the tankard. Machiavelli ruefully described such a place where he wasted time with the village baker, miller and butcher before walking back up the village street to get on with *The Prince*.[52] And alehouses were useful to governments as readily identifiable sources of disorder and valuable look-out points for informers.

The balance between viable control and the indulgence of human appetite was more complex where prostitution was concerned. The most revered of all medieval theologians, St Thomas Aquinas, had compared a brothel in a town to a cesspit in a palace; unpleasant but necessary as a sump for natural impurities. The Borgia Pope Alexander VI's master of ceremonies may have deplored the need to invite prostitutes to entertainments in the Vatican, but German cities were aware that a free night at a brothel would be welcomed during a visit from the Emperor and his retinue. Between them, the search for pleasure on the part of the rich, and the need to canalize sexual activity acknowl-

Jan Sanders van Hermessen (attrib.), *Tavern Scene*, *c.*1540 (Staatliche Museen, Berlin-Dahlem)

edged by both secular and clerical authorities (both accepting the profits from brothels established in properties they owned), combined to support sexual commerce 'for common utility', 'in the interest of the public good', 'for enhancing the good, piety and honour of the whole commune'.[53] These were the reasons given for maintaining municipal brothels in French and German cities, but the arguments for accepting prostitution were European commonplaces: to cut illegitimacy rates at a time when the age of marriage commonly ran ten years or more ahead of the onset of sexual appetite; to prevent the transmission of sexual disease by freelance prostitutes who were not subject to medical inspection by municipally approved midwives; to divert young men from more scandalous homosexual relationships.

As legalized brothels performed a public service, prices were kept low, the keepers or madams recompensing themselves for less than a free market price by selling drink and food. In effect taverns with sex, they immobilized roaming troublemakers for whole evenings at a time.

In return, licensed prostitutes had to accept the discipline of the house, work for a low wage and submit when they went out of doors to wearing a brand: a badge or stripe on their costume or an identifying hat. Their position was anomalous. As a civic amenity they were invited in German cities to festivals which feasted representatives of all the occupations which established the city's repute. In Italy they ran in the races which formed part of carnival celebrations. There were pious institutions which provided a home for ex-prostitutes, though their statutes suggest that in some cases at least they were mainly concerned with institutionalizing women still young and pretty enough to carry temptation through the streets. There are enough instances of former brothel workers marrying and obtaining positions of servants to show that the stigma of their trade could be taken with sympathetic indulgence. Nonetheless, with badge or hat, supervised and segregated church attendance, and a ban at least in theory on sleeping with the respectable sections of society, clerics and married men, they shared with the Jews the status of useful outsiders. Indeed, in some cases only girls and young women who came from outside the city could be employed in municipal brothels. And the parallel with the Jews became even stronger with the moral outrage associated with Reform.

'Is it not a lamentable thing', asked Luther in 1520, 'that we Christians should openly tolerate in our midst common houses of ill-fame, though we all took the oath of chastity at our baptism? I am well aware of the frequent reply . . . that it is better to have such houses than that married women, or maidens . . . should be dishonoured. Nevertheless, ought not the secular but Christian government to consider that that is not the way to get rid of a heathen custom?'[54] It was not long before his view was acted on. Under the year 1532 an Augsburg chronicler noted that 'the Council did away with the brothel at the prompting of the Lutheran preachers.'[55] The Councils of Ulm and Regensburg followed suit in 1527 and 1553. Nuremberg consulted the magistrates of Augsburg as to the effect of their own closures. The reply was that most, though not all, responsible citizens approved, and the Nuremberg house was shut down in 1562. There was some backsliding. Closed in 1537, the brothel at Freiburg in Saxony was reopened by public demand three years later – only to be closed again after the magistrates received a furious letter from Luther: 'those who wish to reestablish such houses should first deny Christ's name and recognize that rather than Christians, they are heathens.'[56]

By then Luther the ex-Catholic priest had married a former nun. For both Luther and Calvin, who was equally insistent that brothels should be closed, it was clear that the strain of enforced celibacy had led clerics both to live openly in sin with women and to be over-tolerant of others' recourse to prostitutes. And alongside its attacks on commercial sex, Protestantism built up by example and pulpit pleading the sacredness of married, family life, and thus the importance of pre-marital chastity. No longer should Christians accept the need for cesspits. When the Lutheran city fathers of Zwickau shut their brothel as early as 1526 they offered as a practical reason 'the fact that so many young journeymen have been poisoned with the French disease', but gave as the chief motive the need for a chaste life before marriage.[57]

It was above all in Germany, Switzerland and France, where brothels were run by and paid taxes to municipalities, that they were the most obvious targets for moralists striving to improve the tone of urban life. And it was in the Protestant areas of such countries that the target was hit hardest; in Catholic Perpignan the Dominicans were still contributing in 1608 to the upkeep of the municipal brothel. When Philip II tightened the regulations of the privately run brothels of Seville in 1570 it was to ensure weekly inspection by a physician and a surgeon with powers to compel infected prostitutes to go to hospital for treatment. In Venice the government occasionally intervened to insist on the wearing of a distinguishing mark, to ban too-open soliciting in the streets or from gondolas, and the wearing of men's clothes. There, in times of plague, brothels were closed to trade and pimps forbidden to seek customers. But no moral crusade was launched with governmental support. A printed list of 1535 which gave the names, prices, specialities and contact addresses of 110 outstanding prostitutes circulated openly, as did a fuller *Catalogue* in 1570 which contained two hundred and fifteen names, among them that of the widely admired poet Veronica Franco, then aged twenty-nine (charge: two ducats).

Such lists dealt with the *cortegiane*, women with houses or apartments of their own, as opposed to the brothel-based or casual *meretrice*; the order of 1578 against cross-dressing, however, was to apply both to '*cortegiane et meretrici*'. The outstanding courtesan-geishas, often the quasi-consorts of rich patrician bachelors, lived in a style not too much guyed by Bandello in his description of the household of the heroine of one of his stories, Imperia. 'Her house was so appointed and in every way provided for that any visitor entering it and noting the furnishings and servants would have thought it the habitation of a princess.'[58] He dwells on the carpets and tapestries, the richly bound books, the shelves of vases of semi-precious stones, the musical instruments laid out on tables. For another real-life Roman courtesan, Faustina, Michelangelo wrote a verse epitaph, praising her beauty but regretting her use of it. Brantôme recorded that on his first visit to Rome he had approached her but 'she was too expensive: ten or twelve écus a night.'[59] Rome and Venice remained exceptionally tolerant. Both had populations with a disproportionate number of influential unmarried men. Both were centres of a lucrative international tourism. More typical of the response to governments supporting the mood of Reform was London. In the mid-sixteenth century brothels were banned in the City of London, and the keepers of others which were set up outside the city limits to replace them, especially in Clerkenwell, Whitechapel and Shoreditch, were increasingly raided and closed – before shifting elsewhere or clandestinely reopening. For London, too, had its foreign visitors and foreign communities for whom life abroad required compensating pleasures. The authorities had, moreover, to cope with brothel-keepers who were offered noble protection. One openly wore the livery of Lord Ambrose Dudley. A prostitute sentenced to prison in 1578 got off when it was shown that she worked for 'Mr Browne which kepeth my Lord of Lecester's house'. That control was tightening, however, emerged from the confession of a pimp in the following year who explained to the justices that when his master, the financier favourite of Queen Elizabeth, had asked him to procure 'some mayden to abuse who had not been dealte with all before', he had had to travel as far as Guildford in order to find one.[60]

The closing or sending underground of brothels could not check prostitution. When public ones were closed their inmates lost the regular pay and protection from violence the private ones seldom afforded. When these in turn were harassed or suppressed, their inmates' position worsened at a time when competition was growing from the increasing number of women who could find no other means of livelihood than travelling to offer themselves at fairs, vintage and harvest-home celebrations and pilgrimage shrines in the countryside or to haunt city taverns and alleys. In around 1500 the lawyer-poet Guillaume Coquillart had written of a familiar figure in the streets of Paris, the

> Woman who goes torch-less by night
> And murmurs to each "so you want me"?[61]

With every subsequent generation such haunting figures became more numerous. Even army regulations reflected – in intention – the changed morality. In the Burgundian army of 1473 companies were allowed thirty 'women' (who foraged for food, laundered, cooked and bound wounds as well as providing sex). German armies up to the 1540s at least, had an official, the *Hurenweibel*, to discipline and protect women camp-followers. Such portable cesspits were taken for granted in itinerant male societies. They also served to prevent the alienation of the societies through which armies moved or among whom they were billeted. All the same, Huguenot commanders tried to honour their Calvinist convictions by excluding them. Ironically congratulated by an old soldier for his puritanical regulations of 1562, the Protestant Count of Coligny replied with equal irony that the exclusion of women was 'very fine – provided that it lasts'.[62] In the Low Countries wars, the establishment of official whores in the Catholic Spanish forces was cut to a maximum of eight per two hundred men.

To what extent such regulations, and the closing of brothels, more vigilant street patrols and greater co-operation from self-righteous neighbours, cut down the incidence of commercialized sex can only be conjectured. It is clearer that for those who provided it, unless they found rich protectors, life became more harassed and degrading, and that for those who sought it, extra-marital sex became more furtive and animalistic and less companionable, less holiday-like, no longer a more-or-less taken for granted rite of passage from adolescence to manhood.

As fellow Deadly Sins of the flesh, Gluttony and Lechery had always been paired. Moralizing paintings and prints continued to link them: the heaped table in the brothel, the alfresco meal for lovers in a garden. Literary descriptions of conversation as a banquet proceeded sometimes showed it – as did those of Rabelais, and of Béroalde de Verville in *c*.1610 – as becoming progressively bawdy. But feasting, indulging immoderately and wonderfully at the table, was above all appreciated as an end in itself.

Overwhelmingly the normal diet was farinaceous: wheat, rye, barley, oats, millet; the commonest meal was bread floating in a thin vegetable soup. Fresh meat was eaten rarely, perhaps a dozen times a year by most families. Because of the concentration on cereals and the difficulty of keeping stock alive during the winter the animal population was small; butchers were only to be found in sizeable towns, their supplies were intermittent and their charges high. Milk and butter and

Anon., *The Prodigal Son*, *c.*1550, oak relief (Rijksmuseum, Amsterdam)

the hard, keeping cheeses were all expensive and the poor townsman probably never tasted them. Eggs and an occasional fowl provided the main variety in the country. A pig was more likely to be sent to town or the local manor for cash than eaten, because of the high cost of salting it. Game was jealously protected by the large landowners. Fresh sea fish was available only near the coast and it is doubtful whether salt fish played a part in the ordinary man's diet; the costs of salting and transport meant that he normally kept his Fridays and other fast days by not varying his normal meatless diet. Rivers and lakes were fished – on the town wall of Constance was a circle showing which fish was best to eat in each month of the year – but fishing rights were restricted to the big riparian landlords and much of the catch channelled to monastic or noble households.

The pattern varied widely. The alert and full-fleshed men and women who gaze from their portraits did not owe their confidence to bread and soup. The dependants of a noble household might have meat every day (twice a day, according to the accounts of the Bavarian count

Joachim von Gettingen), the prosperous bourgeois housewife might use sugar from Sicily not as a medicine, its normal use, but as a substitute for honey as a sweetener. But even though the contrast in diet between rich and poor was extreme, even the most fortunate ate frugally and monotonously and the bouts of indulgence which figure so largely in contemporary records were given prominence because they contrasted with an abstemiousness fostered by high prices and scarcity. The raw glee with which the fifteenth-century aristocratic feast, with its gargantuan catalogue of meats and fowls and fishes is described, is not far in mood from the peasant orgy when a wedding, a death or the harvest home was seized on as an excuse to take holiday from the workaday margins of existence.

Not only the clergy but secular moralists and governments attacked the advantage of their stomach's holidays and their presumed aftermath of bastards, broken heads, resentments by the excluded and illnesses. In the early sixteenth-century play *A Condemnation of Feasting* by the French lawyer Nicholas de la Chesnaye, a French doctor of civil and canon law, DINNER, SUPPER and BANQUET invite GOURMAND, EPICURE, PLEASURE, and GOOD COMPANY to eat. In the midst of their meal they are attacked by a horde of sinister monsters: APOPLEXY, PARALYSIS, EPILEPSY, PLEURISY, COLIC, and GOUT among them. After a violent dance the gourmets expel their unwelcome guests and repair from DINNER's house to SUPPER's where they at once fall to again. The diseases once more invade their potations and this time they are the victors. They have brought DAME EXPERIENCE with them, and when GOOD COMPANY confesses his fault, she hands him over to her servitors, PILL, ENEMA and BLEEDING. SUPPER is sentenced never again to approach nearer than six hours to DINNER and to wear bracelets of lead so that his hands will not fly so readily to his mouth. DINNER escapes with a scolding, but BANQUET, having confessed the grossness of his conduct, is ceremoniously hanged by DIET as a warning to the audience.

It was a warning that only the privileged few needed to take to heart. Nevertheless it was repeated by inference in the recurrent legislation by which governments attempted to limit the number of dishes that might be served at weddings and other occasions of rejoicing; the consumption of the well-to-do must not be such as to excite the jealousy of the poor. And from the publication of such gastronomic works as Platina's *Honest Pleasure and Good Health* in *c.*1474 and the English *Boke of Kerving* of 1508 onwards, there was a growing concern with the decorous order and presentation of grand meals, and the considered relation of one course to another. In Domenico Romoli's *The Steward* of 1560, the noisy, messy, unplanned and unthoughtfully prepared medieval feast has become civilized. There are forks as well as knives, guests no longer use their hands. There are table-cloths, sometimes changed between courses, and napkins. One course is cleared before another is provided. Servants are deft, quiet and carefully rehearsed. As with the design and contents of the garden outside, the meal indoors reflected the chastening influence of civility. Montaigne described how he interviewed an Italian before engaging him as his steward; 'he told me a long, formall and eloquent discourse of the science or skill of epicurisme and gluttonie, with such an oratorie-gravitie, and magistrale countenance, as if he had discoursed of some high mysterious point of divinitie.'[63] Rather than with lechery, gluttony became identified – at least for the discriminating – with eloquent table-talk and displays of learning: Platina had drawn on ancient and Arabic sources; the treatise of 1582 on the history and significance of meals by the Swiss Guilielmus Stuckicus ran to 838 folio pages and cited some 550 authors. Feasting among the wealthy remained a matter for infrequent special occasions as it was for the poor, but its manner, and its more withdrawn privacy, made it more markedly different in kind. The days of adventitious sharing in the noise and warmth within an open palace door and a hand-out of the leavings were over; the populace was firmly excluded from the pleasures of the rich.

A similar withdrawal took place with publicly organized occasions of holiday mood. Bread and circuses: Lorenzo de' Medici was accused of soliciting in the 1470s and 1480s the support of those excluded from a voice in government by lavish public entertainments: tournaments, street pageants. Shortly after Lorenzo's death in 1492, Savonarola wrote generalizingly that 'many times the tyrant . . . occupies the people in spectacles and festivals.'[64] There is no evidence that Lorenzo intended to do more than add panache to Florence's traditional festival occasions. In a republic that had been subtly manipulated into a narrow oligarchy it was natural, however, for opponents of this tendency to remember with alarm how the emperors who subverted the republican constitution of ancient Rome had employed gladiatorial and wild beast combats to occupy simple minds. A century after Lorenzo, however, with the rising price of bread and the popular insurgency that rose with it, the issue of diversion was seen in terms of practical contemporary politics. 'Because the common people are unstable and long for novelty', wrote Giovanni Botero in 1589 in his *Reason of State*, 'they will seek it out for themselves, changing even their government and their rulers if their prince does not provide some kind of diversion for them.'[65]

In reality, governments were neither so cynical – nor so naïve. The more elaborate pageant-tournaments of Elizabethan England, France and ducal Florence were a form of display aimed rather at consolidating local aristocratic support and attracting international admiration than at placating the crowd. The city-sponsored and widely advertised shooting matches in Switzerland and Germany, with their associated public lotteries, were, like trade fairs, designed to bring outsiders' money into the local economy. That they generated a festival atmosphere was a side-issue and, from the point of view of those who had to maintain law and order, a not particularly welcome one.

There were no 'circuses' deliberately contrived to sublimate social discontent. Public spectacles to welcome a monarch into a city or celebrate a royal betrothal or a peace became more esoteric in the imagery provided for their arches and floats, and the side-streets along the route more carefully guarded. The outdoor tournament gave way to the indoor masque and dance. Civility interposed between spectacle and public in the shape of the invitation card.

Nonetheless, wrote in 1604 a French lawyer with long experience of a socially 'difficult' city, Lyon, 'it is sometimes expedient to allow the people to play the fool and make merry, lest by holding them in with too great a rigour, we put them in despair.'[66] What he had in mind was not so much a return to official or privileged celebration which also reached out to a wider, vicarious participation, but the wisdom of non-interference with traditional local rites of excess. Apart from the obstreperousness of popular sports, especially those ritualized into inter-village or urban inter-ward combat games, all over Europe the 'charivari' offered an occasional release of bile and wild humour. The remarriage of a widower, the marriage of a man to a much younger woman, notorious instances of cuckoldry or cravenly suffered nagging and scolding: all were used as an excuse to make an uproar outside the victim's house, with gangs of youths shouting ribald comment, banging saucepans, ringing bells and blowing horns in a cacophony of insult. These disturbances were tolerated because their motivation was basically conservative. Remarriages poached upon the local stock of unmarried young women, and excessive age differences offended against an instinctively felt norm; to be cuckolded or to surrender to a termagant put the reassuring model of a stable marriage in doubt. Though used as an excuse to make an illegal disturbance, the charivari represented a form of rough justice, an expression of a community's wish to police its habitual values in its own way. And, doubtless, the silence of magistrates was helped by a certain *Schadenfreude*.

Moreover, while the seasonal dinners of guild-masters became more formalized, silver bedecked and closed, their juniors, apprentices and journeymen formed groups for their own entertainment. Best known in France, but recorded elsewhere, their leaders too had anarchic titles: Abbot of Misrule, Prince of Pleasure, of Youth, of Fools. Under-officials at Royan included Bishop Meany, Duke Kick-Ass and The Grand Patriarch of Syphlitics. Mainly they ate, drank and rushed through the streets on their own, but their membership could be called on by the charivari to harass a wedding's procession by stretching chains in front of it or to burst into the couple's bedroom to embarrass and delay its consummation. These were the moods that Protestants tried to check ('on Midsomer Day laste at evening prayer the youthe were sumwhat meerie together in crowning of lordes', ran an indict-ment of c.1600 in the church court of Wootton in Oxfordshire[67]), and which Catholic authorities glumly accepted as part of the vast conti-nuity within their own traditional regime.

Alongside individual needs for drink or sex or a copious meal, the socialized euphoria of officially sanctioned holidays reveals the volatility which civility feared, even if some of its representatives enjoyed its licence. Religious festivals, whether of a local saint's name day or the celebration of a major event in the calendar – Corpus Christi, Ascen-sion, St John's Eve, St Bartholomew's Day – were seized on with a verve that reflected the glee with which a community both partook in an act of devotion and stage-managed it – with plays and floats, fire-works and noisy music, food and drink – on its own terms. A Lutheran pastor in Estonia glumly noted that St John's Eve was marked by 'flames of joy over the whole country. Around these bonfires people danced, sang and leaped with great pleasure, and did not spare the big bagpipes . . . many loads of beer were brought . . . what disorder, whoring, fighting and killing and dreadful idolatory took place!'[68] But disorder was the point of festival, however carefully its pageantry was organized.

'The Upside Down World',
engraving by the
Housebook Master
(Rijkprentenkabinett,
Amsterdam)

The themes of the most excited festival of all, the last days of Carnival preceding Lent, showed, through mimes and caperings, the joy in
turning the world of order upside down for a few days: women drew
ploughs, men were dressed as women and vice versa, masters served
their servants (or revellers dressed as servants) in houses that dared
not close their doors to passers-by, masks and costumes showed the
representatives of authority, clerics, lawyers, magistrates, in ridiculous
and humiliating guises. 'The women, too, take their part,' wrote a late
sixteenth-century visitor to Barcelona in Carnival time; 'throughout
the year they are so severely restricted that they are not allowed to talk
to strangers. But at carnival there are no such shackles and hindrance.
They put on masks and run through the streets in complete freedom

. . . So, for more than one husband, the cuckoo sings before the spring comes.'[69]

With a favourite costume being that of the Wild Man, it comes as no surprise that Carnival was the occasion for the violent settlement of quarrels under a veneer of play, for a parading of phallic ornament and the singing of obscene verses, for unbridled onslaughts on stalls full of pies and flagons. It was not only the commonalty that broke loose from normal restraints. The aristocratic Cardinal of Aragon was named by Castiglione in *The Courtier* as a spectator or participant in the Roman carnival sport of pelting passers-by (in this case a friar) with eggs. It was well-born Protestant travellers who were attracted by the licence of the Venetian Carnival. But when the world was turned upside down (and prints extended the notion with fish flying, a town exchanging places with the moon), it was primarily for the delectation of those who daily experienced the restraints of cash, morality and social inferiority, and stored up in *anticipatio* the prospect of temporary release from them.

CHAPTER X

The Taming of Nature

THE LAND

When the conqueror Hernán Cortes wrote that 'it is a universal condition of mankind to want to know',[1] and the man of letters Lodovico Domenichi in 1551 that men have 'an infinite desire to know many things,'[2] they were echoing a classical opinion that had become a medieval commonplace: curiosity, the desire for knowledge, distinguished men from animals.

Carpaccio's painting of about 1502 showing St Augustine in his study sums up the old view: knowledge comes from books and from divine inspiration – the light streaming in from the most realistically rendered of the Trinity of windows beside his desk. But already the idea of knowledge based on practical experience was gaining ground. Machiavelli, though a lover of book-knowledge, stressed the statesman's need to study 'the actual condition of affairs'.[3] Cortes was celebrating the discovery of a new world, Domenichi telling his contemporaries what the Turkish Empire was actually like.

This sort of curiosity was expressed by the investigative mood of the chorographers, and by artists no longer content with careful studies of individual details – a lily, a deer – which they or their assistants could use over and over again. Leonardo wrote of the painter's need to study the changes in atmospheric conditions due to cloud, rain and dust, the changing play of light whether on a landscape or a pebble on a river bed, the curl of a current registered on the surface of a stream. Dürer stressed that the materia for art 'is embedded in nature'.[4] For in no context more than that of the world of nature was the enthusiasm for gaining practical knowledge more constantly expressed.

Its intensity was mildly ridiculed by Rabelais, that master of being garrulous while keeping his tongue in his cheek. 'As for the knowledge of Nature's works', Gargantua gravely advised his son on his educational curriculum, 'I should like you to give careful attention to that, too, so that there may be no sea, river or spring of which you do not know the fish. All the birds of the air, all the trees, shrubs and bushes of the forest, all the herbs of the field, all the metals deep in the bowels of the earth, all the precious stones . . . let none of them be unknown to you.'[5] But only three years later, in 1538, another traditionally educated scholar, the Spaniard Juan Luis Vives, was taking such advice perfectly seriously. For the man who wants to understand nature, he wrote, 'all that is wanted is a certain power of observation. So he will observe the nature of things in the heavens in cloudy and clear weather, in the plains, in the mountains, in the woods. Hence he will seek out and get to know many things about those who inhabit such spots. Let him have recourse to gardeners, husbandmen, shepherds and hunters . . . for no man can possibly make all observations without help in such a multitude and variety of directions.'[6]

This wanting to know was to reinforce the separateness of those who studied nature and those who simply lived in it. A mid-sixteenth-century story made the point. A man crossing a meadow was delighted to find an early violet. But on bringing his mistress to share his pleasure, he found that a peasant had casually covered it with his turds.

Allied to the intellectual impulse to explore nature was the economically-based desire to exploit it. Spenser had identified the barbarous past with a time when the land was 'unmanurd, unprov'd'. And elsewhere in *The Faerie Queene*, allegorizing the fate of the Protestant Netherlands, which had been devoured by a papal-Spanish monster, he described the dreadful fate of Belge, its dispossessed ruler, who had been turned 'into moores and marshes, Out of the pleasant [i.e. cultivated] soyle, and citties glad, In which she had been wont to harbour happily'. Now, she complained to Prince Arthur, her would-be rescuer, she was exiled from civility:

> Onely these marishes, and myrie bogs,
> In which the fearefull ewftes [lizards] do build their bowrs,
> Yeeld me an hostry mongst the croking frogs.[7]

Spenser's own enforced sojourn among the 'meer Irish' added poignancy to his depiction of Belge's plight. But the connection between the civility of 'citties glad' and that of lands reclaimed from 'myrie bogs' was widely representative of his time. Looking back from *c*.1620, Niccolò Contarini, a future doge, reviewed the history of Venice during

Vittore Carpaccio, *St Augustine in his Study*, c.1505 (Scuola di San Giorgio degli Schiavoni, Venice)

the preceding generation. With 'ordered government' he coupled 'a fertile countryside'. 'Those fields which had been the lowest of marshes, deep lakes and ponds, were now transformed by ingenuity, effort and expense into the most fertile terrain, pleasant meadows and charming gardens . . .; forests and hills were subjected not only to the axe but to the plough.'[8] The ideal of a man-made landscape cropped up again a year later in Richard Burton's Utopian vision: 'I will have no bogs, fens, marshes, vast woods, deserts, heaths . . . I will not have a barren acre in all my territories, not so much as the tops of mountains: where Nature fails, it shall be supplied by art.'[9] There could hardly be a clearer statement of the idea that to be civilized was to wish to tame nature into the productive service of man – or to accord with his aesthetic taste: of the countryside near Constantinople Busbecq wrote, 'it is a district the like of which for beauty could not, I think, be found anywhere if only it were cultivated, and art gave a little assistance to nature.'[10]

We have such evidence for a desire to rationalize both the use and the appearance of the land because a large number of cultivated men actually took to cultivating it. The flow of aristocratic landlords to cities and courts for a good part of the year was balanced by wealthy citizens who bought country estates for prestige and profit, as refuges from the contagious diseases of towns during the summer, and for a pleasure heightened by a conscious following of the example of the villa-loving Romans. There was thus a new market for vernacular versions of the texts of classical authors on husbandry, like Varro and Columella, and for contemporary works praising country life and giving advice on agricultural practice: on drainage and irrigation, on the use of animal and mineral (potash, lime) manures, mulches and

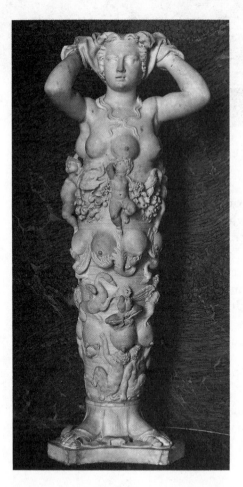

Niccolò Tribolo, *Nature*, c.1528 (Château de Fontainebleau)

composts. For whether the merchant-landowner had acquired country property to enhance his rank, secure a source of produce or diversify his investments, he brought his own approach to the running of the land surrounding his villa or manor house.

Late medieval representations of the labours of the months, which took for granted the unchanging acceptance of traditional seasonal tasks, dwindled towards 1500, though Breughel defiantly restated in the mid-sixteenth century the perennial grip of nature's timetable on that of man. Meanwhile, the idea of nature's bounty became conceptualized. Artists showed Ceres, the goddess of agriculture, with her cornucopia of natural produce as the generalized tutelary deity of the countryside. Niccolò Tribolo's sculpted *Nature*, sent from Florence to Francis I's villa-palace at Fontainebleau, was, with its multiple charitable breasts and the foison of animal and vegetable produce running up its base, a new form of homage to the capacity of nature to be seduced into the service of man.

In 1591 Giuseppe Arcimboldo went so far as to portray the Emperor Rudolf himself in the guise of Vertumnus, the guardian spirit of gardens throughout the changing seasons. His head, neck and chest are entirely composed of fruits, flowers and vegetables: parsnips, onions and pumpkins which supplement the more conventional associations of apples with cheeks and cherries with lips.

Under the earth, most notably in eastern Germany, Bohemia and Poland, shafts were driven deeper than ever before in search of minerals (silver, copper, lead) and salt. Public interest in this exploitation was shown in a full-page miniature in a Bohemian liturgical manuscript of the 1490s which portrayed the mining procedures employed at Kutna Hora for extracting and refining silver. In 1532 a design for a table centre showed a silver cup resting on a hill penetrated by mine-shafts and topped by a winch for hauling the sacks of ore to the surface: an acknowledgement of art's indebtedness to man's penetration of nature. Improved pumping and winching systems made it possible to work seams three hundred metres down. By 1550 the earth was being made to disgorge something like five times the ores that had been prised from it a hundred years earlier. On the surface, the late medieval enclosure of arable land for pasturage continued, but with growing caution because of the social problem caused by the obliteration of peasant holdings. Thanks to improvements in surveying techniques and hydraulic engineering, capital investment was tempted into land reclamation schemes which changed the appearance of the land while increasing its yields.

Giuseppe Arcimboldo,
Rudolph II as Vertumnus,
*c.*1591 (Kunsthistorisches
Museum, Vienna)

Sea margins were dyked against further erosion in the coastal Low Countries. Marshes and boggy wastes were turned into larders or grazing grounds in Italy in the Veneto, around Ravenna and in parts of the Pontine Marshes south of Rome. Vines were planted in the former wetlands surrounding Bordeaux. A start was made on draining the East Anglian fenlands. Save in the Low Countries the areas involved were quite small, but the new alliance between investment and advanced technology represented a changed approach to land control. And it is entirely characteristic of the sixteenth century that for every practical advance (in canal digging, in pumping devices) there was an over-ingenious one: earth-shifting machines too complex to be made to work, perpetual motion pumps that were claimed to produce energy without receiving any. Even the wildest scheme reflected the conviction – and those submitted to the Venetian government, for instance, were examined and often tested in an optimistic spirit – that man should extend his mastery of nature.

Deforestation, caused by the commercial demand for more and larger ships, frameworks for more and taller houses, carbon for the smelting of iron and copper and the refining of steel to satisfy a booming arms industry, was countered patchily by schemes for the protection of mature timber by naval powers like England and Venice. It was also to some extent balanced by a more widespread planting of windbreaks and, in the interest of the silk industry, plantations of mulberries along Italian roads. In southern Europe changes in the appearance of the countryside were also induced by the cultivation of rice, the newly imported maize and, in the Mediterranean islands, sugar. It was, however, through changes in gardens and parklands that the attitude of civility towards nature was most clearly expressed: its self-cherishing proprietorialness, its fears, and its interest in knowledge of the natural world.

The medieval interest in plants for their prettiness and medicinal properties stimulated the traveller's interest in novelties and led Europe to be deluged with exotic imports, seeds and roots packaged in chests

Herri met de Bles, *Copper Mine*, detail, 1540s (Uffizi, Florence)

of earth to try their fortunes at home. The utilitarian monastic plot of useful herbs was overtaken by the deliberately encyclopaedic botanic garden. The first was laid out in Pisa in 1543. Florence and the University of Padua followed suit in 1545, Bologna in 1567. Soon they spread to other countries; Leiden's was founded in 1594. Philip II, who commissioned agents to scour his American territories for specimens, hesitated over the purchase of such a garden established by one of his subjects in Seville in spite of being assured that it was 'one of the outstanding things in Spain . . . Italians and other foreigners have come here just to see this';[11] he bought one instead in Madrid which was handier for the researches of his apothecaries.

The most influential classical writer was the first-century physician Dioscorides, whose *On the Materia Medica* had been the chief source for the medieval herbals which listed plants and described their properties. He had described some five hundred. In 1623 Gaspard Bauhin's *Pinax* described six thousand. The stimulus of imports led to a fresh interest in plants that were native to Europe, and because so many of them had no place in the illustrations to traditional herbals, it became necessary to commission new ones. This drew attention to the inadequacy of images that were already copies of copies. The pioneering work was German, and Otto Brunfels announced it in the title of his *Living Portraits of Plants*, published in 1530 with illustrations by the

versatile Hans Weiditz. This was followed in 1542 by the *History of Plants* by Leonhard Fuchs who made the connection between art and knowledge even clearer by including a woodcut showing his two artists at work and a portrait of the craftsman who translated their drawings into woodcuts.

For well-known plants, both authors followed Dioscorides; their artists, on the other hand, copied the specimens before them. The result was that the text was at odds with the illustrations. It was a problem that occurred, as we shall see, with anatomical illustration. Texts were most objective when they dealt entirely with plants unknown to the Greeks and Romans. 'Don't frighten me with Dioscorides . . . because I am only going to say what I know to be true,' declared the author of a work on Indian plants in 1563.[12] It was the promise of new medicinal cures or palliatives to be derived from American plants that caused a Spanish treatise of 1574 to be translated within three years into English as *Joyfull Newes out of the Newe Found World*.

It is moving to observe the attempts of serious botanists to avoid following two obvious lures: either the mechanical up-dating of ancient knowledge or the classification of plants according to their use in medicine as narcotics, purgatives, salves or cures – such as, conspicuously, an infusion of South American guaiacum wood as a cure for syphilis. New modes of classification were proposed, based on buds and fruit,

Anon., *Polder*, 1590s
(on loan to
Rijksmuseum from
Zuiderzeemuseum,
Enkhuizen)

habit or size or provenance but all were subordinated to the idea of use. Only in 1592, with the Bohemian Adam Zaluziansky's *Method of Treating Plants*, was there a declaration of what the future was to take for granted. 'It is customary', he wrote, 'to connect medicine with botany, yet scientific treatment demands that we should consider each separately . . . In order that botany . . . may form a unit by itself. Before it can be brought into connection with other sciences it must be divided and unyoked from medicine.'[13] While not yet a true science – it lacked the microscope of the seventeenth century – botany was at least becoming a respectable branch of *scientia*, knowledge of the natural world. 'Wise women' still prowled the hedgerows but they were increasingly likely to meet bands of botanizing students fanning out from the universities. And alongside the botanic garden there developed the herbarium, the *hortus siccus*, the library of pressed and dried plants; both called for the artist-illustrators who transformed the relationship between drawn and written description.

None of this *scientia* meant that an interest in nature had become the preserve of scholars. The old love of plant-lore survived the transition from the rambling herbal to the well-trained treatise. 'Artichoke reformeth the savour of the mouth' – it cleansed, that is, bad breath, Thomas Hill in 1586 told the readers of his *The Gardener's Labyrinth*; 'it causeth urine and the venereal act . . . amendeth the hardness of making water and the rank savour of the armpits . . . helpeth the privie places [so] that men children may be conceived.'[14] New plants poured far more widely into ordinary gardens than into botanic ones. Asparagus followed the artichoke as a Mediterranean vegetable that could be acclimatized in the North. The potato began its progress from oddity to staple. Nearly ninety new shrubs and trees were persuaded to grow in English gardens and parks during the sixteenth century. Contacts with Turkey led to the naturalization of lilac and tulips. Hyacinths, anenomes and crocuses joined the long familiar roses, marigolds and violets. Professional nurseries were established to satisfy the amateur demand for imports of plants and shrubs. There were so many of them in England that by 1629 the botanist John Parkinson was complaining about the irresponsible ones 'where of the skirts of our towns are pitifully pestered'.[15] In 1612 Emmanuel Sweert's catalogue of what was available in Amsterdam to feed the current tulipomania listed some hundred varieties. Of these some at least were beyond the purse of all but the rich enthusiast. But the acquisitiveness of the ordinary citizen was well expressed by the Elizabethan London chronicler William Harrison. 'Let

François Clouet, *Pierre Quthe*, 1526 (Musée du Louvre, Paris)

me boast a little of my garden', he wrote, 'which is but small . . . but yet, such hath been my luck in purchase . . . that there are very near three hundred of one sort or another contained therein, no one of them being common or ordinarily to be had.'[16]

Some imported plants refused to take on a new life in Europe and were banished to the *hortus siccus*. A partial exception was tobacco, along with syphilis an aspect of America's revenge on its conquerors. Attempts to naturalize its plants failed but its imported leaf created an international habit. Of its use in late sixteenth-century England,

Thomas Platter observed that after rubbing down the leaf 'the powder is lit in a small pipe, the smoke sucked into the mouth, and the saliva allowed to run freely.' They use it so abundantly, he went on, 'because of the pleasure it gives, that their preachers cry out on them for their self-destruction, and I am told that the insides of one man's veins after death were found to be covered in soot just like a chimney'.[17]

While gardeners turned eagerly to new botanical knowledge (and, by so doing, further stimulated it), the notion grew towards the middle of the sixteenth century that a carefully designed garden represented a Third Nature. That man's ability to tame 'natural' nature by agriculture created a Second Nature had been implied since Cicero wrote of how 'we sow corn and plant trees; we fertilize the soil by irrigation. We dam the rivers – to guide them where we will.'[18] The distinction became clearer as the cultivation of the land was seen as a function of civility. Now, as the design of gardens became a matter of fashion and pride, nature was made to co-operate not just with man's needs but with his idea of beauty; plans made for beds, walks and prospects relied on nature to bring life to art.

The Paradise Garden, in which the Virgin safely played with her child, the Unicorn Garden, where the ideally chaste young woman cradled her symbolic pet's head in her lap, the secular Love Garden in which young people got up to no good in privileged seclusion: all these late medieval pictorial fantasies relied on the notion of a safe, enclosed space within the nature of wild growth and wild beasts and men. It was not until the mid-fifteenth century that actual gardens began to be developed as amenities that deliberately expressed social and aesthetic ideas. The lay-out of plots near the house reflected the patterns of intarsia and embroidered lawns and pleached alleys offered another mirror of indoor life: strolling and conversation grounds akin to the long galleries that were becoming fashionable in great houses. Further out, a carefully contrived 'wilderness' provided a safe version of 'natural' nature. In the largest estates a yet larger zone added a walled park in the interest primarily of poacher-free hunting but in some cases extending the metaphors of the 'wilderness'. Grottoes selected from the natural world shells and crystals and stalactites. The rain-storms of nature were chastened to thin sprays that could be manipulated to drench the unwary promenader.

Statues now comforted visitors by holding up baskets of produce, or now – as with Giambologna's giant *Apennines*, made in 1579 for the park at Pratolino, outside Florence – reminded them of the gaunt

powers that lay beyond man's taming. The desire to keep raw nature
at bay was combined with an urge to play with the dangers, the variety
and the burdens of 'outside'. In 1611 a German visitor to Sir Francis
Carew's estate at Beddington noted how it constituted a microcosm
of the life beyond its walls. Coloured sculpted fish 'swam' in the basins
of its fountains; along its streams were miniature mills, and tiny ships
lay at anchor in cosy reflection of the risky world of commerce outside.

As the taste grew – where there was space and money – to push the
artifice employed on gardens further into the countryside it was natural
to take encouragement from ancient models of the civilized treatment
of an estate. The features described in the first century by Pliny the
Younger in his account of his villa in the Tuscan countryside recur
over and over again in descriptions of sixteenth-century extended gardens. He acknowledges the existence of the nearby Apennines, he takes
pleasure in his intermediate views over man-made meadows, but his
tone is that of the impresario of an outdoor theatre of amenities. On
the side of his house facing the estate is a colonnade, extended at one

Giambologna, *Allegory of the Apennines* (Villa Demidoff, Pratolino)

side into a summer dining room commanding the whole view. In front is a terrace from which a bank slopes down 'with figures of animals cut out of box facing each other on either side'. This leads to the garden proper, laid out 'oval like a racecourse . . . enclosed by a dry-stone wall which is hidden from sight by a box hedge planted in tiers'. Inside are paths, lawns and more topiary work 'and then suddenly in the midst of this ornamental scene is what looks like a piece of rural country planted there'. At one end is 'a curved dining seat of white marble . . . water gushes out through pipes from under the seat as if pressed out by the weight of people sitting there, is caught in a stone cistern and then held in a polished marble basin which is regulated by a hidden device so as to remain full without overflowing. Throughout the garden are fountains and marble chairs for the weary and everywhere can be heard the sound of running streams, the flow of which can be controlled by hand'.[19]

The Plinean garden-estate, with its emphasis on landscaping, water engineering, and the rendering of architectural forms (terrace, circus, theatre) into natural ones, was an influence primarily on Italian gardens from the mid-sixteenth century such as that of the Villa d'Este at Tivoli near Rome, which was built within the grounds of the villa of the Emperor Hadrian. But by then garden design had come to turn its most familiar and practical aspects into art. The garden of Duke Ercole d'Este's villa-palace of Belfiore just outside Ferrara was largely devoted to feeding his large household. But in a description of it in 1497 by Giovanni Sabadino degli Arienti, vegetable and herb plots and fruit trees were laid out with such 'diverse artifice' that they seemed master strokes from 'the brush of the finest of painters'.[20] Walking around on the tidy brick paths, Sabadino was put in mind now of Paradise, now of the secluded garden in which the chaste Susanna was assaulted – in the Apocryphal *Story of Susanna* – by trespassing sex-crazed old men, now of the tranquilly fecund realm of Pomona, the classical goddess of orchards. These were formidable associations to be conjured up by cherries and pears, mint and marjoram and beetroot. Sabadino was writing to flatter his patron, Ercole. Nevertheless, this new way of responding to gardens both reacted to and influenced their design.

Other, unclassical, features were added in the North, where a love of seasonal flowers was stronger than in Italy, and where the horse-cult influenced gardens made by owners who liked to ride as well as prom-enade in man-made nature. In 1517 Antonio de Beatis visited Francis

I's garden at Blois, the work of an Italian, Pacello da Mercoliano, working to French orders. 'The palace overlooks three gardens of fruit-trees and foliage, access to which is by a gallery adorned on either side with real stag's antlers set on imitation stags carved from wood and coloured quite realistically . . . The great garden is completely surrounded by alleys which are wide and long enough to ride horses down at full gallop. They have fine pergolas resting on wooden trellises . . . In the middle is a domed pavillion over a beautiful fountain.' The smaller gardens contained native and imported flowering plants and, de Beatis added, 'there are many plants and herbs for salads.'[21]

In 1575 a description by Robert Laneham of the Earl of Leicester's garden at Kenilworth combines both Italianate and French ideas of how to express the notion of a Third Nature: terrace, statuary, alleys and arbours, orchards, carefully devised plots of 'redolent plants and fragrant earbs and floourz in foorm, coller and quantitee so delicioously variaunt', fountains and concealed water-works drenching the visitor

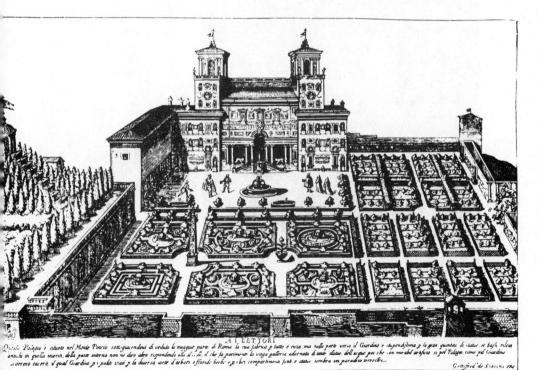

Garden of the Villa Medici, Rome, engraving, Gottefred de' Scaichi, sixteenth century

'with the wreast of a cok'. With its aviary and fish ponds, Kenilworth was a fair representative of the garden planned to be a civilized microcosm of tamed natural energies.

Summing up his impression, Laneham wrote that in spite of its lack of 'fayr rivers', Kenilworth was worthy to be called Paradise, 'yet better a great deal by the lak of so unhappy a tree'.[22] For as well as providing respite from the cares of government and business, and a safe zone of recreation for their owners' womenfolk, the great gardens instilled in their visitors a range of associations which defined the third Nature. The idea of the garden as a reference to Eden was sustained by the Gospel record of Christ appearing to Mary Magdalen in the guise of a gardener, bearing the spade with which Adam had been forced to labour when banished from a garden that had needed no tillage; it was

Hell's Mouth (Bomarzo, near Viterbo)

a theme which artists continued to illustrate throughout the sixteenth century. In this view the garden stood for redemption, the recovery of a time when natural nature itself held no taint of wildness. More commonly the associations, prompted by real and fake ruins, temples and obelisks, were with the orderly rule of Rome or with the enchanted gardens to which the heroes of late medieval chivalric romance and Renaissance epic were transported to give them respite from slaying dragons and giants and blood-crazed paynims in the world outside. Some gardens positively aimed at enchantment.

In Vincenzo Orsini's 'sacred wood' at Bomarzo, nature was left pretty well to its own devices but was filled with a static ballet of stone metaphors: a leaning house, a sphinx hard by a chapel, a dreadful Hell-Mouth with a convenient picnic table inside. This was nature tamed less by spade than by wit.

For the garden as a metaphor of orderly political rule, Shakespeare's Gardener in *Richard II* spoke to every member of the audience who had a cultivable plot of land of his own. 'Go,' he tells his assistants,

> Go, bind thou up yon dangling apricocks,
> Which, like unruly children, make their sire
> Stoop with oppression of their prodigal weight:
> Give some supportance to the bending twigs.
> Go thou, and like an executioner,
> Cut off the heads of too-fast-growing sprays,
> That look too lofty in our commonwealth:
> All must be even in our government.
> You thus employ'd, I will go root away
> The noisome weeds that without profit suck
> The soil's fertility from wholesome flowers.

To which one of his assistants asks, in one of the dramatist's most effective compressions of cloudily perceived common opinion,

> Why should we, in the compass of a pale,
> Keep law and form and due proportion,
> Showing, as in a model, our firm estate
> When our sea-walled garden, the whole land,
> Is full of weeds. . . ?[23]

For in all its guises, the Third Nature of gardened land was taken for a model of both the dreams and the reality of civility.

And while the botanists compiled and classified their lengthening lists, practical gardeners manured, hoed, pruned and grafted and brought everyday craft within the purview of natural science, helping, for instance, the satiny-textured 'Lady's Thigh' pear to grow outside its native soil around Lyon. Love, here and uniquely, combined with a scientific interest in experiment. Francis Bacon's essay *On Gardens* begins, 'God Almighty first planted a garden; and indeed it is the purest of human pleasures'; his own pleasure gives a poetic voice to the northern European response of the senses to the loosening of winter's grip. 'Because the breath of flowers,' he wrote (after giving a long catalogue of those that came to their prime in spring, summer and autumn), 'is far sweeter in the air, where it comes and goes, like the warbling of music, than in the hand, therefore nothing is more fit for that delight, than to know what be the flowers and plants that do best perfume the air . . . Those which perfume the air most delightfully, not passed by as the rest, but being trodden on and crushed, are three; that is burnet, wild thyme, and water mints. Therefore you are to set whole alleys of them, to have the pleasure when you walk or tread.'

Later in the essay, however, he becomes severe about over-subordinating nature to art: 'as for the making of knots or figures . . . they be but toys; you may see as good sights, many times, in tarts.'[24] And in his Utopian *New Atlantis* he brings into the language of the laboratory the hit-or-miss experience of practical gardeners as they grafted, propagated and tried to acclimatize the flowers, shrubs and trees that had caught their or their employers' fancy: 'we practise all conclusions of grafting and innoculating . . . we make . . . trees and flowers to come earlier or later than their seasons and to come up and bear more speedily than by their natural course they do. We make them also by art greater much than their nature, and their fruit greater and sweeter.'[25]

From the fish-ponds of medieval monasteries and the wire-meshed aviaries for pheasants and partridges that de Beatis admired at Gaillon in 1517, the garden as a cabinet version of nature had also offered in its extended parklands enclosures for deer, wild goats, rabbits and hares that may from time to time have been hunted or shot but were primarily there as exemplars of what lay outside. And, as with plants, enclosure encouraged the idea that man could collect and tinker with animal nature. Bacon imagined that New Atlantis vivisectors tried out on animals drugs and regimens to help cure humans of their ailments. Experiments were carried out to dwarf animals, or increase their size or reproductive ability. 'We find means', moreover, 'to make commixtures and copulations of various kinds, which have produced new kinds.'[26]

Here Bacon was ahead of his time. Careful breeding in practice remained restricted, as it had been in the past, to the creatures most used by the aristocracy: horses, hunting dogs and falcons. Though the cosy taste for pets, little fluffy dogs, parrots, canaries and other cagebirds, monkeys, was associated with the demand for domestic comfort and diversions in the growing number of single-family homes, older attitudes to farm animals still prevailed. An ox with a pet-name could without second thought be exposed to a terrified baiting by mastiffs, an ordeal that was supposed to make its meat more tender. Chickens were crammed into dark attics and cellars to satisfy the demand for fowl-flesh. Piglets who had been played with by children in urban streets as well as rural yards grew up to have their intestines wound out as sheaths for sausages. Because the lamp oil derived from seals and whales was more light-productive than wax candles, they were hunted far into the Arctic in one of the great sagas of marine daring. Banquets transformed the natural world into a menu: goat, deer, hedgehog, dormouse, dolphin and porpoise, peacock, gull, robin, stork and bittern. Apart from rats and cats almost everything that walked or flew could be food or, at least, culinary spectacle. Only the creatures that crawled or slithered were off-limits to the trencherman.

Just as botany came to transform the medieval herbal, the reappraisal of ancient scientific knowledge, coupled with the flow of new information from outside Europe, led to a zoological challenge to the view of the animal kingdom expressed in earlier bestiary lore. The bestiary was a compendium of information about animals, birds, fishes and a few insects that drew on biblical references and classical descriptions, often moralistically tuning them to offer lessons to man: the elephant as a model of conjugal fidelity, the spider of industry, the ermine of chastity. They were uncritically hospitable to the medieval love of the marvellous, to unicorn, mer-man and mer-woman. The chief classical authorities were Aristotle, whose aim to explore the purpose of the whole of creation led him to investigate not only man but non-rational beings in his factual *On the Animals* (which included fishes), and the Elder Pliny whose *Natural History* was as hospitable to travellers' tales as to his own observation.

Humanistic criticism from the late fifteenth century, notably the Venetian Ermolao Barbaro's massive *Corrections to Pliny* of 1493, helped to sort fact from legend and show that knowledge derived from Greek and Latin experience of the Mediterranean, Near East and North Africa did not necessarily hold good for northern Europe. And this critical strand was supported by the discovery of forms of animal life that could not have even been heard about in antiquity. The pelts of American animals and birds were brought back with written descriptions to help the artist and taxidermist. Naturalistic reconstruction became a new skill; the paintings of animals and birds from the New World by Jacopo Ligozzi in the 1580s, for instance, though imagined from skins, are astonishingly life-like thanks to his dissection of analogous indigenous creatures.

The twin stimuli – pride in revealing ancient error and a zest for absorbing fresh information – produced a new character, the naturalist. Such a one was the mid-sixteenth century Frenchman Pierre Belon, whose *History of uncommon Fish* and *Natural History of Birds* reflect his concentration on the animal life he encountered both in the wild and in markets and on seashores where fishermen landed their catch during his travels in the Near East. The Swiss Conrad Gesner's *History of Animals* – a direct challenge to Aristotle's – was unfinished at his death in 1558, but the published (and illustrated) volumes set a new standard for encyclopaedic works of natural history, and the questions he had put to his wide circle of friends within the commonwealth of learning produced books which were in effect specialized appendices to his own work. It was as a tardy response to his inquiry, for instance, that the English physician John Kay's *Of English Dogs* was published in 1575, shortly after his own death, with its realistic, if unscientific, division of the animals into social categories: the aristocratic companions of the hunt, the gentrified house-pet, the working companion of shepherd and farmer, and the servile curs who snarled in alleyways and were shut into treadmills to raise weights or to turn spits in kitchens.

There was also a new interest in comparing and illustrating the comparative anatomy of beasts and birds and man. The stimulus here was the contemporary study of human anatomy. Nonetheless, with rare exceptions, such as the Bolognese Carlo Ruini's veterinary treatise *On the Anatomy and Diseases of the Horse*, the analogies between animals and humans – blood, bones, locomotion – made it more difficult for zoology than for botany to throw off medieval preconceptions. In books and in collections of natural curiosities the legendary unicorn survived, and not only its fabled horn (actually the long spirally-twisted tooth of the Arctic narwhal); in London in 1599 Sir Walter Cope proudly showed to his visitors a unicorn's *tail*. Gesner did not reject the vestmented bishop-fish or that scaly animal with a woman's face, the Lamia; in 1607 Edward Topsell, a follower of Gesner, warned his reader to avoid it, for 'when they see a man they lay open their breasts, and by the beauty thereof, entice them to come nearer for conference, and so having them within their compasse, they devoure and kill them.'.[27]

As more readers became travellers, bestiary lore yielded ground to experience. A German who served with Spanish troops in South America from 1534 wrote of the crocodile that 'it has been said to come to life spontaneously, that the only way to kill it is to show it a mirror, when it will die from the horror of its appearance. But all this is fable and nonsense. If it were true I should be countless times dead, for I have captured and eaten more than three thousand of them.'[28] And this bluntness was paralleled by a coming to terms with the natural world, by a radical change in the craft of verbal description. The medieval mode had been to describe what was new in terms of what was already familiar, an approach still present in a laborious attempt in 1540 to report on the appearance of an armadillo. It is, wrote Roger Barlow, 'no bigger than a pig of a moneth old, and the fete the hede and the eares be like a horse, and his bodie and his head is all covered saving his eres with a shell moche like the shell of a tortuga [turtle], but it is the very proportion of an armed horse, for this shelle hangeth downe by his sides . . . moche like the lappes of a complete harneis'.[29] But by then the struggle to get words to follow the eye instead of the mind's wandering in search of inappropriate and out-of-scale comparisons was becoming out-of-date as language, like the artist's brush or pen, came to master a more direct record. Peter Martyr's description of the courtship display of a turkey (another American discovery which he saw in Spain in the 1520s) exemplifies the change, even if he was unable to resist one analogy with human behaviour. 'They preen themselves before their females', he wrote, 'and from time to time, at regular intervals, they shiver like victims of a strong fever when their teeth chatter from cold. They display the different coloured feathers about their necks, sometimes blue, sometimes green or purplish according to the move-ments of their body.'[30]

As with gardens, there was a desire to naturalize nature's extravagances. The late medieval menagerie, chiefly a repository for a city's emblematic animals, Florence's lions, the bears which were displayed both in their pit and on the battle flags of Berne, gave way for a while in the early sixteenth century to the more diverse zoo, like that of Ferrara where Titian studied the cheetahs for his *Bacchus and Ariadne*. But the problems of animal management prevented any continuity being achieved in large collections. The rhinoceros of which Dürer constructed a lumberingly powerful image from accounts that reached him in 1515 of its arrival in Lisbon, was one of the last representations of the great exotic beasts to reach Europe; as relations with Turkey and Islamic North Africa worsened, the arrival of animal gifts – Lorenzo de' Medici's camel, Pope Leo X's elephant – ceased. The royal menageries in the Tower of London and at the Louvre were kept up rather to preserve the traditional association between monarchy and noble animals than for purposes of study, and it was chiefly with his status in mind that the Elector Augustus I of Saxony founded a menagerie at Dresden in 1554. The growing interest in natural history was met, rather, by illustrated books and the establishment of cabinets of curiosities, 'treasure-chambers' where armadillo and crocodile figured among stuffed pelicans and toucans and mummified Egyptian cats, tusks and nuts and strangely shaped roots. And to what moved and grew on the land collectors added what lay beneath: crystal clusters, fossils and polished semi-precious stones.

From the mid-sixteenth century these collections of rare, valuable or merely strange objects from the natural world became common throughout western and central Europe: some the size of a parlour in the house of a lawyer or physician, others large and expensively accumulated through the agents of such collectors as successive dukes of Tuscany or the Emperor Rudolf at Prague and his cousin Ferdinand at Schloss Ambras near Innsbruck. The serious essence of this passion can be gauged by the enterprise, undertaken in the 1620s, of the scholar and occasional diplomat Cassiano dal Pozzo. Living in Rome, a city of patrons and collectors, Cassiano lacked the cash to obtain the objects he thought to be of outstanding interest. So he commissioned draughtsmen to record for him buildings and statues, the works of man, and plants, birds, animals and minerals, the works of nature. What he called his 'Paper Museum' came to comprise some five thousand sheets.

The taste for bringing the broadening knowledge of the world into a small compass, the desire, as Bacon put it, to have 'a model of the universal nature made private' at the convenient disposal of civilized

Ferrante Imperato's museum, from Ferrante Imperato, *Historia naturale* (Naples, 1599)

man whether in his garden and park or in his study, had been expressed in 1531 by Thomas Elyot in his *The Governour*.[31] He celebrated

> the pleasure . . . in one houre to beholde those realmes, cities, sees, ryvers and mountaynes that unneth [scarcely] in an olde mannes life can not be journaide and pursued; what incredible delite is taken in beholding the diversities of people, beastis, foules, fishes, trees, frutes and herbes: to knowe the sondry maners and conditions of people, and the varietie of their natures – and that in a warme studie or perler [parlour], without perill of the see or daunger of longe and painfull journayes: I can nat tell what more pleasure shulde happen to a gentil witte than to beholde in his owne house every thynge that with in all the worlde is contained.[32]

The mood had been expressed visually twenty years before in Carpaccio's portrait of the young Ligurian nobleman Francesco della Rovere.

Armoured, but without spurs, he stands in a pose that reveals his bright red hose and a paper tucked into a pocket in his codpiece. These features, and his wearing a soft cap, make him a combination figure –

a man of letters as well as of arms. He grasps his sword as if prepared to defend both the aristocratic way of life suggested by horse, hound and falcon, and the plants, birds and animals – deer, rabbit, ermine – that are also in the landscape behind him; it is a landscape safely paled in between buildings and a lake, nature made to the measure of man.

There were many obstacles to appreciating the 'natural' nature that lay beyond gardens and crops and pastures. Most obvious was the danger of venturing into mountains, penetrating forests (except in the paramilitary company of a hunting party), walking or riding too far from villages and farmsteads. Countryside crime kept pace with the interest in its wild- and plant-life; God may have created the earth, paused from his labours and seen 'that it was good', but he also permitted the first murder, when Cain struck down Abel in the real landscape outside the tamed park of Eden. This was the viewpoint adopted by Giovanni Bellini when shortly after 1500 he painted the assassination of St Peter Martyr on a country road beside which foresters turned a habitually blind eye to what was none of their business. Most educated travellers saw the landscape sidelong, as it were, from within the sanctuary of an escort or merchant convoy. Moreover, what they saw was filtered through a mental check-list derived from what they had read: classicizing poetry with its emphasis on the well-trained vine and sacred grove, imaginative medieval accounts of the Earthly Paradise, chivalric romances.

As travellers became more literate and calculating their accounts of what they saw became more artificial. For all the joyous spontaneity of his initial response to the colours and foliages of the Caribbean islands, Columbus's later descriptions gave a more calculating parallel to what he had expected to find: thus the estuary waters of the Orinoco had to flow from what his employers would recognize as the Earthly Paradise. A Spanish visitor who rode in company about the reasonably tranquil English home counties in 1554, assured his readers that 'you may be certain that there are more sights to be seen here in England than are described in any book of chivalry: country houses, river-banks, woods, forests, delicious meadows, strong and beautiful castles, and everywhere fresh springs.'[33] One of the loveliest passages in Sir Walter Raleigh's prose has to be read with the awareness that his political fortunes turned on the financial success of his contentious expedition of 1595 to Guiana. 'I never', he defensively claimed on his return,

Vittore Carpaccio,
*Francesco della Rovere in a
Landscape*, 1510 (Thyssen
Collection, Madrid)

saw a more beautiful country, nor more lively [i.e. promising] prospects,
hills so raised here and there over the valleys, the river winding into
diverse branches, the plains adjoining without bush or stubble, all fair
green grass, the ground of hard sand, easy to march on either for horse
or foot; the deer crossing in every path; the birds towards the evening
singing on every tree, with a thousand tunes; cranes and herons of white,
crimson and carnation perching on the river side; the air fresh with a
gentle easterly wind; and every stone that we stooped to pick up
promised either gold or silver by his complexion.[34]

This is an extreme example, but almost every description has to be
examined for its element of deliberate or unconscious artifice. A baffling
obstacle to understanding what people felt when they looked across
the land is the gap in our evidence between reaction in thought and

word and its subsequent record in writing. Occasionally an analogy which comes unconsciously to a writer's mind reveals an aspect of pleasure we would otherwise not have known about. Such a moment comes when an author in 1575 explains that the paths in a country house garden are 'as pleasant to walk on as a seashore when the tide is out'.[35] But almost always the reactions recorded by travellers, painters and literary men and women drop veils of cultural convention between experience and description. When to this is added the difficulty of describing the unfamiliar, and the mental selectivity that prevents a man who is searching for one thing, whether an inn, a plant or evidence of a metalliferous ore, from paying attention to the wider scene, our grasp on contemporaries' reactions to wilder nature is frustratingly restricted.

There is, surely, something disingenuous about the declaration of Konrad Gesner, botanist and zoologist, that 'I have determined for the future . . . each year to ascend a few mountains, or at least one.' He wants, he goes on, to climb 'when the vegetation is flourishing, partly to become acquainted with it, partly for the sake of bodily exercise and the delight of the Spirit. For how great the pleasure, how great, think you, are the joys of the spirit, touched as is fit it should be in wondering at the mighty mass of mountains while gazing upon their immensity and, as it were, in lifting one's head above the clouds. In some way or other the mind is overturned by the dizzying height and is caught up in contemplation of the Supreme Architect'.[36] There is a strong echo here of a famous letter that Petrarch had written as long ago as 1353. In it he described, or purported to describe, his climb of Mont Ventoux in Provence. As he rose further from the habitations of men he felt more aware that his ascent was a moral as well as a foot-sore one. And at the summit he opened a copy of the *Confessions* of St Augustine (which he happened to have brought with him) and hit on the following passage: 'And men go to admire the high mountains, the vast floods of the sea . . . and desert themselves'. For all the impressiveness of the view, Petrarch reflected that 'nothing is admirable besides the mind; compared to its greatness nothing is great.'[37] So Gesner, when he had climbed past the tintinnabulation of cow-bells in his native pastures, felt the need to offer not a careful description of nature but, as an alibi for his secular investigations, a generalized religious response to the grandeur of God's creation. When descriptions ring most true it is because the writer, while looking out towards wild nature, felt at his back the comfort of its tamed state. The hillside clovers of Pembrokeshire, wrote George Owen in 1603, so flourish that 'in the summertime the land will be covered with these flowers . . . with a claret colour mingled with white and red and will yield a most pleasant odour and smell.'[38] This was garden appreciation writ large.

The written evidence of men's response to the land that surrounded them was paralleled in paint. By the 1420s artists had already acquired the skills necessary to show long vistas of countryside, as in the river winding towards distant hills in the background of Jan van Eyck's *Madonna of the Chancellor Rolin*. Following Pliny's descriptions of the ancient Romans' interest in landscape views and Vitruvius's mention of them as suitable for the furnishing of a villa, Alberti in *c*.1452 wrote that

> our minds are cheered beyond measure by the sight of paintings depicting the delightful countryside, harbours, fishing, hunting, swimming, flowers and verdure.[39]

For Leonardo da Vinci, one of the glories of the painter was that 'if he desires valleys or wishes to discover vast tracts of land from mountain peaks and look at the sea on the horizon beyond them, it is in his power . . . In fact, whatever exists in the Universe either potentially or actually or in the imagination, he has it first in his mind and then in his hands.'[40] In spite of these skills and these claims, however, little taste for finished works devoted purely to landscape developed in the fifteenth and sixteenth century save as decorations supplementing views from garden terraces and villa windows.

Art, after all, was a disciplining, order-inducing activity, while nature was wild. An interest in mastering the rendering of natural features (the animals of Pisanello, the flowers of Botticelli, the rock-strata of Leonardo, the trees of Fra Bartolommeo and Titian) did not necessarily fuse with a feeling for nature itself in the raw. The painter of outdoor religious scenes – the Flight into Egypt, the Baptism, San Jerome in the desert, St Anthony in the wilderness – had to provide a landscape setting, but to ring true to the story this did not have to ring true to observation. And at a time of experiment in the rendering of distance by means of atmospheric colour and perspectival composition as in Italy during the second half of the fifteenth century, what lay before the eye was adjusted to the purposes of the mind's eye. Both Piero della Francesca and his contemporary Giovanni di Paolo knew the hills in the countryside around Arezzo and Siena, but the differences

between the individual shapes of the hills do not account for the contrasts that emerged when the two artists' feelings for pattern, atmosphere and colour had finished with them. Based on intense study of
natural phenomena as they were, Leonardo's landscapes, whether the
pierced grotto in the *Virgin of the Rocks* or the hazed mountainscape
that stretches, with such teasing purport, behind *Mona Lisa*, came to
his hand from his imagination. Even when a painter used a recognizable
local background, as Antonio Pollaiuolo did when he deployed the
valley of the Arno behind his *Martyrdom of St Sebastian* of *c*.1475, this
was primarily a way of showing his command of linear perspective as
a foil to the demonstration in the foreground figures of his command
of anatomy. Other Italian artists in the fifteenth century borrowed the
tree shapes and cornfields of Flemish and German landscapes rather
than interpret their own.

It was among German artists of the early sixteenth century, especially
those working, as did Dürer, Albrecht Altdorfer, Hans Baldung and
Wolf Huber, near to the hilly, forested valleys threaded by the Danube,
that an unrestrained empathy with the landscape first declared itself.
They accepted the wild, jagged-outlined, lonely features of the countryside with an impulse that was not so tamed by notions of aesthetic
decorum as in the South. Altdorfer's *St George* is almost lost in the
forest where he comes upon the dragon.

Though there are references to human habitation in Altdorfer's *Landscape with a Footbridge* – the bridge itself, the fortified house it leads to,
the far-off village among the trees – there are no people, no allusion
to a narrative; the subject is the scene itself. Here, as in Dürer's series
of water-colour scenes recording what he saw when he travelled back
from Italy and to the Netherlands, nature is put straight-forwardly
before the viewer.

This degree of rapport was both localized and short-lived. And Altdorfer's paintings were exceptional; for the most part this response to
landscape was expressed in drawings and in the backgrounds of prints.
By the 1530s, under Italian influence, landscape in Germany came to
be seen as little more than a useful accessory to the narrative painting
which demonstrated an artist's most fashionable skills in his own and
his patron's eyes: the expressive rendering of the human figure and
an overall compositional decorum. Yet before the Germanic impulse
accepted this teaching, it had crossed the Alps, chiefly in the form of
engravings and woodcuts. The collector Sabba da Castiglione recalled
in his *Memoirs* (completed and first published in 1545–6) his purchase

as a young man of 'a print by Albrecht Dürer . . . which had recently
arrived from Germany. With delight and great pleasure I admired and
considered the figures, animals, perspectives, houses, distant views and
landscapes'.[41] But as in southern Germany, the new dominance of naturalistic landscape was brief and local. It mainly affected north Italian
artists in the second and third decades of the sixteenth century, and it
produced not so much a record of nature in the raw as an idea: that of
a soothing and tranquil out-of-doors.

In the countryside of Giorgione, Titian and Palma Vecchio there
were common elements. Distant towns or farmsteads, a well-made

Albrecht Altdorfer, *Landscape with a Footbridge*, 1518–20 (National
Gallery, London)

Titian, *Fête Châmpetre*, *c.*1510 (Musée du Louvre, Paris)

bridge (unlike Altdorfer's crude planks) a carved well-head: all indicate that civility is just around the corner in case of need. Commonly the pictured nature-lovers brought with them threads that connected them to urban life: the strings of lutes and viols, counterpoint to the less soothing 'natural' sounds of rustic pipes. And because by venturing even thus far the protagonists of these scenes were entering the rough world of rural occupations, one representative of these was chosen to meet them there, the shepherd, the acceptable face of the peasantry, a figure who did not dig, plough, prune, make horseshoes, sweat or intrude. The shepherd gently led his flock, conversed in low tones with passers-by, or slept. He came into Arcadia not from life but from literature.

Though it was then that the word landscape (*paesaggio*) first came into use to describe this type of picture, it meant no more than a painting in which landscape played an unusually important role. Thus, in a famous case, Giorgione's *Tempest* of *c.*1508 was described in 1530 as a *paesaggio* in spite of the presence of three human figures, a line of buildings defining the presence of a sizeable town and relics of earlier, classical occupation of the site. At the mid-century a north Italian painter, Girolamo Muziano, who had tried establishing himself with landscapes as a self-sufficient genre, gave them up and sought respectability and profit by turning to figure subjects. However, visiting a Venetian patrician's villa at the same time, Anton Francesco Doni described 'a stupendous large room, in which everything is a pleasure . . . easel-paintings by Titian; wall paintings of landscapes by good Flemish masters, marvellously pretty'.[42]

Indeed, overlapping with the German and Italian generation of artists, who expressed a changed attitude to the countryside, was a development in the Low Countries that outlasted both of them. Departing from the carefully realized background to religious subjects that was a local tradition, painters raised their view-points under the influence of cartographic and topographical bird's-eye depictions of tracts of countryside to cover vistas so extensive as practically to absorb their ostensible subjects – Moses and the Burning Bush, St John preaching, Christ carrying the Cross. For some this led to the specialized 'marvellously pretty' pictures that became part of the furnishings of European houses. For others the lofty view-point became a religiously motivated point of view: an invitation to the observer to brood on a segment of the earth's surface as standing for the World Landscape that God had created and in which minuscule man had to justify his role. Naturalism here had to adjust to symbols: the placid meadow, the wild forest, the threatening mountain range, the monitory roar of a cataract. Such visionary landscapes, first consistently employed by Joachim Patinier before his death in 1524, and kept alive until the end of the century by such artists as Gillis Mostaert, aroused the Italianizing streak in Karel van Mander's history of Netherlandish art of 1604. Nature, in his view, whether realistic or symbolic, should be kept in its place.

Referring to Breughel, perhaps especially to his *Conversion of Saul* of 1567, where the protagonist is almost lost in the tramp of his army through a high rocky defile, Van Mander sourly remarked that the artist 'in passing the Alps' in his journey to Italy, 'swallowed the mountains and crags to vomit them up on his return on his canvases and panels'.[43]

Coming from a man who was a painter himself, this remark emphasizes the gap between artists' technical ability to record nature and the preference both of art theory and of patrons' taste to subordinate it to mood or symbol. For while many of those who commissioned paintings had travelled widely, the growing emphasis on civility as a taming, urban-based process, led them to prefer views of nature as it had been reclaimed from its savagery. Even the pleasurable activities of music and love-making that had been placed in a rural setting were brought by 1600 within the walls of a carefully planned garden. Landscape, therefore, except in views commissioned by property-owners, either shrank back into its pre-1450 status as background or reflected a subjective motive. St Matthew's account of how the devil takes Christ up to 'an exceeding high mountain and sheweth him all the kingdoms of the world' parallels the Italian poet Veronica Gambara's reference to 'hidden, reverend and holy groves, and solitary ways', where 'weeping, I have, times over, told my woes'.[44] Cabinets of natural curiosities may have been bursting at the seams, a tulip bulb may have cost as much as – in some cases even more than – a picture, but a reminder of the land whence they came, abandonedly stretched out, unallegorized and uncensored remained difficult to accept.

Imaginative literature was subject to the same restrictions. The idea that country life was more carefree and innocent than that of town or castle or court had been touched on in chivalric writing. The poet Duke René of Anjou, deposed from the throne of Naples in 1442, fell in naturally with it:

> I saw a Sicilian king
> Into a shepherd turn,
> And saw his gentle wife
> Take up the same occupation;
> Carrying the shepherd's pouch,
> The shepherd's crook and hat,
> Dwelling upon the heath
> Near to their flock of sheep.[45]

And as writers came to be more confident of catching the range and tone and intention in classical writing about rural life – the naturalism of Theocritus, Virgil's idealizing *Eclogues*, the acerbic melancholy of Horace's exposure of the ills of over-civilization – praise of the pastoral life became more deliberate. Not long after the wars of Italy began in 1494, Sannazaro, picking the word from Virgil, gave a name to what was rapidly becoming a genre with his *Arcadia* of 1504 with its delicate evocation of a Golden Age of good manners: decorous love play,

Pieter Breughel the Elder, *The Conversion of Saul*, 1567 (Kunsthistorisches Museum, Vienna)

restrained music, uncomplicated acts of piety towards the rural gods. And as wars continued, social tensions increased and moral restrictions became intensified, the yearning for Arcadia led to the production of poems, plays, masques, novels (and, as in *Don Quixote*, interludes in novels) that transposed the non-materialistic concerns of civilized men and women into a carefree zone where nymphs, satyrs, shepherds and shepherdesses could add colour to, at times share, the debates about love and happiness among their betters.

As in painting, literary Arcadia reflected civility: the nearness of the off-stage town, the sophistication of the visitors, the nice sense of social distance from the natives. It is easy to mock. Indeed, it was mocked by Angelo Beolco in his play *La Pastoral* as early as 1520, when the peasant Ruzzante cannot make head or tail of what an Arcadianized shepherd says. But as a metaphor of escape for those who found the threats to civility troubling or its internal controls burdensome, its appeal was strong, and backed by its printed classical prototypes, its charm lasted longer than the pastoral moment in art. Nevertheless, if it led to the Arden of *As You Like It*, or the captivating Perdita of *A Winter's Tale*, it also threw up fake sentimentalities. The 'fair and happy milkmaid' of Sir Thomas Overbury's *Characters* (1616) was intended as a paragon of artlessness to shame city ladies. She uses no 'face-physic', 'her dreams are so chaste that she dare tell them'. But when he refers to the spinning wheel, over which real countrywomen were forced to spend late hours to keep hunger at bay, as 'her merry wheel', the idyll becomes as false as Marie Antoinette's milk pails at Versailles.[46]

Poetry may have offered its invitations; Marlowe's shepherd wooer pleaded:

> Come live with me and be my love,
> And we will all the pleasures prove
> That hills and valleys, dales and fields,
> Woods or steepy mountains yields.[47]

But almost no one who thought themselves civilized had any positive feelings about an actual steepy mountain, or cared to penetrate far into a real wood. Nature imagery, as in Marlowe's erotic symbolism, became richer and more habitual. But save for the colonist or the natural scientist, 'Nature', though explored and exploited as never before, remained within calling distance of a garden or town wall.

THE BODY

Within man's concern for his place in nature, of far more importance than woods and mountains and birds and beasts was the colour of his urine and the texture of his faeces. For those who had survived the ailments of infancy – half to two-thirds of all births – survival depended on avoiding external wounds and infectious diseases, and on preserving from day to day the natural balance of the 'humours', hot and dry, cold and moist, generated by the juices and vapours spreading through their bodies from what they ate. If these were co-operating all would be well. If one was slightly predominant it could affect personality: too much absorption of what was dry made a man choleric, too much undissipated moistness predisposed him to melancholy. If his system radically lost control of the blending process, he became physically ill, and if medication and regimen did not reassert it he died. These humours spread through the veins and arteries so well known to butchers and housewives, to the noble heart and the directing brain;

but after mulching in the stomach, their combined routeing point was the liver, and as there were no diagnosable exudations from the first two, it was on the liver's refuse pits, bowel and bladder, that a diagnosis of imbalance depended.

In Switzerland and Germany, where chronicle illuminations and prints accepted the facts of ordinary life, there are many details of men defecating. They are peasants or common soldiers. But the concern for bodily functions was not restricted to them. In the *De Civilitate*, written for boys of good family, Erasmus remarked that 'to repress the need to urinate is injurious to health; but propriety requires that it be done in private. There are some who lay down the rule that a boy should refrain from breaking wind by constricting his buttocks. But it is no part of good manners to bring illness upon yourself while striving to appear polite. If you may withdraw, do it in private. But if not . . . cover the sound with a cough . . ., it is more dangerous to refrain from breaking wind than it is to constrict the bowels.'[48] By the late fifteenth century doctors had come to discriminate between twenty varieties of colour and density in urine, and the same number for faeces. No wonder that private individuals let alone physicians in hospitals and spas, saw nature largely in terms of the chamberpot. This frequent reminder of the body's contents was reinforced by the habitual recourse to bleeding as a palliative for real or imagined ills. 'I ask you to send me a blood-letting lancet,' wrote a student at the University of Altdorf (near Nuremberg) to his mother in 1578; 'the other students have their own special lancets' so that they do not have to submit at the baths to those 'used to bleed the peasants and everyone else'.[49]

An understanding of the physiology of the human body and the consequential basic approach to diagnosing and curing its ailments was derived with little change from the medical knowledge of classical antiquity. The writings by, or associated with, the Greek physician Hippocrates who was born in 460 BC, contained a formidable range of case studies dealing with the progress of a disease and its treatment by medicine or instrument. The enduring influence of the Hippocratic Corpus was not only based on clinical observations but on its common-sense and humanity. 'Weariness without cause indicates disease,' rang true to doctors in all subsequent ages. All but avaricious charlatans agreed with its emphasis on 'the healing power of nature'. It was within the Corpus that lay the founding document of medical ethics, the Hippocratic Oath.

'The regimen I shall adopt', it ran in part,

shall be for the benefit of the patients according to my ability and judgement, and not for their hurt or any wrong. I will give no deadly drug
to any, though it be asked of me, nor will I counsel such, and especially
I will not aid a woman to procure abortion. Whatsoever house I enter,
there will I go for the benefit of the sick, refraining from all wrongdoing
or corruption, and especially from any act of seduction, of male or
female, of bond or free. Whatsoever things I see or hear concerning the
life of men in my attendance on the sick or even apart therefrom, which
ought not to be noised abroad, I will keep silence thereon, counting such
things to be sacred secrets.[50]

As with so much of ancient Greek learning, the Hippocratic writings
were taken up by the Romans and the Arabic scholars of the eastern
and southern Mediterranean world, and from both sources entered the
mainstream of medical teaching in the universities of medieval Europe.
The same was true of the medical writings of the inescapable Aristotle,
whose dissections of the uterus (in animals) and scrutiny of the growth
of chicks within the egg helped to convince him that an embryo owed
its total form to the mother from the moment of conception, the contribution of the male sperm being probably to jolt the generative process
into starting and certainly to add, in a non-material manner, the soul.
It was theoretically possible, in this view, for conception to take place
without intercourse and the soul to be added by divine intervention.
This explanation of Virgin Birth helped Christian Europe to accept
Aristotelian anatomy just as the church's ethical stance towards the
sacredness of life helped in the absorption of Hippocratic teaching.

Though the humanistic relish for reappraising ancient authors
brought a new prominence to both, it was above all Galen, a Greek of
the second century by birth who served successive Roman emperors,
who had the most influence on Renaissance medical debate and practice.
The volume of his surviving works was enormous. He was one of
those men whose intellectual tediousness wins acclaim because of the
importance of his subject. And he, too, was readily assimilable into a
Christian environment. Whether describing his dissection of an elephant's trunk or of a mollusc, or expatiating on the wonderful convenience of a sweat-deflecting eyebrow or the grasp of a hand, he
celebrated Aristotle's dictum that nature made nothing in vain. How
can man so overpraise the sculptor, he asks, when he can only copy
nature and never rival the marvel of its design not only of the outside
but the inner parts of man and beast? And while admiring them, how

can man not look up from the ignoble earth and its creatures to the
bodies of the heavens, sun, moon and stars? 'It is reasonable to suppose
that the intelligence dwelling in them is as much better and more perfect
than that in earthly bodies as their bodily substance is the purer'. The
study of physiology, he concludes, 'is serviceable not only for the
physician, but much more so for the philosopher who is eager to gain
an understanding of the whole of nature. And I think that all men of
whatever nation or degree who honour the gods should be initiated
into this work'.[51]

In the fifteenth and sixteenth centuries doctors had access to the rich
endowment of their subject by ancient practice and speculation, added
to by later accessions to the medical canon such as the works of the
eleventh-century Persian Avicenna, and the treatise on anatomy of 1316
by the Italian Mondino di Luzzi, which was based – unusually – on
the dissection of human subjects. This accumulation of learning was,
however, more relevant to the status of doctors than to their ability to
cure. Paracelsus, around 1530, was sufficiently influenced by Hippocrates to produce an oath of his own 'to love the sick, each and all of
them, more than if my own body were at stake' and not 'to administer
any medication without understanding, nor to collect any money without earning it'.[52] But he also stated that 'the physician does not learn
everything he must know and master at high colleges alone; from time
to time he must consult old women, gypsies, magicians, wayfarers
and all manner of peasant folk.'[53] Girolamo Cardano, very much the
self-consciously intellectual physician, warned against learned prescriptions that were often written purely in the interest of monetary gain.
Typical of the mood which accompanied the acceptance of the classical-
medieval canon was his advice to avoid having recourse to doctors by
moderating indulgence in food and sex, and to avoiding stress by getting plenty of sleep, mixing with cheerful company, and cultivating an
optimistic frame of mind. But equally typical was his pronouncement in
a work of 1550 that 'when a woman menstruates she will tarnish a
metallic mirror . . . and she will damage the crops through which she
walks.'[54] Both men, the Swiss and the Italian, drew on a common
heritage. Finding it wanting as pronounced from academic lecterns,
they reflected the pseudo-medical lore of the uninstructed. And both,
together with others equally impatient with the gap between knowledge and cure, looked outside the apparent rationalism of the Graeco-
Roman case study and the traditional *materia medica*.

In the 1570s, in his old age, Cardano found himself dwelling on the popular myth of the Fountain of Youth, 'a fountain of water much more precious than wine, by drinking from which anyone who is aged becomes young' – and healthy.[55] The yearning to recover the limberness of young man- and womanhood had made representations of the Fountain a popular subject in fifteenth century art.

It was one of the features looked for by the explorers of new lands. By Cardano's time, indeed, its location had been pinned down to somewhere in Florida. This was to invoke magic. But magic was also a subject to pursue soberly. While the human body was there to be undressed, palpated, bled, cut into, poulticed and medicated, it was also, as Galen had implied, invisibly linked to the rest of the natural world by its chemical composition and the physical principles that theoretically connected the jerk in a muscle to a comet's trail across the heavens. So physicians turned to astrologers' theories connecting the 'complexion' of the planets at any given moment with the skin and pulse of a patient, to aid their diagnosis. And for medication they turned to the acids, alembics and furnaces of alchemists, who experimented with the distillation into quintessences of vegetable and metallic substances and the rendering down of poisons into non-toxic prophylactics.

For all the richness of its endowment with the 'hard' knowledge derived from two millennia of experience, the Renaissance was unprecedented in its serious pursuit of alternative medicine. Even if this contributed little to the saving of lives, it was a sign of renewed vitality within the profession. In only two respects was there an advance which can be called positive. One, whose real gains still lay in the future, was a more pragmatic academic approach to human anatomy. The other was preventive medicine where the advance was due not just to doctors but the decision of public authorities and a changing approach to the hygienic decencies of civilized life.

Anatomical dissections, carried out by the humbler surgeons under the direction of a presiding physician, from being visual demonstrations of information included in classical texts, became more questioning. The valvular system of the heart, the female oviducts (named the Fallopian tubes after their discoverer, Gabriele Falloppio): these discoveries were advances in a knowledge of the workings of the body. The most impressive monument to sixteenth-century anatomy is the publication at Basel in 1543 of Vesalius's *On the Fabric of the human Body*. Though its text remained conservative, following Galenic suggestions, for instance, about the non–circulatory movement of the blood, its illustra-

The Fountain of Youth, anon., fresco (Castello, Manta)

tions set a new standard of accuracy for published depictions of the flayed and dissected parts of the body. Vesalius originated from Brussels and Louvain, but his intellectual formation owed much to the masters at Paris under whom he studied. However, it was as lecturer in surgery at Padua that he, and his subject, reached a wider audience. His dissections became public events.

This interest was not peculiar to Padua. In the medical faculty at Montpellier the public were admitted – the women masked when the subject was a male – to demonstrations. The dissection of a dead body became a salon version of the public spectacle of the dismemberment of a live criminal, adding a pornographic leer to a sense of wonder at the body's intricate composition and of hope that fresh investigation would lead to new cures. The illustrations of the *De Fabrica* owed something, too, to artists' prior interest in anatomy as a way of advancing their own craft. From Antonio Pollaiuolo's dissections of the 1470s and Leonardo's anatomical drawings of the early sixteenth century – unpublished at the time but never surpassed for the working in them of mind and eye and knife together – to the private, preparatory studies

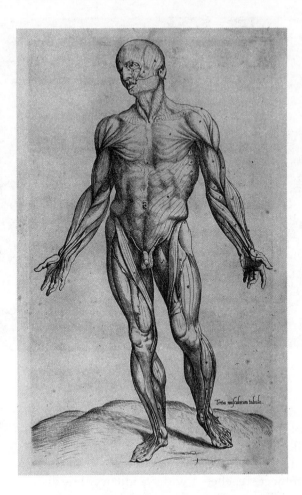

Human muscles, from
Andreas Vesalius, *De humani
corporis fabrica*, Basel, 1543
(Newberry Library, Chicago)

from dissections of Bronzino and Alessandro Allori, and the *ecorché*,
flayed-body statuettes of the mid- and late sixteenth century, the artist's
ability to describe first anticipated and then kept pace with the anatomist's wish to display. Artists' guilds were commonly named after
St Luke, because of the tradition that he had painted the Virgin. In the
1560s, Maerten van Heemskerck combined this theme with St Paul's
description of him as a physician. There is a urinal in the foreground,
in front of the Virgin. In a niche above her are classical medical texts.
As he paints, the evangelist artist's gaze can take in not only the Virgin
and Child but an open volume of anatomical drawings, the inspiration
of his hand just as she is of his faith. But just as anatomically inclined
artists produced no better likenesses of the face or body than did those

who were content to study surfaces, the virtuosity of the dissection room did little to teach doctors how to treat ailments, even where to apply a tourniquet to a spouting artery; it was not until 1628 that the circulation of the blood was explained by William Harvey.

All the same, the demand for dead bodies grew. Medical faculties applied for those of recently executed criminals. Keen medical students risked both secular and ecclesiastical punishment by digging up by night the corpses of innocent citizens who had been buried during the day. Genuine inquiry became confused with the spirit in which books are stolen to help prepare for an exam.

Classical and medieval anatomy, out of deference to religious notions about the sanctity of the human body, had been chiefly restricted to animals; dogs, pigs and, when available, North African apes. It was for this reason that Galen had gone astray, over-emphasizing the resemblance between the organs, and thus the metabolism, of animals and men. And, in turn, even Leonardo da Vinci and Vesalius described the right kidney in humans as being higher than the left, as it was in animals and in Galen. All the same, anatomical studies represented a bold, secularizing attempt to understand Adam dispassionately from the inside out. Comparative anatomy, comparing brute to man, continued, though not so much in the interest of the quest for health as in sustaining the civilized emphasis on man's essential difference from the rest of the animal kingdom. Vesalius celebrated this 'blessed age' which permitted the cleansing of classical medical knowledge from its own and medieval misapprehensions. But glancing from cadaver to ancient text, he still deferred to what he felt he ought to see as well as what he actually did see. Writing of the septum, the membrane separating the ventricles of the heart, in the revised edition (1555) of his great work, he remained cautious.

> In considering the structure of the heart and the use of its parts, I bring my words for the most part into agreement with the teaching of Galen; not because I think these on every point in harmony with the truth, but because . . . I still distrust myself. Not long ago I would not have dared to diverge a hair's breadth from Galen's opinion. But the septum is as thick, dense and compact as the rest of the heart. I do not, therefore, see how even the smallest particle can be transferred from the right to the left ventricle through it. When these and other facts are considered, many doubtful matters arise concerning the blood-vessels.[56]

In the anatomy theatre the body was treated as a text to be explicated. Little positive advantage extended from it to the treatment of disease or the techniques of operation amputation, trepanning, surgically assisted births, the treatment of hernias. And the knife was in any case helpless to explain, let alone cure, the age's great killers, infectious diseases.

Habituation to endemic infections had rendered Europeans less vulnerable to their own infectious and contagious diseases than were the peoples they encountered overseas. Because European contacts with Africa and Asia were mainly in the form of coastal settlements, the damage caused to the native populations by the unfamiliar germs they brought with them was limited. In colonized America the case was different. The Carib population of the West Indies was almost entirely wiped out. The native population of Mexico was reduced from about eleven million to a mere two million by 1600. It is probable that a similar fate overcame the indigenous population of Peru. These catastrophes far exceeded the epidemic casualties in Europe caused by virulently infectious forms of influenza, smallpox, typhus and various forms of dysentery, including the luridly termed 'bloody flux', though it is unlikely that any area in Europe was free from one or another of these in any period of five years. What prompted the greatest alarm and a heightened level of practical precaution was plague.

Announcing itself with especial dreadfulness through a blackish abscess in the groin or armpit or the palm of the hand, and followed with a unique swiftness by death, this was the Black Death which had cut back the population of Europe by over one third on its appearance in 1349. From then on plague remained endemic. It could splutter as well as rage. In 1484 a teacher in Deventer wrote to an acquaintance with some casualness, 'you ask how my school is doing. Well, it is full again now; but in summer the numbers rather fell off. The plague, which killed twenty of the boys, drove many others away, and doubtless kept some from coming to us at all.'[57] Scaliger in 1604 told his friend Isaac Casaubon in Paris that plague had been endemic in Leiden for the past two years. 'Yet though it carries off many every day, the city seems no less populous. Indeed, it appears to me that the more people die, the greater are the numbers in the city. The University has a very large attendance, and the dreadful carnage keeps none away. All around me stand the houses of mourning; I am separated from death only by the thickness of the walls. Amid these woes I await the will of the god of mercy, who from my boyhood even to this day has shielded me from great perils.'[58]

Anon., *The Anatomy Lesson*, after 1581 (Wellcome Trustees, Hunterian Museum, Glasgow)

But these woes were frequently on a scale that called for more positive reactions than passive moral hardihood. Ten per cent of the English population perished in 1471. In the summer of 1527 the average number of deaths was five hundred a day. In Venice Palladio's Redentore celebrates the city's redeeming by God from a plague visitation that had reduced the population by twenty-seven per cent. Baldassare Longhena's church of the Salute rose from the more than one million piles driven into the bank of the Grand Canal to thank Mary the Saviour for the city's release from the still more destructive epidemic of 1630 that had affected the whole of northern Italy. Four years later one ninth of the population of Amsterdam died. It has been noted as a curiosity that 'there is no reliable evidence of plague anywhere in England between 1616 and 1624.'[59] Wherever images of saints were allowed artists turned out paintings showing St Sebastian; the arrows shot at him, which he survived, were identified with the assaults of plague (later he acquired martyrdom through the less aesthetically pleasing means of being clubbed to death). In Italy there was a flourishing cult of St Roch (San Rocco), who caught the plague but recovered and subsequently devoted his life to caring for its victims.

Recourse to fatalism of faith was understandable enough. It was not realized until the nineteenth century that bubonic plague was communicated by the fleas carried by black rats that became domesticated after being brought into Europe in ships trading with the Levant in the fourteenth century. Meanwhile, there was no logical explanation for its existence, or for its erratic incidence which depended on the breeding habits of rats and the movements of men – between houses, between town and village – carrying their fleas. But while populace and preachers saw plague as punishment for sin like other divine punishments, crop failures and wars, and while physicians discussed whether it was contagious, spread by touch, or an infection, spread by spittle, breath or even glance, or was spontaneously generated by freak weather conditions, the only answer appeared to be, to isolate the sick or suspect from those who were well. There was a precedent. Following the Old Testament injunctions of Leviticus's pronouncement that the leper 'is unclean: he shall dwell alone; without the camp shall his habitation be, all his clothes shall be burnt in the fire', by isolating the sufferer, leprosy during the later Middle Ages had been caused practically to disappear. In 1490 Pope Innocent VIII dissolved the Order of Lazarites because the need for the care of lepers for which they had been founded had come to an end. Similar precautions had been adopted during the Black Death, but it was not until the renewed gravity of outbursts of plague from the 1470s that municipal and governmental authorities gave *ad hoc* precautions the force of edicts binding on populations as a whole. Foreign vessels were kept at anchor. Suspect travellers were either turned back by guards posted fifteen or twenty miles from towns or forced to stay in specially constructed hospitals for forty days, the *quarantina* that gave the word quarantine its currency, to see whether the characteristic symptoms developed. In towns the clothes of victims were burned. Those suspected of infection were made to wear a white armband or to carry a whitened stick to warn others not to approach them while they attended to essential business. Markets were closed, church festivals cancelled. Streets were cordoned off, or individual houses barred with planks, their inhabitants, if administration was effective, fed with food poked through the windows; in 1593 a London parish clerk recorded the burial of a man who 'died of grief, being shut up in his house this sickness time'.[60]

Applied with varying degrees of rigour in different parts of Europe, these regulations represented an unprecedented mobilization of legal and human resources to combat disease. They took their own toll among physicians, the members of religious charitable organizations who visited and nursed sufferers, the porters who carried away and buried the dead. They were flouted by those who could afford to suborn frontier and gate-guards to let them pass. They did something to check the spread of the disease from infected areas, very little to control its course within them. There were those who thought it not only useless but sacrilegious to attempt to flout the just indignation of God. All the same doctors, even if they were wrong, had gained a secular point; men could, and should strike back at their scourges.

Plague, too, had a role in tautening the division between those who did and did not represent civility. With food supplies restricted and the law and order agencies diverted to other tasks, civic authorities organized food doles to head off potential looters, and by so doing further pin-pointed the men and women who were a social danger. And coinciding with the identification of good manners with personal cleanliness, this helped the well-off to see the unwashed as a health danger as well. While plague spared neither rich nor poor, the latter proportionately provided the greatest number of victims. Unlike the house rat, which climbed everywhere, the black rat preferred cellars and drains and foraged there or at ground level. Its fleas seldom climbed the social ladder of multi-storey houses. Drainage schemes and street cleansing were concentrated in civic centres rather than in the suburban clusters of hovels where immigrants perched while looking for employment, even though all of them were burrowed by alleys where garbage and human wastes accumulated. The well-off changed their clothing and bed-linen more frequently, used soap, had servants to heat and carry water for bathing, had houses in the country to escape to when plague first announced itself. While this basis was not understood, the facts seemed to speak for themselves: in their threateningly growing numbers, it was the poor who were the contaminators. To help meet their needs with charitable gifts of money and food and medical care, therefore, was not only a sincere Christian duty but yet another precaution. The Florentine government sponsored the confraternity of the Misericordia as an act of piety, and because the brothers, by tending and feeding the sick in their own homes, dissuaded them from coming into the streets to beg.

A disease that did strike all without distinction was the new, uniquely virulent form of sexual infection, syphilis. It was first noticed in 1494 among the French troops then occupying the Kingdom of Naples, whither it had most probably been brought by sailors who had been in contact with prostitutes visited by those who had been on Columbus's first voyage to the West Indies. Syphilis spread with the army's return across the Alps in 1495 and its disbandment. In 1496 its symptoms were reported in Switzerland, Germany and Holland. Quarantine precautions were ordered in France and Scotland in 1497. By 1499 it had passed east of Prague. Dürer, in a woodcut of 1496, illustrated the sores that were an early symptom.

In c.1517, in a powerful drawing, the Swiss artist Niklaus Manuel showed death, wearing the remnants of a soldier's costume, fingering the genitals of a young woman. As time passed and allowed the physical malformations of the tertiary phase of the disease to become familiar, their likeness to those of leprosy added terror; in an anonymous German

Niklaus Manuel, *Death and the Young Woman*, drawing, c.1517 (Kupferstichkabinett, Kunstmuseum, Basel)

Anon., *St Anthony and the
Syphilitics*
(Museum für Kunstgeschichte,
Lübeck)

painting of *c*.1520 a male and female victim with grossly distorted faces
are being brought to St Anthony by the Magdalen to intercede for his
protection, while behind him forms up a small queue of ashamed but
not yet symptom–revealing young women.

There was, nonetheless, no panic. It was realized that this was no
scourge–like epidemic; to risk contracting syphilis was voluntary, like
challenging a man to a duel or breaking into a house to steal. There
was much gossip about its victims: leading political and learned men,

Pope Julius II himself. The belief that its origin lay in the New, unchristian, World became fairly general by the 1530s. There was also the suggestion, trailed with a what-do-you-expect venom, that its progress followed the diaspora of the Jews after their expulsion from Spain in 1492. There was much displacement of responsibility: to Italians it was either the Spanish Disease or – more popularly – the French Disease, to the French it was the Pox of Naples, to the Turks it was the Christian Disease. The initial quarantining of suspect sufferers was soon relaxed. By the mid-sixteenth century it was realized that early manifestation could be checked by medication (including the internal use of mercury) and that it was seldom that the disease advanced to its final mutilations and death. There was some attempt to tighten the medical inspection of brothels; victims were admitted into the charitable hospitals for 'incurables'. But on the whole reactions to the new phenomenon were phlegmatic.

In a similar spirit, painful ailments, hernias, arthritis, gallstones, gout (a generic term for swollen joints) were dreaded but seen as well-nigh inevitable. 'I have had a long life', Erasmus wrote to a friend in 1535, when he was sixty-nine, 'counting in years; but were I to calculate the time wrestling with fever, the stone and the gout, I have not lived long.'[61] More perturbing was the incalculability of fevers whose rages between sweat and chill, while appearing to confirm the theory of the humours, challenged the assumption that their balance could be restored before it was too late.

But medicine remained a conservative profession, responding as much to its university-based syllabus and licensing system as to the popular clamour for cures. Respectability involved re-establishing contact with classical knowledge rather than extending it. There was, for instance, an initial reluctance to admit that syphilis was a new disease. Though not described by the ancients, Niccolò Leoniceno wrote in 1497, it must have been known to them, for 'humanity has the same nature, is born under the same sky, grows up under the same stars.' So 'I must conclude that we have always been subjected to the same illnesses, and I absolutely cannot believe that this illness is born suddenly only now and has infected only our epoch and none of the preceding.'[62] It was partly to protect the reputation of the ancients that there came to be a general acceptance that syphilis had been generated in lands that had been unknown to them. Galen's texts were enshrined in university syllabuses, and the profession closed ranks about them. In the opinion of the Galenists of Paris, Montpellier, where anti-Galenist views were treated with cautious respect, was 'a stinking bog of ignorance and imposture'.[63]

Loyalty to received ancient knowledge concerning the structure and health of the body was strengthened by the alertness of both revived Catholicism and the maturing orthodoxies of the Lutheran and Calvinist faiths to the dangers of heresy, of breaking with authority in order to find personal solution. The defence of Galen and Hippocrates was non-sectarian. But from the College of Physicians in Protestant London to Vesalius's caution in Catholic Padua, the emphasis was on toeing the line; between 1490 and 1598 there were no fewer than six hundred and sixty editions of works by Galen. The direct attacks on him came from radicals like Cornelius Agrippa who were enraged by the pretensions of classicizing physicians or who, like Paracelsus, saw nature as a better teacher, and from a few moderate eirenists like Montaigne who distrusted dogma whether religious or scientific. Moreover, even at reasonably tolerant Montpellier the medical faculty conservatively guarded its rights. 'If an unlicensed doctor is found, or a hawker of ointments', wrote Thomas Platter, recalling his student days there, 'the doctors and the students have the right without further ado to set him backwards on an ass' – symbol of the World Turned Upside-Down – 'with the tail in his hands for a bridle, and to drive him round the town; which delights the populace, who pelt the fellow with mud and rubbish until he is filthy from head to foot. We caught one of these men on the 19th of December 1595. We shut him up in the anatomy theatre while we went to find an ass. His wife ran everywhere, crying out that we were going to dissect her husband alive, and the district was so aroused to compassion that he was taken from us by force.'[64]

Academic medicine took the lead in anatomy, cautiously adding observational marginalia to the Galenic texts that would in the seventeenth century go far towards replacing them. Meanwhile practical advances in operative techniques and medication remained the province of working doctors and the apothecaries who were consulted in the first instance about common ailments: catarrh, ringworm, sprains, cataract, infected cuts and sores. Though the old prejudice against male doctors supervising childbirth persisted, the execution in 1522 of a Hamburg physician for dressing as a woman to gain experience of what happened during delivery was exceptional; by then the taboo had been virtually lifted by books calling attention to the negligence and ignorance of midwives. Much was learned about the treatment of wounds and amputated limbs from the new carnage caused by bullets and cannon-balls:

both Paracelsus and Paré served as army surgeons. Paré described an early experience in the field when he ran out of boiling oil to cauterize gunshot wounds as was the received practice. Embarrassedly he dressed the remaining wounds with a cold salve. Finding next morning that the last patients were in a better state than the first, 'I resolved never so cruelly to burn poor wounded men.'[65] And printing enabled such experience to be widely known and compared with the many popularized versions of Galenic orthodoxy. It was a sign of changing times when a French midwife, Louise Bourgeois, published in 1608 a book both defending her profession against contemporary denigration and criticizing Galen's misleading advice.

All the same, the gap between medical knowledge and cure was hardly narrowed and this gap prolonged the vitality of the old remedies against the advances of the new medicine. Save by hypochondriacs of means, doctors were turned to as a last resort; in any case they seldom practised outside towns or armies (few ships carried a doctor as well as a barber, whose trade included bleeding and the care of wounds). Most people sought relief through local knowledge of the properties of plants and herbs. The traditional emphasis in herbals on the medicinal properties of plants was echoed in cookery books. An English work of the mid-fifteenth century claimed to be the joint work both of 'mayster cokys' and 'maysters of fysyke'. The book of recipes by the Lombard humanist Platina, published c.1474, started with a section on the maintenance of health by a sensible diet. Later, after giving a description of salad dressing ('salt, a little oil and a little more vinegar') he warns against eating salad followed by fruit: 'if they come to be mixed together their moistness and coldness would ruin the digestion' by overloading one of the humours.[66] In 1615 Gervase Markham took it for granted that the readers of his *The English Housewife* would want not only recipes but advice on the concoction of medicines, salves, infusions and broths, that the larder should also be a pharmacy. And alongside this reliance on self-help ran the old belief in the curative efficacy of spells and charms, muttered incantations and written amulets. 'Charming', William Perkins wrote disapprovingly of folk magic in 1608, 'is in as great request as physic, and charmers more sought unto than physicians in time of need.'[67] Well into the seventeenth century and beyond, wax and metal images of eyes and breasts and limbs in Catholic shrines bore and still bear witness to the alternative medicine of prayer.

Doctors, when available, were expensive. And their operations hurt. A combination of university-based anatomy and practical experience had led to a notable improvement of the way in which a common ailment, stones in the neck of the bladder, was treated. There were three treatments. The surgeon could pass crushing implements up the urethra (many of these survive, of chilling size), cut down through the perineum, or open up the bladder above the pubic symphysis. The first left the least risk of subsequent fatal infection. Of all, Paré noted that it was necessary for four strong men to hold the patient motionless. Though the fabric of man, 'the paragon of animals', as Shakespeare made Hamlet put it, and the very reason for the creation of nature itself, was subject to unprecedented scrutiny, far more organized and original effort was expended to promoting the health of the soul than of the body; in this respect Vesalius's 'blessed age', was little more than a continuation of the middle age its spokesmen so frequently scorned.

THE COSMOS

By the 1530s intellectual life was already firmly associated with increasing knowledge of the natural world and the discoveries and inventions that accompanied it. Without these advances, Peter Apianus went so far as to say in 1532, 'life would return to the state of the men of old who lived without laws or civility, like beasts.'[68] He had been born Peter Bienewitz. Latinizing his name in order to proclaim his affiliation to the commonwealth of learning, he adapted the German *Biene* (bee) to the Latin *Apis*. The bee was, indeed, a suitable emblem of the scientific interests of Peter's time. As physician, geographer and astronomer he was more interested in collecting information about the world of nature than in relating fresh knowledge to new explanations of the physical laws that determined its makeup. Scientific interests did not, in themselves, produce science.

Indeed, their very multiplication retarded its emergence as an objective urge to explain natural phenomena. The German Nicholas of Cusa, in a treatise of 1440 entitled, with sophisticated caution, *On Learned Ignorance*, had mooted the possibility that the earth rotated, that it might not be at the absolute centre of the universe, that outer space could be infinite rather than bounded by divine decree, that an understanding of the cosmos was open to rethinking according to mathematical rather than dogmatic rules. His ideas reached a number of later thinkers, Leonardo, Copernicus, Giordano Bruno among them. But the obstacles to rethinking the accepted model of the cosmos were formidable. Data was flowing in at an unprecedented rate: from European chorographers and naturalists, from overseas explorers and colonists. Speculative energy was absorbed into recording and classifying. Again, a number of men with a scientific bent were increasingly interested in studying technological processes. These involved, as well as the better harnessing of the natural power of wind and water, improved methods of mining and extracting ores, of refining them (as in the mercury process for purifying silver) and of assaying metals in order to produce in the case of brass, for instance, alloys more suited to their purpose. Thanks to them even what went on in the sealed-off communities of miners in remote mountain valleys in eastern Germany or in the forest smelting plants of central France could be known from a variety of books, from short how-to-do-it handbooks to formidable, well illustrated treatises. This was an aspect of scientific knowledge that appealed to merchant communities and found a place in gentlemen's libraries.

In 1544 the German Lucas Gassell summed it up in a landscape which placed the sheds and machinery of a mountain mine near a luxurious country house with, in the background, a city. Two years later, in his treatise on mining and metallurgy, Georg Agricola stressed the importance to civilized man of studying not only what grew and moved on the surface of the earth but 'other things which the earth generates in herself which are wholly hidden and unknown'. And he made the more general point that it was through a practical study of 'natural objects . . . that man acquired an indefinable something beyond that which seemingly was allotted to the human species'.[69]

His hands-on approach to knowledge, carried further in a second treatise on methods used in the extraction and treatment of metals ('I have not only described them, but also hired illustrators to delineate their forms'[70]), followed Vesalius's declaration in 1543 that 'the most important . . . branch of the art of medicine . . . is based above all on the investigation of nature.'[71] And it was followed in turn by the cruder claim by the self-taught potter, enamellist and pigment-experimenter Bernard Palissy, whose zoomorphic dishes and platters displayed the acuteness of his interest in plants, animals, fish and fossils. Introducing his *Most Worthy Discourses* in 1580, he wrote that 'through practice I prove that the theories of many philosophers even the most ancient and famous ones, are erroneous in many points. Anyone can ascertain this for himself merely by taking the trouble to visit my workshop

Lucas Gassell, *Landscape with a Mine*, 1544 (Musées Royaux, Brussels)

. . . I assure you, dear reader, that you will learn more about natural history from the facts contained in this book than you would learn in fifty years devoted to the study of the theories of the ancient philosophers.'[72]

Bacon was to urge that a deliberate connection be established between the natural philosopher, the law-seeking scientist, and the artisan. But though deep-mine pumps and canal and weir constructions offered full scale equipment for hydrostatic and hydraulic study, and metal foundries, ceramic, soap and glass works, living laboratories for the chemist, the very stridency of tone adopted by the working technicians and their observers suggests their distance from the thinking scientist's study. An obsession with pulleys and worm-drives led to the design of machines that while demonstrating mechanical principles, were simply too complex or power-hungry to work: this strain ran on from Francesco di Giorgio and Leonardo da Vinci in the late fifteenth century to Agostino Ramelli's beautifully illustrated and perverse *Diverse and Ingenious Machines* published in Italian and French at Paris in 1588. The fascination with ingenious but impractical technology is not to be ignored as a link between artisanship and educated patronage. Francesco di Giorgio's mechanical fantasies were carved into the walls of the ducal palace of Urbino. A financially hard-pressed Florentine government took seriously Leonardo's grandiose plan for diverting the course of the river Arno from the rebel city of Pisa. More remarkable still was the case of Girolamo Maggi. While he was working as a scholarly editor in Venice, it became clear in 1570 that an impending Turkish attack on Cyprus would imperil the imperfectly fortified city of Famagusta. Maggi submitted to the Council of Ten designs for strengthening it and protecting its approaches to the Council of Ten. One showed prefabricated towers within which cannon could be raised by complex levers to shoot outwards by a remote timing device.

Another showed a battery of giant forks, connected to winches turned by oxen in subterranean compartments which, sweeping backwards and forwards across the ramparts, would push away enemy ladders raised against the walls (it was, in fact, an idea that had already occurred to Leonardo). Nonetheless these, and Maggi's other theoretically plausible but impractical ideas were accepted by the wisest council of the soberest government of Europe. He was knighted, given *carte blanche* to order supplies of material from the Arsenal, and sent with them to Famagusta. There his projects failed or proved too complex

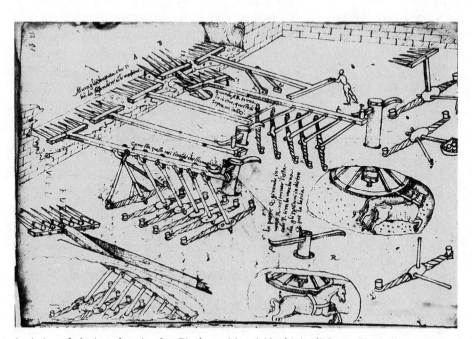

Anti-siege forks in a drawing by Girolamo Maggi (Archivio di Stato, Venice)

to build, and he served, bravely, as a simple soldier. When Famagusta fell in 1571 he was sent as prisoner to Constantinople where he was executed for trying to escape.

Maggi's story becomes less bizarre when set alongside the flood of inventions submitted to governments by men from a wide range of occupations: diving bells for salvage work and diving suits to enable holes to be bored in the bottom of enemy ships; giant earth-shifting machines; multi-barrelled and multi-shot guns too expensive to fabricate in any numbers and liable to jam or misfire; perpetual motion machines that would somehow still keep going when harnessed to irrigation pumps. By the early seventeenth century the inventor had become a figure of popular fun. In Quevedo's *The Swindler* a character produces a plan for sucking up with sponges the water defences of Ostend during the long siege by the Spanish in 1601–4. The same siege prompted Jonson, in *The Staple of News*, to report invented rumours of an 'invisible eel' (a navigable torpedo) and a Spanish project

> To bring an army over in cork-shoes
> And land them here at Harwich. All his horse
> Are shod with cork, and fourscore piece of ordnance,
> Mounted upon cork carriages, with bladders
> Instead of wheels, to run the passage over
> At a spring tide.[73]

Meanwhile, throughout the sixteenth century, technological processes were improved by trial and error among craftsmen responding to market demand, for more accurately bored cannon, for instance, and improved firing mechanisms for sporting guns and military pistols. Water-powered ore-crushers and trip-hammers, wire-drawing and paper mills were developed to increase productivity. So were multiple looms and knitting frames, though their prototypes met with such resistance from piece-workers that their wide use was postponed.

It was above all curiosity, observation and a consideration of the use to which knowledge could be put that occupied the scientific element within intellectual life. Leonardo pictured himself peering into the mouth of a dark cave, hand over narrowed eyes, body swaying from side to side, divided between fear and 'the desire to see if within there was any miraculous thing'.[74] The cave was nature. And if the exploration of it was on the whole descriptive and utilitarian rather than experimental, if increased knowledge did not as a general approach seek to turn fresh conjectures into physical and chemical laws, the sixteenth century scrutiny of nature was an essential prelude to the science of the Newtonian century that followed, with its improved range of precision instruments (microscope, thermometer, barometer, air-pump for producing a partial vacuum) which enabled scientists to refine their investigations and pass them on for replication by others. Old theories had first to be measured against new knowledge. 'I have no knowledge other than that gained through my own eyes,' wrote the industrial chemist Vannoccio Biringuccio in 1540.[75] It was a practical approach endorsed by Bacon: 'the understanding must not be supplied with wings but rather hung with weights to keep it from leaping and flying.'[76]

This accumulative pragmatism goes far to explain why Nicholas of Cusa's radical questioning was left, as it were, suspended over men's investigation of nature. The old model of the universe had stood the test of many centuries of practical experience and was elastic enough to absorb the new evidence fed into it without losing its shape. It comprised a ready-reference system for the allocation by category of every phenomenon to its place in the scheme of things. Matter was divided into four elements, earth, air, fire and water. Each possessed characteristics drawn from four basic qualities: heat, cold, moistness, dryness; thus heat was hot and dry, water moist and cold. These were reflected in the medical humours that determined health, also four: choleric, melancholic, phlegmatic, sanguine. These in turn echoed the characteristics of the planets as they slid past one another within their concentric spheres, the cold and dry Saturn, the moist moon, the fiery Mars. It was a model that, to the senses, made sense. The sailor navigated by it. The doctor prescribed by it. The judge of character selected among its categories – or concentrated on one, as Dürer did in the slumped introspection of his *Melancholia*. It was, moreover, winningly participatory, a cosmos of leakings from above, of sympathetic reactions across space, of correspondences between man and universe which linked a war with a comet, a syphilitic infection with a conjunction of the virile Mars with Saturn, for whom heated pleasure was anathema. It was a model perfectly suited to the two most familiar forms of traditional scientific inquiry, alchemy and astrology. And its inner logic was only shown to be flawed when its outside was broken, when a new vision of celestial mechanics put the whole system of links and correspondences in doubt.

While many industrial processes, whether the use of alum in fulling and dye-fixing or the fusion of glass and of ceramic glazes, involved chemical processes, and had been described in considerable detail by the end of the sixteenth century, there was no new attempt to explain them in terms of the nature of the substances involved. There were occasional references to the classical idea that all material objects were made up of unseeable 'atoms', variously constituted and variously responsive to those in unlike bodies. But without a generally accepted theory of atomic structure, the concern of the 'chymist' could not be to formulate, let alone test, theories about reactions that could lead to chemical laws. All he could do was amass particular examples of what happened when X was added to Y or when Z was subjected to heat.

The 'chymist' was still an alchemist. The first general survey of how to produce compounds, solutions, distillates, crystallizations and fusions – practical chemistry, in fact – was the 1597 *Alchemia* of the German physician Andreas Libau (Libavanus). It was in the laboratories of the alchemist that the equipment of the later chemist *pur sang* was to be found: beakers, retorts, condensers, balances, filters, heat sources. In spite of the cranks and charlatans that gave it a bad name, its suspect secrecy and the mystical mumbo-jumbo of its language and symbolism (rotting hermaphroditic corpses, trees fruited with faces, lions devouring suns and so forth), alchemy was a natural science. The search for the philosopher's stone or elixir (the agent was not necessarily solid) that could transform base metal into gold was an attempt to reproduce the method used by nature itself to isolate gold from less pure substances. Even the hard-headed Libau yielded ground on this point. God had willed nature into being in the laboratory of the cosmos but, leaving it imperfect, had challenged man to detect and concentrate the perfect essences diffused in it.

This notion was put clearly by Paracelsus; 'Nothing is made in the form of ultimate matter . . . alchemy brings to its end that which has not come to its end . . . Learn thus to recognize what alchemy is, that it alone is that which prepares the impure through fire and makes it pure.'[77] He was here thinking of ultimate matter as the pure essences that could be reproduced from impure substances and used in medicine. He saw diseases as being conditioned not by imbalances affecting the whole body as in Galenic humour theory, but by specific organs whose chemical make-up had gone out of kilter. Man's body was not played upon by the humour-conditioning planets as such but by the chemical balance within the universe as a whole. So cures were effected by the correct dosage of the right chemical, distilled or otherwise refined, whether a metallic salt, an acid or a poison like antimony. In the *Advancement of Learning* Bacon had no hesitation in declaring that 'the search and stir to make gold hath brought to light a great number of good and fruitful inventions and experiments, as well for the disclosing of nature, as for the use of man's life.'[78]

The alchemist's belief that terrestrial nature, from man to minerals, was intimately connected with the wider nature of the universe and could use that connection positively, was paralleled by the most popular science of all, astrology. The earth, heavy and motionless, the stage appointed for the playing out of the Christian drama, was surrounded by an unstable atmosphere that could shudder with tempests or flare with comets. From the moon outwards, however, the atmosphere was replaced by closely fitting spheres, each larger than the other and composed of a transparent substance impervious to change. The moon was locked into one, the planets into the one next in size and so on outwards: the spheres of Mercury, Venus, the Sun, Mars, Jupiter, Saturn. All slid past one another and were moved at different speeds by angels, and as they frictionlessly turned they produced unheard sounds, the 'music of the spheres'. An outermost sphere, however, did not move, and into it were studded the fixed, non-planetary stars. This made perfectly adequate sense to anyone looking up into the night sky. Only astronomers, checking the actual position of the 'fixed' stars against observations made in antiquity, noted changes over time; even so, they could 'save the appearances' that threatened the model by sophisticated mathematical explanations of the apparent discrepancies.

With the cosmos a constant, it was possible to work out a reliable model of its terrestrial influences. In the unstable environment of the earth and its atmosphere everything was subject to change. The level of the seas changed relative to the land: hence fossil fish in the sides of mountains. Plants and animals grew and sickened, as did man. One man's temperament differed from another, as did his fortune. All these changes and varying conditions and moods were produced by the influence of the planets as their spheres moved in relationship to the still earth, and to each other, against the background of the twelve zodiacal bands into which the fixed sphere of the stars had been divided. Evolved by the sages of antiquity, hallowed by Christian endorsement, universal nature in this view was brought close to human nature. And, thanks to astrology, man could make use of it.

The more emphasis education placed on the study of man's achievements and secular development, the greater was the recourse to astrology alongside prayer; and this was licit, for though planetary influences could incline a man towards a decision or a physical disposition they could not compel anything to happen contrary to God's will. The revived interest in classical mythology brought the planetary gods alive in literature and art. Printing made astrological lore widely available especially, as we have seen, in the form of almanacs.[79] The night sky was a vast reference book in which the truly skilled found answers to a multitude of questions.

In theory, astrologers, if they got their complex planetary computations right, could explain past and present events and forecast those to come: pestilences, famines, the deaths of princes. The questions put to them, however, mainly related to the present, the recent past or to the immediate future, when the precise time of an expected event, a birth or a journey or a building project could give the consultant a fix on where the planets had been or would be. Inquiries came from all classes, from monarchs and bankers to farmers and servant girls: when to begin a campaign or to try to beget a male heir or to dig the foundations of a palace or fortress; the cure for an ailment; the chance – on the evidence provided – of a wife being unfaithful or of a rich uncle dying; the whereabouts of missing husbands or stolen goods; the putting of a brood mare to a stallion; the chances of success for a business deal.

Of course there were sceptics. After keeping a weather diary in the 1480s, Pico della Mirandola found that astrological predictions had been correct for only seven out of one hundred days. In the same vein a much imitated English pamphlet of 1569 mockingly printed the three differing predictions of contemporaneous almanacs. The gaps between learned prediction and mere fortune-telling, between astrology and magic were embarrassingly small. Whether the intention was to put the audience on the side of Edmund in *King Lear* or, more probably, condemn his disbelief is unclear, but his tirade may have caused some heads to wag, if ruefully:

> This is the excellent foppery of the world that when we are sick in fortune (often the surfeit of our own behaviour) we make guilty of our disasters the sun, the moon and the stars; as if we were villains by necessity, fools by heavenly compulsion; knaves, thieves and treachers by spherical predominance . . . My father compounded with my mother under the dragon's tail, and my nativity was under Ursa Major; so that

it follows I am rough and lecherous. Tut, I should have been that I am, had the maidenliest star in the firmament twinkled on my bastardizing.[80]

About two years after Shakespeare had written these lines, in 1608, John Dee died at his home in Mortlake, on the Thames near London. Elizabeth I had often visited him there; as her court astrologer he had written in 1570 that 'we . . . daily may perceave that man's body, and all other elementall bodies, are altered, disposed, ordred, pleasured and displeasured, by the influentiall working of the Sunne, Mone and other Starres and Planets.'[81] In 1596 Elizabeth appointed him Warden of Christ's College, Manchester. But just before *Lear* was written, he had been forced to resign by increasingly strident accusation of necromancy, the illegal conjuration of spirits to foretell the future, and he died in an atmosphere of disgrace. Elsewhere, as at the courts of Rudolf II and Ferdinand I of Tuscany, astrologers were still held in high regard. But their trade was losing its hold on educated opinion as both faiths increasingly closed ranks against the idea of God working through a material filter and as astronomers challenged the accuracy of the cosmic model on which astrology relied.

Popular belief remained largely intact, leading governments to censor predictions of political change which could excite public opinion and encourage conspiracies, and forecasts of famines, which it was feared could bring them about by encouraging merchants to buy grain in bulk and store it until the price rose. And even among the educated, distrust of astrologers often coexisted with belief in a system which made more comforting sense of man's personal relationship to the universe than any other. Tycho Brahe remained intrigued by astrology while drastically revising the model on which it was based; Galileo, who destroyed it, cast horoscopes for his Medici patrons and their friends. John Napier, the inventor in 1614 of logarithms remained a student of the subject. Their interest suggests the age's reluctance to cast men and women adrift in a universe where flowers opened to the sun and tides rose and fell in obedience to the moon but they themselves were left alone – save in their less calculable relationship with nature's maker.

Rather as industrial chemistry was stimulated by the demand for better soaps, glass and dyestuffs and improved or cheaper weapons, mechanics by the need for more complex machines, and ballistics by the importance of understanding the range and trajectory of cannonballs, astronomy reacted to the post-Columbian appetite for fuller information about the celestial bodies. Rough positions at sea or at landfall could be determined by dead-reckoning, the balancing of estimated speed against the zig-zag of tacking and the slippage from straight lines caused by currents and winds, all seen in the corrective light of compass bearings. Precise locations, needed as much by cartographers as by navigators, relied on conversion tables; these gave the difference between the angle of elevation of sun or star from that measured at the same time-point in a European city where the tables were compiled. Another incentive to celestial observation was the urgent need for reform of the calendar; since Julius Caesar decreed the length of the solar year (the Julian Calendar) a backlog of discrepancies between solar and conventional time measurement had led to a cumulative error of ten days. When a commission that drew on a painstaking analysis of astronomical data was presented to Pope Gregory XIII, he ruled that the ten days should be omitted in 1582 and that thereafter the Gregorian – today's – system of leap years should be implemented. It was a reform fairly quickly adopted outside the areas of Russian and Greek Orthodoxy, not without some popular resentment against what was seen as a filching of ten days from a man's life.

Purposeful star-gazing was not, however, only motivated by these practical considerations. As interest in astrology widened, so did interest in the heavenly bodies: throughout the sixteenth century, indeed, the terms of astrologer and astronomer came commonly to be virtually interchangeable. As the biographer of the physician-turned-astronomer Jean Fernel put it after his death in 1558, 'contemplation of the stars and heavenly bodies excites such a wonder and charm in the human mind that once fascinated by it, we are caught in the toils of an enduring and delighted slavery, which holds us in bondage and serfdom.'[82] And for the born mathematician there was the lure of checking the calculations underlying the second-century contribution to the cosmic model by Ptolemy, or simplifying those that had been introduced later on to 'save the appearances' of it.

When Nicholas Copernicus settled to work in his Frauenburg tower study overlooking the Baltic in Polish-ruled East Prussia after 1512, his calculations were devoted to exploring a notion that had surfaced along with so much else that emerged from the fifteenth century trawl of Greek texts. This was that it might be the sun, rather than the earth, that lay at the centre of the universe. Nicholas of Cusa had played with the possibility. By 1530 Copernicus had proved it to his own satisfaction, though he only agreed to the publication of his findings in 1543. Set out in *On the Revolutions of the Heavenly Spheres* the new model, with the earth and moon placed between the spheres of Venus and Mars, was judged not only shocking but unconvincing. To explain the relationship of the planets and stars to a now moving platform in a new position in space while retaining, as he did, the 'official' picture of concentric spheres revolving in perfect circles, involved such computational complexities as to challenge belief in their purpose. His trapping of the changeable earth and its impure atmosphere among spheres of changeless immaculacy was another challenge to belief. His model was the confusing 'let's suppose' of a thinker of genius, and it acted as a challenge until other astronomers found better reasons for accepting its heliocentric core.

Slowly, always against conservative, at times equally intelligent if less imaginative, opposition, Tycho Brahe broke the whole spheral system up and postulated a common atmosphere pervading the universe as a whole in which accidents like novas and comets could be generated anywhere in space. The spheres, he wrote in 1588, 'which authors have invented to save the appearances, exist only in the imagination in order that the motions of the planets in their courses may be understood by the mind'.[83] But he kept to the assumption that the earth was at or – still a significant break with tradition – near the centre of the universe. With the planets freed from their spheres, Johannes Kepler (another astrological enthusiast) was able to calculate that planetary motion was not circular but elliptical and that it varied in speed according to proximity to the sun. By suggesting, in his *The New Astronomy* of 1609, that the interactions between the magnetic fields of sun, earth and planets formed a self-contained solar system within the universe as a whole, he was able to strengthen the claims of Copernicus and Brahe that the stars were immensely farther from the earth than the old model had supposed. The heaven-abolishing notion of an infinite universe containing a multitude of systems, which might, like the solar one, even be populated, became dismayingly possible to imagine. Lucretius had, indeed, imagined it in the first century BC, and Giordano Bruno, burned at the stake in Rome in 1600, compounded his other heretical opinions by endorsing it in his *On the Infinite Universe and Worlds*. If the idea of God's personal interest in every Christian had been strained by the inclusion of the Amerindians, Africans and Japanese, the idea of plural inhabited worlds put the whole Christian apparatus of belief and organization at risk. Both Protestant and Catholic reforms had been devoted to strengthening the bond between men and God.

The intimacy of the relationship could survive, just, the earth's displacement from creation's centre. But the churches had psychology as well as Genesis on their side when condemning ideas that stripped men and women of their exclusive divine paternity.

The botanist and zoologist could pursue their interests with equanimity. So could the alchemist and astrologer if they were not tempted to supplement their studies with the darker forms of magic. The anatomist and physician had – as in the case of Vesalius – to go on tiptoe when shaking the authority of Galen. But only the astronomer had to take on both divine and classical authority at once.

Copernicus's Lutheran friend Andreas Osiander, who saw his book through the press in Nuremberg on his behalf, felt it necessary to add an unauthorized Preface of his own. In this he pointed out that Copernicus's conclusions were only hypothetical; 'these hypotheses need not be true nor even probable. If they provide a calculus consistent with the observations, that alone is sufficient . . . And if any causes [of movement] are devised by the imagination, as indeed very many are, they are not put forward to convince anyone that they are true, but merely to provide a correct basis for calculation.'[84] Copernicus only saw the book on his death-bed in 1543. It was not until 1566 that a printer risked a second edition.

He had been careful to play down the challenge of his figures to the Ptolomaic form and Aristotelean physics of the consecrated model. Others, buoyed up by the sciences that had shown how ancient knowledge could be extended, were less reticent. When a nova, a bright new star near the constellation of Cassiopeia, suddenly appeared in 1572, Jeronimo Muñoz, professor of Hebrew and astronomy at Valencia, pounced on the opportunity to show that Aristotle's teaching about the nature of space above the moon – that nothing there could corrupt or be generated – was in error. The image of Aristotle on all fours being ridden by Phyllis, the doxy with whom he became (according to legend) infatuated, had been a popular medieval *exemplum* of the dangerous power of women over wisdom.

When it was taken up again in a lively drawing of 1600 by Joseph Heinz the Elder – working then for Rudolf in Prague (as were Brahe and Kepler) he was seen as humiliated for his cosmological errors as well.

Up to then clerics, aware that cosmological theory was mathematically too complicated to corrupt the masses, and not averse to the baiting of pagan authority, were not over-alarmed. It was Galileo, armed with his improvement to the recently developed telescope and his interest in mathematical physics, who most disturbingly re-examined Copernican heliocentricity in the light of Brahe's and to some extent of Kepler's findings. His publications from 1610, with their intentionally iconoclastic asides, challenged classical authority in the skies so pungently that the theological structure which had leaned on it was seen as in danger of collapse. Galileo's telescope revealed that 'the surface of the moon is not perfectly smooth, free from inequalities, and exactly spherical, as a large school of philosophers considered.'[85] This information, and the revelations, also published in his *Starry Messenger* of 1610, that four satellites swung round Jupiter just as the moon circled the earth, and that the number of stars was even greater and more various in their distance from the earth than his predecessors had surmised: all these discoveries led to a revised cosmic theory. It was not, as Isaac Newton was to show in his *Mathematical Principles of*

Joseph Heinz the Elder,
Aristotle and Phyllis,
drawing, 1600 (Fine Arts
Museum, Budapest)

Natural Philosophy of 1687, a true assessment of the potential of all the available evidence. But as extended in Galileo's later works, it was a revised, earth-demoted Copernicanism cogent enough to stir entrenched Aristotelians and clerics into forcing him in 1633 to abjure proselytizing and live under virtual house arrest outside Florence until his death nine years later. By then, as Robert Burton confessed in his *Anatomy of Melancholy* in 1621, rival cosmic theories had left his imagination 'almost giddy with roving about'.[86]

In a catalogue published in 1595, the London bookseller Andrew Maunsell listed over six thousand books printed in England which he divided into three sections. After 'Divinitie' came 'Science' and then 'Humanities', devoted to 'Gramer, Logicke, Rethoricke, Lawe, Historie, Poetrie, Policie, etc which for the most part concern matters of delight and pleasure'. The second term, he explains, 'concerneth the sciences mathematicall, as Arithetick, Geometrie, Astronomy, Astrologie, Musick, the Arte of Warre and Navigation and also . . . Physick and Surgerie'.[87] The section also contained books on architecture and cookery. What all in this mixed bag had in common was their application of knowledge to the actual world of men and nature and, whether a mathematical theorem or a work of architecture of the positioning of an army or a pharmaceutical prescription involved the use of numbers. The quantities given in cook books were imprecisely rounded and timings were subjective: roast a haddock 'til it be enough' was a fifteenth-century English piece of advice; an Italian recipe of 1560 recommended heating cod's roe for as long 'as it takes to say a credo'. All the same, science was the branch of knowledge that used numbers as a tool. Surgery may seem the odd man out, but it was linked to the physicians from whose ranks came so many of those who also described themselves as mathematicians.

Some respect for numeracy was built into elementary education and taken for granted in the *quadrivium* (arithmetic, geometry, astronomy and music) of the early stage of university education. For the shopkeeper and merchant it was essential. Alberti emphasized its importance to the artist. Piero della Francesca wrote two number-drenched treatises on perspective and proportion. In one of his notebooks Leonardo warned, 'let no one read me who does not understand mathematics.'[88] In 1525 Dürer published a treatise on geometry which was cited as late as 1622 in the list of books on mathematics recommended for perusal in Henry Peacham's *The Compleat Gentleman*. Changes in the art of war led to books stressing the need for arithmetic in calculating space for the brigading of armies and geometry for the design of fortifications. In one of them the author, Thomas Digges, referred in 1571 to those who did not appreciate the importance of mathematics as 'two-footed moles and toads whom nature and destiny hath ordained to crawl within the earth and suck upon the muck'.[89] Military mathematics became part of the educational 'finishing' of an active man of birth; Galileo himself lectured on the subject in Padua. The requirements of governmental accountancy and of navigation added to the need for calculating skills.

Holbein's clerical and seigneurial *Ambassadors*, posing in 1533 beside a carefully composed litter of navigational and astronomical instruments, a lute and score (carrying quadrivial mathematical associations in this context) and a German arithmetic book, is only one of a number of portraits in which educated men linked themselves to mathematical competence.

The rediscovery of practically the whole range of ancient mathematical texts led to fruitful controversy – an Italian editor of *Euclid* said in 1505 that the editor of the previous, bungled, edition should have called it not *Euclid* but *Chaos* – and a new zeal for pure mathematics stimulated by the revival of interest in Plato. For him the certainty of mathematics had been essential training for the philosopher 'because he must rise above the world of change and grasp true being'; 'it will tend to draw the soul towards truth and direct upwards the philosophic intelligence which is now wrongly turned earthwards'; 'it forces the mind to arrive at pure truth by the exercise of pure thought.'[90] While usefulness prompted advances in trigonometry and the invention of logarithms, play with the relationships between numbers for its own sake led to the concepts of negative and imaginary numbers and lively, often acrimonious, debate about the theory of cubic and biquadratic equations. The results of this, largely Italian, branch of inquiry were summed up in the *Algebra* of Rafael Bombelli, published in 1572. But the practical role of mathematics as the common denominator among the branches of science is more typically represented by the Englishman Robert Recorde. His first book, on arithmetic, was revealingly called *The Grounde of Artes*. Published in 1540 and six times reprinted by 1561, it reflected the 'grounde' represented by the width of subjects he had taught at Oxford and Cambridge: anatomy and medicine, music, astrology and astronomy (he was the first English writer to mention

Hans Holbein, *The Ambassador Jean de Dinteville with Georges de Selve*, 1533 (National Gallery, London)

Copernicus). In 1557 he published the first English work on algebra, further popularising the use of Arabic numbers for calculation and the symbols for plus, minus and equals.

The investigators of natural laws relied far more on mathematical explanations than on deductions based on the results of true experiments. Amidst the mass of practical observations made by Leonardo only a small handful of set-up experiments can be discerned, chiefly in the field of optics. Though Galileo described at least one experiment, his construction of a low-friction grooved inclined plane in connection with his study of motion, it is by no means clear how far his theoretical physics was buttressed by experimental means. Rather than to test new conjectures, experiments were used to check received opinions and explode old wives' tales. None of Giovambattista della Porta's experiments on the properties of the loadstone were so contrived as to carry the conviction of his explosion of the myth that the aroma of garlic cancelled the effectiveness of the compass ('a common opinion amongst seamen'[91]); having munched a clove he belched on a magnetized needle and found its north-seeking powers unimpaired. It is easy to be misled by the frequent use of 'experiment' as a synonym for 'experience', as when Paracelsus in 1527 claimed that 'if I wish to prove anything, experiment and reason for me take the place of authorities,'[92] or when Jacques Cartier, the explorer of eastern Canada in the 1530s, wrote that 'the common navigators of our day, making real experiments, have learned the opposite of the opinions of the philosophers,' before going on to add, in a remarkable statement that encapsulated the new spirit of inquiry as a whole, 'I would like to ask that nobody try to convince me of something that is contrary to experience.'[93]

It was a spirit that tested and demonstrated opinion rather than sought new explanations of natural phenomena. It is an agreeable legend that Galileo dropped weights of different sizes from the top of the leaning tower of Pisa to show that they hit the earth at the same time. If he had done so, it would have been to convince sceptics of a theory of impetus proposed a generation before by the Venetian Giovanni Battista Benedetti to combat the Aristotelian idea that heavy bodies seek the earth with a speed proportional to their weight. When in 1623 Galileo described how, if you whirl round in a circle holding out a pan of water with a ball in it, the ball will revolve in a contrary direction, he was defending Copernicus's introduction of the idea of contrary rotation to explain celestial mechanics. It was in this spirit that the Netherlander Simon Stevin constructed apparatus to show the relationship between the height of a column of water and the pressure it exerted in order to demonstrate the effectiveness of his practical proposals as a hydraulic engineer.

In spite of Bacon's warning against leaping and flying, however, without some flyers and organizations to sustain their researches, scientific investigation would not have led so suggestively towards science.

In The New Atlantis Bacon imagined a permanent central research centre, which he called Salomon's House, where the results of experiments could be discussed and follow-up ones planned. Until then (1617, or a few years earlier) nothing of the sort existed, though Bacon's idea may have been suggested by the men with scientific interests who met in the London house of Sir Thomas Gresham which in 1597 became Gresham College. Their interests, however, were mainly in the field of applied mathematics. As a ballad 'in honour of the elect company of philosophers and subtle minds who meet on the Wednesday of every week at Gresham College' put it:

> This college will the whole world measure
> Which most impossible conclude,
> And navigation make a pleasure
> By finding out the longitude!
> Every Tarpaulian [common sailor] shall then with ease
> Saile any ship to the Antipodes.[94]

Other informal clusters gathered about leading investigators like John Dee at Mortlake or Federico Cesi in Rome, all pointing towards the establishment in the seventeenth century of the scientific Academies and Societies which were to contribute so much to experiment and publicity.

For the time being, the nearest approach to Salomon's House, and perhaps another influence on it, was Tycho Brahe's purpose-built laboratory palace of Uraniborg on the Danish island of Hveen, with its multiple observatories, giant quadrant, great brass-plated globe for the mapping of observations, its furnaces and alchemical equipment, its staff of assistants and garret suite of rooms for visiting students and colleagues. Its foundation ceremony in 1576 suggests the semi-romantic prestige science had acquired since it had enlisted the interest of merchants, bureaucrats and members of the aristocracy as patrons or students themselves. The stone was laid by the French ambassador to Denmark accompanied by scholars and members of the court 'when the sun was rising together with Jupiter near Regulus, while the moon in Aquarius was setting. Libations were solemnly made with various wines, success was wished to the undertaking and the stone was put in its place.'[95]

While universities cautiously came to accept the new vogue for inquiry alongside their traditional syllabuses, the flyers were either the possessors of non-professorial means (Copernicus from his canonry, 'logarithms' Napier from his Scottish estates, Harvey from his stipend as Royal Physician and his extensive private practice as well as his fees from the College of Physicians, Bacon from his crown legal offices and a shrewd marriage), or were the beneficiaries of patronage. The part this had played in the careers of other men with more talent than means was long familiar; in a board game described by a Spanish author in 1587, if the dice landed a contestant's counter on square forty-three, which was inscribed 'your patron dies', he had to go back to the start.[96] Now it became the scientist's turn.

King Frederick II made Brahe one of the richest men in Denmark, and the astronomer had himself portrayed as very much the gentleman (as, by birth, he was) as he sat beside his wall-quadrant dictating to a secretary while his assistants noted the time and angle of the celestial observation. Kepler's salary as Imperial Mathematician was paid irregularly but at least kept him afloat, and the position enabled him after the death of Rudolf II to obtain a well-paid post under the provincial government of Graz. Galileo owed his release from the chores of university teaching at Padua to his shrewd angling for Medici patronage. Hearing in 1608 of the forthcoming marriage of Cosimo, the heir of the Grand Duke Ferdinand I of Tuscany, he wrote to Cosimo's mother proposing an emblem for a commemorative medal. In a masterly conflation of science and flattery he suggested the image of a loadstone and the motto 'strength causes love', explaining that just as the magnetic force of the loadstone draws iron filings towards it, so the attraction of princely power 'lifts up his subjects' in loving obedience.[97] This he followed by naming the satellites of Jupiter which he had discovered 'the Medicean stars'. Within months he was in Florence as Grand Ducal Mathematician with a stipend which was among the ten highest paid to governmental officials in the whole of Tuscany, soaring above those of the artists, military engineers and ducal secretaries employed by the court.

Patronage was extended in return for the prestige attached to what was patronized. Frederick's favour was based on the European respect gained by Brahe's explanation of the nova of 1572. Cosimo, who succeeded Ferdinand as Grand Duke in 1610, gained repute through his 'stars' and by sending Galilean telescopes and copies of The Starry Messenger as diplomatic gifts. From their princely perches the flyers drew attention to science's ability not only to explain but exploit nature so that 'human life be endowed with new discoveries and power,' to cite Bacon again on the achievement of his own times and his hopes for the future.[98] In a Europe within which scientific information circulated while science was still unorganized, Galileo's stipend was almost as encouraging to others as his new discoveries in the fields of optics, mechanics and astronomy.

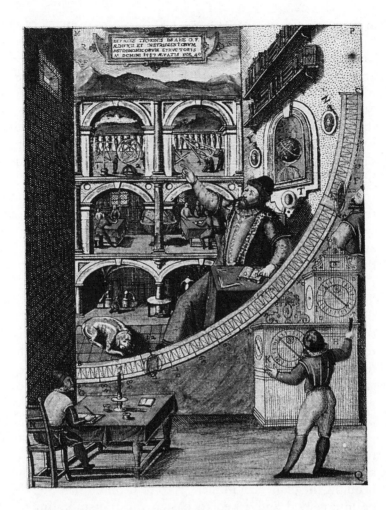

Tycho Brahe at Uraniborg, engraving from Tycho Brahe, *Astronomiae instauratae mechanica*, Nuremberg, 1602

Even this endorsement of his researches, however, did not protect Galileo from clerical persecution. In 1615 one of his early Catholic antagonists declared that his endorsement of Copernicanism was 'a very dangerous thing' which threatened 'to injure the holy faith by suggesting that the Scriptures are false'.[99] He also found himself forced to argue with academic conservatives that the surer methodology of his subject deserved the respect granted to philosophy and theology. In any case, given the inability of scientists as yet to prevent epidemics and sepsis and relieve pain, or produce new sources of energy, or do much more than try to explain what technical workers were already doing, Bacon's optimism could not be widely shared. While most men and women could grasp something of traditional pseudo-science, true, objective science was not sufficiently enough known to be popularized. Stevin was more extensively talked about for his land-yacht of 1600 than for his hydrostatics, Galileo better known for his telescope than for what he had discovered through it. Botany and zoology and mineralogy satisfied curiosity. But of what practical use was the most prestigious branch of science, cosmological astronomy? Especially as those who could understand the calculations involved could not agree amongst themselves? 'What shall we reape by it', asked Montaigne, 'but only what we need not care which of the two [the Ptolomaic and Copernican systems] it be? And who knoweth whether a hundred years hence a third opinion will rise, which happily will overthrow these two praecedent?'[100]

Given the suspicion and scepticism expressed in intellectual circles, the more popular desire to hold on to a vision of the natural world that could be believed in rather than coldly understood is all the easier to grasp. For every book which can be called scientific there continued to be a host of far more congenial compilations which repeated the old encouraging myths about the fountain of youth or the power of amber to detect infidelity in a wife. What most people wanted was not methodology but magic; the science of the non-numerate, the potential power of the unprivileged. This was the helpmeet, too, of those scientists themselves who were in a hurry to break open nature's secrets. If the cosmos was tended by spirits, those who turned the spheres and brought the planetary influences to bear on human life, then they could be intercepted and asked to hasten the transmutation of iron pyrites into gold, to restore the flow of milk to a sick cow. Or they could be persuaded to explain the secret workings of the universe so that men, armed with this knowledge, could worship God with a fuller understanding of His plan – or seek power for themselves.

Natural Magic (the title of a book by Giovambattista della Porta which was widely reprinted and translated after its publication in 1558) was so called because it investigated the forces in nature that could not be seen or touched. In its motivation, such magic was a true investigative science. It did not imagine the spirits that kept everything in the cosmos in place and in touch with everything else as entities that could be conjured up. That aspect of magical belief was left to the folklore of elves and fairies and to the enchanters and enchantresses of poets who could stop a sword in its swing and change men into animals. The practitioners of natural magic were careful to distance themselves from necromancers, who claimed to be able to call up demons to serve them and who, to an excitable witness like Benvenuto Cellini, actually did so one night in the Roman Colosseum. That the devil's agents walked abroad and offered sex, riches and power to men in exchange for their souls was not just a pulpit metaphor. It was enshrined in the Faustus stories that prompted Marlowe's intuitive demonstration of how the scholar's love of knowledge could become contaminated by his lust for occult power.

In his own book on natural magic, the *On Subtlety* of 1551, Girolamo Cardano dealt equably with the problem. Accepting the lure of necromancy, he pointed out that 'no proof has yet been given that demons really exist, nor that they could be controlled by means of a pact if they did. If demons do exist', he went on, 'they probably exist on a higher mental plane than man and will hardly comprehend our vain ambitions and insignificant achievements. After all, humans do not understand the agreements, regulations or discourse governing the life of ants.'[101] And there was in general nothing sensational about the literature of scientific magic. It did have a mystical and esoteric tone, because of the object of its study. It rode on the then fashionable Neo-Platonic emphasis on the indwelling of God in every particle of creation. It accepted the leadership of those who appeared to have read the code, or part of it, aright: the prophets and sybils of the Old Testament days, the Magi whose knowledge had led them to Bethlehem, the God-like sage Hermes Trismegistus, whose riddling ancient Greek writings, translated into Latin by Ficino in 1471 and treated seriously by Pico della Mirandola, were considered a promising key to insert into box after box in the vault of concealed knowledge. Another approach, encouraged by the revived interest in the sixth century BC mathematician Pythagoras, suggested that arithmetical formulae and geometrical forms could break the code that determined the form of the universe. By the theory of sympathies, therefore, the calling on a divine pattern through its man-made simulacrum should turn another type of key to open a door of knowledge – hence the pentograms and circles within which the necromancer stood as he compelled the emergence of the 'legions' of infernal spirits which Cellini claimed if not to have seen at least to have been conscious of.[102]

Magic's role was to be reduced in the course of the seventeenth century to that of a box of clever tricks, or a superstition for the ultra-credulous. As a science it could not survive the gradual replacement of an animistic view of the cosmos by a mechanistic one. But from the generation of Ficino until that of Bacon, advanced scientific thought moved on parallel, often overlapping paths. Both were European in scope. Among others, the branch of science that came to be recognized as the 'true' one was extended by the work of the Pole Copernicus, the Spaniard Muñoz, the Dane Brahe, the German Kepler and the Italian Galileo. Bacon was aware of the magical approach pursued by the German Agrippa of Nettesheim, the Italians della Porta and Cardano and his own fellow-countrymen the astrologer John Dee and the mathematician and physician Robert Fludd. It was not without some hesitation that he finally came down on the other side. While magic could investigate phenomena it could not demonstrate its findings; it contained 'frivolous experiments strange rather by disguisement than in themselves'.[103]

Never had so many men looked down to wonder at the puzzles set by nature as they did from the bridge linking the late fifteenth to the early seventeenth century. 'There are so many astonishing things that remain unexplained,' noted Thomas Platter, an averagely well-educated physician, towards 1600 in his travel journal. He was recording a visit to a spring in the French village of Perois 'full of water constantly boiling as though it were very hot, which is nevertheless found to be cold when you put your hand in it'.[104] And if many compulsively sought explanations for nature's conundrums in mathematics or magic this did not necessarily distance them from the ordinariness of life that the historian finds so difficult to convey. Here is Cardano, physician, mathematician, inventor (of gimbal-mountings for use at sea), hypochondriac and believer in the significance of dreams and the magical path to knowledge. 'Although happiness suggests a state quite contrary to my nature, I can truthfully say that I was privileged from time to time to attain and share a certain measure of felicity. If there is anything good at all in life with which we can adorn this comedy's stage, I have not been cheated of such gifts.' He goes on to list them: 'rest, peace, quiet comfort, self-restraint, orderliness, change, fun, entertainment, pleasant company, coziness, sleep, food and drink, riding, rowing, walking, obtaining the latest news, meditation, contemplation, good education, piety, marriage, merry feasts, a good and well-ordered memory, cleanliness, water, fire, listening to music, beholding the beauty surrounding us, pleasant conversation, tales and stories, liberty, continence, little birds, puppies, cats, the consolation of death and the thought of the eternal flux of time as it flows past happiness and misfortune'. And, he adds, 'there is always the hope for some unexpected good turn of fortune; there is the practice of an art one is skilled in; there are the manifold changes of life, there is the whole wide world!'[105]

EPILOGUE

'OUR AGE'

'O tempora, o mores'. 'Oh, what times. Oh, what behaviour!': ever since Cicero's mournful observation in the first century BC men had expressed the feeling that something, usually of a shocking or deplorable nature, distinguished their own age from former ones. But never before the Renaissance had such references been so habitual, nor included so many that were optimistic. 'Our times since 1400', the cultivated merchant Giovanni Rucellai wrote in 1457, 'have greater reason to be contented than any other since Florence was founded.'[1] For others the pace of change brought a change of mind. Erasmus the scholar buoyantly saluted his age in 1517: all over the world,' – that is, the Europe of humanist studies – 'as if on a given signal, splendid talents are stirring'.[2] Not long before his death in 1536 Erasmus the peace-loving Christian, reflecting on the darkening panorama of political and religious strife, spoke of living in 'the worst age of history'.[3] On the whole, however, the increasing number of references to present or other times – within three stanzas of his *Orlando Furioso* Ariosto wrote of 'our days', 'our age' and contrasted 'ancient' with 'modern', 'old' and 'new' – concerned changes that were felt to be for the better.[4]

Changes in the appearance of Giotto's works and his fame outside Florence had led Dante to compare him with his predecessor Cimabue: 'Cimabue thought he led the field in painting, but now the cry is all for Giotto, and his fame is darkened.'[5] In *Purgatory*, Dante puts this opinion into the mouth of another artist, the manuscript illuminator Oderisi of Gubbio. A century after Dante's death in 1321, another generation of Florentine artists of striking originality, intellectual power and contemporary fame, Masaccio, Brunelleschi and Donatello, artist, architect and sculptor, coincided with the first concerted endorsement of humanistic studies by Florentine scholars and patrons. From then on men of letters associated the evidence of contemporary artistic talent with their own awareness of matching the achievements of antiquity. The arts, if not given prominence, were at least among the reasons the humanistically educated Matteo Palmieri gave in the 1430s to urge 'every thoughtful spirit to thank God that it has been permitted to him to be born in this new age'.[6]

At the mid-century there was a cluster of opinions to similar effect. The Romagnol historian and antiquarian Flavio Biondo wrote that 'this present age' – the Latin *saeculum*, like its Italian derivative, *secolo*, did not have the rigidity of our 'century' – 'has seen the rise of all the arts, notably those of eloquence and letters'.[7] Writing in Naples, Lorenzo Valla referred to 'those arts that are closest to the liberal arts, that is, painting, sculpture and architecture [which] were first so long and so greatly denigrated and almost perished with letters themselves, [are] now being reawakened and revived.'[8] The Sienese Aeneas Silvius Piccolomini added a more precise historical dimension: 'pictures produced two hundred years ago were not refined by [conscious] art; what was written at that time was crude, inept, unpolished. After Petrarch, letters re-emerged; after Giotto, the hands of the painters were raised once more. Now we can see that both the arts have reached perfection.'[9] Later on, in *c*.1490, Raphael's father, the artist Giovanni Santi, wrote of painting in a rhymed chronicle he composed in Urbino that

> In this splendid, noble art
> So many have been famous in our age
> They make any other time seem poor.[10]

And he gave a list of them reaching from Masaccio and Jan van Eyck, through Filippo Lippi and Rogier van der Weyden, to his contemporaries Giovanni Bellini and Leonardo. With no attention to this northern contribution to Renaissance culture Marsilio Ficino wrote in 1492 to a German correspondent, with some patriotic smugness, that 'this age, like a golden age, has restored to light the liberal arts that were almost extinct: grammar, poetry, rhetoric, painting, sculpture, architecture, music.'[11]

It was in the sixteenth century that the sense of intellectual and artistic achievement as the hallmark of an age passed north of the Alps. Erasmus's exclamation of 1517 was followed in the next year by Ulrich von Hutten, recently crowned Poet Laureate of the German Empire: 'Oh age! oh letters! It is a joy to be alive! . . . Woe to you, barbarians!'[12] Dürer published his treatise on human proportion in 1528 'so that our successors may have something to perfect and lead to further progress'.[13] And a few years later Rabelais, though fully aware of the threat to free expression in Erasmus's 'worst age', wrote Gargantua's ringing letter to his son Pantagruel. 'The times when I was a student', declared the author's giant hero, 'were not as fit and favourable to learning as they are today . . . Indeed, the times were still dark . . . But thanks be to God, learning has been restored in my age to its former dignity and enlightenment. Why, the very women and girls aspire to the glory and reach out to the celestial manna of sound learning.'[14]

It was this sense of consistent improvement that led the word 'modern' to be used with increasing frequency. In 1448 the South Italian Luca di Puglia applied to work with Niccolò Pizzolo 'in order to learn to paint in the modern [*in recente*] style'.[15] The bastioned system of defensive architecture was dubbed fortification 'alla moderna'. Vasari praised Michelozzo for arranging the rooms inside the Medici palace with a view to comfort 'in the modern manner'.[16] Taking a longer view of this progress, it was Vasari in 1550 who used the potent word rebirth, *rinascita*, to describe the new enlightenment that had delivered the arts by breaking into their long subjection to Gothic and Byzantine barbarities.[17] For all its secular content, it was a word of powerful religious resonance. St John's Gospel had quoted Jesus: 'except a man be born again, he cannot see the Kingdom of God'. And to those to whom the arts and learning witnessed to man's better part, it was a readily appropriate idea. Dedicating his translation into French of Plutarch's *Lives* to King Henri II in 1559, Jacques Amyot referred to the king's father, Francis I, who 'so fortunately established good letters and caused them to be reborn and to flourish in this noble realm'.[18] In 1571 Jacques Charron edited yet another edition of Erasmus's *Adages*. Their deviser, he wrote, with what would have seemed an exaggeration in Italian eyes, 'was the first who came to the support of eloquent learning [*bonnes lettres*] at a time when it was on its way to rebirth and emergence from its barbarian mud'.[19]

It was not just a fresh start for the fine arts and letters that created the idea of a new cultural epoch. In 1581 Galileo's father Vincenzo represented the recovery of the ability to write and perform music to standards thought to have been reached in the ancient world in similar terms; from the barbarian invasions, 'men had been overcome by a heavy lethargy of ignorance, they lived without any desire of learning and took as little notice of music as of the Western Indies'. It was only in his own age (his references date this to the early sixteenth century) Vincenzo claimed, that man 'began to investigate what music was and so seek to rescue it from the darkness in which it had been buried'.[20]

While fashion kept alive the idea of short-term changes – in 1537 the architect Sebastiano Serlio was already complaining that 'the majority of people have always liked novelty and still do so'[21] – it was the breathtaking disregard of the medieval contribution to music, the arts and learning that influenced the overall notion of picking up each activity afresh from the condition antiquity had left it in.

In 1554 the tutor of the young Genoese noble Giovanni Battista Grimaldi advised his young charge that as he built up a collection of books for his study, he should have those by classical authors bound in red, those by modern ones in green; this would enable him to review the balance of accomplishment each colour represented. This followed expressions of the opinion that with the learning of the ancients digested, the moderns could do better. Guillaume Budé, celebrating the printing press for aiding 'the restoration and perpetuation of antiquity' in 1518 or 1519, went on to say: 'since in our age we see letters restored to life, what prevents us from seeing among us a new Demosthenes, Plato, Thucydides, Cicero?'[22] 'If only we apply our minds sufficiently', wrote the Spaniard Juan Luis Vives in 1531, 'we can judge better over the whole round of life and nature than could Aristotle, Plato, or any of the ancients.'[23] Vasari made it clear that by the death in 1564 of Michelangelo, painter, sculptor and architect, the ancients had been surpassed, for 'the three fine arts have been brought to a state of absolute perfection.'[24] Bacon was in no doubt that after antiquity and the long age that followed it, 'this third period of time will far surpass that of the Graecian and Roman learning.'[25] From the mid-sixteenth century, moreover, the sense of living in a third period was enhanced by the conviction that there was a widening response to the new learning. In his *The Rule of Reason*, a treatise on logic, Thomas Wilson in 1551 wrote of 'the forwardness of this age, wherein the very multitude are prompte and ripe in all sciences [branches of learning]'.[26] In 1599 the German Matthias Quadt declared that 'what in former days even the experts could not master can in our time be understood by plain, ordinary, and scarcely half-learned men. There will come a time', he added, 'when none of the secrets of nature will be out of the reach of the human mind.'[27] And this vision was supported by developments in the natural sciences, especially in the field of medicine. It was public benefit as well as intellectual satisfaction that caused Vesalius and the physician Jean Fernel in the 1540s to speak respectively of a 'blessed age'[28] and 'this age of ours which sees art and science gloriously rerisen after twelve centuries of swoon'.[29]

The third period of time was no mere construct of culture in its narrow sense. Bacon was as much a scientist as a man of letters. Louis Le Roy in 1547 conflated overseas discoveries and inventions alongside letters, painting, sculpture and architecture within the historical change that marked 'the last hundred years'.[30] Postel in 1560 put the discoveries and the use of artillery and the printing press alongside learning and letters as activities in which men 'have made more progress in fifty years than in the previous one thousand'.[31] There had been changes in rigging and ship design. Navigators came to supplement their reliance on the compass with log line and traverse board and, more sceptically, the quadrant. With these aids the survivors of Magellan's expedition from Spain who limped home in 1522 had been able to circumnavigate the globe. Five years later the merchant Robert Thorne spoke for a new age of exploitative maritime enterprise: 'there is no sea unnavigable, no land uninhabitable.'[32] Ficino's celebration of the golden age had gone on to include 'the military arts'. There was not a soldier or a stay-at-home who read about battles and the fortunes of combat who was not aware that the effective use of gunpowder weapons had from the mid-fifteenth century transformed the nature of warfare. No writer or reader was unaware of the imprint of mechanical movable typeface on the age, again from the mid-fifteenth century.

By 1620 the sense of liberation from the schoolroom of antiquity was put with missionary zeal by Alessandro Tassoni in his *A comparison between Ancient and Modern Ingenuity*.

> What did the Greeks and Romans ever invent that can be compared with the printing press . . . Let us pass on to the compass and to the nautical chart . . . what glory is owed to him who taught the Portuguese to navigate to an unknown pole, from one horizon to another? . . . What invention so tremendous was ever imagined that could match that of our artilleries? . . . What would the Greeks and Latins have said of the brilliant invention of wheel clocks that strike and show the hours in a perpetual round, as well as the motions of the planets? The telescope alone, with which you can see things fifteen or twenty miles away as though they were in front of you, and which discovers invisible stars in the sky, surpasses by far any Latin and Greek inventions that were discovered in the whole of their so-much celebrated course of years.[33]

No matter that the compass and gunpowder weapons and mechanical clocks were in fact products of the despised medieval centuries. They had been refined, put habitually to use, become part of a world grown larger and more richly endowed with information and investigative techniques than the ancient one. When Tassoni wrote it was becoming commonplace to link the compass of Columbus with Galileo's telescope; both means towards discovering aspects of nature unknown or misunderstood in antiquity. And this aspect of the age's novelty was refreshed by the links between productive technology and scientific advance. 'I am certain', wrote Vannoccio Biringuccio, the author of the first printed work to deal with every aspect of advances in metallurgy, 'that new information always gives birth in men's minds to new discoveries and so to further information.'[34]

Others, again, saw their age as being primarily defined by events which appeared to them to be of unprecedented significance. The early progress of sectarian Protestantism, which seemed to Erasmus to usher in 'the worst age of history', was seen by Luther in a different but equally epoch-making light: 'in this age everything begins to be restored, as if that day of the restoration of all things were near.'[35] The iconoclastic movements were actual physical assaults on what the past had stood for. When Englishmen in the 1530s were referring to their neighbours in such terms as 'he is of the new sort, he is of the old faith'[36] and Frenchmen from the 1560s to those branded with 'Pope-ism' or to 'Huguenotters', and when international politics had conflicting religious faiths folded deeply into their traditional rancours, it was clear that the links with local, suppressible or containable late medieval heresies – those of the English Lollards and the Bohemian Hussites – had been snapped.

The pace with which political alliances on a European scale were made, broken and re-formed and the more deeply scouring effects of warfare, led Guicciardini, looking back from the 1530s to the French invasion of 1494, to see it as 'a most unhappy year for Italy, and truly the beginning of years of wretchedness because it opened the way for innumerable horrible calamities which later for various reasons affected a great part of the rest of the world'.[37] It was an early statement of what was for centuries to be a habitual chronological break-point at 1494 in histories of European politics and diplomacy. It became increasingly difficult for reflective men to isolate political events from what they saw as defining their age. Referring in *The Courtier* to the period before the mid-fifteenth century, Castiglione said in his own voice 'that the men of those times were, generally speaking, far less capable than those of today; this is fully apparent from the works they have left us in letters as well as in pictures, statues, buildings and everything else.'

But as he set his characters talking among one another he found it impossible to keep the calamities referred to by Guicciardini from breaking into the charmed circle of cultivated topics they passed one to another. When this occurred, he had one of them restore the lightness of mood by saying 'it is better to pass over in silence what we cannot recall without sorrow', or 'I do not want to embark on a tale of woe, so it would be better to discuss the clothes our courtier ought to wear.'[38] Sir Francis Walsingham, the patron of spies, not of men of letters, had only in mind, more narrowly, the international political scene when he wrote of 'our times' and 'our age'.[39] But changes in the attitude to periods within the historical process as a whole twisted the chronology of the arts, of learning and letters, and of events more closely together.

Petrarch and the English scholar Richard of Bury had been contemporaries. But when the latter compared 'the novelties of the moderns' with 'the well-tested labours of the ancients', he was comparing the opinions of Aristotle with those of later Aristotelians.[40] He had no vision, as did Petrarch, of the general nature of classical literary discourse or the personalities of its spokesmen, nor of the long interval of 'darkness' that separated their time from his own. Thanks to this notion of an intervening age, in 1382 Filippo Villani could already refer in his book on illustrious Florentines to the names given to various islands in 'ancient, medieval and modern times'.[41] And as the Italian mode of dividing history into periods became familiar elsewhere in Europe it encouraged the habit of emphasizing the differences between them. Moreover, as the composition of histories became refined under the influence of classical models, which concentrated on political and military events, in both civic and national histories, the international repercussions of the Italian Wars and the Reformation encouraged the writing of contemporary history on a European scale, densely devoted to statecraft, war and religion. And it was increasingly accepted that, as the German Johann Sleidan put it in his *Commentaries* (1555), value judgements should be eschewed; what mattered was tracing each event 'as it actually happened'.[42] Both the writing of contemporary history and the emphasis on accuracy of detail had the same effect: to make the recent past and the present seem sharply different in kind from the previous age, for which reliable evidence was thinner; the middle age appeared ever more wan and irrelevant as a link between on the one hand the more clearly apprehended world of classical antiquity, and on the other the dense experience of 'our Age'.

The notion of living within a separate historical period added a sharpness to men's awareness of time's passing. Thomas Kantzow wrote in the 1530s of his chorography of Pomerania that thanks to him, 'posterity will have a record of the country as it was in my time.'[43] Cardano stressed that 'matters concerning contemporary society which are at present familiar to everyone should not just be mentioned in passing. This is how so many things of our historical past have been obscured.'[44] His autobiography, from which this remark is taken, joined Cellini's and a host of memoirs which, like those of the French soldier Blaise de Monluc, witnessed to an individual's wish to leave a stamp on times that were new and passing. The theme went back at least to Horace in the first century B C, but never before had poets so constantly urged their mistresses to let their rosebuds be gathered before it was too late. Worry about the hurrying impact of events led Giacomo Luccari in 1605 to mourn – in the generation of Donne, Lipsius and Galileo – the demise of 'the human intellect in this all-but-last age of the universe'.[45] He wrote in a Ragusa (Dubrovnik) that was increasingly isolated by the Turks from European contacts. But it was the early conflicts of the Thirty Years War that led Carlo Borromeo to describe the paintings in his collection in 1625 lest words were to remain the only source of knowledge of them, just as Pliny's words alone recalled the ancient works of art lost to the barbarians.

This scattering of opinions, though each was personally motivated and came from among what was in any case the minority of the articulate, does suggest that between the mid-fifteenth and the early seventeenth centuries thoughtful men – at different times and in different places and with different reasons – came to see themselves as living in a period which, for all its dovetailing into the previous centuries, felt different. For some this meant a participation in a period of cultural rebirth and in the fascinating maturity that followed. For most, the sources of awareness were more various. However posterity describes this century and a half, whether selectively as 'the Renaissance' or blandly and neutrally as the 'early modern' phase of European history, to contemporaries it was, cumulatively and naturally enough, 'our age'.

Notes
Bibliography
Index

NOTES

Unless otherwise indicated, references are to the books, articles (op. cit.) and editions of texts (ed. cit.) listed in the Bibliography. 'Quo.' signifies a contemporary quotation cited in the secondary work referred to.

CHAPTER I: THE DISCOVERY
OF EUROPE

1. 'Nos Europäi', *De Augmentis* (the extended Latin version of the 1605 *The Advancement of Learning*). Quo. Gollwitzer, p. 39.
2. Quo. Hutchison, p. 7.
3. *History of Henry VII*, ed. cit., p. 641; *Advancement of Learning*, ed. cit., p. 296.
4. Cochrane and Kirshner, p. 414.
5. *Certain Discourses Military*, ed. Hale, J. R., Ithaca, NY, 1964 passim.
6. Mundy, p. 85.
7. Michele Lauretano, SJ. I owe this reference to Dilwyn Knox.
8. Elliot, J. H. in Parker and Smith, p. 112.
9. Ed. cit., vol. iv, Parte terza, Novella LXII, Dedication.
10. Quo. Hay (1957), p. 109; 'vide Europaei'.
11. Gylford, John, prefatory poem to *Coryat's Crudities*, ed. cit., vol. 1, p. 68.
12. Quo. Law, T. G. in *The Cambridge Modern History*, vol. 3, p. 264.
13. Bussi, Gianandrea, quo. in Lowry, p. 25.
14. *Henry IV*, Part 2, 4. iii.
15. Quo. Hutton, p. 131.
16. Tr. Quint, p. 55.
17. For the 1471 woodcut and this drawing see *Die Verführung der Europa*, exhibition catalogue, ed. Mundt, Barbara, Staatliche Museen, Berlin, 1988, figs. 77, 136.
18. *Cosmograficae disciplinae compendium*, p. 2. Cited in Céard, *La Conscience européenne*, p. 60.
19. Strauss (1959), pp. 118–19, 127.
20. Tr. 1606. Introduction to the map of Europe.
21. Ed. cit., p. 34.
22. Biblioteca Correr, Venice, Portolano 40, 1r.
23. *Henry IV*, Part 1, 3. i.
24. Rowse, p. 50.
25. Part 2, 5. iii.
26. Davies, p. 159.
27. Herberstein, ed. cit., vol. 1, p. clx.
28. Fletcher, ed. cit., p. 58.
29. Herberstein, ed. cit., vol. 2, p. 11.
30. *Plantz, pourtraits et descriptions . . .*, Lyon, 1564, p. 11.
31. Quo. Anderson, M. S., *Britain's Discovery of Russia, 1553–1815*, London, 1958, p. 28.
32. 'To the Reader', English translation of 1606.
33. Rowse, pp. 32–3.
34. Basel, 1553. Quo. Strauss (1959), p. 84.
35. *The Minor Elizabethan Drama*. vol. 2, *Pre-Shakespearean Comedies*, London (Everyman), n. d., pp. 220–2.
36. Tr. Witt, in Kohl, Benjamin G. and Witt, Ronald G., eds., *The Earthly Paradise: Italian Humanists on Government and Society*, Manchester, 1978, p. 139.
37. Strauss (1959), p. 70.
38. Englander, pp. 345, 350.

39. Quo. Hale, ed., *Antonio de Beatis* . . ., p. 44.
40. Strauss (1959), pp. 63–4.
41. Ib., p. 83.
42. *Voyage*, ed. cit., p. 62.
43. Braudel, Fernand, *Identity* . . ., tr. Reynolds, Sian, London, 1989, p. 321.
44. Quo. Ehrensvärd, Ulla, in *Art and Cartography*, ed. Woodward, David, Chicago, 1987, p. 134.
45. Quo. Cochrane, 1981, p. 364.
46. Quo. Cozzi, Gaetano, *Il Doge Niccolò Contarini*, Venice, 1958, pp. 309–10.
47. Hay (1957), pp. 120–1.
48. Ed. cit., p. 197, pp. 120–1.
49. Heath, Michael, 'Unlikely Alliance: Valois and Ottomans' *Renaissance Studies*, vol. 3, no. 3 (1989), pp. 307–8.
50. *De Civilitate* . . ., ed. cit., p. 286.
51. Burien, Orlan, 'Interest of the English in Turkey as reflected in English Literature of the Renaissance', *Oriens*, vol. 5 (1954), p. 214.
52. Ib., p. 210.
53. Matheson, Peter, 'Thomas Müntzer's idea of an Audience', *History*, vol. 76, no. 247 (1991), p. 190, note 28.
54. Ed. cit., p. 20.
55. Ib., p. 135.
56. London, 1608, ed., p. 13.
57. Cooper, p. 222.
58. Ib., p. 180.
59. Ib., pp. 4, 43.
60. Ib., p. 229.
61. Cheyney, vol. 2, pp. 35–6.
62. Quo. Mote, E. W., in Levenson, p. 346.
63. Quo. Honour, p. 3.
64. Quo. Pagden (1987), p. 2.
65. Below, pp. 369–72 seq.
66. Quo. Morison, Samuel Eliot, *Admiral of the Ocean Sea, A Life of Christopher Columbus*, Boston, Mass., 1942, p. 556.
67. Quo. Todorov, Tzvetan, 'Viaggiatori e Indigeni', in Garin, pp. 341–2.
68. Montaigne, ed. cit., vol. 3, pp. 141–4.
69. Ib., vol. 1, p. 219.

CHAPTER II: THE COUNTRIES OF EUROPE

1. Quo. Gutierrez, Asensio, *La France et les français dans la littérature espagnole*, Saint-Etienne, 1977, p. 21.
2. *On the Eve of the Reformation: Letters of Obscure Men*, ed. Holborn, Hajo, 1964, pp. 143–4. Possibly written by one of Hutten's collaborators in the *Letters*.
3. Quo. *Conscience européenne*, p. 225.
4. *The Merchant of Venice*, I, iii.
5. *De Civilitate*, ed. cit., p. 278.
6. *Sei Giornate*, pp. 178–83.
7. Bradford, William, ed., *Correspondence of the Emperor Charles V*, London, 1850, pp. 455–60.
8. *The Works*, ed. McKerrow, R. B., 4 vols., Oxford, 1958, vol. 2, pp. 297–303.
9. Quo. Barycz, Henryk, in Brahmer, Mieczyslav, ed., *Italia, Venezia e Polonia tra Umanesimo e Rinascimento*, Warsaw, 1969, p. 153.
10. *La Oposición y conjunción de los dos grandes Luminares de la Tierra. Obra apazible y curiosa en la qual se trata de la dichosa Alianca* [the 1598 Peace of Vervins] *de Francia y España: con la Antipatia de Españoles y Franceses*. For what follows, see ed. cit., p. 223–35.
11. Ed. cit., p. 64.
12. Ed. cit., p. 38.
13. Quo Yates, Frances, *Astrea, The Imperial Throne in the sixteenth century*, Harmondsworth, 1977, p. 16.

14. *De Civilitate*, ed. cit., p. 276.
15. Quo. Archer, p. 131.
16. Quo. Hale (1963), p. 15.
17. Bächtiger, Franz, 'Andreaskreuz und Schweitzerkreuz: Feindschaft zwischen Landsknechten und Eidgenossen', *Jahrbuch des Bernischen Historischen Museums* (1971–2), pp. 205–70.
18. Ascoli, p. 50.
19. Quo. *Dictionary of National Biography* (Boorde).
20. Quo. Braudel (1981–4), vol. 3, p. 354.
21. Dilwyn Knox in Henry and Hutton, p. 103.
22. Barycz, V., op. cit. in note 9, passim.
23. Fynes Moryson, quo. Hale (1963), pp. 28–9.
24. Tr. Pine-Coffin, R. S., Harmondsworth, 1958, p. 48.
25. Op. cit., 251–2.
26. Tr. Holland, Philemon, quo. Hale (1963), p. 36.
27. 1570. Quo. Wilson, John Dover, *Life in Shakespeare's England*, London, 1964, p. 82–3.
28. Op. cit., p. 176.
29. Quo. Strauss (1971), p. 66.
30. Smith, William. Quo. Ozment (1989), p. 15.
31. Ed. cit. in note 25, p. 101.
32. Quo. Amelung, p. 149.
33. Ed. cit., 292 and 298. On Swiss, p. 364.
34. Quo. Roberts, Michael, *The Swedish Imperial Experience, 1560–1718*, London, 1979, p. 85.
35. Quo. Stechow, p. 16.
36. *Certain Discourses Military*, ed. Hale, J. R., Ithaca, N. Y., 1964, pp. 41–2.
37. *Autobiography*, p. 49.
38. Quo. Chambers, David in Chaney and Mack, p. 99.
39. Quo. Williams, Penry in Dickens, p. 155.
40. Anon., *A Relation . . . of the Island of England*, ed., Sneyd, C. A., Camden Society, 1847, pp. 20–5.
41. Quo. Wilson, op. cit., in note 24, p. 18.
42. Quo. Douglas, David C., ed., *English Historical Documents 1485–1558*, London, 1967, p. 207.
43. Ascoli, p. 102.
44. Bates, p. 134.
45. Quo. Wilson, op. cit., in note 24, p. 92.
46. Ed. cit., vol. 1, p. 10.
47. Ed. cit., p. 29.
48. Tr. in *Two Spanish Picaresque Novels* by Alpert, Michael, Harmondsworth, 1969, p. 106.
49. Platter (1963), p. 227.
50. Quo. Strauss (1959), p. 9.
51. Quo. Klein and Zerner, p. 49.
52. Braudel (1972–3), vol. 1, p. 237.
53. Beatis, pp. 111–12.
54. Quo. Strauss (1959), p. 112.
55. Quo. Stechow, pp. 58–9.
56. *The Discovery of a New World*, pp. 10–11.
57. Ed. cit., p. 295.
58. Possevino, Antonio. Paraphrased in Cochrane (1981), p. 359.
59. Bagrow, fig. 52.
60. Beatis, pp. 115 and 164–9 on 'France proper'.
61. Thomas Bedyll writing to Thomas Cromwell, quo. Brigden, p. 129.
62. Pagden (1990), p. 57–8.
63. *The Prologues and Epilogues of William Caxton*, ed. Crotch, W. J. B., London, 1928, pp. 108–9.
64. Quo. Grayson, Cecil, in *The Fairest Flower*, p. 168.
65. *A Dialogue on Language* in *The Literary Works of Machiavelli*, tr. Hale, J. R., Oxford, 1961, p. 190.
66. Quo. Mallett, M. E. and Hale, J. R., *The Military Organization of a Renaissance State: Venice c. 1400 to 1617*, Cambridge, 1984, p. 435.
67. Rauw, Johann. Quo. Strauss (1559), pp. 41–2.
68. *The Schoolmaster* (1570), by

Ascham, Robert, ed. Ryan, V. Lawrence, Ithaca, N. Y., 1967, p. 137.

69. Picot (1901–5), ii, p. 126.
70. 3, iii and 4, iii.
71. Quo. Honour, p. 123.
72. Quo. Margolin, J. C. in *Conscience européenne*, p. 235.
73. *The Policy of War* in *Early Works*, ed. Ayre, J., London, 1843, pp. 232–5.
74. Ed. cit., p. xxxi.
75. *The Education of a Christian Prince*. Quo. Russell, Joyceline G., *Peacemaking in the Renaissance*, London, 1986, p. 88.
76. Correspondence, ed. cit. in note 7, p. 136.
77. Quo. Frecero in Hollier, vol. 1, pp. 146–7.
78. Quo. Strong (1984), p. 159.
79. *Commentaries*, abridged in *Memoirs of a Renaissance Pope*, tr. Gragg, Florence A., New York, 1959, p. 81.
80. Sir Thomas Overbury. Quo. Hughes, Charles in *Shakespeare's England*, 2 vols., Oxford, 1932, vol. 1, p. 214.
81. Quo. Koenigsberger, H. G. and Mosse, George L., *Europe in the Sixteenth Century*, London, 1968, p. 176.
82. Quo. Cottrell, p. 27.
83. Quo. Hale, J. R., *Florence and the Medici*, London, 1977, p. 169.
84. Quo. Elton, G. R., *Renaissance and Reformation 1300–1648*, London, 2nd ed., 1968, p. 134.
85. Ed. cit., p. 41.
86. Quo. Strong (1984), p. 159.
87. Quo. Bonney, p. 313.
88. *Il Principe*, chap. 3, in *Opere*, cit.
89. Quo. Pagden (1990), p. 65.
90. Quo. Aulard, A., *Le Patriotisme français de la Renaissance à la Revolution*, Paris, 1921, p. 21, note 60.
91. Platter (1963), pp. 48–9.

92. Quo. Strauss (1959), pp. 76–7.
93. Beatis, p. 51.
94. Quo. Strauss (1971), p. 198.
95. Ib., p. 91.
96. Quo. Ozment (1973), p. 143.
97. Quo. Heinemann, Margot in Braunmuller and Hattaway, p. 181.
98. Goodman, David C., *Power and Penury*, Cambridge, 1987, p. 102.
99. Quo. Trevor-Roper (1976), p. 50.
100. Quo. Hale (1983), p. 67.
101. Kelley, Donald in Foster and Teich, p. 134.
102. Platter (1937), p. 228.
103. 3, i.
104. 4, v.

CHAPTER III: THE DIVISIONS OF EUROPE

1. *The Memoirs of Philip de Commines*, tr. Scobie, A. R., 2 vols., London, 1855–6, vol. 1, pp. xlvi and 379.
2. Quo. Ruffman, Karl H., *Das Russbild im England Shakespeares*, Göttingen, 1952, pp. 168–9.
3. 'Instrucciones de Carlos-Quinto à Don Felipe su hijo' in Ch. Weiss, ed., *Papiers d'Etat du Cardinal de Granvelle*, vol. 3, Paris, 1842, pp. 267–318.
4. Ib., paraphrased and abbreviated.
5. Quo. Hutton, p. 115.
6. Stechow, p. 72.
7. Lloyd, Lodowick, *The Stratagems of Jerusalem*, London, 1602.
8. Quo Bouthoul, Gaston, *Les Guerres*, Paris, 1951, pp. 278–9.
9. Quo. Tillyard, E. M. W., *The Elizabethan World Picture*, London, 1950, p. 5.
10. Quo. Davies, p. 143.
11. 'Of bad Meanes emploied to a good End', ed. cit. (1910), vol. 2, p. 409.
12. Ed. cit., p. 77.
13. Tr. Cohen, J. M., Harmondsworth, 1950, p. 341.
14. Quo. Terry, Arthur, in Mulryne and Shewring, p. 116.

15. For these quotations and their context: Hale, J. R., *War and Society in Renaissance Europe*, London, 1985, p. 91.

16. Quo. Hale, J. R. in *The New Cambridge Modern History*, vol. 1, Cambridge, 1957, p. 290.

17. Quo. Terry, Arthur, in Mulryne and Shewring, p. 105.

18. Quo. Hutton, p. 79.

19. Quo. Vasiliev, A. A., *History of the Byzantine Empire*, 2 vols., Madison, Wi., 1958, vol. 2, p. 656.

20. Letter to Francesco Vettori, 10 August, 1513. *Lettere Familiari*, ed. Alvisi, E., Florence, 1883, p. 277.

21. Quo. Mattingly, Garrett, *Renaissance Diplomacy*, London, 1955, p. 109.

22. Quo. Osborn, *Young Philip Sidney*, p. 342.

23. *The Treatise of Lorenzo Valla on the Donation of Constantine*, tr. Coleman, C. B., New Haven, Conn., 1922, p. 167.

24. Quo. Fichtner, Paula Sutter, *Ferdinand I of Austria 1503–1564*, Boulder, 1982, p. 4.

25. Both quoted in Parker, Geoffrey, *The Army of Flanders and the Spanish Road, 1567–1659*, Cambridge, 1972, p. 133.

26. Quo. Koenigsberger, H. G. and Mosse, George C., *Europe in the Sixteenth Century*, London, 1968, p. 198.

27. Sir Ralph Winwood. Quo. Buisseret, David, *Henry IV*, London, 1984, p. 85.

28. *Utopia*, ed. cit., pp. 87–9.

29. Marino Cavalli. Quo. Knecht, R. J., *Francis I*, Cambridge, 1982, pp. 95–6.

30. Quo. Maltby, William S., *Alba. A biography of Fernando Alvarez de Toledo, third Duke of Alba, 1507–1582*, Berkeley, Ca., 1983, p. 82.

31. Marin Sanudo. For context see Mallett, M. E. and Hale, J. R., *The Military Organization of a Renaissance State: Venice c. 1400 to 1617*, Cambridge, 1984, p. 317.

32. Quo. Santillana, Giorgio de, *The Crime of Galileo*, London, 1958, p. 6.

33. Quo. Brown, A., p. 112.

34. Hair, p. 124.

35. Quo. Speroni, Charles, *Wit and Wisdom of the Italian Renaissance*, Los Angeles, 1964, p. 147, note 43.

36. Quo. Ozment (1975), p. 26.

37. Cochrane and Kirshner, p. 327.

38. Brigden, p. 110.

39. Cameron, p. 122.

40. Quo. Dickens, A. G. in Mack and Jacob, p. 206.

41. Brigden, p. 437.

42. Ozment (1973), pp. 140–1.

43. Quo Terry, Arthur, in Mulryne and Shewring, p. 112.

44. Ed. cit., p. 20.

45. Ed. cit., p. 194.

46. *The Apology and Treatise*, Keynes, Geoffrey, London, 1951, p. 49.

47. Quo. Terry, Arthur, in Mulryne and Shewring, p. 113.

48. Both quotations in Braudel, *The Identity of France*, vol. 1, pp. 121–2.

49. Quo. Douglas, David C., *English Historical Documents 1485–1558*, London, 1967, p. 177.

50. Quo. (from tr. London, 1548) by Yates, *Astraea: The Imperial Theme in the Sixteenth Century*, pp. 55–6.

51. Stanley of Alderley, Lord, ed., *The First Voyage round the World by Magellan*, Hakluyt Society, 1874, p. xxix.

52. *My Voyage round the World*, tr. Weinstock, Herbert, London, 1965, p. 201.

53. *Four Years at the Court of Henry VIII. Despatches written by the Venetian Ambassador, Sebastian Giustinian*, ed. Brown, R., 2 vols., London, 1954, vol. 2, p. 57.

54. François Duaren. Quo. Fulbecke,

William, *The Pandectes of the Law of Nations*, London, 1602, p. 41v.
55. Ed. cit., p. 163.
56. Quo. Pagden (1990), p. 49.
57. Quo. Mattingly, op. cit. in note 21, p. 292.
58. *De Jure Belli Libri Tres*, Rolfe, W. John C., Oxford, 1933, p. 3.
59. Quo. Ozment (1973), p. 222.
60. Émeric Crucé, *The New Cyneas*, tr. Balch, T. W., Philadelphia, 1909, p. 4.
61. Quo. Bouwsma, p. 130.
62. Quo. Saitta, p. 25.
63. Ib., pp. 28 seq. Derek Heater kindly showed me the typescript chapter on Henri IV and Sully for his forthcoming *The Idea of European Unity*.
64. Ed. cit., p. 66.
65. Ib., p. 10.
66. Ib., p. 104.
67. Ib., p. 114.
68. Quo. Parker, Geoffrey, *Europe in Crisis, 1598–1648*, London, 1979, p. 14.
69. Ib., *The Thirty Years War*, London, 1984, p. xiv.

CHAPTER IV: TRAFFIC

1. Platter (1937), pp. 229–30.
2. Sastrow, p. 172.
3. Quo. Braudel (1981–3), vol. 2, p. 48.
4. His letter describing 'the whole tragi-comedy of my journey' from Basel to Louvain is translated in Huizinga, J., *Erasmus of Rotterdam*, London, 1952, pp. 223–9.
5. Quo. Braudel (1981–4), vol. 3, p. 27.
6. Ed. cit., p. 19.
7. Ed. cit., pp. xii-xiii.
8. Geanakoplos, Deno, 'La Colonia greca di Venezia e il Rinascimento' in Pertusi, A., ed., *Venezia e l'Oriente fra tardo medioevo e Rinascimento*, Florence, 1966, p. 186.

9. Ed. cit., p. 318.
10. Monga, p. 115.
11. Elliott (1970), p. 73.
12. Ib., pp. 75, 96.
13. Nicander Nucius. Quo. Platter (1937) p. 95.
14. Quo. Simonin, M., in *Conscience européenne*, p. 384.
15. Ed. cit., p. 320.
16. *De Liberorum Educatione*, tr. Nelson, J. S., Washington, 1940, p. 137.
17. 5, ii.
18. Clark, Sir George, *A History of the Royal College of Physicians of London*, Oxford, vol. 1, 1964, p. 170.
19. *Queen Elizabeth's Academy*, ed. Furnivall, F. J., Early English Text Society, extra series, vol. viii.
20. Quo. Wright, Louis B., *Middle-Class Culture in Elizabethan England*, Chapel Hill, 1935, p. 365.
21. Spitz, p. 241.
22. Vettori, Francesco, *Viaggio in Alemagna* in *Scritti storici e politici*, ed. Niccolini, E., Bari, 1972, p. 105.
23. Tr. Alpert, Michael, Harmondsworth, 1969, p. 67.
24. Quo Rouillard, p. 222.
25. Quo. Ozment (1990), p. 25.
26. Quo. Hale (1963), pp. 18–9.
27. Quo. Kohn, Hans, *The Idea of Nationalism*, New York, 1940, p. 159.
28. Jerome Horsey. Quo. *Of the Russe Commonwealth by Giles Fletcher 1591*, ed. Pipes, Richard and Fine, J. V. A., Hakluyt Society, 1966, p. 13.
29. Quo. (from *First Fruites*) Rossi, Sergio and Savoia, Daniella, *Italy and the English Renaissance*, Milan, 1989, p. 17.
30. Ed. cit., p. 322.
31. Ozment (1989), p. 108.
32. Quo. Picot (1906), vol. 1, p. 51.
33. Ed. cit. (1942), p. 234.
34. Ed. cit. (1910), vol. 2, p. 256.
35. Quo. *Canon Pietro Casola's*

*Pilgrimage to Jerusalem in the Year
1494*, ed. Newett, M. Margaret,
Manchester, 1907, p. 92.
36. Quo. Prescott, H. F. M., *Jerusalem
Journey: Pilgrimage to the Holy Land
in the Fifteenth Century*, London,
1954, pp. 69–70.
37. Op. cit. in note 35, p. 230.
38. Quo. Braudel, *The Identity of
France*, vol. 1, p. 158.
39. Cochrane (1981), p. 253.
40. Quo. Elliott (1970), p. 76.
41. Quo. Kagan, Richard L. in
Levenson, p. 60.
42. Quo. Davies, p. 441.
43. Quo. Braudel (1981–4), vol. 2,
p. 166.
44. Quo. Israel, p. 11.
45. Ib., p. 15.
46. Ib., vol. 3, p. 187.
47. *Autobiography*, pp. 50–51.
48. 5, v.
49. Quo. Ozment (1989), p. 80.
50. Quo. Letts, Malcolm, *Bruges and its
Past*, London, 1924, p. 133.
51. Platter (1963), p. 117.
52. 4, i.
53. Quo. Koenigsberger, H. G. and
Mosse, George L., *Europe in the
Sixteenth Century*, London, 1968,
p. 203.
54. Quo. Roberts (1968), p. 8.
55. Quo. Hamilton, H., *The English
Brass and Copper Industries to 1880*,
London (reprint), 1967, p. 6.
56. Ed. cit., p. 300.
57. Quo. Bates, p. 10.
58. *The Travels of Leo of Rozmital*, tr.
and ed. Letts, Malcolm, Hakluyt
Society, 1957, p. 19.
59. Op. cit. in note 22, pp. 203–4.
60. Quo. Eisenstein, p. 472.
61. Quo. Bates, pp. 33–4.
62. Quo. Dionisotti, Carlo, *Europe in
Sixteenth-Century Italian Literature*,
Taylorian Lecture, Oxford, 1971,
pp. 11–12.
63. Ed. cit., p. 43.
64. 'Frons aperta, lingua parca, mens

clausa'. Quo. Bates, op. cit. in note
58, from Sir Robert Dallington's
1606 *A Method for Travell.*
65. Quo. Matthiesson, F. O.,
Translation: an Elizabethan Art,
Massachusetts, 1931, p. 20.
66. Beatis, p. 57.
67. Ed. cit., p. 46.

CHAPTER V:
TRANSFORMATIONS

1. Ed. cit. (1955), book 4, chapters 55–6.
2. Quo. Whitfield, J. H., in
Hainsworth, Peter, ed., *The
Language of Literature in Renaissance
Italy*, Oxford, 1988, p. 37.
3. *The Literary Works of Machiavelli*, tr.
Hale, J. R., Oxford, 1961, p. 139.
4. Quo. Matthiesson, p. 54.
5. Ib., p. 181.
6. *De varietate fortunae*, extract in
Valentini, R., and Zucchetti, G.,
Codice topografico della città di Roma,
IV, Rome, 1953, p. 231.
7. Quo. Mitchell, Charles, in Jacob,
E. F., ed., *Italian Renaissance Studies*,
London, 1960, p. 470.
8. *Tutte le Opere*, ed. Mazzoni, G.,
Casella, M., p. 56.
9. Quo. Martines (1991), p. 111.
Lauro Martines kindly showed me
this article 'The Protean Face of
Renaissance Humanism' before
publication.
10. *The Conquest of New Spain*, tr.
Cohen, J. M., Harmondsworth,
1963, p. 131.
11. Quo. Lynn, Caro, *A College
Professor of the Renaissance*,
Chicago, 1937, p. 110.
12. Quo. Eisenstein, p. 396.
13. *Institutio Oratoria*, Loeb edn., IV,
p. 509.
14. *Letters*, translated under the title *On
the Eve of the Reformation: Letters of
Obscure Men by Ulrich von Hutten*,
et al., New York, 1964, p. 210.
15. Vives, J. L., *In Pseudo Dialecticos*, tr.

Fantazzi, C., Leiden, 1979,
p. 88–90.
16. King, p. 205.
17. Quo. Brown, p. 70.
18. *Familiar Colloquies*, tr. Bailey, N.,
Glasgow, 1877, p. 96 (amended).
19. Quo. Dickens, A. G., in Mack and
Jacob, p. 209.
20. Quo. Holberton, p. 63.
21. 2, ii.
22. Quo. Golzio, Vincenzo, *Raffaello
nei Documenti*, Rome, 1936, p. 30.
23. Thornton, P., p. 394, note 16.
24. Platter (1963), p. 66.
25. Quo. Hope, Charles, in *Andrea
Mantegna*, catalogue, ed., Martineau,
Jane, London, 1992, pp. 350–1.
26. Tr. Cohen, J. M., book 1, chap. 48,
Harmondsworth, 1950, p. 429.
27. 2, ii.
28. Wickham, Glynne, *A History of the
Theatre*, 2nd edn., London, 1992,
p. 138.
29. Dreyer, p. 74.
30. King, p. 199.
31. Ed. cit., p. 343.
32. 2, ii.
33. Garin, p. 195.
34. Ed. cit., vol. 1, p. 55.
35. Ed. cit., vol. 3, p. 167.
36. Seneca, *Letters*, ed. cit., pp. 237–8,
note 49.
37. *Discorsi del Poema eroica*. I owe this
reference to Hellmut Wohl.
38. *Letters*, ed. cit., p. 171.
39. Quo. Cameron, James K., in
Goodman and MacKay, p. 145.
40. Quo. Oestreich, p. 26.
41. Ib., p. 33.
42. Saunders, p. 22.
43. Quo. ib., p. 55.
44. *Lives*, ed. cit., vol. 1, p. 245.
45. Quo in Beatis, p. 46.
46. Quo. ib., p. 47.
47. Beatis, p. 96.
48. Ib., p. 182.
49. Quo. Mainz, Valerie, in Weston
and Davies, p. 143.
50. Quo. Honour, p. 1.

51. Ed. cit., vol. 1, p. 57.
52. Ed. cit., vol. 1, pp. 249–52.
53. Vasari, Giorgio, *Le Vite*, ed.
Milanesi, Gaetano, 9 vols., Florence,
1875–85, vol. 5, p. 224.
54. Stechow, p. 38.
55. Boschini, quo. Hope, Charles,
Titian, London, 1980, p. 163–4.
56. Quo. Würtenberger, p. 107.
57. Both quotations from Murray,
Peter J., *The Architecture of the Italian
Renaissance*, London, 1963, p. 6.
58. Ed. cit., vol. 1, p. 248.
59. Quo. Hutchison, p. 138.
60. Quo. Thornton, Peter, p. 369, note 30.
61. Ed. cit., pp. 16–7.
62. Quo. Campbell, p. 202.
63. Quo. ib., p. 204.
64. Quo. ib., p. 193.
65. Quo. Thornton, Dora, vol. 1, p. 74.
66. *On the Art of Building*, cit., p. 149.
67. Quo. Pedretti, Carlo, in *Le Lieu
Théâtral à la Renaissance*, Paris,
1964, p. 26.
68. Quo. Thornton, Dora, vol. 1,
pp. 45–6.
69. Tr. Alpert, Michael, in *Two Spanish
Picaresque Novels*, Harmondsworth,
1969, p. 159.
70. Quo. Cochrane et al., 1987, p. 10.
71. Quo. Dreyer, p. 311.
72. Quo. Ozment (1983), p. 65.
73. Quo. Perjéz, pp. 268–9.
74. Quo. Ozment, 1989, p. 80.
75. Quo. Friedman, p. 50.
76. Quo. Ozment, 1983, p. 55.
77. See Braudel, *Civilisation and
Capitalism*, tr. Reynolds, Sian,
London, 1982, vol. 2, chapter 6 and
passim.
78. Wright, p. 341.
79. Ed. cit., vol. 1, p. 7.
80. Quo. Strauss (1959), p. 137.
81. Quo. Jordan, Constance,
*Renaissance Feminism. Literary
Texts and Political Models*, Ithaca,
N. Y., 1990, p. 174.
82. *Catalogue*, p. 10, item 17.
83. Quo. Salinger, p. 6.

84. Ib., p. 5.
85. I owe this information to Tommaso Astarita.
86. Ed. cit., vol. 1, p. 91.

CHAPTER VI: TRANSMISSIONS

1. In Weinstein, Donald, ed., *The Renaissance and the Reformation, 1300–1600*, New York, 1965, p. 120.
2. *Catalogue*, p. 11, Lot 24.
3. *Album*, p. 25
4. Quo. Kohn, Hans, *The Idea of Nationalism*, New York, 1944, p. 158.
5. *Autobiography*, p. 53.
6. Spitz, p. 13.
7. Trevor-Roper (1986), p. 151.
8. Cochrane, p. 350.
9. Lowry, p. 165.
10. Kemp, p. 279.
11. *The Fugger News-Letters*, ed. Klarwill, Victor von, London, 1928, pp. 59–60.
12. Quo. Campbell, p. 165.
13. Quo. Rosand, David, 'Dialogues and Apologies: Sidney and Venice', *Studies in Philology*, 1991, 236–49.
14. Quo. Philips, Margaret Mann, *Erasmus and the Northern Renaissance*, London, 1949, p. 206.
15. Quo. Rowse, pp. 46–7, from the 1573 translation of Lluyd's *Commentarioli*.
16. Sastrow, p. 262.
17. Quo. Matthiesson, F. O., *Translation: an Elizabethan Art*, Cambridge, Mass., 1931, p. 25.
18. Quo. Wright, Louis B., *Middle-Class Culture in Elizabethan England*, Chapel Hill, 1935, p. 347.
19. *Catalogue*, p. 24, lot 70.
20. Ed. London, Everyman, n. d., p. 7.
21. Quo. Hutchison, p. 141.
22. Campbell, p. 183.
23. Jacobowitz, Ellen S., and Stepanek, Stephanie, *The Prints of Lucas van Leyden and his Contemporaries*,

Catalogue, National Gallery, Washington, 1983, p. 13.
24. Quo. Gombrich, p. 110.
25. Vasari, *Le Vite*, ed. Milanesi, Gaetano, 9 vols., Florence, 1875–85, vol. 5, p. 430.
26. Quo. Gilbert, Creighton E., *Italian Art 1400–1500*, Englewood Cliffs, 1980, p. 112.
27. Chambers, p. 134.
28. Quo. Elam, Caroline, 'Art and Diplomacy in Renaissance Florence', *Journal of the Royal Society of Arts*, October, 1988, p. 821.
29. Ib., p. 821.
30. Quo. Stechow, pp. 56–7.
31. Quo. White, Christopher, *Peter Paul Rubens*, New Haven, Conn., 1987, p. 11.
32. Beatis, p. 132.
33. Quo. Wittkower, Rudolf and Margot, *Born under Saturn*, London, 1963, p. 60.
34. Ed. cit., vol. 2, p. 183.
35. Ib., vol. 2, p. 299.
36. Ed. cit., n. 25 above, vol. 7, p. 309. It was in one of the compositions made for Michelangelo's funeral obsequies.
37. Quo. Furnivall, F. J. ed., *Early English Meals and Manners*, Early English Text Society, vol. 32, 1968, p. xix.
38. *Autobiography*, tr. Bull, George, Harmondsworth, 1956, p. 21.
39. Beatis, p. 51.
40. Quo. *New Oxford History of Music*, vol. 3, ed. Hughes, Dom Anselm and Abraham, Gerald, Oxford, 1960, p. 372, note 1.
41. Quo. Bridgman, p. 202.
42. Quo. Scarisbrick, J. J., *Henry VIII*, Harmondsworth, 1971, p. 32.
43. Quo. Cummings, Anthony M., *The Politicized Muse: Music for Medici Festivals, 1512–1537*, Princeton, 1992, p. 128.
44. Quo. Bridgman, Nanie in *Ars Nova and the Renaissance 1300–1540*, ed.

Hughes, Dom Anselm and Abraham, Gerald, Oxford, 1960, p. 283.

45. Ed. cit., p. 145.

46. Quo. Arnold, Denis, 'Josquin des Prez' in Hale, J. R., ed., *Concise Encyclopaedia of the Italian Renaissance*, London, 1981, p. 179.

47. Quo. Kubler, George, *Portuguese plain Architecture . . . 1521–1706*, Middletown, Conn., 1972, p. 17 and note 26.

48. Quo. Klaniczay, Tibor, in Porter and Teich, p. 167.

49. Quo. Bircher, Martin, in *Fairest Flower*, p. 123.

50. Quo. Ed. Evans, Marice, Harmondsworth, 1977, p. 10.

51. Both this and the following quotation, from Germaine Greer, *Shakespeare*, Oxford, 1986.

52. *Fratris Felicis Fabri Evagatorium*, ed. Hassler, C. D., Stuttgart, 1843, I, pp. 95–6.

53. Quo. Gombrich, E. H., *The Heritage of Apelles: Studies in the Art of the Renaissance*, Oxford, 1976, p. 112.

54. Quo. McFarlane, p. 5.

55. Paolo Giovio, referring fastidiously to a life of Marcus Aurelius by a Spanish monk. Quo. Cochrane (1981) p. 319.

56. Quo. Grayson, Cecil, in Chastel, André et al., eds., *The Renaissance. Essays in Interpretation*, London, 1982, p. 218.

57. Quo. Panofsky, Erwin, *The Life and Art of Albrecht Dürer*, Princeton, 1955, p. 245.

58. Quo. Englander, p. 478.

59. Quo. Benesch, Otto, in Gundersheimer, Werner, ed., *French Humanism 1470–1600*, London, 1969, p. 216.

60. Quo. Cruikshank, J., ed., *French Literature and its Background*, vol. 1, *The Sixteenth Century*, Oxford, 1968, p. 98.

61. Ed. cit., p. 14, 'Les petitz corps. . .'.

62. 'Si tu veux que je meure. . .' in McFarlane, p. 278.

63. Tr. Lobb, Frances, *The Twenty-Four Love Sonnets: Louise Labé 1525–1566*, London, 1950, p. 41.

64. Ed. cit., p. 108. 'Amour, je ne me plans. . .'.

65. No. xxxi.

66. Quo. Armstrong, Elizabeth, *Ronsard and the Age of Gold*, Cambridge, 1968, p. 15.

67. Ib., p. 43.

68. Quo. Dorsten, J. A. Van, *Poets, Patrons and Professors: Sir Philip Sidney, Daniel Rogers and the Leiden Humanists*, Oxford, 1962, p. 117.

69. 3, ii.

70. Quo. Black, J. B., *The Reign of Elizabeth 1558–1603*, Oxford, 1976, p. 257.

71. Ib., p. 244.

72. *Second Frutes*. Quo. Rossi, Sergio, in Rossi and Savoia, *Italy and the English Renaissance*, Milan, 1989, p. 13.

73. Part Two, 4, iv.

74. Quo. Gurr, p. 35.

75. 5, ii.

76. 4, i.

CHAPTER VII: CIVILITY

1. *Life of Johnson*, ed. Chapman, R. W., Oxford, 1980, p. 466. I owe this reference to Stuart Proffitt.

2. Ed. cit., pp. 6–7.

3. Vitruvius, *Ten Books of Architecture*, II, i.

4. *On the Good Life*, tr. Grant, Michael, Harmondsworth, 1971, p. 242.

5. Quo. Le Goff, Jacques, *Time, Work and Culture in the Middle Ages*, Chicago, 1980, pp. 225–6.

6. Quo. Rubinstein, Nicolai, in Pagden (1987), p. 55.

7. Quo. Elliott (1970), p. 94.
8. *The Politics of Aristotle*, ed. and tr. Barker, Ernest, Oxford, 1948, p. 14.
9. Ed. cit., p. 298.
10. Hanke, p. 133.
11. Ed. cit., pp. 101–2.
12. Cottrell, p. 68.
13. *Six Bookes of Politickes*, tr. Jones, William, London, 1594, p. 17.
14. Menavino, Giovanni Antonio. Quo. Cochrane, p. 331.
15. Quo. Barthelemy, Anthony Gerard, *Black Face maligned Race. The Representation of Blacks in English Drama from Shakespeare to Southerne*, Baton Rouge, 1987, pp. 4–5.
16. Quo. Honour, p. 56.
17. Quo. Kamen, p. 5.
18. Quo. Elliott (1970), p. 45.
19. Quo. Fletcher, p. 10.
20. Quo. Jardine (1990), p. 78.
21. Ed. cit., p. 199.
22. Quo. Bates, pp. 177–8.
23. Op. cit., pp. 36, 117.
24. Quo. Brown, p. 116.
25. Ed. cit., p. 261.
26. Book 2, 10, v.
27. Hutton, p. 86.
28. Quo. Yates, p. 60.
29. Book 6, 1, i.
30. Ed. cit., pp. 56, 174–5.
31. *Civilis conversationis libri duo*, Hanover, 1611, p. 1. I owe this reference to Dilwyn Knox.
32. Quo. Huppert, pp. 766–7.
33. Fletcher, p. 115v.
34. E.g. Machiavelli, *Discorsi sopra la prima Deca di Tito Livio*, lib. 2, cap. xxiv; the extent to which the phrase was in the air is suggested by its use by the architect Michele Sanmicheli: Mallett, M. E. and Hale, J. R., *The Military Organization of a Renaissance State: Venice c. 1400–1617*, Cambridge, 1984, p. 421.
35. Grendler, 1989, p. 63.
36. Quo. Elam, Caroline and Gombrich, E. H. in Denley and Elam. London, 1988, p. 481.
37. Tr. Price, Russell, ed. Skinner, Quentin, Cambridge, 1988, p. 52.
38. *Arte della Guerra*, ed. Bertelli, Sergio, Milan, 1961, p. 518.
39. Ed. cit., p. 284.
40. Quo. de la Barre-Duparcq, E., 'L'Art Militaire pendant les Guerres de Religion 1562–1598', *Séances et Travaux de l'Académie des Sciences Morales et Politiques*, 1864, p. 290.
41. *Correspondence of the Emperor Charles V*, ed. Bradford, William, London, 1850, p. 457.
42. Quo. Simon, Joan, *Education and Society in Tudor England*, Cambridge, 1966, p. 369.
43. Quo. Chilton, Paul, in Mulryne and Shewring, p. 132.
44. Cafritz, p. 21.
45. Ed. cit., vol. 1, p. 219.
46. Elliott (1970), p. 26.
47. 2, i.
48. *Method for the easy Comprehension of History*, tr. Reynolds, Beatrice, New York, 1966, p. 298.
49. Quo. Cipolla, Carlo, *European Culture and Overseas Expansion*, Harmondsworth, 1970, p. 100.
50. Quo. Wright, p. 530.
51. 'Loves Growth'.
52. I owe much to the explication by Yamey, pp. 115 seq.
53. Quo. Cochrane and Kirshner, p. 411.
54. Quo. Mitchell, R. J., *The Spring Voyage*, 1964, p. 19.
55. *The Voyages and Colonising Enterprises of Sir Humphrey Gilbert*, ed. Quinn, D. B., Hakluyt Society, London, 1940, II, p. 387.
56. Quo. Skrine, Peter, 'Images of the Merchant in German Renaissance Literature', *Bulletin of the John Rylands Library*, vol. 72, 1990, p. 189.
57. Quo. Ferguson, Wallace K., *Europe

in Transition, 1300–1520, London, 1962, p. 434.

58. *The Prince*, ch. xvii.
59. Illus. in ed. Levenson, p. 647, fig. 1.
60. *Sommario della Storia d'Italia in Scritti storici e politici*, ed. Niccolini, E., Bari, 1972, p. 152.
61. Ed. cit., p. 40.
62. Quo. Ozment (1990), p. 90.
63. Above, p. 288.
64. Quo. Bennett, H. S., *English Books and Readers 1475 to 1557*, Cambridge, 1952, pp. 121–2.
65. Quo. Thornton, Peter, p. 393, column 3, note 9.
66. Long, pp. 328, 332, 339.
67. Quo. Cochrane and Kirshner, pp. 248–9.
68. Quo. Skrine, op. cit. in note 56, p. 188.
69. Quo. Kent, F. W. and Lillie, Amanda in Denley and Elam, p. 352.
70. *I Diarii*, ed. Cessi, Roberto, 4 vols., Bologna, 1912–38, vol. 4, p. 24.
71. Quo. Brigden, p. 471.
72. Quo. Jardine (1983), pp. 147–8.
73. Ed. cit., p. 206.
74. Yamey, p. 20.
75. *The Literary Works of Machiavelli*, tr. Hale, J. R., Oxford, 1961, pp. 84–5.
76. Quo. Schama, Simon, *The Embarrassment of Riches*, London, 1987, p. 7.
77. Quo. Elliott (1986), p. 305.
78. Quo. Stone, Lawrence, *The Crisis of the Aristocracy*, Oxford, 1965, p. 50.
79. Platter (1963), p. 47.
80. Quo. Lowry, p. 8.
81. Facsimile ed. with introduction by Cholakian, Rouben C., 2 vols., New York, 1973, vol. 2, p. 501v.
82. Ib. vol. 2, p. 540.
83. Ib., vol. 1, p. 55v.
84. Quo. Cochrane (1981), p. 235.

85. Paruta, P., *Discorsi Politici*, Venice, 1599, p. 569.
86. Quo. Mann, Nicholas, *Petrarch*, Oxford, 1984, p. 28.
87. Quo. Englander, p. 149.
88. Quo. Woodward, W. H., *Studies in Education during the Age of the Renaissance*, Cambridge, 1924, p. 67.
89. Quo. Harbison, E. Harris, *The Christian Scholar in the Age of the Reformation*, New York, 1956, p. 87.
90. Guazzo, vol. 1, p. 8.
91. Quo. Pagden (1990), p. 47.
92. Henry Dowes. Quo. Furnivall, F. J., *Early English Meals and Manners*, cit., pp. xxi–xxii.
93. Quo. Cohn, Henry, in Mulryne and Shewring, pp. 25–6.
94. Starkey, p. 126.
95. *Journal*, ed. cit., p. vi.
96. Quo. Spitz, pp. 163, 165.
97. I, v.
98. Quo. Simon, p. 15.
99. Quo. Burke (1978), p. 253.
100. Alberti, *De re Aedificatoria*, Bk. IX, chap. ix, trans. Bartoli, C., Leoni, J., ed. Rykwert, J., *Ten Books on Architecture* (reprint from 1755 edn.), London, 1965, p. 205.
101. Frommel, p. 41.
102. Thornton, Peter, p. 323, column 2.
103. Quo. Seward, Desmond, *Naples: A Traveller's Companion*, London, 1984, pp. 113–5.
104. Quo. Brown, Alison, pp. 109–10.
105. *The Ten Books on Architecture*, tr. Morgan, Morris Hicky, New York, 1960, pp. 5–6.
106. Quo. Chastel, André, in Garin, E., ed., *L'Uomo del Rinascimento*, Bari, 1988, p. 254.
107. Quo. Stechow, pp. 112–3.
108. Ib., p. 114.
109. *The Elder Pliny's Chapters on the History of Art*, tr. Jex-Blake, K., London (reprint), 1968, pp. 108–9.
110. Ib., pp. 118–9.

111. Quo. Ames-Lewis, Francis in *Bulletin of the Society for Renaissance Studies*, October, 1989, p. 25.
112. Op. cit. in note 109, p. 168–9.
113. Stechow, p. 116.
114. Quo. Chastel in op. cit. in note 106, p. 254.
115. Quo. Brown, Alison, p. 115.
116. Quo. Gombrich, p. 110.
117. Quo. Thornton, Dora, vol. 1, p. 131.
118. Quo. Stechow, p. 34. But see also Ristori, Renzo, in *Rinascimento*, 2nd ser, XXVI (1986), pp. 77–97.
119. Ib., p. 146.
120. Ib., p. 147.
121. Quo. Smart, Alistair, *The Renaissance and Mannerism outside Italy*, London, 1972, p. 175.
122. Quo. Stechow, p. 132.
123. Quo. Ib., p. 171.
124. Diálogas em Roma, ed. Felicidade, Alves J. da, Lisbon, 1984, pp. 89–90. John Bury drew my attention to this list and provided me with a transcript.
125. Quo. Levey, p. 124.
126. Quo. Rosand (1991) p. 245.
127. Quo. Thornton, Dora, vol. 1, p. 97.
128. Ed. cit., p. 101.
129. Ed. cit., p. 28.
130. Ed. cit., vol. 1, pp. 347–8.
131. Quo. Richter, pp. 52–3.
132. Quo. Hutton, p. 104.
133. Repro. *Prag um 1600*, cit., vol. 1, cat. no. 96.
134. Quo. Aston (1988), p. 1.
135. Quo. Strauss (1966), p. 237.
136. Quo. Smith, p. 87.
137. Quo. Tafuri, p. 2.
138. Ed. cit., p. 115.
139. Ib., p. 195.
140. Ib., p. 127.
141. Ed. cit., p. 65.
142. Quo. Widmar, Bruno, *Scrittori politici del '500 e '600*, Milan, 1964, p. 845.
143. Ed. cit., p. 173.
144. Ib., p. 187.
145. Ed. cit., p. 201–3.
146. Quo. Curcio, Carlo, *Utopisti italiani del Cinquecento*, n. p., 1944, p. 73.
147. Campanella, ed. cit., pp. 67, 85–7.
148. Ib., p. 105.
149. *Utopia*, ed. cit., p. 245.
150. *The Education of a Christian Prince*, ed. Born, L. K., New York (reprint), 1965, p. 197.
151. Ed. cit., p. 107.

CHAPTER VIII: CIVILITY IN DANGER?

1. Quo. Strauss (1971), p. 209.
2. Quo. Potter, Lois, *Times Literary Supplement*, 1988, p. 673.
3. Quo. *Tudor Royal Proclamations*, eds. Hughes, F. L. and Larkin, J. F., vol. 1, New Haven, Conn., 1964, p. 106.
4. *Journal*, ed. cit., p. 10.
5. Quo. Mandrou, Robert, *Introduction à la France Moderne: Essai de Psychologie Historique*, Paris, 1961, p. 81.
6. Quo. Rossi, P. in Chaney and Mack, p. 175.
7. Platter (1961), p. 93.
8. Quo. Schildhauer, p. 111.
9. Ed. cit., pp. 70, 52, 206–8.
10. Quo. Brigden, p. 539.
11. Quo. Thomas, Keith, 'Age and Authority in Early Modern England', *Proceedings of the British Academy*, vol. 62, 1977, p. 217.
12. Platter (1961), p. 127.
13. Mundy, p. 78.
14. Ed. Sowards, p. xxxvi.
15. Op. cit., p. 279.
16. Fletcher, p. 116.
17. Quo. Brown, Alison, p. 118.
18. Quo. Onians, John, *Bearers of Meaning: The Classical Orders in Antiquity, the Middle Ages and the Renaissance*, Princeton, 1988, p. 166.
19. E.g. Hale, J. R., *War and Society in Renaissance Europe*, London, 1985, pp. 192–3.

20. *Lenten Stuffe* in ed. cit., vol. 3, p. 183.
21. Quo. Garin, Eugenio, *Scienza e vita civile nel Rinascimento italiano*, Bari, 1965, pp. 33–4.
22. 4, ii.
23. Quo. Hale (1983), pp. 340–1.
24. Quo. ib., p. 343.
25. Quo. Santore, pp. 57–8.
26. Hair, p. 83.
27. Ib., pp. 55–6.
28. *De Subtilitate*, quo. Fierz, p. 102.
29. *Voyage*, ed. cit., pp. 289–93.
30. Quo. Lowry, p. 33.
31. Tr. Kitchen, Laurence, *Love Sonnets of the Renaissance*, London, 1990, p. 31.
32. Ib., p. 29.
33. Quo. Delumeau, J., *La Civilisation de la Renaissance*, Paris, 1967, p. 468.
34. Quo. Jenneret, J., 1991, p. 239, with other examples.
35. Quo. Cottrell, p. 50.
36. Quo. Freedberg, p. 346.
37. Ib., p. 361.
38. Klein and Zerner, p. 123.
39. Quo. Freedberg, p. 357.
40. Quo. Fierz, p. 103.
41. Induction, i.
42. Quo. Freedberg, p. 30.
43. Moxey, p. 117.
44. See below, pp. 496–501.
45. Quo. Elliott (1963), p. 294.
46. Quo. Davis (1975), p. 24.
47. Tr. Alpert, Michael, Harmondsworth, 1969, p. 83.
48. Quo. Cheyney, Edward P., *A History of England from the Defeat of the Armada to the Death of Elizabeth*, 2 vols., New York, 1948, vol. 2, p. 5.
49. Quo. Speroni, Charles, *Wit and Wisdom of the Italian Renaissance*, Berkeley, Ca., 1964, p. 93.
50. Luca Landucci. Quo. Camporesi, p. 22.
51. Sastrow, p. 38.
52. Quo. Strauss (1971), pp. 218–22.

53. *The Countess of Pembroke's Arcadia*, ed. Evans, Maurice, Harmondsworth, 1977, p. 383.
54. Quo. Knecht, R. J. in Mulryne and Shewring, p. 14.
55. Quo. Stan, A. E. and Mendy K., 'Speculum Britanniae'. *Regional Study, Antiquarianism and Science in Britain to 1700*, Toronto, 1989, p. 92.
56. Above, p. 362.
57. Ed. cit., p. 269.
58. Quo. Herford, C. H., *Studies in the Literary Relations of England and Germany in the Sixteenth Century*, Cambridge, 1886, p. 247.
59. *Henry IV. Part 1*, 4, ii.
60. Brant, p. 270.
61. Quo. Wilson, pp. 164–5.
62. Quo. Le Goff, Jacques, *Medieval Civilization 400–1500*, tr. Barrow, Julia, Oxford, 1989, p. 168.
63. Quo. Elliott, J. H., in Clark, ed., 1985, p. 308.
64. Quo. Camporesi, p. 85.
65. Sancho Panza's grandmother in *Don Quixote*, ed. cit. p. 600.
66. Henry Chettle. Quo. Koenigsberger, H. G. and Mosse, George L. *Europe in the Sixteenth Century*, London, 1968, p. 56.
67. Quo. Elliott (1970), p. 63.
68. Strauss (1971), pp. 177–8.
69. Quo. Koenigsberger and Mosse (1968), p. 23.
70. Quo. Kamen, p. 59.
71. Quo. Heinemann, Margaret, in Braunmuller and Hattaway, p. 175.
72. Quo. Moxey, p. 96.
73. Quo. Davidson in Clark, p. 157.
74. Quo. Aston (1988), p. 38.
75. Ib., p. 39, note 68.
76. Quo. Davidson (1982), pp. 94, 93.
77. Quo. Lightbown, R. in Chaney and Mack, p. 248.
78. Quo. Bush, Douglas, *English Literature in the Earlier Seventeenth Century 1600–1660*, Oxford, 1945, p. 282.

CHAPTER IX: THE CONTROL OF MAN

1. Quo. Tillyard, E. M. W., *The Elizabethan World Picture*, London, 1950, p. 91.
2. Quo. Bercé, p. 54.
3. Quo. Tillyard, op. cit., in note 1, p. 88.
4. 2. i.
5. Quo. Rowse, p. 37.
6. Quo. Englander, p. 262.
7. Quo. Parker, Geoffrey, *Europe in Crisis 1598–1648*, London, 1979, p. 128.
8. Quo. Bercé, p. 43.
9. Quo. Archer, p. 1.
10. Quo. Strauss (1971), p. 145.
11. Quo. Kamen, p. 336.
12. Quo. ib., p. 337.
13. Quo. Bercé, p. 11.
14. Quo. Camporesi, p. 31.
15. Quo. Bonney, p. 410.
16. Quo. Englander, p. 241.
17. Quo. Black, J. B., *The Reign of Elizabeth 1558–1603*, Oxford, 1936, p. 161.
18. Quo. Davidson (1982), p. 88.
19. Platter (1963), pp. 28–9.
20. Quo. Davidson (1982), p. 92.
21. Quo. Englander, p. 168.
22. Quo. Klein and Zerner, p. 132.
23. Quo. *Tudor Royal Proclamations*, eds. Hughes and Larkin, vol. 1, New Haven, Conn., 1944, p. 329.
24. Quo. Englander, pp. 301–2.
25. Quo. Cochrane and Kirshner, p. 425.
26. Ib., p. 381.
27. Quo. Hair, p. 57.
28. Sastrow, p. 285.
29. Quo. Mandrou, Robert, *Introduction à la France Moderne: Essai de Psychologie historique 1500–1640*, Paris, 1961, p. 229.
30. Quo. Kemp, pp. 225–7.
31. Ed. cit., p. 69.
32. Quo. DNB, 'Boorde'.
33. Quo. Davis (1975), p. 37.
34. Ib., p. 17.
35. Quo. Hale (1971), p. 122, from Benassar, B., *Valladolid au siècle d'or: une ville de Castille et sa campagne au XVIe siècle*, Paris, 1967.
36. Tr. Pine-Coffin, R. S., Harmondsworth, 1958, pp. 22–3.
37. *Maxims and Reflections of a Renaissance Statesman*, tr. Domandi, Mario, New York, 1965, p. 86.
38. Ed. cit., p. 273.
39. *Discours Politiques et Militaires* [1587], ed. Sutcliffe, F. E., Paris, 1967, p. 235.
40. Quo. Brown, Alison, 'Between Curial Rome and Convivial Florence: literary patronage in the 1480s', *Renaissance Studies*, vol. 2, no. 2, 1988, p. 213.
41. Elton, G. R., *Renaissance and Reformation 1300–1648*, London (2nd edn.), 1968, p. 137.
42. Matthiesson, p. 11.
43. Ed. cit., pp. 283, 275.
44. *Galateo*, tr. cit. in note 36, p. 26.
45. Quo. Knox, p. 134.
46. Ed. Smith, J. C., 2 vols., Oxford (reprint), 1968, vol. 2, p. 485.
47. Quo. Ozment (1983), pp. 142–3.
48. 2, iii.
49. *The Prince*, chap. 14.
50. Quo. Hale (1983), p. 234.
51. Ib., p. 234.
52. Letter to F. Vettori, 10 December 1513 (*Opere*, ed. cit., p. 885).
53. Quo. Rossiaud, p. 9 and Roper, p. 4.
54. Quo. Roper, p. 12.
55. Quo. Roper, p. 1.
56. Quo. Otis, p. 43.
57. Karant-Nunn, p. 24.
58. Ed. cit., vol. 4, pp. 130–1.
59. Quo. Cottrell, p. 30.
60. Quo. Archer, p. 232.
61. *Oeuvres*, 2 vols., Paris, 1857, vol. 1, p. 106.
62. Quo. Hale, J. R., *War and Society in Renaissance Europe*, London, 1985, p. 162.
63. Ed. cit., vol. 1, p. 347.

64. Quo. Bontempelli, Massimo, *Il Poliziano, Il Magnifico: Lirici del Quattrocento*, Florence, 1917, p. 289.
65. Quo. Bercé, p. 125.
66. Quo. Davis (1971), p. 41.
67. Hair, p. 64.
68. Quo. Burke (1978), p. 195.
69. Platter (1963), p. 224.

CHAPTER X: THE TAMING OF NATURE

1. Quo. Elliott (1989), p. 31.
2. Quo. Cochrane, p. 319, note.
3. *The Prince*, chap. 15.
4. Quo. Stechow, p. 118.
5. Ed. cit., p. 195.
6. Quo. Eisenstein, p. 473.
7. Book 5, canto x, verse 23.
8. Holberton, pp. 12–13.
9. Quo. Trevor-Roper (1986), p. 252–3.
10. Ed. cit., p. 26.
11. Quo. Goodman, p. 238.
12. Garcia d'Orta. Quo. Debus, p. 47.
13. Ib., p. 51.
14. Quo. Strong (1991), p. 195.
15. Quo. Thomas (1984), p. 224.
16. Quo. Intro. to Platter (1937), p. 26.
17. Ib., pp. 170–1.
18. *De Natura Deorum*, quo. Lazzaro, p. 9.
19. Ed. cit., pp. 140–3.
20. Quo. Gundersheimer (1972), pp. 52–5.
21. Beatis, pp. 134–5.
22. Quo. Strong (1991), pp. 304–6.
23. 3, iv.
24. Ed. cit., pp. 118–19.
25. Ed. cit., p. 207.
26. Ed. cit., p. 208.
27. Quo. Debus, p. 37.
28. Quo. Céard and Margolin, p. 104.
29. Quo. Honour, p. 39.
30. Ib., p. 37.
31. Quo. Impey and Macgregor, p. 1.
32. Ed. cit., p. 43.
33. Quo. Douglas, David C., *English Historical Documents 1485–1558*, London, 1967, p. 210.
34. *The Discovery of Guiana*, London, 1887, p. 103.
35. Quo. Strong (1991), p. 305.
36. Quo. Strauss (1959), p. 144.
37. Letter in *The Renaissance Philosophy of Man*, ed. Cassirer, Ernst et al., Chicago, 1948, p. 44.
38. Quo. Rowse, p. 45.
39. Alberti, *On Architecture*, Bk. IX, Chap. iv. Quo. Gibson, Walter S., 'Mirror of the Earth', *The World Landscape in Sixteenth-Century Flemish Painting*, Princeton, 1989, p. xix.
40. Quo. Klein and Zerner, p. 8.
41. Quo. Thornton, D., vol. 1, p. 30.
42. Quo. Holberton, p. 127.
43. Quo. Smart, Alistair, *The Renaissance and Mannerism outside Italy*, London, 1972, p. 122.
44. Quo. Turner, A. Richard, *The Vision of Landscape in Renaissance Italy*, Princeton, 1966, p. 117.
45. Quo. Huizinga, p. 84.
46. Quo. Wilson, pp. 32–3.
47. 'The Passionate Shepherd to his Love'.
48. Ed. cit., pp. 277–8.
49. Quo. Ozment (1990), p. 103.
50. Quo. Singer, p. 18.
51. Ed. cit., vol. 2, p. 734.
52. Ed. cit., p. 79.
53. Ib., p. 131.
54. Quo. Fierz, p. 99.
55. Quo. Camporesi, p. 32.
56. Quo. Singer, pp. 89–90.
57. Letter from Hegius to Rudolf Agricola, quo. Allen, P. S., *The Age of Erasmus*, Oxford, 1914, p. 27.
58. *Autobiography*, pp. 46–7.
59. Slack, p. 175.
60. Quo. ib., p. 183.
61. Letter in Huizinga, J., *Erasmus of Rotterdam*, London, 1952, p. 252.
62. Quo. Foa, Anna in Muir and Ruggiero, p. 29.
63. Quo. Trevor-Roper (1986), p. 171.

64. Platter (1963), p. 38.
65. Quo. Singer, p. 94.
66. Ed. cit., pp. 85–6.
67. Quo. Thomas (1971), p. 7.
68. Quo. Rossi, p. 71.
69. Ib., p. 48, note.
70. Ib., p. 48.
71. Ib., p. 8.
72. Ib., p. 2.
73. 3, i.
74. Quo. Garin, p. 174.
75. *Pirotechnia*, Boston, 1966, p. 70.
76. Quo. Rabb, p. 50.
77. Quo. Boas, pp. 177–8.
78. Ed. cit., pp. 246–7.
79. Above, p. 143.
80. 1, ii.
81. Quo. French, Peter J. in Dee, John, *The World of an Elizabethan Magus*, London, 1972, p. 92.
82. Quo. Boas, p. 168.
83. Ib., p. 114.
84. Quo. Koyré, p. 36.
85. Quo. Smith, p. 118.
86. Ib., p. 165.
87. Quo. Eisenstein, pp. 106–7.
88. Quo. Wind, Edgar, 'Mathematics and Sensibility', *The Listener*, 1 May 1952, p. 705.
89. Quo. Hale (1983), p. 214.
90. *The Republic of Plato*, tr. Cornford, T. M., Oxford, 1941, pp. 235–9.
91. Quo. Boas, p. 188.
92. Quo. Smith, p. 136.
93. Quo. Rossi, p. 66.
94. Ib., p. 140.
95. Quo. Dreyer, p. 93.
96. Quo. Biagioli, p. 16.
97. Biagioli, Mario, 'Galileo the Emblem Maker', *Isis*, 81, 1990, p. 240.
98. Quo. Smith, p. 74.
99. Quo. Davidson, N. S., *The Counter-Reformation*, Oxford, 1987, p. 17.
100. Quo. Boas, p. 104.
101. Quo. Fierz, p. 109.
102. *Autobiography*, tr. Bull, George, Harmondsworth, 1956, pp. 121–2.
103. Ed. cit. (*Advancement of Learning*, Book II), p. 322.
104. Platter (1963), pp. 89–90.
105. *The Book of My Life*, quo. Fierz, p. 30.

EPILOGUE: 'OUR AGE'

1. Ed. Perosa, A., *Giovanni Rucellai ed il suo Zibaldone*, I, London, 1960, p. 60.
2. Quo. Harbison, E. Harris, *The Christian Scholar in the Age of the Reformation*, New York, 1956, P. 87.
3. Quo. Trevor-Roper (1986), p. 74.
4. Canto 33, stanzas 2–5.
5. *Divine Comedy*, Purgatory, canto xi.
6. Quo. Woodward, W. H., *Studies in Education during the Age of the Renaissance*, Cambridge (1906), 1924, p. 67.
7. Quo. Strauss (1959), p. 18.
8. Quo. Huizinga, 'The Problem of the Renaissance' in *Men and Ideas*, London, 1960, pp. 245–6.
9. Quo. Panofsky, Erwin, *Renaissance and Renascences in Western Art*, London, 1970, p. 16.
10. Quo. Baxandall, Michael, *Painting and Experience in Fifteenth-Century Italy*, Oxford, 1972, p. 113.
11. Quo. Brown, A., p. 94.
12. Quo. Spitz, p. 111.
13. Quo. Rossi, p. 71.
14. Ed. cit., pp. 194–5.
15. Martineau, Jane, ed., *Andrea Mantegna*, London, 1992, p. 99.
16. Quo. Thornton, Peter, p. 392, col. 2, note 15.
17. See above, p. 218.
18. Quo. Delumeau (1967), p. 96.
19. Ib., p. 96.
20. Cochrane and Kirschner, p. 309.
21. *Tutte le opere d'Architettura*, IV, cap. 6, Venice, 1619 edn., p. 147v.
22. Kelley, Donald R. in Porter and Teich, p. 131.

23. Quo. Simon, p. 116.
24. Ed. cit., vol. 1, p. 254.
25. *Advancement of Learning*, ed. cit., p. 433.
26. Quo. Wright, p. 343.
27. Quo. Strauss (1959), p. 147.
28. Quo. Eisenstein, p. 571.
29. Quo. Sarton, p. 195.
30. Quo. Rossi, p. 68.
31. Quo. Bouwsma, p. 271.
32. Hakluyt, Richard, *Voyages*, vol. 1, *The English Voyages*, London, 1907, p. 228.
33. Quo. Rossi, p. 89.
34. Quo. Long, p. 333.
35. Quo. Aston (1988). p. 5.
36. Quo. Brigden, p. 3.
37. *History of Italy and History of Florence*, tr. Grayson, Cecil, ed. Hale, J. R., New York, 1966, p. 124.
38. Ed. cit., pp. 110, 99, 135.
39. See above, p. 192.
40. Quo. Bolgar, R. R., *The Classical Heritage*, New York, 1964, p. 240.
41. Quo. McLaughlin, M. L., 'Humanist Concepts of Renaissance and Middle Ages in the Tre- and Quattrocento', *Renaissance Studies*, vol. 2, no. 2, 1988, p. 135.
42. Quo. Burke, Peter, *Sarpi*, New York, 1967, p. xxix.
43. Quo. Strauss (1959), p. 63.
44. Quo. Fierz, p. 36.
45. Quo. Cochrane (1981), p. 322.

BIBLIOGRAPHY

The literature generated by an interest in the period is enormous. The list that follows is restricted to works I have found directly useful while planning this book and above all to those from which I have taken quotations from contemporary sources.
General coverage is best provided by four volumes in the paperback Fontana History of Europe.

J. R. Hale, *Renaissance Europe, 1480–1520*
G. R. Elton, *Reformation Europe, 1517–1559*
J. H. Elliott, *Europe Divided, 1559–1598*
Geoffrey Parker, *Europe in Crisis, 1598–1648*

Single volume surveys include:

J. Delumeau, *La Civilisation de la Renaissance*, Paris 1967
Jean-Claude Margolin, *L'Avènement des Temps Modernes*, Paris 1977
H. G. Koenigsberger, and George C. Mosse, *Europe in the sixteenth Century*, London 1968

The outstanding collections of sources are two volumes in the series *University of Chicago Readings in Western Civilization* published by the University of Chicago Press:

Vol. 5 *The Renaissance*, ed. Eric Cochrane and Julius Kirshner, 1986
Vol. 6 *Early Modern Europe: Crisis of Authority*, ed. Eric Cochrane, Charles M. Gray and Mark A. Kishlansly, 1987.

Alberti, Leon Battista, *The Family in Renaissance Florence (Della Famiglia)*, tr. Renée Neu Watkins, Columbia, S. C., 1969.
—— *On the Art of Building in Ten Books*, tr. Joseph Rykwert, Neil Leach, Robert Tavernor, Boston, Mass., 1988.
Amelung, Peter, *Das Bild des Deutschen in der Literatur der italienischen Renaissance, 1400–1559*, Munich, 1964.
Anderson, M. S., *Britain's Discovery of Russia, 1553–1815*, London, 1958.
Andersson, Christiane, 'Polemical Prints during the Reformation', in the catalogue *Censorship: 500 Years of Conflict*, New York, 1984.

Anglo, Sydney, *Images of Tudor Kingship*, London, 1992.
Archer, Ian W., *The Pursuit of Stability: Social Relations in Elizabethan London*, Cambridge, 1991.
Aretino, Pietro, *Sei Giornate*, ed. Giovanni Aquilecchia, Bari, 1975.
Armstrong, Elizabeth, *Ronsard and the Age of Gold*, Cambridge, 1968.
Ascoli, Georges, *La Grande-Bretagne devant l'opinion française depuis la Guerre de Cent Ans jusqu' à la fin du XVIe siècle*, reprint Geneva, 1971.
Aston, Margaret, *England's Iconoclasts*, vol. 1, *Laws against Images*, Oxford, 1988.
—— 'Iconoclasm in England: Rites of Destruction by Fire', *Wolfenbütteler Forschungen*, vol. 46, 1990.
Bacon, Francis, *Essays . . . with other Writings*, London, 1902.
Bagrow, Leo, *History of Cartography*, revised R. A. Skelton, London, 1964.
Bandello, Matteo, *Le Novelle*, Florence, 1930, 4 vols.
Bates, E. S., *Touring in 1600*, London, 1911.
Beatis, Antonio de, *The Travel Journal . . . 1517–1518*, ed J. R. Hale, Hakluyt Society, London, 1979.
Bercé, Yves-Marie, *Revolt and Revolution in Early Modern Europe*, tr. Joseph Bergin, Manchester, 1987.
Biagioli, Mario, 'Galileo's System of Patronage', *History of Science*, xxviii (1990), pp. 1–61.
Blunt, Anthony, *Art and Architecture in France 1500 to 1700*, Harmondsworth, 1957.
Boas, Marie, *The Scientific Renaissance 1450–1630*, London, 1962.
Bodin, Jean, *Six Livres de la République*, facsimile of 1606, tr. Richard Knolles, Cambridge, Mass., 1962.
Bonney, Richard, *The European Dynastic States 1494–1660*, Oxford, 1991.
Boorde, Andrew, *The Fyrst Boke of the Introduction to Knowledge*, London [before 1542].
Botero, Giovanni, *The Reason of State* and *The Greatness of Cities*, tr. Robert Peterson (1606) and P. J. and D. P. Waley, London, 1956.
Bouwsma, William, *Concordia Mundi: the Career and Thought of Guillaume Postel (1510–1581)*, Cambridge, Mass., 1957.
Bradford, William, ed., *Correspondence of the Emperor Charles V*, London, 1850.
Brady, Thomas, *Turning Swiss: Cities and Empire 1450–1550*, Cambridge, 1985.
Brant, Sebastian, *The Ship of Fools*, tr. Edwin H. Zeydel, New York, 1944.
Braudel, Fernand, *The Mediterranean and the Mediterranean World in the Age of Philip II*, tr. Siân Reynolds, 2 vols., London, 1972–3.
—— 'L'Italia fuori d'Italia', in *Storia d'Italia*, vol.2, part ii, Milan, 1974, pp. 2091–2248.
—— *Civilization and Capitalism*, tr. Siân Reynolds, 3 vols., London, 1981–4.
—— *Le Modèle italien*, Paris, 1989.

—— The Identity of France, vol. I, History and Environment, tr. Siân Reynolds, London, 1989.

Braunmuller, A. R., and Hattaway, Michael, The Cambridge Companion to English Renaissance Drama, Cambridge, 1991.

Bridgman, Nanie, La Vie musicale au Quattrocento, Paris 1964.

Brigden, Susan, London and the Reformation, Oxford, 1991.

Broockmann, Hartmut, Die Stadt in späten Mittelalter, Munich, 1987.

Brown, Alison, The Renaissance, London, 1988.

Brown, Jonathan, The Golden Age of Painting in Spain, New Haven, Conn., 1991.

Burckhardt, Jacob, The Civilization of the Renaissance in Italy, tr. S. G. C. Middlemore, London, 1944.

Burke, Peter, Popular Culture in Modern Europe, London, 1978.

—— 'Did Europe exist before 1700?', History of European Ideas, vol. I, no. I (1980), pp. 21–9.

—— The Renaissance, London, 1987.

—— The Historical Anthropology of Early Modern Italy: Essays on Perception and Communication, Cambridge, 1987.

Busbecq: The Turkish Letters of Ogier Ghirlain de Busbecq, tr. E. S. Forster, Oxford, 1927.

Bush, Michael, 'Tax Reform and Rebellion in Early Tudor England', History, lxxvi, October 1991, pp. 379–400.

Cafritz, Robert, Gowing, Lawrence and Rosand, David, Places of Delight: The Pastoral Landscape, catalogue, The Phillips Collection, Washington, 1988.

Cameron, Euan, The European Reformation, Oxford, 1991.

Campanella, Tommaso, The City of the Sun: a Poetical Dialogue, ed. and tr., Daniel J. Donno, Berkeley, Ca., 1981.

Campbell, Lorne, Renaissance Portraits: European Portrait Painting in the 14th, 15th and 16th Centuries, New Haven, Conn., 1990.

Camporesi, Piero, Bread of Dreams, tr. David Gentilcore, Cambridge, 1989.

Cardano, Girolamo, The Book of My Life, tr. J. Stoner, London, 1931.

Carletti, Francesco, My Voyage around the World, tr. Herbert Weinstock, London, 1965.

Casey, Paul F., ' "Formed not Born": Vernacular Reading and Books of Manners in Sixteenth-Century Germany', German Life and Letters, xlii, 1989, pp. 91–100.

Castiglione, Baldassare, The Book of the Courtier, tr. George Bull, Harmondsworth, 1967.

Céard, Jean and Margolin, Jean-Claude, eds., Voyager à la Renaissance, Paris, 1987.

Céard, Jean, 'L'image de l'Europe dans la littérature cosmographique de la Renaissance', in La Conscience européenne (see below), pp. 49–63.

Cervantes, Miguel de, Don Quixote, tr. J. M. Cohen, Harmondsworth, 1950.

Chambers, David, *Patrons and Artists in the Italian Renaissance*, London, 1970.

Chaney, Edward and Mack, Peter, eds., *England and the Continental Renaissance: Essays in Honour of J. B. Trapp*, Woodbridge, 1990.

Charles, V., 'Instrucciones de Carlos-Quinto à Don Felipe su Hijo', in *Papiers d'Etat du Cardinal de Granvelle*, ed. Charles Weiss, vol. 3, Paris, 1942, pp. 267–318.

Chartier, Roger, ed., *A History of Private Life*, vol. 3, *Passions of the Renaissance*, tr. Arthur Goldman, Cambridge, Mass., 1989.

Chastel, André et al., *The Renaissance: Essays in Interpretation*, London, 1982.

Cheyney, Edward P., *A History of England from the Defeat of the Armada to the Death of Elizabeth*, 2 vols., New York, 1948.

Cipolla, Carlo, *European Culture and Overseas Expansion*, Harmondsworth, 1970.

—— *Public Health and the Medical Profession in the Renaissance*, Cambridge, 1976.

Clark, Sir George, *A History of the Royal College of Physicians of London*, vol. 1, Oxford, 1964.

Clark, Peter, ed., *The European Crisis of the 1590s: Essays in Comparative History*, London, 1985.

Cochrane, Eric, *Historians and Historiography in the Italian Renaissance*, Chicago, 1981.

La Conscience européenne au XVᶜ et au XVIᶜ Siècle. Actes du Colloque international organisé à l'Ecole Normale Supérieure de Jeunes Filles, Paris, 1982.

Cooper, Michael SJ, *They Came to Japan: An Anthology of European Reports on Japan, 1543–1640*, London, 1965.

Coryat, Thomas, *Coryat's Crudities*, 2 vols., Glasgow, 1905.

Cottrell, R. D., *Brantôme, The Writer as Portraitist of his Age*, Geneva, 1970.

Crucé, Émeric, *The New Cyneas*, tr. T. W. Balch, Philadelphia, 1909.

Cummings, Anthony M., *The Politicized Muse: Music for Medici Festivals 1512–1573*, Princeton, NJ, 1992.

Curcio, Carlo, *Utopisti italiani del Cinquecento*, n.p., 1944.

Davidson, N. S., 'Northern Italy in the 1590s', in Clark, Peter, cit.

—— 'Il Sant' Ufficio e la Tutela del Culto a Venezia nell' 500', *Studi Veneziani*, N.S. VI (1982), 87–101.

Davies, N., *God's Playground: A History of Poland*, vol. 1, *The Origins to 1795*, London, 1981.

Davis, Natalie Zemon, 'The Reasons of Misrule: Youth Groups and Charivaris in Sixteenth-Century France', *Past and Present*, l, 1971, pp. 41–75.

—— *Society and Culture in Early Modern France*, Stanford, Ca., 1975.

Debus, Allen G., *Man and Nature in the Renaissance*, Cambridge, 1978.

Della Valle, Pietro, *Pilgrim: The Journeys of Pietro della Valle*, tr. George Bull, London, 1989.

Denley, Peter and Elam, Caroline, *Florence and Italy: Renaissance Studies in Honour of Nicolai Rubinstein*, London, 1988.

Dickens, A. G., ed., *The Courts of Europe: Politics, Patronage and Royalty, 1400–1800*, London, 1977.

Dollinger, Philippe, *The German Hansa*, tr. D. S. Ault and S. H. Steinberg, London, 1970.

Doesten, J. A. van, *Poets, Patrons and Professors: Sir Philip Sidney, Daniel Rogers and the Leiden humanists*, Oxford, 1962.

Dreyer, J. L., *Tycho Brahe: a Picture of Scientific Life and Work in the Sixteenth Century*, reprint (from 1890 ed.), New York, 1963.

Eisenstein, Elizabeth L., *The Printing Press as an Agent of Change: Communications and Cultural Transformations in Early-Modern Europe*, Cambridge, 1980.

Elias, Norbert, *The Civilizing Process*, vol. 2., *State Formation and Civilization*, tr. Edmund Jephcott, Oxford, 1982.

Elliott, J. H., *Imperial Spain, 1469–1716*, London, 1963.

—— *Europe Divided, 1559–1598*, London, 1968.

—— *The Old World and the New, 1492–1650*, Cambridge, 1970.

—— *Spain and its World, 1500–1700*, New Haven, Conn., 1989.

—— *National and Comparative History: An Inaugural Lecture*, Oxford, 1991.

Ellis, Harold, *A History of the Bladder Stone*, Oxford, 1969.

Elyot, Sir Thomas, *The Boke named the Governour* (1531), London, Everyman ed., n.d.

Englander, David et al., *Culture and Belief in Europe 1450–1600: An Anthology of Sources*, Oxford, 1990.

Eörsi, Anna, *International Gothic Style in Painting*, Budapest, 1986.

Erasmus, Desiderius, *De Civilitate Morum Puerilium Libellus*, tr. Brian McGregor, Toronto, 1985.

—— *Literary and Educational Writings*, ed. J. K. Sowards, Toronto, 1985.

Evans, R. J. W., *Rudolf II and his World*, Oxford, 1973.

Febvre, Lucien, 'Frontière: le mot et la notion', in id., *Pour une histoire à part entiére*, Paris, 1962, pp. 11–52.

—— 'Civilisation: évolution d'un mot et d'un groupe d'idées', ib., pp. 479–528.

The Fairest Flower; the Emergence of Linguistic National Consciousness in Renaissance Europe, Accademia della Crusca, Florence, 1986.

Ferguson, W. K., *The Renaissance in Historical Thought: Four Centuries of Interpretation*, Cambridge, Mass., 1948.

Fierz, Markus, *Girolamo Cardano 1501–1576*, Boston, 1983.

Fletcher, Giles, *Of the Russe Commonwealth*, ed. Richard Pipes and J. V. A. Fine, Cambridge, Mass., 1966.

Freedberg, David, *The Power of Images: Studies in the History and Theory of Response*, Chicago, 1989.

Friedman, Alice T., *House and Household in Elizabethan England: Wollaton Hall and the Willoughby Family*, Chicago, 1989.

Frommel, Christoph L., 'Papal Policy: the Planning of Rome during the Renaissance', in Rotberg, Robert L. and Rabb, Theodore K., eds., *Art and History: Images and their Meaning*, Cambridge, 1981, pp. 39–66.

Galen, *On the Usefulness of the Parts of the Body*, tr. Margaret Tallmadge May, 2 vols., Ithaca, NY, 1968.

Garcia, Carlos, *La Antipatia des Franceses y Españoles*, ed. Michel Bareau, Edmonton, 1979.

Garin, Eugenio, ed., *L'Uomo del Rinascimento*, Bari, 1988.

Geneakoplos, Deno, 'La Colonia greca di Venezia e il Rinascimento', in Pertusi, Augustino, ed., *Venezia e L'Oriente fra tardo Medioevo e Rinascimento*, Florence, 1966.

Gibson, Walter S., *'Mirror of the Earth': The World Landscape in Sixteenth-Century Flemish Painting*, Princeton, NJ, 1989.

Gollwitzer, H., *Europabild und Europagedanke*, Munich, 1964.

Gombrich, E. H., *Norm and Form: Studies in the Art of the Renaissance*, London, 1966.

Goodman, Anthony and Mackay, Angus, *The Impact of Humanism on Western Europe*, London, 1966.

Goris, J. A., *Etude sur les Colonies marchandes méridionales à Anvers de 1488 à 1567*, Louvain, 1925.

Grafton, Anthony and Jardine, Lisa, eds., *From Humanism to the Humanities: Education and Liberal Arts in Fifteenth- and Sixteenth-Century Europe*, Cambridge, Mass., 1986.

Grafton, Anthony and Blair, Ann, eds., *The Transmission of Culture in Early Modern Europe*, Philadelphia, 1990.

Grendler, Paul F., *Schooling in Renaissance Italy: Literacy and Learning 1300–1600*, Baltimore, 1989.

—— *Culture and Censorship in late Renaissance Italy and France*, London, 1981.

Guazzo, Stefano, *The Civil Conversation*, tr. George Pettie, London, 2 vols., 1925.

Gundersheimer, Werner L., ed., *French Humanism 1470–1600*, London 1969.

—— *Art and Life at the Court of Ercole I d'Este: the 'De Triumphis Religionis' of Giovanni Sabadino degli Arienti*, Geneva, 1972.

Gurr, Andrew, *Playgoing in Shakespeare's London*, Cambridge, 1987.

Gutierrez, Asensio, *La France et les français dans la littérature espagnole. Un aspect de la xenophobie en Espagne (1589–1665)*, Saint Etienne, 1977.

Hair, Paul, ed., *Before the Bawdy Court*, New York, 1972.

Haitsma Mulier, E. O. G., *The Myth of Venice and Dutch Republican Thought in the Seventeenth Century*, Assen, 1980.

Hale, J. R., *England and the Italian Renaissance*, London, revised edn., 1963.

—— *Renaissance Europe, 1480–1520*, London, 1971.

—— *Renaissance War Studies*, London, 1983.

Hampe, T., *Das Trachtenbuch des Christoph Weiditz*, Berlin-Leipzig, 1927.

Hanke, L., *All Mankind is One: A Study of the Disputation . . .in 1550 on the Intellectual and Religious Capacity of the American Indians*, Dekalb, Ill., 1974.

Hay, Denys, *Europe—the Emergence of an Idea*, 1957, 2nd revised edn., Edinburgh 1968.

—— 'England, Scotland and Europe: the Problem of the Frontier', *Transactions of the Royal Historical Society*, 5th ser, xxv, 1975, 77–91.

—— *Renaissance Essays*, London, 1988.

Heater, Derek, *The Idea of European Unity*, Leicester, 1992.

Henderson, John, 'Epidemics in Renaissance Florence', in Bulet, Neithard and Delort, Robert, *Maladies et Société*, Paris, 1989.

Henry, John and Hutton, Sarah, *New Perspectives on Renaissance Thought: Essays in the History of Science, Education and Philosophy in Memory of Charles B. Schmitt*, London, 1990.

Herberstein, S. von, *Notes upon Russia*, tr. R. H. Major, Hakluyt Society, 2 vols., 1851–2.

Holberton, Paul, *Palladio's Villas. Life in the Renaissance Countryside*, London, 1990.

Hollier, Denis, ed., *A New History of French Literature*, vol. 1, Cambridge, Mass., 1989.

Honour, Hugh, *The New Golden Land: European Images of America from the Discoveries to the Present Time*, London, 1976.

Hope, Charles, 'Tiziano e la committenza', in catalogue, *Tiziano*, Palazzo Ducale, Venice, 1990.

Hsia, Ronnie Po-Chia, *Social Discipline in the Reformation: Central Europe 1500–1750*, London, 1989.

Hughes, Dom Anselm and Abraham, Gerald, *Ars Nova and the Renaissance 1300–1540*, New Oxford History of Music, vol. 3, Oxford, 1960.

Huizinga, J., *The Waning of the Middle Ages*, London, 1924.

Huppert, George, 'The Idea of Civilization in the Sixteenth Century', in A. Molho and J. A. Tedeschi, eds., *Renaissance Studies in Honor of Hans Baron*, Florence, 1971, pp. 759–69.

Husa, Václav, *Traditional Crafts and Skills: Life and Work in Medieval and Renaissance Times*, Prague, 1967.

Hutchison, Jane Campbell, *Albrecht Dürer: A Biography,* Princeton, NJ, 1990.

Hutton, James, *Themes of Peace in Renaissance Poetry*, ed. R. Guerlac, Ithaca, NY, 1984.

Impey, Oliver and Macgregor, Arthur, eds., *The Origins of Museums: The Cabinet of Curiosities in Sixteenth- and Seventeenth-Century Europe*, Oxford, 1985.

Israel, Jonathan, *European Jewry in the Age of Mercantilism*, 1550–1750, revised edn., Oxford, 1985.

Jacob, E. F., ed., *Italian Renaissance Studies*, London, 1960.

Jardine, Lisa, 'Mastering the uncouth: Gabriel Harvey, Edmund Spenser and the English Experience in Ireland', in Henry and Hutton, eds., pp. 68–82.

—— *Still Harping on Daughters: Women and Drama in the Age of Shakespeare*, Brighton, 1983.

Jeanneret, Michel, *A Feast of Words: Banquets and Table Talk in the Renaissance*, Chicago, 1991.

Jones, E. L., *The European Miracle: Environments, Economies and Geopolitics in the History of Europe and Asia*, Cambridge, 1981.

Jordan, Constance, *Renaissance Feminism: Literary Texts and Political Models*, Ithaca, NY, 1990.

Kagan, Richard L., 'Philip II and the Art of Cityscape', in Rotberg, Robert T., and Rabb, Theodore K., eds., *Art and History. Images and their Meaning*, Cambridge, 1988, pp. 115–135.

Kamen, Henry, *The Iron Century: Social Change in Europe 1550–1660*, London, 1971.

Karant-Nunn, Susan C., 'Continuity and Change: Some Effects of the Reformation on the Women of Zwickau', *Sixteenth-Century Journal*, vol. xiii, no. 2, 1982, pp. 17–42.

Kauffman, Thomas Da Costa, *L'Ecole de Prague; la peinture à la cour de Rodolphe II*, Paris, 1985.

Kearney, Hugh F., *Origins of the Scientific Revolution*, London, 1964.

Kemp, Martin, ed., *Leonardo on Painting*, New Haven, Conn. 1989.

Kent, F. W., and Simons, Patricia, *Patronage, Art and Society in Renaissance Italy*, Oxford, 1987.

Kibre, Pearl, *The Nations in the Medieval Universities*, Cambridge, Mass., 1948.

Kiernan, V. G., *The Duel in European History*, Oxford, 1989.

King, Margaret L., *Women of the Renaissance*, Chicago, 1991.

Kitchen, Laurence, tr., *Love Sonnets of the Renaissance*, London, 1990.

Klein, Robert and Zerner, Henri, *Italian Art 1500–1600: Sources and Documents*, Englewood Cliffs, NJ, 1966.

Knox, Dilwyn, '*Disciplina*: the Monastic and Clerical Origins of European Civility', in *Renaissance Society and Culture: Essays in Honor of Eugene F. Rice Jr.*, ed. John Monfasani and Ronald G. Musto, New York, 1991, pp. 107–35.

Koyré, Alexandre, *The Astronomical Revolution*, London, 1973.

Krailsheimer, A. J., ed., *The Continental Renaissance 1500–1600*, Harmondsworth, 1971.

Kristeller, Paul, 'The Modern System of the Arts', in id., *Renaissance Thought*, vol. 2, New York, 1965, pp. 163–227.

Kubler, George, *Portuguese Plain Architecture: between Spices and Diamonds 1521–1706*, Middletown, Conn., 1972.

—— and Soria, Martin, *Art and Architecture in Spain and Portugal and their American Dominions*, Harmondsworth, 1959.

Labé, Louise, tr. Frances Lobb, *The Twenty-Four Love Sonnets*, London, 1950.

Lewner, Lynne, *I Modi*, Milan, 1984.

Lazzaro, Claudia, *The Italian Renaissance Garden*, Cambridge, Mass., 1990.

Levenson, Jay A., ed., *Circa 1492: Art in the Age of Exploration*, catalogue, National Gallery, Washington, New Haven, Conn., 1992.

Levey, Michael, *The Soul of the Eye: An Anthology of Painters and Painting*, London, 1990.

Lievsay, J. L., *The Elizabethan Image of Italy*, Ithaca, NY, 1964.

Long, Pamela O., 'The Openness of Knowledge: an Ideal and its Context in Sixteenth-Century Writings on Mining and Metallurgy', *Technology and Culture*, vol. 32, April 1991, pp. 318–55.

Lowry, Martin, *The World of Aldus Manutius: Business and Scholarship in Renaissance Venice*, Oxford, 1979.

MacCurtain, Margaret, *Tudor and Stuart Ireland*, Dublin, 1972.

McFarlane, I. D., *A Literary History of France. Renaissance France 1470–1589*, London, 1974.

Machiavelli, Niccolò, *Tutte le Opere*, ed. Guido Mazzoni and Mario Casella, Florence, 1929.

Mack, Phyllis and Jacob, Margaret C., *Politics and Culture in Early Modern Europe: Essays in Honour of H.G.Koenigsberger*, Cambridge, 1987.

McLaren, Angus, *A History of Contraception from Antiquity to the Present Day*, Oxford, 1990.

McLaughlin, M. L., 'Humanist Concepts of Renaissance and Middle Ages in the tre- and quattrocento', *Renaissance Studies*, II, 1988, pp. 131–42.

McNeill, William H., *Europe's Steppe Frontier 1500–1800*, Chicago, 1964.

Manley, Lawrence, 'Fictions of Settlement: London 1590', *Studies in Philology*, 1991, pp. 207–24.

Martines, Lauro, 'The Protean Face of Renaissance Humanism', *Modern Language Quarterly*, li, 1991, pp. 105–21.

Matthiesson, F. O., *Translation: An Elizabethan Art*, Cambridge, Mass., 1931.

Mattingly, G., 'An Early Non-Aggression Pact', *Journal of Modern History*, x (1938) pp. 1–30.

—— *Renaissance Diplomacy*, London, 1955.

Mendyk, Stan, A. E., *'Speculum Britanniae': Regional Study, Antiquarianism and Science in Britain to 1700*, Toronto, 1989.

Monga, Luigi, ed., *Discours viatique de Paris à Rome et de Rome à Naples et Sicile (1588–1589)*, Geneva, 1983.

Montaigne, *Essayes*, tr. John Florio, 3 vols., London, 1910.

—— *Journal du Voyage en Italie en 1580 et 1581*, ed. A. d'Ancona, Città di Castello, 1889.

—— *Journal de Voyage en Italie par la Suisse et l'Allemagne en 1580 et 1581*, ed., Maurice Rat, Paris, 1942.

Monter, E. William, *Calvin's Geneva*, New York, 1967.

More, Thomas, *Utopia*, ed. Edward Surtz and J. H. Hexter, New Haven, Conn., 1965.

Moryson, Fynes, *Shakespeare's Europe*, ed. Charles Hughes, London, 1903.

Moxey, Keith, *Peasants, Warriors and Wives: Popular Imagery in the Renaissance*, Chicago, 1989.

Muir, Edward and Ruggiero, Guido, eds., *Sex and Gender in Historical Perspective*, Baltimore, 1990.

Mulryne, J. R. and Shewring, Margaret, eds., *War, Literature and the Arts in Sixteenth-Century Europe*, London, 1989.

Mundy, Peter, *The Travels of Peter Mundy in Europe and Asia 1608–1667*, vol. 1, *Travels in Europe, 1608–1628*, ed. R.C.Temple, Hakluyt Society, London, 1907.

Musikgeschichte in Bildern, Leipzig, 1976.

Nashe, Thomas, *The Works*, ed. R. B. McKerrow, vol. 3, Oxford, 1958.

Oestreich, Gerhard, *Neostoicism and the Early Modern State*, ed., Brigitta Oestreich and H. G. Koenigsberger, tr., David McLintock, Cambridge, 1982.

Olson, Roberta J. M., *Italian Renaissance Sculpture*, London, 1992.

Ortelius, Abraham, *Theatrum Orbis Terrarum*, Antwerp, 1570.

—— ed., Puraye, Jean, *Album Amicorum Abraham Ortelius*, Amsterdam, 1969.

—— *Catalogue of the . . . Correspondence of Abraham Ortelius*, Amsterdam, 1969.

Otis, Leah Lydia, *Prostitution in Medieval Society: The History of an Urban Institution in Languedoc*, Chicago, 1985.

Ozment, Steven, *The Reformation in the Cities*, New Haven, Conn., 1975.

—— *When Fathers Ruled: Family Life in Reformation Europe*, Cambridge, Mass., 1983.

—— *Magdalena and Balthasar: An Intimate Portrait of Life in Sixteenth-Century Europe revealed in the Letters of a Nuremberg Husband and Wife*, New Haven, Conn., 1989.

—— *Mysticism and Dissent. Religious Ideology and Social Protest in the Sixteenth Century*, New Haven, Conn., 1973.

—— *Three Behaim Boys: Growing up in early modern Germany. A Chronicle of their Lives*, New Haven, Conn., 1990.

Pagden, Anthony, 'The Impact of the New World on the Old: The History of an Idea', *Renaissance and Modern Studies*, xxx (1986).

—— ed., *The Languages of Political Theory in Early-Modern Europe*, Cambridge, 1987.

—— *Spanish Imperialism and the Political Imagination: Studies in European and Spanish-American Social and Political Theory 1513–1830*, New Haven, Conn., 1990.

Paquet, Jacques and Ijsewijn, Jozef, eds., *Les Universités à la fin du Moyen Age*, Louvain, 1978.

Panofsky, Erwin, *Studies in Iconology*, New York, 1939.
—— *Renaissance and Renascences in Western Art*, London, 1970.
Paracelsus, *Selected Writings*, ed., Jolande Jacobi, New York, 1951.
Parker, Geoffrey, *The Military Revolution: Military Innovation and the Rise of the West, 1500–1800*, Cambridge, 1988.
—— and Smith, Lesley, *The General Crisis of the Seventeenth Century*, London, 1978.
Penrose, Boise, *The Sherleian Odyssey*, Taunton, 1938.
Perjés, Géza, *The Fall of the Medieval Kingdom of Hungary: Mohacs 1526–Buda 1541*, tr., Mario D. Fenyö, New York, 1989.
Phillips, J. R. S., *The Medieval Expansion of Europe*, Oxford, 1988.
Piccolomini, Aeneas Silvius, *La Germania*, tr. and ed., Gioacchino Paperelli, Florence, 1949.
Picot, Emile, 'Les italiens en France au XVI^c siècle', *Bulletin Italian*, i–iv (Bordeaux, 1901–1905).
—— *Les français italianisants au XVI^c siècle*, 2 vols., Paris, 1906.
Pirotta, N., *Music and Culture in Italy from the Middle Ages to the Baroque*, Cambridge, Mass., 1984.
Platina (Sacchi, Bartolomeo), *Il Piacere onesto e la buona Salute*, ed. Emilio Faccioli, Turin, 1985.
Platter, Felix, *Beloved son Felix: The Journal of Felix Platter a Medical Student in Montpellier in the Sixteenth Century, 1552–7*, tr. Seán Jennett, London, 1963.
—— *Thomas Platter's Travels in England*, tr. and ed. Clare Williams, London, 1937.
Pliny the Younger, *The Letters*, tr. Betty Radice, Harmondsworth, 1963.
Poliziano, Angelo, *The Stanze*, tr. David Quint, Massachusetts, 1979.
Pontano, Giovanni, *I trattati delle virtu sociali*, ed. Francesco Tateo, Rome, 1965.
Pope-Hennessy, John, *The Piero della Francesca Trail*, London, 1991.
Porter, R. and Teich, M., eds., *The Renaissance in National Context*, Oxford, 1992.
Prag um 1600. Kunst und Kultur am Hofe Kaiser Rudolfs II, catalogue, 2 vols., Kulturstiftung Ruhr Essen and Kunsthistorisches Museum, Vienna, 1988.
Rabb, Theodore K., *The Struggle for Stability in Early Modern Europe*, Oxford, 1975.
Rabelais, François, *Les Epitres . . . escrites pendant son voyage d'Italie*, ed. L. and S. de Sainte-Marthe, Paris, 1651.
—— *Gargantua and Pantagruel*, tr. J. M. Cohen, Harmondsworth, 1955.
Rabil, Albert, Jr., ed., *Renaissance Humanism: Foundations, Forms and Legacy*, 3 vols., Philadelphia, 1988.
Richter, Irma, A., ed., *Paragone: A Comparison of the Arts by Leonardo da Vinci*, London, 1949.

Roberts, Michael, ed., *Sweden as a Great Power*, London, 1968.
—— *The Swedish Imperial Experience*, London, 1979.
Robb, Nesca, 'The Fare of Princes: A Renaissance Manual of Domestic Economy', *Italian Studies*, VII, 1952, pp. 36–61.
Ronsard, Pierre de, *Poems of Love*, ed. Grahame Castor and Terence Cave, Manchester, 1975.
Roper, Lyndal, 'Discipline and Respectability: Prostitution and the Reformation in Augsburg', *History Workshop Journal*, 19, 1985, pp. 3–28.
Rosand, David, 'Dialogues and Apologies: Sidney and Venice', *Studies in Philology*, 1991, pp. 236–49.
Rosand, David and Muraro, Michelangelo, *Titian and the Venetian Woodcut*, catalogue, National Gallery, Washington, 1976.
Rose, Paul Laurence, *The Italian Renaissance of Mathematics*, Geneva, 1975.
Rosenthal, Earle E., *The Palace of Charles V in Granada*, Princeton, 1985.
Rossi, Paolo, *Philosophy, Technology and the Arts in the Early Modern Era*, tr. Salvator Attenasio, New York, 1970.
Rossiaud, Jacques, *Medieval Prostitution*, tr. Lydia G. Cochrane, Oxford, 1988.
Rouillard, C. D., *The Turk in French History, Thought and Literature, 1520–1660*, Paris, 1941.
Rowse, A. L., *The England of Elizabeth: The Structure of Society*, London, 1950.
Rubinstein, N., 'The History of the Word *politicus*', in Pagden, 1987.
Ruffman, Karl H., *Das Russlandbild im England Shakespeares*, Göttingen, 1952.
Russell, Joycelyne G., *The Field of Cloth of Gold: Men and Manners in 1520*, London, 1969.
—— *Peacemaking in the Renaissance*, London, 1986.
Saitta, Armando, *Dalla Res Publica Cristiana agli Stati Uniti di Europa*, Rome, 1948.
Salinger, Leo, 'Jacobean Playwrights and "Judicious" Spectators', *Proceedings of the British Academy*, lxxv (1989), pp. 1–23.
Santore, Cathy, 'Julia Lombardo, "somtuosa meretrize": a Portrait by Property', *Renaissance Quarterly*, xlv, no.1 (1988), pp. 44–83.
Sarton, George, *Six Wings: Men of Science in the Renaissance*, London, 1957.
Sastrow, B., *Social Germany in Luther's Time: Being the Memoirs of Bartholomew Sastrow*, tr. A. B. Vandam, London, 1902.
Saunders, J. L., *Justus Lipsius*, New York, 1958.
Scaliger, Joseph Justus, *Autobiography*, tr. George W. Robinson, Cambridge, Mass., 1927.
Scammell, G. V., *The First Imperial Age: European Expansion c.1400–1715*, London, 1959.
Schama, Simon, *The Embarrassment of Riches*, London, 1987.
Schildhauer, Johannes, *Die Hanse: Geschichte und Kultur*, Leipzig, 1984.
Schmitt, Antje, *Daniel Frese's Pictures of Justice in the Lüneburg Town Hall*, MA Dissertation, The Warburg Institute, University of London, 1991.

Scribner, R. W., *Popular Culture and Popular Movements in Reformation Germany*, London, 1987.

Seneca, Lucius Annaeus, *Letters from a Stoic: Epistolae morales ad Lucilium*, tr., Robin Campbell, Harmondsworth, 1969.

Sharpe, Kevin, *Politics and Ideas in Early Stuart England: Essays and Studies*, London, 1989.

Sher, Stephen K., 'Veritas odium parit', *The Medal*, vol. 14, Spring, 1989, pp. 4–11.

Simon, Joan, *Education and Society in Tudor England*, Cambridge, 1969.

Singer, Charles, *A Short History of Medicine*, Oxford, 1928.

Sixsmith, G. M., *The Painted City: A Survey of External Painted Decorations on Secular Buildings in the Venetian Area in the Fifteenth and Sixteenth Centuries*, D.Phil. Thesis, University of Nottingham, 1981.

Skrine, Peter, 'Images of the Merchant in German Renaissance Literature', *Bulletin of the John Rylands Library*, lxxii, no. 3 (1990), pp. 185–96.

Slack, Paul, 'The Response to the Plague in Early Modern England: Public Policies and their Consequences', in *Famine, Disease and the Social Order in Early Modern Society*, ed. John Walter and Roger Schofield, Cambridge, 1989.

Smart, Alistair, *The Renaissance and Mannerism outside Italy*, London, 1972.

Smith, Alan, G. R., *Science and Society in the Sixteenth and Seventeenth Centuries*, London, 1970.

Smith, Pauline M., *The Anti-Courtier Trend in Sixteenth Century French Literature*, Geneva, 1966.

Spitz, Lewis W., *The Religious Renaissance of the German Humanists*, Cambridge, Mass., 1963.

Starkey, Thomas, *A Dialogue between Pole and Lupset*, ed. T. F. Mayer, London, 1989.

Stechow, Wolfgang, *Northern Renaissance Art 1400–1600: Sources and Documents*, Englewood Cliffs, NJ, 1966.

Stone, Lawrence, 'The Educational Revolution in England, 1560–1640', *Past and Present*, xxviii (1964), pp. 41–80.

—— *The Crisis of the Aristocracy*, Oxford, 1965.

Strauss, Gerald, *Sixteenth Century Germany: Its Topography and Topographers*, Madison, Wi., 1959.

—— *Manifestations of Discontent in Germany on the Eve of the Reformation*, Bloomington, Ind., 1971.

Stricchia, Santoro F., 'Arte italiana e arte straniera', in *Storia dell'Arte Italiana*, pt. 1, vol. 3, Turin, 1979, pp. 71–171.

Strong, Roy, *Art and Power: Renaissance Festivals 1450–1650*, Woodbridge, 1984 (2nd edn.).

—— *A Celebration of Gardens*, London, 1991.

Tafuri, Manfredo, *Venice and the Renaissance*, tr. Jessica Levine, Boston, Mass., 1989.

Tetel, Marcel, Witt, Ronald G., Goffen, Rona, eds., *Life and Death in Fifteenth-Century Florence*, Durham, NC, 1989.

Thevet, André, *Les vrais Pourtraits et Vies des Hommes illustres*, Paris, 1584, facsimile, New York, 2 vols., 1973.

Thomas, Keith, *Religion and the Decline of Magic*, London, 1971.

—— *Man and the Natural World: Changing Attitudes in England 1500–1800*, Harmondsworth, 1984.

Thornton, Dora, *The Study Room in Renaissance Italy*, Ph.D. Thesis, The Warburg Institute, University of London, 2 vols., 1990.

Thornton, Peter, *The Italian Renaissance Interior 1400–1600*, London, 1991.

Torresan, Paolo, *Il dipingere di Fiandra. La pittura neerlandese nella letteratura artistica italiana del Quattro e Cinquecento*, Modena, 1981.

Trevor-Roper, Hugh, ed., *The Age of Expansion: Europe and the World 1559–1660*, London, 1968.

—— *Princes and Artists: Patronage and Ideology at Four Habsburg Courts, 1517–1633*, London, 1976.

—— *Renaissance Essays*, London, 1986.

Ullman, Ernst, ed., *Geschichte der Deutschen Kunst 1470–15*, Leipzig, 1985.

Vasari, Giorgio, *Lives of the Artists*, tr. George Bull [selected lives], 2 vols., Harmondsworth, 1965, 1987.

Veldman, Ilja, *Maerten van Heemskerck and Dutch Humanism in the Sixteenth Century*, Maarssen, 1977.

Die Verführung der Europa, catalogue, Kunstgewerbe Museum, Berlin, 1988.

Vickers, Brian, 'Leisure and idleness in the Renaissance: the Ambivalence of Otium', *Renaissance Studies*, iv (1990), pp. 107–154.

Waddington, Raymond B., 'Before Arcimboldo. Composite Portraits on Italian Medals', *The Medal*, vol. xiv, spring 1989, pp. 13–23.

Weinstein, Donald, ed., *The Renaissance and the Reformation 1300–1600*, New York, 1965.

Weiss, Roberto, *The Renaissance Discovery of Classical Antiquity*, Oxford, 1969.

Weston, Helen and Davies, David, eds., *Studies in Honour of John White*, London, 1990.

Whitfield, Clovis and Martineau, Jane, *Painting in Naples 1606–1705: From Caravaggio to Giordano*, catalogue, Royal Academy, London, 1982.

Wilson, John Dover, *Life in Shakespeare's England*, Harmondsworth, 1944.

Wittkower, Rudolf, *Selected Lectures: The Impact of Non-European Civilization on the Art of the West*, ed. Donald Martin Reynolds, Cambridge, 1989.

Würtenberger, Frazepp, *Mannerism: The European Style in the Sixteenth Century*, London, 1962.

Yates, Frances A., *The French Academies in the Sixteenth Century*, London, new edn., 1988.

INDEX

Photographic Credits

All photographs courtesy of the museums credited except for the following: